The Very Young

FOURTH EDITION

The Very Young

Guiding Children from Infancy
Through the Early Years

George W. Maxim
West Chester University

Merrill, an imprint of
Macmillan Publishing Company
NEW YORK

Maxwell Macmillan Canada
TORONTO

Maxwell Macmillan International
NEW YORK   OXFORD   SINGAPORE   SYDNEY

Editor: Linda Sullivan
Production Supervisor: Publication Services, Inc.
Production Manager: Aliza Greenblatt
Text Designer: Publication Services, Inc.
Cover Designer: Proof Positive/Farrowlyne Associates
Cover Art: Beach Buddies © Ivan Anderson, 1060 Flamingo Road, Laguna Beach, CA 92651

This book was set in 10/12 Galliard by Publication Services, Inc.,
and printed and bound by R.R. Donnelley & Sons.
The cover was printed by Lehigh Press.

Macmillan Publishing Company
866 Third Avenue, New York, New York 10022

Macmillan Publishing Company is
part of the Maxwell Communication
Group of Companies.

Maxwell Macmillan Canada, Inc.
1200 Eglinton Avenue East
Suite 200
Don Mills, Ontario M3C 3N1

Library of Congress Cataloging-in-Publication Data
Maxim, George W.
    The very young: guiding children from infancy through the early
years / by George W. Maxim. — 4th ed.
        p.   cm.
    Includes bibliographical references and index.
    ISBN 0-02-378171-8
    1. Early childhood education—United States.   2. Child
development—United States.   3. Socialization.   I. Title.
    LB1139.25.M39   1992
    372.21—dc20   92-19461
                                                   CIP

Printing: 1 2 3 4 5 6 7   Year: 3 4 5 6 7 8 9
Photo credits appears on page 557 which constitutes a continuation of this copyright page.

To
Stanley and Rose
Libby, Michael, and Jeff

The lifeblood of parenthood
is to love what you're doing.

Preface

The spotlight of professional attention has unquestionably fixed its focus on the task of creating programs and formulating practices corresponding to the unique developmental characteristics of young children. The focus encompasses the many challenges faced by early childhood professionals as they attempt to associate significant developmental information with developmentally appropriate practices. NAEYC, ACEI, and other influential professional groups have helped sharpen the focus by establishing clear, reasonable goals for programs designed to help youngsters flourish. In keeping with the spirit of their recommendations, the revisions of this textbook were planned to help to take into account the latest research, theory, and practice that contribute to a developmentally appropriate, child-centered, bias-free experience for children in quality group settings.

FOCUS

One of the central aims of this edition is to help the student of early childhood education understand how theory and research can be translated into child-centered, developmentally appropriate practices for youngsters as they grow from infancy through the preschool/kindergarten years. Separate, chapter-length coverage is given to developmental concepts (Chapter Three) and to the notion of developmentally appropriate practice (Chapter Four). After reading these chapters, individuals should acquire a conceptual framework essential for organizing and establishing a nurturing, respectful environment for young children. Although these key areas are detailed in those early chapters, they are not limited therein; they are linked continually to the specific recommendations discussed throughout the subsequent chapters of the book.

CHAPTER STRUCTURE

Each chapter begins with a photo to highlight the topic under discussion. Following the chapter-opening photo is a brief list of questions designed to guide the reader's thinking. Short "Episodes to Ponder" lead the reader into the actual content of each chapter. These episodes are enjoyable, conversation-type stories that entice the reader into the topical coverage of the chapters. Throughout each chapter, practical ideas are highlighted in boxed displays. Students will appreciate these "nuts-and-bolts" suggestions for working with young children. A brief summary of the major topics within each chapter as well as thoughts for reflection are featured in a "Some Final Thoughts" segment at the end of each chapter.

SPECIAL FEATURES

This textbook was written with consideration of the basic needs of students on their way to becoming professionals in the field of early childhood education. For that reason, special attention was directed to the design elements of the text. Appealing charts, tables, and figures highlight and summarize key information and ideas. Delightful photographs depict childhood scenes with clarity and sentiment. Boxed sections within chapters embrace scores of sample activities for easy reference. In addition, the opening questions, episodes to ponder, and end-of-chapter thoughts help to reinforce important information communicated within each chapter.

The text offers a meticulous introduction to the process of teaching and caring for the very young. It offers a comprehensive overview of current theory and practice, as well as a perspective on the historical evolution of the field of early childhood education. Central to the book is a strong concern for applying theory to appropriate practice.

In addition to fundamental topics such as play, music, art, Piagetian theory, the role of the family, and managing the environment, this text includes topics and chapters that are not usually covered in such breadth or depth:

- An entire chapter devoted to the concept of developmentally appropriate practice

- Rejection of some traditional subject matter headings such as "science" and "social studies" and, instead, examining the child's intellectual and physical efforts to unlock the mysteries of her world through exploration and problem solving

- A strong emphasis on thematic approaches to curriculum planning

- The importance of providing appropriate experiences to promote emergent literacy and associated language abilities

- Special attention to children with unique developmental challenges, including giftednesses

- A concentrated treatment of infancy that helps the reader understand the full range of developmental needs as individuals grow through childhood

FOURTH EDITION MODIFICATIONS

The fourth edition has experienced a considerable revision in response to significant changes in the realm of early childhood education. Following is a brief summary of the principal alterations:

- A chapter on developmentally appropriate practices has been added (Chapter Four), encouraging students to consider how children's development is best supported in preschool settings.

- New topics have been added—gifted children, Montessori, constructivist early education, physical knowledge, and professional ethics.

- The treatment of the topic of child development (Chapter Three) has received major attention. Central concepts are clearly introduced and supported with sound research and theory.

- The chapters have been rearranged into a more logical pedagogical sequence. Chapters One through Five should be read first, but the remaining chapters stand alone and could easily be reordered to fit various instructional frameworks.

- The text has been extensively updated throughout to reflect the most current research in early childhood education and to incorporate emerging emphases in the field.

- All chapters have been substantially reorganized and rewritten. Some have changed emphases; the chapters on the child's physical and social worlds (Chapters Six and Eleven)—while retaining their focus on the child's interest in his world—have been greatly modified and retitled. They now emphasize a more child-centered, exploration-based pattern of learning.

- Finally, the book has received extensive design changes. It has been transformed from a double-column to a single-column design, new photos have been added, illustrations have been updated, and the internal heading structure has been significantly transformed.

These extensive changes give the text a more appealing, lucid, practical, and scholarly quality than the previous edition.

ACKNOWLEDGMENTS

Although only the author's name is prominently displayed on the cover of a book, its final form results from the contributions of many people. I was especially fortunate to have the support and assistance of many whose names deserve special mention here. I am principally grateful to my wife, Libby. Her patience and understanding during those long hours when I was locked away in my writing room were truly appreciated. And, her discreet prodding and motivating pep talks often provided the inspiration I needed whenever those dreaded "writing day blues" began to descend. Libby was also the principal photographer for this project. She did all these things while fulfilling a role much more important than my writing duties—as caring mother to our two sensational sons, Michael and Jeffrey. I don't really know how she did all of that, but I am certain how much it means to me.

Although they didn't realize it, Michael and Jeffrey were of great help during the writing period, too. They always brought a spirit of freshness to my day that helped me meet the challenges of writing with renewed energy and a special tenderness for the early years. Their special smiles, hugs, and loving responses have been locked into my memory forever.

I am also deeply indebted to my parents, Rose and Stanley Maxim. Their honorable work ethic instilled in me the value of persistence in tackling a job as immense as writing a book. Their love of parenthood was an important model for me throughout my career in early childhood education.

I wish to thank Linda Sullivan, administrative editor, for her confidence in me and in *The Very Young*. Her vision and professional abilities helped transform this edition into a vastly improved book. Words of special appreciation must also be offered to others at Macmillan Publishing for their superior leadership throughout the evolution of this text: Jeff Johnston, editor-in-chief of the Education Division; Anne Vega, photo editor; and Claire Huismann, production coordinator from Publication Services.

I would like to extend my sincere gratitude to the directors and teachers of the following early childhood facilities for allowing us into their classrooms to take photographs for this text: Goshen Friends Meeting and School, Nursery School of the First Presbyterian Church, Central Chester County YMCA Children's Center, and the East Bradford Elementary School.

Typing for this edition was done by Gail Habbersett. I am deeply appreciative of the hours she spent deciphering my handwritten, cut-and-paste copy and skillfully transforming it into expertly typed drafts.

The form of the fourth edition was greatly influenced by the insightful suggestions and critical comments offered by its accomplished reviewers:

Jerold P. Bauch, Vanderbilt University

Anita Brehm, East Carolina University

Natalie Delcamp, Rollins College—School for Delcamp

Betty Hathaway, Wright State University

Diane M. Kohl, University of Georgia, Athens

Elaine Lyons, Luzerne County Community College

Donna Castle Richardson, Oklahoma City University

Janice Sherman, Winona State University

Brief Contents

Contents

CHAPTER 6:   Facilitating the Discovery of Physical Knowledge   193

CHAPTER 7:   Offering Cognitive and Mathematical Experiences   221

The Very Young

CHAPTER 1

A Career in Early Childhood Education

Good teachers enrich the lives of young children by filling their early years with an abundance of happiness, confidence, and respect. Good teachers are aware of the special qualities of childhood and use their genuinely sensitive, affectionate personalities to make children's early years as delightful and productive as possible. You may wish to find out if (or show that) you have what it takes to become a quality member of the time-honored profession of teaching. You should begin by (1) examining the personal and professional elements (described in this chapter) that predict successful teaching, and (2) assessing how to effectively acquire or enhance those elements. As you read, use the following questions to guide your thinking:

- Of what importance is personal motivation to successful teaching?

- How does a teacher's personality influence good teaching?

- What does the professional program contribute toward a person's development as a teacher?

- How does a teacher gain certification for public or private schools?

- What career opportunities await those who satisfy the basic competencies required of certified teachers?

- What levels of compensation for early childhood positions are common within the profession?

An Episode to Ponder

We are tops of red and blue.
We spin 'round and 'round for you.
We twirl 'round and 'round some more,
'til we tumble to the floor.

"Let's do it again, teacher...please?" the children call, as the last youngster plops to the floor with glee. "Let's be 'helipropters' this time," giggles Tracy, "watch out for my 'frobellers'!" The teacher and children climb back up and joyously agree to repeat the activity as helicopters. "Rrmmm, rrmmm, rrmmm," the whirring engines clatter as everyone flutters around and around the room in small shuffling steps until it is time to land and, perhaps, start all over again.

Do you see yourself in this scene? Surely, the joy, spirit, energy, humor, sharing, and inventiveness illustrated in this anecdote are contagious. You must value such intimate, delicate exchanges of openness and enthusiasm—that's probably one reason why you decided that teaching young children is the field for you. It is easy to take your place in this scene and to become part of the shared spirit that serves as a deep-rooted foundation for all constructive behavior in the preschool setting.

But how about less pleasant situations? Let us suppose that, just after the last "helicopter" lands, everything that can go wrong does go wrong. Michelle plows her truck into Larissa's block structure and sends building blocks tumbling into a heap. "My house! My house!" shrieks Larissa as she examines the ruins of her budding architectural wonder. Ethan yanks on Jamielle's homemade beaded necklace and sends beads rolling in every direction. A tide of tears wells in Jamielle's eyes as he wails, "I want my mama....I want to go home!" As you attempt to resolve these problems, new ones develop: Blaine wets his pants during outdoor play, Carrie throws up while eating a snack, and Wendy spills a container of paint at the art table. Are you eagerly a part of these scenes? Instead, you may think: "What am I doing here? Maybe I should have majored in something like geography, where the possibility of being bitten on the arm by a disgruntled toddler is a bit more remote than it is in early childhood education!" Don't worry about your mixed reactions; it is quite normal for individuals beginning the study of any profession—medicine, law, engineering, education, and so on—to examine their career choice critically. But, since you *have* made a choice, jump into your studies with complete dedication. Only by plunging yourself totally into your work will you accurately perceive the realities, the joys, and the hardships awaiting you in a career in early childhood education. And, only by giving your best effort at all times will you develop the sensitivity and skill required to offer appropriate experiences for children at their

Affectionate, responsive interactions between adult and child are crucial ingredients of the developmental process.

most delicate stage of development. Some experts have considered the quality of adult-child relationships so important that they have singled it out from all other pressing issues—drug abuse, war, environmental concerns, crime, and so on—as the major factor influencing social change. Lloyd DeMause, a respected authority on the history of childhood, argued: "The major dynamic in historical change is ultimately neither technology nor economics. More important are the changes in personality that grow from differences between generations in quality of the relationships between [adult] and child."[1] What a powerful thought! And, what a challenge to you—to affirm your devotion to children by pledging to work to your fullest potential. You will want to strive all you can to develop the deep sensitivities similar to those of highly skilled artists. It is said, for example, that Michelangelo once peered intently at a monumental slab of Carrara marble and saw within it the Pieta, waiting to be released. Like a talented sculptor, you will use your emerging skills to help each child reach his or her fullest potential—to create a masterpiece that has never been and never will be duplicated.

YOUR MOTIVATION FOR TEACHING

You must have some very special reasons for having decided to become a teacher of young children. Perhaps you made your decision after someone said that you have an excellent way of working with children. You may want to emulate a good teacher you've seen in the past, or feel you have something special to contribute to young children's lives. You may even feel that belonging to such a noble profession as teaching will bring you personal fulfillment. Your reasons for wanting to teach are highly personal—they explain to a great extent how you will behave and feel during your professional training. Stop and reflect about your motives for becoming a teacher. You will find that motivations often fall into one or more of three general categories: **intrinsic, extrinsic,** or **imposed.** Intrinsically motivated students choose teaching because of the personal satisfaction it brings, not for salary or any other outside rewards. These individuals enjoy helping people and work well with others because they enjoy doing so. On the other hand, extrinsically motivated students are mainly guided by perceived personal or material rewards, such as good salary and long vacation time. Imposed motivation is the pressure others place on an individual to choose teaching as a career. Such a choice is not based on the joys or rewards of teaching but, rather, on a desire to please others. For example, some individuals may be encouraged by guidance counselors or parents to consider a career in early childhood education.

How can this information be used to clarify your commitment to teaching young children? Before exploring that question directly, you should understand that your motivation was a highly personal phenomenon, based on previous life experiences unique to you. Because what you are and what you will become are products of your life experiences, it would be unfair to assign a "right" or "wrong" designation to any motives you have identified. It is clear, however, that the kind of teacher young children need has a high degree of intrinsic motivation. If your motivation is intrinsic, chances are that you will prize your educational experiences and try your best to accomplish them successfully. You will work hard, want to learn more, and be able to perceive clearly the purpose of your education program as it relates to your future career. On the other hand, those who fail to list even one intrinsic motivator may eventually become disenchanted with their program, or fail to see its applicability to future career goals. Consequently, they often lose interest in their education. In the absence of intrinsic motivation, it is unlikely that an individual will become a successful teacher. This is not meant to serve as an idealistic or romantic image of career motivation; rather, it is meant to clarify the implications of your work for the lives of young children. A child's early years are too important to entrust to someone whose major reasons for entering the teaching profession do not include an inner drive to make those years as rich and productive as possible.

Motivations are important but, by themselves, are not enough to help you become a quality teacher. If teaching were a simple task, motivation might suffice until trial-and-error experiences gave you the insight you needed. But teaching is a highly sophisticated responsibility—one that must meet the myriad of standards and expectations of parents and other social forces. Those standards and expectations are usually classified into two major categories: **personal** and **professional** characteristics.

PERSONAL CHARACTERISTICS OF GOOD TEACHERS

All of us, at one time or another, have had the pleasure of learning from excellent teachers, people who enjoyed their work and the children they taught. They may have been **entertainers,** free enough to have fun with the children and bring a flair of the dramatic to their work. They may have been **intellectuals,** intensely interested in knowledge and its transmission to children. They may have been **directors,** shouting out, "You're in my classroom now, and we'll operate by my rules." They may have been **recapitulators,** repeating everything they taught until they were sure everyone understood. You may have had one of these teachers or other unique individuals who found special ways of making their teaching successful. Who were those people? What special characteristics did they exhibit? After discussing your ideas with your peers, you may wonder how there could be so many different yet successful teachers. Essentially, they were successful because they allowed their true personalities to emerge as they applied professionally and developmentally sound principles of teaching. Albert Cullum emphasized the importance of teachers being themselves with this example from his teaching career:

> When I first began teaching, there was Al Cullum the teacher and Al Cullum the person. I soon discovered that this split personality was not a healthy one for the children nor for me. I realized I had better bury Al Cullum the teacher and present Al Cullum the person, or else the school year would become monotonous months of trivia.[2]

It is difficult to determine exactly which personal qualities are most valued in good teachers. Researchers since the late 1800s have attempted to describe the characteristics that separated outstanding teachers from the rest, but to this day it has been impossible to agree upon one list of such characteristics. And yet a number of personal characteristics can be observed in people who, like teachers, deal with feelings as a part of their work. Table 1–1 lists some of the possibilities.

Much can be said about each item in this list, but one deserves special elaboration. That is the first item: "I respect the children entrusted to me." How do you show respect for young children? Stacie G. Goffin[3] defines *respect* for children as all the things we do *with* them. To elaborate, Goffin described 12 active categories that frame the ways early childhood educators can display their respect to children.

- *Action #1: Showing respect for childhood:* paying attention to and showing esteem for the separate, developmental period of life called "childhood."
  EXAMPLE: Teachers who respect childhood accept "childish" behavior such as negativism (e.g., "No, me do it!") as developmentally appropriate behavior for two-year-olds. Even though respectful adults will want to help two-year-olds learn other ways of expressing their feelings, they also recognize that children behave differently than adults because of their maturational level and life experiences.
- *Action #2: Responding with sensitivity to children's individuality:* acknowledging the unique characteristics of individual children and the way their uniqueness is revealed in decisions, choices, preferences, and styles of responding to and interacting with objects and people.

Table 1–1 Personal characteristics of good teachers

- I display a deep regard for all children through my actions and words—respect the children entrusted to me.
- I am freely and sincerely myself, not playing a role.
- I express realistic feelings of security and self-confidence.
- I seek knowledge about child development and apply that knowledge to the child's play and curriculum.
- I get along well with people.
- I am a hard worker.
- I am willing to put in extra time to complete a job.
- I am punctual and dependable.
- I can keep secrets regarding confidential matters.
- I admit mistakes and work hard to correct them.
- I observe the rules of the groups to which I belong.
- I leave my problems at home and do not let them affect my work.
- I ignore rumors and refuse to gossip.
- I keep myself groomed and neat.
- I keep my work area in order.
- I use supplies and equipment as carefully as if I had purchased them myself.
- I take pride in my work.
- I follow directions and respect the leadership of others.
- I have a good sense of humor; I can laugh with others.
- I am a flexible person; I can vary my approach if the situation calls for it.
- I am curious and want to explore new ideas for working with young children.
- I know youngsters are active, so I eat and sleep well and exercise in order to stay physically fit, energetic, and healthy.

EXAMPLE: Teachers who are sensitive to individuality are flexible people. When Maria, in her dress-up clothes (long skirt, adult shoes, purse, and flowery hat) is allowed to talk into the toy telephone after several signals were given to clean up, a teacher is responding to individuality. The teacher has no idea what Maria may be saying during her call, but she does know through Maria's actions that Maria's need to talk is certainly far greater than her interest in the activity scheduled to follow.

Classrooms that respect young children are clearly human.

- *Action #3: Developing nurturing relationships with children:* realizing that, even though children are dependent upon adults and have less knowledge and fewer skills, they are still entitled to respect as human beings.
  EXAMPLE: Nurturing teachers strive to encourage success by suggesting coping strategies to those who may become frustrated with an activity: "Try

moving your straw closer to the paint before you puff. Now, does that help scatter the paint about your paper?"

- *Action #4: Using adult authority with wisdom to facilitate children's growth into caring adults:* A wise adult uses positive directions rather than the negative; she always tells the child the correct thing to do in a particular situation rather than dwell on a mistake.
  EXAMPLE: Rather than saying, "Don't run in the classroom," a teacher should comment, "Please walk in the classroom. You may run outdoors." Such positively stated comments direct the child's attention toward something she can do that is acceptable.

- *Action #5: Considering how day-to-day practices influence children:* facilitating children's involvement in personally meaningful activities and experiences.
  EXAMPLE: Teachers are sensitive to the cumulative impact of daily interactions with children, so they are careful to utilize developmentally appropriate practices. Thus, a teacher would involve the children in the use of invented spelling while writing a story about a recent trip to the apple orchard, not in a predictable outcome project such as pasting precut apples on a dittoed apple tree shape.

- *Action #6: Recognizing discipline as a learning experience for children and viewing mistakes as potential learning opportunities:* using sound principles of guidance and discipline to help children understand adult expectations and develop control from within.
  EXAMPLE: A respectful teacher does not resort to an abuse of power ("Do it because I said so; that's why!") to coerce children, but uses techniques of positive guidance: "If you are not wearing a coat, you may not go outdoors. It is cold out there."

- *Action #7: Acknowledging children's competencies:* showing esteem in children's growing capabilities.
  EXAMPLE: A respectful teacher uses sincere praise that focuses upon the child's special accomplishment, not phony or superficial glorification. She does not say, "What an excellent worker you are today!" The child may have no clue as to what he did to be singled out as an "excellent worker." Instead, the teacher comments, "I like the way you placed each block into its proper section on the shelf. The block center is in order again."

- *Action #8: Organizing a curriculum that provides children with interesting things to think about:* offering activities and experiences that are engrossing and that permit the teacher to challenge children's thinking.
  EXAMPLE: One teacher sets aside an hour each week to cook with her class. The children help set up the space, read the recipe, gather and measure ingredients, and prepare the food according to the recipes.

- *Action #9: Supporting and strengthening parents in their childrearing responsibilities:* showing consideration for the importance of family in a child's life and expressing esteem for the challenge of parenthood.

EXAMPLE: Teachers plan conferences during which they gather information that will help them better understand each child and his or her family circumstances. They ask questions such as, "What does your child enjoy most about our classroom?" "What ways of handling your child are most successful at home?" "What are your expectations for your child's future?" "How can our center/school help you reach those goals?"

- *Action #10: Acknowledging the expertise needed to be a professional in early childhood education:* being convinced that early childhood education has a distinctive, professional knowledge base that makes possible programming specific to children's needs and interests.
  EXAMPLE: New articles, books, conferences, and discussions keep teachers busy revising, trying out, throwing away, and updating. An unquenchable thirst for improvement keeps these teachers well-informed and acts as a catalyst to motivate others to spend time gathering new ideas.

- *Action #11: Speaking out on behalf of the profession of early childhood education:* articulating our purposes and advising educational decision makers and others of the unique characteristics of early childhood education.
  EXAMPLE: Teachers must believe that, next to being a parent, there is no greater calling than to influence the next generation with care and compassion. Teachers are convinced of this crucial responsibility and are not afraid to become vocal advocates of quality care and education of the very young.

- *Action #12: Speaking out on behalf of children's needs to parents, school administrators, business and community representatives, and policymakers.*
  EXAMPLE: Teachers join professional organizations such as the National Association for the Education of Young Children, Association for Childhood Education International, or Day Care and Child Development Council of America. Teachers also join specialized child advocacy groups such as the Children's Defense Fund or the Alliance for Better Child Care as a means to exert political power and ensure the well-being of young children.

Respect for children encompasses all we do and implies a concern that regularly results in special moments of satisfaction. As a respectful teacher, you will find extraordinary joy, excitement, and personal fulfillment as each day unfolds. One of the most flattering compliments you will receive is to have someone sense your respect and call you a "gentle" or "caring" teacher—a teacher like the one described by James L. Hymes, Jr., in the following passage.

There is a gift each and every young child would love—the gift of gentleness. Your soft voice . . . your friendly eyes . . . the reassuring set of your whole body, unhurried and pleased and supporting. Each and every child would love—and needs—the gentle gift of your best and nicest and cheeriest self. Your gift of gentleness warms children about themselves, and they have to live with themselves their whole life long. Your gift warms children about people, and they must live with people all their lives. Your praise, your smile, your personalized attention, the time you make to chat alone with

We demonstrate respect for children through our actions and words.

a child; your quiet, intimate explanation instead of the public rebuke...your good humor that saves a situation...these are the great gifts. They please a child and help make a world.[4]

Teachers who are able to offer children such gifts and gain pleasure from the process of doing so reflect a personal characteristic that is especially difficult to describe with any commonly agreed upon list of criteria. But, simply put, they are all *good people*. Teachers of young children must be among the best people we know, for everything they do—even the most seemingly insignificant chore—really makes a difference in young children's lives. Conversely, people without good intentions often display behaviors and temperament detrimental to positive growth and development.

Good teachers realize their responsibility and use every approach at their disposal to bring a young child's world to life. They guide the youngsters and help them reach their fullest potential through techniques, activities, and strategies that grow from plentiful knowledge, creativity, and sensitivity. Good teachers never achieve total satisfaction with the job they do. They have a spirit of inquiry, realizing that there is always so much more to know. Good teachers can never stop; their minds must constantly seek to learn more and more. As a good teacher you must sacrifice, but you will find it worth the effort when, for example, a little child asks you to bend down, and plants an apple-juice-and-cracker-crumb kiss on your cheek, declaring, "I really like you lots."

As an individual interested in a career with young children, you become trusted by parents, colleagues, and the community as someone who can make a significantly positive contribution to the growth and development of young children. You must prepare for this responsibility by examining and reexamining your personal characteristics as you progress through your training. By doing so, you will enter the profession as a confident, responsible, happy person, willing and able to move forward in the development of a unique teaching style.

PROFESSIONAL CHARACTERISTICS OF GOOD TEACHERS

Have you ever been so swayed by an individual's ability to engage the interest of young children that you categorized the individual as a "natural teacher"? The implication of such an assertion is that the individual's personality automatically allows him or her to achieve the same degree of success in teaching young children as another individual who has received sound professional training. Although this emphasis on the value of an individual's personality in the making of a successful teacher is good, the approach does not do justice to the importance of professional training. L. B. Graham and B. A. Persky offer the following example of how an untrained person, although well meaning, may lack some of the specific knowledge or skills necessary to maximize developmental opportunities for the very young.

> The untrained person, recognizing the importance of establishing rapport and communication with a child, will show a book to a toddler and ask, "Do you like the pretty pictures?" She does not realize that a question asked in this way boxes the child into a "yes" or "no" response. The person who understands that there is a relationship between thought and language and that verbal interaction can promote thinking skills will word her comments so that they evoke a more thoughtful and complex response—e.g., "Why do you think the puppy is running after the little boy?" This can be the beginning of a conversation and an exchange of ideas rather than a simple question and answer episode.[5]

In early childhood settings, situations arise each day that call for informed, highly constructive, professional responses. Learning how to make sense out of the complicated world of teaching is a tough job. Similarly, you have probably heard the cynicism of individuals who look only at the surface of things and underestimate the colossal importance of your professional program. They may say, in essence, "Preschool's only play; this is just a fun time until 'real' school begins." Or you may hear, "Anybody can teach preschoolers. What do teachers do all day . . . set out puzzles? Mix the paint? Stand out on the playground while the kids scurry around for awhile? Why, anybody can do that!" In the following passage, James L. Hymes, Jr., points out that one way of coping with such accusations is to admit their validity.

> Anybody *can* mix the paints—you can learn how in a jiffy. Anybody *can* set out the puzzles; there is nothing very complex here. Almost anybody can learn to read a story and supervise blocks and watch dramatic play. The accusation is true. There is only one thing wrong with it: It misses the whole point of [early childhood] education! Paints, blocks, stories, puzzles, boards, barrels, boxes—these are simply the means to an end! These are the gadgets we use.[6]

Well-informed teachers look deeper into what goes into their work and profoundly understand that there is much more to those "gadgets" than many would believe. Materials are the substance of the program. Existing by themselves, they are of little or no benefit, but in the hands of a skilled teacher, they are the items necessary for creating happy, strong, content, informed individuals. All the materials we use involve the children in serious work and, with proper guidance, help them acquire important skills, knowledge, and sensitivities. What can the teacher accomplish through the use of these materials? Among the multitude of possibilities, we can expect children to learn that:

1. A group setting is a pleasant place to be.
2. They are accepted with friendliness and respect by the teacher and their peers.
3. They can satisfy their eager minds by getting new ideas, broadening the ideas they have, discovering new relationships, and deepening their zest for learning.
4. They are able freely and creatively to communicate their ideas, feelings, and impressions about the world around them through the use of words and other media.
5. Their strong drive to be physically active can be satisfied through a variety of large-muscle activities.
6. Their strong quest for independence is encouraged, but now somewhat curbed by a growing realization that they must share and work along with others.
7. They can do things for themselves: button buttons, tie shoes, pour juice, and wipe up a spill.
8. Their bodies require rest, exercise, good nutrition, and safe, healthful behavior in order to achieve maximum potential for growth.

Special child development and methods courses will focus on the skills, understandings, and sensitivities required to help young children accomplish these important learnings. In these courses, instructors will acquaint you with the nature of young children, various techniques and approaches to working with them, and special circumstances teachers typically encounter while working with children and their families. Field experiences, which are often at the heart of early childhood professional preparation programs, will give you an opportunity to move out of your college classroom and into the real world of children. Here you will have the opportunity to actually be with and learn from young children, in-service teachers,

Your professional training helps you acquire skills and sensitivities for working with children at various stages of development.

administrators, and parents. Ideally, these early classroom and field experiences will combine to help you develop the professional characteristics necessary to become a well-informed, respectful professional.

In 1991 the Association of Teacher Educators (ATE) and the National Association for the Education of Young Children (NAEYC) jointly developed a set of guidelines to inform decision makers about certification standards for teachers in programs serving children from birth through eight years of age. Their document does not promote any single approach to the attainment of early childhood teacher certification, but it does call for all teachers of children from birth through age eight to be adequately prepared with the knowledge, skills, and understandings specific to their teaching specialization, regardless of where they are employed. The joint committee identified at least five characteristics essential for an early childhood teacher preparation program:

1. Teachers must be educated in the liberal arts and knowledgeable about a variety of disciplines in order to recognize the learning embedded in children's activity. Early childhood teachers must be knowledgeable in various subject matter pedagogies to be skillful in interactive teaching strategies that advance children's developing understandings.
2. Early childhood teachers must be well informed about developmental theories and their implications for practice.
3. Early childhood teachers must understand the significance of play to children's educational development and develop skills in facilitating enriching play in early childhood classrooms.
4. Early childhood teachers must understand families as the primary context for children's learning and development, respect diversity in family structure and values, and develop skills in interacting with parents in ways that enhance children's educational success.
5. Early childhood teachers need to acquire the ability to supervise and coordinate their teaching with other adults. With the expansion of shared decision making in these settings, early childhood teachers also should be able to reflect on their own professional development.[7]

The intent of this position statement is to ensure that all young children and their families have access to qualified early childhood teachers. State departments of education, state certification agencies, and other responsible organizations are strongly urged to review existing certification programs in light of these recommendations. Because institutions of higher learning such as yours typically plan professional programs to meet established standards, the essential characteristics of the position statement should be a part of its policies and practices. The joint committee's standards for early childhood teacher certification are fully described in Appendix A.

It is intended that your professional training will furnish you with the knowledge and skills necessary to make the transition from college student to teacher effectively. It will help you act in ways that promote children's growth and learning within a safe, healthy, stimulating environment. It will help you exercise sound judgment while selecting and defending teaching goals as well as methods of interaction and instruction. It will help you view teaching from a professional perspective rather than from a student's.

As you study children, you will become increasingly aware of their needs for feeling adequate and happy, for exploring their world with active mind and spirit, for creating with a variety of materials, for freedom and physical activity, for protection and promotion of personal health and safety, and for living together as effective members of a group. The materials others may classify as "just for play" are used by trained professionals in highly skilled ways to help meet important developmental interests and needs.

We want to help you develop an image of yourself as a teacher, to push you toward the potential you have brought to this course. We want you to find *your* professional self by examining and comprehending valid information about teaching as you create a personal philosophy of working with youngsters. We do not want to coerce you into accepting any particular style, recognizing that we all achieve whatever degree of success we may experience in our own way. We hope you will combine your unique personalities with acceptable professional practices to originate something successful—take pride in knowing that it is your own.

CAREERS IN EARLY CHILDHOOD EDUCATION

Early childhood education is a broad term referring to programs designed for children "from birth through age eight in part-day or full-day group programs centers, homes, and institutions; kindergartens and primary schools, and recreational programs."[8] When we hear the term *early childhood education,* the specific types of programs we think of usually come under the labels *preschool, child care,* and *kindergarten*.

Preschool programs are mostly commonly half-day experiences designed for children between two and five years of age. They offer developmental learning activities, opportunities for socialization, and many occasions for play. You may often hear preschools referred to as nursery schools or play schools. **Child care** has been introduced recently as a term to replace the more familiar "day care" designation because of its more accurate reference to programs designed for the children themselves. Child care programs operate on a full-day basis to provide center- or home-based comprehensive care for children from infancy through age six; or for school-age children of working parents who need before- and after-school care. **Kindergartens** are programs designed for five-year-olds either on a half- or full-day basis in public or private settings. Traditionally, kindergartens were much like preschools—emphasizing spontaneous learning, socialization, and play—but they are undergoing controversial transitions that focus attention on academic instruction and an extension from half-day to full-day programs.

Child care and preschool or kindergarten programs are often found in such common settings as homes, churches, and schools, but nontraditional settings now show interesting growth potential: shopping centers, hospitals, health clubs, business and industry, and recreation facilities, for example. Regardless of where they are located, these specialized programs are popularly designated as "early childhood education." Because the emphasis of this book is on infants and preschool children (through age six), infant, preschool/kindergarten, and child care strategies will be given primary attention.

CAREER OPPORTUNITIES

The field of early childhood education is a complex one, requiring a vast number of individuals to fulfill varied responsibilities. Most of you are probably preparing for careers as teachers of young children, but there is a much wider range of possibilities available to those granted degrees in early childhood education. Seaver, Cartwright, Ward, and Heasley identified five possible career options, with only one being specified as teacher (see Figure 1–1). However, since this book addresses the distinct

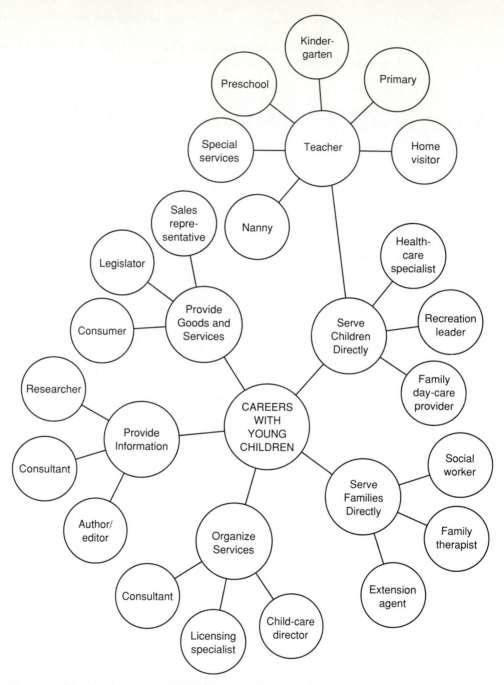

Figure 1–1 Careers with young children. From Judith W. Seaver, Carol A. Cartwright, Cecelia B. Ward, and C. Annette Heasley, *Careers With Young Children: Making Your Decision* (Washington, DC: NAEYC, 1979), p. 8.

professional skills and attitudes associated with working with children in a group setting, *teacher* will be used as the term to describe the roles in which most of you will become involved as you enter a career in early childhood education.

The field of early childhood education provides much flexibility for specialization as a teacher. You may choose to open your own center, manage an operation owned by someone else, or become a teacher or assistant teacher in either public or private schools—a vital, direct link with children. Depending upon your professional motivation and goals in life, the career options for teachers in the field of early childhood education are varied and plentiful. The National Association for the Education of Young Children (NAEYC), the foremost professional organization in early childhood education, has designated four hierarchical (arranged by rank) levels of early childhood teachers (see Figure 1–2). These positions are quite typical of most preschools, child care centers, and kindergartens.

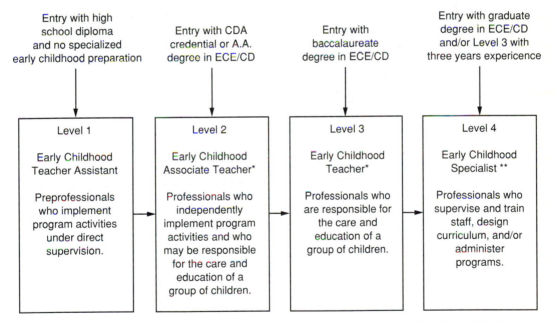

* Early childhood associate teachers and early childhood teachers may perform similar roles and functions. The different titles reflect the different patterns of formal education received and the extent of background knowledge of child development.
** The early childhood specialist can become qualified to perform a number of optional roles (such as program administrator in agencies with multiple programs, resource and referral specialist, parent educator, researcher, policy analyst) with successful completion of specialized education through college courses or formal credit for life experience.

Figure 1–2 Levels of rank for early childhood teachers. From "NAEYC Position Statement on Nomenclature, Salaries, Benefits, and Status of the Early Childhood Profession," *Young Children, 40,* no. 1 (November 1984): 52–54.

CERTIFICATION REQUIREMENTS

To care for and educate young children is an admirable career goal; the responsibilities you must fulfill in meeting this goal requires special teaching and caregiving skills that go far beyond those of "naturally gifted" teachers. Most states recognize the value of specialized training for early childhood teachers and have established formal certification requirements that must be met prior to entrance into the profession. These certification requirements are usually accomplished as students complete bachelor's degree programs offered by approved colleges; therefore, certification may be earned concurrently with a bachelor's degree and a major in the area of specialization—in our case, early childhood education. According to Pamela Lesiak Granucci, however, teachers become certified in early childhood education not after completing programs in early childhood education, but in elementary education.[9] As a result, many preschool and kindergarten teachers fail to provide developmentally appropriate instruction. Instead, they would choose to use workbooks; large-group, teacher-directed instruction; and other didactic methods filtered down from teachers of the higher grades—techniques disdained by teachers with a solid early childhood background. Therefore, Granucci argues that, as it applies to young children, "certified" does not necessarily mean "qualified." Granucci and others have taken forceful positions to encourage state departments of education to recognize the critical uniqueness of early childhood teachers by offering separate certification programs (or special endorsements) with a designation such as "Preschool-Grade 3." In 1988 the National Association of State Boards of Education (NASBE) recognized the importance of specialized certification in early childhood education by making the recommendations that: "Early childhood units should be established in elementary schools to provide a new pedagogy [methodology] for working with children ages 4–8 and a focal point for enhanced services to preschool children and their parents,"[10] and that, "Central to the implementation of the early childhood unit is a *well-trained staff* [italics mine] supported by knowledgeable and sensitive administrators."[11] The NASBE elaborates on the meaning of "well-trained staff" by stating that, "New efforts are needed at the local and state level to make preservice qualifications for teachers of young children more appropriate."[12] In 1990 Granucci found that only 11 states offered special early childhood certification programs; 24 offered only K-6 or K-8 certification; and the rest either did not report or had some combination of the aforementioned.[13] Obviously, the need for specialized early childhood certification programs is necessary if we are to expect developmentally appropriate practices on a large scale in our schools. Many early childhood educators are now sensing this connection and have begun taking an active role in articulating the need for specialized certification programs.

In addition to the four- or five-year college programs that prepare individuals as teachers, many two-year programs help prepare students with specialized training to meet state certification requirements. Graduates of these programs receive an associate degree that qualifies them to work as associate teachers, assistant teachers, primary child care workers, or aides. The degree, combined with a specified number of years of teaching experience, even makes it possible for individuals in some states to become teachers or primary caregivers in *private* early childhood settings. Although the associate degree indicates valued, specialized training in a chosen field of study, it does not culminate in certification to teach in *public* schools. However, individuals with associate degrees skillfully assume extremely responsible roles in private preschools and child care settings, as well as in public school settings where many work as **paraprofessionals.** The value of an associate degree is well recognized among early childhood professionals who point to findings such as those of the National Day Care Study to support their claims. In a comparison of programs the National Day Care Study found that programs having a higher proportion of staff with child-related training produced children who developed better social relationships, were more likely to persist at projects, showed significant gains in knowledge and skills, talked more, and became more involved in general classroom activities. And, surprisingly, the study found that the general educational level of the staff was not as crucial as the amount of child-related training.

CDA (Child Development Associate) credentialing programs offer a third opportunity for becoming certified to work with young children. Not specifically associated with colleges or universities, the CDA National Credentialing Program is a nationwide program initiated in 1971 by the Office of Child Development (now the Administration for Children, Youth, and Families) in response to the great need for trained teachers and caregivers in preschool or center-based programs. The goal of the CDA program is to develop a strong core of child care workers who are uniquely qualified in the early childhood profession. The one-year training program is open to individuals 18 years or older with a high-school diploma or GED. Previous early childhood experience is not required. The Council for Early Childhood Professional Recognition (created by NAEYC) currently administers the program; it designates a model curriculum for early childhood training built around six competency goals:

1. To establish a safe, healthy learning environment
2. To advance physical and intellectual competence
3. To support social and emotional development and provide guidance
4. To establish positive and productive relationships with families
5. To ensure a well-run, purposeful program responsive to participant needs
6. To maintain a commitment to professionalism[14]

These competencies are developed through the program's three-phase training program. Phase 1 involves **fieldwork.** During fieldwork, students observe and participate in child care programs on a daily basis. Phase 2 involves **instructional coursework.** Candidates attend a series of group seminars offered by a local college, university, or other postsecondary educational institution to attain command of the curriculum content as specified by the Council. Phase 3, which occurs at the end of the year of study, offers students an opportunity to *integrate their fieldwork* with their instructional course work and *participate in a final evaluation.* Successful candidates

Every certified teacher's responsibility is to help each child reach his or her fullest developmental potential.

Table 1–2 Types of early childhood certificates

Certifying Agency	Type of Certificate
Four-year college through the state department of education	Certificate allowing one to work as an associate teacher, teacher, or director in public or private schools (baccalaureate degree)
Two-year college through the state department of education	Certificate allowing one to work as an associate teacher, assistant teacher, teacher, or director in private preschools/or child care centers (associate degree)
CDA National Credentialing	Noncollege, competency-based credential allowing one to work in child care settings (CDA credential)

receive the CDA credential, which is valid for life. For information about the CDA program, contact:

Council for Early Childhood Professional Recognition
1718 Connecticut Avenue, NW, Suite 500
Washington, DC 20009
(202)265-9090   (800)424-4310

A summary of certification programs is found in Table 1–2.

NON-CERTIFIED WORKERS IN EARLY CHILDHOOD PROGRAMS

In addition to the positions requiring specialized certification, some programs employ personnel (aides) for the purpose of assisting with daily routines under the guidance of a certified professional. The kinds and numbers of aides and other personnel are usually determined by the number of children attending the preschool or child care facility. Recommendations for suitable adult–child ratios are presented in Table 1–3.

Table 1–3   NAEYC Accreditation Criteria Recommended Staff-Child Ratios Within Group Size

| Age of children | Size of Group | | | | | | | | | | |
	6	8	10	12	14	16	18	20	22	24	28
Infants (birth–12 mo.)	1:3	1:4									
Toddlers (12–24 mo.)	1:3	1:4	1:5	1:4							
Two-year-olds (24–30 mo.)			1:4	1:5	1:6						
Two-and-a-half years (30–36 mo.)				1:6	1:7						
Three-year-olds					1:7	1:8	1:9	1:10			
Four-year-olds						1:8	1:9	1:10			
Five-year-olds						1:8	1:9	1:10			
Six- to eight-year-olds								1:10	1:11	1:12	
Nine- to twelve-year-olds										1:12	1:14

Smaller group sizes and lower staff-child ratios have been found to be strong predictors of compliance with indicators of quality such as positive interactions among staff and children and developmentally appropriate curriculum. Variations in group sizes and ratios are acceptable only in cases where the program demonstrates a very high level of compliance with criteria for interactions, curriculum, staff qualifications,health and safety, and physical environment.
Source: Barbara Willer, Ed., *Reaching the Full Cost of Quality* (Washington, DC: NAEYC, 1990), p. 64.

In addition to these paid personnel, many schools and centers encourage the involvement of supervised **volunteers** to work directly with the children. These volunteers, usually parents, help the teachers with daily routines so that the children's needs can more adequately be met. They also serve to lower the adult–child ratios in centers with limited funds and have an important function in helping to interpret the varying cultural patterns and expectancies of the children for the teacher. Most states require volunteers to be at least 16 or 18 years old and able to read and write.

The personnel described to this point, then, are those who work directly with the youngsters in providing school or caregiving services to children. This category includes the director, teachers, associate teachers, aides, and volunteers. A second category of personnel, **nonprogram personnel,** also plays important roles in the success of early childhood programs, as these individuals furnish services that support or facilitate the programs. This group includes dietitians, food service personnel, medical staff, psychologists, caseworkers, maintenance staff, office staff, and transportation staff. Their professional qualifications will not be discussed at this point because most of you will be entering the professions mentioned earlier. However, all must meet the licensing standards of their states and the qualifications established by their respective professions.

Some nonprogram personnel may be hired directly by the school or center, while others are retained on a need basis. For example, special funds may be set aside in order to make medical attention available on a daily basis for those children who need it (the physician is paid only as services are required). However, a permanent cook or maintenance worker is necessary in child care centers because of the need for quality nutrition and for the cleaning and maintenance of a healthy, safe environment. Nonetheless, the major success of a preschool or child care center depends on a clear commitment from all program and nonprogram personnel, whether full or part time, to the welfare of young children.

SALARIES

Let us assume that you have satisfactorily attained the minimum qualifications necessary for a position in early childhood education. Enthusiastically you initiate a job search by checking the career development center at your college, by reading want ads of newspapers in the communities in which you wish to live, or by making personal contacts with administrators of centers or schools. Several places ask you to fill out an application. Should your qualifications merit further consideration, you may be invited to an interview. Interviews are carefully planned by the administrators in charge, not as inquisitions, but as comfortable discussions during which the organization gets to know you and you get to know the organization. Questions are usually designed to elicit all of the personal and professional information about the applicants that the organization needs to make its decision. Generally, you will be given a careful explanation of the position and its requirements, along with salary expectations.

It is this last area—salary expectations—that we in the field of early childhood education have been extremely concerned about over the years. Poor salaries, especially in the private sector, have had their apparent ramifications: Child care centers around the country report great difficulty in recruiting and retaining adequately trained staff; and nearly half of all child care teachers leave their jobs each year to seek better-paying jobs. In 1989 a report of the National Child Care Staffing Study compared the wages of child care teaching staff to those of the civilian labor force.[15] The average annual earnings of child care teaching staff holding a bachelor's degree or more was $11,568. The average annual earnings of the civilian labor force with comparable education was $26,066 for women and $42,422 for men. Salaries vary greatly within the field of early childhood education, depending on the sponsorship and type of program. In private preschool and child care programs located throughout the Philadelphia, Pennsylvania area, beginning teachers with a bachelor's degree could expect to start anywhere from $8,000 to $18,000 for full-time employment on a September through June calendar. Beginning salaries from prekindergarten, kindergarten, and primary grade teachers in public elementary schools throughout the same area were as high as $36,000 with full benefits. The NAEYC studied salaries for different roles within early childhood education along with those of comparable professions. Table 1–4 reflects the national averages.

Although public school personnel are paid relatively well, we should be extremely concerned about the conditions facing most teachers in the private sector. We must all be advocates for better compensation of early childhood teachers—our profession and our nation depend on high-quality services provided by adequately trained and compensated teachers. In 1990 NAEYC called for all sectors of society—families, employers, communities, and the nation as a whole—to further their efforts to improve compensation for early childhood professionals. Among its recommendations, NAEYC suggests that the following guidelines be used in making decisions related to compensation for early childhood professionals.

- Early childhood professionals with comparable qualifications, experience, and job responsibilities should receive comparable compensation regardless of the setting of their job. This means that a teacher working in a community child care center, a family child care provider, and an elementary school teacher who each hold comparable professional qualifications should also receive comparable compensation for their work.

- The provision of an adequate benefits package is a crucial component of compensation for early childhood staff.[16]

Given the importance of the early childhood years, it is crucial that programs employ individuals with the knowledge, abilities, and sensitivities to care for and educate

Table 1–4 Salary comparability across professions

Program director	
Early Childhood Program Director (GAO)	$24,340
Public School Principal Elementary Secondary$52,900	$45,900
Educational Administrators	$35,000
Health Services Managers	$30,524
Personnel Managers	$34,600
Teacher	
Early childhood teacher (GAO)	$14,100
Public School Teacher	$28,900
Registered Nurse Experienced; in Hospitals	$32,100
Entry; in Hospitals	$23,100
Median; in Nursing Homes	$21,300
Social Worker Median	$22,000
With M.S.W.	$27,700
Personnel, Training, and Labor Relations Specialists	$26,400
Teacher Assistants/aides	
Early Childhood Assistant (GAO)	$10,200
Licensed Practical Nurse In Hospitals	$17,500
In Nursing Homes	$15,000
Teacher Aide	$14,664
Nursing Aide	$11,500

Unless otherwise noted, all salaries are annual median salaries for the profession. The source of these data is the 1990 Occupational Outlook Handbook, U.S. Department of Labor. Salaries are reported salaries; for many school personnel, salary is based on a school year not a full year; annualized data would be higher.
Source: Barbara Willer, Ed., *Reaching the Full Cost of Quality* (Washington DC: NAEYC, 1990), p. 70.

young children. Once these teachers are adequately trained, they should be considered to have achieved a professional status and financial reward commensurate with others having the same or similar preparation requirements, experiences, and job responsibilities.

PROFESSIONAL ETHICS

The skills you develop in your professional training program equip you with the competencies necessary to plan and execute a program for young children. Important as they are, however, these competencies are not the only significant factors for your success in teaching. Equally influential is the code of conduct you accept as a guide to determine what you should or should not do while working your way through sensitive daily responsibilities. Situations will arise every day that call for you to choose from among two or more alternative actions, either of which may be a troublesome choice. Here is one example of such a daily situation (see box below). Read it carefully and try to arrive at a responsible decision about what a good early childhood educator should do. Discuss your response with your classmates and critically examine each solution.

Teachers are regularly faced with dilemmas similar to that of the working mother: "Should I do what is profitable (or what will result in the least amount of trouble) for me or what is right?" The choices in the sample are painful—to support the wish of a parent who has primary responsibility for nurturing the child or to maintain a commitment to satisfying the child's physical needs. The difficult issues confronting teachers during their daily routines are referred to as **ethical dilemmas,** times when conflict arises between two or more **core values.** Core values are those principles that form the moral basis of a profession's practices.

Conflicts among core values are quite difficult to conciliate; it is hard for any individual to release or compromise a prized value when situations involving strong beliefs are involved. This is especially true when something as important as the needs of a young child are debated. In our field, these five situations are consistently mentioned as problem conditions involving conflicts of values:

1. Discussing a child or family in a nonprofessional setting.
2. Implementing policies you feel are not good for children because the program requires them.
3. Letting children do an activity that may not be worthwhile or appropriate.
4. Knowing that a program is in violation of state regulations.
5. Dealing with conflicting requests from divorced or separated parents.[17]

▶▶▶▶▶▶

THE WORKING MOTHER

Timothy's mother has asked you not to allow her four-year-old son to nap in the afternoon. She says, "Whenever he naps he stays up until 10:00 at night. I have to get up at 5:00 in the morning to go to work. I am not getting enough sleep." Along with the rest of the children, Timothy takes a one-hour nap almost every day. He seems to need it in order to stay in good spirits in the afternoon.[18]

How do we resolve such powerful conflicts involving the needs of a child, the needs of a family, and the needs of a teacher? That is not an easy question to answer. A special Ethics Commission of NAEYC struggled for over five years with that issue and, realizing that many daily decisions required of those who work with young children are of a moral and ethical nature, eventually framed its Code of Ethical Conduct.[19] The code offers guidelines for responsible behavior and sets forth a common basis for resolving the primary ethical dilemmas encountered in early childhood education. The code is based on the principle that the well-being of any child is the highest order of concern to the good early childhood educator. Ethical behavior, therefore, is based on a commitment to the core values that are deeply rooted in the history of our profession. The spirit of those core values is reflected in NAEYC's Statement of Commitment (see Figure 1–3). The Code of Ethical Conduct is reprinted in Appendix B.

To see how the code can be used to help resolve ethical dilemmas, let us return to a consideration of the "Working Mother" dilemma presented earlier in this sec-

---

The National Association for the Education of Young Children
Statement of Commitment*

As an individual who works with young children, I commit myself to furthering the values of early childhood education as they are reflected in the NAEYC Code of Ethical Conduct.

To the best of my ability I will:

- Ensure that programs for young children are based on current knowledge of child development and early childhood eduction.
- Respect and support families in their task of nurturing children.

* The Statement of Commitment expresses those basic personal commitments that individuals must make in order to align themselves with the profession's responsibilities as set forth in the NAEYC Code of Ethical Conduct.

- Respect colleagues in early childhood education and support them in maintaining the NAEYC Code of Ethical Conduct.
- Serve as an advocate for children, their families, and their teachers in community and society.
- Maintain high standards of professional conduct.
- Recognize how personal values, opinions, and biases can affect professional judgment.
- Be open to new ideas and be willing to learn from the suggestions of others.
- Honor the ideals and principles of the NAEYC Code of Ethical Conduct.

Figure 1–3 NAEYC Statement of Commitment[20]

Teaching young children is a rewarding, if sometimes exhausting, career.

tion. According to Lilian G. Katz, one of the distinguished members of the Ethics Commission, the dilemma should be handled in this manner:

> In cases when parental preferences require a child to be excepted from standard program procedures and the teacher judges the exception to jeopardize the child's well-being, the teacher must respectfully decline to honor the parents' wishes. . . . [and] the teacher shall explain to the parents her professional judgment concerning appropriate practice and its implications for the child, respectfully, without rancor or hint of demeaning.[21]

Kenneth Kipnis, a renowned expert in the study of ethics, was asked to offer a philosopher's view of the incident. His response was:

> It is a cardinal principle of medical ethics that physicians not knowingly injure a patient. It ought to be the same for early childhood education. In my opinion, it ought to be a principle of professional ethics that early childhood educators not participate in practices that are dangerous, harmful, or psychologically damaging to children. There is a clear ethical limit to respecting parental authority. With firm politeness and as a matter of professional responsibility, the teacher should decline to honor the working mother's request.[22]

Both responses indicate that solutions to many of the difficult dilemmas faced by early childhood educators cannot be based solely on personal values, preferences, or predictions. They must be derived from the shared values and ethical commitments of all individuals within the profession. The NAEYC Code of Professional Conduct affirms the core values of our field and provides specific direction for sound professional judgments as ethical dilemmas are encountered. You are urged to seek guidance from the applicable parts of the code whenever faced with ethical dilemmas involving daily practice with children and their families.

YOUR FIRST YEAR OF TEACHING

Picture yourself ready to start your first job, full of high hopes and expectations to do well. You have a clear vision of succeeding and of exerting a positive impact on the lives of the children you touch. Successful teachers are made of such dreams; let these ideals guide you throughout your entire professional career. As Clark and Cutler advise, "Experience will tell you which to abandon or modify and which are beacons to steer by."[23] So, let your dreams flow as you anticipate a successful career; hopefully your optimism will be realized. The rapture of success will be yours as steady accomplishments dot your career. Note the joy this first-year teacher expresses as she recounts some initial accomplishments:

> It is working! My dreams are coming true. I found a teaching job and it's going well. Not perfectly, but well. I say things and they listen. I tell them to do things and they do them...I ask them to stop talking or to lower their voices and they actually do it. Or at least most of them usually do it. I feel like I am becoming an adult, like I am taking my place in society. And after all the schooling and all the worries and dreaming, it feels good.[24]

How to Grow as a Professional

This new teacher feels good about herself because she has successfully progressed through the first of four career challenges. These challenges have been described by Lilian G. Katz.[25] Katz studied the development of preschool teachers and described the first of four professional stages as a quest for survival. She elaborated as follows:

> *Stage 1:* You are preoccupied with survival. You ask yourself questions such as "Can I get through the day in one piece? Without losing a child? Can I make it until the end of the week? Until the next vacation? Can I really do this kind of work day after day? Will I be accepted by my colleagues?" (first year)

During this period, according to Katz, teachers need support, understanding, encouragement, reassurance, comfort, and guidance. They need instruction in specific ways of handling complex behavior in children, especially since classroom management problems can cause intense feelings of inadequacy at this stage. Katz went on to characterize the remaining three developmental stages of teachers:

Stage 2: You decide you *can* survive. You begin to focus on individual children who pose problems and on troublesome situations, and you ask yourself these or similar questions: "How can I help a shy child? How can I help a child who does not seem to be learning?" (second year)

Stage 3: You begin to tire of doing the same things with the children. You like to meet with other teachers, scan magazines, and search through other sources of information in order to discover new projects and activities to provide for the children. You ask questions about new developments in the field: "Who is doing what? Where? What are some of the new materials, techniques, approaches, and ideas?" (third and fourth years)

Stage 4: This is the stage of maturity. You now have enough experience to ask deeper, more abstract questions calling for introspective and researched replies: "What are my historical and philosophical roots? What is the nature of growth and learning? How are educational decisions made? Can schools change societies? Is teaching really a profession?"

The point Katz made in describing the four stages of preschool teachers is that the need for furthering your education and becoming exposed to new ideas changes as you gain experience. Just because you have completed a specialized professional program and begun your first job, your concern for further training should not come to a halt. Administrators usually realize this and follow a plan for staff development in order to make their operation more effective and efficient.

Commonly, administrators attempt to help new teachers face their challenges by assigning mentors. **Mentors** are experienced teachers who have gone through the same struggles and offer informal help during this start-up phase of professional development. Oftentimes, the mentor and beginning teacher work together to address concerns such as:

1. *Classroom management.* "Are you having trouble getting your group started, scheduling transitions, encouraging free interaction with equipment and materials, establishing routines, or handling conflicts?"

2. *Time management.* "Do you have enough (or too much) time to accomplish what you have planned?"

3. *Knowledge of children.* "Do you have a firm grasp of the developmental characteristics of the children you are teaching?"

4. *Appropriate instruction.* "Are you aware of the value of play and its central role in the lives of children?"

5. *Interpersonal relationships.* "Are you comfortable working with other teachers, administrators, or parents?"

A mentor might, for example, engage the first-year teacher in a simulation activity prior to the first parent-teacher conference if she feels this is an area in need of attention. Playing the role of a parent, the mentor approaches the teacher with a variety of questions or concerns. After each exchange, they discuss how a parent might react and examine other alternatives, if appropriate.

In addition to these training programs, your personal effort to keep abreast of innovations in the field can be enhanced by seeking membership in major professional groups. Three of those groups especially influential in advancing programs and policies for young children are given below:

Association for Childhood Education
   International (ACEI)
11141 Georgia Avenue
Suite 200
Wheaton, MD 20902
Journal: *Childhood Education*

National Association for the Education of
   Young Children (NAEYC)
1834 Connecticut Avenue, NW
Washington, DC 20009
Journal: *Young Children*

Day Care and Child Development Council of America
1401 K Street, NW
Washington, DC 20005

Participation in professional groups keeps you up-to-date with the latest developments in early childhood practice, research, and theory. This knowledge is important not only for your benefit as a dedicated classroom teacher, but also for fulfilling your growing responsibility as an early childhood professional—becoming a **child advocate.** Advocates assume active roles defending programs and influencing public opinion about those practices believed to be in the best interest of children, families, and the profession. They may do so by communicating with their legislators, but, as a single voice, each feels powerless to change anything. Consequently, they become interested in joining professional groups or other organized networks that lobby for the profession. These groups know the legislative and administrative process and can influence the path of legislation more effectively than any single individual. Our profession needs people interested in its organizations, for it is mainly through these organizations that policymakers listen.

By working hard to further your personal and professional dreams, you will be bound for success. For the ambitious, mediocrity has no place. One consistent thread running through the careers of teachers who excelled is not only that they learned, but that they were also willing to take risks. They tried new ideas, spoke out for their beliefs, and tackled assignments with uncertain prospects for success. They demonstrated, without timidity, that they would rather be challenged than safe and bored. It's a good idea to accept as much risk as you can early in your career; succeeding in risky situations helps identify potential greatness more clearly than any other factor. Those who take risks have a high degree of self-confidence, and self-confidence is a distinctive quality of most outstanding teachers. As someone once said, having a positive sense of self-worth is worth **50 IQ** points. So work hard, dream a lot, and muster up the intestinal fortitude to establish a point of view. However, risks cannot, and should not, be taken unless your fundamentals are solid. Risks are never taken blindly by outstanding teachers; they are founded on a deep foundational core of knowledge and skill. Build that foundation in early childhood education and take your risks there, for it is the one area of education that most openly invites the ideas and dreams of imaginative innovators.

SOME FINAL THOUGHTS

The most important ingredient of a successful early childhood program is a good teacher. The physical setting is important, but the skills and enthusiasm of the teacher are of overriding importance. The teacher's personality, attitude, and behavior determine the tone of the environment and make a lasting impact on the children, on their families, and indirectly on society in general. Few individuals are more important in the lives of young children than their parents, close relatives, and teachers. Teachers are admired and imitated; they are expected to display courage, cleanliness, honesty, openmindedness, generosity, faithfulness, sensitivity, tact, and other admirable qualities. Teachers of young children should be among the finest people we can imagine. But being a fine person does not in itself guarantee success in teaching. A superior teacher must also possess a sound educational background. The successful teacher is a person and a professional who considers it a privilege to be an early childhood educator.

Professional skills develop through an effective combination of education and experience. As they grow, teachers constantly reevaluate themselves, their children, and their techniques; so that they can provide the best-balanced, most educationally sound environment possible. As you are faced with career choices throughout the next few years, you will undoubtedly ask yourself two questions: Am I happy with what I am? With the skills I now possess, what can I become? The early childhood field can answer these questions because it offers many careers involving young children. In deciding which career is most appropriate for you, consider these questions now and as you progress in your professional training:

- Why am I interested in a career with young children?

- What do I enjoy most about working with young children?

- What special experiences, skills, and abilities will I bring to my work with young children?

- With what age child do I feel most comfortable?

- Can I work with children demonstrating special needs?

- Am I sensitive to the differences of children from racial, cultural, ethnic, or socioeconomic groups other than mine?

- What kind of early childhood setting is most attractive to me?

- How much responsibility can I handle while working with young children? Other adults?

- Do I find the contributions of early childhood professional groups and organizations to be of value to my career?

- How will I continue to accumulate specific learning experiences and educational background as I grow into my career serving young children and their families?

NOTES

1. Lloyd DeMause, "Our Forebears Made Childhood a Nightmare," *Psychology Today, 8,* no. 11 (April 1975): 85.
2. Albert Cullum, *Push Back the Desks* (New York: Citation Press, 1967), p. 19.
3. Stacie G. Goffin, "How Well Do We Respect the Children in Our Care?" *Childhood Education, 66,* no. 2 (Winter 1989): 68–74.
4. James L. Hymes, Jr., *Worth Repeating* (Carmel, CA: Hacienda Press, 1985), p. 7.
5. L. B. Graham and B. A. Persky, "Who Should Work With Young children?" in L. B. Graham and B. A. Persky, *Early Childhood* (Wayne, NJ: Avery Publishing Group, 1977), p. 336.
6. Hymes, *Worth Repeating,* pp. 4–5.
7. "Early Childhood Teacher Certification," *Young Children, 47,* no. 1 (November 1991): 16–21.
8. National Association for the Education of Young Children, *Early Childhood Teacher Education Guidelines* (Washington: NAEYC, 1982), p. xii.
9. Pamela Lesiak Granucci, "Kindergarten Teachers: Working Through Our Identity Crisis," *Young Children, 45,* no. 3 (March 1990): 6–11.
10. Tom Schultz and Joan Lombardi, "Right From the Start: A Report on the NASBE Task Force on Early Childhood Education," *Young Children, 44,* no. 2 (January 1989): 7.
11. Ibid., p. 8.
12. Ibid., p. 8.
13. Granucci, "Kindergarten Teachers: Working Through Our Identity Crisis," p. 9.
14. Carol Brunson Phillips, "The Child Development Associate Program: Entering a New Era," *Young Children, 45,* no. 3 (March 1990): 26.
15. Marci Whitebrook, Carollee Howes, Deborah Phillips, and Caro Pemberton, "Who Cares? Child Care Teachers and the Quality of Care in America," *Young Children, 45,* no. 1 (November 1989): 41–45.
16. "NAEYC Position Statement on Guidelines for Compensation of Early Childhood Professionals," *Young Children, 46,* no. 1 (November 1990): 30–32.

17. Stephanie Feeney and Lynda Sysko, "Professional Ethics in Early Childhood Education: Survey Results," *Young Children, 42,* no. 1 (November 1986): 15.

18. Stephanie Feeney, "The Working Mother," *Young Children, 43,* no. 1 (November 1987): 16.

19. Stephanie Feeney and Kenneth Kipnis, "Code of Ethical Conduct and Statement of Commitment," *Young Children, 45,* no. 1 (November 1989): 24–29.

20. "NAEYC Code of Ethical Conduct," *Young Children, 45,* no. 1 (November 1989): 29.

21. Lilian G. Katz, "Ethics Commission Member's Comment," *Young Children, 43,* no. 1 (November 1987): 18.

22. Kenneth Kipnis, "Philosopher's Comment," *Young Children, 43,* no. 1 (November 1987): 19.

23. D. Cecil Clark and and Beverly Romney Cutler, *Teaching: An Introduction* (New York: Harcourt Brace Jovanovich, 1990), p. 19.

24. Kevin Ryan, *The Induction of New Teachers* (Fastback 237) (Bloomington, IN: Phi Delta Kappa Educational Foundation, 1986), p. 13.

25. Lilian G. Katz, "Developmental Stages of Preschool Teachers," *Elementary School Journal, 58,* no. 2 (October 1972): 50–54.

CHAPTER 2

Our Historical Roots

Americans are a proud people. We consider ours one of the strongest, wealthiest, most virtuous nations in the world. Our national pride is often reflected in our educational system: Early childhood educators have historically reacted swiftly to prevailing social concerns by establishing and maintaining quality preschools, child care centers, and kindergartens. These dauntless "friends of children" (child advocates) have spoken out in a variety of forums to generate support for top-notch education and care of the very young. As someone entering our proud profession, you must not be content to confine your energies to the classroom; rather, you must be committed to the active support of excellent programs for whatever part of a day or week the child's or family's needs require. To understand this better, let us examine how influential child advocates have reacted to prevailing social conditions through the years to create the myriad early childhood programs available today. As you read, use the following questions to guide your thinking.

- How have popular views of childhood changed throughout the years?

- Among the many determined pioneers who have helped shape early childhood education into what it is today are Margaret McMillan, Abigail Eliot, Maria Montessori, Arnold Gesell, Sigmund Freud, James Hymes, Jr., Jerome Bruner, J. McVicker Hunt, Benjamin Bloom, Friedrich Froebel, Margarethe Schurz, Elizabeth Peabody, Susan Blow, Patty Smith Hill, G. Stanley Hall, and John Dewey. What were their influential contributions?

- What major efforts of the federal government have stirred growth and innovation in early childhood programming?

- How do we presently characterize and differentiate among programs commonly referred to today as *preschool, child care,* and *kindergarten?*

- What contemporary issues confront contemporary professionals in preschools, child care centers, and kindergartens?

▶▶▶▶▶▶▶

An Episode to Ponder

Picture three people, on their lunch break, sitting on three separate park benches beside a river that runs through their community. These three people do not know each other. For the purpose of our story we will call them: "Wise," "Care," and "Indifferent." "Wise," "Care," and "Indifferent" are reading the paper and eating a bag lunch when they hear a child crying.

In the river they see a 4-year-old child desperately clinging to a *log* trying to keep above water. The person named "Care" doesn't hesitate at all before jumping into the water and swimming with the child to safety.

Only a few minutes later, they hear the cry of another child and spot a 2-year-old in the river wearing a *defective life preserver.* Again the person named "Care" jumps in the river and saves the child.

"Care," exhausted from two rescue missions, barely makes it to the river bank before having to swim back out to save a child in a *rubber raft* that is quickly deflating from ineffective patches.

By this time "Care" is exhausted and when another child cries for help, "Care" asks the other two people to help.

The person named "Indifferent" replies, "It's not my problem; it's not my child."

The person named "Wise" says, "I'm going to help all right, but not by jumping in the river to save drowning children. I'm running up the river bank to prevent people from putting these children in the river without adequate equipment and supervision."[1]

The river scene described by Marilyn M. Smith is a vivid representation of the condition of early childhood education as it has existed throughout the years. The *river* represents the flow of life during the childhood years and the varied *flotation devices* symbolize the efforts of adults to provide suitable environments for children to help them successfully navigate the river. The contrived flotation devices didn't always work, but, as we watched the historical panorama float by, we realized that—as crude as some efforts may have been—the major goal of keeping children afloat was commendable in itself. Now imagine that we've floated into the future. It is the year 2000; we're going to replay the river scene and "if we have achieved excellence for young children, we would see them in safely constructed boats, equipped with a variety of educational materials, supervised by adequate numbers of adults who have special training to make the children's time in the boat productive, constructive, safe, and pleasant."[2] The joyous vista reveals that we have achieved the ability to arrange safe passage for all children.

Naturally, all of us who are concerned about young children hope that our vision for the year 2000 becomes reality. Herein lies the challenge: to help "Caring" people (who kept jumping in the river to save the children from drowning) become "Wise" people (who run up the river bank to stop people from putting children in without adequate protection, and to help "Indifferent" people become caring and wise people who have a stake in stimulating improvements for early childhood practices and policies. To do this we must first be able to stand by the shore of the proverbial river, take out our binoculars and attempt to fix a sharp focus on the children riding in each boat. A clear understanding of childhood, of course, is basic to all adult-child relationships. Our generation is not unique in this endeavor. Historically, our profession has attempted to fix a clear focus of children from "binoculars" fashioned by prevailing political, social, or religious influences. Currently, images are said to be truer because they are more scientific in origin; but, history has witnessed the interpretation of many different images of childhood, each influenced by those who had been "holding and focusing" the binoculars at the time. Some images have been more beneficial to the child's care and education than others. A review of these images is instructive and will be the focus of the remainder of this chapter. The purpose for offering such a detailed account is, in the words of David Elkind, to tell us "that the image of the child at any point in history never goes unchallenged and that the challengers in the past, as today, often come from the ranks of early childhood educators."[3]

OUR PRESCHOOL/CHILD CARE HERITAGE

Early childhood education in the United States can admirably trace its roots to Europe where revolutionary ideas regarding the status of childhood motivated caring individuals to initiate major efforts in support of the care and education of young children. European ideas of early childhood education were brought to our shores primarily by immigrants who ventured to America during the Industrial Revolution of the late 1800's and early 1900's to find jobs in factories and to search for a better way of life. But their dreams faded before the harsh realities of life in a new world when widows, mothers abandoned by their husbands, and immigrants with large families soon realized their incomes were not sufficient for survival. Many mothers were forced to go to work, which created serious dilemmas in their lives. Mothers were considered negligent during this time if they were not at home caring for their children. But could a mother be considered any less negligent if she failed to utilize her economic potential to earn money for her children's food, clothing, and shelter?

Some mothers, especially those who were widowed or abandoned, addressed this dilemma by sending their children to orphanages or foster homes. They were then free to enter the work force. For the large majority, however, the thought of giving up their children was incomprehensible. Instead, they searched for alternatives, such as the **day nursery.** The first day nurseries were funded primarily by wealthy philanthropists (charitable individuals) concerned about the plight of women and the lives of young children. The centers were staffed by women who provided nutritious food, adequate rest, sanitary conditions, and a healthful environment for up to 12 hours a day while mothers worked. Such basic group care that is designed primarily to address health and safety needs is today often referred to as **custodial care.**

Margaret McMillan's Nursery School

Not finding the limited custodial care appropriate, some leading child advocates in the United States turned to the emerging **nursery school movement** in England. This movement began in 1911 when Margaret McMillan opened her first school in Deptford, a highly industrialized slum of London. Like her contemporaries in the United States, McMillan was concerned primarily with the physical health of the young children; her studies showed, for example, that although 80 percent of the babies in England were well at birth, only 20 percent came to school in good health. She wondered what happened to cause so many healthy children to contract maladies such as rickets, measles, scabies, ringworm, and impetigo.

Convinced that such problems had already advanced too far by school age, McMillan chose to open "nurseries" for children younger than school age. Her nurseries, however, were designed to offer services going far beyond the physical care normally provided by the day nurseries of her time—by including provisions for emotional, social, and educational growth. For that reason, she called her facility a **nursery school** and her caregivers were called **nurse-teachers** to signify their combined educational and health care duties.

In an effort to compensate for the neglect that the children of the poor received at home, McMillan designed the school's full-day program to emphasize qualities of child rearing characteristic of more affluent homes. Central to her program was a self-caring aspect (buttoning, lacing, tying, washing, dressing, hair brushing, etc.). The self-care responsibilities included keeping clean—children were often bathed in waist-high tubs (a dozen or more children at a time)—wearing clean clothes, eating nourishing meals, and getting fresh air and exercise. This last concern motivated McMillan to design an "Open Shed," or open-air nursery school. The building had one side that opened into a garden or play area; children were encouraged to play in that outdoor area for most of the day. They romped in herb, vegetable, or flower gardens as well as in nontraditional play areas, such as "junk piles" containing mounds of ashes or nuts and bolts. McMillan valued these play activities not only for their physical benefits but also because she saw them helping children to control their muscles and develop sensory images (taste, touch, smell, hearing, and sight), as well as to acquire basic intellectual skills. Supplementing these outdoor experiences, McMillan provided children with many creative self-expression activities including clay modeling, coloring, drawing, and block play. Rhythmic movement and other musical activities encouraged the children to move creatively and extend their physical skills.

Margaret McMillan was a strong person who spearheaded the nursery school movement with boundless energy. Her book, *The Nursery School,* influenced educators for decades and was partially responsible for spreading the nursery school movement to the United States.

Abigail Eliot's First American Nursery School

Nursery schools, then, were created as full-day alternatives to custodial day nurseries, not as the half-day preschool programs we know today. In the 1920s, young women in the United States were given the opportunity to study at the McMillan Nursery School in London with the goal of opening bona fide nursery schools for young children in the United States. In the following passage, Abigail Adams Eliot, one of these early pioneers, describes how she applied what she learned from McMillan as she assumed leadership of Boston's Ruggles Street Day Nursery, and transformed it into one of our nation's first nursery schools.

When I walked into 147 Ruggles Street in Roxbury on January 2, 1922, the registered nurse who had been head of the Day Nursery there walked out. There were about 30 children, ranging in age from a few weeks to 14 years! The place was clean, and it was neat, but it was *dull*. Walls were dull green and bare; tables were covered with clean, shiny oilcloth—white! There were some irregular-sized blocks and a few worn-out toys in a box in the closet. No pictures, no rugs, no flowers—nothing pretty. And on a shelf in the closet we found some [educational games]—never used.

There was much to do. First of all we had to place the babies and the school-age children elsewhere. We painted the walls a soft, light yellow. We got some color into the place with pictures for the walls, flowers for the tables, colorful smocks for the workers. But most of all, we let the children use the equipment, and gradually we acquired more.[4]

Eliot went on to replace the adult-size furniture with child-size furniture and set up a garden and sandbox in the playground. Large group activities included music, art, water play, sand play, games and stories; independently chosen activities included play with materials such as blocks and chalk. The children were provided with sound nutrition during a daily lunch period and were given about two hours of quiet sleep or rest each day. Nursery schools similar to Ruggles Street soon appeared in various styles throughout the country. The distinction between a *day nursery* and a *nursery school* now became clear—the day nursery simply offered custodial care ("babysitting"), whereas the nursery school supplemented basic physical care with a planned daily program that included an educational component. Both offered full-day services.

Abigail Eliot believed that young children should use a variety of play equipment and projects—a value we continue to hold in early childhood education.

Despite the progressive dreams and good intentions of the nursery school movement, it grew slowly during the 1920s. By 1931, for example, only about two hundred nursery schools were in operation throughout the United States; most had been established for children of the poor from the inner city.

Maria Montessori's Children's Houses

At about the same time the nursery school movement grew in England and spread to the United States, a young woman named Maria Montessori originated a new system of caring for and educating young children in Italy. Montessori's glorious career as an educator has made her name as recognizable as any name in the field. Montessori, who was born and raised in Italy, was known throughout her life as a woman of many roles. As a young woman, for example, Montessori had no intention of becoming an educator. Her great interest was directed toward biology and medicine. Despite the fact that females had been traditionally excluded from medical practice in Italy, Montessori overcame all barriers and emerged as the country's first woman to win a medical degree. Her initial appointment as a physician was with the Psychiatric Clinic at the University of Rome, where she was responsible for caring for the insane. At this time, insanity was popularly explained as having physical causes. Because the behavioral sciences of psychiatry and psychology were not yet accepted as professional fields, the care of the insane came under the auspices of medical doctors such as Montessori. Also, because insanity and mental retardation were considered to be the same, Montessori came into frequent contact with retarded youngsters who were unmercifully called "idiot children," a harsh but scientifically acceptable label at this time. Montessori's original plans were to observe the children carefully and study their maladies, with hope that she could more effectively treat them. Her observations eventually led her to believe that educational principles rather than medical care would be most effective in curing such childhood problems as rickets, paralysis, deafness, and "idiocy."

First, Montessori observed the children carefully in an effort to diagnose their problems. Then she created an innovative, activity-centered, sensory method of education using **didactic** (designed to teach) materials as the focus of her program. Her efforts were so successful that all her children passed an achievement test that they took along with the children from regular Roman schools; not all of the "normal" children passed this same test. While others were admiring the "miracle" she had accomplished, Montessori began to search for the reasons that brought normal children to such a low level as to allow her unfortunate children to equal or surpass them. Thus she spent several years modifying her method for use with normal children. She was granted an opportunity to apply her methods when Edoardo Talamo, the director general of the Roman Association for Good Building, asked her to organize a school for young children from families living in Roman tenements. Montessori accepted, and her "Casa dei Bambini," or "Children's House," for children aged three to seven, opened in 1907. The school began opening branches in other locations as her successes became known.

Montessori's method was based on her ideas of child development. She believed that children move through "sensitive periods," stages of life during which they are able to learn certain skills or behaviors more easily than they can during others. Using this idea, she devised an environment with activities and materials designed specifically for the special needs of children during three basic periods of growth: (1) the period of practical life experiences, (2) the period of sensory education, and (3) the period of academic education.

Practical Life Experiences   Montessori saw care of the self as an extremely important initial stage in the educative process. Therefore, the first phase of her program was designed to address the following important self-care areas.

Care of the Person   Montessori advised that children be inspected for cleanliness as soon as they enter school. This included an examination of the hands, nails, neck, ears, face, teeth, and hair. Also, clothing was checked for rips, soil marks, or missing buttons; shoes are checked for dirt or scuffs. By encouraging teachers to do this, Montessori hoped that the children would soon begin to take interest in their own appearance. From this point, children were taught to button, lace, fasten, zip, snap, or buckle their clothing. In addition, children were encouraged to polish their shoes. wash their hands, clean their nails, comb their hair, brush their teeth, and so on.

Care of the Environment   As Montessori observed children, she noted that they appeared to take a great deal of interest in watching adults prepare the classroom for their activity or clean up once they were finished. Capitalizing on this interest, Montessori included activities such as dusting, sweeping, washing table tops, raking leaves, mopping, shoveling, setting the table for a snack, caring for plants and animals, and so on. Importantly, the children carried out these activities with scaled-down brooms, mops, rakes, and other instruments, not with toy-type reproductions of adult tools. Here we sense Montessori's strong commitment to a respect for children and their activity.

Muscular Education   Montessori sought to organize and control the children's natural movements through planned exercises such as walking, marching, running, kneeling, rising, bending, breathing, jumping, swinging, rhythmically moving and other simple gymnastics. She felt that muscular education was extremely important, not only because of its physiological advantages, but also because of its influence on learning. For example, she considered breathing activities important because they helped the child develop control necessary for the exact articulation of words. She felt finger exercises were necessary because they readied the fingers for buttoning, lacing, manipulating objects, and, later, for writing. According to Montessori, without such motor coordination, the acquisition of higher mental processes later would not be as effective.

Sensory Education   Sensory education was designed to help the child develop discrimination in sight, taste, touch, and sound through the use of graded didactic materials. The children were deemed ready to move from the earlier practical life experiences to the sensory materials only when they showed an eagerness to work with these materials. Following the children's lead, the teacher then slowly introduced them to the didactic materials. Each piece of sensory equipment exhibited two important characteristics: *gradedness* and *error control*. The *graded materials* increased in difficulty following the normal cognitive development that Montessori observed. *Error control* allowed the material itself to reveal an error. She considered these two characteristics important because they helped the children become autonomous, or self-motivated, learners. The following are examples of didactic sensory materials. Illustrations of the manipulative activities are shown in Figure 2–1.

- *Knobbed cylinder blocks.* Three separate wooden blocks with holes and three corresponding sets of wooden cylinders (with knobs on top) that fit into

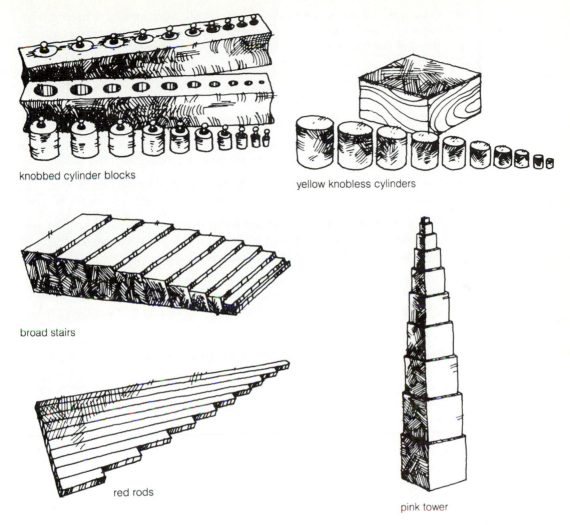

knobbed cylinder blocks

yellow knobless cylinders

broad stairs

red rods

pink tower

Figure 2–1 Sensory materials found in Montessori classrooms *(Nienhuis Montessori catalogue)*

the holes. One block has holes that vary in diameter only while the depth remains constant; another block varies in depth only while the diameter remains constant; and the third block varies in both diameter and depth. The children remove the knobbed cylinders from the wooden blocks, arrange the cylinders in mixed order, and then attempt to match each to its proper hole.

- *Pink tower.* A set of ten pink wooden cubes that diminish in size from ten cubic centimeters to one cubic centimeter. The child begins with the largest block and attempts to build a graduated tower so that the smallest block is at the top.

- *Broad stairs.* A set of ten blocks of wood, each 20 centimeters in length but varying in height and width (from one to ten square centimeters). The child arranges the blocks in order, from largest to smallest, so that they resemble a staircase.

- *Sound cylinders.* Two sets of closed wooden cylinders that are filled with materials such as sand or rice. The child shakes the cylinders, using sound quality to match each cylinder from one set to its match in the other set.

- *Musical bells.* Two sets of bells, one white and one brown, that are alike in shape and size. The child matches the bells according to tonal quality.

- *Sandpaper tablets.* Two sets of sandpaper tablets that vary in texture. The child rubs his or her fingertips over the tablets to identify two of the textures.

- *Herb jars.* Two identical sets of jars made of white opaque glass. The tops allow odors to pass but do not allow the children to see inside. The child matches pairs of jars according to likeness of smell.

- *Red rods.* Ten red wooden rods increasing in length from 10 to 100 centimeters. The child arranges the rods next to each other from largest to smallest.

Montessori's lesson technique was highly prescriptive; the teacher was advised to use each piece of material in a planned, systematic way:

1. *Isolate the object:* Children are exposed only to the object they will be working with. Everything else is to be cleared from the table so there will be no distraction.
2. *Work exactly.* The teacher is to show the children the proper use of the material, performing the activity once or twice so they can develop a complete understanding of its use.
3. *Rouse the attention.* The teacher is to display a lively interest as the object is offered to the children. The goal is to attract their attention to the new material.
4. *Finish well.* The teacher is to show the children how to put the finished material back on the shelf. Children are to carry each item securely in both hands and replace it exactly where it belongs.

This sequence gives some idea of the degree of organization that characterizes the Montessori approach. The sensory materials were not considered toys, but tools necessary to develop the concentration needed for later learning.

Academic Education   The final area of Montessori's approach involved academic learning. Montessori found that once the children had appropriate early experiences with the sensory materials, they were ready to be led from sensations to the internalization of ideas. An essential component of this process was the use of exact nomenclature as new ideas were presented to the child. The following example illustrates the procedure.

1. The children associate sensations with a letter sound. The teacher says, "This is *b;* this is *a.*" Immediately, the children trace these letters, which are mounted on cards. Once they master this skill, they attempt to repeat it with their eyes closed. The goal of the activity is to enhance muscular memory.

2. The children recognize letter shapes when they hear the corresponding sounds. The teacher says, "Give me *b;* give me *a.*" If the children recognize the correct letter, they hand it to the teacher. If not, the lesson is ended and begun again on another day.

3. The children recognize the letter and generate its name. The teacher spreads out the letters on the table and asks, "What is this?" They are expected to respond with the appropriate letter name.

Academic concepts were introduced as early as age four through this three-step lesson and through the use of a variety of didactic, concrete teaching materials. Some of those materials are as follows:

- *Geometric insets.* Ten geometric shapes that introduce writing skills. The children choose one alphabet letter inset and trace around it. Then they fill in the letter outline with a colored pencil.

- *Activity cards.* A set of red cards with an action word printed on each. The children read the word on the card and perform the identified command— "jump" or "sing," for example.

- *Sandpaper letters and numerals.* Letters or numerals cut from sandpaper and mounted on individual cards. The teacher uses these letters or numerals in the three-stage lesson just described.

The Montessori method became extremely popular in the United States during the first part of this century; hundreds of Children's Houses sprouted up in urban areas throughout the country. By popular demand, Montessori made visits to our nation to deliver lectures on her system of education. This popularity was short-lived, however, as discontent with her emphasis on academics grew among "child-centered" early childhood educators, who believed a higher value should be placed on expressive activities such as play, music, and art. Since the 1960s a revival of interest in academic instruction has led to what many have described as "the rediscovery of Montessori." Nancy Rambusch also provided much of this impetus with her "Americanization" of Montessori. Rambusch opened a Montessori school in Connecticut in 1958 and changed the curriculum to include greater opportunities for music, art, imaginative play, and social activity. Others followed Rambusch's lead and the movement eventually led to the formation of the **American Montessori Society** (AMS). Because the Montessori program is very specialized and requires at least one year of formal training from Montessori specialists, it is not described in greater detail in this text. Nevertheless, you should become aware of the basic components of the program and of its impact on early childhood education today. If you are interested in knowing more about either the international Montessori program—**Association Montessori Internationale** (AMI)—or the American program, write to the following addresses:

The American Montessori Society
150 Fifth Avenue
New York, NY 10010

Association Montessori Internationale (USA)
170 West Scholfield Road
Rochester, NY 14617

Growth During the Depression

After 1931 the steady growth of McMillan-influenced nursery schools continued; and by 1935 the number of nursery schools in operation had increased from only about two hundred to over nineteen hundred. What caused such significant growth? One factor was the **Works Progress Administration** (WPA), an agency established by the federal government in 1933 (and later renamed the Works Projects Administration) to combat the problems brought about by the Great Depression. The WPA appropriated funds to various groups throughout the nation to create jobs for the unemployed and to combat the conditions the Great Depression imposed upon young children. Nursery schools and day nurseries benefited from this funding; they not only provided for the care of children while mothers worked, but also became a major source of jobs for unemployed teachers. Although custodial day nurseries remained the most popular form of child care during this time, nursery schools gradually grew in popularity, for several reasons. One is that nursery school education gained status as a "profession" because its teachers had formal training, just as all other teachers had. The first of these nursery school training programs, which were usually located in departments of home economics, began in 1924 at Iowa State University. Another reason for the popularization of the nursery school movement was the eminently popular idea of child development being advanced by Arnold Gesell. Dr. Gesell wrote in 1923, shortly after the first nursery schools were founded, that:

The preschool period is biologically the most important period in the development of an individual for the simple but sufficient reason that *it comes first*. Coming first in a dynamic sequence, it inevitably influences all subsequent development.... This remarkable velocity of mental development parallels the equal velocity of physical growth during these early years.

The character of this mental development is by no means purely or preeminently intellectual. Almost from the beginning it is social, emotional, moral and denotes the organization of a personality.[5]

Gesell, often credited with initiating formal study into the characteristics of young children, made a strong case for the planned program of the nursery school.

Sigmund Freud's elaborate work describing the effects of experiences during the early years on an individual's future personality also captured the nation's interest during this time. Popular among the more affluent and informed members of the community, Freud viewed the first six years of life as a period of tremendous influence upon the adult personality. Freud explained that it is during this time that children are neither exclusively active nor passive, but always in flux between the two states. The flux is created by a constant battle between two forces: (1) satisfying unbridled natural instincts representative of different stages of psychosexual development, and (2) controlling them according to the constraints imposed by adult society.

The ways by which adults lead children through the conflicts associated with each stage determines whether or not a healthy adult personality will emerge. "Normal" development occurs when neither excessive gratification nor excessive suppression of sexual urges occurs during any stage.

Despite recent criticisms of Freud's theory, his original ideas made an immense impact on the nursery schools of the time. People became keenly aware of the nature of emotional functioning and of the importance of the early years. But, as important to the growth of nursery schools as this new information on childhood was, it had a devastating effect on Montessori schools. Critics viewed the specific, rigid learning experience as contrary to the recommended use of make-believe and play so currently popular. As a result, parents withdrew their children from Montessori schools at such a rapid pace that, by the 1950s, it was estimated that fewer than one-half dozen were in existence.

To concerned parents, the ideas of Gesell and Freud were a revelation about the importance of the early years. Not wanting to send their children to the publicly funded nursery schools for the needy, however, middle- and upper-income families preferred to organize private nursery schools where they established programs directed toward meeting the special needs of children as described by Gesell and Freud. Those programs emphasized play and a warm, loving environment as their major characteristics. Not sharing the need for five-day, full-day programs, these parents shortened the standard nursery school week to the two- or three-day per week, one-half day program as we know it today. In effect, the nursery school (today's preschool) served the children's needs, while the day nursery (today's child care) served the parents'.

The Influence of World War II

As the nursery school movement grew, day-long child care—so dependent upon public financial support for its existence—slowly began to wane, especially as WPA funds were phased out. This pattern continued for a few years until the start of

World War II, when women were forced back into the labor force to assume the jobs vacated by men entering the armed services. Once again, day-long child care became a serious problem. The federal government intervened once more and passed the Lanham Act, which provided funds for the establishment and staffing of more child care facilities. Like those of the Great Depression, these wartime centers provided children with food, rest, shelter, and a kind, loving mother substitute. There was little or no desire among working mothers to go beyond this basic custodial care. However, some notable efforts were made to adapt the nursery school philosophy to child care programming. Prominent among these efforts were the Kaiser Shipyard programs which began in 1943 at the massive Kaiser Shipyards in Portland, Oregon. At that time, Edgar Kaiser asked government agencies to name the best qualified people in the country to operate his centers so that women could enter the work force and help turn out the ships needed for our war effort. Acting on their advice, Kaiser hired Lois Meek Stolz as consulting director and James Hymes, Jr., as on-site manager. Although the centers were in operation for only two years, the attractive facilities, trained professionals, sound health and educational programs, and constructive play activities provide a model of excellent child care even today. In many regards, this concept was so popular that it served as a model for other facilities and paved the way for future child care formats.

Shortly after the war, the Lanham Act was phased out, and federal support for child care services stopped. The Kaiser Shipyard program and other special child care programs slowly faded from the American scene. Once more it became the prevailing attitude that a mother's place was not at work but in the home with her children. But because the war convinced many that children were the hope of the future, parents and educators agreed that the child's early years should not be totally ignored. Therefore, preschools, with their established half-day programs, continued to grow in popularity through the 1980s.

Head Start

Custodial care remained the norm for child care programs into the decade of the 1960s; play-oriented environments best characterized the half-day preschool programs. But this trend was destined to change. In 1964 the federal government passed the Economic Opportunity Act as an attempt to break intergenerational cycles of poverty in the United States. A major outcome of the act was the creation of the Office For Economic Opportunity, an agency under which Project Head Start was administered. Head Start provided funds for the establishment of child development centers that were to offer educational opportunities for children from low-income families.

Head Start *funds* were disbursed to community-action agencies throughout the country in order to promote the traditional goals of improving physical health and guiding positive emotional and social growth. Head Start *guidelines* went a

Head Start was conceived as a comprehensive federally funded program.

step further and suggested that, in order to prevent failure in later schooling, these traditional goals be supplemented with provisions for improving children's mental skills. The arguments for this provision were:

(a) The earlier we start a child in the formal academic path, the earlier he will finish and the cheaper the total educational cost; (b) learning comes easy to the young child and we should take advantage of the preschooler's learning facility and eagerness to learn; (c) intellectual growth is rapid in the preschool years and instruction will help to maximize that growth while failure to provide appropriate intellectual stimulation may curtail the child's ultimate level of achievement and (d) traditional preschool experience is too soft, too directed toward emotional well-being and too little concerned with cognitive stimulation.[6]

Experimental Head Start programs sprang up around the country. Social workers, medical personnel, parents, and teachers worked together in this nationwide effort to develop comprehensive programs. Each group assumed special responsibilities. *Social workers* identified the need for clothing, food, toys, and learning materials that were absent from the home. Where child-rearing practices were involved, they were responsible for conducting parent or parent-child counseling sessions. *Medical personnel* examined the children and provided care when needed. In addition, they stressed good nutritional practices. *Parents* did volunteer work in the classroom and helped establish programs and formulate policies for the community preschools. They were also often asked to try learning activities with their children at home. *Teachers* were responsible for planning and providing the high-priority learning activities and for coordinating the efforts of the supporting personnel at Head Start centers.

The Effectiveness of Head Start   Early short-range studies of the effectiveness of various Head Start programs were predominantly positive. The short-range data showed evidence of growing interest in school, gains in I.Q. scores, better results on reading readiness or language tests, and even growth in initiative, imagination, and expressiveness. Although encouraged, project directors and researchers were, nevertheless, looking for long-range studies; these would give a better idea of the lasting effectiveness of Head Start experiences. But these findings were disappointing: They did not show the positive results most had anticipated. Researchers found that the original gains were short-lived. The programs failed to produce any growth that persisted into the early elementary grades. Since these early studies, the effectiveness of early intervention programs such as Head Start has been hotly debated. New evidence based on the longitudinal studies of Schweinhart and Weikart suggests that the effects of early intervention programs last for years, past the early elementary school grades. One study followed 123 low-income African-American children with low I.Q.'s from their preschool years through age 19. Half the group attended preschool at the Perry Elementary School in Ypsilanti, Michigan, and the other half received no preschool education. The results indicated that the preschoolers spent less time in special education classes, had higher attendance rates, graduated from high school in greater numbers, received less public assistance, and stayed out of trouble with the law. Those results once again stressed the importance of the early years and provided increased interest in federal funding for early intervention programs.

Head Start, now well over 25 years old, continues to be a viable comprehensive program that provides health, educational, and social services to low socioeconomic groups. As such, it has influenced child care programs by seeking to extend its services to accommodate the need for full-day care for infants, toddlers, and preschool children—so that unemployed mothers, especially those in single-parent homes, can work and become self-sufficient. The research and innovative practices spurred by the fascination with "compensatory" education (intellectual stimulation to overcome the effects of poverty) has resulted in increased interest in providing academic instruction in today's preschools, especially for children from middle and upper socioeconomic groups.

Most of the interest in early academics comes today from middle and upper socioeconomic couples who were the "baby boom" babies of the 1950s and have waited until they were successful in their careers before starting a family. These parents, often having planned for only one child, have looked at what preschool education can do for the children from low-income families and ask, "If enriching the environment can do so much to raise the intelligence of underprivileged children, what about ours?" During the 1980s these success-driven families invaded preschools around the country, each trying to "raise the smartest kid in America." These competitive contemporary parents possess a great drive to perform their jobs well and to raise their children successfully. These parents are not only older and more competitive; they are richer, as well. They are identified by what they have achieved and want their children to be a part of their success. They will settle for no less than the best money can buy, and they immerse their children in whatever early experiences they deem necessary for future success. They have become the single greatest group influencing preschool education today. You will read more about the influence of these parents on the early childhood curriculum in Chapter 3.

Head Start raised some serious questions in the public's mind; among the most crucial was the question, "What is the role of play in early education?"

OUR KINDERGARTEN HERITAGE

Kindergarten, although emerging from the same era as the original day nurseries and nursery schools, has a unique origin and notable history. It was started in 1837 by Friedrich Froebel, a man of varied life experiences. Froebel satisfied a lifelong interest in children with a school that placed high priority upon the active nature of children and their spirit to learn. Concerned with the overwhelmingly restrictive child-rearing and educational practices of his time, Froebel sought alternatives. Unlike today's kindergarten programs, which accept children of five, Froebel's first kindergarten accepted children from one to seven years of age. Froebel chose the word *Kindergarten* ("children's garden") for his school because he frequently compared the development of young children to leaves, plants, or gardens. With proper love and care, the child grows naturally and blooms into full beauty.

Friedrich Froebel's Kindergarten

Friedrich Froebel's philosophy can be readily understood by examining the poem (see box below) that he wrote for his program. In it, he utilizes "thirsty plants" as a metaphor for children.

Froebel developed a carefully planned, systematic program in which the teacher was responsible for "cultivating and nurturing" the child. He based his curriculum on the idea of play—a revolutionary idea in 1837. During Froebel's time, play was not completely understood; most who did believe in its value saw it only as an activity having no particular educational benefit. But Froebel believed in the educational value of play. With this goal in mind, he designed three basic elements for his curriculum: *Gifts, Occupations,* and *Mother Plays.*

> ▶▶▶▶▶▶
>
> Now the garden-beds are blooming,
> Water-pot in hand we're coming,
> All the thirsty plants to sprinkle,
> All the birds begin to twinkle,
> Scatter now their perfume rare,
> They open their petals one by one,
> They roll out their cups to the glowing sun,
> Rewarding all our tender care.
>
> From *Mother-Play and Nursery Songs*
> by Friedrich Froebel (1878)

Gifts were concrete objects to be manipulated by the children in accordance with the teacher's instructions. They were to be used for learning colors, shapes, and concepts of counting, measuring, contrasting, and comparing. The first Gift, originally intended for infants and toddlers, was a set of six colored worsted (smooth, hard woolen surface) balls with six lengths of yarn the same colors as the balls. The Gift was to teach color recognition and to serve as a valuable plaything. Froebel's **law of universal unity** was abstractly applied to the use of the balls and to the other Gifts as well. In this instance, by moving their hands over the smooth, hard surface, children would begin to sense the ball as a symbol of unity between man and the divine. The following song was used in a learning activity involving colorful cloth-covered balls:

> Now take this little ball
> And do not let it fall,
> Balls of yellow, red, and blue
> Some for me and some for you.
> Now take this little ball
> And do not let it fall
> Hold it in your hand
> Then quite still let it stand
> Balls of yellow, blue, and red
> You are round just like my head.
> Hold it in your hand
> Then quite still let it stand.[7]

Notice how concepts of size, shape, and color were introduced and reinforced through this hands-on, joyful learning experience.

The second Gift consisted of a wooden ball, a cube, and a cylinder. Each object was to be used repeatedly in situations such as the following:

Step 1: Hide the cube in your hand and sing to the child:
"I see now the hand alone.
Where, oh, where can cube be gone?"
Purpose: To encourage the child to fix his attention in an effort to find the cube.

Step 2: Open the concealing hand and sing to the child:
"Aha! Aha!
My hand has hid the cube with care.
While you looked for it everywhere.
See, it is here!
Look at it, dear."
Purpose: To encourage the child to look at the cube sharply and compare it to the hand.

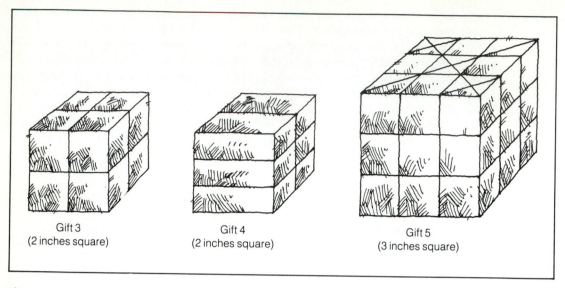

Gift 3
(2 inches square)

Gift 4
(2 inches square)

Gift 5
(3 inches square)

Figure 2–2 Froebel's Gifts 3 through 5

Step 3: Clasp the cube again, allowing one surface to be seen, and sing to the child:
"Only one side here you see.
Where can now the others be?"
Purpose: To understand that several parts compose the whole.[8]

As this passage illustrates, Froebel encouraged children to observe the Gifts carefully and to recognize similarities and differences through their use. The third through sixth Gifts were sets of wooden cubes, each set subdivided into smaller blocks of different sizes and shapes (see Figure 2–2).

Notice that the fifth Gift consisted of 27 one-inch cubes (three bisected and three quadrasected). The sixth Gift was also a three-inch cube, but with an even more sophisticated division—three bisected one-inch squares and six quadrasected squares! The third through sixth Gifts were presented as whole cubes to the children, separated into parts according to Froebel's directions, and always returned to the whole. Gifts 7 through 10 consisted of various other mathematics-oriented materials:

- Gift 7: colored square and triangular tablets
- Gift 8: small wooden sticks
- Gift 9: circular metal rings
- Gift 10: beans, pebbles, seeds, and other natural objects

Because Froebel's philosophy reflected a strong belief that mathematics should be the starting point of all education, the Gifts were specifically designed as basic materials to gain mathematics experiences. Initially, the child would be encouraged

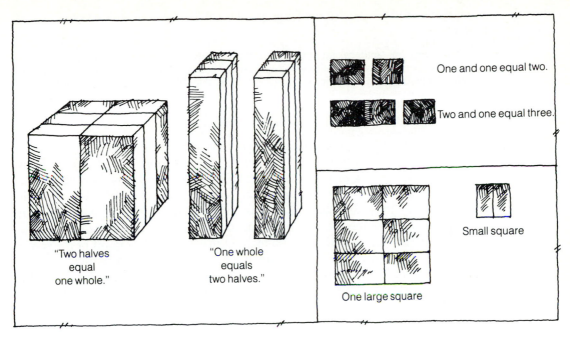

One and one equal two.

Two and one equal three.

"Two halves equal one whole."

"One whole equals two halves."

Small square

One large square

Figure 2–3 Mathematical concepts taught by Froebel's Gift 4

to explore the Gifts freely, but then, with the teacher's guidance, the child would manipulate the Gifts in predetermined ways. For example, the child would divide Gift 4 into two equal parts while accompanying the action with the words, "One whole equals two halves; two halves equal one whole." Because Froebel recognized the relationship between language and learning, words always accompanied action in his approach.

As Figure 2–3 illustrates, the mathematical concepts presented by the Gifts were not limited to fractions. Number combinations and geometry were also taught in this innovative manner.

Occupations were basically such craft-type activities as making designs by poking holes in paper with sharply pointed sticks, sewing outlines on pattern cards, cutting with scissors, folding paper, weaving, drawing, and modeling with clay. **Mother Plays** were simple songs, poems, or games that Froebel suggested for use with very young children. These included rhymes (e.g., pat-a-cake) and other appropriate interactive activities for either teachers or mothers to use with their children.

Froebel's recognition of the educational value of play and his gentle approach to the teaching of young children were received with a great deal of respect and enthusiasm by teachers throughout Germany. Carrying a large box containing his materials, Froebel visited schools throughout the country to describe his kindergarten ideas. His natural magnetism and enthusiasm for the program resulted in eager acceptance of the kindergarten. Wherever possible Froebel demonstrated his methods and materials with children, but sometimes he used adults when children were not available. Kristina Leeb-Lundberg cites Froebel's firsthand account of one such session:

> There being not children enough present, I said, "If we want to educate children, we must become children ourselves." There was no getting out of it; all the dignified school masters had to become children again. They felt rather strange at it at first, but were soon so completely filled with the joyous spirit of the occasion that all worked together in perfect harmony. . . . It was not until eleven at night that we parted in a cheerful mood, and resolved to meet again the next day.[9]

Froebel's kindergarten program sounds innocent; yet in 1851, not 15 years after it first became a reality, the Prussian minister of education banned kindergartens because he believed they promoted socialism. The probable reason for such drastic action was that the minister had apparently confused Friedrich Froebel with his nephew Karl, a radical and outspoken critic of the Prussian government. Though that possibility was pointed out to the minister, he did not rescind his decree. The action so affected Froebel that his death in 1852 may have been a result of the severe disappointment and depression accompanying the ban on his kindergarten.

Throughout Europe and into the United States, however, educators promoted Froebel's ideas. The swiftness and completeness with which the kindergarten swept into the United States is discussed in the next section.

Kindergartens in America

Immigrants coming to American from Eastern European countries during the mid-1800s were often well-educated and, naturally, had strong feelings about the care of their children. As they moved into urban neighborhoods and searched for schools for their youngsters (younger than age six), they found to their dismay that there were few. The only schools available were for older children, and disappointingly, the prevailing concept of childhood in America at that time dictated that the children be taught in a strict, moralistic manner. Fortunately, however, the immigration movement brought a number of German women trained by Froebel to teach kindergarten children in a manner consistent with emerging European philosophies. They set up private kindergartens in their homes to serve their families and those of close friends and relatives. Soon word of the revolutionary kindergarten began to spread as American educators sought to learn more about that new view of childhood and method of child care.

The first American kindergarten was opened in Watertown, Wisconsin, in 1855 by Mrs. Margarethe Schurz, who had been a student of Froebel's in Germany. This German-speaking kindergarten was originally intended only for Schurz's own children and those of close relatives, but it soon became known to others. Schurz's application of Froebel's teaching materials, creative activities, and warm classroom technique attracted other parents, and her school gained widespread interest. The greatest opportunity for spreading Froebel's program throughout America, however, came when Mrs. Schurz and her statesman husband, Carl, attended a social gathering

Today's kindergartens offer a careful mix of free and structured activities.

with their five-year-old daughter, Agathe. Also present at the gathering was Elizabeth Peabody, a prominent socialite who was noted for her strong interest in the conditions of young children. Peabody was very impressed by Agathe's demeanor while at play with the other children, calling her enchanting behavior a "miracle" and asking how the girl had been raised. Mrs. Schurz told Elizabeth Peabody about the kindergarten, introduced her to the ideas of Froebel, and later sent her a copy of Froebel's book *The Education of Man*. Peabody became so convinced by what she learned that she established the first English-speaking kindergarten in Boston in 1860, and became one of the leading proponents of kindergartens in the United States.

The kindergarten movement spread rapidly from this beginning. In 1870 fewer than a dozen such private kindergartens existed in the United States, but by 1892 the number of classrooms had risen to approximately twenty-five hundred and involved over 33,000 pupils. Rapid growth was confined mainly to the large cities of the East and Midwest, where there was support from private associations like mothers' clubs and other philanthropic agencies concerned with the lives of young children. Interest in the movement spread to public school systems, too. Encouraged by supporting letters from Elizabeth Peabody, Susan Blow opened the first public school kindergarten in St. Louis in 1873. Although attendance at public kindergartens was not mandatory, enrollments surged to over 130,000 children by 1900. Professional organizations whose main interest was educating kindergarten children also arose at this time. The largest of these organizations, the International Kindergarten Union, became the third largest educational organization in the world by 1918.

Why was Froebel's impact in the United States so monumental during the early 1900s? Patty Smith Hill offered these thoughts about the kindergarten movement's being "in the right place at the right time":

> The kindergarten appeared on the horizon at the right moment. . . . Society turned to the young child as the one great hope, and kindergartens opened under religious and philanthropic influences all over America. They were located in the worst slums of the cities, and highly cultured and intelligent young women prepared themselves in normal schools [teacher-training schools] supported by philanthropists. These young women entered upon the work with rare enthusiasm and consecration to the cause. No neighborhood was too criminal, no family too degenerate, no child too bad. Into Little Italy, Little Russia, Little Egypt, and the Ghettos they went, offering daily care to humanity in its early years.[10]

Unfortunately, this initial enthusiasm about the Froebelian kindergarten in America was hindered by the fact that the followers of Schurz, Peabody, and Blow were unable to study Froebel's program directly. (Remember that Froebel had died in 1852, and his program had been banned in Germany.) Instead, they could study only under proponents of Froebel's theories in the United States, and these followers often advocated a more rigid use of materials than was originally intended. Programs in the United States gradually lost the freedom and activity that characterized earlier kindergartens, and interest in Froebel waned. An example of how formalized the instruction became is offered by Joseph Mayer Rice:

> Before the lesson there was passed to each child a little flag, on which had been pasted various forms and colors, such as a square piece of green paper, a triangular piece of red paper, etc. When each child had been supplied, a signal was given by the teacher. Upon receiving the signal, the first child sprang up, gave the name of the geometrical form upon his flag, loudly and rapidly defined the form, mentioned the name of the color, and fell back into his seat to make way for the second child, thus: "A square; a square has four equal sides and four corners; green" (down). Second child (up): "A triangle; a triangle has three sides and three corners; red" (down). Third child (up): "A trapezium; a trapezium has four sides, none of which are parallel, and four corners; yellow" (down) . . . This process continued until each child in the class had recited.[11]

Patty Smith Hill's Kindergarten

Groups of educators in the United States reacted against the rigid formalism that had crept into kindergartens, and sought to return to the more flexible, play-oriented settings originally conceived for five-year-old children. They turned for the first time to new educational reformers from America rather than to European philosophers and educators. Teachers were now searching for a scientific approach to study the characteristics of young children, an approach emphasizing formal observation and data collection instead of speculation on the uniqueness of childhood. Their interest in scientific information was given great impetus by G. Stanley Hall, commonly referred to as the "father of the child study movement."

Beginning in 1891 with a formal study of children's thinking, Hall verified that children are not miniature adults—they have skills and abilities much different from those of adults. Hall's students adopted his point of view and became interested in studying all aspects of children's growth and development. Arnold Gesell was among the most prominent of Hall's students. He and his coworkers Louise Bates Ames and Frances Ilg extended Hall's original research by observing large numbers of children and describing their intricate development in terms of normal developmental stages.

A popular educator, John Dewey, embraced these new views about the value of the early childhood years. He urged the immediate application of these findings to school programs for young children. His suggested program, often referred to as "progressive education," emphasized learning through real experiences and an atmosphere that encouraged healthy social and emotional growth in young children. This progressive philosophy was very close to that of earlier European educators, but it had one major difference. As Martin Dworkin explained, "In education, progressivism brought...a romantic emphasis upon the needs of interests of the child, in the tradition of Rousseau, Pestalozzi, and Froebel—but now colored and given scientific authority by the new psychology of learning and behavior."[12]

A "Progressive" Program   Patty Smith Hill, who became a leader in the "progressive" kindergarten movement, embraced the new philosophy and dedicated herself to reintroducing the concepts of play and purposeful activity into the kindergarten setting. Hill developed her concept of the "progressive" kindergarten while teaching at the Louisville Free Kindergarten with Anna Bryan. Together, Hill and Bryan proposed a program that used the child's personal experiences as a basis for learning. The program involved concrete, child-oriented activities and classroom play based on the natural activities of childhood, set in a free, informal atmosphere. It was similar to Froebel's original program, except that blocks, dolls, and other toys replaced his "Gifts," and more time was devoted to expressive activities like housekeeping, art, and music. Hill's creative music activities were so outstanding that some of her works remain popular today. She was the composer of "Happy Birthday," which was originally sung, "Good morning to you. Good morning to you. Good morning, dear children. Good morning to you." The basic form of Hill's progressive kindergarten became extremely popular and eventually became known as a **traditional approach** to early childhood education. The types of activities provided during a typical day are shown in the box on traditional program activities.

Dolores Durkin offers this explanation of why Hill's program resisted change for so many years:

> The reason might have been the general tendency of people to resist what is new and different, but it might also have been the tendency to hang on to what was difficult to achieve. Here I refer to the great effort required in earlier years to break out of the Froebelian rut. It is easy to believe that once the new ideas won approval and the new program was accepted, those who worked hard for the approval and acceptance would not be eager to abandon what they had achieved in favor of something else. Further, it is also likely that once the newer ideas became a program, inertia took over. How much simpler to do what was done last year than to try something different![13]

▷▷▷▷▷▷▷

TRADITIONAL PROGRAM ACTIVITIES

Work Period   The children choose their own activity—painting, working with clay, building with blocks, or participating in dramatic play at the housekeeping center.

Story Time   The children listen while the teacher reads or tells a story. The story is usually about children their own age or about animals.

Music Time   The teacher leads the children in singing short, simple songs in which the children are encouraged to move their bodies rhythmically or to experiment with rhythm instruments.

Outdoor Play   The children spend a generous amount (30–40 minutes) of time on the playground, using equipment such as boxes, slides, swings, tricycles, and digging equipment.

Rest Time and Cleanup   The children return to the room, where they are encouraged to use the bathroom facilities and to wash up. The room is then darkened and the children are encouraged to stretch out, relax, and sometimes take a short nap.

Snack Time   The children gather around small tables and have a half-pint of milk or glass of juice along with a cookie or cracker.

Real Experiences   Field trips, resource people, and other active experiences help the children acquire information and develop increasingly sophisticated ideas about their growing world.

Until the 1960s, the kindergarten existed much in the form conceptualized by Patty Smith Hill and created for itself a fairly comfortable niche in the educational establishment. Presently, although kindergarten attendance is mandatory in only seven states, approximately 97 percent of all kindergarten age children are enrolled in a program.[14]

KINDERGARTEN IN TRANSITION

The traditional half-day kindergarten has changed character during the past 15 years, subject to the same social and educational forces (e.g., the changing American family, working mothers, a demand for "high quality" education) that have affected preschool and child care programs. As a result of these forces, many new questions about the kindergarten have surfaced: What should be the nature of the curriculum? At what age should children be tested prior to kindergarten entrance? What is the value of a full-day kindergarten experience?

The importance of play was richly recognized by early kindergarten programs.

The Nature of the Curriculum

The issue of what constitutes an appropriate kindergarten curriculum has provoked widespread contemporary debate. Because of the same forces that impacted preschool curricula and caused a shift in orientation from a developmental orientation toward an academic orientation, we have witnessed a dramatic shift in kindergarten philosophy. The child-centered, traditional program has been replaced by a skills-oriented, academic kindergarten utilizing educational practices labeled by professionals as "developmentally inappropriate"—reliance on paper-pencil tasks, teacher-directed instructional strategies, use of workbooks and worksheets, children working alone on assigned seatwork, and a curriculum divided into separate subjects. In short, the kindergarten has become a "miniature elementary school." Through its influential publications NAEYC contends that academic kindergartens do not serve the best interests of young children.[15] They have issued position statements on the academic kindergarten and have offered suggestions for what is described as "developmentally appropriate practices."[16] As a result, many kindergarten programs are reconsidering their current practices and are returning traditional concepts of play, creativity, curiosity, self-esteem, and interest to kindergarten classroom. In Chapter 4 you will read more about the kindergarten child in the developmentally appropriate classroom.

Entry Age

Because of the shift to academic kindergartens, and new "developmentally inappropriate" demands placed on the children, the entry age of youngsters has been dramatically affected. Historically, the entrance criterion for kindergarten was that a child needed to be five by December or January to enter that academic year. Currently, 30 states require children to be five by September or October,[17] and one (Missouri) requires a July birthdate.[18] The purpose for this widespread three- to six-month shift is that children were often considered not ready for the academic demands they would face in the kindergarten. This "youngness problem" was complicated by the fact that many parents have chosen to voluntarily hold back their children if they were young (i.e., have a summer birthday). As a result, many kindergartens today are made up of 6- and young 7-year-olds as opposed to 5- and 6-year-olds in programs of the past. Most educators today react strongly to this trend. They say that we should allow children to be children and to adjust the program to their developmental characteristics rather than require the children to adjust to unreasonable academic pressures.

Testing for Entrance into Kindergarten

In addition to raising the age for entry, many schools require testing young children to assess their skills prior to kindergarten entrance. As with the issue of entrance age, this testing process has come under strong attack in recent years.[19] Evelyn B. Freeman states that, "Although many tests were designed for screening or curriculum planning purposes, they are now being used to determine such critical decisions as retention or placement in a junior kindergarten or pre-first grade. Concern has been voiced regarding the accuracy of these tests in identifying children for special programs."[20] If the tests are administered prior to the beginning of the academic year, results are often used as recommendation that children enter one of two different programs: *kindergarten* for those who are labeled as ready to begin; **developmental kindergarten** for those who are labeled as developmentally delayed (these programs usually span two years in length). If the tests are administered during or at the end of the kindergarten year, results are often used to recommend that the child be "passed" to first grade, retained, or placed in a **transitional class**—a placement between kindergarten and first grade where the children can continue to practice delayed skills and developmental abilities. There appears to be widespread acceptance of these practices today, especially by those who believe that children should be driven by academic competence. But, in reviewing the research on children who have had two years of kindergarten, Shepard and Smith concluded that: "Children in these programs show virtually no academic advantage over equally at-risk children

It is important that the kindergarten offer experiences appropriate for the child's developmental characteristics.

who have not had the extra year . . . There is often an emotional cost associated with staying back."[21] In today's society, then, children are judged as "flops" very early in life; there is little room left for the "late bloomer." As concerned professionals, we must not support such policies and must not wilfully set up roadblocks in our children's lives. Instead, we must be willing to work for change; to actively advocate change for more effective, appropriate kindergarten for young children.

Full-Day Kindergarten

The traditional half-day kindergarten is starting to give way to the all-day kindergarten in many areas of the country. Historically, schools have operated half-day kindergarten programs—one session in the morning and one in the afternoon. The rationale for this pattern is that five-year-olds lacked the physical and emotional endurance to attend school any longer. However, with contemporary influences such as the desire to offer more comprehensive programs and changing family needs, we are finding that more and more schools are moving in the direction of full-day kindergarten. A national survey of elementary school principals reported that 67 percent of the kindergartens in America are still half-day ones; however, 22 percent are now full-day, and 7 percent alternate the weekly schedule with half-days and full-days.

Table 2–1 Contrasting kindergarten schedules

| Full-Day Programs | | Half-Day Programs | |
Advantages	Disadvantages	Advantages	Disadvantages
Provide increased learning time	Cost more	Offer the most developmentally appropriate introduction to school	Do not provide enough instructional time
Offer more opportunities for working on one-to-one basis	Cause fatique among children	Provide for a healthier separation process from parent	Cause problems at home if no adult is present for the other half-day
Free up time to include neglected areas such as science, art, or music	Frustate slower learners	Allow parents to spend more time with children at home, assuming they can be there	Does not offer adequate child care for working mothers
Provide child care for working mothers	Invite too much academic exposure	Are less expensive for the district to operate	
	Require more space and resources		

Many surveys, although inconclusive in their findings, present the advantages and disadvantages of full-day and half-day kindergartens (see Table 2–1).

Mary Renck Jalongo[22] contends that, instead of prolonging the debate, educators should work toward creating a more constructive approach to designing excellent kindergarten programs, whether half-day or full-day. The *quantity* of time spent in school is far less important than the *quality* of the experience. She summarizes the major recommendations of the two most influential early childhood professional groups today (National Association for the Education of Young Children and Association for Childhood Education International) while describing these characteristics of excellent kindergarten programs:

1. *Careful planning and preparation.* Involve the input of parents and provide for in-service education of teachers as part of the planning process. Maintain a teacher–child ratio of 1:20 and expect to delegate many routine matters to qualified teacher aides.

2. *Curriculum development.* Recognize the special developmental needs of kindergarten children. Do not make the full-day program a longer version of the half-day program or a watered-down first-grade curriculum. Play and rest should be valued as vital developmental needs rather than as time fillers.

3. *Comprehensive and continuous evaluation.* Successful kindergarten programs do not limit their evaluation processes to sets of standardized test scores. In-

formation about the children's self-concept, psychomotor skills, and socio-emotional growth must be valued and supported.

These issues are central to kindergarten education today and will be significant for society in the future. Although most agree about the importance of kindergarten, there is considerable disagreement about which course to follow: formal, teacher-directed academic instruction, or spontaneous, self-directed learning; half-day or full-day sessions.

SOME FINAL THOUGHTS

Early childhood education enjoys a rich past, a fascinating present, and an exciting future. I have heard its early years described as a *playground*, the 1960s era as a *training ground*, and the present as a *battleground*. Regardless of changing feelings about what is right or wrong for young children, early childhood education has proven to be a responsive field, one that is keenly aware of its ever-widening responsibilities. Its crises are not new; as far back as the 1850s, day nurseries were a radical solution to the problems of one segment of society. In the 1870s there were those who began a struggle to spread the Froebel kindergarten, and later the Hill kindergarten, as a beneficial childhood experience prior to entrance into elementary school. Social reformers of the early 1900s worked feverishly to implement the nursery school ideas of McMillan and Montessori for this nation's centers. The ideas of Gesell and Freud during the 1930s influenced the development of social-emotional/play-oriented nursery schools, while altered family circumstances resulting from the Great Depression and World War II encouraged innovative day care changes. The 1960s focused a nation's attention on the plight of the poor; Head Start and other federally sponsored programs flourished. The 1970s and 1980s found the educational spotlight focused upon the importance of learning during infant, preschool, and kindergarten years. Inevitably, the future will present even more exciting challenges. What is controversial now will become mellow, and enticing new dilemmas will spring up.

How our profession will react depends on *you*. What new possibilities might *you* offer for what has been described as public child care for the poor, private preschools or child care centers for the affluent, and potluck for families in neither category? How will *you* evaluate the avalanche of professional and public opinion while recognizing what is appropriate or questionable? You will not be able to meet such future challenges by limiting your professional growth only to finding new ideas to enrich your curriculum. Certainly, you must do those things in order to grow as a teacher. But the future demands that you develop a genuine interest in social issues in our country and in theoretical arguments that are offered to support or criticize what is being done with the very young. Make every effort to keep up in the field. Look for advanced course work, professional organizations, or journals and magazines to help you emerge as a productive professional responsible for helping our young children and their families.

NOTES

1. Marilyn M. Smith, "Excellence and Equity for America's Children," *Tennessee's Children* (Spring 1989): 5–12.

2. Ibid., p. 7.

3. David Elkind, "The Child Yesterday, Today, and Tomorrow," *Young Children, 43* no. 4 (May 1987): p. 7.

4. Abigail Adams Eliot, "Nursery Schools Fifty Years Ago," *Young Children, 27,* no. 4 (April 1972): 212.

5. Arnold Gesell, *The Pre-School Child: From the Standpoint of Public Hygiene and Education* (Boston: Houghton Mifflin, 1923, pp. 2–8.

6. David Elkind, "The Case for the Academic Preschool: Fact or Fiction?" *Young Children, 25,* no. 3 (January 1970): 133.

7. E. O. Chandler, verses taken from her handwritten notebook. In S. J. Braun and E. P. Edwards, *History and Theory of Early Childhood Education* (Belmont, CA: Wadsworth Publishing, 1972), p. 72.

8. George S. Morrison, *Early Childhood Education Today,* 5th ed. (Columbus, OH: Merrill Publishing, 1991), p. 50.

9. Kristina Leeb-Lundberg, "Friedrich Froebel: A Friend," *Childhood Education, 53* (April/May 1977): 302–307.

10. Patty Smith Hill, "Kindergarten," in *American Education's Encyclopedia* (Lake Bluff, IL: United Educators, 1941), pp. 1948–1972.

11. Joseph Mayer Rice, "A General Consideration of the American School System," in *The Public School System of the United States* (New York: Century, 1893), pp. 39–46.

12. Martin S. Dworkin, *Dewey on Education* (New York: Teachers College Bureau of Publications, 1959), p. 9.

13. Dolores Durkin, *Teaching Young Children to Read* (Boston: Allyn and Bacon, 1976), pp. 12–13.

14. National Association of Elementary School Principals, "The Statistical Trends," *Principal, 64,* no. 5 (May 1985): 16–17.

15. Johanne T. Peck, Ginny McCaig, and Mary Ellen Sapp, *Kindergarten Policies: What Is Best for Children?* (Washington, DC: National Association for the Education of Young Children, 1988).

16. Sue Bredekamp (ed.), *Developmentally Appropriate Practice in Early Childhood Programs Serving Children From Birth Through Age Eight* (Washington, DC: National Association for the Education of Young Children, 1987).

17. Nancy Karweit, "Quality and Quantity of Learning Time in Preprimary Programs," *Elementary School Journal, 89,* no. 2 (1988): 119–133.

18. D. J. Walsh, "Changes in Kindergarten: Why Here? Why Now?" *Early Childhood Research Quarterly, 4,* (1989): 377–391.

19. National Association for the Education of Young Children, "NAEYC Position Statement on Standardized Testing of Young Children 3–8 Years of Age," *Young Children, 43,* no. 3 (March 1988): 42–47.

20. Evelyn B. Freeman, "Issues in Kindergarten Policy and Practice," *Young Children, 45,* no. 4 (May 1990): 29.

21. Lorrie A. Shepard and Mary Lee Smith, "Effects of Kindergarten Retention at the End of First Grade," *Psychology in the Schools, 24,* no. 4 (1987): 346–357.

22. Mary Renck Jalongo, "What is Happening to Kindergarten?" *Childhood Education, 62,* no. 3 (January/February 1986): 155–160.

CHAPTER 3

Who Are the Very Young?

Young children are special people. They come to your classroom brimming with a powerful exuberance for life, a matchless eagerness to unlock all of life's mysteries, and an intense desire to become the object of your respect and admiration. These are but a few of the unique traits of the very young—good teachers know such distinctive features and concentrate on them as they interact with children and design developmentally appropriate practices. They realize, however, that each child has his or her own special style and that to stamp labels of description on all children of a particular age range would be a professional disservice. Instead, teachers patiently tailor their classrooms to fit the needs of individuals. They understand that all children have much in common, but they also understand that each child possesses unique qualities that set him or her apart. Take pride in learning about children and creating a classroom environment geared for each distinctive youngster. As you read, use the following questions to guide your thinking.

- Why is it easy to become confused when studying the field of child development?

- To what extent do heredity and environment influence child development?

- What are some prominent research and theoretical convictions that help us understand maturation within the realms of physical and motor development, affective development, and intellectual development?

- What is meant by the term *at-risk*?

- What are Public Laws 94–142 and 99–457, and how have they influenced preschool programs in recent years?

- What categories of "at-risk" children are included under Public Laws 94–142 and 99–457?

- How do "gifted" preschoolers differ from other children of the same age?

- How can teachers adapt the curriculum to meet the special needs of "at-risk" and "gifted" youngsters?

▶▶▶▶▶▶

An Episode to Ponder

That Little Child Who Follows Me

A careful person I want to be,
A little child follows me.
I'll carefully guard what I do and say
And hope to show the proper way.

I cannot once escape his eyes.
Whate'er he sees me do he tries.
Like ME he says he's going to be.
That little child who follows me.

He thinks that I am tender and fine
And believes in every word of mine.
The best in me he must always see
That little child who follows me.

But after all, it's easier,
That brighter road to climb,
With the little hands behind me
To push me all the time.

And I reckon I'm a better person
Than what I used to be
Because I have this child at school
Who thinks the world o' me.

—-Adapted by George Maxim
from That Little Chap Who
Follows Me (author unknown)

Many lucky youngsters get off to a good start in school by experiencing the gentleness, patience, kindness, support, and understanding of teachers who truly care about them. The children's classrooms are saturated with tenderness and sensitivity, for their teachers realize that "lessons" are best "taught" through the interactions that occur with warmhearted adults—those "big people" in whom the children place their total trust. Young children are life's neophytes—relative newcomers who have not yet accumulated experiences to the point where they are able to discriminate the motives of adults around them. They accept events as they come and consider any routine interaction as the way things must be. Because they have no other yardstick with which to measure the suitability of care, young children look to you, the teacher, for a helping hand. You are one of the most significant influences in their lives, and they must count on you to help guide them through their formative years. You have accepted this breathtaking task willingly; you will soon assume the responsibility of taking a group of human beings, hand-in-hand, and guiding them on one of life's most cherished journeys—that delightfully thrilling excursion through early existence that we popularly refer to as childhood. You have taken this trip, but may now be facing your first encounter as a "tour guide." Certainly, you will have anxieties and fears as you assume this leadership role, but your itinerary for this remarkable expedition is most effectively supported by the wealth of knowledge that is available about young children today. Knowing young children is a primary consideration for your trip, but it is also critical to understand that children are all different from one another. Each develops at a unique pace. The children may not arrive at the point of departure together; they will not demonstrate identical needs, interests, and abilities along the way; and they will not be able to reach the destination simultaneously. They cannot all be transported through their early years with the same means of conveyance—some will walk through childhood, many will cruise, and others will fly. As a tour guide, your primary concern should be to discover the "mode of transportation" most apropos for each child's trip and to make the resulting voyage as productive, purposeful, and happy as possible. Do not hurry them along the way; allow them time to relish this priceless stage of their lives—for if they cannot be children now, when will they be? Istar Schwager elaborates:

> Just the way some babies cut their teeth earlier and some later, children mature socially, physically, and intellectually at different rates. And when it comes to growing up, faster is not necessarily better. None of us would consider pulling our children's baby teeth out at age six to make the kids more grown up. Yet some [teachers] do the equivalent in rushing children through essential stages of emotional and intellectual growth, before the "new teeth"—or the new skills and competencies—have evolved to the point where they are ready to serve the child.[1]

As your travel plan will vary for each child, so will their reactions to the trip. Never expect a "textbook child." As a matter of fact, if we were to do a true service for young children, a separate text would need to be published for *each* child; no single source can ever have all the answers for all your children. By the same token, don't expect to be a "textbook teacher." Each child is unique, and so is the relationship that child has with the significant adults around him—parents, siblings, grandparents, and teachers. Don't be afraid to supplement the professional knowledge and skills you gain from this course with your own instincts and common sense. The most astonishing thing about teaching is how truly personalized it can be.

This chapter, then, is an attempt to help you appreciate the richness and excitement of childhood. It recognizes that—although timetables vary considerably from child to child—certain developmental characteristics remain somewhat similar. This chapter attempts to combine information about children as offered in child development texts with material based on the personal observations that I have made during countless hours of experience and observation in preschools, child care centers, and kindergartens. Specific suggestions for enhancing social, emotional, physical, and intellectual development will be offered in their respective chapters.

CONCEPTS OF CHILD DEVELOPMENT

As you have read in Chapter 2, the scientific study of childhood had a noteworthy beginning in the 1920s with the pioneering works of Arnold Gesell and his associates. Since that time, attempts to add to our understanding of the complexities of childhood have attracted investigators from many fields of study—education, psychology, medicine, sociology, nutrition, and genetics, among others. As careful as most of these studies have been, the deep intricacies of life have yet to be explained with an all-inclusive, precise, completely agreed-upon description. Nancy Lauter-Klatell characterizes the uncertainty new students in the field of education must experience when faced with the myriad of explanations about developmental influences.

> How do we decide what factors influence the development of any child? Is development driven by biological endowment, so that some infants are born to become great leaders, while others will never amount to much? Or does environment (the settings, interpersonal relationships, cultural values, and experiences of daily life) shape if and when a child will be successful? Is development continuous, so that skills and behavioral patterns developed early in life remain? Or is it discontinuous: can behaviors not acquired early (such as an ability to form relationships with others) be learned later in life? Can a preschooler whose language development is delayed later become captain of the high school debating team?[2]

There are no simple answers to these questions. Uncertainties that perplex you now will only become more confusing in the years to come. There are many doubts, and few simple answers, about what factors influence children to develop as they do. The best answer we can offer the student at this point is that most early childhood authorities align themselves with the belief that human development is influenced by a complex series of interactions between the individual and the environment. But, that view has not always been popular. Early in this century, for example, the dominant view was that inherited factors alone accounted for one's lot in life. According to this view, if you were born "on the wrong side of the tracks" and your parents were uneducated and unskilled, that would probably be your life's condition, too. There would be very little you could do to overcome your inherited traits. Challenges to this belief emerged during the 1930s with the proposals of behaviorists such as John Watson, Edward Thorndike, and B. F. Skinner, whose views purported that one's environment could be controlled in such a way as to overcome genetic influences. As Watson asserted:

> Give me a dozen healthy infants, well-formed, and my own specified world to bring them up in and I'll guarantee to take any one at random and train him to become any type of specialist I might select—doctor, lawyer, artist, merchant, chief and, yes, even beggar-man and thief, regardless of his talents, penchants, tendencies, abilities, vocations, and race of his ancestors.... Please note that when this experiment is made I am to be allowed to specify the way the children are to be brought up and the type of world they have to live in.[3]

Early childhood educators responded with various reactions; for years, a nature/nurture controversy existed. However, as we now stand at the threshold of the 21st century, we find substantial agreement that heredity and environment interact in complex ways throughout life to jointly influence development. Such ideas were prompted by the instrumental work of Jean Piaget and supported by the research and theoretical convictions of other significant authorities. Many of these prominent contributions will now be described.

Finding time for vigorous outdoor activity is important for enhancing physical growth.

PHYSICAL AND MOTOR DEVELOPMENT

The least controversial of all developmental descriptions generated by child development specialists are those of physical growth: Typical heights, weights, and other **physical traits** are relatively simple to observe and evaluate. The characteristic physical measurements for each age, as well as the distinctive stages of motor development, are well known and anticipated by most parents and teachers. Knowing about these distinctive patterns and stages can be of tremendous help to educators; after all, the process of judging growth and providing developmentally appropriate experiences is greatly enhanced when we are assisted by specific guidelines. It must be emphasized, however, that within specific parameters, children vary considerably in their physical development. One child, for example, may walk with help at 11 months and another may not until 14 months; one child may feed himself at 18 months and another not until several months later. We must take into account that not all children will do the same thing at any given age—a combination of genetic and environmental factors will prevent that from happening. However, we know it is still possible to develop a general outline of what a child is expected to do at a given age.

Principles of Physical Development

Physical development is usually discussed in terms of what is "normal" for children at a certain age. For example, the average height and weight of newborn boys has been determined to be 20 inches and just over seven pounds. These figures were established through a process of carefully measuring and observing thousands of infants and arriving at an *average* weight and height figure. The average newborn girl measures 19.75 inches and weighs in at an even seven pounds. Both boys and girls double their birth weight by five months and triple it by a year, at which time their height will have increased by seven to ten inches. By two years of age, most children have grown another four or five inches and put on another five pounds, and most children settle into a regular growth pattern that enables us to predict their adult height. This rule of thumb for determining height seems to be as valid as the many other formulas that exist: double a girl's height at eighteen months and a boy's at twenty-four months. After the age of two, growth slows down to a steady two to three inches per year. You can expect a "typical" five-year-old boy to be somewhere between 39 and 45 inches in height, while a "typical" girl is between 39 and 44 inches. The measurements discussed up to this point should be considered only as *typical* levels of growth. Be careful not to think of them as *ideal,* for such a misinterpretation often leads to unfair expectations.

What is happening to the children's bodies as they experience these years of rapid physical change? A number of developmental principles help us understand, and that knowledge assists teachers in establishing realistic expectations for children in their care. Researchers and child development specialists have classified these developmental principles in a number of ways. I have chosen to condense their perceptions into the following categories.

1. *Directional growth.* In general, this principle of physical growth states that growth proceeds from the head down to the toes and from the center of the body outwards. The principle divides the body in two different ways:

   - *Cephalocaudal.* This Latin term meaning "from head to tail" describes the development that proceeds from the head to the toes. For instance, the child's head at birth comprises about one-quarter of its body, the rest being evenly divided between trunk and legs. In contrast, the adult's body is made up of about one-eighth head, one-half legs, and one-third trunk. The muscles closest to the head are the first the child is able to control. Therefore, infants placed in a lying position are first able to raise their heads, then—as shoulder, arm, and stomach muscles develop—they become able to raise their shoulders. Eventually they are able to raise the entire upper part of their bodies. Gradually, as leg and thigh muscles develop, children can raise their hips from the surface.

   - *Proximodistal.* Another Latin term, this one meaning "from near to far," refers to the physical development that works its way from the center of the body to the extremities. The child first learns to control the shoulders and pelvis, then the elbows, wrists, knees, and ankles. For example, infants first use their shoulder muscles when reaching for an object, but by the end of the first year they begin to use and control their arms at the elbows, wrists, hands, and fingers.

2. *General to specific growth.* This principle of development explains that the baby's original reflexive reactions progress from general to specific behaviors. For example, a pinprick to the bottom of a baby's foot may initially result in a whole-body reaction—kicking, thrashing, and screaming. Later the same stimulus may evoke a more specific, coordinated response, such as a quick withdrawal of the foot. The overall tendency in physical development is toward minimal, specific muscular involvement: large-muscle to small-muscle control. The child gradually moves from the large, random movements of arms and legs typical of infancy to the refinement of specific movements necessary for special skills like cutting, pasting, or drawing.

3. *Differentiation and integration in growth. Differentiation* refers to the process through which the child eventually gains control over specific parts of the body. For example, even into toddlerhood young children have great difficulty controlling and coordinating their movements in order to catch a ball. However, if a five-year-old is thrown a ball, it is very likely that she will catch it. Once children have discovered, or differentiated, which parts of the body can do certain things, they are ready to perform more complex activities that involve coordinating movements in different parts of the body (*integration*). Climbing a stair, drawing a picture, and building a block tower are all complex activities for certain children—depending upon their abilities to understand which parts of their bodies are involved in the control of certain movements and how those movements can be coordinated to achieve a specific goal. Some movements, such as crawling,

walking, sitting, or grasping, develop naturally if the environment allows the child a reasonable degree of freedom. Others, such as riding a bicycle, skipping (for some children), or roller skating, require some instructions.

4. *Variations in growth.* Growth rates vary in two ways. They vary from person to person, and the various organs and systems within each individual grow at different rates. Anyone who has ever observed children recognizes that rates of growth vary from one child to another. Some grow quickly, others more slowly. One of the most apparent demonstrations of this principle is that girls grow faster than boys until adolescence.

5. *Optimal tendency in growth.* Individuals seek to reach their full potential for development. For example, suppose growth during a certain period is interrupted by a lack of food or exercise. The child attempts to make up for that lean period as soon as adequate provisions are available. He soon catches up to normal growth expectancies and then resumes his characteristic growth pattern. Only if the deprivation is severe will the child exhibit permanent effects from it.

   For children afflicted with a physical disability, this principle is especially apparent. Blind children, for example, learn to compensate for their lack of sight by sharpening other senses.

6. *Sequential growth.* This principle, mainly influenced by the work of Gesell, explains that physical growth evolves through an orderly sequence. Children must learn to crawl before they can walk. Sequential patterns of growth have been described for nearly all physical skills, including locomotion, use of the hands, and other abilities. Gesell's original work described such sequential growth as a natural "unfolding" process, but the current view is that the child's environment, together with heredity factors, is basic to the process of physical development.

7. *Growth during critical periods.* There are certain key times in a child's development during which the presence or absence of specific interactions can be especially important. For example, the first three months of an infant's life are extremely critical for the development of the eyes, ears, and brain. In order to foster optimal development of these organs, the child should be provided with a rich variety of visual and verbal stimulation. A critical period, then, is the time when a certain kind of development can be most readily enhanced.

Individual differences make it imperative that teachers avoid establishing rigid expectations for physical growth and appearance. Each child grows differently. Each is distinguished by body build, size and shape, hair color, eye color, skin color, physical abilities, and different levels of physical maturity.

Our genes help determine body size, build, facial characteristics, hair color, and so on. However, heredity determines only the *potential* for development; the *actual* growth and maturation process must be considered within an environmental context.

Directing her hands to stack a pile of small blocks helps this child master fine motor skills.

Principles of Motor Development

Basic changes in the body—height, weight, muscles, bones, nervous system, and hormones—are commonly dealt with in courses on child development, so they will not be treated here. However, all these changes operate together to influence how infants, toddlers, and young children are able to use their bodies. This process is referred to as **motor (muscular) development.** For parents as well as teachers, the development of a child's motor skills offers some truly exciting moments—such as seeing an infant take a first faltering step or a three-year-old child learn to catch a ball. All children require physical activity to exercise their growing muscles. A child can learn to ride a bike or to skip only when these new skills are supported by a great number of prerequisite and less obvious skills. For that reason, we will break down motor development into two distinct categories: (1) large-muscle control (**gross motor development**) and (2) small-muscle control (**fine motor development**). Gross motor development involves the use of large muscles like those in the arms, legs, and trunk. Fine motor development involves the use of smaller muscles, like the ones in the fingers. Acquisition of both gross motor skills and fine motor skills follows certain predictable patterns.

Motor development during infancy progresses very rapidly. The child advances in two years from an uncoordinated individual capable of reflex actions to a walking, toddling, exploring wonder. Mary M. Shirley conducted a study of infants that illustrates the predictable sequence of gross motor development during infancy. Her results are illustrated in Figure 3–1. Through the preschool years, most children are captivated by activity helping to promote these and other large motor skills: running, jumping, galloping, hopping, climbing, skipping, and throwing, catching, and kicking a ball. (See Table 3–1.)

Children enjoy practicing these skills. A child will stand on a balance board or kick a ball, trying out many different techniques until he finds one that actually works. It gives him confidence to develop skills through such active self-initiated play. Some large-muscle play activities with which children may be involved during a normal preschool day include swinging on a swing, climbing on a jungle gym, digging with a shovel in sand or dirt, throwing and catching a ball, jumping with a rope, walking on low balance beams, riding a tricycle, sliding down the slide, pulling a wagon, pushing a small wheelbarrow, painting with water, running through fresh grass, pounding nails, sawing, planing, and sanding.

During these activities, a child builds not only muscle control but self-confidence, too. He gains when he is "in tune" with his own body, when he is able to use it freely. Physical activity heightens curiosity, too; it evokes a natural childhood urge to look at things, grasp them, taste them, bang them together, shake them, drop them, and put them in and take them out of containers. All we have to do is provide safe, simple objects or toys. Motor activities challenge the child's creativity and imagination; each is part of the child's mental development. Spirited physical activity stimulates all physiological processes, such as circulation, respiration, and elimination. Eating habits improve, and rest is more welcome. Physical activity has values that go beyond mere physical gains: It enhances the emotional, creative, and intellectual areas as well.

AFFECTIVE DEVELOPMENT

Affective development, as defined by Rosalind Charlesworth, is "the area that centers on the self-concept and the development of social, emotional and personality characteristics."[4] It encompasses all aspects of interactions among individuals that deal with feelings and relationships. Affective concerns are met by teachers when, for example, they say to each child—through gentle hugs, playful pats, friendly smiles, and kind words—"you're important to me!" In turn, every boy and girl leaves school with the attitude, "I'm extra-special!" Helping a child acquire such brimming self-confidence strengthens her sense of self as an individual who can feel happy, sad, helpful, or angry—but who knows that someone is near who can help her cope with these feelings without being overwhelmed.

Figure 3–1 Motor development in infants. *Source:* From *The First Two Years,* Institute of Child Welfare Monograph No. 7 by M. M. Shirley, 1933, Minneapolis University of Minnesota Press. Reprinted by permission of the University of Minnesota Press.

Table 3–1 Physical characteristics of the child from two to five years old

At Two Years Begins to	At Three Years Begins to	At Four Years Begins to	At Five Years Begins to
Walk	Jump and hop on one foot	Run, jump, and climb with close adult supervision	Gain good body control
Run	Climb stairs by alternating feet on each stair	Dress self using buttons, zippers, laces, and so on	Throw and catch a ball, climb, jump, skip with good coordination
Actively explore his environment			
Sit in a chair without support	Dress and undress self somewhat	Use more sophisticated eating utensils such as knives to cut meat or spread butter	Coordinate movements to music
Climb stairs with help (two feet on each stair)	Walk a reasonably straight path on floor		Put on snowpants, boots, and tie shoes
Build block towers	Walk on balance beam	Walk balance beam with ease	Skip
Feed self with fork and spoon	Ride a tricycle	Walk down stairs alone	Jump rope, walk in a straight line
Stand on balance beam	Stand on one foot for a short time	Bound and catch ball	Ride a two-wheel bike
Throw ball	Catch large balls	Push/pull wagon	Roller skate
Catch	Hop	Cut, following lines	Fold paper
Jump	Gallop	Copy figure ×	Reproduce alphabet and numbers
Push and pull	Kick ball	Print first name	
Hang on bar	Hit ball		Trace
Slide	Paste		
	String beads		
	Cut paper with scissors		
	Copy figures ○ and +		

Personality Development

"What a friendly guy!" Donald's teacher said, as she stopped what she was doing to watch Donald share some of his toys with Richard. It was true—Donald seemed to be a vivacious, warmhearted lad who tended to congregate with others, share materials and experiences, and show an awareness of the feelings of other children. "Here," he said to his tearful friend Richard as he freely handed over the toy to share. "Thanks," replied Richard as he accepted Donald's offer and slowly stopped crying. Donald obviously delighted in the company of other children and adults. What makes children like Donald so friendly and other children less friendly? What makes some children shy and others outgoing? Many experts have speculated about the development of these and other **personality** characteristics—the traits that give each person a unique style of reacting to other people, places, things, and events. The difficulty is that there is much disagreement in the explanations of these experts. Some, for example, cite biological influences; others weigh social, economic, cognitive, or environmental factors more heavily. The problem is compounded when we realize that personality development may have multiple causes and require a combination of theories to explain it.

Natural Temperament

Although any single or conglomerate theory could have been used in this text, I have chosen to base my recommendations on the works of Alexander Thomas, Stella Chess, and Herbert Birch. Substantiating what mothers for thousands of years must have known, these researchers have identified nine natural characteristic temperaments that vary from individual to individual.[5] They have categorized those nine temperaments into three basic personality types that are apparent from infancy:

1. *Easy children.* These are the constantly happy youngsters. They are adaptable, approachable, have predictable body functions, and adapt well to regular routines. About 40 percent fit this description.
2. *Slow-to-warm-up children.* These youngsters take longer to adapt to new situations than "easy children." They tend to be less active and less predictable, and they tend to have a lower intensity level (energy level). About 15 percent fit this description.
3. *Difficult children.* These children are often unhappy; they fuss, sob, and complain. They adapt slowly to change, are unpredictable (there is no telling when they are ready for a nap), and exhibit sudden, intense reactions. About 10 percent fit this category.

The researchers had difficulty placing the remaining 35 percent into any category. A flurry of responses followed the publication of the Thomas, Chess, and Birch study—some supportive and others challenging. The interesting implication, however, is that babies appear to be born with natural temperaments. Instead of expecting all youngsters to fit into a preconceived model of behavior, adults need to employ tactics that best meet the needs of each child's innate personality. For example, the "regular" baby can be given a consistent feeding schedule, whereas the "irregular" baby can have a flexible schedule based on his needs. The "quick-to-adapt" baby could be given more independence, whereas the "slow adapter" could be given more time to warm up to new situations. As a teacher, you will realize that your interaction patterns are crucial to the development of each child.

Achieving "Rhythmic" Interactions

T. Berry Brazelton and his colleagues at Children's Hospital in Boston have assumed a philosophy of innate personality very closely aligned with that of Thomas, Chess, and Birch. Brazelton believes that a significant adult's ability to achieve a satisfactory "rhythm" with an infant forms the basis for all subsequent positive social interaction. But, in order to achieve this rhythm, Brazelton advises that adults must work to find special ways to interact with their babies. Each adult and each baby is an individual—as such, each pair is "stuck" with its own ways of interacting. Therefore, the adult is challenged to chart out her own course toward achieving a rhythm via the "markers" (natural temperament) set out by the baby. Brazelton's popular book, *Infants and Mothers*, was an attempt to show how normal babies can be quite different in personality makeup and how their unique personality characteristics affect those who care for them. In the introduction to the book, Brazelton states the following:

> Normal babies are not all alike. However obvious, this fact is invariably overlooked by the literature for new parents. It is therefore, together with its extensive implications for child rearing, the principal reason for this book. I have described the normal developmental paths of three very different infants, as well as the very different ways in which they affected their environments. These are not actual biographies of any one baby. Instead, they are composites of many of each type—the active, the average, and the quiet babies—seen over fifteen years of pediatric practice.... From the very moment of birth these differences become apparent and begin to determine the tone of the parents' reactions.[6]

Although he does not use the same three categories of temperament as Thomas, Chess, and Birch, Brazelton recognizes that babies do have distinct personalities and that a magical "coming together" of positive interchange, or a coordinated meshing of behaviors (rhythm), is essential for positive personality growth. Kathleen Stassen Berger describes that coordination:

> To be sure, the specific behaviors of caregivers playing with their babies are not impressive in themselves: mothers and fathers open their eyes and mouths wide in expressions of mock surprise, make rapid clucking noises or repeated one-syllable sounds ("ba-ba-ba-ba-ba,"...etc.), raise and lower the pitch of their voice, change the pace of their movements...tickle, lift, and rock the baby, and do many other simple things. Nor are the infants' behaviors very complex: babies stare at their parent partner or look away, vocalize, widen their eyes, smile and laugh, move forward or back, or turn aside.

> But what is fascinating to observers is the coordination of parts in the unwritten script that the parent and infant seem to follow, a coordination that becomes more impressive the more carefully one examines it.[7]

The research of Thomas, Chess, and Birch, as well as the insightful observations of Brazelton, highlight the need to observe and follow a child's "markers," or cues. Guidelines are not suitable for governing such interactions (e.g., amount and type of vocalization, touching, movement, and distance) but we do know that bonds of attachment are strengthened when important people in the child's life find uniquely special ways to say, "you're a special person to me." To explain the process of achieving rhythm more deeply is nearly impossible. As Jerome Bruner explains, "The first time the child sustains his look into his mother's eyes [he] begins on a career of social exchange of such complexity that no grammar has yet been devised to explicate it."[8] Such a complicated process, although elusive to describe, still composes a crucial foundation of understanding necessary for establishing warm, rewarding social and emotional relationships.

Social/Emotional Development

The ways that children relate to others and the ways they handle their feelings are referred to as **social/emotional development.** I have chosen to combine these two critical developmental areas into one topic of discussion because the dynamics of both interact with each other in such a way as to actually form a wholeness. Take, for example, the neonate who exhibits her first **emotional expression** at birth—that is, crying. It is a powerful emotional message signaling the entrance of life into this world. And, during the first few weeks of life, it is a clear form of communication—a cue from the baby that something needs to be attended to. There are few sounds that concern parents or teachers more than a baby's cry. Picking up the baby, hugging her, singing to her, or rocking her are all frequent rhythmic **social expressions** that lead to strong emotional ties. Babies quickly recognize those responsible for their care. As time goes on and the care becomes consistent, babies begin to develop feelings about their encounters. Desperate cries accompany the absence of immediate help, whereas pleasant coos and babbles are indications of the baby's satisfaction. From these early experiences, infants go through a special developmental process called social-emotional development.

The term **social** refers to the establishing of relationships between two or more people, through which they influence each other's behavior. The term **emotional** refers to the personal expression of feelings. Some emotions, like love and happiness, are rewarding aspects of adult-child interactions. On the other hand, childhood expressions of anger and fear signal matters of strong concern. Several important theories of social/emotional development have furnished us with support for learning what kinds of interactions are most appropriate for individuals as they grow through infancy into young childhood. We will now examine the works of several theorists who have had a significant impact on early childhood programming today.

Erik Erikson

Erik Erikson declares that a person's social-emotional character is determined by the ways particular crises are resolved during specific periods of development. Erikson's theory described eight stages through which we all pass as we advance from birth through adulthood. During these stages we are confronted with unique conflicts that

Sympathy, sharing, and other social behaviors increase dramatically through the preschool years.

demand an adjustment of personal desires to the social expectation of the culture in which we live. Erikson described each stage as a **crisis period,** or a time when individuals experience stresses and strains in attempts to regulate their behaviors to the demands of those around them. In each crisis period, Erikson describes pairs of competing biological drives fighting for control of the individual. The first pair of competing biological drives is referred to as the stage of **trust versus mistrust.** This stage occurs during infancy, when the child learns (or fails to learn) that she can establish close relationships with others, that others will provide for basic needs gratification, and that she is valued and important ("trust"). At the same time, the baby also learns that her every need cannot be anticipated by the adults in her environment; and that she must acquire strategies to elicit desired responses from them for basic self-protection ("mistrust"). Erikson emphasizes that a proper mix of trust and mistrust must be forged during infancy if a healthy personality is to emerge (with trust predominant).

If the first crisis is resolved satisfactorily, the child will recognize her own self-worth and acquire the confidence to become independent. During this stage of **autonomy versus shame and doubt,** children are faced with choices of holding on or letting go, deciding what is safe to try, and determining what they might not yet be ready for. They shift from the dependency of babyhood into a notion of invincibility: "I can do anything and everything. Let me do it myself!" Children must find the right balance between what is realistic and what is beyond their capabilities; although autonomy should be encouraged, a certain amount of doubt is necessary.

The third crisis period descriptive of the development of preschoolers is **initiative versus guilt.** At about three years of age, children start to be even more interested in trying out new things and exploring the world around them. However, rather than attempting these challenges primarily as a means to satisfy personal desires, young children become interested in the effects their efforts have on other people. Through initiative, the child plans and carries out activities; the effects of her actions may result in guilt: "I shouldn't have taken the last cookie. Jerry likes Fig Newtons just as much as I do." This is a stage where teachers must allow children opportunities to make decisions and try things on their own but also guide them with sensitive leadership and decisive control when the children exercise poor judgment. Table 3–2 summarizes these three periods as well as the period immediately following the preschool years.

Of what significance is Erikson's thinking to planning developmentally appropriate programs for young children? Foremost, teachers must be committed to creating an environment where healthy social-emotional attributes can develop. The basic climate of the school or center should reflect a strong feeling of trust among adults and children. By knowing when to let go and, at the same time, informing the children that they can depend on you, you will be able to achieve this goal. Trust is also established as you plan a consistent daily schedule or as you react to children's behaviors with regularity and fairness. Children's growing sense of independence must be

Table 3–2 Erikson's first four crisis periods

Stage	Age	Positive Outcome	Negative Outcome
Trust vs. mistrust	Birth–1 $\frac{1}{2}$ years	Learns to place faith in others and have confidence in them. Develops feelings of security and comfort	is fearful and unsure of the environment. Fear, anxiety, and apprehension characterize the personality.
Autonomy vs. shame and doubt	1 $\frac{1}{2}$ years– 3 years	Accepts independence, learns to make decisions, does things for herself.	Overcontrol leads to inhibitions, shame, and loss of self-esteem.
Initiative vs. guilt	3–6 years	Plans and carries out own activities, tests new powers confidently, enjoys achievement, and attempts to master new challenges.	Fears failure in trying new things. Failure may lead to punishment, leading to guilt feelings.
Industry vs. inferiority	6–12 years	Learns to seek recognition by learning the skills of a culture or by producing things. These successes help the child develop a positive self-concept	Consistent failure or lack of recognition leads to feelings of frustration, inadequacy, and inferiority. Neglects forming relationships with others.

supported with skillful guidance. Children must be given many opportunities to do things for themselves and to take part in meaningful decisions. At the same time, a supportive adult must be near to offer control when necessary. After all, young children are sometimes unsure of their abilities to perform all the actions necessary to complete a project; they are often better "starters" than "finishers." In all instances, however, children must be made to feel adequate; a positive sense of worth is an irreplaceable element in the child's development. As a teacher, you should attempt to provide an environment rich in opportunities for making plans and to take the risk of attempting challenging goals. All of these factors are crucial in the development of a healthy personality.

Abraham Maslow

Unlike Erik Erikson, Abraham Maslow is not a stage theorist. Instead of describing the child as moving through specific levels of development, Maslow focuses upon the environmental influences that determine the effectiveness of social/emotional interactions. To describe these influences, Maslow advanced a hierarchy (arranged in order) of needs that all individuals need to resolve in order to become self-actualized (develop a positive self-concept).[9] This hierarchy is represented in Figure 3–2. Each lower level must be satisfied in order to reach the upper needs. Maslow's hierarchy encompasses the following needs, beginning with the most basic:

Physiological needs—needs of security and survival: eating, breathing, warmth, activity, and other essentials necessary to maintain life.

Safety needs—routine, rhythm and order in life; protection from dangerous situations.

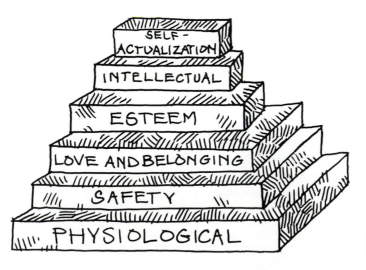

Figure 3–2 Maslow's hierarchy of needs

Love and belonging needs—desire for affectionate relationships with people and for acceptance in a group.

Esteem needs—being recognized as a worthwhile individual; developing confidence and self-worth.

Intellectual needs—curiosity, exploration, and the desire for knowledge; wanting to know about things.

Self-actualization needs—striving to fulfill one's potential; being a fully functioning person.

Maslow's ideas have very important implications for early childhood programs. Children who are consistently deprived of nutritious meals, for example, may find it difficult to establish strong positive relationships with their peers; those who are often subjected to harsh disciplinary measures may tend to avoid intellectually stimulating tasks because they are "energized" (motivated) to satisfy stronger needs of love and acceptance. Children come to you hoping, or expecting, to have their most basic needs met. Know what they are and respect those needs throughout all aspects of your program.

Lawrence Kohlberg and Judy Corder-Bolz

The developmental process of identifying oneself as male or female and adopting the various behaviors and attitudes considered normal for each gender is called *gender identification,* or *gender typing*. Like most other aspects of child development, gender identification emerges from dynamic interactions of biological and environmental forces. There is no debate, for example, that there are basic chromosomal, physiological, and hormonal differences between males and females that biologically determine sexual differentiation. John W. Santrock and Steven R. Yussen examined biology's influence on gender identification and reported that Sigmund Freud and Erik Erikson assigned it primary importance:

> One of Freud's basic assumptions is that human behavior and history are directly related to the reproductive processes. From this assumption arises the belief that sexuality is essentially unlearned and instinctual. Erikson extended this argument, claiming that the psychological differences between males and females stem from anatomical differences. Erikson argued that—because of genital structure—males are more intrusive and aggressive, females more inclusive and passive. Erikson's belief has become known as "anatomy is destiny." Critics of the anatomy-is-destiny view believe that Erikson has not given experience adequate importance. They argue that males and females are more free to choose their gender role than Erikson would allow. In response to the critics, Erikson has modified his view, saying that females in today's world are transcending their biological heritage and correcting society's overemphasis on male intrusiveness.[10]

Unquestionably, biology sets the stage for gender identification. However, biology by itself does not determine what is acceptable male or female behavior in various cultures. We exert social influences on gender identification shortly after a baby's birth, for example. Girls are adorned in pink blankets or clothing, whereas boys are routinely bedecked in blue. Boy babies are commonly referred to with terms such as "robust" or "strong," whereas girls are quite often described as "pretty" or "dainty". Soon afterward, differences in toys, clothing, and hairstyles continue to influence gender identification.

As young children become aware of the fact that they belong to the group called "boys" or "girls", they work hard at finding out exactly what each gender does that is so different from the other group. Lawrence Kolhberg describes this growing awareness of gender understanding as evolving through three developmental levels:

1. *Basic gender identity* describes the initial stage where the infant recognizes simply that he is a boy or she is a girl.
2. *Gender stability* refers to the realization that gender is permanent and unchangeable.
3. *Gender constancy* reflects the child's eventual understanding that superficial changes [in ways of behaving or dressing, for example] are irrelevant to one's basic gender.[11]

Kolhberg asserts that once children become aware of their gender and understand what it means, they work hard at trying to conform to gender-appropriate behaviors. Judy Corder-Bolz, a sociologist specializing in gender identification, believes that society's traditional attitudes about gender behaviors have a powerful influence on moving children from an awareness of gender identity toward some degree of sexism. Corder-Bolz asserts that this process begins with a fascinating stage she labels as "developmental sexism." What this means is that children are enormously sexist in their gender-role perception and choice of play activities. Despite adults' most systematic attempts to shape a nonsexist environment, at this age most boys still remain pilots and girls do the dishes. Developmental sexism is viewed as a natural phenomenon influenced by something called "gender constancy." That is, children understand that they belong to a certain sex, and that a person's sex cannot change. Prior to about age five, children are unsure about whether or not boys can change into girls or vice versa.

Once they grasp the concept that one's sex cannot change, they begin to organize the world into "girl" or "boy" categories. Such a connection to gender identity helps solidify the sense of self that children began to form during infancy. When observing children stereotyping through play, many parents and teachers attempt to reason with them in order to create more objective attitudes about gender roles. For example, if the child says, "Only boys can grow up to be carpenters," teachers may say something like, "That's not true. Women are carpenters, too." This approach often fails. The child's way of classifying the world into male and female is new and not open to exceptions. A child may even become upset that the teacher fails to see the world in the same light and defend his case even more strongly. We can compound the problem, therefore, by trying to reason with a child. This presents us with an interesting dilemma: We want children to experience a nonsexist world, but they tend to resist our efforts of objectivity. What *can* we do? First, let the children know you understand and accept their unique system of trying to make sense of the world. Their willingness to come to you and share an excitement about new discoveries should always be accepted with openness and sincere interest. You do have, however, a responsibility to help them understand that choices should be open to each person, regardless of gender. In responding to the "carpenter" comment, for example, a teacher might say, "I know you've never seen a woman carpenter before, so it's hard to understand that women can be carpenters, too." On the other hand, reasoned comment such as, "It's okay for women to be carpenters, too. Many women are very skilled carpenters," often brings about a response such as, "Well, they shouldn't be!"

Just as you lead young children toward understanding the idea of equality through your conversations, the activities and materials you choose for your classroom should resist gender stereotyping. A program offering opportunities for both sexes to participate in classroom experiences should transcend obsolete sex-role expectations such as boys playing with blocks and tools and girls with dolls or kitchen utensils.

As important as these suggestions is that teachers assume the position of a positive role model. Be sensitive to your choice of words to describe occupations; for example, police *officer* replaces police*man*, fire*fighter* replaces fire*man,* and mail *carrier* replaces mail*man.* Additionally, be aware of how actions can convey sex-role coequality consciousness. For example, the children may learn to understand gender roles less rigidly if they see their male teacher sing a soothing lullaby to a baby doll at the dramatic play center, or their female teacher tighten a loose bolt on the favorite riding toy.

Schools that foster positive gender roles will help children value the likenesses and differences in themselves, thereby taking an important step toward alleviating the damage resulting from long-ingrained patterns of sexism so common in our society. It is this unconditional positive regard for children that lies at the heart of early childhood education.

Mildred Parten

Of all the natural aspects of childhood, play appears to be the most integral; it dominates a great portion of each child's day. The play process has fascinated researchers for years, and—despite differences in orientation—all agree that play is an esteemed, indispensable part of childhood. One especially respected view of play is Mildred Parten's time-honored description of social play. In her classic study, Parten discovered that social participation among two- to five-year olds increases with the child's age through six stages of development, beginning with a desire to play alone and growing into a desire to play and cooperate with others.[12]

1. *Unoccupied behavior.* The children are not actually playing, but they occupy themselves by watching anything of momentary interest. When nothing interests the children, they loll around, play with their own bodies, follow an adult, or simply sit in one spot glancing around the room. (pre–two-year-olds)

2. *Onlooker behavior.* One child spends his time watching the other children play. He may talk to the others, ask them questions, or give suggestions, but he does not enter into the play situation itself. This stage differs from the preceding one in that the child is specifically observing a group of children at play rather than anything that happens to be exciting at the moment. (two-year-olds)

3. *Solitary play.* The child actually engages in play activity, but by herself. She may choose toys that are different from those used by the children within speaking distance and makes no effort to move near the others. She pursues her own activity without concern for what others are doing. (two- to two-and-one-half-year-old children)

4. *Parallel play.* The child still plays by himself, but deliberately chooses a toy or activity that will bring him among the other children, where he can enjoy other children's company. He may choose a toy that is like those the other children are using but play with it the way he wants, not as the others may be playing. Likewise, he does not try to influence or modify the play of the children near him. He plays near to, not with, the other children. (two-and-one-half- to three-and-one-half-year-old children)

5. *Associative play.* The child begins to play with other children in groups. There is borrowing and lending of play materials; following one another with wagons or trains; and mild attempts to control who may or may not play in the group. All the group members engage in a similar activity,

Preschoolers engage in significant amounts of play with their peers.

but there is no organization of the activity around any specific purpose, materials, or individual. Therefore, a group of children may flock together in the sandbox, each doing his or her own activity. The children do not subordinate their individual interests to those of the group; each child plays as he or she wishes. The interest is obviously in developing interpersonal associations rather than in the play activity itself. (three-and-one-half- to four-and-one-half-year-old children)

6. *Cooperative play.* The child plays in a group that is organized for some specific purpose. That purpose may be to make something, to dramatize situations of adult or group life, or to play a formal game. Regardless of the purpose, the major social significance is that there is a marked sense of group membership. (four-and-one-half-year-olds and onward)

Since the 1930s, Parten's research has excited great interest and has resulted in many more studies—some supporting her findings and others challenging them. One of the most interesting aspects of current research into Parten's work is the finding that three- and four-year-olds in today's society display significantly more unoccupied, solitary, and onlooker activity and significantly less associative and cooperative play than Parten's children.[13] The reasons for the change are not clear, but some have cited cultural and class differences over the years. Among researchers who have supported Parten's classifications of play, some have questioned her conclusion that solitary play is less mature than succeeding kinds. They argue that the child who plays alone may be exhibiting very mature behavior. Independence may be a sign of growing independence and maturity rather than poor social adjustment. In light of these developments the traditional application of Parten's categories needs to be reconsidered. We must be aware that children's play progresses from playing alone to playing with others. Even as children develop greater social maturity, they do not outgrow their need for solitary, individual play.

INTELLECTUAL DEVELOPMENT

Intellectual development refers to the changes in mental structures that occur as children explore the world around them. Of all the theories of intellectual development proposed so far, the most influential have been those of Jean Piaget. As early as 1920, Piaget began his studies of human intelligence—explorations, mainly of his own children, suggesting that the roots of intelligence were firmly established during infancy.

The Influence of Jean Piaget

According to Piaget, intelligence begins with the reflex capacities all infants possess at birth. These involuntary reactions help the infant cope with the environment. Knowledge of why some of the reflexes stay with us (coughing or blinking, for example) and others leave (the rooting reflex in which a baby's head turns and the mouth opens to suck when the cheek is stroked) as we grow into adulthood is not fully complete. However, Piaget describes infant learning as a process beginning with such reflexes and evolving into higher processes of thought.

Piaget talks about intelligence in a broad biological framework: Some organisms have more complex biological structures, which accounts for higher levels of intelligence. For example, one-celled organisms do not explore their environment, but human babies certainly do. Humans have hands that immeasurably increase their capacity to manipulate and explore objects.

Piaget used this concept of a child's acting on and manipulating things in the environment to form his own general definition of intelligence. He said that intelligence was a form of "equilibrium" which all individuals seek. The term **equilibrium,** taken from physics, implies seeking a balance between the person's existing mental structures and those things yet to be understood. To Piaget, this self-regulatory process is the most fundamental of all factors of intelligence. Through this process, children encounter something that is new to them and actively work toward relating that entity to something they already know. As they are able to resolve such discord, they reach a new level of equilibrium (intelligence).

The growth of intelligence can be viewed as an ascent up a flight of stairs, each stair representing a balanced state of equilibrium. As people progress through each stair, they are using a process called **adaptation,** adjusting themselves to their surroundings. Adaptation involves combining two processes, **assimilation** and **accommodation.** Assimilation deals with the environment in terms of current intellectual or physical structures. Accommodation changes existing structures in ways that fit the new situation more effectively. The following example illustrates the process of adaptation, illustrating how the grasping reflex leads to intellectual growth.

▶▶▶▶▶▶▶

Suppose an infant is presented with a rattle for the very first time. The infant reaches out and tries to grasp the rattle. He has grasped things like plastic rings and his bottle before, and when he sees the rattle he attempts to pick it up by curving his fingers in one way and then another, trying to use the same grasping patterns he used to fit the shapes of the bottle and rings. The child is comparing the new object with things that he is already familiar with—things that can be grasped. This is *assimilation.*

The child finds, however, that his grasp must be modified if he is ever to pick up the rattle and hear its pleasing sounds. He eventually curves his fingers in a new way—a way that fits the long, slender handle of the rattle instead of the more substantial shapes previously experienced. The child has now *accommodated* previous grasping reflexes to a shape never before experienced.

The simultaneous process of assimilation and accommodation is called adaptation. Equilibrium is achieved, and the child has grown to a new level of knowledge.

Assimilation and accommodation are constantly working in harmony to produce changes in the child's world and in the ways the child reacts to it. This is an active process; it requires interaction between the child and something or someone. The child's reflexes become refined as planned sensory or motor activity are experienced: for example, making sounds; listening to and gazing at objects; grasping and handling objects; physical mobility; and knowledge of one's own body.

Young children learn much during their early years. They progress from the natural reflexes of infancy to the wondrous development of complex cognitive structures in several short years. All of this is accomplished in an environment full of direct experiences in which the child is free to explore, manipulate, and experiment. Children, however, do not learn by being placed somewhere with objects to explore, and then left alone. They need adults to interact with them; point out shapes, sizes, and colors; help them perceive relationships among things; and lend a hand as they attempt to make sense out of their world. Preschoolers learn much by doing, but they need someone to be near to provide stimulation and encouragement.

MAJOR DEVELOPMENTAL DIFFERENCES

We have stressed that all children have their unique ways of growing; they all have special differences that are appreciated by parents and teachers alike. Some of these differences can be explained primarily by heredity. The distinctive genetic composition we acquire from our parents is responsible for some variation—hair and eye color, height, and gender, for example. The environment is primarily responsible for other variations; excessive drug or alcohol use during pregnancy, for example, has a detrimental effect on the development of the fetus. Still other differences may be accounted for by the interaction of heredity and environment—that is, the inborn potential of the child and what she actually does become. For example, a child with inborn potential for an average level of language acquisition will not achieve that level unless she is exposed to the richness of the language of the culture into which she was born. Ever-widening ranges of factors influence the miracle of individual growth and development.

When trying to provide services for our young children, early childhood educators are especially interested in knowing what has been determined to be "typical development"—because such descriptions provide standards by which individuals can be judged. Subsequently, appropriate services can be provided. We, as a profession, take pride in our desire and ability to meet the needs of all children and their families, even those who vary greatly from the norm. Children who function well below the norms ("at-risk" children) must be guaranteed the same basic educational opportunities as other children.

"At-Risk" Children

One of the major dilemmas faced by early childhood educators involves the difficulty of providing equal services for all children, regardless of personal needs. Educators sometimes feel reluctant to categorize children who might benefit from special programs because of the psychological effect labels might have on them. We have, for example, referred to children with learning problems as "retarded," "disadvantaged," or "learning disabled." Currently, the term "at-risk" seems to be the accepted expression in identifying children in need of early intervention. Elizabeth J. Hrncir and Corinne E. Eisenhart advise that we must use the term with caution for, when misused, this label, like any other, may be harmful and undermine our best intentions. Who is the "at-risk" child? Hrncir and Eisenhart answer this question in the following passage.

> the term "at-risk" is ambiguous. Indeed this classification has multiple definitions because it is used to label children with a great variety of strengths and weaknesses. It has been applied to: children who are from minority groups, low-income homes, or one-parent families; children who were born prematurely or with mental and/or physical disabilities; children who have parents with low IQ's, minimal job skills, or a substance abuse problem; children who are developmentally delayed (cognitively, physically, and/or emotionally); and children who speak English as a second language. ...Even boys, when compared to girls, are often viewed as at risk for failure.[14]

Attach this confusing label judiciously; it should be used to identify children with potential problems who would benefit from an early intervention program rather than as an indiscriminate label. Two significant milestones of federal legislation provided funds to offer services for children with unique needs: PL 94-142 and PL 99-457.

THE EDUCATION FOR ALL HANDICAPPED CHILDREN ACT (P.L. 94–142)

Public Law 94–142, signed by President Ford in 1975 and implemented in the fall of 1978, was a valuable outcome of social efforts during the early 1970s to prevent the segregation of any child from regular classrooms, whether because of special needs or race. Specifically, Public law 94–142 made free public education mandatory for all children older than age five who were identified as having special needs. Such education was to take place within a "least restrictive environment." A least restrictive environment is not a place where children are permitted to do anything they want, but one where the same opportunities as those available to any other child are offered to children with special needs.

In order to offer programs for special-needs youngsters within a least restrictive environment, the public schools first needed to identify and classify those children in need of special services. Who were these children variously described as having "special needs," "handicaps," "impairments," or "exceptionalities"? These were children who needed special attention to overcome conditions that could delay normal growth and development, distort normal growth and development, or have a severe negative effect on normal growth and development and adjustment to life. Public Law 94–142 divided this diverse group with its distinct categories of handicapping conditions.[15] See Table 3–3.

Children with major handicaps were easily identified, but those with borderline or more subtle needs were more difficult to detect. Public Law 94–142 required every state to initiate a plan for identifying, locating, evaluating, and providing special services for all children with disabilities. Children with obviously or severely handicapping conditions were usually identified during a nationwide Child Find program. The Child Find program consisted of placing notices in newspapers and public places, offering public service messages on radio and television, and sending letters home from school with all children. Children with more subtle handicaps were more difficult to identify. Philip L. Safford explains:

> One of the most difficult tasks . . . is that of determining which among the varying patterns of individual differences among children constitute "problems." A 4-year-old boy seems to be acting out themes of anger and destruction in his play with dolls. A 6-year-old frequently reverses the direction of certain numerals and letters of the alphabet as he learns to copy them from the board. A 3-year-old makes essentially no use of expressive language. Do such patterns of behavior indicate the presence of problems or handicaps, or are they within the bounds of normalcy, given the individuality of children's development?[16]

Developmental screening tests were administered by teachers and other professionals. If the screening tests indicated special needs, a comprehensive evaluation was administered by a multidisciplinary team to determine the extent of the disability. From there, possible remediation strategies could be proposed. The comprehensive evaluation was conducted by a local or regional team consisting of the child's regular teacher and whatever specialists were deemed necessary: psychologists, speech therapists, physicians, or other professionals in child development agencies. Nancy H. Fallen and Warren Umansky have described the following minimum components of a comprehensive evaluation:

> Educational: a written report describing current educational performance and identifying precise instructional needs in academic (developmental) skills and language performance

> Medical: a written report from a licensed physician indicating general medical history and any medical/health problems that may impede optimal learning

> Sociocultural: a written report describing background and adaptive behavior in home and school

> Psychological: a written report from an approved psychologist based on the use of a battery of appropriate instruments including individual intelligence test(s). . . . Also, when appropriate, a clinical/psychiatric evaluation should be included.[17]

Once this process is completed, the school schedules a meeting where the prospective teacher, the child's parents, a representative from the school district

Table 3–3   Categories of handicapped children: Public Law 94–142

Public Law 94–142 defines categories of handicapped children as including the following:

Deaf means a hearing impairment which is so severe that the child is impaired in processing linguistic information through hearing, with or without amplification, which adversely affects educational performance.

Deaf-blind means a concomitant hearing and visual impairment, the combination of which causes such severe communication and other developmental and educational problems that such children cannot be accommodated in special education programs solely for deaf or blind children.

Hard-of-hearing means a hearing impairment, whether permanent or fluctuating, which adversely affects a child's educational performance but is not included under the definition of *deaf* in this section.

Mentally retarded means significantly subaverage general intellectual function existing concurrently with deficiencies in adaptive behavior and manifested during the developmental period, which adversely affects a child's educational performance.

Multihandicapped means concomitant impairments (such as mentally retarded-blind, mentally retarded-orthopedically impaired, and so on), the combination of which causes such severe educational problems that these children cannot be accommodated in special education programs solely for one of the impairments. The term does not include deaf-blind children.

Orthopedically impaired means a severe orthopedic impairment which adversely affects a child's educational performance. The term includes impairments caused by congenital anomaly (for example, clubfoot, absence of some member, and so on), impairments caused by disease (for example, poliomyelitis, bone tuberculosis, and so on), and impairments from other causes (for example, cerebral palsy, amputations and fractures, or burns which cause contractures).

Other health impaired means limited strength, vitality, or alertness, due to chronic or acute health problems, such as a heart condition, tuberculosis, rheumatic fever, nephritis, asthma, sickle-cell anemia, hemophilia, epilepsy, lead poisoning, leukemia, or diabetes, which adversely affects a child's educational performance.

Seriously emotionally disturbed means a condition which exhibits one or more of the following characteristics over a long period of time and to a marked degree, which adversely affects educational performance: (a) an inability to learn, which cannot be explained by intellectual, sensory, or health factors, (b) an inability to build or maintain satisfactory interpersonal relationships with peers and teachers, (c) inappropriate types of behavior or feelings under normal circumstances, (d) a general pervasive mood of unhappiness or depression, or (e) a tendency to develop physical symptoms or fears associated with personal or school problems. The term includes children who are schizophrenic or autistic. The term does not include children who are socially maladjusted, unless it is determined that they are seriously emotionally disturbed.

Specific learning disability means a disorder in one or more of the basic psychological processes involved in understanding or using language, spoken or written, which may manifest itself in an imperfect ability to listen, think, speak, read, write, spell, or do mathematical calculations. The term includes such conditions as perceptual handicaps, brain injury, minimal brain dysfunction, dyslexia, and developmental aphasia. The term does not include children who have learning problems which are primarily the result of visual, hearing, or motor handicaps; or mental retardation; or environmental, culture, or economic disadvantage.

Speech impaired means a communication disorder, such as stuttering impaired articulation, language impairment, or a voice impairment, which adversely affects a child's educational performance.

Visually handicapped means a visual impairment which, even with correction, adversely affects a child's educational performance. The term includes both partially seeing and blind children.

(usually a special educator), and a member of the assessment team are present. All information is shared and a special education plan, the **individualized education program (IEP),** is developed by the team. It is estimated that between 10 and 12 percent of all children in the United States fall into the special needs category; they deviate in at least one respect far enough from the typical that they need an individualized school program to address their needs.

The IEP is a carefully written plan that includes the following information:[18]

1. A statement of the child's present level of performance
2. A statement of long- and short-term goals
3. A statement of special services to be provided and the extent to which the child will participate in regular school programs
4. Dates identifying the duration of services
5. Evaluation procedures that determine the extent to which the goals are being met

Although it is not possible in all instances, the least restrictive environment for carrying out the IEP with the special needs child is the regular classroom. This

Mainstreamed children can be effectively assimilated into early childhood programs.

process of offering special educational services to handicapped children in regular classrooms is called **mainstreaming.** Through mainstreaming, the child is able to participate in regular school activities in addition to receiving the special help he needs because of his handicapping condition. Most children with special needs may be mainstreamed for all or part of the day, while some may require the services available only from specialists in a separate classroom. The decision about which placement is most appropriate for any child is made by the IEP team.

The process of placing children with special needs into the regular school program may sound as though it is time consuming and replete with paperwork. It is! But when we consider that the intent of P.L. 94–142 is to protect the right of special needs children to a free public education, the value of our extra work is certainly apparent. P.L. 94–142 was a landmark piece of legislation that benefited children older than age five but, unfortunately, was not made as beneficial for younger children. It did, however, offer *incentive grants* to states for offering services to children under five with special needs. The states would be paid up to $300 for each child if they voluntarily offered programs for preschool children. Over half of the states did so. However, the only programs that were *required* to offer services for children with special needs were those like Head Start, which receives federal funds.

Public Law 99–457

The provisions of P.L. 94–142 were adhered to closely by school districts throughout the country as they conformed to the spirit and intent of the law. Additional possibilities for handicapped children aged three through five years, though, came about in 1986 with the passage of P.L. 99–457. This critical legislation mandated that all the rights and protection of P.L. 94–142 would extend to children between the ages of three and five beginning with the 1990–91 school year. To achieve this objective, P.L. 94–142 was revised to reflect authorization of dramatically increased federal fiscal contributions for this age group. By the school year 1990–91, all states applying for P.L. 94–142 funds had to prove that they were providing free appropriate education to all handicapped children three through five.

The early intervention services provided by programs funded through P.L. 99–457 must include, for each eligible child, an assessment of needs and a written **individualized family service plan (IFSP)** developed by a multidisciplinary team consisting of specialists, the child's teachers, and the parents. The IFSP explains the exact intervention program offered at no cost to the parents except where federal or state law provides for a system of sliding fees (fees based upon parents' ability to pay).

Like the IEP, the IFSP must contain these essential elements:[19]

1. A statement of the child's present levels of development
2. A statement of the family's strengths and needs related to enhancing the child's development

3. A statement of major outcomes expected to be achieved for the child and family
4. Criteria, procedures, and timelines for determining progress
5. Specific early intervention services necessary to meet the unique needs of the child and family
6. Projected dates for the initiation of services and their expected duration
7. The name of the case manager
8. Procedures for transition from special early intervention programs into the regular preschool program

Notice that the IFSP recognizes the crucial importance of the family during the early intervention process. P.L. 99–457 goes as far as to stipulate that whenever appropriate, and to the extent desired by the parents, the preschooler's individualized program will include instruction for parents.

Penny Low Deiner advises that, as teachers confronting mainstreaming, we must access our own feelings toward and understandings of children with impairments.[20] How would you feel, and what would you do, in each of the following situations?

Sarah had a convulsion and you were the only adult around.

David got lost and couldn't hear you calling him.

Jane fell and hurt herself on something you had forgotten to pick up.

Deiner comments that the way most people choose to "deal" with problems like these is to avoid them. How many of us tend to avoid children with handicaps because we feel inadequate around them? You cannot, however, take this approach as a teacher of young children today. You must replace your feelings of inadequacy by confronting your feelings and replacing them with positive attitudes based upon accurate knowledge. Deiner explains:

> Such knowledge not only gives us the confidence to work with special needs children; it enables us to help average children accept their exceptional classmates. If knowledge about strengths and needs is passed on to them, young children can learn to deal with their peers as individuals: "Hey, if Sam isn't looking at you, he can't hear you." Integration provides children with the opportunity for positive experiences that build a good foundation for lifelong learning about others.[21]

Certainly it is not possible to know everything about all the exceptional needs you will face during your teaching career. Nor is it possible to acquire a framework for dealing with every exceptional need as part of the training you are now receiving. You will have to learn about each as you encounter it. That is why the relevant public laws stipulate that a team of specialists be involved in the formulation of each IEP. However, you should become familiar with the overall idea of exceptionality and mainstreaming and of the ways you can accept, understand, and become sensitive to the needs of every child. To help in this regard, you should begin to

- View the child as a whole child with strengths as well as weaknesses. Do not assume that the mainstreamed child is different in that regard. We all have strengths and weaknesses.

- Learn all you can about the mainstreamed child's specific disability. Become aware of therapy techniques and terminology.

- Involve parents in dealing with their child both in the school and at home. They should learn what you are doing in school so that your practices can be reinforced and extended in the home.

- Maximize interactions between the handicapped and nonhandicapped children. Give simple explanations about a child's handicap, when needed. Youngsters are curious; they want to know about a new child and will be satisfied with an open, honest explanation. ("Jeannie's legs don't work well so she needs a wheelchair.") Read books or tell stories about children with differences. Encourage the handicapped child to share strong capabilities. For example, the wheelchair-bound youngster can help another child in a project that demands manual dexterity and soon gain that child's appreciation for outstanding manual skill.

- Individualize your program. Start where the child is and plan a sequential program to encourage him to build one skill upon another. Build on continuous success.

- Visit classrooms where exceptional children have been successfully mainstreamed. Look for ways teachers individualize their instruction. How is peer interaction stimulated? Are parents involved in the classroom activities? Are peer questions about a child's disability answered openly and honestly?

- Attend special conferences, workshops, and other in-service training sessions designed to assist you in IEP writing and/or designing special learning materials and teaching techniques.

- Talk to handicapped children's parents and previous teachers. They can offer valuable suggestions and advice.

- Seek special assistance through publications—*Exceptional Children* or the *Journal of Learning Disabilities* are two examples—and nonprint media (speakers, films, and so forth) from local, state, or national agencies, such as the Council for Exceptional Children.

- Look for special programs designed to introduce regular students to the special needs of the handicapped. Barbara Aiello has developed a special program called "Kids on the Block," which includes puppets with different types of impairments. Each puppet displays a vibrant personality. "The Great

Renaldo," for example, jauntily announces that he "sees nothing and knows all," carrying his white cane and happily describing how he can tell time with his Braille wristwatch. Mark explains how his wheelchair ("cruiser," as he calls it) helps him enjoy life—he once went to a Halloween party as a tractor (only a "handicapped kid" can do that!). Children can ask the puppets questions. Mark, for example, is often asked how he can go to the bathroom. He explains that bathrooms are equipped with special rails to help him get up and down. Life-sized and dressed in real clothes, these puppets become ideal educators in every way. For more information on this complete curriculum on disabilities, contact Kids on the Block, Inc., Suite 510, Washington Building, Washington, DC 20005.

Mainstreaming requires changes in attitudes, behaviors, and teaching style. Because you will be part of this movement, you must gain the skills and attitudes necessary to help all children function effectively in society. What better place to start this process than in a social classroom?

Plan your program to fit your children's needs. No single chapter can give you a complete idea of the innumerable factors that influence your planning. If you truly want to be a successful teacher, you must build an awareness and sensitivity to the real world of children—one that includes careful, day-by-day observation and evaluation to serve as a basis for effective instruction.

Gifted Children

Exceptionally talented or intelligent children were given little special attention in our preschools prior to the 1970s. The general consensus was that these youngsters could succeed with very little or no help; their exceptional intelligence or skills alone ensured success in life. Little or no information was brought forward in regard to the specific needs of gifted preschoolers. To single out and offer special planning for these youngsters was considered by many to be elitist and somewhat un-American. "Why," people inquired, "should we channel extra money and resources for their education when they can do it so well on their own?" Most serious considerations for exceptional children, therefore, were focused on "at-risk" children through programs such as Head Start. However, educators are starting to realize the importance of accommodating young gifted children's needs, too. Jane Wolfle underscored this realization effectively when she argued, "Every child deserves a developmentally appropriate education, not just 'average' children and children who are behind."[22]

The Gifted Preschooler

How do you know when you have an exceptionally gifted or talented youngster in your class? Originally, giftedness was defined primarily in terms of intelligence. Some educators examined scores of IQ tests and identified those with scores of 120 or more as gifted because they made up only 10 percent of the population. Others suggested a 130 IQ score because only 2.27 percent had scores that high. Still others suggested a score of 140 or over because it would restrict giftedness to only 0.5 percent of the total population. Although IQ scores offer a relatively stable, direct source of evidence for giftedness, there are many other traits that separate the intellectually gifted preschooler from others. What are some of the gifts and talents that characterize this unique population? One way to begin answering this question is to examine your children for exceptional characteristics:

1. *Verbal skills*—uses advanced vocabulary; spontaneously creates stories; modifies language to the level of person being spoken to; explains complex processes; influences the behavior of others; exchanges ideas and information fluently.

2. *Abstractions*—remembers and understands letters, words, and numbers; puts together difficult puzzles; sees relationships and patterns; makes interesting things from media such as blocks, drawing materials, or playdough.

3. *Power of concentration*—attentive to features of a new environment or experience; becomes totally absorbed in an activity.

4. *Intellect*—has great skill in ordering or grouping items; carries out complex instructions; focuses on problems and deliberately seeks solutions; stores and recalls information easily; explains ideas in novel ways; learns rapidly; is curious; asks questions; masters academics at an earlier age; has multiple interests.

5. *Creativity*—generates large quantities of ideas as possible solutions to problems (The child who responds to the question, "What things are red?" with "apple, book, car, beet, crayon, and shoes," is more flexible than a child who says, "fire engine and candy."); offers a variety of different categories of responses (The child who indicates that a pencil may be used for such diverse purposes as writing, holding up a window, tapping on a drum, or conducting an orchestra is more flexible than a child who suggests it might be used to draw pictures, write numbers, or compose a story.); proposes highly unusual or clever responses to a problem (A child who finishes the incomplete sentence, "He opened the bag and found..." with "...a giant, black-and-orange, spotted butterfly," is more original than a child who says, "...an apple."); adds on to or expands simple ideas to make them more "elegant" (A child who responds to a teacher's request to add more information to the sentence, "The cat sat on the porch," with "The lazy black and white alley cat sat on the rotten old porch," is more creative than the child who says, "The black cat sat on the old porch.").

6. *Sense of humor*—laughs at things not normally perceived by children of the same age; tells jokes.

7. *Behavior*—sensitive to the needs and feelings of other children and adults; has strong feelings of self-confidence; influences others.

These major areas describe the intellectually gifted, but remember that gifted-ness may extend to other dimensions of development, too. For example, if a child seems to have outstanding physical, musical, or artistic talents, he or she should be recommended for special assessment. A variety of tests and other measures could be used to identify these children.

A Program for Gifted Preschoolers

It makes sense that teachers of gifted children follow the guidelines for establishing a personalized curriculum as described for children at risk. As with "at-risk" children, no single method will work with all gifted children; individual strengths and interests dictate several approaches. Jane Wolfle advises that as we consider special programs, above all else, we must not remove childhood from the lives of gifted preschoolers. She elaborates, "The gifted preschooler is a child and should be treated like a child. Most three-year-olds have simple areas of interest whether they are gifted or not, but gifted children often show an interest in learning *more* about a topic or material."[23] So, like their peers, gifted youngsters will want to play with airplanes and trucks but are motivated to investigate them in more detail (how high airplanes fly or how trucks transport goods from a terminal to the final destination, for example). Wolfle explains how this can be done:

> After "playing airplanes," this child should be encouraged to draw, paint, or mold the plane he had been "flying," and to tell a story about his art. Gifted preschoolers are more goal directed and may enjoy cooperative play earlier than their agemates; sharing their work and ideas with the class will fulfill both these capacities. . . . These children might also enjoy tape recording their stories so they can listen to them over and over. An additional activity might be actually reading their stories after dictating them to an adult. . . . Supplying children with materials that will stimulate them (books, computers, art materials) and at the same time allow them to remain part of the group will help their skill development while providing intellectual challenge.[24]

The object of working with gifted preschoolers, then, is not to isolate them with the materials and activities only they can use; rather, it is to provide enrichment and acceleration experiences within the classroom for all children. We must allow gifted preschoolers to grow to their fullest by building on their interests and talents in developmentally appropriate ways.

SOME FINAL THOUGHTS

I wonder how many of you reading this book have ever attended a social gathering of people your own age and found everyone to be just like you. The thought is ludicrous, isn't it? We take the idea of our individuality for granted, and we certainly recognize our friends and acquaintances as unique people. But in school we often overlook this concept. Faced with a new group of four-year-olds, it is often tempting to recall theorists from child development class—Piaget, Erikson, Gesell, and others—and assume that our children will all be like the four-year-olds described by these respected authorities. With that notion in mind, we often plan for and interact with children in ways expected of "all" four-year-olds.

Generalizing to any particular age group in this manner is potentially dangerous. There is at least as much variation among the characteristics of any group of young children as there is in a group of your friends, and probably more. A typical group of young children will differ in these ways, among others:

temperament	behavior
race	enthusiasm
life experiences	self-confidence
language	ethnic background
sex	mental age
background motivation	self-perception
family background	handicaps
chronological age	height
learning style	physical health
interests	intelligence
thinking processes	

Children differ from each other from the time they enter this world; their differences are accentuated as their environment and heredity interact. They may be alike in some ways—infants, toddlers, and young children certainly share many common characteristics, or they wouldn't be categorized in separate stages of development by all childhood authorities—but they differ in others. For that reason we must certainly get to know the general features of "oneness," "twoness," "threeness," "fourness," and "fiveness," as they are described in child development courses and other authoritative learning resources, but we must also use our knowledge as a base for making and defending appropriate curriculum decisions for any individual within a specific group. Good teachers do not just know many facts about the development of children. They must also be willing and able to accurately and effectively apply their learnings in designing curricula best suited to the uniqueness of any child entrusted to their care.

NOTES

1. Istar Schwager, "Stages, Not Ages," *Parent's Guide: Sesame Street Magazine* (March 1987): 6.
2. Nancy Lauter-Klatell, *Readings in Child Development* (Mountain View, CA: Mayfield Publishing Company, 1991), p. 1.

3. John B. Watson, *Behaviorism* (Chicago: University of Chicago Press, 1924), p. 104.

4. Rosalind Charlesworth, *Understanding Child Development,* 2nd ed. (Albany, NY: Delmar Publishers, 1987), p. 382.

5. Alexander Thomas, Stella Chess, and Herbert Birch, *Temperament and Behavior Disorders in Children* (New York: New York University Press, 1968).

6. T. Berry Brazelton, *Infants and Mothers* (New York: Dell, 1969), p. xvii.

7. Kathleen Stassen Berger, *The Developing Person Through Childhood and Adolescence,* 2nd ed. (New York: Worth Publishers, 1986), p. 228.

8. Jerome Bruner, foreword to T. Berry Brazelton, *Infants and Mothers* (New York: Dell, 1969), p. iii.

9. Abraham H. Maslow, *Motivation and Personality,* 2nd ed. (New York: Harper & Row, 1970).

10. John W. Santrock and Stephen R. Yussen, *Child Development: An Introduction,* 5th ed. (Dubuque, IA: Wm. C. Brown, 1992), p. 551.

11. Erik Erikson, in Guy R. Lefrançois, *Of Children,* 7th ed. (Belmont, CA: Wadsworth, 1992), p. 403.

12. Mildred Parten, "Social Participation Among Preschool Children," *Journal of Abnormal and Social Psychology, 33,* no. 2 (April 1932): 243–369.

13. Keith Barnes, "Preschool Play Norms: A Replication," *Developmental Psychology, 5,* no. 1 (July 1971): 99–103.

14. Elizabeth J. Hrncir and Corinne E. Eisenhart, "Use With Caution: The 'At-Risk,' " *Young Children, 46,* no. 2 (January 1991): 24.

15. U.S. Office of Education, "Education of Handicapped Children," *Federal Register* (part 2) (Washington, DC: Department of Health, Education and Welfare, 1977).

16. Philip L. Safford, *Teaching Young Children With Special Needs* (St. Louis, MO: C. V. Mosby, 1978), p. 11.

17. Nancy H. Fallen and Warren Umansky, *Young Children With Special Needs,* 2nd ed. (Columbus, OH: Merrill/Macmillan, 1985), p. 81.

18. U.S. Office of Education, "Education of Handicapped Children."

19. Department of Governmental Relations of the Council for Exceptional Children, "New Federal Preschool Program under PL 99–457" (Reston, VA: The Council for Exceptional Children, 1986).

20. Penny Low Deiner, *Resources for Teaching Young Children With Special Needs* (New York: Harcourt Brace Jovanovich, 1983), pp. 13–14.

21. Ibid.

22. Jane Wolfle, "The Gifted Preschooler: Developmentally Different But Still 3 or 4 Years Old," *Young Children, 44,* no. 3 (March 1989): 42.

23. Ibid., p. 45.

24. Ibid., pp. 45–46.

CHAPTER 4

The Concept of Developmentally Appropriate Practice

Children have a natural curiosity about their world; they are fascinated by all its wonders. They enjoy being told about things, of course, but derive greatest meaning and pleasure from confronting new objects, living beings, or events with their eyes, ears, noses, mouths, and fingers. Young children need to lift, feel, taste, smell, hear, observe, drop, shake, roll, and rattle to find out about their world.

Observing this strong hunger to learn has inspired many parents and teachers to view children as little sponges, eager to soak up the academic world. These adults have sought to formalize the teaching of basic academic skills in many early childhood programs with workbooks, dittoed material and a strong emphasis on learning words and numbers. Although early formalized academics may be the rage in various communities throughout the country, many experts condemn its use. They firmly maintain that the preschool period is not developmentally suited for explicit academic instruction. Instead, they have rallied around the cry of "developmentally appropriate practices," the focus of this chapter. As you read, use the following questions to guide your thinking.

- How is the concept of *developmentally appropriate practice* described?

- What is the conception of the learner, the learning process, and the goals of education for those who espouse developmentally appropriate practices?

- What authoritative evidence supports the call for developmentally appropriate practices in our nation's early childhood programs?

- What are the implications of this educational philosophy for choosing and utilizing materials and activities?

- How are assessment procedures influenced by the use of developmentally appropriate practices?

▶▶▶▶▶▶

An Episode to Ponder

I have taught kindergarten children for twelve years. During most of that time I worked in an academically oriented school. I remember my first year—the children arrived so eager to learn. Yet, there I stood knowing very little about what to do. I was informed that the curriculum was a given; the director handed me a thick manual and two workbooks (plus a folder of ditto sheets) for each child. Being new, I felt pressured to follow the program precisely. Children spent most of their day at their desks filling in workbooks. Even their "art" time turned into an exercise in coloring or pasting according to specific directions; the end product was to conform to an adult's preconceived pattern rather than encourage creative freehand artwork. I even found myself setting unreasonable controls on what was supposed to be a twenty minute "play time." I limited the materials, required minimal noise, and even took away their freedom of choice—remembering that it was best for young children to stay "on task." Although I was rewarded by my director for doing a good job (class discipline as well as scores on the California Test of Basic Skills were considered "outstanding"), something seemed to be wrong. I didn't know what it was until after my sixth year. Suddenly and shockingly I found it in the children's faces. Every class entered the year as eager, happy children. However, as the year unfolded, facial expressions slowly took on different looks—fear, boredom, anxiety. The classroom was not theirs; they were not happy. Was I the best person for the job? I got to thinking about it very deeply and began to read a lot about the harms of excessive academic pressures during the early years. I even took an evening course in child development at a local university. What I learned was astonishing. I was constantly controlling children, turning them into passive learners. Surely, they did well on standardized achievement tests, but could they think? Did they enjoy school? Did I value child-initiated learning? Did I appreciate individuality? It was a lot for me to think about, and did I ever think! Many changes, including a new teaching job, came into my life. However, the most important was a conviction that it is our professional duty to tailor early childhood programs to the child rather than the reverse.

This first-hand account of one teacher's experiences could be duplicated in schools around the country many times over. Countless newcomers entering into the profession with a love for teaching and for children find that their efforts to tailor a program to the developmental characteristics of young children are thwarted by those who passionately seek to stimulate early intelligence through every means possible, including rigid drill and practice exercises. Pressures placed on preschool and kindergarten administrators by parents who are driven to "raise the brightest child in America" (see Chapter 2), have resulted in curricula that offer intensive academic challenges. Expectant mothers enter their "Baby Smiths" for desired programs before the tots are even born. Tuition for such exclusive programs is often in excess of $4000 per year, but competitive parents are willing to pay the price. "There's so much pressure to get into college," contends one mother. "You have to start them young and push them on toward their goal. They have to be aware of everything—the alphabet, numbers, reading. I want to fill these little sponges as much as possible."[1] Because of the pressures on parents to get their toddlers into prestigious preschools, some entrepreneurs have even established special "prep" courses for two-year-olds, explicitly geared to help them pass the entrance examinations.

This trend toward pushing young children to achieve academically has been deplored by a majority of the early childhood establishment on the grounds that it places the children in a pressure cooker situation that increases the chances of educational burnout, as well as leading to the introduction of inappropriate teaching methods. David Elkind, a prominent child-psychologist, envisions both short- and long-term harm resulting from too early formalized learning. *Short-term* risks derive from the stress that formal education places on young children. Some stress-related danger signals are already evident—fatigue, headaches, loss of appetite, and stomachaches. Chicago psychologist Myra Leifer has seen 'several' distressed two- and three-year-olds who have pulled out clumps of hair or their eyelashes. Other signs of disturbance may not surface for years.[2] *Long-term* risks are of three kinds, according to Elkind: motivational, intellectual, and social. Formal instruction, he argues, ignores the spontaneous, self-directed nature of young children's learning. When adults interfere with the child's natural need to explore and manipulate, children become dependent upon adult direction and gradually lose their personal motivation to learn. Early formal instruction puts the child at *intellectual* risk because it requires rote learning by memorization and teacher-initiated instruction instead of self-initiated activity and exploration. The children may master the content to be learned, but they have very little opportunity to ask questions and find answers on their own. When their natural desires to learn are thwarted through too much teacher direction, children often lose spontaneity and initiative in learning. Introducing formal instruction too early also puts the child at *social* risk. It introduces the notions *correct* and *incorrect* as denoting degrees of social comparison. One child gets an answer right, and another gets it wrong; one is smarter, somehow better. Such comparisons are especially damaging among preschoolers. T. Berry Brazelton argues that if one line of development (mental abilities) is placed out of proportion, the child will not have a chance to learn the other two (physical and social). Brazelton is especially concerned about the child's ability to cope socially:

> Being precocious is not likely to make for a well-rounded child or even for one who is acceptable to his classmates. When straining so hard to master tasks that are beyond his age level, he may not have the time or emotional energy left over to care whether they like him or whether he likes them. He may become too self-centered, too self-critical and, ultimately, too emotionally upset to deal successfully with the realities of living. And that's not what caring parents would ever want for their child.[3]

A vocal critic of early formalized learning, Burton White, expressed his concerns for the total well-being of the child:

> During the early years some of a child's most important learning is in the social realm. Children learn to relate to people in fundamental ways during the first six years of life. They learn to use their bodies. And they go through experiences that are not dictated by any lesson plan but nevertheless seem to be an important part of healthy early development. Any program that promises precocity ultimately has to be evaluated in the light of all its effects on the broad pattern of development in the child.[4]

Thus, the competing forces fervently volley arguments back and forth on their philosophical battlefield, each side attempting to wrest control of the direction into which early childhood education should proceed. The conflict remains heated to this day; it will certainly remain so during the years to come, when you will enter the profession and become involved in deciding what form your curriculum should take. There are many labels associated with each philosophical front; for the purposes of this book, we will refer to the competing forces as the **psychometric philosophy** (supporting early formalized learning experiences) and the **developmental philosophy** (advocating informal learning through play). Currently, the early childhood profession stands solidly behind the developmental philosophy and wholeheartedly supports its basic tenets through an appeal for "developmentally appropriate practices." Many parents, however, cite the positive gains made during the 1960s and 1970s by children of poverty through academically-oriented "compensatory" programs. These parents see developmental learning as a "soft" approach and demand schools that push their children to learn. "If children from 'underprivileged' circumstances can make such gains from early intervention, just imagine what ours can do!" they claim.

How does a beginning professional sort out the confusion associated with this controversy? Perhaps the best way to start is to consider the factors involved in establishing a philosophy of education.

DEVELOPING A PHILOSOPHY OF EDUCATION

When educators express strong feelings about how children should be taught, they are communicating their **philosophies of education.** Philosophies of education incorporate our strong beliefs about how children grow and learn; in turn, they help us determine the activities and materials we consider most beneficial. Philosophies are important because they give us direction for what we do and help explain why children do what they do. Our philosophies do not emerge instinctively; they are based on strong beliefs that emerge as one becomes attached to a particular set of **theories** (underlying principles of developmental phenomena). Presently, there are two major, sharply contrasting philosophies (models) of the learner—the psychometric and developmental. David Elkind describes the psychometric model of the learner as being composed of specific **measurable abilities.**[5] Children learn best by being screened, evaluated, and moved through a predetermined sequence of teacher-directed learning experiences having predictable outcomes that can be measured and

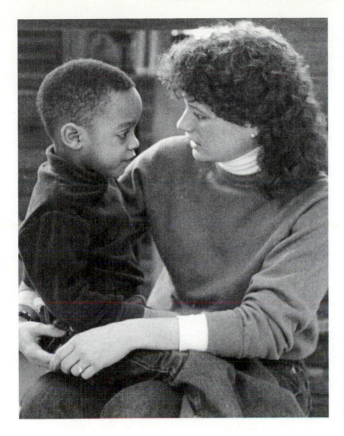

Regardless of what philosophy is chosen, teachers must maintain a close, caring relationship with children.

quantified (tested). Developmental learning, on the other hand, characterizes learners as developing at different rates of intellectual growth. Children must be active, make choices, discover, create, discuss, and greet a variety of new challenges while constructing understandings, each at his or her own rate. These are two extremes of a continuum, and many variations can be placed at various points between the two. (See Figure 4–1). At this point of your professional preparation, where would you

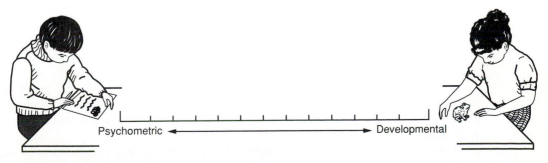

Psychometric ⟵⟶ Developmental

Figure 4–1   A continuum of educational philosophies

take a position on the continuum? According to Polly Greenberg, "Seldom do we see *excellent* examples of *either* philosophy. The majority of excellent programs mix aspects of each model."[6] Because the conflict between these two philosophies is so current and important in terms of your professional development, this chapter will explore the subject comprehensively.

THE PSYCHOMETRIC PHILOSOPHY

Academically-oriented teaching practices gain their support from the psychometric philosophy, whose conception of the learner is rooted in the acquisition of discrete learning abilities. The philosophy postulates that any existing ability must exist in some amount and, therefore, can be measured; the most common form of measurement found in academically oriented programs is the standardized test. The three most popular forms of standardized tests are these varieties: (1) *developmental,* (2) *diagnostic,* and (3) *readiness.*

Developmental tests are quick, easy-to-use instruments designed to assess the skills and behaviors children have acquired at any specific chronological age. One of the most easily administered developmental tests is the **Denver Developmental Screening Test (DDST).** It consists of over one hundred items classified into four separate categories: personal-social, fine motor-adaptive, language, and gross motor development. See Figure 4–2. The screening test itself is part of a two-step process. It follows the utilization of the Revised Prescreening Developmental Questionnaire, a parent-answered questionnaire related to age-appropriate accomplishments and an examination of the child. The second step consists of utilizing the full DDST as a more objective developmental screen.

Developmental tests are popularly called "developmental screening tests" because they are the first step in the process of determining whether any particular child may have a disability or potential handicap.

As a first step in an evaluation process, developmental screening tests should never be used to make any decision other than whether or not a child should be referred for further developmental assessment. When the results of a developmental screening test indicate that a child's ability to learn may be affected by a specific liability, a referral for a diagnostic assessment is recommended.

Diagnostic tests offer a more detailed evaluation of the child's developmental needs. They are usually administered by trained professionals and require much more time and expertise to conduct than the developmental tests. Diagnostic tests provide insight into a child's specific strengths and weaknesses and comprise the informational support needed to design possible remediation strategies.

Readiness tests are designed to assess the degree to which a child is prepared to benefit from a specific academic or preacademic program. The results of readiness tests are meant to be used as guidelines to identify a child's potential to benefit from a program of instruction.

Many factors are involved in readiness to learn, and readiness tests offer a broad selection of items and materials for testing purposes. Some contain manipulative

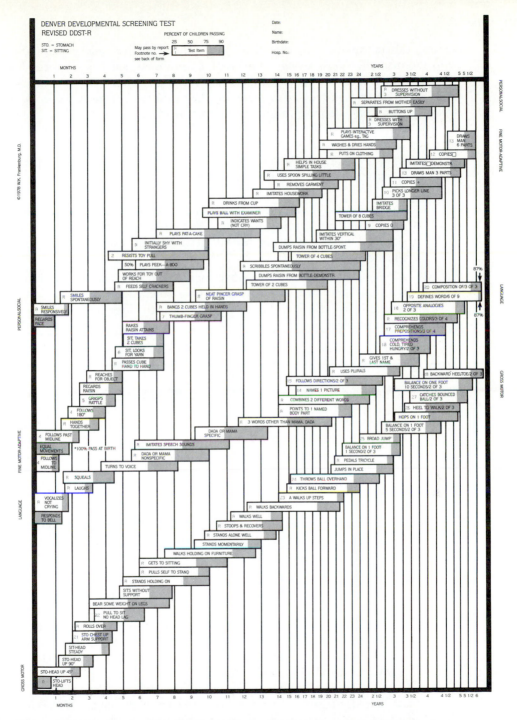

Figure 4–2 The Denver Developmental Screening Test. From Denver Developmental Screening Test by W. K. Frankenburg, J. B. Dodds, and A Fandal, 1975, Denver, CO: LADOCA Project and Publishing Foundation. Reprinted by permission.

devices; others, kits of activities; while still others involve only paper-and-pencil items. Some address only a single dimension of readiness, such as intellectual development; others cover several areas, including social awareness. Of course, some are much more effective in measuring readiness than others—but most, taken by themselves, are far from adequate in giving the total readiness picture of the child. You may wish to examine and compare some popular readiness tests. Two well-known examples are the *Metropolitan Readiness Tests* (Psychological Corporation) and the *Preschool Inventory* (Addison-Wesley). Readiness tests in general are administered as group tests and typically include items like these:

1. *Associating the spoken word with pictured objects.* Four or five pictures are displayed in a line across the page. The child must put a cross on the one corresponding to what the teacher describes. For example, "Put a cross on the clown."

2. *Visual discrimination.* Four or five similar objects or shapes are shown in a row. The first one has a cross on it. One other picture or shape in the row is exactly like the first one. The child marks the identical picture or shape. For example,

3. *Sentence comprehension.* Before the child is a row of pictures. For example, a calendar, lawnmower, clock, and automobile may be illustrated in one row. The teacher may say, "Mary's mother told her to be home at two o'clock. Mark the picture that tells Mary the time to come home."

4. *Copying a design.* A series of geometric figures or alphabet letters serve as models. The child copies the model.

5. *Auditory discrimination.* A row of four or five pictures is placed on the page. At the left is a stimulus picture; for example, a dog. The child marks each picture that beings with the same sound; for example, doll and duck.

6. *Drawing a human figure.* By examining the amount of detail, the teacher can estimate the stage of the child's physical and mental development.

7. *Ability to count and write numbers.* The child is asked to put a cross on a numeral; to mark the first, second, or third object in a row; or to solve a simple mathematical problem such as, "Marlene had four cookies and gave one to each of her two friends. Put a cross on the number that shows how many cookies Marlene had left."

Educators today have two primary concerns about the abuse of developmental and readiness tests with preschool and kindergarten children. First, Samuel G. Meisels[7] criticized the tests because teachers are quick to use the results to label children as "young," "developmentally immature," or "not ready" to benefit from a specific academic program. Moreover, Meisels added, countless schools are using readiness tests to make placement decisions (e.g., whether a child should be admitted to a particular preschool on the basis of his or her test scores). As a result, anxious parents have resorted to desperate measures to ensure that their children are placed in the most highly attractive preschool or kindergarten situation possible. One school district, for example, established a policy whereby a certain readiness test would be administered to all entering kindergarten children to determine which should be assigned to the morning session (least mature) and which should go in the afternoon (most mature). In this particular community, fierce competition developed among the parents to see whose child would be assigned to the most "prestigious" session. Teachers were amazed at the cutthroat nature of the session conflict; parents even formed social groups on the basis of session assignment of their children. Matters finally reached a head late one summer when all the children from the same geographical area near the school not only ended up in the top group of all children taking the test, but displayed a phenomenal command of each task. An informal investigation unearthed the fact that the parents had actually acquired a copy of the readiness test and secretly tutored their children over the summer! It is alarming that schools are using readiness tests alone for making such crucial decisions, especially when, according to Meisels, "labels have been assigned on the basis of tests with unknown validity by testers who have had little training and usually no supervision." [8] As a matter of interest, readiness tests have error rates in the range of 50 percent, meaning that half of the children placed in any program on the basis of readiness test scores are done so in potential error. We could achieve the same accuracy in placing children by flipping a coin (and it would be less expensive and time consuming)!

A second concern about readiness tests is that we ignore very special characteristics of children at this stage of development. According to Peck, McCaig, and Sapp, educators should be aware that

- Most young children will never before have taken a test—paper-and-pencil or any other type—and they may well be scared of the procedure, the intimidating room, other children, and the strange adults. Therefore, the results will in no way resemble a complete or accurate picture of what these children can do.
- Most children have no idea what is expected of them in a testing situation. They may use the pencil or marker awkwardly, be more interested in what is going on around them, or just be bored. Most children are not accustomed to performing for adults on command. Even if they try, few children pay attention to things that have no interest for them.
- The time of day, what children have heard about tests from parents or other children, their lack of familiarity with following specific instructions, and many other factors can drastically affect test results.
- Children's first impression of school may be that of the test. If the test is difficult or seems too easy, or the people are not friendly, or the room is overwhelmingly large or noisy, children's impressions may not be positive.
- Even if tests are valid and reliable, if they are administered just prior to the opening of school or during the first few weeks, the teacher has little time to prepare for the needs of students as identified by the test. On the other hand, children's abilities change so rapidly that tests administered in the spring may not reflect the child's status when school starts in the fall.

- Children vary greatly in development and come from a variety of backgrounds. Their behaviors cover a wide range, all of which may be typical and perfectly natural for their age. Ideas, language, the setting, and the tasks and materials may be unfamiliar or incongruent with the child's experiences. Other tests of children's abilities have been shown to be culturally biased....

- Parents, who know the child best, are rarely asked to participate or to provide information about the child. Parents can provide a medical history, alert the school to any potential problems, give a broader picture of the child's early development, and discuss personality characteristics relevant to learning (perseverance, interests, etc.). Test data should never be used without knowledge of sociobiographical information about the child...the child's responses must be considered in context.[9]

NAEYC has expressed a strong concern for the improper use of standardized tests and has endorsed a set of guidelines for standardized testing. Their guidelines apply to all forms of standardized testing but, for preschoolers and kindergartners, primarily address the uses and abuses of readiness and developmental screening tests. (See Table 4–1).

NAEYC's position on standardized testing during the early years restricts testing only for purposes of ensuring that children's special individual needs can be addressed accurately and objectively. In addition, multiple sources of information should be considered when making decisions having a profound effect on a child's life. Samuel J. Meisels supported this claim and suggested that standardized tests be used only

> to make better and more appropriate services available to the largest number of children.... Children who need special services can be identified by developmental screening and assessment. Children in need of modified classroom programming or individualized attention in preschool or kindergarten can be identified by readiness tests and, to a certain extent, by developmental screening inventories. Tests that exclude children from public education services or that delay their access to the educational mainstream, however, are antithetical to legal and constitutional rights to free education and equal protection.[10]

Instructional strategies emerging from psychometric philosophies tend to encourage the acquisition of specific academic skills. Teachers place children in situations where they are carefully and deliberately led through learning episodes (see box on page 118). Educators aligning themselves with this position place children in situations where they are carefully and deliberately led by the teacher through learning episodes over which the teacher has direct control. The children are often taught in groups where they are required to sit and listen to the teacher. Occasionally, they may be asked to imitate the teacher or respond in predetermined ways while the teacher approves or praises correct answers. The emphasis on learning is placed on subskills associated with reading, writing, and math. Learning is reinforced with an abundant supply of workbooks and worksheets; paper-and-pencil seatwork focuses upon memorization of letters, words, numerals, and number facts. Children's efforts may be recognized with "stars," "smile faces," and other such material rewards. Even art projects must imitate a pattern displayed by the teacher. Psychometric classrooms find little time for play, creative thinking, group or individual problem solving, risk,

Table 4–1 NAEYC Position Statement on Standardized Testing

1. All standardized tests used in early childhood programs must be reliable and valid according to the technical standards of test development.

2. Decisions that have a major impact on children such as enrollment, retention, or assignment to remedial or special classes should never be based on a single test score.

   Appropriate sources of information may include combinations of the following:

   - Systematic observations, by teachers and other professionals, that are objective, carefully recorded, reliable (produce similar results over time and among different observers), and valid (produce accurate measures of carefully defined, mutually exclusive categories of observable behavior).

   - Samples of children's work such as drawings, paintings, dictated stories, writing samples, projects, and other activities (not limited to worksheets).

   - Observations and anecdotes related by parents and other family members.

   - Test scores, if and only if appropriate, reliable, and valid tests have been used.

3. It is the professional responsibility of administrators and teachers to critically evaluate, carefully select, and use standardized tests only for the purposes for which they are intended and for which data exists demonstrating the test's validity (the degree to which the test accurately measures what it purports to measure).

4. It is the professional responsibility of administrators and teachers to be knowledgeable about testing and to interpret test results accurately and cautiously to parents, school personnel, and the media.

5. Selection of standardized tests to assess achievement and/or evaluate how well a program is meeting its goals should be based on how well a given test matches the locally determined theory, philosophy, and objectives of the specific program.

6. Testing of young children must be conducted by individuals who are knowledgeable about and sensitive to the developmental needs of young children and who are qualified to administer tests.

7. Testing of young children must recognize and be sensitive to individual diversity.

Source: "NAEYC Position Statement on Standardized Testing of Young Children 3 Through 8 Years of Age," *Young Children, 43,* no. 3 (March 1988): 42–47.

or exploration; these are peripheral activities, not a central part of the program. Polly Greenberg shared this letter, written by an excellent teacher of three-year-olds, as a description of life in an academic preschool classroom:

> When I started work, it was in a preschool I later learned would be called an academic preschool, but until all the debate began in the mid-1980s, I thought it was the way all preschools were. It was a top-of-the-line private school. So all the wrong ideas and strategies I had learned were reinforced. I spent my days chiding children. If my aide and I had a child who refused to "perform," we pursued him like furies. I remember the frightened little faces of those who never did well. If tears troubled their eyes, I felt I was reaching them, motivating them. I look back now and feel it was an affront to childhood, just pure intimidation and pretension (which cynics say is the aim of most human behavior anyway). I worry now, praying I didn't char any little hearts with my predictions about how they would never amount to anything if they didn't work harder. They were only 3 years old![11]

> > > > > > >

A Classroom Based on the Psychometric Philosophy

Seated at a table with a small group of children, Mr. Koh enthusiastically announces, "We are really going to have fun today." The children meet his announcement with an approving, "Hooray!"

"I want you all to be good listeners and lookers while I show you a picture. What am I going to do?"

"Show us a picture," reply the children in unison.

"You are all very good listeners today," says Mr. Koh. "Look at the picture and tell me what kind of animal you see."

"Bunnies," offer the children.

"Very, very good," replies Mr. Koh. "Now I will count the number of bunnies in the picture. Follow my finger as I point to each bunny...one bunny...two bunnies. How many bunnies did I count?"

"Two bunnies!" exclaim the children.

"I like your answers," compliments Mr. Koh. "Now you count the bunnies while I point."

"One bunny...two bunnies," count the children in unison.

"Oh, you are so smart today," says Mr. Koh. "Now let me see if I can fool you. Here is another picture—a picture of some kittens. There is one kitten in the picture."

"No!" counter the children.

"No?" questions Mr. Koh. "Show me! I'll point to the kittens and you help me count."

"One kitten...two kittens," chant the children. "See you can't fool us."

"You're right," admits Mr. Koh. "You're too sharp for me today."

Following this rapid-fire dialogue, Mr. Koh distributed a worksheet to the children. On it, they were directed to circle each set of two items.

THE DEVELOPMENTAL PHILOSOPHY

Early childhood authorities today have nearly unanimously sent forth the message to eradicate the rigid, formalized practices of the psychometric philosophy that have crept into preschool and kindergarten programs and to replace it with a curriculum that gives children a chance to be children. These reformers argue that quality programs do not place a lopsided emphasis on academics, but seek to offer a safe and nurturing environment that promotes the *whole child: physical, affective, and intellec-*

Young children must be provided with rich opportunities that enhance all areas of development.

tual development. Many factors influence the success of early childhood programs, but, according to NAEYC, "a major determinant of program quality is the degree to which the program is *developmentally appropriate.*[12] NAEYC defined the concept of developmental appropriateness as having two dimensions: age appropriateness and individual appropriateness.

1. *Age appropriateness.* Human development research indicates that there are universal, predictable sequences of growth and change that occur in children during the first 9 years of life. These predictable changes occur in all domains of development—physical, emotional, social, and cognitive. Knowledge of typical development of children within the age span served by the program provides a framework from which teachers prepare the learning environment and plan appropriate experience.

2. *Individual appropriateness.* Each child is a unique person with an individual pattern and timing of growth, as well as individual personality, learning style, and family background. Both the curriculum and adults' interactions with children should be responsive to individual differences. Learning in young children is the result of interaction between the child's thoughts and experiences with materials, ideas, and people. These experiences should match the child's developing abilities, while also challenging the child's interest and understanding.[13]

To translate these two dimensions into actual classroom instruction requires a sound theoretical base—one that is today drawn primarily from the influential works of Jean Piaget and Lev S. Vygotsky.

The Influence of Piaget and Vygotsky

Our present-day concerns for developmentally appropriate practice have caused a marked revival of interest in the work of Jean Piaget. Although his work is not free of controversy, Piaget has furnished educators with enlightened ideas about the nature of children's thought (see Chapter 3). Piaget asserts that young children develop cognitive structures (intelligence) by becoming involved in and by thinking about physical actions performed on objects in their environment. This exploratory behavior begins during infancy, when thought is not possible without action. Table 4–2 describes how the sensory and motor explorations of infants eventually evolve into increasingly mature thought processes.

Table 4–2   Intellectual Achievement During Piaget's Sensorimotor Period

Stage	Characteristics of Intellectual Achievement
1. Reflexes (birth–1 month)	Infants respond to the environment only with reflexes. They suck to receive nourishment or grasp objects placed in their hands.
2. Primary circular reactions (1–4 months)	Reflexes become elaborated upon and coordinated. Sucking, for example, is an inborn behavior intended to help the baby ingest food. However, if a safe object is placed near the infant's mouth, the inborn reflex would cause her to suck the object and, perhaps, enjoy the experience. The infant would then repeatedly seek out the object, not for food-getting, but for pleasure. The change in purpose from food-getting to pleasure is elaboration, whereas the process of grasping and bringing the object to one's mouth is an example of a higher order of coordination. Active repetition, "habituation," of such activity is characteristic of this period.
3. Secondary circular reactions (4–8 months)	In stage 2, babies repeat actions because of the pleasure they bring. Now they repeat actions for the purpose of seeing what will happen. The first shake of a rattle may startle a child, but with experimentation the child soon knows that certain regular movements of his arm will cause a sound. Once the child shakes the rattle for the purpose of producing the sound, he is demonstrating a specific skill or repeating actions not only for the pleasure it brings but also to experience the consequence of the action itself.
4. Coordination of schemes (8–12 months)	The child's reactions are now becoming more purposeful. She may initiate an action now because she has a specific goal in mind. For example, if a desired toy is shown to the child and then placed beneath a scarf out of a child's sight, the child will look for it, lift off the scarf, and grasp the toy. This is an example of object permanence, or knowing that an object exists even though it cannot be seen. Object permanence exists only in a rudimentary form at this stage, however. If the toy were taken by the adult from beneath the first scarf and placed beneath a second scarf (even while the baby was watching), the baby would still look under the first scarf and look in wonderment as to why it was no longer there.

Table 4–2 *(Continued)*

Stage	Characteristics of Intellectual Achievement
5. Discovery of new schemes (12–18 months)	Infants begin to demonstrate a rudimentary form of purposeful, trial-and-error activity at this stage. They sill make accidental discoveries of actions as they explore their world, but now they no longer exactly repeat those actions for pleasurable results only. They seem to be "experimenting" with the objects or actions for the purpose of seeing what makes them different than others. Infants also begin to discover new ways of attaining certain goals. For example, instead of crawling to a toy and grasping it to play, the baby may now pull it to herself by means of an attached string. Finally, the concept of object permanence is complete except for multiple displacements. For example, if you put a small toy in your hand, put your hand inside a box, and brought your hand out for the baby to see, the baby would look for the toy in your hand.
6. Invention (18–24 months)	Children now have a fairly good understanding of the nature of objects and the results of their actions upon objects. They no longer need to perform trial-and-error actions with objects in order to "understand," but can now picture events in their minds in order to solve new problems. In essence, they are learning to think, and words become attached to the mental pictures. For example, an 18-month-old baby is pushing and pulling a sliding screen door back and forth. All is going well until a toy block becomes wedged in the door track and hinders the door's movement. Without needing to experiment in order to determine how to get the door to slide again, the baby visualizes the problem and removes the block from the track. In addition to the development of thought processes, the child is now beginning to use language. The concept of object permanence is also complete at this stage.

This Piagetian description of how infants begin to distinguish between themselves and their world and gain the ability to organize and coordinate sensations with physical movements is the best example of what might happen during early stages of cognitive development. The cognitive world of the preschooler evolves from this beginning into what Piaget refers to as the period of **preoperational thought** (ages two to seven years). During this time, stable concepts are formed, mental reasoning emerges, and magical beliefs are constructed.

Preoperational Thought

Infants pursue much self-initiated activity "just for fun." This characteristic continues during the early years as the children learn much more about their world through play and sensory exploration. Children learn a lot through these avenues, but does *all* knowledge come from rousing the five senses? Is knowledge limited only to a child's ability to organize the sights, sounds, smells, tastes, and sensations of touch? Piaget says no. Certainly, a great deal of what young children learn happens through sensory exploration; humans are unique from other life forms in that they are able to develop *mental schema* (structures) that help interpret and organize sensory stimulation as it is received from the environment. The environment is viewed as the activating agent and the child is seen as the ambitious seeker of knowledge. Piaget

Babies are explorers and adventurers. They learn much through sensory exploration.

sees the knowledge of objects gained from individual actions on objects as only one type of knowledge: **physical knowledge.** For example, a child learns about the weight of a series of containers by picking them up. In order to obtain this information, she must be able to focus on only one property and ignore all others (color, size, and shape). Piaget refers to the acquisition of information about objects themselves gained by the initiation of individual action on those objects as **simple** or **empirical abstractions.** Knowledge gained through the physical experience is important, but is joined by two other important types of experiences: *logico-mathematical experiences* and *social-conventional experiences.*

Logico-mathematical knowledge is gained as children are able to perform actions on objects that help them perceive characteristics not physically present in the objects themselves. For example, when given a choice of a red or blue ball, the child may consistently choose the red one. She makes her selection based on a physical property (color) of the ball and uses that criterion as her basis of choice. Choosing on the basis of a single observable quality of objects is rooted in physical knowledge. As the child's cognitive skills grow and she is able to perceive characteristics that are not physically discernable in the objects themselves, she may call for "two balls." *Twoness* does not exist as a physical characteristic gained through action on the objects themselves, but is based on a relationship that must be constructed in one's mind. Relationships among objects that are constructed by the learner herself is logico-mathematical knowledge. Piaget refers to the understanding of relationships constructed by individuals as **reflective abstractions.**

Social-conventional experience differs from physical and logico-mathematical knowledge in that it has other people as its source. Social-conventional knowledge includes arbitrary truths that have been agreed upon and accepted by a cultural group as convention. Piaget asserts that culture is an important source of knowledge; it would not be desirable, for example, to learn through experience only that cars must stop at an intersection when the light is red. We learn the names of objects, too, not by inventing our own language system, but by accepting the conventional word labels commonly agreed upon by our culture. That is why most children in the United States associate the word "chicken" to a particular mealtime favorite, whereas their counterparts in Spain use the word *pollo* (pō-yō).

Often, there is an interaction between two or more of Piaget's three sources of knowledge. I recall an example where an inquisitive four-year-old was touching many objects on the beach. A jellyfish washed ashore and immediately caught the child's attention. As he ambled over to the blob, his mother called, "No! That's a jellyfish. It can sting and hurt." At a safe distance, the child warily looked at the long hanging tentacles and jellylike substance, not venturing to touch it. He eventually went about collecting a variety of shells, seaweed, driftwood, and sea glass, putting each into separate buckets. But, he refused to go near the jellyfish. Obviously, the child learned in three ways: (1) he learned through his own actions on the various seashore objects, (2) he classified the objects by constructing relationships, and (3) some knowledge was given to him. It is difficult to say how much knowledge children gain from performing their own actions on objects as opposed to obtaining knowledge from people, but Piaget contends that children learn through various experiences.

Thus, for Piaget, thinking begins during infancy as the child performs physical actions on objects and matures into sophisticated forms of reasoning abilities. The period of life when the child learns by empirical abstractions (constructs knowledge by pushing, pulling, shaking, dropping, and other actions on objects) is called the **sensorimotor period** (birth to two years). During the next period, the **preoperational period** (two to seven years), the child's thinking is considered unstable. It is during this stage that children begin to use primitive reasoning abilities, referred to as "intuitive" thought by Piaget. Piaget used the term *intuitive* because children seem so sure about their understandings, but are unaware of how they know what they know. One characteristic of preoperational thought is called **classification.** Classification involves a child's ability to group objects based on some common criterion. For example, from a group of geometric figures we may ask the child to "put together the things that you believe go together in some way." (See Figure 4–3.) The sorting might look something like that shown in Figure 4–4. When asked, however, whether the objects could be sorted as shown in Figure 4–5, the preoperational child would be unlikely to agree. The understanding that objects could be cross-classified simultaneously has not yet evolved.

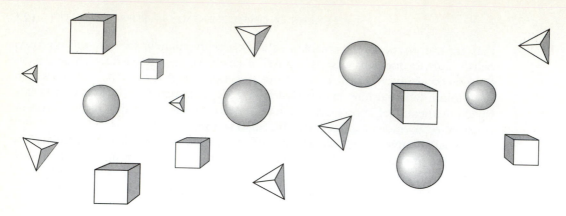

Figure 4–3

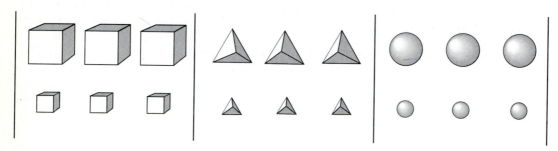

Figure 4–4

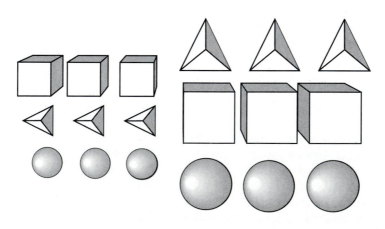

Figure 4–5

This example shows a characteristic of preoperational thought called **centration,** or the focusing of attention on one characteristic to the exclusion of all others. Another evidence of centration is the preoperational child's lack of **conservation.** Conservation is an understanding that the quantitative aspects of objects do not change unless something has been added or taken away from them (despite other changes in the objects). Some popular tests of conservation skills are shown in Figure 4–6. In Piaget's theory, failing the conservation tasks indicates that the child is at the preoperational stage of cognitive development. Passing the test (this usually happens around seven years) indicates that the child is at the concrete operational stage. The **period of concrete operations** (7 to 11 years) finds the consolidation of thinking abilities into true logico-mathematical skills. The child can reason beyond the limitations of characteristics directly observable in physical objects.

Lev Vygotsky's ideas about how young children learn are quite similar to Piaget's, but he does not ascribe to a sequence of developmental stages as described by Piaget. Vygotsky, instead, distinguishes primarily between two types of concepts that young children construct through experience: **spontaneous concepts** and **school-related concepts.** Spontaneous concepts are those that children construct through direct experience, such as that a cork floats in a container of water, whereas a marble sinks. These are concepts that children are able to construct free of instruction by an adult. School-related concepts are much different; they originate in a culture and represent arbitrary (commonly agreed upon) knowledge from past generations; as examples, the spoken or written word symbol "cat" stands for the real animal and the numeral "4" represents a specific amount. These conventional concepts must be communicated in a school-type social experience because they would be virtually impossible to construct solely from direct personal experiences.

A close examination of Piaget and Vygotsky indicates strikingly similar tenets. For example, Vygotsky's view of spontaneous concepts closely parallels Piaget's notion of constructing physical and logico-mathematical knowledge. And, Piaget's ideas regarding social-conventional knowledge is comparable to Vygotsky's school-learned concepts. These theoretical frameworks are quite important in helping early childhood educators establish a sound philosophy to support what they call "developmentally appropriate practices."

NAEYC use Piaget's and Vygotsky's theories as support for an interactionist, constructivist philosophy of learning, as described in its acclaimed *Guidelines for Developmentally Appropriate Practice:*

- *Curriculum planning emphasizes learning as an interactive process. Teachers prepare the environment for children to learn through active exploration and interaction with adults, other children, and materials.*

   The process of interacting with materials and people results in learning. Finished products or "correct" solutions that conform the adult standards are not very accurate criteria for judging whether learning has occurred. Much of young children's learning takes place when they direct their own play activities. During play, children feel successful when they engage in a task they have defined for themselves, such as finding their way through an obstacle course with a friend or pouring water into and out of various containers. Such learning should not be inhibited by adult-established concepts of completion, achievement, and

	Have the children agree that there are:	Then make this change:	And ask the children:
Conservation of liquids	two equal glasses of liquid. 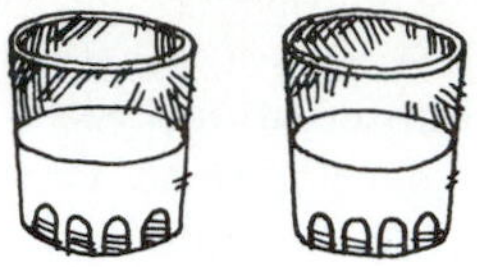	Pour one into a taller, thinner glass. 	Do the glasses contain more, less, or the same amount? Why do you think so?
Conservation of number	two equal lines of coins. 	Lengthen the spaces between the coins on one line. 	Do both lines have the same number of checkers or does one line have more? Why do you think so?
Conservation of matter	two equal balls of clay. 	Squeeze one ball into a long thin shape. 	Which piece has more clay—the ball or the snake? Why do you think so?
Conservation of length	two pencils of equal length. 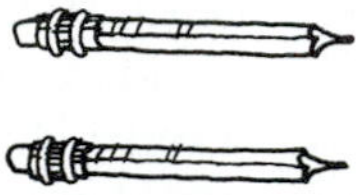	Move one pencil. 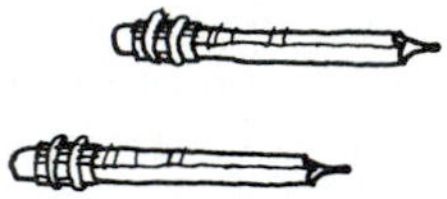	Would two ants starting a hike at the end of the pencils and walking at the same speed both travel the same distance? Why do you think so?
Conservation of area	two identical pieces of green construction paper representing a field of grass on which are placed the same number of red blocks representing barns. Add a toy horse to each field. Establish that both animals have same amount of grass to eat.	Rearrange the barns. 	Do the animals still have the same amount of grass to eat? Which has more? Why do you think so?

Figure 4–6 Piagetian conservation tasks

126

failure. Activities should be designed to concentrate on furthering emerging skills through creative activity and intense involvement.

- *Learning activities and materials should be concrete, real, and relevant to the lives of young children.*

    Children need years of play with real objects and events before they are able to understand the meaning of symbols such as letters and numbers. Learning takes place as young children touch, manipulate, and experiment with things and interact with people. Throughout early childhood, children's concepts and language gradually develop to enable them to understand more abstract or symbolic information. Pictures and stories should be used frequently to build upon children's real experiences.

    Workbooks, worksheets, coloring books, and adult-made models of art products for children to copy are *not* appropriate for young children, especially those younger than 6. Children older than 5 show increasing abilities to learn through written exercises, oral presentations, and other adult-directed teaching strategies. However, the child's active participation in self-directed play with concrete, real-life experiences continues to be a key to motivated, meaningful learning in kindergarten and the primary grades. . . .

- *Teachers provide a variety of activities and materials; teachers increase the difficulty, complexity, and challenge of any activity as children are involved with it and as children develop understanding and skills.*

    As children work with materials or activities, teachers listen, observe, and interpret children's behavior. Teachers can then facilitate children's involvement and learning by asking questions, making suggestions, or adding more complex materials or ideas to a situation. During a program year, as well as from one year to another, activities and environments for children should change in arrangement and inventory, and special events should also be planned.[14]

To further support a developmental approach to early childhood education, NAEYC formulated a position statement specifically focused upon the processes through which children learn most appropriately: "Guidelines for Appropriate Curriculum Content and Assessment in Programs Serving Children Ages 3 Through 8." In answering the question, "What does it mean to approach children developmentally?" NAEYC utilized the theories of Piaget and Vygotsky to suggest this explicit framework:

1. Children learn best when their physical needs are met and they feel psychologically safe and secure.
2. Children construct knowledge. . . . children construct their own knowledge through repeated experiences involving interaction with people and materials.
3. Children learn through social interaction with adults and other children.
4. Children's learning reflects a recurring cycle that begins in awareness, and moves to exploration, to inquiry, and finally, to utilization.
5. Children learn through play.
6. Children's interests and "need to know" motivate learning.
7. Human development and learning are characterized by individual variation.[15]

The basic law of application for Piaget and Vygotsky, then, is that the child constructs his own knowledge through physical *and* mental activity. Active methods presuppose direct movement and manipulation of real objects as well as opportunities to mentally organize the specific content of the experience. In this text, we will examine situations to stimulate children's cognitive development in developmentally appropriate ways. Chapter 6 will consider active methods for stimulating *physical knowledge;* Chapter 7 will address approaches appropriate for *logico-mathematical knowledge;* and Chapters 8 and 11 will deal with *social-conventional knowledge.*

A Classroom Based on the Developmental Philosophy

To help you understand how the developmental philosophy influences classroom practices, consider the scene described below.

This scene depicts learning as an engaging interaction of the child within a challenging environment. Youngsters learn best in a happy, safe, supportive environment where teachers guide and facilitate learning (rather than transmit knowledge to the children) and where children are able to construct their own knowledge.

The interactive/constructive philosophy recognizes the need for child-initiated, spontaneous acitivity because the nature of learning during childhood is active. Anyone who has worked with the very young understands that children spend most of their waking hours inspecting, probing, touching, exploring, questioning, and trying to find out about all the marvelous mysteries of the fascinating new world into which they have been so recently thrust. Their curiosity is intense; it fuels their eager efforts to obtain information from every source possible. It is a rare youngster who is not interested in learning about new things.

▶▶▶▶▶▶

Mrs. Corrado is watching two children playing with the plastic bowling set. One child keeps missing the bowling target by rolling the ball too far to the left. Not perceiving his need to adjust his aim, the child tries once again and misses by the same margin.

Mrs. Corrado sees that the child is beginning to lose initiative, so she is ready with ideas to suggest. "What will happen if you aim the bowling ball just a bit more this way?" asks Mrs. Corrado. Through encouraging the child by asking this type of question, Mrs. Corrado fostered an experimental attitude.

Mrs. Corrado kept teacher-initiated verbalization to a minimum during the play activity, but, afterward, found it desirable to ask the child to reflect on what he had found out—to see how adjustments to his actions may (or may not) have produced desired effects. For example, Mrs. Corrado asked: "What did you have to do to knock over the bowling pins?" and "What will you try next time?"

Helping children by supporting their self-initiated efforts to learn is an important teaching responsibility.

Young children are impassioned learners because they feel good about themselves as learners. They have confidence in their ability to learn. Youngsters react to mysterious elements in their environment with natural intrigue and fascination. For example, consider the child who discovers a strange rock on the playground, picks it up, inspects it, and, in the course of time, asks the teacher questions about it. Her persistence grows as she continues her attempts to find out more. She may compare the features of her new rock with other rocks; ask more questions; smell, bang, or scrape the rock; and, if so skilled, look at rock books to gain more information. Children act much like the playful storybook monkey, Curious George: they confront novel elements in the environment with great energy, seek intense sensory stimulation during their explorations, and even make unintended mistakes. These spirited investigators let very little stand in their way when confronted by curious situations around them. Teachers must be sensitive to their inborn curiosity, for the experiences they have during their early years not only help satisfy their present developmental needs, but help form a framework of more complex thinking behaviors such as logical reasoning and problem solving. In short, teachers must be prepared to ask: "How can I create an environment for learning where the child will feel free to learn from the surroundings, peers, and from me? How can I help him continue the excitement of learning that is so much a natural part of childhood?" John Holt offered a concise, meaningful response to these questions:

> We do not need to "motivate" children into learning by wheedling, bribing, or bullying. We do not need to keep picking away at their minds to make sure they are learning.

> What we need to do, and all we need to do, is bring as much of the world as we can into the school and the classroom; give children as much help and guidance as they need and ask for; listen respectfully when they feel like talking; and then get out of the way. We can trust them to do the rest.[16]

Developmentally Appropriate Practices

By and large, the most vocal cry of early childhood educators today has been in the direction of taking back the curriculum and resisting practices that they feel are not in the best interests of young children. Mainly, experts assert that the curriculum should be cultivated to meet the developmental needs and interests of the children, rather than necessitating the children to meet the demands of a "pushed down," unreasonable curriculum. Advocates of **developmentally appropriate practices (DAP)** advise that child-initiated activities that appeal to natural childhood inclinations—play, exploration, problem solving—must return to the preschool classroom. Nearly every allied professional group in the country has supported this philosophy. NAEYC, for example, has led the assault with its acclaimed "Guidelines for Developmentally Appropriate Practice." The organization asserts that "A developmentally appropriate curriculum for young children is planned to be appropriate for the age span of the children within the group and is implemented with attention to the different needs, interests, and developmental levels of those individual children."[17] The major highlights of NAEYC's position for establishing a developmentally appropriate curriculum are shown in Table 4–3.

A second influential early childhood professional organization, the Association for Childhood Education International (ACEI), has also issued a position statement regarding developmentally appropriate preschool practices. The ACEI addressed the especially strong academic orientation in kindergarten programs, and made the recommendation found in Table 4–4.

Certainly, professional organizations composed mainly of early childhood educators would be likely to promote such similar child-centered views. Meanwhile

Table 4–3 Guidelines for Developmentally Appropriate Practice for Children from Birth Through Age 8 (The Curriculum)

A. Developmentally appropriate curriculum provides for all areas of a child's development: physical, emotional, social, and cognitive through an integrated approach.

B. Appropriate curriculum planning is based on teachers' observations and recordings of each child's special interests and developmental process.

C. Curriculum planning emphasizes learning as an interactive process. Teachers prepare the environment for children to learn through active exploration and interaction with adults, other children, and materials.

D. Learning activities and materials should be concrete, real, and relevant to the lives of young children.

E. Programs provide for a wider range of developmental interests and abilities than chronological age range of the group would suggest. Adults are prepared to meet the needs of children who exhibit unusual interests and skills outside the normal developmental range.

F. Teachers provide a variety of activities and materials; teachers increase the difficulty, complexity, and challenge of an activity as children are involved with it and as children develop understanding and skills.

G. Adults provide opportunities for children to choose from among a variety of activities, materials, and equipment; and time to explore through active involvement. Adults facilitate children's engagement with materials and activities and extend the child's learning by asking questions or making suggestions that stimulate children's thinking.

H. Multicultural and nonsexist experiences, materials, and equipment should be provided for children of all ages.

I. Adults provide a balance of rest and active movement for children throughout the program day.

J. Outdoor experiences should be provided for children of all ages.

Source: "NAEYC Position Statement on Developmentally Appropriate Practice in Early Childhood Programs Serving Children From Birth Through Age 8" in Sue Bredekamp, Ed., *Developmentally Appropriate Practice in Early Childhood Programs Serving Children From Birth Through Age 8* (Washington, DC: NAEYC, 1987): 3–8.

other educators and policymakers have likewise become disturbed by the academic preschool. In a report entitled *Right From the Start,* the National Association of State Boards of Education took a surprisingly assertive stand on the status of education for four- to eight-year-olds:

> Preschool, kindergarten and primary grade teachers report an increasing use of standardized tests, worksheets and workbooks, ability grouping, retention and other practices that focus on academic skills too early and in inappropriate ways.
>
> ...Policies have been adopted that, while perhaps appropriate for improving high schools, may be less helpful for elementary schools and very young children. For example, it may well be the case that making high school students work harder is an appropriate formulation. However, lack of effort is not the problem for kindergarten students.

Table 4–4 The ACEI Child-Centered Kindergarten[18]

An effective, developmentally appropriate kindergarten program (both curriculum and learning environment):

- Recognizes and accepts individual differences in children's growth patterns and rates by setting realistic curriculum goals that are appropriate to their developmental levels.

- Educates the whole child—with attention to physical, social/emotional and intellectual developmental needs and interests.

- Responds to the needs of children as developing, thinking individuals by focusing on the processes of learning rather than disparate skills, content and products.

- Provides multiple opportunities for learning with concrete, manipulative materials that 1) are relevant to children's experiential background and 2) keep them actively engaged in learning and discovering through use of all the senses, leading to more input upon which thought is constructed.

- Provides a variety of activities and materials by incorporating 1) learning activities that encourage active participation through "hands-on" activity, communication and dialogue; 2) large blocks of time to pursue interests; 3) time to ask questions and receive answers that develop concepts and ideas for use at varying levels of difficulty and complexity; and 4) time to reflect upon and abstract information when encountering different viewpoints from peers.

- Views play as fundamental to children's learning, growth and development, enabling them to develop and clarify concepts, roles and ideas by testing and evaluating them through use of open-ended materials and role-enactment. Play further enables children to develop fine and gross motor skills, to learn to share with others, to see others' point of view and to be in control of their thoughts and feelings.

- Provides opportunities for the use of multicultural and nonsexist experiences, materials and equipment that enhance children's acceptance of self and others and enables them to accept differences and similarities among people, including those who are handicapped in some way.

- Embraces the teaching of all content areas, presented as integrated experiences that develop and extend concepts, strengthen skills and provide a solid foundation for learning in language, literacy, math, science, health, art and music.

- Allows children to make choices and decisions within the limits of materials provided, resulting in increased independence, attention, joy in learning and feelings of success necessary for growth and development.

The legitimate concern about the link between our economic future and the quality of schooling has fostered a competitive mentality for our educational enterprise, with unfortunate consequences for early segments of schooling. If education is seen as a contest that pits children against their peers, or race against our foreign competitors, we risk teaching very young children the wrong academic tasks in an appropriate fashion before they are ready, and we stimulate fears and pressure among parents.

...Thinking in young children is directly tied to their interactions with people and materials. Young children learn best and most by actively exploring their environment, using hands-on materials and building upon their natural curiosity and desire to make sense of the world around them.[19]

It's clear that preschool children learn through many activities commonly considered "play."

Other national organizations such as the Association for Supervision and Curriculum Development,[20] the National Association of Early Childhood Teacher Educators,[21] National Association of Elementary School Principals,[22] the National Council of Teachers of English,[23] and the National Council of Teachers of Mathematics[24] have offered similar testimony calling for a halt to formal academic instruction.

In a developmentally appropriate program, learning is not defined by narrow subject areas, but through spontaneous encounters with interesting or puzzling things. Children are encouraged to discover, make choices, move at will, discuss, and grapple with personal challenges. The major goal in curriculum implementation is to interact with people and materials in a richly prepared indoor and outdoor environment. Much learning takes place during play activities. While engaged in play, children exercise opportunities to develop creativity and imagination while learning much about math, science, social studies, language, literature, and the arts. In order to implement such a program, teachers must develop sophisticated guidance and enrichment skills intended to enhance the type of free play that is chosen. Polly Greenberg elaborates:

> This philosophy of education assumes that what children learn casually and naturally as they live their lives and play their days away is valuable learning, nature's way of educating children...if you will; and that though it can be improved upon by the careful craftswomen that expert childhood practitioners are, adults should not *deprive* children of natural learning by making them sit down and be taught at. This philosophy believes not *only* in preparing the environment for excellent play, but *also* that for the child to have optional learning opportunities, adults (parents or teachers) need to **enrich** the play, **plan** projects, and **teach** children many things somewhat in the same way that one **naturalizes** plants. You carefully arrange your purposeful additions to the landscape here and there and all around in the midst of what's happening there naturally so that to a person stumbling into it, all seems relaxed and natural. We **naturalize** "subjects" and "skills" and the conventional knowledge that we expect children to learn, throughout the children's learning environments (home, school, community).[25]

Myths Associated with Developmentally Appropriate Programs

Because DAP is such a complex phenomenon, myths have sprung up as people have attempted to explain what it all means. Marjorie J. Kostelnik has explained those myths and false assumptions that have become the products of fallacious reasoning. Kostelnik's common myths follow, accompanied by her impressions of reality.[27]

> *MYTH: There is one right way to implement a developmentally appropriate program.* There is no "one right way," because what was optimal for last year's class may not be appropriate for this year. We need not search for one "right" answer, but for the best *answers* to meet the needs of children representing a wide range of abilities, learning styles, interests, and backgrounds.
>
> *MYTH: Developmentally appropriate practice requires teachers to abandon all their prior knowledge and experience. Nothing they have learned or done in the past is acceptable in the new philosophy.* Few experienced teachers require total "overhauls" to become more developmentally appropriate. The knowledge gained from previous experience will serve as a foundation to examine past practices. Some may only need confidence to continue the fine job they have been doing.
>
> *MYTH: Developmentally appropriate classrooms are unstructured classrooms.* Developmentally appropriate classrooms are active ones where many people are talking at once or where several children are moving about the room at the same time. To the untrained eye these conditions may appear chaotic, but a closer look should reveal children on-task, constructively involved in their own learning. If children are wandering aimlessly or racing from place to place,

the environment is not conducive to learning, and so it is developmentally inappropriate.

MYTH: In developmentally appropriate classrooms, teachers don't teach. Teachers in developmentally appropriate programs do not fit the stereotype of standing up in front of a group of students and telling them all they need to know. Instead, curricular goals are frequently addressed through regular classroom routines such as dressing to go outside, preparing for snack time, or cleaning up. Although some whole group instruction takes place, teachers spend most of their classroom time moving throughout the room working with children individually or in small groups.

MYTH: Developmentally appropriate programs can be defined according to dichotomous positions. One position is always right, the other position is always wrong. Developmentally appropriate programming is not an "all-or-nothing" position. For example, process learning is very important to children and should be highly valued. However, anyone who has watched young children proudly show off their work knows that products are sometimes important, too. Planning a program is therefore a matter of balance. Developmentally appropriate programs are both varied and comprehensive.

MYTH: Academics have no place in developmentally appropriate programs. Academics must not be equated with technical subskills (e.g., reciting the ABCs or number sequences) or with rote instruction (e.g., masses of worksheets). Children are interested in numbers and words, but manifest their desire to learn these skills in ways that go beyond rote learning. Small group instruction, active manipulation of relevant, concrete materials, and interactive learning provide a solid foundation for academics within a context of meaningful learning.

MYTH: Developmentally appropriate programs are suitable for only certain kinds of children. Although specific details concerning what is appropriate for children will vary from population to population and from child to child, the principles of guiding developmentally appropriate programs are universally applicable.

MYTH: Developmental appropriateness is just a fad, soon to be replaced by another, perhaps opposite, trend. If developmental appropriateness is conceived of as a philosophy, it will not fade away. Certain basic assumptions and beliefs will prevail, regardless of how we choose to operationalize them. In other words, the essence of developmental appropriateness is not simply what we do, but how we think: how we think about children and programs, what we value children doing and learning, and how we define effectiveness and success.

Special Teaching Skills

For children to learn optimally through developmentally appropriate practices, teachers must cultivate a specific set of skills that are direct implications of the philosophy.

Those teaching skills, listed below, compose the bulk of what the rest of this text is about:

1. Providing many direct experiences and concrete, manipulative materials
2. Creating a stimulating, manageable learning environment
3. Offering enriched free play opportunities
4. Fostering learning through teacher-guided, integrated, thematic projects that take place in meaningful contexts rather than as subjects, like "math" or "science"
5. Working effectively with families
6. Learning how to interject thought-stirring questions or comments while children approach the solution of a new problem, the acquisition of new knowledge, or the development of a new skill
7. Helping children acquire healthy self-discipline through fair, firm guidance procedures
8. Establishing a multicultural, nonsexist environment

By working hard to acquire these skills, you will be among those extraordinary professionals who regard the child as an active learner with steadily growing abilities. You will understand how to facilitate the overall development of children by encouraging them to construct their own understandings—each at their own rate of intellectual development—instead of forcing youngsters to master a predetermined set of skills or understandings. In short, you will help develop individuals who are, as described by Piaget, "capable of doing new things, not simply repeating what other generations have done—[individuals] who are creative, inventive, and discoverers."[26] Early childhood professionals will have to unite and insist that programs for young children be staffed with teachers mindful of the special nature of the very young. They must be able to base instruction not exclusively on the chronological age of the child, but on an assessment of each child's stage of development. We must keep in mind that a true early childhood education does not happen only with rote transmission of shapes, colors, letters, numbers, and words. To truly educate, early childhood teachers must walk a fine line between the "dribble down" problem (moving content and instructional practices down from the elementary school) and the "play only" problem (no content; goals and objectives are unclear). Developmentally appropriate teaching avoids both extremes. It is neither overly academic nor just play. It provides young children with meaningful interactions with adults as well as opportunities to explore and discover.

SOME FINAL THOUGHTS

With increasing information about how children learn, parents and teachers sometimes overemphasize the child's intellectual growth. As a consequence, a number of early childhood programs have tended to transfer the traditional elementary school program to the preschool classroom by teaching facts and skills associated with reading, writing, and mathematics. These schools, based on the psychometric philosophy, believe that the acquisition of knowledge and skills is the most important goal in early childhood education. In turn, they teach with highly directed methods, with the hope that the children will score high on standardized tests of achievement. However, most preschoolers are not ready for such abstract thinking. They want to form wet sand, observe ant colonies, group seashells, and investigate the world through their senses. Children want to figure out what things are, how they work, and how they fit into their lives.

Those advocating developmentally appropriate practices capitalize on young children's natural capacity to learn by organizing an environment in which children interact and explore with enjoyment. You do not need a great variety of expensive materials to do this—common objects like spools of thread, pebbles, or pots and pans will suffice. The world outside the classroom is a great resource, too. Just consider the possibilities for learning associated with leaves (shapes, sizes, colors, and textures). Children, however, do not learn simply by being placed in an environment with all these things and left alone. They need adults who talk with them; point out shapes, sizes, and colors; help them perceive relationships among things; and assist them to organize their world in ways that will aid them when they begin formal learning. Talking with children is a very important part of the program, because it helps them to acquire and refine the language skills so essential for the growth of higher mental abilities.

Preschoolers learn so much by doing. Be near to provide stimulation and encouragement. If you are there, the youngster will associate enjoyment and success with increasingly sophisticated learnings. The overall goal of developmental learning, then, is to produce active, creative, independent thinkers who pursue learning not for its external reward but for deep internal satisfaction. True and meaningful learning, according to the overwhelming majority of early childhood experts today, can be experienced only when children are actively engaged in age- and individually-appropriate educational opportunities.

NOTES

1. Lynn Langway, et al., "Bringing Up Superbaby," *Newsweek* (March 28, 1983): 62.
2. David Elkind, "Formal Education and Early Childhood Education: An Essential Difference," *Phi Delta Kappan, 67,* no. 9 (May 1986): 631–636.
3. T. Berry Brazelton, "Do You Really Want a Superbaby?" *Family Circle* (December 3, 1985): 75.
4. Burton White, quoted in Sue Berkman, "See the Baby. See the Better Baby," *American Baby* (May 1984): 79–80.
5. David Elkind, "Developmentally Appropriate Practice: Philosophical and Practical Implications," *Phi Delta Kappan* (October 1989): 113–117.

6. Polly Greenberg, "Why Not Academic Preschool? (Part 1)," *Young Children, 45,* no. 2 (January 1990): 70.

7. Samuel J. Meisels, "Uses and Abuses of Developmental Screening and School Readiness Testing," *Young Children, 42,* no. 2 (January 1987): 4–6; 68–73.

8. Ibid., p. 4.

9. Johanne T. Peck, Ginny McCaig, and Mary Ellen Sapp, *Kindergarten Policies: What is Best for Children?* (Washington, DC: National Association for the Education of Young Children, 1988), pp. 21–22.

10. Samuel J. Meisels, "Uses and Abuses of Developmental Screening and School Readiness Testing," p. 71.

11. Polly Greenberg, "Why Not Academic Preschool? (Part 1)," p. 70.

12. Sue Bredekamp (ed.), *Developmentally Appropriate Practice in Early Childhood Programs Serving Children From Birth Through Age 8* (Washington, DC: National Association for the Education of Young Children, 1987), pp. 1–2.

13. Ibid., p. 2.

14. "NAEYC Position Statement on Developmentally Appropriate Practice in Early Childhood Programs Serving Children From Birth Through Age 8," in Sue Bredekamp, ed., *Developmentally Appropriate Practice in Early Childhood Programs Serving Children From Birth Through Age 8* (Washington, DC: National Association for the Education of Young Children, 1987), p. 3.

15. "Guidelines for Appropriate Curriculum Content and Assessment in Programs Serving Children Ages 3 Through 8," *Young Children, 46,* no. 3 (March 1991): 21–38.

16. John Holt, *How Children Learn* (New York: Pittman, 1967), p. 187.

17. "NAEYC Position Statement on Developmentally Appropriate Practice in Early Childhood Programs Serving Children From Birth Through Age 8," in Sue Bredekamp, ed., *Developmentally Appropriate Practice in Early Childhood Programs Serving Children From Birth Through Age 8* (Washington, DC: National Association for the Education of Young Children, 1987), p. 3.

18. J. Moyer, H. Egertson, and J. Isenberg, "The Child-Centered Kindergarten." *Childhood Education, 63* (1987): 235–242.

19. National Association of State Boards of Education, *Right From the Start* (Alexandria, VA: Author, 1988), pp. 3–5.

20. Association for Supervision and Curriculum Development, "Testing Concerns," in *Forty Years of Leadership: A Synthesis of ASCD Resolutions Through 1987* (Alexandria, VA: Author, 1987), pp. 17–19.

21. National Association of Early Childhood Teacher Educators, "Resolution: Testing in the Early Years," *The Journal of Early Childhood Teacher Education, 10,* no. 1 (1989): 16–17.

22. National Association of Elementary School Principals, "Standardized Tests." In *Platform 1988-1989* (Alexandria, VA: Author, 1989), p. 7.

23. National Council of Teachers of English, "Testing and Evaluation." In *NCTE Forum: Position Statements on Issues in Education from the National Council of Teachers of English* (Urbana, IL: Author, 1989), pp. VI:1–VI:4.

24. National Council of Teachers of Mathematics, *Curriculum and Evaluation Standards for School Mathematics* (Reston, VA: Author, 1989).

25. Polly Greenberg, "Why Not Academic Preschool?" pp. 71–72.

26. Quoted in Richard E. Ripple and Verne E. Rockcastle, eds., *Piaget Rediscovered* (Ithaca, NY: School of Education, Cornell University, 1964), p. 5.

27. Marjorie J. Kostelnik, "Myths Associated with Developmentally Appropriate Programs," *Young Children, 47*, no. 4 (May 1992): 17–23.

CHAPTER 5

The Significance of Play

Play is a spontaneous activity that begins shortly after birth and becomes an important activity for young children throughout their preschool years. It influences all areas of development: intellectual, social, emotional, and physical. Play is an enjoyable pursuit, but it is also an important device by which children practice skills, solve problems, socialize, cooperate, discover, communicate, and exercise all the essential abilities central to childhood. Play is something on which children spend a lot of time and expend a great deal of energy; most children spend a great portion of their waking hours in play. Adequate materials and sensitive adults promote good play in the early childhood setting. This chapter examines the topic of play as it contributes to a developmentally appropriate program for young children and offers suggestions for encouraging play among youngsters. As you read, use the following questions to guide your thinking.

- What is play? How does it contribute to the total development of the child?
- What is the role of play in developmentally appropriate programs?
- What are the major dimensions of play? How have Mildred Parten, Jean Piaget, and Sara Smilansky helped distinguish the characteristics of these dimensions?
- How do infants play? What do they play with or at?
- How does the play of toddlers and young children differ from the play of infants?
- What is creativity? How does it relate to play?
- How do teachers provide guidance during play times but still allow enough freedom to encourage children to experiment and investigate freely?

An Episode to Ponder

Eleven-month-old Jed crawls over to an empty cup, takes a few loud gulps, and grins at his parents.

Two-year-old Carrie puts her doll in its cradle, says "night-night," then picks it up and starts again.

Three-year-olds Lynn and Alexis take a pretend car trip together. On the way, they put on various hats and jewelry, run out of gas, get into car crashes, stop to care for sick babies, and negotiate over who gets to drive.

From its first isolated appearances at the age of about one year to its rich flowering years later into scenes with complex plots and roles, pretend play occupies an important place in a child's development.

—Wendy Schuman

Do you remember playing as a young child: climbing trees, jumping in leaf piles, sliding down a snowy hill, sitting in a cardboard box "space shuttle" zooming through outer space, rocking your favorite doll or stuffed animal to sleep, molding a chunk of clay or mud into a funny shape, building a magic castle with blocks, sloshing your hands through a container of sudsy water, or eating pretend soup with a toy spoon? Can you recall how you did these things "just for the fun of it"? These are surely among our most pleasant childhood memories. If you were like most other children, you had a strong need to play. A boundless supply of energy and a wealth of ideas constantly poured forth into a fountain of activity providing endless opportunities for exploration, discovery, creativity, and fun. Through play, you learned from your environment as you never will again. Supportive guidance opened up the doors to a world where you grew to understand yourself and those with whom you lived. It is likely that no one ever told you as a child that play was so valuable; you probably would not have understood if someone had. The environment we establish for the children will say to them more clearly than we can ever express in words, "Here is a place to explore, to discover, to express your feelings, to create, to learn, and yes, to have fun."

WHAT IS PLAY?

Early childhood educators have long understood and valued the unique contributions of play to all aspects of childhood. Recall, for example, the pioneering efforts of educational leaders such as McMillan, Froebel, Montessori, and Hill. Each believed that appropriate activities for young children should reflect a powerful play component. Their essential belief in play dominated the preschool curriculum well into the 1960s. At that time, however, strong resistance to play-oriented early childhood programs surfaced. The main reason for this opposition was an intense concern for children raised in conditions created by poverty. It was felt that these children lacked sufficient early experiences of the type necessary for success in school and that, since so much of their early years were neglected, a streamlined, no-nonsense, highly structured format would be required to make up for lost time. One of the major developers of strict, drill-type, academic programs designed to overcome the effects of poverty was Siegfried Engelmann. Defending his program, Engelmann said, "Our motto in trying to work out a successful [learning] approach was simply, keep the baloney [play] out of the program."[1]

As you have read in Chapter 2, early achievement results of these academically oriented preschool programs were quite positive; they even encouraged parents of more economically successful families to think about the gains their children could make if they experienced such intense instruction, too. Parents observing play-oriented preschools during the 1970s and 1980s often expressed concerns similar to those of Deborah Burnett Strother:

> When I started working at my child's cooperative day-care center, I was dismayed by the lack of "structure." Each week I came with activities, projects, and worksheets to keep fingers busy and territorial and toy fights to a minimum. I was disappointed when the children preferred to play independently or changed my ideas to suit their purposes.[2]

Deborah Burnett Strother's original attitude toward play underwent a swift transformation as she gained experience and understanding in that center. Now she relates that, "I feel sad that when my child enters school his playtime will be more structured, ordered, or even missing."[3] Why do some people feel as Strother originally did about the role of play in an early childhood setting?

One major reason is that some people simply do not understand play. They often think of play in rather elementary ways—either as a way of burning off excessive energy or as a recreational pursuit valuable only for its enjoyment. With such a limited knowledge of play, critics consider it to be something the children can do on weekends or at other times when they are home from school. They regard academic learning to be of primary significance for the early childhood program and regard anything that falls short of direct instruction a waste of valuable time. Sue Spayth Riley offers this example of how some have overemphasized their desire for children's academic success:

> A nursery school recently ran into considerable difficulty because the parents were disturbed by the "free play" period. As earnest parents concerned by the academic demands to be made on their children later, they felt this hour was a waste. If Johnny was to get ahead he must not delay learning. He could play on Saturday. The result was that this contested first hour was renamed—"work period." Everyone was satisfied, and the children continued to play.[4]

By participating and observing as Strother did in a children's program, however, these skeptics soon learn that play occupies an important place in a child's life. For children, play is a way of assimilating knowledge and making sense of the world. Play should be understood as an existential need for young children, an innate activity that is crucial for wholesome growth.

Despite this small "bubble-in-time" of excitement about offering formal academics in preschool settings during the 1970s and 1980s, there is a very intense 1990s movement to return play to its developmentally appropriate place in young children's lives. NAEYC's "Guidelines for Developmentally Appropriate Practice" spearheads this movement; it has supported the role of play not only as it contributes to cognitive development, but also as it is a vital link enhancing growth in all realms of development:

> Children's play is a primary vehicle for and indicator of their mental growth. Play enables children to progress along the developmental sequence from the sensorimotor intelligence of infancy to preoperational thought in the preschool years to the concrete operational thinking exhibited by primary children.... In addition to its role in cognitive development, play also serves important functions in children's physical, emotional, and social development.... *Therefore, child-initiated, child-directed, teacher-supported play is an essential component of developmentally appropriate practice.*[5] [italics mine]

NAEYC and other prestigious professional groups have been exceedingly forceful in their advocacy of play; people are convinced of play's potency more today than ever before. Play has returned to its proper position as the very essence of childhood. What is play? No one knows definitely. Sue Spayth Riley says: "It cannot be dissected, catalogued and wrapped up in a neat package for marketing. It is too complex, too subjective, too variable an experience to lend itself to cool, precise definition."[6] B. Tyler adds: "Play, like love, defies description."[7] Carol Seefeldt and Nita Barbour concur: "As with love, there is something almost magical about children's play that mystifies even intellectuals."[8]

DEFINING PLAY

Of all the aspects of this book, the challenge of defining play is perhaps the greatest, because play is such an integral part of every child's life. It is natural, enjoyable, voluntary, spontaneous, and non–goal directed. It can, however, be set apart from other childhood pursuits on the basis of five identifiable characteristics.

> *Intrinsic motivation.* Activities are pursued for the pleasure they bring the child; motivation comes from within. Children are not attracted to play because they will receive praise from a significant adult, for example, but because it is something they like to do.
>
> *Attention to process rather than product.* Children direct their attention to the activity itself rather than to the end product. For that reason, roles constantly shift without causing any worry about how a play episode turns out at the end. A "wife" may have as many as four "husbands" during any play episode; a child may be a "puppy," "sea monster," or "superhero" all in the same morning.
>
> *Nonliteral behavior.* Children use their amazing powers to pretend during play. They can easily become kings, construction workers, mothers, monkeys, or

whatever else suits them in their make-believe world. Play transports children beyond reality.

Freedom of choice. Children choose the activity themselves rather than having it assigned by an adult.

Intense pleasure. Children become passionately involved in their play and pursue it for its special inward pleasures rather than for some type of external motivation or reward.

Play helps children develop in all basic areas: physical, intellectual, social, and emotional. In the physical realm, play develops the large muscles as children lift blocks, ride trikes, dig with shovels, climb ladders, or throw balls. It develops small muscles as the children cut with scissors, draw with crayons, paint with brushes, complete puzzles, or button, lace, zipper, and tie articles of clothing. Play develops intellectual skills as children share and communicate thoughts through language; examine colors, shapes, sizes, and relationships through block play, sand play, painting, and other experiences; make decisions and solve problems; and interact with the environment in many distinctive ways. Play develops social skills when numbers of children cooperate with each other to achieve a common goal. Whenever one child becomes involved with another, that child must learn how to be accepted, how to get along with the other so that everyone enjoys the activity, how to give and take, and how to develop empathy and consideration for others. Finally, children learn to express, control, and manage their feelings; play out tensions, frustrations, and fears; or simply take comfort in knowing that it's okay to "act like a child."

Play is considered a synergetic activity; that is, it is a combined force whose separate features work together into a correlated wholeness. Take block play, for example. All aspects are interwoven in the child's play experience and become separated only when play is analyzed for academic purposes and broken down into its components. Let us examine block play to illustrate some of the benefits children derive from it.

- *Physical development.*
  - Large motor. Lifting, stacking, pushing, pulling, and climbing efforts all contribute to large motor growth and coordination.
  - Small motor. Manipulating toy cars and trucks, cutting a construction paper road, or stacking a pile of blocks develop small muscle control as well as eye-hand integration.
- *Intellectual development.* Perceiving size and weight relationships, counting, matching, sorting, communicating with others, and understanding that blocks are symbolic representations of the real world are among the important learning experiences acquired through block play.
- *Social development.* Sharing responsibility, coordinating group efforts, cooperating, achieving satisfying friendships, and building self-confidence result from individual and combined efforts.

- *Emotional development.* Deriving pleasure from completing an enjoyable activity, sustaining interest, overcoming frustrations, and expressing an openness of feelings (frustration and joy) accompany the use and mastery of blocks.

Play begins with the exploratory behavior of infants and continues as a central part of our lives even into adulthood, as we become involved in our competitive games or recreational pursuits. Although its basic characteristics change as we get older, the enjoyment of play doesn't change. Play is necessary in the lives of youngsters and is vital to all aspects of their development. In fact, as Jerome Bruner has stated, "Play is . . . the principal business of childhood."[9]

THE DIMENSIONS OF PLAY

According to the available research on play, there are two major categories, or dimensions, of play. The **social dimension** deals with the ways that children progress from solitary pursuits to an interest and skill in collaborating and cooperating with others. The **content dimension** refers to the composition of play, or what children play with, such as sand and blocks; or what the children play at, for example, serving tea. The key point to remember about the two dimensions is that each is developmental. The patterns of play enjoyed during infancy develop into new models as the children grow older and accumulate new experiences. But the earlier patterns do not disappear suddenly as new characteristics emerge; play becomes different as behaviors gradually change throughout childhood. Rosalind Charlesworth offers a fitting example of how play with objects emerges during infancy and develops throughout the early childhood years:

> Interaction with objects begins in infancy. The nine-month-old infant grasps an object and puts it in his mouth. He waves the object and bangs it. By twelve months of age, the child usually looks at the object, turns it over, touches it, and then puts it in his mouth, waves it and/or bangs it. By fifteen months, the child visually inspects an object before he does other activities with it. By the time he reaches three years of age, he is acting out themes with objects, such as feeding a doll using a toy cup and saucer or having a doll drive a toy truck.[10]

As the child grew from stage to stage, some behaviors from previous stages were left behind and others were carried on. Children never leave a complete set of behaviors as they develop new ones. Development through play is continuous; what comes before influences what follows as interactions with the environment cause the child to adapt and change.

THE SOCIAL DIMENSION

Social play is play that entails social interactions with peers. Mildred Parten's historically recognized categories of social play, which were described in Chapter 3,

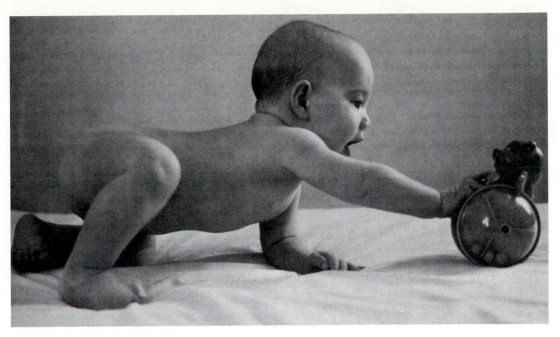

What is the value of this play activity for a baby?

compose the most widely accepted theory explaining how social play evolves from infancy throughout the preschool years. During these years, children progress from patterns of play that are quite solitary to those that are increasingly social. Very young children may or may not want to become involved with others as they play with a watering can, wagon, doll, stick, or truck. But as they seek to extend the possibilities inherent in their play, youngsters eventually look for other children to play with. These significant peers are very important to children because only they can share the imaginative thinking that is so much a part of the early years. Do adults understand that the empty orange crate is really a race car, that the pile of leaves is obviously a nest of baby birds, or that the mud patty is the juiciest, tastiest cherry pie ever made? This private world of make-believe appears to be the exclusive property of children. The border between reality and fantasy is very fluid for the very young, and they move back and forth freely. For this reason, youngsters bring wide ranges of behavior to their play situations.

As children become increasingly aware of their environment, they begin to realize that others must be involved in their play activity to portray that environment most effectively. Think how limited our "fire fighter" would be if there were no "kitty" on top of a burning building to save, or how restricted our "baby birds" would be if there were no "mama" or "papa" bird to feed them their "worms." The need for playmates must be met in the early childhood setting. However, these play opportunities may present critical interpersonal conflicts as the children stubbornly refuse to participate in ways their companions deem as suitable. For example, Kacie, who had been content for weeks to be Nikki's "mommy," now wants to move away from the housekeeping center and toward the block center, where she sets up shop as a gas station attendant. Nikki, sensing the loss of a crucial play partner, pleads with Kacie, "But I *need* a mommy. The baby *needs* her mommy!" and breaks into tears.

During play youngsters learn to give and take, solve conflicts, and perceive things from others' points of view. Your leadership in this area is critical, for inherent in the idea of social growth through play is the children's ability to learn about their place in the world from each other. They must learn how much to expect from others and how much of their own desire they will need to compromise in order to become a functioning group member. Learning these things is not a major problem for many, but it may be painful for some children. Conflicts will arise over play areas, sharing or using equipment, or how group projects can best be carried out. You must be able to help children solve such conflicts and work toward acceptable group behavior. More information on this topic is presented in Chapter 12.

THE CONTENT DIMENSION

The social dimension of play does not explain by itself all the major facets of the play experience. We must now examine what children play with or at—the content dimension. As described earlier, play enables children to transform or explain their world. They are communicating a level of understanding as they fit their play to the degree of experience they bring to it. If they have had very limited experiences, children will not have rich play opportunities, because they will have very little to express through their play. Conversely, children with full, varied life experiences will find much to play with or at. The content dimension of play reflects the experiences children have had in their lives, beginning in infancy. What kinds of play do children normally enjoy at various developmental stages? Perhaps the best way to answer this important question is to combine the shared features of two of the most popular current explanations of the content dimension of play, based on the teachings of Jean Piaget and Sara Smilanksy.[11] These explanations divide the content dimension into three basic categories: *sensorimotor play, symbolic play,* and *games with rules.*

Sensorimotor Play

Sensorimotor play is engaged in by infants as they gain pleasure from exploring the environment through their senses and emerging motor skills. The term **sensorimotor** was chosen as a label for this type of play because it is descriptive of the kinds of play experiences infants enjoy—organizing and coordinating sensory stimuli with physical movements and actions. Annie L. Butler, Edward Earl Gotts, and Nancy L. Quisenberry describe these two play activities as follows:

> Sensorimotor play is the earliest form of play. It appears in infancy and is typically prominent until about age two. The word *sensory* emphasizes the roles of (a) sucking

Through play, infants learn to control their actions to make many interesting things happen.

and mouthing, (b) making sounds and listening, and (c) gazing at and following moving objects visually, including one's own hands and feet. The word *motor* emphasizes those simple movements of infancy which result in (a) control of grasping and handling objects, (b) physical mobility from sitting up to eventual walking and running, (c) production of speech sounds and the formation of words, and (d) exploration and knowledge of one's own body. Play in this period of life is accordingly referred to as *sensorimotor play.*[12]

Muscular movement and sensory stimulation gained through interactions with play objects become a framework upon which new play behaviors are built. The banging together of pots and pans by a nine-month-old, therefore, serves to stimulate the senses (making sounds and listening) and motor skills (grasping and handling objects). But in addition, the skills gained by repeating such actions will help the child gain confidence in his own abilities and eventually lead to more mature forms of exploration and problem solving. Rosalind Charlesworth found that, when children meet new objects, which are refinements of the sensory and motor play of infancy: (1) they usually go through a sequence of four activities, many of exploration,

(2) manipulation, (3) practice, and (4) repetition.[13] Charlesworth used an example from the work of Catherine Garvey,[14] in which she described the behaviors of a three-year-old boy approaching a large wooden car he had never seen before.

1. *Exploration:* He paused, inspected it and touched it.
2. *Manipulation:* He then tried to find out what it can do. He turned the steering wheel, felt the license plate, looked for a horn and tried to get on the car.
3. *Practice:* Having figured out what the object was and what it could do, he got to work on what *he* could do with *it*. He put telephones on it, took them off, next put cups and dishes on it. Now he knew what could be done with the car.
4. *Repetition:* He then climbed on it and drove furiously back and forth with suitable motor and horn noises.[15]

The child's beginning exploratory efforts were sensory and motor in nature. He touched, poked, and prodded throughout the first three activities until he found out what the object was and what it was capable of doing. Once the experimentation helped the boy solve his problem, dramatic play activity followed. In this example, it can be observed that the sensorimotor orientation of infancy remains as a play behavior into the early childhood years and serves as an avenue of solving Problems.

Sensorimotor Play Opportunities

Every caregiver is eager to provide the best possible attention during the baby's first years of life. Special relationships between caregiver and child develop from their day-to-day routines. Through these relationships the baby learns to explore his surroundings and remain alert and curious. His responsiveness—smiles, gurgles, coos, and waves—indicate to all that he craves attention. He seeks to be touched, to be held, to move, to hear, and to be played with—he needs stimulation of all his senses.

Babies learn about the world through sensory play. Watch how a baby explores everything within reach by handing her a stuffed animal with a bell inside. She will touch it gingerly, pick it up, try to put it in her mouth, and shake it vigorously. As she hears a jingling sound, she will gurgle with glee and go on to try something new. These actions are done for fun, but they are also attempts to put things together—to learn. When her curiosity has been satisfied about one toy, she will briskly push it aside and seek something else. Give her a plastic key ring; she will chew on it, bang it on the floor, toss it, and study it carefully. All the time, the active, interested baby is learning more and more. Before the age of seven or nine months, the baby does not understand that her play objects are independent of her, so when she shakes a rattle, she does it for the action itself, not to explore or find out about the objects involved. In fact, the baby may not even look at the object when she plays with it, and if a toy falls from view she does not search for it. But between about seven and nine months, babies reach an enormous mental milestone. They begin to realize that the world is separate from their own existence. They develop "object permanence," understanding that objects exist even when they cannot be seen or heard. Now when the baby drops a toy, she will actively search for it, knowing that it is somewhere and can be retrieved. Objects begin to replace physical actions as the focus of the baby's activity. The baby may shake a noisemaker and look at it at the same time, delighting in the effect she has caused. She continues to explore with the same object: "What will happen if I drop it on the floor?" These explorations continue throughout infancy and are a precursor to language. For example, babies attach names to their toys ("ball") or can find toys when asked to ("Where is your ball?").

Watch your infants play, for sensory activities are among the most important processes of infancy. They occur spontaneously in normal, healthy babies. Even during the earliest weeks of life, before he can perform the exploratory actions described above, baby's play begins with the senses of seeing and hearing. Mobiles or objects hanging above the crib are excellent first playthings. They should be constructed safely and firmly fastened to the crib so they won't fall. Select mobiles with designs or figures on the bottom that the baby can see.

When the baby learns how to sit up, he is beginning to see the world from a new angle. Let him visually explore his new environment while sitting in a safe infant seat. He can watch you perform your duties, view the outdoors, or look at older children playing. When the baby begins to lift his head up while lying on his tummy, you may want to encourage crawling by placing a colorful toy just out of his reach and tempting him to reach out for it.

Babies delight in opportunities to touch, wave, bang, and push objects around. They love to explore color, shape, texture, movement, and sound qualities. You don't need expensive toys—pots and pans, old cereal boxes, and other common household items easily amuse them and naturally captivate their interest. They need toys and interactions that appeal to many different sensory stimulations—soft "clutch balls" or figures to grasp, feel, and let go of; a clean spoon that can be held in the hand or put in the mouth; multicolored rattles of different sizes and shapes. Babies love bath time and water toys. They enjoy pushing toys in the tub, watching them sink and float, and feeling the wet, warm water. They will pat and splash the water gleefully for quite some time.

After about six months, babies are starting to control finger movements a little better, and "busy-box" activity toys can be introduced. These toys have knobs, switches, wheels, or other features that can be pulled, pushed, turned, or dialed to make a noise or change their appearance. The baby can now manipulate toys, and she will especially enjoy balls to throw, items that can be stacked, and simple puzzles, plastic bottles, or boxes in which items can be placed, pop beads, or play workbenches. Don't expect the baby to use these toys as they are intended, for a particular skill or interest may not yet be developed. For example, she will enjoy putting stacking rings on a post, but not in order. Similarly, the baby may enjoy pulling pop beads apart but not possess the eye-hand coordination necessary to put them back together again.

Developmentally appropriate toys bring great satisfaction and joy.

At about one-and-a-half years, the baby may begin a transition to symbolic play by using toys in make-believe play. He is still interested in banging a cup, for example, but now he may also pretend to drink from it. He may grasp a clean spoon and put it in his mouth, or use it to "feed" you some cereal. He may dial a play phone and pretend to be listening to someone talk to him. He uses toy objects as they are meant to be used, either in play by himself or with dolls and stuffed animals. As he progresses through toddlerhood, though, he will begin to imagine that these toys are something else.

Throughout infancy, babies learn to play at their own pace. Some will sit and play with one object for quite some time. Others will throw something down and go from one toy to another quickly. Some will be serious, others more relaxed. Some will exaggerate their actions; others will be more contained. It is important to recognize these individual differences and adjust your interactions to the roles the children enjoy during play. By your involvement and sensitivity, you must communicate to the child that you accept and value play and that it appeals to you. Watch the baby carefully to see how she responds to the play activity. Never force her to respond; don't push her; don't force her to change her play to something else just because you think it's time to go on. Her enjoyment will be fullest if she is allowed to follow her own play rhythm and interests. A summary of play interests during infancy is shown in Table 5–1.

Table 5-1 Sample play interests during the sensorimotor stage

- Rub smooth satin on the child's cheek.

- Tickle the baby's lips with a soft piece of terry cloth.

- Hold a favorite toy in front of the baby and encourage him to reach for it.

- Suspend a favorite toy above the baby with elastic so she can look at it, reach out and bat it, and watch it move.

- Get a toy that can be attached to a flat surface by means of a suction cup. Encourage the baby to reach for and grasp it.

- Hold the baby on your lap. Place a favorite squeaky toy in front of him so he must reach for it. Squeak the toy and reinforce the baby's efforts with praise and smiles.

- Occasionally place a brightly patterned sheet on baby's crib so she can be visually stimulated.

- Babies are attracted by bright objects. Move a bright object or penlight across the baby's line of vision until she follows the light with her eyes.

- Place a mirror above the child in the crib.

- Lay the baby on a variety of surfaces during feeding, changing, rest, or play.

- Provide toys with different kinds of surfaces— plastic, cloth, furry, soft, smooth.

- Stimulate the baby's hearing by tying a bell to his bootie or around his wrist, putting a rattle in his hand, setting a metronome near him, talking or singing, rustling paper near his ear, or playing soft music periodically.

- Say a series of babbles (*ma, pa, ba, ga*) so the child hears them easily. Say these sounds or the baby's name in various situations. Reward the baby's attempts to imitate you.

- Call the baby's name from the side of the crib opposite where she is looking. If she doesn't respond, gently turn her toward you and offer a bright smile.

- Say the baby's name to her over and over again. Sometimes sing it, and sometimes vary your pitch and inflection. Try to get her to look at you when you do this.

- Smile and talk as you hold the baby. Hold him between 12 and 18 inches from your face. Tickle him or toss him gently, trying to make him laugh and gurgle.

- Use a pull toy that makes some type of sound. Pull it slowly back and forth in front of the baby.

- Seat the child upright in a soft chair and support his head with pillows. Hold a toy or bright object in front of the baby and encourage him to initiate head support. Gradually reduce the support until you see how well the baby keeps his balance. Repeat the procedure.

- Place a soft, small object (sponge or soft cloth) in the baby's hand and wrap her fingers around it. Take your hand away. Repeat the procedure if she drops it. Then vary the texture of the objects placed in the baby's hand.

- Seat the child on your lap facing you and pull her up by having her grasp your fingers.

- Stand the baby on your lap and bounce him up and down, smiling and saying a series of babbles.

- Help the child to stand by placing his hands on the corners of the crib.

Symbolic Play

The sensorimotor stage lasts to about two years of age—at which point children begin transforming objects in the physical environment into symbols. The exact age at which this stage begins varies from child to child, but somewhere between the age of nine and thirty months, children begin turning objects into other objects through their imagination and acting toward them as if they actually were those objects. For example, a child might treat a large packing box as if it were a powerful truck struggling up a hill with a heavy payload. The interaction between the child and truck takes on a deeper meaning than simply the action involved in manipulating the truck for sensory or motor purposes. It becomes an avenue by which the child can show what he understands about his physical and social world. Likewise, dolls, blocks, and other materials help children develop a greater and more accurate understanding of their environment by allowing them to reproduce the realities of people, places, and events within their experiences.

Typical symbolic play among young children involves experiential themes such as house, school, farm, zoo, doctor, dentist, place of worship, animals, community helpers (fire fighter, police officer, sanitation worker, street sweeper), construction workers, bus driver, bride and groom, television characters, and innumerable other possibilities. The variety and content of the children's play are valid indicators of the amount and the quality of firsthand experiences that the children have had. Children from a remote Kentucky mountain home bring different content and materials to their play episodes than do children from an urban environment, who are exposed to traffic, crowds, tall buildings, and concrete.

The nature and function of symbolic play are derived from the work of Sara Smilansky. According to Smilansky, there is a special type of symbolic play that children use to tie together different experiences, interpret them, and utilize them in problem-solving situations. This she calls *sociodramatic play*.[16] The criteria for sociodramatic play are that

1. The child should be interacting with at least one other person.
2. Make-believe roles are taken by each participant.
3. The roles are expressed through imitation of actions and words.
4. Actions and verbalizations substitute for real objects and concrete situations.
5. There is sustained verbal interaction related to the play episode.
6. The play episode persists for upwards of ten minutes.

Although other forms of play may have some of these characteristics, they do not have all of the characteristics. Smilansky's "rule of thumb" for using sociodramatic play are that

1. The theme should allow for boys and girls to assume roles of either gender—there should be no gender stereotyping.
2. Themes should appeal to the children.
3. Children should have had some experience with which to relate the roles required in the play situation.

The beginnings of symbolic play can be thought of as an experimental stage during which children continue to enjoy sensory play (rubbing, patting, hearing, tasting) and motor play (pushing, pulling, lifting, dropping; playing with shape sorters and pop beads). They remain fascinated by textures and forms as well as by experimenting with cause-and-effect relationships (dropping a ball and watching it dribble away). However, they are developing more complex play behaviors, too. As they begin to talk and learn to organize their activities, they eventually direct their play actions toward *imitating* others: using the toy vacuum as you sweep the rug, changing a doll's diapers as you change another child's. Toward the end of two years, however, the child becomes interested in *pretending*. This is a slightly more complicated form of play, one which incorporates some aspects of imitation but now advances toward using play materials in ways that go beyond convention—large cartons become houses, blocks become trains or stores, and "grown-up" clothes transform children into all kinds of fascinating people. Children easily become other people, animals, automobiles, trucks, or even the wind and trees. They develop a strong interest in experimenting and exploring—turning wet sand into different shapes, for example—playfully examining and manipulating things around them. These creative instincts are common to all children, but only by providing rich opportunities to explore and experiment can we help them derive the maximum delight from their playthings. Between the ages of two and three, then, you will notice many changes in *what* your children like to play with and in *how* they play. The toy shopping cart she pushed around at age two for the sheer joy of using her muscles becomes, at age three, a holder filled with the supplies necessary to cook a complete meal for her family.

Among the greatest joys expressed by experienced preschool teachers is observing the creative interactions of their children as they become involved in symbolic play. These teachers, like a great majority of early childhood educators, consider the preschool years as the "golden age" of play during which children's interests become dramatic or sociodramatic in nature. This type of play reaches a peak at about five or six years of age and then gradually declines.

The play equipment we provide for young children should offer endless opportunities for exploration and creativity. What attributes should be considered in selecting good play materials?

Select simple play materials that can be used in various ways, for those are among the things that interest young children most. Someone who has not worked with children might find it difficult to believe the sustained attention a three-year-old can give to something like pouring sand from one container to another. Yet children will spend a great deal of time doing things just like that because they are sensory and manipulative, and serve as an avenue for pretending: The sand can be mentally transformed into pancake batter being poured on a griddle, or any number of other things. Surely toys of unique color, function, size, or shape may initially attract some children, but that initial interest may not continue. Children naturally play with toys longer and more creatively when they, not the play material, dictate the course of action.

A child's rich world of fantasy bursts forth during opportunities for play.

Young children's play must center around objects that have a range of play possibilities. A toy car with a minimum of details, for example, can be used to transport people, race down an inclined plane, or rush a traffic officer along to ticket a speeding driver. Imagination dictates the use of the toy. Too specific toys force children to use them in the same way again and again, eventually becoming of less interest. Equipment that makes the child a spectator—mechanical dogs that sit up and bark after being activated with batteries, or a talking animal that reads children stories—may entertain for the moment, but have very little real play value. Such toys do not actively involve children in play; they mainly divert their attention.

Children need much freedom to use a variety of play materials in the early childhood setting; this informs children that their world of fantasy and imagination is valued and that you are willing to offer uninterrupted time to bring their play activities to satisfactory completion. Play equipment in preschool classrooms is usually divided into separate thematic areas called activity centers (sometimes interest centers). Teachers do this for two main reasons. First, young children function more effectively in small groups. By creating areas of activity, you limit the number of children who can play together at any one time. Second, a subdivided classroom offers children opportunities to make choices. An area set up for books, for example, invites a child who might prefer a quiet activity, whereas a block-building area would appeal more to a child in need of more physical activity. Developmentally appropriate classrooms, then, are divided into separate activity centers, giving children clear choices of where they wish to play.

It is possible to arrange many kinds of activity centers in typical early childhood classrooms, but the following are typically offered to children each day: *housekeeping, blocks, table toys, books, art, sand and water,* and in most kindergartens, *learning stations.* If the indoor space or supervisory help is limited, areas for other activities may be made available periodically: *woodworking center, large-motor space, exploratory center,* and *computer center.*

Dramatic Play

The best play for young children happens spontaneously, when the youngsters are relaxed and receptive. The dramatic play corner, housing equipment for play activities such as dress-up or housekeeping, is one center that has traditionally offered a wealth of opportunities for spontaneous play. Usually organized as a separate "room" within the classroom, the dramatic play center is often set apart by locating it in an alcove or by making walls of low screens or shelves. This gives the children a degree of privacy while still making their play visible to the teacher.

Basic equipment for the dramatic play center includes child-size furniture such as a wooden or plastic sink, table, refrigerator, stove, and cupboard. Sometimes doll beds, cradles, doll-size carriages, chest of drawers, rocking chairs, ironing boards, or play telephones are added. Unbreakable dolls, simple doll clothes, doll blankets, and other accessories are often included. Male and female clothing as well as purses, briefcases, and other dress-up items provide endless opportunities for play enhancement.

Most children recreate family experiences and roles during initial efforts at dramatic play, but as they become exposed to new experiences, they move into other imaginative situations involving doctors, nurses, gas station attendants, fire fighters, police officers, construction workers, taxicab drivers, truck drivers, pilots, or dentists. Children normally enjoy depicting occupations in which specific active functions are apparent rather than those in which a person's role is somewhat general or sedentary. A lawyer or a bookkeeper, for instance, holds little appeal for dramatic play. Because of this strong desire to dramatize events recently experienced, some teachers prefer to equip a permanent housekeeping center *and* a second dramatic play center that changes periodically. Creative possibilities for role playing include shoe repair persons, launderers, jewelers, service station attendants, fire fighters, police officers, factory workers, secretaries, farmers, barbers, postal workers, race car drivers, and the like. It is important to remember, though, that four-year-olds are more likely to engage in domestic play themes. Five-year olds are more interested in expanded themes.

While arranging dramatic play centers, teachers usually try to fight the tendency to supply the children with every piece of material needed for a given role. Even five-year-olds must be encouraged to be inventive in adapting unrelated materials to suit new purposes. Teachers usually organize dramatic play centers according to one of these three plans:

1. Some teachers have only a permanent *housekeeping center* where the children are provided hats, dresses, vests, jackets, shoes, and a variety of other garments worn by household members. The children are encouraged to try on the clothes, regardless of sex, and to assume the roles of interest. Boys may become "mommies," and girls become "daddies." Luncheons, tea parties, baby's bath time, telephone calls, and even reenactments of unpleasant arguments involve the children. This fantasy outlet permits the children to reduce the intensity of emotion associated with real experiences or to redefine and clarify the meanings of real-life experiences. In addition to clothing, common household items make great vehicles for dramatic expression: old electric shavers, lunch boxes, pots and pans, sweepers, magazines, briefcases, alarm clocks, toasters, purses, clip-on earrings, and a variety of other easily obtained, inexpensive materials.

2. Other teachers have a permanent housekeeping center *and* a second dramatic play center that varies with the children's interests. In this second center, there are garments and props associated with particular experiences. For example, your group may have recently visited the fire station or have had regular medical exams. The children may be particularly interested in a popular movie or television show, or a special story may have fanned an interest in space exploration. The play materials in these special centers usually are not as plentiful as those in the housekeeping area, but they provide a nice variation for children who need and enjoy them.

3. Finally, some teachers prefer to gather a variety of dramatic play kits for the children and introduce them one at a time throughout the year, keeping only one center equipped at a time. A housekeeping center may be one possibility, but it may not be available for the entire year, as it was in the previous examples. Under this plan the teacher observes the children's level of interest and changes the materials as the children's needs dictate.

Regardless of the pattern you choose, it is important to arrange attractive, neat areas. Display the materials invitingly, and hang the special costumes neatly so they can be easily seen. Children respond more positively to clean, fresh costumes. Whatever the design of the area at any one time, furniture and equipment should be child-size whenever possible. The housekeeping corner generally includes a table and chairs, wooden kitchen equipment such as a stove, refrigerator, or sink, a wide selection of dolls, and cupboards containing cups, saucers, pots, spoons, pitchers, and so on. These materials do not need to be purchased—a little imagination turns orange crates into stoves or storage cabinets, and a little resourcefulness leads you to

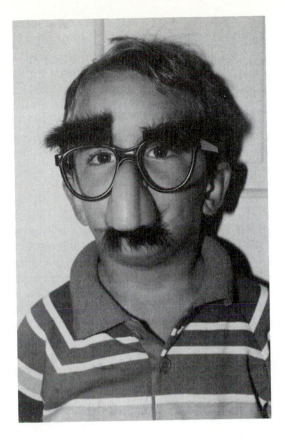

Children love to laugh; their humorous costumes during creative play delight teachers and peers.

used and outgrown toys. The *dramatic play center* offers children a wide variety of creative possibilities. New items should be provided so that children can change roles when they want to. In this area children can explore the lives of people in various occupations and locations. For example, the following locations can be depicted (with their equipment):

- *Ice cream store*. Ice cream scoops, empty ice cream containers, white aprons and caps, a table with chairs.

- *Automobile repair shop*. Overalls, work caps, tools, hose for gasoline, miniature vehicles or crates to represent cars and trucks.

- *Food stand*. Aprons, caps, paper bags, napkins, food containers, pad and pencil, cash register, play money, trays.

- *Hospital*. Doctor's bag, stethoscope, bandages, doctor or nurse uniforms, bed, crutches.

- *Tailor's shop*. Table, measuring tape, variety of cloth, scissors, needle, thread, dolls to be fitted with clothes.

- *Hairdresser's shop.* Hair curlers, aprons, shampoo and makeup bottles, hair dryer, old electric shaver, mirror.
- *Bakery.* Cookie cutters, bowls, baker's apron and cap, flour sacks, rolling pin, pie tins, cash register, play money.

One interesting variation on this approach to the dramatic play center is to invite your children to take turns making it into an area that represents their lifestyle, hobby, interest, or fantasy by bringing in materials from home. This activity offers a child a chance to share something personal with the other children. Creative play is one of the most effective forms of children's communication.

Superhero Fantasy Play   An area of dramatic expression that has received some attention recently is superhero play. Suppose you are watching as three-year-old Matt charges over to David, lifts a long stick out from the back collar of his shirt, raises it into the air, and shouts, "Fire power gazegaw!" ("By the power of Grayskull!") After making a few sputtering sound effects, Matt once more shouts, "I have the power! Let's go get that bonk head (bone head), Skeleporp (Skeletor)." Although Matt was unsure of some of the correct words used on a popular television program, he did display a great deal of interest in his pretend superhero role. How would you react to allowing such play in *your* classroom? Although it is criticized by some because of its violence, Marjorie Kostelnik, Alice Whiren, and Laura Stein describe the young child's penchant for assuming superhero roles as constructive experiences for young children.[17] Even though some teachers object to the rowdiness of the play and to the difficulty some youngsters have in shedding their superhero identities during nonpretend activities such as snack or group time, these writers view superhero play as an important play activity.

The positive qualities of superhero play are related to the fact that superhero images are attractive ones to imitate: all are unquestionably good; they are wise, fearless, and strong; superheroes possess speed and strength that the children would like to have; they solve problems by overcoming seemingly insurmountable obstacles. The authors go on to point out that children benefit in these ways from imitating superheroes:

1. They have little power in their real world, so, through their play, children can become powerful and dominating with no real risk to themselves.
2. Feelings of fear, vulnerability, and uncertainty are transformed into courage, strength, and wisdom through superhero play.
3. It helps children develop self-confidence at a time when they are struggle with such real-life obstacles as dressing themselves or eating without making a mess.
4. Superhero fantasy allows children to pretend to be someone they admire but whom they are not equipped to imitate fully from real life.

5. Because superheroes are *all good* and antiheroes are *all bad,* children have clear, precise models for imitation.

6. As with all types of dramatic play, superhero play allows children to improve language skills, problem solving, and cooperation.

John M. Johnston recognizes that many teachers are bothered by the high noise level and frenzied physical activity of superhero play, but advises them that it should be allowed because of its many benefits for young children. His suggestion is to offer opportunities for superhero play as a tabletop activity rather than in a running or yelling group:

> If we allow superhero play, but limit it to a small figure, table-top activity, then the environmental structure will control and eliminate most of the undesirable features of such play. The many superhero characters supplied by television and movies are available in a variety of sizes. . . . Just as we provide table-top space for other beneficial activities, providing a table for superhero play will allow children to realize the many social, emotional, cognitive, and linguistic benefits possible from this activity. . . . By allowing this activity *only* while sitting at a table, running and crashing bodies cease to be a problem.[18]

Superhero play should be considered a normal form of dramatic play in early childhood settings if it is not carried to excess. It offers a sound way for the children to express their interests and provides an avenue by which they can balance the demands of the real world with their need to fantasize.

Blocks

While some children become involved at the dramatic play centers, others will be playing at another historically popular activity center—the block center. A well-equipped block center should have a variety of building materials differing in size, shape, color, texture, and material of construction. Basic to most classrooms are **unit blocks,** first developed by the early childhood pioneer, Caroline Pratt. Unit blocks are durable, their natural wood color is pleasing to the eye, and the smooth finish makes them pleasant to touch. They may be purchased in complete sets (over 750 blocks), half sets, or individual pieces. Each set of blocks contains many different shapes so that children at various levels of ability may use a set with success. These blocks are made in multiples of a unit (5 1/2 inches $\times$ 2 3/4 inches $\times$ 1 3/8 inches), with increasing size along one dimension only—length—to the size of 22 inches $\times$ 2 3/4 inches $\times$ 1 3/8 inches. Also part of the unit block assortment are pillars, cylinders, curves, arches, and hardwood boards of various sizes (see Figure 5–1).

Unit blocks should be made of unvarnished durable hardwood; all corners and edges should be rounded and smooth, and, above all, accurate to avoid frustration in building. **Hollow blocks** are often used as a supplement to unit blocks in an early childhood facility. These are large, wooden blocks that allow children to make

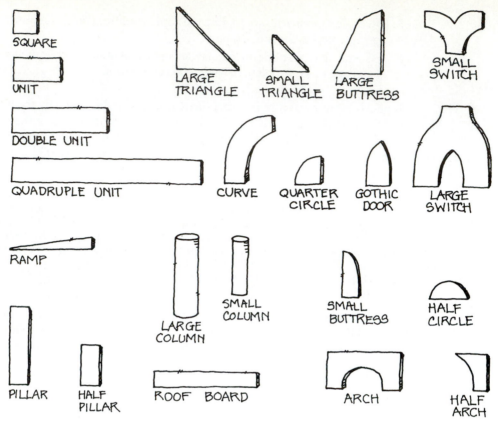

Figure 5-1   Unit building blocks

a variety of structures—some even large enough to play within (see Figure 5–2). Despite their size, hollow blocks are light to handle and easy for small hands to grip. When selecting hollow blocks, be sure to choose those made from unvarnished wood such as oak or maple which are durable enough to resist splintering or cracking. They

Figure 5–2   Hollow blocks

should have rounded edges and corners to facilitate picking up and handling comfort. Hollow blocks come in the following sizes and shapes:

- *Square:* 5 1/2 inches × 11 inches × 11 inches (28 in a full set)
- *Double square:* 5 1/2 inches × 11 inches × 22 inches (16)
- *Half square:* 5 1/2 inches × 5 1/2 inches × 11 inches (16)
- *Short board:* 5/8 inches × 3 3/4 inches × 22 inches (8)
- *Ramp:* 22 inches long × 5 1/2 inches high × 11 inches wide (4)

A complete set of hollow blocks contains 80 pieces. Other popular plastic or wooden block-type construction toys include *Duplo, Legos, bristle blocks, Tinkertoys,* and *Lincoln logs.* Their small size invites a different kind of play. These miniature structures are ideal for use on tabletops or in areas where space is limited. Examine these and other types as you select block play equipment for your youngsters.

Because most early childhood facilities operate on limited budgets, teachers often find that they are not able to purchase all the blocks they would like. You don't have to buy everything; discarded, donated, or homemade equipment can serve your needs well. Some excellent materials of this type include milk cartons, cans, boards, spools, styrofoam, lumber scraps, boxes, barrels, shoeboxes, and cardboard tubes. As children have greater opportunities for block building, they welcome more variety in their play. They still enjoy making the block structures, but begin to augment them with various figures of people, animals, or things. Jessie Stanton and Alma Weisberg listed the materials appearing to provide the most satisfaction due to their ability to represent a great variety of popularly recurring play themes:

> *Rubber, plastic, or wooden figures* (adults about 5″ high)
> 2 varying ethnic families: mother, father, boy, girl, baby, grandparents
> 12 community figures: farmers, workers, doctors, firefighters, etc.
> 16 farm and domestic animals: cow, bull, calf, 2 horses, colt, sheep, ram, lamb, 2 pigs, piglets, cat, dog, etc.
> 1 set zoo animals
> *Vehicles:* (Plastic, rubber, or wood is recommended. . . .)
> 2 sets trains and tracks
> 24 small cars, airplanes, buses, assorted trucks, and tractor (according to environment)
> 4 jumbo trucks (if floor space permits)
> 6 small and large boats (tugboats, barges, liners, ferries, etc., according to environment)[19]

Arrange the block corner in a protected area of the room, out of the flow of traffic, but where the children can move freely and be safe from distractions or accidents caused by other children in unrelated play. For example, don't put the block center near riding toys or climbing equipment. Likewise, the sand or water table invites problems if it is located near the block area. Place storage shelves or cabinets

Whether using table top blocks or large boxes, children enjoy building structures of various designs.

on the perimeter of the area to separate it from other areas of activity. Be sure the children have a flat, steady surface on which to work; a wobbly table or a carpeted floor is too unstable for building large structures like towers. Store the blocks on low shelves so that the children can easily take them out and put them back. Be sure to inform the children that all blocks are assigned a special position on the storage shelf and that the appropriate blocks should always be returned to that place. Organize the blocks by size, shape, or some other quality, and label the shelves with outlines or pictures of the blocks that belong in each section. This makes cleanup time go smoothly and gives children practice in grouping and ordering objects. Illustrated labels help children find correct shelves when putting blocks away.

Maja Apelman condensed Harriet Johnson's description of the stages of block building that children seem to pass through as they play with blocks. Children progress through the stages regardless of whether the blocks are introduced to them at age two or six. The only difference is that the older children go through the early stages much more quickly as they move toward the stage appropriate for their age.

Stage 1. Blocks are carried around, not used for construction. This applies to the very young child.

Stage 2. Building begins. Children make mostly rows, either horizontal (on the floor) or vertical (stacking). There is much repetition in this early building pattern.

Stage 3. Bridging: two blocks with a space between them, connected by a third block.

Stage 4. Enclosures: blocks placed in such a way that they enclose a space....

Stage 5. When facility with blocks is acquired, decorative patterns appear. Much symmetry can be observed. Buildings, generally, are not yet named.

Stage 6. Naming of structures for dramatic play begins. Before that children may also have named their structures, but the names were not necessarily related to the function of the building.

Stage 7. Children's buildings often reproduce or symbolize actual structures they know, and there is a strong impulse toward dramatic play around the block structures.[20]

The values children derive from block play were lucidly expressed by Harriet Johnson, a pioneer in early childhood education. She made three major points: "The power to deal effectively with his environment accrues to a child through the free use of constructive material"; second, "Possibilities are offered by blocks and similar materials for expressing rhythm, pattern, design"; and third, "By means of these materials, children may review, rehearse, and play out their past experience."[21]

Block play, then, offers three avenues of expression encompassing major principles of child growth: (1) it provides for active physical exercise and motor coordination, (2) it encourages experimentation and creativity, and (3) it provides a means of expression through which ideas and feelings can be dramatized or transformed into other depictions of reality. All schools and centers should bring children opportunities to exercise the processes presented by block play. Faith in the children and belief in the value of blocks are of prime importance in carrying out a successful program.

Table Toys

Most early childhood classrooms have special areas where children are offered activities designed to build small-muscle skills, eye-hand coordination, and cognitive abilities. *Puzzles* are among the most popular manipulative toys available. Simple wooden or durable cardboard puzzles should be matched to the children's developmental level; one- or two-piece puzzles are appropriate for two-year-olds, whereas five-year-olds will be able to complete 24-, 60-, or even 100-piece puzzles. *Dressing frames* that help children develop skills like lacing, typing, buttoning, zipping, and snapping are challenging to most young children. *Commercial table toys* (such as Tinkertoys, Duplo or Lego blocks) stacking toys, wooden beads for stringing, snap-lock plastic beads that snap together and pop apart, shape sorters, Lotto games, Parquetry, pegboards, and other action or movement activities are not only inherently pleasing to young children, but also serve as the raw material for intellectual growth. Before young children can be expected to hold a pencil to write, for example, they must be able to control the movements of their wrists and finger muscles. They gain this control as they pour, cut, build, drill, mix, construct puzzles, paste, button, zip, grasp, and lace. As these small-muscle skills evolve, children learn to coordinate the movements of the hand and eye. Children who easily thread a wooden bead on a string, for example, demonstrate good eye-hand coordination: they are able to make the eyes and hands work together. All these actions help increase the children's intellectual growth.

As a teacher, you should avoid placing too many manipulative toys out at one time. Arrange a few materials clearly, at the child's eye level, and rotate them on a weekly basis. It is important to check your materials daily—nothing is more frustrating than trying to complete a puzzle with pieces missing. Many teachers code puzzle pieces by placing small numbers or letters on the back of each puzzle piece that correspond to a number assigned to a particular puzzle. Other teachers carefully label plastic tubs—such as those that contain margarine or popcorn—for storing toys with small parts. By doing so, teachers not only maintain their materials, but also help the children develop effective organizational skills.

Books

Cozy chairs, cushions, stuffed animals, a couch, a rocking chair, or carpet squares help make this area cheerful and inviting. Located as far as possible from the distraction of the noisy, active areas, the book center contains a wide variety of reading materials that arouse curiosity and imagination. Books, magazines, and other reading materials can respond to the many "whys" of your children as well as to their rich fantasy.

Your book center should have racks or shelves on which books can be displayed in such a way that the children can readily see what is available. If you are among the lucky ones, your room will have a record player or tape recorder with a set of earphones. This makes it easy for the children to listen to commercially produced or teacher-made audiotapes whenever they feel like hearing a story.

As you select story materials, remember to start with the children's interests. Carefully plan a program to broaden those interests and expand the children's experiences. Look for books with colorful illustrations clearly relating to story lines that intrigue children and stimulate their imaginations. You might begin by recalling favorites from your own childhood or choosing books that were shared in your professional prepatory courses. You should also be aware of other sources that can aid in identifying the best books (see page 266). Examine the popular award books; they have been identified as excellent examples of literary and artistic merit. A highly regarded prize is the Caldecott Award, an annual award of the American Library Association presented for best illustrated book.

Many awards for excellence in the field of early childhood literature are offered each year. You may be interested in the book that names the awards as you seek to build your first quality children's library:

Children's Book Council, *Children's Books: Awards and Prizes* (New York: The Children's Book Council), published every two years since 1969.

It is best not to organize your book corner as a "library" by displaying your entire collection. Children become confused when confronted by too many choices, so arrange only part of your collection on tables or tops of shelves and change it periodically. Have duplicates of favorite books so that some youngsters will not feel left out if they can't read what they would like to, and others won't need to be reprimanded for grabbing another's book in their impatience.

Sand and Water Play

Sand and water play is an area of sensory stimulation, social interaction, and physical exercise involving wonderfully messy, squishy, sticky materials. Experiences with water and sand are probably among the most memorable of our lives, but often we forget their pleasures and deny them to youngsters because "they're dirty," "they get wet," or "they take so much time." Anyone who has ever observed children at the beach, however, can testify to the enjoyment children experience from sand and water.

Sand play is a soothing sensory activity that results in many learning outcomes.

Sand play usually takes place outdoors in a sandbox, although some preschools have indoor sand play areas. The sandbox should be fairly large (about ten feet square) with a wide ledge around it to serve as a seat for the children or as a table for different activities. The ledge also keeps loose sand from spilling over the edges. It is wise to locate the sandbox as far away from the classroom door as possible so that much of the accumulation on children's clothes can fall or be brushed off on their way in. Keep the sandbox covered when it is not being used to prevent it from becoming contaminated with animal elimination or excess rainwater.

Children enjoy sand for many reasons. It pours; it forms into shapes; and it smells, looks, and feels good. Children enjoy pouring sand, molding it into castles, building roads, digging rivers or lakes, and making sand cookies or cakes. Imagination flows freely during such activity. Children almost always accompany their construction with the "brrm, brrm," of a steam shovel, the "whoosh" of a jet plane, or some other inventive expression. Small dump trucks, pails, shovels, funnels, refrigerator trays, road graders, animals, and other props encourage children to dramatize and verbalize events within their sandbox environment.

Water play is often feared by teachers because of their concern that the children may become overstimulated, resulting in a wet and messy area. The opposite is usually true, however. If the water play experience is carefully planned and organized, the children become so absorbed that their cooperativeness and behavior is more controlled than during most other daily activities. Water play usually takes place with a water table—a raised, rectangular galvanized container resembling a table in appearance. A washtub or other large container holding up to 25 gallons of water to a depth of eight to ten inches is suitable for water play either indoors or out. Protect the children with full-length plastic aprons, boots or plastic bags over the shoes, and sleeves pushed up over the elbows. Cover the floor with plastic if you are indoors, and then add several layers of newspaper. Rugs or mats may also be used. Also, good preparation includes provision for cleanup when accidents occur: Sponges, mops, and paper towels should be handy. Once these steps are taken, you are ready to try a variety of activities involving water. Check the "water play" box for some suggestions to get you started.

There should always be an adult present whenever sand or water play is in progress—not to participate in the play with the children or to tell them how to play, but to keep a watchful eye for problems. One of the most frequent problems is a tendency to throw sand or splash water. Another problem is that youngsters need a great deal of room while using shovels, sand rakes, or other tools. They may become so enthusiastic in their play that they sometimes bang another child with their tools. A third problem is the propensity of some two- and three-year-olds for putting sand into their mouths or rubbing their eyes while sand is sticking to their hands. Be near to forestall these problems before they happen. Otherwise, sand and water play should be among the freest play activities we can provide for children. Such play is absorbing, soothing, and free from pressures and tension. Besides, sand and water play are excellent in stimulating social interaction.

Learning Stations

All the activity centers you have been reading about are designed to initiate and foster growth in all areas of development—physical, social, emotional, and intellectual. Activity centers are broadly conceptualized areas of child-initiated activity that help

▷▷▷▷▷▷▷

WATER PLAY ACTIVITIES

Straight Water Play

Children love to experiment with the water itself:

- Measuring cups, funnels, egg beaters, medicine droppers, strainers, watering cans, squeeze bottles, sieves, ladles, sponges, and brushes help children observe and feel water as they experiment with it.

- Encourage the children to swish their hands through the water, swirl their hands in circles, try to grab a handful of water, stir it with a spoon, and so on.

Water and Soap

Add a mild nondetergent soap to the water and try these activities:

- Blow bubbles with a straw.

- Beat the water with an eggbeater or whip.

- Wash dolls, furniture, dishes, and other materials.

- Add glycerine to the soapy water. It will make larger and stronger bubbles from a bubble ring.

Floating and Sinking

Collect a variety of objects and see what will sink or float. Beverage bottle caps, bits of wood, paper clips, rubber bands, styrofoam shapes, and other materials can be used.

Water and Color

Add food coloring to the water and try these activities:

- Try a drop or two at a time into a small container to see how vivid it becomes as more coloring is added.

- Dip fabrics or a sponge into the water to see how the water is absorbed.

- Drop one color onto wax paper. Add other drops from different colors to see, for example, what happens when a red and yellow drop come together.

- Get a number of jars with watertight lids. Fill the jars halfway with colored water and fill it the rest of the way with vegetable oil. Have the children screw the lids on tightly and rock the jars back and forth to see the changing designs.

Fitting puzzle pieces together offers a challenging opportunity to exercise physical and intellectual skills.

attain all goals of the early childhood program. Teachers who choose to use learning stations, however, have much more specific purposes in mind—primarily to reinforce or extend stated learning goals. Learning stations are found in many preschool and kindergarten programs and, because they deal specifically with intellectual objectives, should not be confused with activity centers.

There does not seem to be one common definition today for the term *learning station*. Perhaps a major reason for this is that learning stations are designed to meet children's needs in unique ways. Because of this personalization, learning stations differ from one another in much the same way that children do: It is as difficult to describe a typical learning station as it is to describe a typical child. As they apply to the ideas presented in this book, learning stations are areas in which organized learning materials motivate and enable children to assume individual responsibility for their own learning.

According to Barbara Kimes Myers and Karen Maurer, learning stations (sometimes called learning centers) may be described as *self-directing/self-correcting; self-directing/open-ended;* or *teacher-instructed/exploratory.*

> *Self-directing/self-correcting* centers have obvious and prescribed uses; the material tells the learner whether a given action is correct or incorrect. Puzzles and other toys with parts that fit together in one specific way are self-directing/self-correcting. . . .

> *Self-directing/open-ended* learning centers allow for a variety of learning outcomes, including some that teachers may not initially consider appropriate. A unit block or hollow block center is self-directing because the blocks invite building and creative possibilities are limited only by the children's experience and imagination. An egg carton with objects to place in the hollows may motivate children to drop one object in each hollow for one to one correspondence. . . .

> *Teacher-instructed/exploratory* centers can provide opportunities for children to further explore techniques or concepts that have been presented earlier in a teacher-directed activity. Following a teacher-presented experiment in which a cork, a rock, a coin, and a piece of wood are tested to see whether each will sink or float, children may extend the possibilities beyond the initial four items.[22]

Examples of each of these three major types of learning centers are provided in Table 5–2. In designing your own classroom learning centers, it is advisable to follow this sequential procedure:

- Select a *purpose* for the station. Will it be used to reinforce some skill? Will it extend a previous learning? Will it foster creativity? Will it clarify a concept? Each station must have a clearly defined purpose. *Example:* To reinforce knowledge of colors and color names.

- Choose an *attractive learning activity* that interests the children, that can be done independently, and that invites the children to manipulate and explore special learning materials. *Example:* Construct a "Color Clown." Draw a large clown and place him where he can be easily reached by the children. Extend colorful construction paper balloons from the clown's hand with pieces of bright yarn. Glue a small magnet to each balloon. Cut a corresponding set of colorful balloons from construction paper, print the color name on each and attach magnet strips to their backs. Have the children match the colors of the clown's balloons to the color-word balloons.

- Provide a means of *self-correction*. The children should be able to tell immediately after completing the task whether or not they were correct. *Example:* The children check to see if the two sets of balloons match in color. The correct color words will be printed on the back. The children will check to see if the color words on the balloons match the color words on the cards.

Table 5–2 Types of learning centers

Self-directing/self-correcting centers		
Educational objectives	Defined space	Materials
1. Auditory discrimination, preparation for paper and pencil matching	Rug samples or carpet squares	Direction cards with correct match illustrated on back, object pairs that can be matched by some criterion (e.g., initial sound, rhyme), lengths of yarn
2. Auditory discrimination, verbal interaction and cooperation when two or more children work together	Table	Boxes labeled with upper- and lower-case letters, pictures on individual cards to be sorted into boxes according to the same initial sound (same center may be varied so that sorting is by final sound or by rhyme)
3. Understanding and audio discrimination of rhyme to sharpen audio discrimination, opportunity for verbal interaction and cooperation when children work together	Table, rug	A puzzle having pairs of rhyming objects

Self-directing/open-ended centers		
Educational objectives	Defined space	Materials
1. Audio discrimination, listening pleasure, motivation for children to practice rhyming or making up stories of their own	Table	Tape recorder, headsets, audio tape with recordings of stories written in rhyme
2. Representation of experiences and feelings with oral and written language	Tables near display of children's paintings	12″ × 18″ paper, pencils, markers (This center will need a couple of parent volunteers or older students from the 5th or 6th grade who can write down the children's dictations about their pictures. Children who are writing independently with conventional or invented spelling, of course, write their own stories.)
3. Visual discrimination, practice in formation of letters	Table	Rubber stamp letters, ink pad, pencils and paper
4. Opportunity for oral language and verbal and nonverbal cooperation, representation of experience through pretend play	Family living center	Child-sized furniture, clothes for dress up, other props for dramatic play

Table 5–2 *(Continued)*

Teacher-instructed/exploratory centers		
Educational objectives	Defined space	Materials
1. Practice in rhyming, audio discrimination, exploring and sharing own ideas	Table	Tape recorder, headsets, teacher-made audio tapes of rhymes with time on the tape for children to add their own examples
2. Idea that experience can be represented in visual form, opportunity for children to explore and share feelings and experiences with others, expansion of vocabulary as children mix paints in various colors and tones	Tables or easel	Tempera paint (the three primary colors, black, and white), 12″ × 18″ paper, 1/2-inch wide brushes (teacher initiates the activity with conversation about sensory memories related to a common experience the children have recently had)
3. Concept of writing as meaningful marks on paper and of stories as something that can be written down	Table next to bulletin board where children's original stories are displayed as well as library display of picture books (teachers have previously written the children's original stories with them)	Magazine pictures mounted on 12″ × 18″ sheets of unlined paper, pencils or felt-tipped markers, stapler (for those who may want to make a book)

Source: Barbara Kimes Myers and Karen Maurer, "Teaching with Less Talking: Learning Centers in the Kindergarten," *Young Children, 42,* no. 5 (July 1987): 20–27.

- Each activity should be *uncomplicated.* Children should be able to use the materials by themselves with little or no teacher direction.

- Construct an *appealing background* that will draw the children to the learning station.

- *Change activities frequently.* Sometimes one activity will be sufficient for the purpose of your station, but at other times several will be needed. The specific content, as well as the needs and interests of your students, will dictate the number you need. Don't overwhelm the children by planning more than they can handle. On the other hand, don't make the activity so unchallenging that children will be bored by the learning station.

The Woodworking Center

As children gradually gain control of their fingers and hands and learn to coordinate their movements, they should be given chances to work with real tools two or three times per week.

How many of us recall such pleasant childhood memories as exploring a grand-father's garage workshop with all of its exciting tools and materials? Our memories may include the joy we experienced at being shown how to use the tools or the fun we had while making something out of wood. For some, this initial interest grew into a stimulating adult hobby. Woodworking is a wonderful experience—a process

Woodworking opportunities help children acquire many concepts and skills.

that offers many benefits for children: creative expression, emotional release, and opportunities for small- and large-muscle growth and coordination.

The tools most often used in a preschool woodworking program include claw hammers, large-head nails, hand drills, crosscut and back saws, miter box, clamps, sandpaper blocks, and wood glue. These must be quality tools. Toy tools frustrate children because they constantly break or fail to do the job efficiently. The activities in which the children use the tools are outlined below.

Hammering   Children love to hammer. They will spend up to half an hour at a time hammering if they are given the opportunity. But in order to hammer well children must be deliberately introduced to the proper technique. Many youngsters are not yet ready to use real tools, so their carpentry experiences should be of the "readiness" type—that is, hammering wooden pegs into holes with mallets. These experiences help children to control eye and hand movements as well as to practice the vertical wrist action necessary to hammer. Another experience appropriate for this inital hammering stage is using the mallet to drive golf tees into pieces of styrofoam. Be sure to show the child how to use the mallet or hammer properly if she is having trouble. It should be grasped about two or three inches from the end of the handle. Instruct the child to keep her eye on the head of the object to be hammered. Tap it lightly until it has been started and then take the nail-holding hand away. Then the object can be hammered in a more forceful manner. Be sure to emphasize the importance of using the vertical wrist movement as the main source of power. It is much easier to hammer with the wrist than with elbow or shoulder, and the children will be able to control their hammering motions to a finer degree.

Once the children have shown a basic skill in the proper use of a hammer, you will want to introduce a real hammer. The typical hammer weights about 16 ounces, much too heavy for most preschoolers. You should find one that weighs between 8 and 10 ounces. The handle should be small enough for the child to grip easily, and the face should be free of any pit marks or dents. Some hammers have sharp claws on top that help remove nails. Ball peen hammers are favored by teachers who are concerned about the unrefined hammering skills of their inexperienced children. Ball peen hammers have a rounded, ball-shaped top in place of the claw and are not as dangerous if the child is accidentally struck. A common method to help children drive their first nails is to start the nail yourself by tapping it lightly into the wood (make sure the nail is straight). After a few starts, the children will want to try by themsleves. Advise them to tap the nail lightly a few times while holding it straight. Then tell them to move their fingers out of the way and drive the nail into the wood, using the recommended vertical wrist action described earlier. A second useful technique for starting nails (especially small ones) involves the use of a small piece of heavy paper. First push the nail through the heavy paper. The paper will hold the nail in place as it is started with a few light taps. Slide the paper away after the nail becomes firmly embedded in the wood. Nails for beginners should have large heads and very thin shanks for ease of driving. Be sure that shanks are strong enough to drive the nail into the wood without bending easily. Flooring or wallboard nails are especially good.

Old tree stumps are interesting objects for hammering practice. Remember, the children are just beginning to learn how to use a hammer, so they are not yet interested in actually using it to make it something. They are quite thrilled at their ability to use a hammer to drive a nail into wood. As a result, they are content to spend concentrated amounts of time just hammering large numbers of nails into softwood—your tree stump will be totally covered with nails in a very short time. A major advantage of the tree stump is that children hammer their nails into the end grain, which makes it much easier to drive the nails without bending them. Other than tree stumps, only softwoods should should be used for driving nails. Pine, fir, cedar, or redwood are ideal choices. The $2'' \times 4''$ size should be used for initial hammering practice, and scraps of one-inch-thick lumber work well when children want to nail pieces of wood together.

Sawing   Most preschool programs generally offer two types of saws for their children: the *crosscut saw* and the *back saw*. Both are easy to use if introduced properly and provide countless hours of enjoyment for young children.

Perhaps the safest way of intiating sawing practice with a real saw is to attach a miter box securely to the work table with C-clamps (4″ clamps work best). Miter boxes are three-sided (the top is open), U-framed, box-shaped devices generally made of solid hardwood. They have two sets of grooves cut into the sides for guiding straight cuts and two sets for guiding straight cuts and two sets for guiding cuts at a 45° angle. Miter boxes are good for young children because they are relatively safe and help children learn to saw correctly. To use the miter box, place the wood to be cut into the box and either hold it against the edge closest to you with your nonsawing hand or clamp it securely. Insert the back saw (it has a reinforced top that ensures a straight cut) into the pair of miter box grooves that will give your desired cut and begin a slow back-and-forth stroke to get the cutting groove started. The stroke can then be speeded up, but be careful not to put too much pressure on the

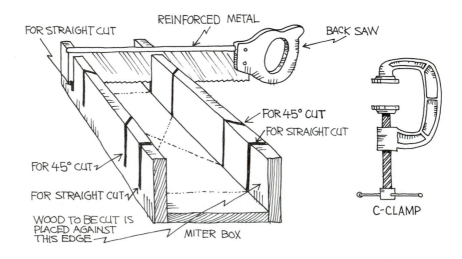

Using these big saws takes a lot of concentration and muscle power!

saw, or it may pinch or bind in the wood. Let the saw do the work; pressure is more of a hindrance than a help. You should cut smoothly and safely in this manner.

Once the children have acquired confidence by sawing successfully with miter boxes, you can introduce the crosscut saw. Crosscut saws have teeth much like the back saw's but are somewhat longer and lack the reinforcing strip of metal on the top of the blade. Look for crosscut saws 16 to 20 inches in length for young children. They are the easiest to handle. As with all sawing, the wood to be cut must be clamped to a secure base. *Vises* that are permanently mounted to the work table can be used by the children to hold their wood steady. Stanley® brand *Work-Mates* also work well. They offer a secure base for sawing and an adjustable top that can be easily regulated by knobs to hold almost any size or shape of wood.

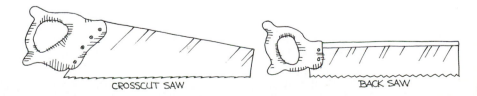

CROSSCUT SAW   BACK SAW

Children often have a more difficult time starting a cutting groove with a crosscut saw than with a back saw. Two major reasons for this are that (1) the crosscut saw lacks the reinforced top, so its blade tends to bend as the children exert pressure sideways, and (2) the grooves of the miter box no longer guide the saw, so the children tend to force the crosscut saw against the edge of the cutting groove. This results in troublesome binding against the wood and a sporadic, rather than a smooth, cutting motion. You may want to start a cutting groove for the children and remind them to hold the saw straight without forcing its direction. Again, let the saw do the work.

Drilling   Turning hand drills to make holes in wood is an enjoyable activity that fascinates nearly all young children. A good hand drill should have a handle that the child can grip comfortably and, if possible, a convenient removable cap that stores various sizes of drill bits. Children are not able to change the bits, so the teacher must do that when necessary.

Before drilling, secure a thick $2'' \times 10'' \times 30''$ plank painted bright red to the top of a work table. Clamp the piece being drilled to the red plank, and tell your children that when they see red sawdust they should stop drilling. Make a starter hole for the children with a large nail. Then the child can guide the bit to the starter and begin drilling. The child should hold the drill handle with one hand and turn the pinion with the other. Be sure the child's body is well above the drill so she is able to exert ample downward pressure. The drill should be in a straight vertical position at all times and the drilling movement should be rhythmical and smooth.

A second tree stump might be designated as a drilling station. The hammering stump will not work because the driven nails will tend to dull the drill bits. A word of caution as the children drill into the stump, however: Always make sure the child's body is above the drill and that the drill bit is pointed away from the body. Constant supervision and adherence to firmly established safety standards are critical to a successful woodworking center.

Gluing   Before being given opportunities to glue together pieces of wood, young children must have ample opportunities to glue and paste other materials. With such experience they should understand some basic gluing considerations: The table surface should be protected with newspapers, the glue should be applied sparingly (too much results in a longer drying time), and a damp washcloth or sponge should be near to remove glue from hands while the child is working.

Yellowish wood glue in squeezable plastic containers is the best glue to use on wood, since it is resistant to water. Once children begin gluing or nailing pieces of wood together, their imaginations often become engaged, and they use their creations in other activities. A child's block of wood with a spool glued on becomes a more durable "ocean-liner" if the proper glue is used. In order to achieve the best bonding, the pieces should be clamped together or weighted until dry. Drying time varies, but it might be best to allow the project to dry overnight before using it.

Sanding   Sanding a piece of wood is an absorbing experience for young children, especially because the wood constantly changes appearance as the grain is brought out.

Choose a coarse grade of sandpaper—it is much less difficult to use. Sanding will be more successful if the children attach the sandpaper to sanding blocks. Fold a piece of sandpaper around a wooden block large enough for the children to grip easily. Tack the sandpaper to the block so it will not slip. Clamp the wood to be sanded to a work table and instruct the children how to make smooth, steady sweeps of the arm along the grain of the wood.

Children progress through a sequence of interests and skills beginning with the sensory pleasure derived from woodworking to the desire to make things. Of course, their creations will be primitive, but just imagine the joy when a child becomes aware that the piece of wood she just sawed would make an excellent train engine just by driving a nail in the right place! The values of experimentation, creativity, muscular coordination, emotional pleasure, planning, and social exchange far outweigh the need for accuracy in the final product.

Two excellent resources that provide information about tools and offer sugggestions for woodworking projects are:

Patsy Skeen et al., *Woodworking for Young Children* (Washington, D.C.: National Association for the Education of Young Children, 1984).

David Thompson, *Easy Woodstuff for Kids* (Mount Rainier, Md.: Gryphon House, 1981).

The woodworking area should be under careful supervision whenever children are working there. At no time should children be allowed to use the tools unless an adult is present. Tools can be dangerous objects in anyone's hands (I'm sure we've all watched a thumb grow swollen and purple after whacking it with a hammer), but young children's hands move especially quickly and erratically when excited. For that reason, a calm adult who carefully and deliberately introduces children to the proper way of doing things and watches over them as they experience woodworking opportunities is vital. That person must have the insight to praise children for using tools properly and to stop whatever is going on when tools are being used unsafely. Children should not be sent away from the center if they are using the tools improperly, but firmly reminded of the proper procedure. Then allow a moment or two for the child to regain his composure before he uses the tool again.

If an injury does occur, you should have a first aid kit readily accessible. Most injuries involve hitting a finger with a hammer or getting splinters while handling pieces of wood. Whenever either of those happens, the children should know what to do about it—personal responsibility is an important part of woodworking. Running cold water over a finger that was inadvertently struck by a hammer is a widely recommended treatment. Getting the splinter remover for the teacher, running cold water over the area from which the splinter was removed, and washing the affected area thoroughly with soap and water should take care of splinter problems.

Of all the special centers described in this chapter, woodworking is the one most often neglected by preschool teachers. Many are unwilling to invest the time and effort necessary to include woodworking, possibly because they are unaware of the valuable experiences children gain from these activities.

Large-Motor Space

Young children's days are full of active movement, for the energy contained in their fresh bodies is boundless. Young children need much time during the day to release this energy, to learn what they can do with their bodies, and to practice developing large-muscle skills: climbing, jumping, sliding, crawling, and walking freely. Most classrooms provide indoor wooden climbers if they have room. Mats are usually placed beneath the climber for protection. Some classrooms have lofts where children are able to crawl through small passages, climb ladders, jump down elevated platforms, or glide down slides or poles. If you are not fortunate enough to have this equipment, you can make crawling tunnels from planks and small crates, or an obstacle course from cardboard boxes. Similarly, other ordinary equipment can be adapted for active use by the children.

Exploratory Center

Young children prefer active exploration with real things, so the classroom should offer an environment where children are able to interact physically with a variety of novel materials. Such materials exist in many forms, colors, weights, textures, and states. Plants to grow and animals to care for fascinate children and open up new vistas of understanding. Ordinary objects—wood, stones, feathers, seeds, leaves, and seashells—invite active exploration. Magnets, scales, machines, experiments with water, and a world of things for seeing, touching, hearing, smelling, and tasting are important additions. Arrangements of real things are treated much like exhibits in the best child-oriented public museums—not with a hands-off policy, but with one that invites touching and exploring. Children's natural curiosity must be allowed to surface in the classroom. By arranging opportunities for this to happen, you "inform" the children that you value and welcome their curiosity, an important pre-requisite to further learning.

Computer Center

Fifteen years ago, only a few early childhood educators would have deemed it appropriate to expose young children to computers. Those who felt this way believed that the cost of making computers available far outweighed the educational benefits, that most computer programs were no better than "electronic worksheets," and that children would become isolated from their peers as they used the computer alone. However, advocates of computers in early childhood settings argue that computer technology has clearly made a significant impact in our society. According to Susan W. Haugland and Daniel D. Shade, "To insist that children be protected from computers is like claiming they must be protected from electric lights."[23] Perhaps the best way to look at computers is to consider them as neither good nor bad, but rather as a tool that becomes useful only as teachers use them wisely. Haugland and Shade offered 10 criteria for selecting computer software for preschool classrooms. Choosing software on the basis of these criteria can help computer activities result in outcomes that are both relevant and worthwhile.[24]

1. *Age appropriateness.* The concepts taught and their presentation reflect realistic expectations for the children.
2. *Child control.* Children, not the computers, are active participants who initiate and decide the sequence of events.
3. *Clear instructions.* Because the majority of preschoolers are nonreaders, directions must be simple and precise. Directions must be communicated verbally, but if printed directions must be used, they must be accompanied by spoken directions.

Fascinating new processes and discoveries can be experienced with developmentally appropriate computer software.

4. *Expanding complexity.* Software begins at a comfortable developmental level for the children, then gradually expands as children explore, teaching the children the skills as they become ready to learn them.

5. *Independent exploration.* The children are able to use the software with minimal adult intervention.

6. *Process orientation.* The intrinsic joy of learning by discovery should be what motivates children to use the computer. Printouts of the completed work are certainly enjoyable but are secondary to the process.

7. *Real world representation.* The software simply and reliably models some aspect of the real world, exposing children to representations of real objects and their functions.

8. *Technical features.* Children's attention is captured by software of high technical quality—colorful, with uncluttered, realistic animated features. Software loads quickly and runs fast.

9. *Trial and error.* Children are able to explore varieties of solutions or answers within a problem-solving framework.

10. *Visible transformations.* Children are able to change objects or situations through their responses, and see the effects of their actions.

Much commercial software is available for young children today. Unfortunately, most of it falls short of the criteria listed above and does not reflect a developmental approach to learning. Be sure to examine software you are considering for your children carefully and do not use it only because it allows the use of computers in your classroom. Inappropriate software holds no more educational value than all other types of mindless drills and practice (worksheets, flash cards, etc.).

Art

Art has been considered a valuable part of early childhood programs throughout the history of our field. Young children have always enjoyed the opportunity to express themselves openly and creatively through various art media—painting, drawing, print making, or sculpting. Young children do not use these materials to produce "master-pieces," but to experience the pleasure and creative outlet that only these forms of expression can provide. For that reason, an art center containing a variety of well-organized materials should be available each day—a place where children are free to express the feelings and ideas inside of them. Art areas can be very basic or extensive, but their primary mission should be to encourage the spontaneous creative expression of the very young. The art center might include any of the follwing materials.

Easels   A classic art medium, easels are found in almost all early childhood settings. Children of all ages enjoy swooping, swirling, tapping, or swishing their brushes over newsprint paper until the creamy paint becomes a creative design.

Crayons, Marking Pens, Pencils, Chalk   Handy containers holding a variety of drawing tools should also be a staple at the art center. Most children enjoy scribbling and creating crude pictures and shapes with these tools; the real pleasure, though, seems to come from the activity itself, rather than from what is produced. Because creativity is the major reason for the existence of the art center, you should make every effort to avoid offering coloring books or worksheets. Most early childhood educators advise against their use for two major reasons: (1) they inhibit the creative process in young children, and (2) children of preschool age lack the fine motor control to stay within the lines.

Clay and Play-Doh   These modeling materials give children many rich opportunities to create as they pull, push, squeeze, roll, stretch, and pound to create original three-dimensional shapes and sculptures. Typical examples of children's efforts include rolled balls, stretched-out snakes, coiled bird's nests, hollowed-out pots, or a variety of human and animal figures. Include a variety of materials at this area—rolling pins, cookie cutters, plastic knives, and a variety of other implements that shape or leave imprints.

Prints   Printing or stamping utensils give children many rich opportunities to express their creativity as well as develop a sense of design. Children accomplish this by dipping into paint an object that will leave an imprint when pressed upon a sheet of paper. A variety of print-making objects can be used, such as commercially made rubber stamps, cookie cutters, bits of sponge cut up into a variety of shapes, potato stamps, corks, different kitchen utensils, or even fingers (or other parts of the hand).

Collages   Collages are creative combinations of material attached together by glue or some other binding medium. Collages can be one of the most creative of all forms of artistic expression because almost any materials can be used to create a collage. Some collages are two-dimensional (such as paper glued on paper) and others are three-dimensional (buttons, beads, toothpicks, twigs, shells, pebbles, yarn, string, scraps of foil, packaging "popcorn," straws, pipe cleaners, etc.). Children should be encouraged to create collages freely, so a great variety of well-organized materials should be provided at the art center for frequent use.

Games with Rules

According to Piaget and Smilansky, children remain content to express themselves through symbolic play during the preschool years and into the primary grades. As a matter of fact, it is not until about six or seven years of age that children leave the major thrust of symbolic play and begin to govern their activities with rules. The following example illustrates this transition: If we give a one-year-old a ball, he would roll it on the floor or grasp it (sensorimotor play); a three-year-old might place it on a pillow, lie on it and "pretend she is an eagle in her nest" waiting for the baby bird to hatch (symbolic play); a six-year-old, however, would probably gather a group of friends for a game regulated by an agreed-upon set of rules (game with rules). The rules are serious business for these youngsters, and any violation is usually met with verbal abuse or even physical aggression by the others. Because children themselves are establishing guidelines for their behaviors, rather than having restrictions placed upon them by others, games with rules are usually considered the highest form of play activity.

However, because we are primarily addressing the teaching of children through the kindergarten level in this book, we will examine the teacher's role in providing for sensorimotor and symbolic play only. Your role in these areas is crucial and goes far beyond the directing and controlling aspect discussed earlier. You must learn two very important skills: providing for play areas inside and out, and supplying the materials necessary for the children to bring out their ideas effectively.

THE TEACHER'S ROLE

The natural type of play behavior emerging throughout childhood has been given several different labels, but regardless of what we call it, play is a *spontaneous* activity. The motivation to play comes from within each child and is not bound to adult approval or reward. Because play is internally motivated, children are free to engage in situations full of pretending and imagination. Janice J. Beaty focused on the importance of originality and novelty in children's play:

> When we speak of a creative person, we generally mean someone who has original ideas, who does things in new and different ways, who uses imagination and inventiveness to bring about novel forms. Can young children be creative like this?
>
> Not only can they be, they are. Creativity seems to be intuitive in young children, something they are born with. From the very beginning they have the capacity to look at things, to hear, smell, taste, and touch things from an entirely original perspective—their own. . . .
>
> Young children bring to any activity a spirit of wonder, great curiosity, and a spontaneous drive to explore, experiment, and manipulate in a playful and original fashion. This is creativity. It is the same impulse that artists, writers, musicians, and scientists have.[25]

Whenever children express their thoughts or actions in inventive, self-initiated, original ways, they are being creative. Creative thinkers are those who react uniquely to their environment. The reactions may be similar to those discovered by millions of children before them, but the characteristic that makes any reaction creative is that it is *new to them*. This may show up in infants as they discover different ways to play with their toys, or in adults as they seek to find an easier way to perform a household chore. Each person has some innovative way of meeting a situation, but some people apparently feel freer to search for and express their ideas than do others.

E. Paul Torrance feels that a great deal of what contributes to a person's ultimate ability to exhibit open-ended, original thinking as opposed to rigid, closed thinking occurs during the preschool years:

> Creative imagination during early childhood seems to reach a peak between four- and four-and-a-half-years, and is followed by a drop at about age five when the child enters school for the first time. This drop has generally been regarded as the inevitable phenomenon in nature. There are now indications, however, that this drop in five-year-olds is a man-made rather than a natural phenomenon.[26]

Some people argue that the drop occurs because some preschools and kinder-gartens clamp down and limit the freedom of children. Expectations to conform to rigid routines and behaviors often thwart adventuresome attempts at self-expression. Most children eventually conform to the growing rigidity of the school structure, but a few are reluctant to change. They clearly keep a bit of the child in them, continuing to meet life's challenges in independent, adventurous ways.

The noted Russian psychologist Kornei Chukovsky believes that creative thought is extremely important: "without imaginative fantasy there would be complete stagnation in both physics and chemistry, because the formulation of new hypotheses, the invention of new implements, the discovery of new methods of experimental research, the conjecturing of new chemical fusions—all these are products of imagination and fantasy."[27]

Creative thinking is obvious among children in most preschool settings. We can see a steady progression in their ingenuity, imagination, and mastery of ways to use the things available to them. They first understand the ways that materials can be used normally and then eagerly explore ways to find new uses for them. Children do this with many things in their environment. Plastic cups are not to be used merely for drinking liquids, for they make wonderful scoops for the sand area; can hold a pet hermit crab while its cage is being prepared; can be used in pairs to simulate binoculars; and can even be decorated with glue, sand, seashells, spangles, and pebbles, and sent home as colorful pencil holders. Paper clips, napkins, rubber bands, paper bags, straws, water, clay, paints, blocks, saws, hammers, leaves, twigs, and rhythm instruments are all fuel for the child's creative engine. The teacher is the key that turns on that engine and encourages it to continue running.

Teachers can and should encourage creative play endeavors in young children. Although all children will not become Mozarts, Michelangelos, Einsteins, or Curies as a result of their creative experiences, most educators believe that creative thinking is a valuable cognitive tool. Researchers have attempted to identify the conditions under which creativity seems to flourish in the schools and have come up with these general conditions:

- Time limits are removed from activities in which children are deeply involved.

- A free, accepting atmosphere is established where open expression is encouraged.

- The children are allowed to share ideas and to stimulate one another's thinking.

- Conditions leading to stress and anxiety are removed.

In order to establish such conditions, every teacher must become an astute observer.

Observing Children's Play

According to James Johnson, James Christie, and Thomas Yawkey, all the adult needs to do is

> to provide adequate time, space and materials for play.... Once that is done, the adult can step back and observe the ongoing free play. If all children are engaging in high-quality, creative play activities, nothing more needs to be done. If, on the other hand, observation reveals that some children are not playing at all, or only exhibit low social and cognitive levels of play, or are bogged down in repetitive play episodes, the adult might want to intervene.[28]

Observation of play behaviors is the key to providing successful play opportunities. From observation you will learn when additional time, space, or play materials are needed to extend play opportunities. It can show you that certain play materials are beyond a child's ability, or that the play situation does not stimulate some children. Whenever play gets bogged down for one of these reasons, it can be appropriate for an adult to intervene. However, before entering children's play, you must spend some time watching it. Without careful observation, the mood of a play episode can be destroyed. Gail Bjorklund offers this example.

> Miss Miller noticed several children busily at play in the housekeeping corner. She walked over, sat in one of the chairs surrounding the small table, and asked Julee, "What are we having for dinner?" The children all paused in their play and seemed confused. Although Julee responded, "We're not having dinner. We're getting dressed to go shopping," the children's interest and enthusiasm seemed to decline.
>
> Miss Miller's remark to Julee seemed to make the children uncomfortable with their play decision to go shopping. A few seconds of observation would have quickly informed Miss Miller of the content of the children's play. How much differently the children might have received a remark like, "Don't you look lovely for your trip to go shopping. What are you going to buy?"[29]

Adults can become involved in several different ways. Johnson, Christie, and Yawkey synthesized the work of several researchers and developed a description of four different types of involvement: *parallel playing, coplaying, play tutoring,* and *being a spokesperson for reality.*[30] The following descriptions are based on their work.

Parallel Playing   This occurs when an adult comes near the child and plays with the same materials but does not interact with the child. For example, if the very young child is playing with snaplock beads, the adult can come near the child, choose some beads, and snap them together. He can also make occasional comments ("My beads are all yellow"), but no attempt to engage the child in conversation should be made. This type of involvement is most appropriate for construction or sensorimotor play.

Bjorklund advises teachers to enter into parallel play because they are significant figures in the children's lives and serve as important models of behavior—and we cannot take for granted that all children know how to play merely because they are children. They must observe the teacher's behavior, imitate it, and eventually expand on their imitations. Of course, there are some play experiences where teachers should avoid providing models; the most obvious is art. If the teacher patterns designs with crayons, for example, the child may hesitate to design his own creations. So if the children already have adequate play skills in any certain area, be careful not to reduce their creativity by asking them to model your behaviors.

Keeping this word of caution in mind, however, you should understand that parallel play is valued beyond its modeling aspect, because children enjoy teachers who come together with them in their play. They show the children that they like to play, too, and that play is valued in their classroom. This can reinforce the children's interest in play and encourage increasingly active roles. Finally, parallel play is important where special procedures are necessary in order to ensure proper use of equipment. At the carpentry center, for example, a teacher will want to model proper tool use. At the water play center, children may benefit from watching the teacher demonstrate how to pour from one container into another without spilling water on the floor. When participating in parallel play, however, teachers should always play as the children's peers. They should never become actors and the children spectators.

Coplaying   This occurs when adults join in the play episode but allow the children to maintain control. The role of the adult is to make comments or ask questions that can stimulate the children to extend the possibilities of their play. Here is an example of coplaying.

Audrey:	Do you want to join our tea party?
Adult:	Sure. It sounds like fun.
Audrey:	Here's some tea. (Gives the teacher an empty, small plastic cup and saucer.)
Adult:	This tea is delicious!
Martin:	Here, have some sugar.
Adult:	Thanks, I'll have just a tiny bit. By the way, do you have any lemon?
Audrey:	Yes, I'll get it for you.
Martin:	Lemons are in the refrigerator.
Audrey:	I've got one. Let me squeeze some for you. (Pretends to squeeze an imaginary lemon into the adult's empty cup.) How does it taste?
Adult:	The tea is great. . . . What should I do with the squeezed lemon?
Martin:	Give it to me. I'll throw it away.

Notice that the teacher did not control the play, but delicately influenced its direction by adding a new element: a lemon. Then she used three common types of comments often offered by adults during coplaying episodes:

1.   Asking for information: "Do you have any lemon?"
2.   Asking for instruction: "What should I do with the squeezed lemon?"

3. Responding to the children's actions and comments: "Sure. It sounds like fun." "This tea is delicious." And so on.

Coplaying is most successful during dramatic play or construction activities.

Play Tutoring The teacher supplements the play activity with additional lines, material, or information when she feels the children need to expand their play to new levels or that parallel playing or coplaying are not enough. Johnson, Christie, and Yawkey describe three kinds of play tutoring:[31]

1. Outside intervention. The adult remains outside the play episode but enters to make general comments and suggestions designed to extend the play. For example:

   > *Adult:* Miss Car Lady, you really have some great-looking cars for sale. How many have you sold?
   >
   > *Amanda:* None, yet.
   >
   > *Adult:* Try moving the wheel toys out of the corner a bit so the children can see them. Meanwhile, I'll run over to the block center and see if I can find you a customer.

2. Inside intervention. The adult takes on a role and joins the play, modeling desired behaviors and skills. For example:

   > *Adult:* Miss Car Lady, you really have some great-looking cars for sale. My old one broke down and I need a new one very badly.
   >
   > *Amanda:* What kind of car do you want?
   >
   > *Adult:* I'd really like a shiny new station wagon. (Walks over to a trike and looks it over.)
   >
   > *Amanda:* This one is thirty million dollars.
   >
   > *Adult:* Wow, that's a bit more than I can afford.
   >
   > *Amanda:* How about sixty dollars?
   >
   > *Adult:* Sold! When can I pick it up?

   Inside intervention, because it involves the teacher more directly, is more obtrusive than outside intervention, where the teacher is involved less directly and is less likely to disrupt the flow of the children's play. However, both are appropriate in certain situations.

3. Thematic-fantasy training. This helps children act out stories that have simple, repetitive plots and a small number of characters (e.g., Three Little Pigs or Three Billy Goats Gruff). The training process involves a three-step sequence that often extends over a period of several days:

   a. The adult reads or tells the story and discusses it with the children.

   b. The adult assigns roles to the children and helps them do a preliminary reenactment, prompting when needed. (Keep costumes and props to a minimum.)

   c. The story is enacted several more times as adult assistance is phased out.

This is a more structured approach than any discussed to this point, but play tutoring is recommended for children who have never before experienced sociodramatic play.

Spokesperson for Reality   This involvement places the adult in the position of encouraging children to suspend make-believe during their play episodes and interjecting reality. The adult attempts to get the children to think about the real-life consequences of their play.

This type of play has been used often by teachers, but not with overwhelmingly positive results. The adult's questions or comments may disrupt the make-believe nature of the play, restrict the children's conversations, and cause them to stop playing altogether. Because of its disruptive influence on children's play, it is recommended that the spokesperson for reality stance be used rarely.

The following example illustrates how an adult intervened as a spokesperson for reality in children's dramatic play:

Mark:	"C'mon Eric, you can play with us. You be a seller."
Eric:	"What's a seller?"
Mark:	"The one who sells the apples."
Eric:	"Okay, here are my apples." *[Eric uses beanbags to represent apples.]* "Apples for sale . . . apples for sale!"
Adult:	"How many apples do you have to sell, Eric?"
Eric:	"Let me look . . . five."
Adult:	"If I buy one from you, how many would you have left?"
Eric:	*[Examines the collection carefully and shrugs his shoulders.]*

A problem with this spokesperson-for-reality exchange is that in an attempt to teach Eric about numbers, the adult had a very restrictive, closed-ended effect on the child's responses; that often happens when adults attempt to intervene as spokespersons for reality. As a result, children's comments will often shrink from phrases and sentences to one- or two-word expressions. Because the richness and spontaneity of the children's play diminish as adults assume spokesperson-for-reality roles, this posture should be used as sparingly as possible. When used sparingly and cautiously, however, this role is an ideal way to infuse academic content into classroom play. The ability to integrate play and learning activities is a very complicated one—a professional role calling for a great deal of skill and understanding. And, because any play episode is a learning episode, teachers must be aware of when and how learnings can be extracted and enlarged upon during creative play endeavors. The acquisition of these skills and understandings is a topic addressed more completely in Chapter 8.

Although children should feel free to experiment and create, play time does not mean an uncontrolled free-for-all environment where anything goes. Realistically, it needs to be a rich experience for children—one in which there is a great deal of supervision, guidance, and organization.

Alert *supervision* implies a system of guiding children that allows them to participate in their active experiences confidently and safely. This means that careful observation of the children and their equipment is necessary at all times.

SOME FINAL THOUGHTS

Play is a need of every child. Children virtually overflow with all the prerequisites for play ... a vast reservoir of energy and curiosity, excitingly new experiences, ripe ideas, and a rich supply of imagination that pours forth freely as a constant stream of activity. And when we observe children at play, we often see enjoyment and delight. Because of this fun aspect, adults sometimes think of play as a form of amusement or fun only, not as something to be taken seriously. However, play is an important childhood activity that helps children master all developmental needs.

The first step in encouraging spontaneous play is preparing the physical environment with abundant play materials in centers that are easily accessible to the children. Youngsters should have extended periods of time during which they can become involved in self-chosen, self-directed play. Some children may choose blocks, others may decide to use the housekeeping center. Whatever their choice, however, they are encouraged to explore and experiment as they learn about themselves and others.

Children must be offered many opportunities for self-directed, spontaneous play. But just giving children toys, a place to play, and a time to play is not enough. Children need a responsive teacher—someone who knows how to interact with and stimulate them not only to help them in their own play initiatives, but also to expand the scope of their play.

We must all recognize the value of play in a young child's life and be able to defend the use of play in our programs. By doing this, we will be able to develop programs attuned to the real needs of childhood.

NOTES

1. Siegfried Engelmann, in Robert C. Ankermann, *Approaches to Beginning Reading* (New York: John Wiley, 1971), p. 449.
2. Deborah Burnett Strother, "The Importance of Play," *Practical Applications of Research* (newsletter of Phi Delta Kappa's Center on Evaluation, Development, and Research), *5,* no. 2 (December 1982): 1. Reprinted with permission of Phi Delta Kappa.
3. Ibid.
4. Sue Spayth Riley, "Some Reflections on the Value of Children's Play," *Young Children, 28,* no. 3 (February 1973): 148.
5. "NAEYC Position on Developmentally Appropriate Practice in Early Childhood Programs Serving Children From Birth Through Age 8," in Sue Bredekamp, ed., *Developmentally Appropriate Practice in Early Childhood Programs Serving Children From Birth Through Age 8* (Washington, DC: National Association for the Education of Young Children, 1987), p. 3.
6. Sue Spayth Riley, "Some Reflections on the Value of Children's Play," p. 148.
7. B. Tyler, "Play," in Carol Seefeldt, ed., *Curriculum for the Preschool/Primary Child: A Review of the Research* (Columbus, OH: Merrill, 1976), p. 225.
8. Carol Seefeldt and Nita Barbour, *Early Childhood Education: An Introduction,* 2nd ed. (Columbus, OH: Merrill/Macmillan, 1990), p. 251.

9. Jerome S. Bruner, "Play Is Serious Business," *Psychology Today, 8,* no. 8 (January 1975): 83.

10. Rosalind Charlesworth, *Understanding Child Development,* 2nd ed. (Albany, NY: Delmar Publishers, 1987), p. 474.

11. Jean Piaget, *Play, Dreams, and Imitation in Childhood* (New York: W.W. Norton, 1962); and Sara Smilansky, *The Effects of Sociodramatic Play on Disadvantaged Pre-school Children* (New York: John Wiley & Sons, 1968).

12. Annie L. Butler, Edward Earl Gotts, and Nancy L. Quisenberry, *Play as Development* (Columbus, OH: Merrill, 1978), p. 27.

13. Rosalind Charlesworth, *Understanding Child Development,* p. 475.

14. Catherine Garvey, *Play* (Cambridge, MA: Harvard University Press, 1977), p. 47.

15. Rosalind Charlesworth, *Understanding Child Development,* p. 475.

16. Sara Smilansky, *The Effects of Sociodramatic Play on Disadvantaged Pre-School Children*

17. Marjorie J. Kostelnik, Alice P. Whiren, and Laura C. Stein, "Living With He-Man," *Young Children, 42,* no. 4 (May 1986): 3–9.

18. John M. Johnston, "Harnessing the Power of Superheroes: An Alternative View," *Day Care and Early Education, 15,* no. 1 (Fall 1987): 16–17.

19. Jessie Stanton and Alma Weisberg, "Block Accessories," in Elisabeth S. Hirsch, ed., *The Block Book* (Washington, DC: National Association for the Education of Young Children, 1984), p. 204.

20. Maja Apelman, "Appendix 1: Stages of Block Building," in Hirsch, *The Block Book,* pp. 193–200.

21. Harriet Johnson, *Children in the Nursery School* (New York: Agathon Press, 1972), pp. 183, 189.

22. Barbara Kimes Myers and Karen Maurer, "Teaching with Less Talking: Learning Centers in the Kindergarten," *Young Children, 42,* no. 5 (July 1987): 24–25.

23. Susan W. Haugland and Daniel D. Shade, "Developmentally Appropriate Software for Young Children," *Young Children, 43,* no. 4 (May 1988): 37.

24. Ibid., p.39.

25. Janice J. Beaty, *Skills for Preschool Teachers,* 4th ed. (Columbus, OH: Merrill/Macmillan, 1992, p. 145.

26. E. Paul Torrance, "Adventuring in Creativity," *Childhood Education, 40,* no. 2 (October 1963): 79–87.

27. Kornei Chukovsky, *From Two to Five* (Berkeley, CA: University of California Press, 1968), p. 116.

28. James E. Johnson, James F. Christie, and Thomas D. Yawkey, *Play and Early Childhood Development* (Glenview, IL: Scott, Foresman, 1987), p. 182.

29. Gail Bjorklund, *Planning for Play* (Columbus, OH: Merrill, 1987), p. 73.

30. James E. Johnson, James F. Christie, and Thomas D. Yawkey, *Play and Early Childhood Development,* pp. 30–39.

31. Ibid.

CHAPTER 6

Facilitating the Discovery of Physical Knowledge

Busy from dawn to dusk, with reluctant stops for eating and resting, the very young stay on the go. At the end of a breathless day, adults may wonder what their little marvels have been up to. But that's no secret; the very young have a lot to learn and they don't want to wait around until someone decides to teach them.

Children of preschool age spend their days actively learning much through play. While playing, they eagerly work on "lessons" appropriate to their age; or, as one youngster described his preschool: "I like it here. We teach ourselves!" Young children learn best by interacting with their environment and constructing their own knowledge. This chapter considers how play and other interactions within the environment help children learn many concepts about their physical surroundings in developmentally appropriate ways. As you read, use the following questions to guide your thinking.

- How have the theories of Jean Piaget and Lev Vygotsky inspired developmentally appropriate practices?

- How does the pursuit of physical knowledge in the preschool classroom differ from "subject matter" learning?

- What are the major types of physical-knowledge activity commonly offered to young children?

- How does the teacher function within each of these major types of activity?

- What are the characteristics of a "psychologically safe" environment?

An Episode to Ponder

"We saw a big halo," Jeffy announced as his big brown eyes peered intently at the teacher in apparent solicitation of approval. "A halo," he repeated. Thus began among a group of kindergarteners a great discussion of their recent field trip to a farm. "The halo holds lots of corn," Jeffy continued. His caring teacher, realizing that a wonderfully creative thinking act had begun, encouraged Jeffy to talk about the "halo." She was convinced that the youngster had ingeniously interwoven the concepts of "hay," "halo," and "silo" into a fascinating new symbol to express his ideas. Jeffy was thrilled with the teacher's reaction to his story and proceeded to draw a picture of the "halo" to share with his family at home. The teacher encouraged Jeffy to "write with his ears" (use invented spelling) as he composed a short story to accompany his picture.

Jeffy is a learner in a kindergarten where the teacher utilizes educational practices founded on solid developmental theory. She understood that Jeffy's excitement of exploring a very interesting place had resulted in the creative use of language so commonly found in early linguistic development. She helped Jeffy by motivating him to draw a picture of what he saw and make a record of his observation. She realized that Jeffy interpreted what he saw in his own way, and that her role was to help Jeffy build an enthusiasm for learning.

When offered such a nonthreatening, "psychologically safe" environment, the very young openly and spontaneously express themselves about the many stirring phenomena experienced in their expanding world:

"Look, those ants are carrying small rocks (crumbs) in their mouths."

"Does the ocean ever get tired of making waves? When does it stop?"

"The hoofs on this reindeer's head are just like the hoofs on a moose."

"Look, that man has a hole in his hair!" (He is bald.)

"The water dust (spray mist) got me all wet!"

Their questions and comments, as openly honest as they are, are real in their lives and therefore are meaningful to them. For the three-year-old who is trying to negotiate an obstacle course without touching any of the impediments, and for the five-year-old who is absorbed in finding a way to make food out of clay for her supermarket, life's complexities are wondrous. The child's environment is a thrilling one, inducing deep thought about a variety of observed happenings.

Children bask in an environment where they are able to take action on and observe the reactions of objects in their physical world. They poke, prod, shake, and move things in attempts to verify what they think should happen or to actuate what they want to have happen. In the course of such activity, misconceptions are often cleared up and relationships between actions and reactions are effectively constructed.

Intense sensory-motor experimentation and exploration begins during infancy as children encounter new objects in their environment. Watch babies as they approach anything new. They will squeeze the object, bang it, shake it, put it into their mouths, or fling it. Coming into this world equipped with vestigial motor and sensory apparatus, as well as an insatiable drive to explore, infants strive from the time they are born to gain an understanding of the new environment surrounding them. First learnings emerge from reflexive motor responses such as sucking—an inborn response to sensory stimuli that causes a baby to suck or mouth anything touching the lips. Consider what a wondrous process it is when babies gradually internalize all of the physical interactions they experience with objects brought to their mouths and eventually mature to the point when they are able to classify objects into two categories: "things that can be sucked" and "things that cannot be sucked." A reflexive motor response (sucking) compels babies to unthinkingly put everything to their mouths. Gradually, though, repeated experiences cause that reflexive response to evolve into a conscious thought element that helps the child understand which objects are suitable for sucking. Repeated sensory and motoric experiences throughout infancy help babies construct deeper knowledge of their exciting world of objects.

Because knowledge of objects gained by the toddler and preschooler are likewise deeply rooted in physical action, activities to promote increasingly mature levels of thought must appeal to children's inborn need to figure out for themselves what makes the world tick.

THE CONCEPT OF PHYSICAL KNOWLEDGE

Jean Piaget refers to the type of understandings children acquire about the objects surrounding them by sensory and motor experimentation (pushing, poking, dropping, etc.) as **physical knowledge.** Physical knowledge is gained as children perform actions on the objects in their environment and observe the reactions of those objects.

Even infants learn about the wonders of their physical environment by manipulating and experimenting with objects.

During the course of their activity children not only build a knowledge of the physical world, but also construct higher levels of intellectual functioning. For example, the smoothness and slipperiness of finger paint are distinctive physical properties of that material that can be known only by wiggling one's fingers or sliding one's hands over it. These properties cannot meaningfully be known in any other way. Likewise, the spring of a ball cannot be known unless one picks it up, lets it go, and allows it to fall to the ground. These are examples of physical knowledge.

Physical knowledge begins with sensory action but is not limited to it. In the Piagetian scheme, the term *action* refers to two types of action—physical activity and mental activity—that must accompany each other if true knowledge is to result. For example, when we move our fingers over a sheet of sandpaper to find out how rough it is, we do so because we want to know something about the sandpaper. We gain information about the object by touching the object purposefully and by interpreting the resulting sensory sensations mentally. Anything less than this two-faceted mental-physical activity would be mindless manipulation. Physical knowledge is important because it not only conveys specific knowledge of the child's expanding world, but also helps promote the acquisition of increasingly mature thought processes.

Because physical knowledge involves information children build when they act on their **physical environment,** some confuse the process with "science education." However, many early childhood educators prefer not to compartmentalize preschool learnings into subject matter categories similar to those found in elementary and subsequent schooling. In this text, we will think of physical knowledge as something that accumulates everywhere and at all times, not just during "science class." Children should be encouraged throughout the day to use all their senses in unlocking the surprises found in their daily lives. James L. Hymes refers to such opportunities not as "science", but as "happenings":

> The teacher teaches subject matter but the subject-matter labels are primarily in her mind. They do not show on the outsides. The teacher thinks in terms of...science ...the children cook, plant, or build a house. Inside her mind the teacher points out the facts, concepts, and skills that lie embedded in the experiences. But the daily program only shows, and the children can only tell about, the *happening:* They are digging a garden; they are feeding the birds; they are going to the shoe repair shop. An alert teacher can pull the subject-matter learning out of any significant activity, but the activity has to be going on in the first place for her to do her job.... The labels are simply administrative devices. They did not come from heaven and they do not exist in reality.... Life comes in big bundles, with the contents all mixed up. Experiences never can be neatly compartmentalized.[1]

Hymes goes on to describe how one activity (a trip to a farm) can help to promote "subject-matter" learning.

> A group of four-year-olds takes a trip to a farm to learn where milk comes from. If you make the teacher put a label on the experience, she will probably call it science. Or if that is too general, biology. Or if not specific enough, animal biology. But what about the conversation in connection with the trip; before, during, and after? That should be called the language arts. The stories before and after the trip are literature. The singing—"Old MacDonald Had a Farm" is fated to be sung!—must be called music. Rules for conduct are developed. This is what civics, government, and politics are all about. The teacher recalls what happened the last time the group took a trip: "You remember how we all crowded around and some people could

not see." The lessons of the past are usually labeled history. A child misbehaves; the teacher's response is a lesson in psychology. Someone counts the children to be sure no one is left at the farm: arithmetic. The trip costs money; that is when the (children) take a brief course in economics. The cow is probably pretty, even if the farmer and the highway are not. The presence of beauty and the absence of it are matters of aesthetics. When the teacher soothes a disappointed child—"Things don't always work out the way we want"—the lesson is one in philosophy. And if, on such a trip, the children drink some milk, that experience is labeled nutrition. Yet the whole trip was labeled Science![2]

Hymes advises that teachers must keep subject matter labels in the background and focus on the experience. Knowing the learning involved in the activity helps the teacher develop a content focus on what to teach, but the label does not have to show. With young children, learning is a continuous, integrated whole. They want to explore the environment simply because it's there; not because they will acquire some type of astounding science knowledge. They care only about the action itself—the experience.

Rheta DeVries and Lawrence Kohlberg criticize many "science education" components of preschool/kindergarten programs because the chosen science experiences are not developmentally suitable.[3] The authors contrasted a "science education" approach with a "physical-knowledge" activity to illustrate how the two approaches differ. The first approach focuses principally on the acquisition of subject matter (see box below).

Kamii and DeVries described how this subject matter-oriented activity was modified by Maureen Ellis into a physical-knowledge experience (see box on page 198).

▶▶▶▶▶▶▶

Theme: Crystals

Behavioral objective:

At the end of the experience, the child will be able to:

1. Pick out crystals when shown a variety of things.
2. Define what a crystal is.
3. Discuss the steps in making crystals at school.

Learning activities:

The teacher will show the children different crystals and rocks. She will explain what a crystal is and what things are crystals (sand, sugar, salt, etc.). Then she will show some crystals she made previously. The children are given materials...so they can make crystals to take home. A magnifying glass is used so the children can examine the crystals.

Method 1: Mix 1/2 cup each of salt, bluing, water, and 1 T (tablespoon) ammonia. Pour over crumpled paper towels. In 1 hour crystals begin to form. They reach a peak in about 4 hours and last for a couple of days.[4]

▶▶▶▶▶▶

While looking through an early-education text, I found the "recipe" for making crystals. I decided to try it, but not as a science project...we used it like a cooking activity. I told them that we didn't know why it happened, but they got the idea that when some things mix together, something extraordinary happens. The activity was such a success that for days individual children were showing others how to make crystals, and some made their "own" to take home.

This experiment inspired other experiments and a whole atmosphere of experimentation. One boy, during cleanup, decided to pour the grease from the popcorn pan into a cup with water and food coloring. He put it on the windowsill until the next day. He was sure "something" would happen and was surprised when nothing much did. Another child said she knew an experiment with salt, soap, and pepper (which she had seen on television). She demonstrated for those who were interested. A third child was inspired by the soap experiment to fill a cup with water and put a bar of soap in. She was astonished by the change in water level and then tested other things in the water—a pair of scissors, chalk, crayon, and her hand to see the change in water level.[5]

In the "subject matter" ("science") approach, the objective is to communicate information about crystals. In the "physical-knowledge" approach, the objective is to encourage children to solve problems and to generate their own spontaneous activities and questions. The entire crystals experience was not offered to teach information about crystals per se, but to get children to think. The physical-knowledge approach emphasized the children's initiative, actions on objects, and social interaction.

Although you will be given many general suggestions for applying Piaget's theory, Piaget himself had never designed a method of teaching. However, I have had the opportunity to listen to Piaget speak to groups and have sensed his uneasiness whenever individuals concerned about methodology asked questions about the value of presenting tasks directly designed for accelerating children through the stages of cognitive development. Piaget consistently commented that only in America were such questions about acceleration asked, and that the use of his tasks as teaching tools to speed children through the stages was "idiotic". Instead, he emphasized the value of direct experience with real things in an environment that stressed exploration and discovery. The developmentally appropriate nature of early childhood programs is easily adaptable to this mission.

Piaget's concept of "activity" is to foster physical *and* mental activity. Active methods must involve the use of experiences that interest the child and serve to motivate genuine experimentation and exploration. Just what those experiences might be, however, has been a subject of debate among educators for decades. Jean Pi-

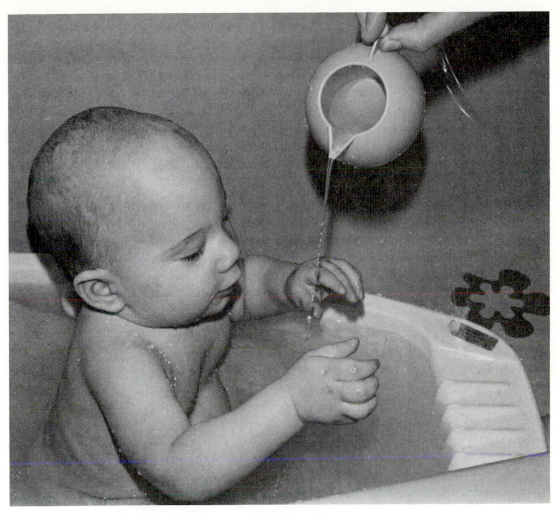

The bathtub becomes a place to experience thrilling physical phenomena.

aget has even admitted that, "There is nothing more difficult for the adult than to know how to appeal to the spontaneous and real activity of the child."[6] Our task is made somewhat easier with knowledge of things we should *not* do: lectures, worksheets, drills, or teacher demonstrations. These methods are only intended to transmit knowledge. DeVries and Kohlberg contrast a Piagetian perspective with unsuitable teaching practices:

> Methods permitting rediscovery or reconstruction . . . are very different from methods focused upon transmitting a body of correct knowledge. By definition, experimentation inevitably involves many efforts that do not succeed in attaining "truth" as adults interpret it.

> A central and revolutionary aspect of Piaget's thought on education is the view that children's "erroneous" ideas are necessary to the construction of knowledge and intelligence.... Such valuing of "erroneous ideas" is revolutionary because it is counter to commonsense intuition and the classic approach to teaching "correct" facts...through social transmissions.[7]

Piaget sees spontaneous activity, stimulated by the teacher, as the primary path leading to intellectual growth.

TYPES OF PHYSICAL-KNOWLEDGE ACTIVITIES

The world of the very young should be considered a huge "hands-on" museum—a perpetual field trip. Children should be led happily and eagerly to discover the natural wonders around them. This is not hard work for the teacher; children are innately curious and alert, actively engaging in serious experimentations with objects in their environment. They want to pick up any twig they see, touch the moss growing on a rock, listen to a june bug's piercing late spring call, or take apart a toy to see what makes it work. Nothing escapes their attention—the tiniest ant or the largest tree dominates their thoughts and actions. In the time it takes to walk from one end of a playground to another, children not only discover the differences in the grassy, dirt-covered, or paved surfaces, but unearth other interesting phenomena as well: a shadow is cast from all objects—including themselves—onto a sunny log; it is cooler in the shade of a tree than it is on the pavement; the branch of the tree has a bud ready to burst open; a robin cocks its head as it listens intently to the ground in search for its baby's food; a few buzzing bees dart from flower to flower looking for nectar; ants surround an inviting cookie crumb. The child continues active examinations of the natural world whether indoors or out. Impelled by wonder, children are constantly exploring and investigating things all around them.

Children are able to discover many things about their world by diving headlong into its mysteries. When they do figure out something on their own, their entire being lets you know. A confident smile and a brisk, "Wow! Look what I just did," communicate a feeling of self-confidence and contentment that's difficult to achieve in other ways. Consequently, a great deal of the fulfillment early childhood teachers experience from their work is watching the satisfaction and happiness children express while discovering something special.

OFFERING HANDS-ON EXPERIENCES

Preoperational children learn by acting on objects. It is therefore important to build early concepts or skills with hands-on experiences with things in the real world and with opportunities for active thinking. Ann C. Howe has made a strong case for children's having such experiences, noting that they provide the structure for the formation of concepts.

Researchers are convinced that growing up is not enough to cause children to give up (characteristics of preoperational thought) and to arrive at a scientific world view; they need contacts with adults and peers who will question and challenge their ideas. They also need much experience with living things: rocks, running water, sunshine, the wind. [Physical knowledge] is not a set of skills and behaviors nor a group of processes. It is knowledge and a way of knowing, knowledge of the universe, of the earth, of living organisms. It is the belief that the world is knowable and worth knowing, and that we can, by our actions, attain some knowledge of it.[8]

Eugene Grant's story of Peter and the rabbit (see box on pages 202–203) underscores the idea that children cannot be "taught" physical knowledge, but that it is something that must be discovered through direct experience. Peter is a child who has great difficulty with the demands of a learning task because he is unable to match new ideas with his background of experiences.

Base Learning on Actual Experiences

Much like Peter, all children must be offered a profusion of situations that are personally meaningful. Mixing red and white paints to get pink motivates children much more than being told about it. Likewise, measuring the ingredients for vegetable soup means more than finding out the answer to a worksheet problem. Compare the thinking required by a child involved in the following experiences to that taking place when a child is faced with a dittoed worksheet:

- Looking into a microscope or magnifying glass
- Setting up an aquarium
- Planting a vegetable garden
- Sawing or nailing pieces of wood
- Digging in the dirt
- Sifting sand
- Making popcorn
- Watering the classroom plants
- Cleaning the guinea pig cage
- Dropping food coloring into water

Each of these activities engage the children's minds and results in learnings that permeate the entire early childhood curriculum. When children are asked to design a den for an animal using building blocks, they are provided with endless possibilities for problem solving as well as for socialization, mathematics, and language. While playing in the water, children discover that some objects sink and others float. Testing the sounds made by strumming an assortment of rubber bands stretched over a box

▶▶▶▶▶▶

"Class, look at the picture, and tell me what you see," said the teacher.

Hands went up, but the teacher called on Peter, whose hand had not been one of them.

"Peter, what is it?"

"It looks like a rat."

The class laughed. Someone said, "Peter is so stupid. He doesn't know a rat from a rabbit."

The teacher said, "Peter, what's the matter with your eyes? Can't you see that it has long ears?"

"Yes," he said.

"Today's story is about a rabbit," said the teacher, pointing to the picture and then the word. "It's a story about a *hungry* white rabbit. What do you suppose a rabbit eats when he's hungry?"

"Lettuce," said Mary.

"Carrots," said Suzy.

"Meat," said Peter.

The class laughed. Someone said, "Peter is so stupid. He doesn't know what rabbits eat."

"Peter, you know very well that rabbits don't eat meat," said the teacher.

"That depends on how hungry they are," said Peter. "When I'm hungry, I'll eat anything my mother gives me, even when I don't like it."

"Don't argue, Peter," said the teacher. "Now, class, how does a rabbit's fur feel when you pet him?" asked the teacher.

"Soft," said Suzy.

"Silky," said Mary.

"I don't know," said Peter.

"Why?" asked the teacher.

"Cause I wouldn't pet one. He might bite me and make me sick, like what happened to my little brother the time a hungry one got on his bed when we was sleeping."

The class laughed. Someone said, "Peter is fibbing. He knows his mother doesn't allow rabbits in bed."

After the class had read the story and had their recess, the teacher said to the supervisor, "I hate to sound prejudiced, but I'm not sure that this busing from one neighborhood to the other is good for the children."

The supervisor shook his head sadly and said to the teacher, "Your lesson lacked one very important ingredient."

"What was that?" asked the teacher.

"A rabbit," said the supervisor.[9]

offers a lesson in science, but also appeals to musical interests. Putting on a record and spinning to its rhythmic beat not only encourages creative movement, but also offers an informal "lesson" about how and why we lose our sense of balance. Starting a seed collection is a fine way to encourage children to observe and classify, but what about the possibility of using the seeds to create an artistic collage?

Teachers must know both how to help the children enjoy their experiences and how to draw out learning from them. The way teachers extract learnings from the child's experiences will gradually lead the child toward the development of more complex thinking styles. Be aware of the numerous opportunities that allow children to explore and question. For example, the following event occurred one day on the playground of a private nursery school.

Helping children learn through such self-initiated activity is an important focus of early childhood education today. Teachers are challenged to capitalize upon the

Direct experiences within the environment form the foundation for meaningful learning.

▶▶▶▶▶▶

On a bright, warm morning, the children were allowed to spend a great deal of time in outdoor activities. They moved from one play activity to another and seemed to enjoy the weather. After a while, three children moved to the shade of a large tree for a short rest period. When the teacher noticed that the children had remained in the shade for longer than usual, she moved to the area to see if there was some problem. There wasn't. The teacher found the three children concentrating intently on the busy efforts of a swarm of ants. "Look at that hole—that's where they live," said Jana. "They live under the ground?" questioned Will. "Yep, and that's where those ants are dragging the food," offered Carrie. "Mrs. Long, do the ants really live underground?" asked Will. Mrs. Long, in an effort to maintain the curiosity already so effectively raised, simply answered, "Let's watch them carefully and see if Jana and Carrie are right."

To capitalize on this incidental experience, Mrs. Long later went to another area populated by ants and dug up a shovelful of dirt and ants. She placed the mixture in a gallon jar, secured the lid carefully, and wrapped the jar with construction paper so that no light could get inside. The darkness would make the ants think that they were underground and that it was safe to begin digging new tunnels. When the dark paper was removed, Will, Carrie, and Jana all became enthusiastic about the passageways constructed by the ants. Other children began to ask: "What do they eat?" "Can we feed them?" "Do they drink water?" and other questions that increased their understanding.

The project continued for some time. Children fed the ants in small quantities: dead insects, food scraps, and almost any other organic substance. They also occasionally gave them small amounts of water. When their interest waned, the teacher helped the children return the ants to the place where they were found.

children's discoveries in order to promote higher-order thinking skills such as those involved in solving problems. If teachers are not aware of such possibilities, they sometimes miss opportunities for learning through real-life situations. These learning situations cannot be concocted by the teacher; most emerge during a child's play. Tegano, Sawyers, and Moran advise:

> Play is *real life* for young children. Problems encountered in play situations represent real problems in their lives and therefore are meaningful to them. For the 3-year-old who is busy looking for a way to make a diaper stay on the doll, the problem is real—it is important. Skills learned in real-life play situations will more likely be generalized to other situations in a child's life . . . for example, discovering that masking tape can be reused more times than Scotch tape in securing a doll's diaper. . . . Real-life problems encountered in play have consequences that *really* matter to the children involved.[10]

A caterpillar wiggling to get off its back, curling up, and rolling over may be all that is needed to initiate a quick, spontaneous learning situation. These wonderful sources of learning arise each day. And, Verna Hildebrand explains, these situations must be seized upon:

> For example, the children find a caterpillar. While other plans wait, this furry creature becomes the focus of learning for several days. The children observe how the caterpillar moves, how it eats, and finally how it spins a cocoon. The teacher tells about the stages of metamorphosis. Good teaching results when a teacher is able to capitalize on a spontaneous interest such as this one.[11]

Spontaneous happenings are advantageous because they are surely related to the children's interests and, therefore, they will be bound to enjoy them. However, Joanne Hendrick warns, overreliance on spontaneous activities may result in a number of real problems:

> The real problem with spontaneity, or excessive reliance on spur-of-the-moment curriculum, is that the children may gain only small pepperings of factual knowledge on a multitude of subjects and lack an overall sense of integration and direction in what they learn. In addition, it may mean that some valuable opportunities for practice of more specific reasoning abilities are not provided, since the fortuitous nature of these curriculum "happenings" makes advance planning impossible.[12]

What happens if your children never discover a caterpillar? Does that mean they will miss out on all the interesting discoveries associated with these fuzzy creatures? Certainly not; the children will benefit from having a caterpillar introduced by their teacher. Hildebrand explains:

> The motivation may not be as high as when they discover something themselves, but if they are allowed to watch and hold the caterpillar the teacher brings to them, their knowledge will be enhanced. Later, when they find a caterpillar, they may recognize it and learn new facts.... Concepts worth learning should be introduced numerous times and in a variety of ways.[13]

Present Appropriate Materials and Activities

Thus, informal experimentation and developmentally appropriate instruction are important ways of gaining physical knowledge. However, when teachers must bring experiences to the children, it is important to remember that all learning must be based on actual experiences involving the child as an active participant. Rheta DeVries and Lawrence Kohlberg offer these criteria for good physical-knowledge activities:

1. *The child must be able to produce the phenomenon by his own action....* The essence of physical-knowledge activities is the child's action on objects and his observation of the object's reaction. The phenomenon selected must therefore be something the child can produce by his own action. The movement of a piece of Kleenex in reaction to the child's blowing or sucking on it through a straw meets this criterion. The movement of objects caused by a magnet, on the other hand, is an example of a phenomenon that is produced only indirectly by the child's action and primarily by magnetic attraction. This does not imply that magnets should be omitted from a classroom. It does imply that we should recognize the educational limitations of experimenting with magnets.

2. *The child must be able to vary his action.* When the variations in the child's action result in corresponding variations of the object's reaction, the child has the opportunity to structure these regularities. In a pool game, for example, if the child misses the target by hitting a ball too far to the left, he can adjust the next attempt accordingly. In a pinball-type game, by contrast, the child's action is limited to pulling a lever, and there is very little variation possible in how he releases the lever. The child thus cannot significantly affect the outcome. Without a direct correspondence between the variations in actions and reactions, a phenomenon offers little opportunity for structuring.

3. *The reaction of the object must be observable.* If the child cannot observe a reaction to his actions on objects, there is no content for him to structure. For example, an opaque tube in waterplay prevents observation of the water inside, and provides less material for structuring than a transparent tube.

4. *The reaction of the object must be immediate.* Correspondences are much easier to establish when the object's reaction is immediate. For example, when a child rolls a ball toward a target, she can immediately observe whether the target is hit or

Mixing ingredients and carrying out the baking process offer direct evidence of how physical properties of objects can be changed.

not, and if so, how it specifically reacts. In contrast, the reaction of a plant to water is not immediately observable, and its action on the water is only indirectly the result of the child's action. This does not imply that growing plants should be omitted from the classroom. In light of the immediacy criterion, sprouting beans on wet paper towels is a better activity to promote such understanding than watering a houseplant.[14]

Activities involving *movement of objects* (pulling, pushing, rolling, kicking, jumping, blowing, throwing, swinging, twirling, balancing, and dropping) meet the criteria in especially satisfactory ways. Blowing hard or softly to speed up an object's motion or rolling a ball in a specific direction to knock over a bowling pin are examples of ways children discover how their physical actions initiate changes in their environment. In addition to activities involving the movement of objects, those involving *changes in objects* are especially beneficial, too. Examples include cooking (making applesauce from apples and other ingredients result in several meaningful changes from the objects in their original form), mixing two hues of paint to achieve a third, or freezing and thawing water. In addition to activities in the two major classifications, there are those activities that cannot be categorized so neatly: finding out whether an object sinks or floats, producing echoes, sifting sand, or looking at leaves through a magnifying glass. These activities share characteristics of the other two categories, but cannot be placed into either of them.

Some of the most creative suggestions for offering physical-knowledge activities to young children are contained in the resource *Constructive Play: Applying Piaget in the Preschool* (Menlo Park, CA: Addison-Wesley, 1984) by George Forman and Fleet Hill. It would also be helpful to consult the book *Constructivist Early Education: Overview and Comparison With Other Programs* (Washington, DC: National Association for the Education of Young Children, 1990) by Rheta DeVries and Lawrence Kohlberg.

Create Centers of Interest

Developmentally appropriate programs for young children place a great deal of emphasis on experience with objects in the child's everyday world. Many of these experiences occur daily as children become involved with materials found in the regular classroom activity centers—sand and water play, mixing paints, or pounding playdough. Barbara Biber explains how these sensory experiences emerge:

> The variety of materials in the schoolroom offers opportunity for a wealth of sensory experience—rough sand in the box; smooth soft covers for the doll bed; hard wooden blocks; soft playdough; effervescent soap suds; contrasting colors on the paint easel and in the crayon box; multishaped pieces in the form boards; and musical instruments with a range of sounds. The possibilities for manipulative kinds of play with these materials are endless—pounding away the roundness of a ball of clay, making mud out of sand and water, making purple with blue and red paint, covering an empty paper with green circles, and filling up the emptiness of a pail with pebbles and listening to the sound as they are dumped out.[15]

Through such activities, children make observations of their environment and initiate actions that lead to transformations of those objects. In addition to these special learning experiences associated with regular classroom activity centers, teachers help support curiosity by structuring special centers and room displays that invite children to question and explore. Magnifying glasses, fans, acorns, feathers, bones, and a host of other "stuff" are usually collected into special corners or sections of the room designated as "exploratory" or "manipulative" centers. In these areas, teachers select materials that children may wish to explore and experiment with. There should be no predetermined teaching objectives or specific directions for the children to follow. Your role is minimal. You serve mainly to set up and maintain materials in the center and to make sure that the children are free to work on their own. Of course, you should always be aware of what is going on in the center. You may need to intervene if one child seems to be approaching frustration with an activity or another child is doing something potentially dangerous. Your presence may also be needed to help clarify concepts or to help address children's questions and concerns.

Many early childhood teachers choose to organize special display areas in the classroom designed to encourage conversation, information-seeking questions, and general interest in something about the children's world. These areas are often referred to by names such as "Our Look and Find Table." These exhibits, whatever they are called, should be treated like exhibits in the best child-oriented museums—with a policy that invites touching and exploring.

The center should encourage a child's free exploration. The teacher will want to model behaviors, words, and attitudes she feels the children should incorporate into their own exploration, but it is critical that the children design their experiments by themselves. For example, in a center dealing with floating and sinking, a teacher will give the children the lead as far as how to find out whether certain objects sink or float, but be nearby to suggest or demonstrate how to record their findings by placing the floating objects on a "Float Chart" and the sinking on a "Sink Chart."

Many interesting collections of objects may be offered at the exploratory center. Sometimes teachers make collections of objects and store them in boxes that can be easily made available for use. Diane Suskind and Jeanie Kittel suggested many possible discovery boxes, including those described in Table 6–1.[16]

In addition to these various manipulative devices, stimulating classrooms for young children should offer direct experiences with live plants and animals. Feeding and watering plants and pets, cleaning cages, collecting bugs to feed to the classroom toad, and watching tiny guppies being born and dying—all of these activities inspire children with fascination and awe.

Animals Young children are fascinated by all kinds of animals, from imaginary storybook animals with human characteristics to real animals with cold, wet noses— so exciting to touch. Children can be observed watching in surprise and wonder as a mother robin feeds and cares for her young. Similarly, they might be captivated by the industriousness and strength of ants as they gather food or materials for their growing colony, and stand watching for long periods of time.

Table 6–1 Possible ideas for discovery boxes

QUILT BOX
Goals
Fine motor skills, problem solving

Contents
An assortment of fabric squares (all the same size) with snaps on each corner (top and bottom) that children snap together to make their own quilt

EXPLORE BOX
Goals
Manipulation, science, tactile awareness, visual discrimination

Contents
Magnifying glasses, sea shells, rocks, laminated leaves, laminated dried flowers, pieces of bark

SEWING BOX
Goals
Fine motor skills, problem solving, eye/hand co-ordination

Contents
Fabric scraps with holes punched through; large, safe yarn needles with yarn threaded; scraps with buttons sewed on and buttonholes; scraps with zippers or snaps sewed on

PLASTIC LIDS BOX
Goals
Rolling, sorting, stacking, music (banging) manip-ulation
Note: large quantities are useful for this activity box.

Contents
Pink "baby wipe" lids; assorted baby food lids; gray film canister lids; beige Tupperware lid; yel-low coffee can lid; margarine tub lid; square clear lid; large and small caps; clear Tupperware lid; clear round cap

METAL OBJECTS BOX
Goals
Visual discrimination, manipulation, dramatic play

Contents
Combination lock, license plate, large coffee grounds holder with lid, small coffee grounds holder, percolator stand, small tray with picture, large tray with picture, aspirin box, screw-on lids, jar top inserts, bracelet, metal ball necklace, spice container

ICE BOX
Goals
Exploration, discovery, science, visual discrimina-tion
Note: This activity box is great for outdoors.

Contents
Freeze water with objects in the ice at different levels; add different colors of food coloring to some containers

PLASTIC OBJECTS BOX
Goals
Dramatic play, pouring, stirring, language skills

Contents
Soda pop bottle; milk bottle; bubble bottle; small, transparent, square container; condiment dishes; lotion bottle; various different bottles; plates; bowls with lids; pitcher with lid; cups; film con-tainers; cookie cutters; measuring spoons; ice container

THINGS THAT MEASURE BOX
Goals
Problem solving, measuring/math, language skills

Contents
Ruler, tape measure, hourglass, measuring cups, measuring spoons

The preschool environment should reflect these childhood interests and provide for many experiences with all kinds of animals. In addition to becoming aware of the physical characteristics of other living organisms, young children acquire strong feelings of importance as they feed the classroom animals and provide for their care. Rarely do young children have opportunities to practice for themselves the care and

Children wonder about everything: "Why don't I have fur like our guinea pig?"

treatment they receive from their own parents. With animals, however, they become directly involved in caring for other living beings, and soon develop an awareness of the value of good diet, cleanliness, and protection. If given good care, animals will become interesting and valuable additions to your classroom.

To obtain the greatest value from having animals in the preschool classroom—either indoors or out—you must constantly watch out for the animals' health and safety. Negligence in this area may serve to foster feelings of disrespect in the children and lead to abuse of the animal, followed by its injury, sickness, or death. If the children are to respect animal life, they must learn to understand and appreciate suitable environments and patterns of care; they must understand that all living things depend upon each other for survival.

Children can learn many important things from animals kept within their classrooms. New worlds open up to them as they observe and care for such small animals as rabbits, guinea pigs, hamsters, gerbils, mice, aquarium fish, ants, earthworms, parakeets, and hermit crabs. If you choose any of these potential pets, be sure to provide suitable housing and a regular diet of appropriate food and water. It would be a good idea to read from related reference books so that you are familiar with the needs and care requirements of any animal before it becomes a part of your classroom.

Some teachers prefer to bring to the children larger pets such as dogs, cats, or even ponies. These animals, too, can provide a richness of experience for youngsters. However, before you plan to add larger animals to your classroom, check into any restrictions or limitations that might be set forth in your local licensing regulations.

Plants Plants are often used in the preschool program for three main purposes: (1) to beautify the classroom, (2) to involve the children in caring for and nurturing them, and (3) to help children learn about plant life through experimentation and observation. Plants can brighten the preschool environment and make it an attractive and pleasant place for the children. However, because plants are often placed in hanging baskets or on tall shelves, the children rarely have opportunities to look at them closely. They become, unintentionally, the *teacher's plants* as they blend into the environment and are ignored by the children. To be *children's plants*—a more worthwhile part of the children's environment—they must be brought down to the level of the children, where they can be watched, touched, and cared for by the children themselves. Children's initial experiences with plants will undoubtedly involve accidents; the children may overwater, break off leaves or branches, pull up the plant with the roots, or even destroy a plant. However, if the children are going to learn to treat plants properly and to respect them, they must be taught to do so through experience. In any event, most of the accidents will occur not from mischievousness but from lack of knowledge about how to treat plants properly. A child's actual experiences while looking after and observing plants go a long way toward helping him understand why it is important to protect the environment around him. Some good plants to have in the preschool classroom include spider plants, geraniums, snake plants, ferns, or jade plants.

All these plants are easy to grow and care for. Their light and temperature requirements cover a wide range of conditions but are not unnecessarily exacting. Once these plants have adjusted to your room—its light, temperature, and humidity—they can be fed and watered routinely by the children with your guidance.

Generally, plants offer children important knowledge of their physical environment. Some plants, however, may be found to contain toxic elements. All the plants should be cleared by your local poison control center.

Physical-knowledge activities involve all the experiences that help children develop knowledge about their fascinating world. They involve observing, predicting, testing, and communicating ideas. A creative physical-knowledge classroom does not become a mere storehouse of facts, but attempts to be a laboratory where learning *happens.*

FACILITATING ACQUISITION OF PHYSICAL KNOWLEDGE

Children should be allowed to explore materials freely as they generate ideas or solutions to situations that arise. Teachers should understand how children do this so that they are best able to encourage and enlarge upon children's interests. Tegano, Sawyers, and Moran described how children's exploration and play contribute to learning.

Mary...has spotted the playdough on the table. This is Mary's first week at school and she has not had much exposure to playdough. She is intrigued by its color, consistency and taste (of course!). A skilled teacher can almost see her thinking, "What is this? How does it feel? How does it taste? What can it do?" [This phase is called *exploration.*]

The next day Mary again explores the playdough and then moves into a more playful mode, poking her finger through a piece of playdough and fashioning a ring for her thumb. Delighted with her own invention, she then makes rings for each of her fingers. At this point Mary is no longer asking herself, "What can this *playdough* do?" but rather, "What can *I* do with this playdough?" She has moved into...*diversive exploration*...the *play phase.*[17]

Your understanding of the difference between exploration and play is critical to the role of learning. *Exploration* is the time of finding out about an object—discovering its critical attributes. During exploration, the child is asking, "What can *it* do?" The exploratory phase provides the information that will be used as a basis for play. "It seems logical, then," Tegano, Sawyers, and Moran suggest, "that the more information acquired by a child in exploration, the richer the quality of his subsequent play."[18]

Play is when the child asks, "What can *I* do with the object?" It is during the play phase that Tegano, Sawyers, and Moran believe actual problem solving occurs: "For instance, after Mary discovers the malleability of playdough by poking her finger through it (exploration), she moves into play where the problem becomes 'How can *I* make more rings?' "[19]

In this situation, Mary discovered her *own* problem. She had a personal stake in its solution; the consequences really mattered to her. Mary could have solved her problem differently, and may have done so if she were given more time to explore her ideas. Periods of uninterrupted exploration and play are crucial for supporting intellectual growth in young children.

Asking Good Questions

It is unreasonable to assume that all learning will occur naturally in every preschool situation. Oftentimes you will need to intervene in order to build enthusiasm, heighten interest, or influence deeper exploration. If, as Vygotsky and Piaget contend, a large part of learning is composed of a relationship between physical experience and thought, the teacher's ability to interact with children is extremely crucial to the learning process. Vygotsky stresses the importance of adult-child interactions during the learning experience. He suggests that those interactions must be closely monitored and guided by the adult during the early stages of the learning experience. This could be accomplished by offering appropriate verbalizations or by helping the child manipulate the material. As the child demonstrates increasing awareness of the situation, the adult gradually relinquishes a leadership role and eventually relinquishes the management of the learning experience to the child.

As an example of how Vygotsky's ideas may be applied to actual classroom learning experiences, consider the episode described by Deborah J. Cassidy (see box at top of page 213).

▶▶▶▶▶▶▶

Beth (age 3.6) and her teacher engaged in a joint game of pendulum bowling, in which the ball is suspended from the ceiling on a long string and bowling pins are located within striking distance. Beth pulls the ball back and the teacher asks, "Which pin do you think the ball will hit, Beth?" Beth shrugs her shoulders and releases the ball. The ball misses all of the pins and hits the wall. Beth repeats this action once again. She then looks to the teacher with some confusion. The teacher responds, "What could you do to hit the pins?" Beth shrugs once again. "What would happen if you stood over here?" "I don't know," Beth responds. Beth chooses a spot near where the teacher indicated and releases the ball. The ball knocks over 2 pins. Beth smiles. She repeats her release from the same spot and once again 2 pins fall. "How could you get more pins to fall, Beth?" Beth moves 2 steps to the left, looks to her teacher for approval (the teacher smiles) and releases the ball. Eight pins fall this time. "Where do you think you should stand to get all of the pins to fall, Beth?" Beth continues to experiment with the bowling ball and pins as the teacher asks questions that structure the learning experience.[20]

Eventually, Beth's teacher observes Beth gradually assume greater responsibility for her learning:

▶▶▶▶▶▶▶

(Several days later) Beth once again approaches the pendulum bowling game. As Beth takes aim, the teacher asks, "Which pin do you think the ball will hit, Beth?" Beth points to a pin and then releases; the ball hits the pin next to the pin Beth had predicted would be hit. The teacher then asks, "What could you do to knock down all of the pins?" This time Beth independently moves 3 steps to her left and releases the ball, tumbling 9 of the 10 pins to the floor. Beth smiles and repeatedly attempts to knock all of the pins down by moving one step to the left and $1/2$ step to the left, etc.[21]

Eventually, as the teacher relinquishes full control, the teacher's questions will become internalized. Notice, however, that throughout the entire progression of experience, the teacher did not give the child any answers, but rather led the child to solve her own problem. While this exact sequence of teacher-initiated verbal interaction cannot be used for each learning experience in the preschool classroom, it does illustrate how the process of questioning assists the child during learning experiences.

All teachers of the very young must become familiar with the types of questions that are most likely to create a positive impact on the learning situation. One of the most important considerations in formulating questions to lead the children's learning is, "Will my comments encourage further exploration, or do they guarantee immediate closure?" When working with preservice teachers during early field experience, I often find that they habitually ask questions resulting in yes-or-no answers—for example, "Did you have fun with the marbles?" In the interest of provoking deeper thought, however, teachers should try to ask questions that require more than a simple, pat answer. Figuring out what the child is thinking is one of the most intricate challenges of experiential teaching. The kinds of questions we ask will often give us a clue and help us to enhance the child's construction of knowledge. Rheta DeVries and Lawrence Kohlberg have suggested these kinds of questions to ask as children act on objects in either of four different ways:

1. "Acting on objects and seeing how they react" suggests questions that involve predictions, such as, "What do you think will happen if you do X?"
2. "Acting on objects to produce a desired effect" suggests questions of the type, "Can you do X?" and, "Can you find anything else that you can do X with?"
3. "Becoming aware of how one produced the desired effect" suggests questions such as, "How did you do X?" The teacher can also encourage comparisons by raising questions such as, "Which way works better (or is easier)?" "How is (another child) doing X differently?" and, "Does it make any difference if you do X?"
4. "Explaining causes" suggests asking, "Why does X happen?" or saying, "I wonder why X happened?"[22]

Several of these sample questions, of course, were designed to help the children observe an object or event; others were designed to encourage higher thought processes like prediction and finding relationships. Through such questions and comments, the teacher helps the children to evaluate and extend their experiences.

Being a Good Listener

Everyone agrees that good teachers know how to ask good questions. As a matter of fact, practice in asking good questions is an important part of all teacher training programs. But how many of us have ever been given help in becoming good *listeners* to the children's questions? We often cut off interest and a spirit of communication by not listening. But when we do listen, we can often get children to offer more details, to clarify experiences, and to grow in creative expressiveness. The following is an example of how one teacher demonstrated the characteristic of nonlistening to a high degree. The teacher was nearby while children were observing a jar-type worm environment. They exchanged comments about the worms until one child turned to the teacher and asked, "Do worms have bones?" The teacher looked at the child coldly and responded, "What kind of question is that? Can't you see that they don't?" This type of response is uncalled for, of course, and does nothing to encourage children to explore the new world into which they have been placed. Because of their tremendous curiosity, children's questions will often furnish rich material for exploration and imagination:

- Are babies born with brains?
- What makes this rock sparkle?
- Why don't airplanes flap their wings?
- Where does the water go when I flush the toilet?
- How do those white clouds get so clean?
- What makes the sky blue?
- Why do puppies have tails?
- Why can't my dog talk?

Children have a lot of questions of their own to ask. For example, Thomas Edison's last day in school came when he asked, "How can water run uphill?" after he noticed that a river in Ohio did just that. Young Tom was then expelled for expressing himself in ways that were unacceptable at the time. Children come to us with a strong need to ask questions. Respect that fact and guide them in exercising this childhood gift. Whenever a child approaches you with a question, ask yourself, "Am I listening as carefully and sensitively as I am able?" When you do listen, you communicate to the child that he or she is a worthwhile individual whose thoughts are valued regardless of how silly they might seem. This is something the children need to know.

Investigation Together

As you choose developmentally appropriate experiences for your children, you will find in the children a sense of wonder and enjoyment. We do not "teach" children about their physical environment; we turn them loose and seek to investigate it together. Asking good questions and being a good listener are important parts of that responsibility, but— in order to be truly helpful—teachers must be tuned in to learning, too. They should be bright and informed; their background should include a strong liberal arts foundation. It will not be necessary for you to known everything about each phenomenon that captures a child's interest, but you should have enough knowledge to support children whenever they need your help. Teachers should constantly read and search for new life experiences related to typical preschool encounters. It is amazing how enthusiastic young teachers are to pass on the knowledge that they steadily accumulate. As R. Carson once said, "If a child is to keep alive his inborn sense of wonder, he needs the companionship of at least one adult who can share it, rediscovering with him the joy, excitement and mystery of the world we live in."[23]

Having the basic knowledge required to talk with children is only one part of the teacher's responsibility; the other part is to develop skill in *communicating* that information to the children when necessary. Often children's observations, questions, and experiments will need to be enlarged upon and verbalized by the teacher. But note that sometimes the teacher's comments can be too involved, as in this case:

Karen: Why did the puddle go away?

Teacher: The heat from the sun made the water disappear into the air. That's called evaporation.

Instead of this confusing answer, the teacher should have offered a simple explanation:

Karen: Why did the puddle go away?

Teacher: The heat from the sun dried it up.

Teachers sometimes cause problems, too, when they fabricate stories in an attempt to explain scientific concepts. Consider this situation, for example.

Richard: What happens to our dead gerbil?

Teacher: He goes to gerbil heaven—where all the good little gerbils go.

Richard: Is it nice there?

Teacher: Oh yes. He will have a clean, comfortable home and plenty of food to eat. And, even better, our gerbil will see his mother and father, along with many of his friends who have died, too.

Obviously, there is a better approach:

Richard: What happens to our dead gerbil?

Teacher: The gerbil died because it was very old. If we keep it here it will start to smell. Let's get the shovel and bury it outdoors.

The teacher's interpretations of scientific events for the children should be free of intricate explanation and mystical descriptions. Your role is a challenging one—to find the balance and sensitivity needed to make an experience uncomplicated and fascinating. Anything that goes beyond these characteristics causes misunderstandings and frustrations that may be difficult or impossible to eradicate later on. Remember to stick to facts and keep fantasy in its proper place; otherwise children may continue to think of new phenomena as magic, rather than as facets of the physical environment.

We have discussed the idea that children learn while they play. A teacher might choose to ask questions to guide children's thinking and encourage them to find their own solutions to problems encountered in play. During this process, however, it is important not to generalize for them. Sally Cartwright offers this example of a wonderful discovery episode that ended with a teacher's fruitless attempt to generalize the learnings her children experienced:

A strip of paper, which Jason, aged 4, had cut, fell onto the hot air register. Retrieving it by one end, he saw the other end lift upwards and float suspended above the grate.

"Magic!" he cried. Five children joined him. "How does that work?" "There are scary faces down there." "Yup, monsters are down there in the dark. They're doing it." "Are they blowing your paper?" Much discussion. Different shapes and colors of paper were tried. Different places. Ty tried a piece of rope. "It doesn't work," he said.

"Only mine works," explained Jason. "Mine is magic. Here, try it." Ty held Jason's thin strip of paper over the register, fascinated.

Finally the children themselves agreed that warm air came out of the register to heat our classroom. They listened in rapt silence for the furnace. When it hummed, the hot air blew up through the floor grate.

This led to a group trip into the basement. We saw the oil furnace and the ducts, and we traced a large duct to our classroom register. Again the children pooled their thoughts and together figured out that the furnace heats air. A blower sends the air to our classroom.

One at a time, with great care, we held strips of paper over the hot wood stove in the nearby kitchen. They lifted like the paper held over our heating register. But I did not hear any child generalize about hot air rising and lifting the paper, even *without* a fan to blow it. I asked many questions: "Why does the paper lift over the hot wood stove with no fan to blow it? Why is it warmer up in the balcony where you play? Why is the floor cold sometimes, while the air above seems warm?"[24]

Lack of success in getting the children to respond to her questions convinced this teacher that the children were not ready to explore in the direction she had hoped to lead them. Only when they are ready, she learned, will they discover the broad concept that hot air rises. At that point, the children were satisfied in knowing that the paper strips lifted up over both the hot stove and the hot air register. Children will let you know how far they want to go with a learning episode; resist the temptation to push them further.

You should always *convey a positive attitude toward the children's interests.* Their world is filled with objects and experiences that fascinate them. But children do not always receive reinforcement and encouragement from the adults around them as they explore these new wonders. Those adults may either frown on certain types of active exploration or simply lack interest in a particular area that engages the child. For those reasons, you may often hear comments or see reactions like the one described in this hypothetical situation (see box below).

Although you cannot treat every area of the children's interest with equal time and enthusiasm, you should be prepared to make new experiences pleasant for them. If you cringe at the sight of worms and other crawling creatures, you must learn to overcome your fears. Children's lives are full of bugs, worms, and other crawling, creeping creatures. Your queasiness in these situations will, of course, be sensed by the children and have an effect on their enthusiasm about future explorations. When situations arise by chance, you should have enough insight and self-control to show interest in a child's discovery.

▶▶▶▶▶▶

Digging in the garden, Marcianne and Dennis uncovered two small, white, wiggling, wormlike creatures. Calling to their teacher, the youngsters each picked up one of the Japanese beetle grubs, held them in their hands, and asked what they were. Her face turning ashen, the teacher drew back and commanded, "Put those things right back where you found them and get inside to wash your hands right now."

How can seasonal changes be exploited for their contributions to the acquisition of physical knowledge?

Children's encounters with their physical world should be spontaneous and active. Because children are not able to use adult logic, David Elkind recommends that, "Instruction in controlled experimentation probably should not be introduced until adolescence when young people can deal with multiple simultaneous variations."[25] Instead, children should be offered concrete experiences in their own environment—where they are able to see the world from their own perspective and begin to sense and discover relationships. It is only through self-initiated exploration that preschool children build ways of thinking about patterns and connections in their physical world.

SOME FINAL THOUGHTS

Children have a deep interest in their physical world; they eagerly explore and experiment while satisfying their curiosity about all its wonders. Our children must be given every opportunity to channel this interest through experiences that are active—both physically and mentally. Children construct important learning, especially physical knowledge, through child-initiated, spontaneous activity. Informal and planned happenings are the major types of personal involvement experiences through which children conduct their own spontaneous research, that is, discovering knowledge in the preschool setting.

The development of exploratory interests begins during infancy with sensorimotor play. As experiences accumulate, children acquire increasingly sophisticated cognitive skills. It is only by acting on the environment that children build a meaningful understanding of their world. Therefore, preschool children must be offered many opportunities to find things out for themselves—not in "subjects" that are traditionally taught in the elementary school, but in "happenings" that help children satisfy their curiosities. We must open up the world to the children, allowing them to experience worms, ants, trees, fire trucks, driftwood, pupae, adobe, pagodas, mesquite, and other enthralling features of our world. These experiences not only fulfill a deep quest to know, but also stimulate further interests as children gain a growing understanding of their world.

NOTES

1. James L. Hymes, Jr., *Teaching The Child Under Six,* 3rd ed. (Columbus, OH: Merrill, 1981), pp. 80–81.

2. Ibid, pp. 80–81.

3. Rheta DeVries and Lawrence Kohlberg, *Constructivist Early Education*: *Overview and Comparison with Other Programs* (Washington, DC: NAEYC, 1990), pp. 103–104.

4. B. Taylor, *A Child Goes Forth* (Provo, Utah: Brigham Young University Press, 1964), pp. 80–81.

5. Constance Kamii and Rheta DeVries, *Physical Knowledge in Preschool Education: Implications of Piaget's Theory* (Englewood Cliffs, NJ: Prentice Hall, 1978), p. 4. Reprinted by permission of Allyn & Bacon.

6. Jean Piaget, *To Understand is to Invent* (New York: Grossman, 1978), p. 105.

7. Rheta DeVries and Lawrence Kohlberg, *Constructivist Early Education,* p. 29.

8. Ann C. Howe, "Childhood Experiences in Science," *Instructor, 84,* no. 1 (January 1975): 58.

9. Eugene Grant, "The Tale of Peter and the Rabbit," *Phi Delta Kappan, 44,* no. 3 (November 1967), back cover. Copyright November 1967 by Phi Delta Kappa, Inc.

10. Deborah W. Tegano, Janet K. Sawyers, and James D. Moran, III, "Problem- Finding and Solving in Play: The Teacher's Role," *Childhood Education, 66,* no. 2 (Winter 1989): 93.

11. Verna Hildebrand, *Introduction to Early Childhood Education,* 4th ed. (New York: Macmillan, 1986), pp. 222–23.

12. Joanne Hendrick, *The Whole Child: Developmental Education for the Early Years,* 5th ed. (Columbus, OH: Merrill/Macmillan, 1992), p. 463.

13. Verna Hildebrand, *Introduction to Early Childhood Education,* p. 223.

14. Rheta DeVries and Lawrence Kohlberg, *Constructivist Early Education,* pp. 92–93.

15. Barbara Biber, "A Developmental-Interaction Approach: Bank Street College of Education." In M. Day and R. Parker (eds.), *The Preschool in Action,* 2nd ed. (Boston: Allyn & Bacon, 1977), pp. 435–436.

16. Diane Suskind and Jeanie Kittel, "Clocks, Cameras, and Chatter, Chatter, Chatter: Activity Boxes as Curriculum," *Young Children, 44,* no. 2 (January 1989): 48–49.

17. Deborah W. Tegano, Janet K. Sawyers, and James D. Moran, III, "Problem- Finding and Solving in Play," p. 93.

18. Ibid., p. 95.

19. Ibid., p. 95.

20. Deborah J. Cassidy, "Questioning the Young Child: Process and Function," *Childhood Education, 65,* no. 3 (Spring 1989): 148–149.

21. Ibid., p. 149.

22. Rheta DeVries and Lawrence Kohlberg, *Constructivist Early Education,* p. 98.

23. R. Carson, *The Sense of Wonder* (New York: Harper & Row, 1965), p. 45.

24. Sally Cartwright, "Group Endeavor in Nursery School Can Be Valuable Learning," *Young Children, 42,* no. 5 (July 1987): 11.

25. David Elkind, "Piaget and Science Education," *Science and Children, 10,* no. 3 (November 1972): 10.

CHAPTER 7

Offering Cognitive and Mathematical Experiences

Developmentally appropriate classrooms enable children to engage in activities designed to address all areas of development, including those normally described as "academics." To most people, the term *academics* represents the typical selection of concepts and skills normally associated with the subject matter of schools, such as reading, math, and spelling. The academic scene suggests a teacher standing in front of a group of children, directing them through lessons designed to teach them "all they need to know." To further develop this portrait, the teacher is at center stage; children are passively seated at their desks, working hard to generate correct answers through drills and rote learning of facts.

People who envision "academics" this way are not familiar with what goes on in developmentally appropriate classrooms. Academic goals are approached with a variety of instructional strategies, including small-group instruction, active manipulation of concrete materials, and lively exploration. Teachers sing songs, read stories, recite action rhymes, play games, and challenge the children's thinking. They give children material to sort, put together, and take apart. They introduce materials that stimulate children to question, to experiment, and to form their own conclusions. Teachers regularly address academics during classroom routines—eating snacks, cleaning up, playing outdoors, and so on. In developmentally appropriate classrooms, teachers present children with challenges that help them move beyond their current competencies toward the development of increasingly sophisticated levels of cognitive abilities.

This chapter examines the kinds of conceptual learnings that are considered appropriate for young children and suggests techniques that help children thrive. As you read, use the following questions to guide your thinking:

- What basic conceptual skills are recommended to be taught in developmentally appropriate programs?

- How can play and teacher-designed games and activities contribute to conceptual growth?

- How do children become naturally aware of numbers and their functions?

- What is the difference between rote counting and meaningful counting?

- How do teachers help children learn about numbers informally?

- Should teachers organize instruction to introduce mathematics concepts? If so, what is the teacher's role?

- Besides the concepts of number, numeral, and sequence, what other mathematics concepts are appropriate for preschoolers?

▶▶▶▶▶▶

An Episode to Ponder

Mr. Cohen is sitting with a group of three children at a work table. He has just introduced them to a set of materials—pictures of objects that had been pasted on tagboard so that three belong to one class and one belongs to another. For example, three squares and one triangle composed one set; three flowers and one tree composed another; and three smiling faces and one frowning face composed the third. Mr. Cohen briefly described the activity with his own set of cards—three had pictures of crayons and one had a picture of a pencil. "Can you find the pictures that go together?" he asks. "Which one does not belong to the group?" Mr. Cohen is sure to ask the children to explain their reasoning as they go along. He then initiates a challenge: "One child told me that all the pictures go together because crayons *and* pencils can be used for drawing *or* writing. What would you say to that child?"

Following the discussion, Mr. Cohen gives a set of four cards to each child and asks the children to find which things belong together and which one does not belong to the group. During the discussion, he constantly asks the children to explain their reasoning.

Small group learning experiences are a regular part of the daily routine of most preschools and kindergartens. Groups usually include three to five children who meet regularly with the teacher for 20 or 30 minutes each day to participate in activities that focus on the development of different thinking skills. Teachers often plan their days with group considerations in mind, but fully understand that children acquire cognitive skills in *everything* they do. As you learned in Chapter 6, children continually strive to explore and examine everything around them. When they spontaneously divide a set of seashells into "small" and "large" groups, for example, they have exercised a cognitive skill (classification). When they hear the word "butterfly" and learn to use it as a label for the fluttering wonder being observed, children are applying cognitive skills. A child's cognitive skills emerge and grow not only at group time, but throughout the entire day.

Whenever we talk about the area of preschool programs dealing with thinking or reasoning skills, we refer to promoting the child's **cognitive development.** We have learned a great deal about cognitive development from the work of Jean Piaget. In previous chapters, you have read that Piaget defined the stages of intelligence through which children pass until they reach maturity. According to Piaget, three kinds of knowledge are constructed as the children mature: physical knowledge, logico-mathematical knowledge, and social-conventional knowledge. *Physical knowledge* (Chapter 6) consists of children's individual actions on objects that lead to an understanding of those objects themselves. This chapter, by contrast, explores a second dimension of cognitive development: the **logico-mathematical experience,** which deals with aspects of objects that cannot be directly observed. It consists of relationships that must be created by the child. Physical knowledge is best acquired when teachers provide opportunities for children to use all their senses while exploring the physical environment. Such activity may lead to logico-mathematical knowledge, but a larger part of logical-mathematical thinking is enhanced during episodes where teachers create game-type materials and puzzling situations that offer challenging problems for the learners. Teachers, therefore, help children acquire cognitive skills by (1) offering opportunities for free exploration and (2) selecting and organizing developmentally appropriate games and activities. Children are not left with unlimited freedom to work on their own; they are provided a mixture of direction and freedom.

PROMOTING COGNITIVE DEVELOPMENT

Children learn a great deal by themselves, but they often need help in putting those learnings together to form more complex concepts. For that reason, early childhood teachers often arrange classroom activities that are focused on getting the children to develop and refine specific thinking skills. Children must be offered many opportunities for playful exploration of the environment; most respond to environmental stimuli in highly constructive ways—they organize information in their brains in predictable patterns from a very early age. Yet, if children are offered only activity with little or no guidance, they sometimes have difficulty clarifying and understanding what they have seen and explored. As young children gain more experiences with the world around them, they often need help in organizing specific learning episodes centered around specially selected concepts. Janice J. Beaty has organized a sequence of conceptual development that appears systematically throughout many early childhood programs.[1]

- *Shape.* Shape is one of the earliest concepts to be formed: young children can discriminate objects on the basis of shape earlier than any other quality. It is best, then, to begin a cognitive program by presenting activities that allow children to distinguish among objects on the basis of shape, beginning with one shape at a time.

- *Color.* Although children often talk about the colors of objects first, Beaty points out that children develop concepts of color after that of shape. Color concepts are best developed by starting out with one color at a time and offering many interesting games and activities relating to that color.

- *Size.* As children gain more experience with things in their environment, they begin to pay special attention to relationships among those things. Size is one of the first properties children give special attention to. Oftentimes, these size relationships are taught in terms of opposites: big versus little, tall versus short, wide versus narrow, and long versus short. Young children can relate to only one property of an object at a time, so they must learn "big" first, then "little", and finally they are asked to contrast the two.

- *Classification.* When children sort objects, people, events, or ideas into groups on the basis of some common trait such as color, size, or shape, we say the children are classifying. Children as young three are able to classify objects. We can see the process clearly when they separate plush toys into groups of "big animals" and "little animals." Children classify things in many ways; a box of buttons, for example, may be sorted according to size, shape, or color.

- *Seriation.* Seriation is the ability to put things in a certain order according to a specific rule; for example, from short to tall or from loud to soft. Many of the Montessori learning materials described in Chapter 2 are seriation activities.

These areas of the preschool curriculum enable children to organize their understandings of the world around them by encouraging the development of mental constructs that describe similar things in certain ways. Children develop these mental constructs (concepts) through real activities appealing to a wide range of sensory experiences. All of the information extracted through playful exploration is filed away into predetermined patterns within the brain. Through their activity, children

When children are given opportunities to put objects that are alike together, they are classifying.

build mental representations of real objects, differentiate among things by outward appearance, and decide how things fit together to form a pattern or sequence. In short, Beaty's categories describe the types of concepts preschools usually identify as appropriate for organizing the data about the real world that the child constantly assimilates.

In Piaget's theory, the ability to conceptualize properties of objects by using color, shape, or size categories is quite different from an ability to conceptualize number. He viewed the two abilities as being so different that he referred to them by separate terms; **empirical (simple) abstractions** refer to the concept categories delineated by Beaty, whereas **reflective abstractions** refer to number concepts. In empirical abstractions, the child focuses on a single property of an object—for example, color—and ignores all others. Empirical abstractions have an existence in *external* reality—the color, size, and shape of objects. By contrast, reflective abstractions are more mature thought processes that are constructed *internally*. When we place two blue chips together, the child can readily form an empirical abstraction (*blue* chips) through observation, but must internalize the fact that *two* chips are there. Nowhere is the idea of "twoness" communicated to the child by the objects themselves. That concept must be formed in the mind. He must *perceive* it, for it is not outwardly there for him to observe directly, as is color.

Because mathematical concepts are reflective abstractions, children must be given opportunities to observe the properties of objects and to learn to form relationships by distinguishing among their common features. Children need help, initially, in perceiving the world around them and organizing their perceptions. Helping children form accurate empirical abstractions is an important way that preschools can encourage more sophisticated mental processes, such as forming reflective abstractions. This chapter, therefore, is divided into two separate sections. This first section, "Promoting Cognitive Development," describes the acquisition of empirical abstractions; the second section, "Developing Mathematics Skills," deals with the attainment of reflective abstractions.

OPPORTUNITIES FOR PLAY

From our understanding of Piaget, we know that children's intellectual growth begins during infancy when babies become involved in sensorimotor play. As they grow, children expand upon it as the play process assumes new characteristics. Dramatic play, for example, enters the life of the three-year-old.

Dramatic play, during which children imitate what they have experienced, offers many benefits. For the purposes of this chapter, we will consider dramatic play as it stimulates children to think creatively and improves their cognitive abilities. Constance Kamii, an educator who has successfully applied Piaget's theories to the early childhood classroom, explains how play activities help the young child gain knowledge of his physical world:

> In a simple situation like pretending to have coffee with friends, children represent their knowledge of reality in all areas of the cognitive framework. For example, they represent their *physical knowledge* by heating the coffee, pouring it, spilling it, stirring it, and burning oneself with it. They represent the idea of pouring more coffee than cream, or giving a lot of cream and sugar to some people, and less or none to other people (*pre-seriation*). They construct elementary *number concepts* as they get just enough cups, saucers, napkins, and spoons for everybody. They represent the *temporal sequence* of making coffee, getting the cups and saucers out, pouring coffee, drinking it, and then cleaning up. They learn to serve the guests first (*social knowledge*). Sometimes, they invite people by phoning them beforehand. In this situation, some children's temporal sequence has been observed to consist of accepting an invitation first before being invited, or dialing first before picking up the receiver![2]

Such play-oriented situations should be kept open-ended and eventually you will see some very important learnings emerge. Ann Hammerman and Susan Morse use an informal classification example to illustrate this process.

> In the course of her play, Judy began grouping objects by color, making a red group and a white group. She noticed a red pencil with a white end. She put it first into the red group and then into the white group. She was noticeably perturbed. Neither solution satisfied her. Finally, she placed the pencil so that the red end was near the other red objects and the white end was near the white objects. The pencil formed a bridge between the two groups. She was experiencing a moment of tension between a more rigid view that an object can belong to only one group at a time and a realization that groups can overlap.[3]

When children begin to develop an increasing awareness of the objects around them, the teacher may do some systematic questioning leading to problem solving. Hammerman and Morse described the following situation, in which a preschool teacher encouraged problem solving.

> Teddy approaches the table. The objects available to him are: a rectangular plastic container, funnel, sticks, wooden and plastic discs of different sizes, aluminum tart tins, different shapes and sizes of blocks (rectangular, cylindrical), marbles, different kinds of paper, beads, spools, straws and plastic airplanes.
>
> Teddy begins making a tower alternating metal tins and paper cups. He is ordering the items in a specific way, as well as testing out the balance of forces. I say, "I'll make a tower too. Let's see if I can make mine taller." I decide to bring in the comparison of heights to see if Teddy will pursue this aspect of tower building. Then he picks up the whole pile of cups to add them to the tower. I ask him, "What do you think will happen if you put all the cups on top there?" Since he is silent, I ask, "Do you think it will fall?" He nods. "Do you want it to fall over?" He shakes his head no. "Well, what could you do so that it will not fall over?" He considers the pile of cups. He takes part of the pile and puts it on the tower. I say, "That's an idea, taking some away." The tower does not fall. He has considered a problem and figured out a solution. He now adds the rest of the cups. The pile topples.
>
> He rebuilds the pile in the same spatial pattern as before. When he is at the point of wanting to add the whole pile of cups, he pauses to consider the situation. He places the entire pile of cups on top of the tower pushing down from the top as he does so to compress the pile. I say, "Another good idea, to press down on the cups." He has considered another solution to the problem. This is a sophisticated solution, intuitively using the laws of physical science. This time the tower does not fall.[4]

Play activities contain many situations where children find and solve problems. Play provides opportunities to explore and experiment with a variety of solutions to very real problems.

The Teacher's Role

Perhaps the single most effective way to expand and enrich children's cognitive growth is to offer many play opportunities in a nonthreatening environment and to know the kinds of questions or statements that best extend children's play. Tegano, Sawyers, and Moran point out the importance of offering many play opportunities:

> Unlike play, teacher-presented hypothetical problem situations are more contrived and less likely to have meaning for the child, and they often have one right answer. ... Real-life problems encountered in play have consequences that *really* matter to the children involved.[5]

Through observation, teachers are able to recognize whether or not intervention to enhance thinking skills is necessary. How the child interacts with the material determines whether the teacher should use a **nondirective** or a **directive** response. For example, if an activity is becoming repetitious, you might want to use directive interactions such as the following to renew interest:

"You've added two drops of food coloring to the playdough. What would happen if you added two more?"

"You've built a tall building with the unit blocks. Who lives in your building?"

A variety of traditional early childhood materials helps children understand basic concepts through play.

"I see you've made a pattern with all of the beads. What other patterns could you make with the same beads?"

"Can you make a necklace with two red beads, two blue beads, and two green beads?"

"Can you think of another way to make designs on your clay 'pancake'?"

Nondirective intervention would be most effective when you push to reinforce appropriate play behaviors: for example, "Your idea to make the block tower wider at the bottom helped keep it from toppling over." A skillful teacher allows the children to have control over their play experiences, but is near to provide help and encouragement when necessary. Dorothy Anker and her colleagues have offered teachers a wealth of intervention possibilities to consider in the block area. See Table 7–1.

Perhaps the best way to contribute to the refinement of specific concepts is by offering children materials to explore and by interacting appropriately with them in their experiences. Additionally, good teachers display a strong interest in the world around them. They model an excitement about things and hope that their enthusiasm will spill over to the children.

TEACHER-FASHIONED GAMES

Certainly, a great deal of what young children learn occurs during direct experiences and spontaneous play. It is unrealistic, however, to think that all learning will occur naturally in every preschool situation. Teachers can set the scene for enhanced learning by creating their own games and activities. For example, a common game enjoyed by preschoolers is the "feely bag" game. In this game, the teacher uses a drawstring cloth bag that the children can reach into without seeing in. A selection of geometric shapes (start with two contrasting shapes—a circle and square—and add more as the children become familiar with the game) is placed in the bag. A child is given a shape to see and feel. Then the child is asked to reach into the bag and, without looking, find a similar shape. The child brings out the shape to compare with the one in her hand. The teacher and child then talk about the shape, how it feels, and its name.

Teachers can offer much help to children as they develop concepts by involving them in such game-type activity. We can use the same basic format to help children learn about colors. Let us suppose that a teacher shows a child a box containing small plastic toys and says, "Look at the toys in this box. Let's dump them on the rug and see what we have." The child is allowed to play for a time with the toys, then is invited to join the teacher in a game: "Let's play a sorting game with these toys. We'll put the red toy on this red rug (sample) because it is the same color, the blue toy on the blue rug, and the yellow toy on the yellow rug. Ready? Show me a toy. Where will you put it? The blue toys all go together.... You sorted all the toys by color. Please tell me the names of the colors we sorted. You did very well. Let's mix the toys and play the game again." The teacher continues

Table 7–1 Verbal intervention possibilities in the block area[6]

"This block is square." (labeling, mathematical concepts)

"You've used all rectangles in your building." (classifying by shape, labeling)

"Can you find another block just like this one?" (matching, classifying according to size and shape)

"Let's see how many round blocks we can find." (labeling, number concepts, classifying by shape)

"How can you make this road as long as that one?" "How can you make this side as high as that one?" (language development, measurement, defining spatial relationships, problem solving)

"Here, this truck will fit through your garage door." (language development, measurement, size discrimination, spatial relationships)

"I wonder what would happen if we put this block here." (experimentation, testing)

"How can we connect these two blocks?" (problem solving, language development)

"Look, two square blocks are as long as, or equal to, one rectangle." "This rectangle is half as long as this rectangle." (fractions, measurement, spatial relationships, language development, labeling)

"When you put these two triangles together, they make the same shape as the square." (mathematical concepts, language development, experimenting)

"Which block feels heavier?" "Do these blocks weigh the same?" (weight concepts, language development)

"Let's put the big blocks on this shelf." (classifying by size and shape during cleanup)

"This is not a big block." "This is not a square block." (the concept of "not" in classifying)

"Could we build a house with round blocks?" (hypothesizing, problem solving, classifying by shape)

Often children build enclosures with no doors or windows: "How will the people get into your house?" (language development, problem solving)

"Does your road have a curve or is it straight?" (language development, shape distinction, spatial relationships)

"Which is the shortest way from the house to the store?" (measurement, spatial relationships)

"Let's make a bridge over the road." (expanding possibilities, new ideas, developing abstract concepts)

"Will the car go under the bridge or over the bridge?" (language development, prepositions)

"You used a lot of blocks." "He has only a few blocks." "He needs five more blocks." (number concepts, language development, comparison of quantity)

"What would you do if he closed the road?" (problem solving, verbalizing alternatives, experimenting with ideas)

"You made it balance." "Let's balance this block with another one on this side." (language development, structural relationships)

"Will it fall down if we put this large block on top?" (Concepts of balance, gravity, relationship of base to height)

"My foot is five blocks long. How many blocks long is your foot?" (concepts of size, numbers, measurement)

"Let's see if this tower is as tall as you are." (height size comparison)

"Is there room enough for that big truck in your garage?" (spatial relationships, language development)

"John's road has a pattern. Let's make his road longer using the same pattern." (discrimination, sequencing, imitation)

"How does it feel when you walk down the inclined plane? When you walk up?" (language development, gravity, force)

"How will the car (the rubber animal, the handkerchief, the crayon) go down (or up) the ramp?" (language development, concepts of force, gravity, motion) playing until the child's interest wanes. Analyzing this teacher's strategy, we find that he:

1. Arranged a special set of manipulative play materials
2. Encouraged the child to play freely with them
3. Demonstrated an activity with the materials that led to understanding
4. Invited the child to perform the same action until mastery was achieved
5. Continued the activity until the child lost interest

Remember that this suggested sequence doesn't need to be followed rigidly. The exact amount of teacher involvement, as well as the number and order of play experiences, should always remain open so they can be made to match the child's changing interests and needs.

Working with Groups

Once we begin to work with young children in group-oriented intellectual tasks, it may be important to provide some structure to the available time, so that maximum benefit can be derived by all. Small-group time devoted to intellectual pursuits becomes a part of the daily routine for some four-year-old groups, and by kindergarten

Teacher-led group games are often used to enrich or reinforce particular skills.

most teachers plan structured group time. Groups usually consist of three to five children who meet regularly for about half an hour each day. The teacher or another adult leads the group.

Setting Objectives   A learning objective is usually specified for each group session. This gives the lesson a focus and professional support for choosing the activity for the group. Examples of objectives include exploring with the senses, comparing contrasting objects, and recognizing colors.

Organizing the Activity   There are two features of objectives that you should remember whenever you are called upon to plan for group sessions: *First,* the objectives are stated in terms of the *children:* "The children will describe the relative position of a set of objects." An inappropriate objective would be one that describes the behavior of the *teacher:* "The teacher will furnish the children with information about basic geometric shapes." When you identify objectives, your statements must describe what you want the children to accomplish; your goal is to make sure the objectives are attained. *Second,* there should be only one or two objectives for each group session. A characteristic problem of many beginning teachers is to state too many objectives; they seek to accomplish too much. Remember that young children need a special focus, and that including too many objectives causes your session to lose focus.

Some educators believe that broad objectives are often stated in such indefinite ways that they lose their meaning. For example, an objective such as "The children will understand the four basic geometric shapes" lacks any real point. Such a statement could apply just as well to the study of plane geometry as it could to the simple recognition of basic geometric figures.

For that reason, some educators prefer to state objectives in terms of direct, observable behaviors. These objectives are called *behavioral objectives.* Behavioral objectives identify the specific behaviors that you hope the children will demonstrate as they progress through the learning activities planned. Behavioral objectives consist of three major parts:

1. Identifying the *input process,* or the activity you will provide
2. Describing *what the child is to do* during the activity
3. Stating the minimum acceptable *level of performance.*

Behavioral objectives are frequently used to give more specificity to broader objectives. For example,

- *General objective:* The children will distinguish among specific sounds made by the teacher.

- *Behavioral objective:* After listening to five common sounds with their eyes shut (*input*), the children will name the source (*what they are to do*) of at least four sounds (*minimum performance*).

Regardless of what objective you have as you plan for small-group learning activities, it is essential that you give that objective careful thought. Objectives give you a reason for providing the session for the children and for choosing the learning activity to which the children are exposed. Instead of aimlessly searching through teachers' idea books for a cute, gimmicky, or fun activity to share with the children, start with a purpose for the session. Ask yourself, "Why is this lesson so important?" or "What is it going to do for the children?" Once you have answered this satisfactorily, you are on the right road to selecting an appropriate activity. Cute, gimmicky, and fun activities now have a purpose. If you go through this process, you are using a sophisticated professional reasoning skill—making *if-then* connections. For example, you may be thinking along these lines:

- *If* we want the children to describe spatial relationships, *then* we may want to place a toy bear at one end of an elaborate construction paper path and a toy house at the other. We'll ask the children to describe how the bear can get home by using spatial terms like going "over" hills or "under" bridges.

- *If* we want to develop small-muscle control for beginning writing, *then* we may want to encourage the children to use knobbed wooden inlay puzzles so that they use the two fingers and thumb in much the same way that they must be coordinated for writing.

Once you have decided what your objectives are and have chosen materials the children will enjoy, you must develop a session, or lesson, framework. Such frameworks are most effective when thoght of in three clearcut parts: *beginnings, bodies,* and *ends.*

Beginning   In order to prepare a good beginning, keep these tips in mind:

- Have the necessary materials ready at the place they are going to be used.

- Have the material divided into portions for each child, if necessary.

- Get everyone's attention in an interesting way. For example, "I'm going to tell you a secret," or "What do you think happened to this carrot today?"

- Give a brief description of the activity, for example: "Here are some toys. Does anyone have an idea how we can find out which ones will sink and which ones will float?"

- Have the childen enter into the activity as soon as they understand what they are to do.

Body   Your role during the actual work time includes these responsibilities:

- Watch and listen to see if things are going smoothly and as anticipated.

- Talk with each child, making sure to stimulate thinking and help them describe the activity with words.

- Challenge the children to solve special problems: "Could we use this piece of styrofoam to help the paper clip float?"

- Give special suggestions to children who may be having trouble.

Ending   To ensure that the children will feel good about the activity, end it well:

- Caution the children that the activity will soon be coming to an end.

- Ask each child to tell about or show what she has done (a summary).

- Throw out a question for the children to reflect upon.

- Make a connection to what will be coming next.

- Make cleanup a part of the activity: "After you put everything away, we can look at books until everyone is ready for the story circle."

- Encourage the children to try the materials again if you have your classroom arranged with interest centers.

Designing Lesson Plans

This sequence of presenting planned cognitive lessons to young children should be studied carefully. You will probably be asked sometime soon to plan an organizational sequence for learning activities. Such a blueprint enables you to predict the proper course of action for the identified area of instruction. Although forms and styles differ markedly among college instructors and classroom teachers, a lesson plan usually contains sections in which objectives, methods and materials, and techniques for evaluation are specified. Depending on the nature of the lesson, some provisions for individual differences must be indicated. The accompanying box contains a sample lesson plan, which applies the ideas shared thus far. This is my style of planning, and it is intended only as a suggestion. Your instructor may express a personal preference, too.

Because we have so carefully considered descriptions of guided learning, we must also point out a common trap that captures many early childhood professionals. This misunderstanding equates preschool instruction with some commonly abused elementary school approaches—all the children sitting at their seats, using workbooks, reciting facts, and so on. Do not bring dull routines and dreariness into the children's lives, but challenge their minds with appealing methods of teaching. The teacher's concern is not to cram information into children, but to help children develop an interest in learning that will last all their lives.

Planned programs recommended by most early childhood educators differ markedly from what many nonprofessionals believe to be "learning." The popular misconception of early learning is that it is much like what we may have experienced during the early elementary grades—acquiring information primarily from books, films, or from listening to teachers tell us about things. These sources of learning do eventually become an important component of the child's educational experience, but the preschool teacher's role is, rather, to encourage the kind of developmental learning most suitable for young children before they enter the elementary school. Such a role entails planning and carrying out those experiences by involving youngsters in exploring, experimenting, and action.

LESSON PLAN

- Group size: 3–5
- Age level: Four-year-olds
- Teacher: Miss Ginny

Objectives

- *General Objective:* The children will understand the concept of "same."
- *Behavioral Objective:* After observing ten common objects, the children will sort all five pairs that are the same.

Methods and Materials

1. Arrange on a large table as many boxes containing five pairs of common objects as there are children in the group: styrofoam cups, pencils, crayons, scissors, and paintbrushes, for example. Also, have a separate box for the teacher containing five pairs of different objects.

2. Encourage the children to explore the objects by saying: "Look at all the things in these boxes. Let's take them out to see what we have."

3. Allow the children to play for a short period of time.

4. Invite the children to join along in a game: "Let's play a sorting game with these toys." Start off by placing one block from the teacher's box on the table and saying, "I'm going to find another that is the *same*." Then place a second block with the first.

5. Ask the children to show a styrofoam cup from their boxes and place it in front of them. Then invite the children to find the matching cup. Once that is done, reinforce the concept by saying, "These are the same."

6. Encourage the children to pull one other toy from their boxes and find the other that is the same. Continue until all five pairs are matched.

7. Ask the children to tell you what they have done.

8. Invite the children to put away the materials they have used: "After you put the toys back into the boxes, place them on the shelf and get ready for the playground."

Evaluation

Observe the children during the activity to determine whether all five pairs were accurate.

Having analyzed the skills and concepts for cognitive learning, teachers are in a position to provide opportunities for a variety of learning experiences. Most times, materials are arranged around the classroom like bait, so that the child is attracted to them. The teacher may encourage and invite the child to explore materials. As a teacher, you should promote active involvement, manipulation of materials, problem solving, and exploration. You should help the child develop a sense of mastery and confidence in his abilities through rich and varied learning experiences. The teacher is always near to clarify and give support during learning activities in order to prevent misinterpretations and misconceptions. In order to learn, young children must have an environment of stimulation within a climate of emotional support.

DEVELOPING MATHEMATICS SKILLS

The basic conceptual skills discussed to this point help children learn mental operations that follow a logical scheme and lead to higher-order thought processes. Classification skills, for example, are prerequisite to an understanding of such mathematical

What math skills might be encouraged through this child's sandbox adventures?

operations as set arrangement and problem solving. For example, when playing with blocks, children may classify (put together) the blocks that are alike into one group (line up all the square blocks). At a more advanced level, a child may declare, "I put the square blocks in a tower and the cylinder blocks in a line." An even more advanced child might state, "I have five square blocks in my tower. I have three cylinder blocks in a line."

Despite the fact that many adults want children to master certain mathematical skills and concepts by the time they finish kindergarten, most preschoolers are not overly interested in such learning. As newcomers to life, they glory in all its *big lessons:* following a frog, watching a developing storm, smelling freshly cut grass, hearing the gush of a hot-air balloon, or tasting a new cookie for the first time. A natural urge to ask questions, to explore, and to experience helps them learn about all that surrounds them. They like to take their time with things that fascinate them. Teachers must have patience and allow children to take the time they need to gain understandings from their wealth of concrete life experiences. When children enter the world of mathematics, they move into a new dimension. As teachers, we must ask children to make a drastic change from the concrete learning so much a part of their lives to the strange world of abstract thinking. This change comes about slowly. How can this process be directed by the early childhood teacher? The basic answer is to provide the child with interesting and realistic experiences that are appropriate for each level of development. We must understand not only the characteristics of mathematics-related thought during stages of children's development, but also the types of experiences most conducive to growth during each stage.

Children do not enter early childhood programs totally devoid of mathematical understanding. Just watch a two-year-old as he approaches his third birthday. Proudly, he announces to everyone in sight, "Hi, I'm Jeffy. I'm this many." (He tries to coordinate his fingers to show two.) "Pretty soon I'll be this many." (Again he struggles until three fingers stand up.)

Children hear many mathematical terms at home and in the classroom long before they understand them. To illustrate this point, imagine that you are touring a preschool setting and are listening for all the references made by children to the field of mathematics. You would probably hear comments like these:

"My new ball cost *60 cents.*"

"We start school at *nine o'clock.*"

"It snowed *yesterday.*"

"We have *two* hammers, Arnie: *one* for you and *one* for Ginnie."

"My little sister is *two-and-a-half* years old."

"I want the *square* block."

"*One, two,* buckle my shoe. *Three, four,* shut the door. . . ."

"My car needs gas—give me a *hundred dollars'* worth."

"My glass is only *half* full."

"My teacher is *bigger* than me."

"*Tomorrow* is Charlene's birthday. She'll be *five* years old."

"Good boy, Charlie. You put *two* glasses on the snack table."

"My mommy gave me a *dime*."

"I want *three* books."

"Jimmy is using *two* paintbrushes."

"Val painted *four* pictures."

"He has *more* blocks *than* you."

"I need *one more* piece to finish my puzzle."

"I can count to *ten*. Wanna hear me? One . . . two . . . three . . ."

Numbers permeate the daily activities of young children. But just how much mathematical understanding do children bring to such comments? Let us look more fully into the experiences of three youngsters involved in serious endeavors to understand.

EARLY MATHEMATICAL CONCEPTS

Concept of Number

Little Jeffrey places one block on top of two others as he busily constructs an elaborate block city. Although he is only two-and-a-half years old, Jeffrey understands that he has just made a "bigger" building by adding one block to two others. He understands this even though he does not yet know how to use the terms *one, two,* and *three.* But by acting on his environment, Jeffrey is encountering basic ideas that will evolve into more sophisticated mathematical concepts. Only after repeated experiences of this type can Jeffrey develop the logical thinking skills necessary to express in words what has happened to his block structure.

Jeffrey's brother Michael, five years old, gathers an acorn collection in his hand and asks his six-year-old friend Libby to do the same. "Who has the most?" he asks. Michael places his in an orderly row like this.

Libby drops her acorns onto the ground in front of her, and they land in the configuration shown below.

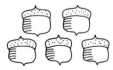

"I have more," shouts Michael. "Look how big my line is." "You don't have more," retorts Libby. "Your acorns are spread out in a line, but I have just as many. They're just all bunched up. Here, I'll show you." With that, Libby picks up her acorns and arranges them one by one in front of Michael's, as shown below. Then she counts each row, saying, "See, we both have five." Surprised by this discovery, Michael says only, "It *looked* like I had more."

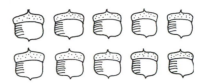

To be sure, Michael and Libby both understood that the word "five" was an appropriate label for their collections of acorns, but their abilities to conceptualize differing configurations as the same number differed markedly. Children who come to school with an ability to count from one to ten or to attach numerical labels to collections of objects may even lack the logical thinking abilities necessary for true mathematical understanding. Their skills were often picked up through repeated imitation of others in their environment, but, if you observe closely, you will often find that these accomplishments fall somewhat short of an accurate portrayal of number. Kristina Leeb-Lundberg provided the following illustration to clarify this point.

> Five-year-old Mary was walking through the park with her parents and some of their friends. It was spring, and on the pond a mother duck was swimming with some ducklings behind her. The proud parents, knowing that Mary could count beyond twenty and "knew her numbers," wished to show her ability to their friends. Her father asked her, "How many ducklings are there swimming behind the mother duck?" Mary, fearful and reluctant, was not able to tell her father how many ducklings there were. Her father seeing her upset wished to help her and said, "But Mary, you know that the mother duck has five ducklings." Mary burst into tears and said, "There is no one in the middle." Mary's mother and father were confused. They could not understand why Mary could not count the ducklings and decided to speak with Mary's teacher. Monday morning, as they entered the kindergarten classroom, there on the wall was the answer to the puzzle. They saw big cards with domino pictures of numbers from one to ten. This pattern represented the number five. This domino pattern of five was the only thing Mary knew about the number five. It became clear to her parents that Mary did not understand the concept of five—the fiveness of five in different pattern situations. When the pattern changed, she could no longer recognize five.[7]

Mary's concept of fiveness was obviously limited because her experiences with five were primarily associated with an abstract domino representation displayed in her classroom. She did not form the concept by building upon a variety of direct experiences, so she had difficulty with a basic mathematical understanding. Children need to recognize the properties of "fiveness" in varieties of ways so that they become capable of understanding that whatever the configuration, any of these abstractions represents five:

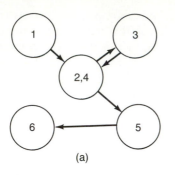

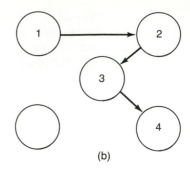

(a)   (b)

Figure 7–1   Examples of double counting and skip counting

Children with limited experiences, like Mary, can often recite correctly up to ten, but may demonstrate confusion when asked to count the circles in the order shown above in Figure 7–1.

They may either count some objects more than once (a) or skip some altogether (b). Teachers of three- and four-year-olds frequently observe such behaviors and realize that children of this age may not sense the need to put the objects in some type of ordered relationship in order to count. Some children, then, cannot perform the mental actions necessary to arrange the objects in their minds as a single display of a number. Biggs and MacLean illustrate the problem of assigning "names" to collections of objects:

> A young boy was counting 5 pieces of candy. He picked each up in turn saying, "1, 2, 3, 4, 5." Accidentally, the parent knocked 2 of the pieces onto the floor. Seeing this he asked the boy, "How many pieces of candy do you have now?" The boy replied, "1, 2, 5," again picking each piece up in turn. The helpful parent then told the child that he had three pieces of candy: "1, 2, 3." The boy, now quite upset with his parent said, "3 is on the floor."[8]

Rote counting is clearly evident in many preschool children. However, the logical numerical notions necessary for true mathematics concepts are not apparent in most preschoolers, who are at this stage more suited to learning by observing the real world.

The Influence of Conservation

What we must understand, then, is that young children think differently about numbers than adults do. Two-year-olds see a row of blocks differently than five-year-olds; five-year-olds perceive them differently than adults. How do individuals gain maturity in understanding numbers? Piaget offered a meaningful explanation to that query when he designed the *conservation* task for young children. With this task, he showed that children generally do not conserve number before five years of age. Thus, number is not an innate concept in human beings but an abstraction that takes many years to understand. To describe the conservation task, suppose that a teacher and a child each have twelve counters. The teacher puts down eight of his spaced evenly in a straight line. Then he asks the child to put out as many as he has. Younger children (two- to three-year olds) cannot do so—they set out their markers unevenly, try to use all twelve instead of only eight, and tend to tail off at the end somewhat confused as shown below. The four- or five-year-old child, on the other hand, can make an equal set by placing one counter *in front of each* of the teacher's, but has trouble with conservation. Kamii outlined the procedure for testing conservation of number:

> The experimenter modifies the layout in front of the child's watchful eyes by spacing out the counters in one of the rows. . . . The following questions are then asked: "Are there as many (the same number of) blue ones as red ones, or are there more here (blue) or more here (red)? How do you know?"

> . . . If the child has given a correct conversation answer, the experimenter says, "Look how long this line is. Another child said there are more counters in it because this row is longer. Who is right, you or the other child?"

> If the child's answer was wrong, however, the experimenter reminds him of the initial equality: "But don't you remember, before, we put one red counter in front of each blue one. Another child said that there is the same number of red and blue ones now. Who do you think is right, you or the other child?"[9]

The challenges are intended to engage children actively in thinking about the various configurations. When children are able to give correct conservation answers and defend their choices against the teacher's challenge, they have achieved the ability to conserve. All precise mathematical reasoning is based on the ability to conserve number. Figure 7–2 summarizes conservation of number: a child is able to see that the number of items in a set remains "three" regardless of change in size or position of the members of the set.

Older children are conservers. They answer each conservation question and are not swayed by your challenges. Nonconservers, though, cannot keep two different qualities in their heads at the same time. This is normal for most children through the age of five years. Educators have found that children cannot be taught number by asking them to *think* about quantities only in their minds, but that children must

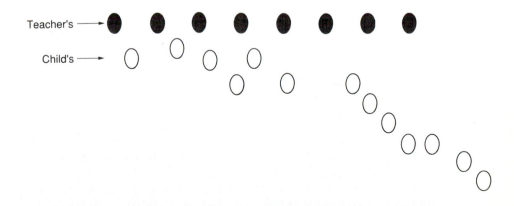

Teacher's ⟶

Child's ⟶

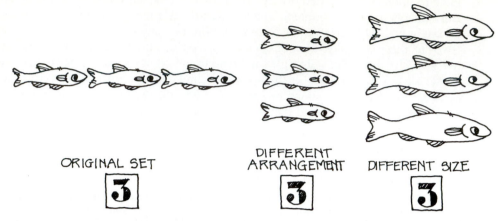

ORIGINAL SET

DIFFERENT ARRANGEMENT

DIFFERENT SIZE

Figure 7–2 The ability to conserve number

act on their environment with concrete materials in many different situations as they learn about relationships among objects.

Informally Helping Children Acquire Early Mathematical Concepts

Piaget does not define "acting on the environment" as learning to count or learning to add, and he does not advocate formal lesson teaching for the preschool or kindergarten child as a way to develop mathematical concepts. What he means by "acting on the environment" is seizing on the experiences that happen to children every day for the mathematical concepts that they present. Some of the first mathematical concepts that children acquire are what I refer to as *indefinite concepts.* They are not precise, but only vague notions of something. Consider young toddlers, for example. Their teachers are very good at helping children enlarge upon indefinite concepts. Mrs. Bryan, for example, rarely says anything like, "You may have some cookies if you wish." Instead, she wants her children's everyday experiences to enrich and strengthen their vague mathematical concepts, so she might instead say, "You may have *two* cookies today—would you like *round* ones or *square* ones?" She realizes that mathematics is not just a process of memorizing correct answers. It is a study of the relationships between different things. For that reason, Mrs. Bryan is extremely careful: If a toddler picks four cookies instead of two, she does not say: "I told you to take only two. Here, I'll take two back." This type of response does not allow the child to think about the situation. Instead she says, "You took *four* cookies, but you may have only two." The child may then ponder the situation and put one cookie back. Instead of now telling him he is wrong, Mrs. Bryan chooses to focus on his correct mathematical idea and praises him for it: "That's very good, Stanley. You knew some cookies had to be put back, didn't you? You knew you had to take some cookies away from four to make two. Put one more back and you'll have two." Mrs.

Bryan, knowing such situations should be kept as open-ended as possible, decided that accurate mathematical facts and processes were not as important at this age as the child's ability to sense relationships among sets of objects.

Although this example featured a toddler, preschool educators should realize that even most three-year-olds find it difficult to really understand what they're doing when they count up to five. They need as much practice as our toddler; they must be able to play and use numbers whenever opportunities present themselves or are created by imaginative teachers. Good teachers give children those chances by offering a multitude of experiences involving numbers—for example, cooking, water play, sand play, blocks, dramatic play, puzzles, and table toys. This has often been referred to as *incidental learning*.

Through incidental learning, one teaches mathematics skills in the context of the child's play activities, instead of structuring specific mathematics lessons. At the snack table, for example, the teacher may say, "There are four chairs, one for each of you." She may singly count the cups or cookies as they are passed out to each child. Children at the sandbox or water table may fill containers, empty them, and experiment with how much more sand or water is needed to fill a larger container than it takes to fill a smaller one. Cooking activities give the children practice in measuring ingredients with cups and measuring spoons. Size relationships are begun as the teacher asks the children to cut the pieces of celery "just as big as this one." During an informal tea party in the kitchen play area, the children match the number of cups and saucers to the number of children participating. Boys or girls at the woodworking area plan to "measure" a piece of wood and saw it so that it is the same length as another piece. Block construction leads other children to choose the biggest block for the base of a building and the smallest for the top. Separate shelves are provided for blocks of different shapes, so the children practice shape recognition as they remove and replace blocks used for construction projects. Number concepts are developed as children look for "one more piece to finish my puzzle."

Dozens of daily experiences can be capitalized upon for their mathematical value. The teacher takes advantage of these opportunities because she believes children are naturally curious and eager to find things out for themselves. With the guidance and support of an alert teacher, the day's normal activities can be utilized for their contribution to mathematics learning, and can form the basis for the entire curriculum.

In order to do this, teachers must be attuned to the kinds of experiences that can be used for their mathematical benefits. Likewise, they should be able to generate interesting phenomena that will stimulate the child's curiosity. Once stimulated, the child attacks a problem and seeks to solve it for himself. Martin L. Johnson and John W. Wilson explained further:

> While some modern proponents of this position...must be viewed as extreme, the common thread found...is that the curriculum for the child...should be developed from the interests of the child. In the case of mathematics, this approach has at different times in history given support to the "incidental learning" theory of arithmetic. That is, the introduction, development, maintenance, and extension of mathematical content and skills were a function of the incidental need for them in connection with what was usually an activity unit.[10]

PLANNED TEACHING OF MATHEMATICAL SKILLS AND CONCEPTS

Teaching Number, Numeral, and Sequence

Up to this point, we have considered the natural experiences within a child's environment as contributing to indirect ways of developing mathematical knowledge. The goal of such instruction is to help children use their strong intellectual curiosity for sound learning in mathematics. We have not yet considered "group teaching" because current methods of group instruction are frequently uninteresting, unmotivating, and therefore, unsuccessful. As Albert Einstein commented:

> It is in fact nothing short of a miracle that the modern methods of instruction have not yet entirely strangled the holy curiosity of inquiry....It is a very grave mistake to think that the enjoyment of seeing and searching can be promoted by means of coercion and a sense of duty.[11]

Although this statement was made decades ago, we hear similar arguments today: children must be freed from structured, adult-directed activities and be offered concrete, meaningful experiences upon which complex concepts can be built. The early childhood mathematics program, then, must have as its base process-oriented

Sometimes teachers plan special small-group activities designed to address the acquisition of number concepts.

activity. The end product is, of course, important, but the processes of manipulating, experimenting, and verifying are much more so.

When we wish to have groups of children focus on one specific mathematical concept, we must do it through hands-on experience, where children continue to learn by doing. They should not be passive observers but should move, manipulate, and sort things. Workbooks, worksheets, and other rigid exercises are undesirable because they turn children into passive learners.

The following example describes how one teacher helped her children learn mathematical concepts actively. She organized her instruction so as to introduce these mathematics skills:

1. Recognizing how many objects are in a set (**number**)
2. Recognizing the number names (**numeral**)
3. Recognizing the proper ordering of the numerals (**sequence**)

▶▶▶▶▶▶

Miss Kramer, a kindergarten teacher, realized that the best vehicle for developing the concept of number was the set (a well-defined collection of objects). So, she planned the children's first experiences with sets of concrete objects. She decided that the way to begin would be to have the children make collections of things that were alike. Miss Kramer gave each of four children one paper clip and two rubber bands and asked them to separate the objects that belonged together.

With the goal of comparing objects in a set, Miss Kramer asked the children questions designed to help them observe which group had "more than" and which group had "fewer than." At this point, the children were not yet ready for counting, so she asked them only to compare sets of different objects with one another. Gradually, she added sets of three erasers, four pencils, five crayons, and so on, and asked the children to group the objects. Through one-to-one matching and comparison activities, the children's concept of number grew as they grouped objects and determined which set had more (or fewer) elements than another.

After Miss Kramer had provided numerous chances for set comparison, she introduced her children to number names (numerals). To prevent rote memorization of numerals, Miss Kramer decided to select numbers randomly to present to the group. For the sake of discussion, let us say that she selected the number three. She then proceeded through this sequence of activities:

1. Ask the child to place the same number of objects in front of him as you have in front of you. (visual recognition/matching)
2. Present the child with a card containing three squares. Ask him to place three counters on the card, one in each square. (visual and verbal stimuli)

3. Present the child with a card containing three squares and the numeral. Ask him to place three counters on the card. (numerical symbol introduced)
4. Present the child with the symbol only and ask him to place as many counters on the table as indicated. (numerical symbol only)

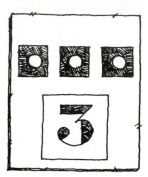

5. After each numeral is introduced in this way, give the child a card on which the numeral is cut in sandpaper. Teacher and child use the sandpaper numerals in three ways.
   a. The teacher shows the card to the child, asks him to move his fingers over the numeral, and says to the child, "This is three," or "This is four," and so forth.
   b. The teacher places the cards in front of the child and has him say, "Give me the three," "Give me the four," and so on.
   c. Still using the sandpaper numerals, the teacher asks, "What is this?" The child generates the number game.
6. For reinforcement, the teacher regularly arranges the classroom with several center-based follow-up activities. For example, the children count the number of objects in each picture and match it to the appropriate numeral strip. (See the illustration on page 247.)

As a final step in the counting procedures, Miss Kramer moved to the ordering of numbers. While she was establishing the number names, Miss Kramer had stimulated exploration of size relationships between numbers (more than, fewer than, and so on). Now she sought to encourage finer discrimination among sets by developing the concept "one more than." She began by asking the children to stack blocks and order such number sticks as Cuisenaire rods. She started with one block and asked the children to make a stack that had one more block than she had. Then she asked them to look at the stack of two blocks and make another stack with one block more than two. When the children had ordered the objects in sequence, she asked them to place a numeral card below each set. A number of creative, individual reinforcement activities were organized into learning stations for use following this initial introduction.

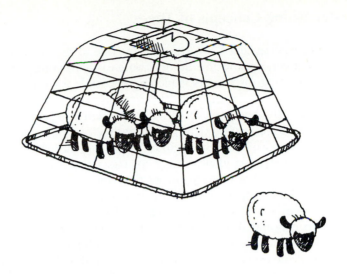

Zoo Animals

Collect a set of ten plastic strawberry containers and place a numeral from 1 to 10 on the bottom of each. These will serve as the zoo cages when turned upside down. Buy a set of plastic or rubber animals and ask the children to place the appropriate number of animals beneath the cages.

Miss Kramer's major concern was to develop *meaningful* counting skills in an environment where the children were involved with concrete, manipulative materials, and where they could explore and experiment while making new discoveries. Her basic strategy followed this plan:

1. Compare and contrast sets: "more than," "fewer than," and "same as."
2. Introduce number names (numerals).
3. Order numbers in sequence.

Active approaches to learning benefit children greatly, helping them progress through normal developmental processes to the point where they are able to understand the twoness or fiveness of items in sets. The sensitive teacher will be careful not to rush the process, but to take cues from the children and let them grow from within.

Establishing Concepts of Time

Anyone experiencing a situation like the one in the box below can certainly corroborate that concepts of time do not come easily to young children.

If waiting three hours is incomprehensible for young children, we cannot reasonably expect them to grasp the time-related concepts of minutes, hours, days, weeks, months, and years when we teach them in a preschool classroom. These concepts are very difficult to teach because they cannot be made concrete—the passage of time is invisible and intangible. When they are learning to read, the children's original experiences involve them in associating words in print with real objects through labeling or through stories that deal with the real world. In learning numbers, children compare sets of concrete objects with numerals, as skills are developed and refined. But with time, teachers are faced with the monumental task of helping children conceptualize an abstract phenomenon, with the use of abstract materials like clocks and calendars. Asking preschool children to read clocks and calendars is an unrealistic expectation. Most are not ready for that type of instruction until they approach Piaget's stage of concrete operations (seven to eight years).

This does not mean, however, that the topic of time should be avoided by preschool teachers. There is more to time than knowing how to read a watch or interpret a calendar. Children often hear references to time and must be led to sense its importance—yet they are just beginning to understand. They are reminded: "It's time to get up to go to school. . . . It's time to go outdoors and play. . . . Snack time. . . . Time for a story. . . . Time to go home. . . . Time for lunch. . . . Just a minute and I'll be with you." How long is a minute to a four-year-old? It may be a fleeting moment if spent frolicking outdoors in an enjoyable game, or it may be an eternity if spent in line awaiting a turn on a playground swing. How much is an hour, a day, a month, or a year? As we grow and mature, even our (adult) concepts of time change. For example, when you were five years old, ten years old was old to you, and to a ten-year-old, fifteen is old. But to a fifteen-year-old, perish the thought of becoming an old-timer of twenty! Time concepts are interesting and challenging. Someone once said that old is always five years older than your present age, and maybe that is right. Time is a difficult concept not only for preschoolers but for all of us. Because our lives are so intertwined with concepts of time, it is of vital importance that these concepts be introduced in early childhood learning. Some of the time-related vocabulary terms usually dealt with in preschool setting are on the following page.

▶▶▶▶▶▶▶

The Jones family, during an automobile trip to visit relatives, stopped at a diner for a quick lunch. Returning to the car, five-year-old Clarice inquired of her father, "Daddy, how much longer to grandma's?" "Only three more hours, honey," replied Mr. Jones. Five minutes after resuming their driving, Clarice suddenly questioned, "Is it three hours yet?"

yesterday	day	last night
today	week	long ago
tomorrow	month	never
morning	year	always
afternoon	minute	now
tonight	hour	early
next week	clock	late
next time	calendar	birthday

Some ideas for teaching these concepts are given in the Time Activities box.

TIME ACTIVITIES

1. Use time vocabulary during your daily dialogues with the children. Look at your watch or clock occasionally and show the children where the hands will be when it is time to go home, for example. Help the children plan events with you—for example, a special birthday party *later in the day* for Tammy's birthday, or a special field trip *tomorrow*, or Santa Claus's arrival *next week*. Ask the children to identify the television show they will want to watch *tonight*. These beginning time descriptions should first be given in terms of day and night and tied into routine activities, such as mealtimes, naps, or time to go home. They will soon begin to tell the difference between school days and weekends, school days and holidays, afternoon and morning, and so on.

2. Display a large, colorful calendar for each month and include days of special significance to the children—birthdays, holidays, special events, weekends, and so on.

3. Make a large clock with movable minute and hour hands. Set the hands to indicate what the real room clock will look like when it is time for a story, snack, nap, or any other special event.

4. Keep time records of special activities in your classroom. Count the days that pass between the time a seed was planted and when the sprout first appeared. Keep track of how many days must elapse before it is time to water the plants again. Observe the time it takes for a chicken egg to hatch. Count the number of days until Christmas or Halloween. Use a cooking timer to guide the children in estimating how long it will be until a batch of cookies is ready. In similar ways, teachers have put to good use various timekeeping paraphernalia such as hourglasses, stopwatches, or old alarm clocks.

Developing Measurement Skills

The preschool classroom should provide many opportunities to experience linear measurement (length, width, height), volume, and weight. Such beginning experiences should be informal and should deal with *arbitrary measurements* rather than with formal terminology such as inch, foot, meter, gram, ounce, pound, pint, liter, and so on. Some arbitrary measurements that often come up during water or sand play, for example, are "the *big* bottle," "the *small* spoon," "the *long* stick," and "the *heaviest* pail." The measurement program should begin with such simple arbitrary comparisons and proceed to informal measurements with meaningful *nonstandard units*. An example of measurement with a nonstandard unit is to give a child a piece of string (the nonstandard unit) and ask him to sort from a group of objects those items that are *longer than*, *shorter than*, or the *same* length as his string.

When planning a program designed to foster skills in nonstandard measuring, it is important to begin with simple comparisons, such as the one just illustrated, and to use concrete materials. With such a basic background, the child will form a sound foundation upon which formal measurement with *standard units* can be introduced later in the primary grades (see Figure 7–3).

The development of measurement skills in the preschool years, then, is based on the idea of *comparison*. The child makes simple, direct comparisons among objects through linear measurements, estimates of volume, and weighing various objects in his environment.

Some suggested activities for each of these areas are given in the Measurement Activities box on pages 251–252.

Figure 7–3 A developmental strategy for teaching concepts of measurement

MEASUREMENT ACTIVITIES

Linear Measurements

1. Compare the height of several children. Have them compare feet to see whose are longest or shortest.

2. Compare the length of different objects in the room. Have them guess which would be longer—for example, two straws laid end to end or five paper clips. Their guess can be verified by actual experimentation.

3. Have the children walk heel to toe from one area of the room or playground to another area and count the number of steps. Have them guess which of two objects is farthest from where they are standing, and then pace off the distances to see if they were correct.

4. Have the child use the width of his index finger to measure the length of a crayon, book, toy, or any other handy object.

Volume Measurements

1. Give the children a spoon with which they can scoop sand from a small sandbox. Have them spoon out the sand from the box into a cup, glass, and jar while counting the number of spoons necessary to fill each.

2. Have the children try to arrange four different containers in order by capacity. They can test their guess by pouring small cups of liquid or sand into the containers and counting which container held the most, which the next, and so on.

3. Have the children use a small cup as a measure and find out how many cups of rice, beans, and sand it would take to fill the same pot.

Weight Measurement

Make a simple balance scale from two lengths of wood, some string, and a pair of pie tins. Comparison activities can be carried out on this simple scale.

1. Children often will judge the larger object to be heavier when asked to distinguish between two items. They believe that the bigger the object is, the heavier it will be. Have the children use the scale to compare the weight of a large styrofoam ball with a smaller ball of clay. They will find that the clay is heavier than the styrofoam and that weight cannot always be determined by visual estimates.

2. Fill five cans with varying amounts of sand. Have the children use the scale to order the cans from lightest to heaviest.

3. Have the children experiment to see how many metal washers balance a cup, how many beans balance a crayon, how many nails balance a block, and so on.

4. Have the children measure one object in comparison to a number of other objects. For example, a block compared to nails, pencils, chalkboard erasers, and so on.

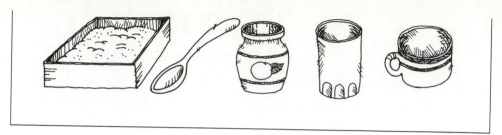

SOME FINAL THOUGHTS

Outlined in this section were three basic areas of mathematics skills usually contained in programs for preschool children: (1) *building counting skills,* (2) *establishing concepts of time* and (3) *developing measurement skills.* You should take advantage of informal play experiences, as well as organized classroom activities, to foster the growth and development of these skills. Varieties of experiences help preschool children build a foundation of understandings that will support and reinforce these sophisticated thinking abilities. The work of Jean Piaget has convinced early childhood educators that the ability to form reflective abstractions (logico-mathematical thought) occurs only after many experiences have helped children acquire the ability to sort information gathered from observable qualities of objects in the environment (empirical abstractions) into meaningful conceptual categories. Although spontaneous mathematical learnings are valuable, carefully planned and executed activities are also necessary for mathematics learning to be complete. Piaget advises against paper-and-pencil activities that confine the children to a right answer, suggesting instead a system of manipulative activities with problem-solving characteristics. These kinds of activities are most appropriate for the young child because they build knowledge and skills by elaborating on what has been originally created by the child. Every new learning is built on earlier learning and will become integrated into later ones. Children are not taught mathematics by rote, but through a sequential program that energizes them to attain developmentally appropriate skills and concepts and that stimulates their curiosity about new ideas.

NOTES

1. Janice J. Beaty, *Skills for Preschool Teachers,* 4th ed. (Columbus, OH: Merrill/Macmillan, 1992), pp. 117–120.
2. From Constance Kamii, "A Sketch of the Piaget-Derived Preschool Curriculum Developed by the Ypsilanti Early Education Program," Ypsilanti Public Schools, Ypsilanti, MI. August 1971. Copyright 1972 by the Charles A. Jones Publishing Company. Reprinted by permission of Wadsworth Publishing Company, Belmont, CA 94002.
3. Ann Hammerman and Susan Morse, "Open Teaching: Classroom," *Young Children, 28,* no. 1 (October 1972): 43–44, 51.

4. Ibid., pp. 43–44.
5. Deborah W. Tegano, Janet K. Sawyers, and James D. Moran, III, "Problem-Finding and Solving in Play: The Teacher's Role," *Childhood Education, 66,* no. 2 (Winter 1989): 93.
6. Dorothy Anker et al., "Teaching Children As They Play," *Young Children, 29,* no. 4 (May 1974): 207–209.
7. Kristina Leeb-Lundberg, *Mathematics Is More Than Counting* (Wheaton, MD: Association for Childhood Education International, 1985), p. 9.
8. E. Biggs and J. MacLean, *Freedom to Learn: An Active Approach to Mathematics* (Don Mills, Ont.: Addison-Wesley [Canada], 1969), p. 111.
9. Constance Kamii, *Number in Preschool and Kindergarten* (Washington, DC.: National Association for the Education of Young Children, 1982), pp. 2–3.
10. Martin L. Johnson and John W. Wilson, "Mathematics," in Carol Seefeldt, ed., *Curriculum for the Preschool-Primary Child* (Columbus, OH: Merrill/Macmillan, 1976): p. 169.
11. Albert Einstein, "Autobiographic Notes," in P.A. Schilpp. ed., *Albert Einstein: Philosopher Scientist* (Evanston, IL: Library of Living Philosophers, 1949), p. 17.

CHAPTER 8

Exploring the Wonders of Language and Literacy

If you have ever tried to learn a second language, you certainly know that the process of language acquisition is a complex task. Yet think of the little baby on the brink of learning her first system of communication with little of the insight you are able to bring to your mastery of a second language. What a herculean task! It's no wonder that so many people have compared the child acquiring language to a genius at work. In the past few years, experts from a range of disciplines—including education, linguistics, and psychology—have discovered exciting information with wide-ranging implications for language instruction. Central to their research is the recognition that children learn to read in much the same way as they learn to speak—through warm interactions with their family and other significant individuals. Immersed in such a nurturing environment, the child becomes aware of the conventions of oral language and print, and develops an intrinsic motivation to use spoken, printed, or written words in order to make sense out of his surroundings. This chapter is designed to help you learn how to capitalize on the child's natural desire to learn language. In doing so, you will be able to set up developmentally appropriate conditions that invite children to take responsibility for their own learning in stimulating and enjoyable ways. As you read, use the following questions to guide your thinking.

- What are some typical patterns of communication found during infancy? How can caregivers help stimulate early language acquisition?

- When does the use of actual words enter a child's system of communication? How do these words eventually become strung together into phrases and sentences?

- What are some types of language experiences that give children a chance to develop their emerging linguistic skills? What is the teacher's role in each?

- What is the teacher's responsibility in the informal language experiences that come up during the day?

- How are the processes of oral and written language acquisition interrelated?

- What conditions help children become aware of the functions of print?

- What strategies or techniques are popularly recommended to stimulate reading skills in a developmentally appropriate, natural environment?

- How do children develop skills in writing? How can the preschool environment contribute to the growth of such skills?

▶▶▶▶▶▶

An Episode to Ponder

Rebecca, a four-month-old, is sleeping peacefully in her crib during one of her daily nap periods. Slowly, she starts to stir and squirm; then she wriggles her arms and legs. As she awakens, she senses a bit of discomfort in her tummy. Rebecca is hungry. No one is around to help, so how can Rebecca's hunger needs be satisfied? She initiates a universal form of communication mastered by babies throughout the world. She begins with a soft whimper, follows up with a bit more thrashing of the arms and legs, and culminates with a slow, rhythmic cry. This is Rebecca's strategy of communicating the very delicate problem that she is experiencing.

Mommy's footsteps deliberately approach the nursery, so Rebecca knows help is on the way. Rebecca's mother picks her up, hugs her, and comforts her with reassurance: "Rebecca sounds very hungry. Mommy will help you." Rebecca takes comfort in the security of her mother's arms and quickly finds herself part of a familiar sequence of action. "Here is your food, Rebecca. Open your mouth wide . . . oh, that's a good girl. Yes, yes—Rebecca *was* hungry."

Her stomach now full, Rebecca delights in being held over her mother's shoulder while being gently patted on the back. The accompanying humming and singing give Rebecca a very warm feeling indeed. She responds in ways that communicate how secure she feels; as tiny bubbles of gas that developed during feeding burble up, Rebecca smiles, gurgles, and babbles with delight. Rebecca's responses elicit smiles and hugs with her mother—completing a sophisticated cycle of parent-child actions and reactions. Through the entire experience, effective patterns of two-way communication transmitted feelings of love and trust between parent and baby.

From patterns of communication during infancy, the difficult task of learning a language begins. The first months of an individual's life are spent in self-imposed practice. The baby listens to sounds and learns to discern their likenesses and differences. Long before he can say words himself, the infant learns how to interpret what others are saying: his caregiver's voice, the sound of his name, and soothing tones of voice all bring him pleasure. The infant can also *express* feelings of pleasure and discomfort during these early months. Loud crying or quick arm and leg movements help communicate a need for relief of discomfort. Soft babbling, cooing, and smiling show strong positive feelings of comfort and satisfaction. How infants grow beyond these initial phases of communication to acquire and retain formal language is a complex

Beginning speech thrives in situations where there is pleasurable verbal interaction.

and varied process. You have probably noticed how valuable it is for the baby to be taken care of (fed, bathed, etc.) by an adult who warmly and pleasantly vocalizes. This gives the baby comfort and a feeling of trust, and also motivates the baby to try to talk himself. Beginning speech flourishes under these pleasurable conditions.

Table 8–1   Patterns of Normal Language Growth During Infancy

Age in Months	Listening	Speaking
1–2	Is calmed by familiar voices Listens to voices Listens to noises made by toys	Exhibits undifferentiated crying as a reflexive response to discomfort Makes throaty vocalizations while crying Coos and babbles—undifferentiated vocalizations
2–4	Looks toward sound Moves head and eyes to follow sound	Differentiates cries for different types of discomfort, such as hunger cry or pain cry Babbles in repeated sounds of two syllables: "ba-ba," "goo-goo" Begins loud laughter
4–6	Distinguishes between friendly and angry sounds	Vocalizes, somewhat randomly, over a sustained period of time Imitates the sounds of others Repeats vowel sounds ("a-a-a")
6–12	Responds to hearing own name Looks at other familiar objects when they are named Enjoys listening to own voice Responds to requests ("Give me the rattle.") Understands commonly used words	Begins to say "mama" or "dada" Imitates words or syllables Begins to expand vocabulary to one or two other words
12–24	Follows simple verbal instructions; points to parts of object when named Listens to simple stories of a few sentences, especially about self	Begins to acquire more words by imitating the sounds of others (at 12 months has 10- to 15-word vocabulary; at 24 months 20 to 50 words) Begins to use personal pronouns "I" and "me" or own name Asks for objects by name: "ball" or "cookie" Begins to string two words together into simple sentences ("Me go.")

The wise parent or caregiver should be encouraged to spend time with the child in verbal interaction. The child should be given many opportunities to practice his growing ability to communicate, and he should receive continuing reinforcement from his parents. Before long, the infant delights in vocalizations and begins to experiment with volume, pitch, and different sounds. He begins to listen more intently to words spoken by others and tries to repeat them. After six to nine months, the child may be crudely naming things with word labels. It is at this time—when verbal sounds are associated with objects, people, or activities—that the first true language is spoken. Robert Armstrong and W. J. Gage say that "from that time on, from a linguistic point of view, he never looks back. He listens and tries to imitate what he hears. He receives responses in the form of warm milk, dry diapers, or approval. He modifies his speech, listens again, adds words and structures, and when success seems obvious a pattern of language becomes habitual."[1]

Table 8–1 presents patterns of normal language growth during infancy. You should be aware of these patterns, for they will help you anticipate normal development at different stages.

LANGUAGE GROWTH DURING THE PRESCHOOL YEARS

By the time children are two years old, they are experiencing a rapid growth in vocabulary and are starting to combine two or three words into rudimentary sentences. Kornei Chukovsky, a famous Russian writer and linguist, wrote: "It seems to me that, beginning with the age of two, every child becomes for a short period of time a *linguistic genius*" [italics mine].[2]

Children begin to feel comfortable with words and use them freely. By the time they are two-and-a-half, children's vocabulary is likely to explode to the point where it includes four hundred words or more. At this age they begin to ask endless questions, and their favorite word seems to be "Why?" Although these constant questions frustrate some adults, they do help children clarify their understandings and feelings.

Also by two-and-a-half years, children have moved from one-word noun utterances to simple combinations of nouns with verbs. Their first combinations take place at about age two. The following list shows word combinations commonly uttered by children during this early phase of language acquisition:

Sit chair	There doggie
Timmy go boom	It choo-choo
Me go	Cars go bye-bye
Janie hungry	Where mitten?
Pretty dolly	See baby
Papa work	He go out
Shoes off	No nap now
More play	Cookie allgone

How do the simple utterances of infancy and early toddlerhood evolve into combinations such as the preceding, and eventually into more complex sentences? David McNeill speculates that a set of "templates" (patterns) in the neural system, collectively called a *language acquisition device (LAD),* allows the child to develop language naturally. He says, "It is as if he were equipped with a set of 'templates' against which he can compare the speech he happens to hear from his parents."[3] First attempts at duplicating adult speech result in shortened versions of the adult's language, but the basic sentence and thought forms remain the same. Some function words—articles, prepositions, conjunctions, and so on—are eliminated. With increased exposure and practice, the child gradually acquires an ability to use different forms of verbs, nouns, prepositions, pronouns, and other function words ("Ryan is helping daddy wash the car.").

A process that should be used by all teachers and parents to encourage children to acquire more complex sentence patterns is *expansion.* When the child says a sentence fragment, an adult expands it by adding appropriate elements. For example:

CHILD'S FRAGMENT	ADULT'S SENTENCE
"Joey eat."	"Joey is eating his breakfast."
"Doggie bark."	"The dog is barking."
"Daddy cookie."	"Daddy has a cookie, too."
"No more play."	"Joey doesn't want to play any longer."

Children love to experiment with language throughout their preschool years in these and similar ways; through such interaction they acquire increased skills in sentence formation. The practice they receive often results in a highly creative and imaginative use of the language. Consider the youngster who inquired about a long word he saw on a sign during a field trip—"pedestrian." Informed by his teacher that the word meant a person who was walking, the child later referred to a "foot-a-tarian" during their classroom discussion.

By three years of age, children's speech patterns have gone beyond the simple two- or three-word phrases uttered earlier. Now they begin to form four- and five-word sentences, such as "The dog is barking." By the age of four or five, most children have acquired all of the basic, common sentence structures of the English language. Although we do not know when and exactly in what order these sentence patterns are learned, we do know that most young children are fairly sophisticated linguistic beings by age three.

TECHNIQUES FOR ENHANCING ORAL LANGUAGE GROWTH

Because the most crucial language learning seems to take place before the child is six, most educators feel that it is the role of the preschool to create programs to facilitate growth in language skills. What helpful advice can be given by early childhood educators and students of language? Alvina Burrows says, "One admonition leaps out beyond most others: *Use the oral efficiency that children bring to school as the means of developing* [further] *efficiency in* [language]. To extend, refine, and enhance the oral arts and skills children already possess is the first obligation."[4] To achieve this goal, children must be given opportunities to practice language. They must be able to speak in a variety of situations, and they must be exposed to good language as it is spoken by a good model. The following sections discuss activities to help children achieve language competence that go beyond simply providing opportunities to talk.

Informal Conversation

Children will talk with one another informally and naturally if you establish the conditions for them to do so. They will talk about their experiences—what happened last evening on television, a new piece of living room furniture, or what their cat did to the bird's nest in the back bush—as they enter the room, take off their coats and boots, play at the interest centers, clean up the room, cavort outdoors, or work

Preschoolers should be encouraged to use their growing oral language skills to share their thoughts and knowledge with each other.

on special activities. Children should be offered many opportunities for free-flowing conversation. Whatever the situation, they will openly talk about their meaningful experiences. Soon, and with very little or no prodding, the children will bring twigs, pine cones, rocks, and countless other objects to the classroom. They will also develop many new ideas, and consequently many new words and sentence patterns for their growing language ability. Language development is stimulated most powerfully by encouraging the children to engage in conversations about all the experiences that mean something to them. You can help the children by encouraging them to recall their experiences, offering words when they become stuck, and helping to clarify ideas.

Marjorie J. Kostelnik, Laura C. Stein, and Alice P. Whiren advised that adults create a positive verbal environment when their verbal exchanges with children have the following attributes:

1. *Adults use words to show affection for children and sincere interest in them.* They greet children when they arrive, take the time to become engaged in children's activities and also respond to their queries. In addition, they make remarks showing children they care about them and are aware of what they are doing: "You've been really working hard to get the dinosaur puzzle together." "You seem to be enjoying that game." They laugh with children, respond to their humor and tell children they enjoy being with them.

2. *Adults send congruent verbal and nonverbal messages.* When they are showing interest verbally, they position themselves near the child at a similar height from the floor, maintain eye contact and thoroughly pay attention. Other actions, such as smiling or giving a pat, reinforce praise and words of positive regard. Incongruent messages, such as following through on a limit while smiling or pinching a child's cheek hard while giving praise, are avoided.

3. *Adults extend invitations to children to interact with them.* They may say, "Here's a place for you right next to Sylvia" or "Let's take a minute to talk. I want to find out more about your day." When children seek them out, grownups accept the invitation enthusiastically: "That sounds like fun." "Oh good, now I'll have a chance to work with you."

4. *Teachers listen attentively to what children have to say.* They show their interest through eye contact, smiling and nodding. They encourage children to elaborate on what they are saying by using such statements as "Tell me more about that" or "Then what happened?" Moreover, adults pause long enough after making a comment or asking a question for children to reply, giving them time to gather their thoughts before responding. Such reactions make children feel valued and interesting.

5. *Adults speak courteously to children.* They refrain from interrupting children and allow them to finish what they are saying, either to the adult or another child. The voice tone used by adults is patient and friendly, and social amenities such as "Please," "Thank you," and "Excuse me" are part of the verbal interchange.

6. *Adults use children's interests as a basis for conversations.* They speak with them about the things youngsters want to talk about. This is manifested in two ways. First, they follow the child's lead in conversations. Second, they bring up subjects known to be of interest to a particular child based on past experience.

7. *Adults plan or take advantage of spontaneous opportunities to talk with each child informally.* In the course of a day, children have many chances to talk with adults about matters that interest or concern them. Eating, toileting, dressing, waiting for the bus, settling down for a nap and just waiting until the group

is called to order are treated as occasions for adult-child conversation. Adults do not wait for special, planned time to talk with youngsters.

8. *Teachers avoid making judgmental comments about children either to them or within their hearing.* Children are treated as sensitive, aware human beings whose feelings are respected. Discussions about children's problems or family situations are held in private between the appropriate parties.

9. *Adults refrain from speaking when talk would destroy the mood of the interaction.* When they see children deeply absorbed in activity or engrossed in conversation with one another, staff members allow the natural course of the interaction to continue. In these situations they treat silence as a sign of warmth and respect and refrain from too much talk at the wrong time.

10. *Grownups focus their attention on children when they professionally engage with them.* They put off housekeeping tasks and personal socializing so that they are fully available for interaction with children. When possible, adults involve children in maintenance tasks and interact with them. In a positive environment, adults are available, alert and prepared to respond to children.[5]

Positive verbal interactions communicate to children a message that they are important, thereby enhancing their perceptions of self-worth. As a result, children are likely to express themselves more openly and interact more spontaneously with other children and adults. The positive verbal environment is characterized by adult behaviors that show warmth, acceptance, respect, and compassion.

GROUP-ORIENTED CONVERSATION

During most of the day, children should be encouraged to speak freely to the teacher and to one another as they plan and execute their daily activities. When we observe four- and five-year-olds, we are often astounded at how free and open they are with their verbalization. They talk to themselves, verbalize to others and listen to their ideas, make up stories or rhymes, and generally participate in a variety of give-and-take situations. Through such practice, children steadily improve their vocabularies, sentence patterns, and clarity of expression.

First attempts at having children speak to others in more controlled situations should also be somewhat informal. Many preschool teachers arrange for a special talking time during the day, when children are free to share anything of interest with the others. Perhaps the best way to describe an informal sharing period is to provide the illustration shown in the box on page 264.

The principle of developing good language experiences through informal conversation is apparent in Mr. Roberts's technique. He allowed Belinda to talk about her toy, but not in the context of a formal presentation. She simply responded to his question about Hippo. The other children were asked to contribute their own individual experiences as Belinda's toy was shared, so that their interest level stayed high. In a few short minutes, Mr. Roberts succeeded in involving several members of the group in the conversation, rather than confining the conversation to the input of only one child. The experience was important not only for its conversational value but also for its contribution to intellectual growth.

▶▶▶▶▶▶

When she arrived at school this morning, Belinda was smiling brightly and clutching a colorful stuffed toy hippopotamus. Mr. Roberts noted the pride with which Belinda shared her new toy with him.

"His name is Hippo," offered Belinda.

"He's cute," said Mr. Roberts. "Do you know what kind of an animal Hippo is, Belinda?"

"A hippopa...hippopapa...apotamus," stuttered Belinda.

"Oh, yes," replied Mr. Roberts. "A hippopotamus. You're a lucky girl to get a nice friend like Hippo. Please show everyone what a nice toy you have."

"Daddy gave him to me. Daddy was away yesterday, and when he came home he gave me Hippo," said Belinda.

"Hippo is a nice gift, Belinda," Mr. Roberts said. "Let's see if anyone can think of another animal that looks like Hippo."

"An elephant," volunteered James. "He's as big as an elephant—I saw one at the zoo."

"That's right, James," commented Mr. Roberts. "I see you remember our trip to the zoo last week."

"I think it looks like a rhino," declared Sally.

"Yeah," "Me too," chimed in the others.

"Does anyone have a toy rhino or toy elephant?" asked Mr. Roberts.

"I think I have a toy elephant—I'm not sure," said Warren. "It's almost as big as Hippo."

"I have a toy elephant!" exclaimed Marty. "I can wind him up and he wiggles his ears!"

Mr. Roberts saw that the interest was still high and allowed the children to talk for several minutes. Then, when he sensed it was time to bring the informal conversation to a close, he simply stated, "Hippo was a wonderful gift for you, Belinda. Thank you for bringing him to school today for all of us to see."

WORD PLAY

Good conversation should not be regarded solely as an ability to converse according to adult standards. Through play experiences especially, children often express patterns of words and ideas that go far beyond the limits imposed by adult speech.

Children speak in rhythm, in pleasing sounds, or even in melodious tones simply for the delight it brings during free play. For instance, while acting as a "daddy" at the housekeeping center, a child may suddenly blurt out a wonderfully creative, melodious rhyme while preparing to feed his "baby": "Daggies, doggles, goo-goo-geeze, too-too-too-too tykle geeze!" Another youngster created this rhythmic non-sense rhyme while playing alone in a quiet section of the playground: "Ka-chinka, chinka, chinka, Ka-chinka, chinka, choo. Ka-chinka, chinka, chinka, moo, moo, moo, moo, moo!" Young children acquire language through imitation, reinforcement, and repetition, as suggested earlier in this chapter, but they also develop linguistic skills by having fun and playing with the language. Children enjoy experimenting with everything, including language. The preschool period is a time of rich word play; children enjoy using word sounds in unusual and original ways. They experiment with rhymes and rhythms, often with sounds that bring pleasure to their tongue—rather than understanding to adult ears. Many times, as the child on the playground did, preschoolers even invent "languages" all their own. Encourage children to make up their own strings of creative words, for their growing language power is enhanced by experimentation and creativity.

Play is necessary for enhancing language growth throughout the early years.

STORY TIME

Stories, either told or read aloud, have an extremely important place in the language program of preschool classrooms. Storytelling is one of the most effective ways of exposing children to rich and varied language, and it is basic to the effective development of speaking vocabularies. Children enjoy listening to stories; it enables them to discover new words and meanings, develop understandings, and engage in imaginative thought.

Stories Children Like Of course, the best source of stories for children is good literature. It is important to know what kinds of stories appeal to young children so the stories you choose will meet their developmental interests. Preschool children delight in hearing many kinds of stories, but they especially enjoy stories about things they are already familiar with. Make-believe, humor, new places, animals, family, Mother Goose rhymes, fables, and fairy tales are also favorites. It is difficult to generalize about the type of story enjoyed by all young children, though, because they demonstrate such a wide variety of interests in stories. They empathize with Dr. Seuss's imaginative Horton as he faithfully attempts to hatch an egg; and their hatred for Seuss's dreaded Grinch changes to love as he brings the Christmas loot back to the citizens of Whoville. Children imagine themselves hitching up their belts and joining the fight with the courageous operator and his brave machine in "Mike Mulligan and His Steam Shovel."

You can locate quality literature by examining several different sources of information:

- Follow the children's book awards and place special orders for the award winners at your local bookstore or at the library. Some of the most influential awards are the Caldecott Award, the Kate Greenaway Medal, and the Canadian Book Award.

- Examine children's book reviews in professional journals such as *Young Children* (the journal of the NAEYC) or *Language Arts* (the journal of the National Council of Teachers of English).

- Choose a source that recommends books according to children's ages. Jim Trelease's *The New Read-Aloud Handbook* (New York: Penguin, 1989) is one source. The Children's Book Council (67 Irving Place, New York, NY 10003) is a clearinghouse for information on children's literature. The American Library Association (50 East Huron Street, Chicago, IL 60611) publishes many helpful aids, including *Notable Children's Books of the Year.*

Marjorie V. Fields and Dorris Lee advise that, despite all our care and diligence in choosing good books, the final "proof of the pudding" lies with the teacher:

Teachers cannot possibly find an expert opinion on every book, nor should they. Instructors must develop their own criteria for what constitutes a good book and then form an opinion about which books are right for certain children and in which specific situations. One simple guide is to decide if you like a book yourself. Good children's literature isn't just interesting to children; it is timeless. Have you picked up a child's story book and found that you couldn't put it down until you finished it? That's definitely a good book.[6]

A rich environment that exposes children to books enhances a child's language abilities. By being in contact with good books, children learn that books are enjoyable and satisfying, and that the print on the page represents spoken words. Children learn what books are like and how they should be handled. When teachers take time to read to children, they provide an invaluable language experience.

Fingerplays and Action Rhymes

Fingerplays and action rhymes are short rhymes, songs, or chants that can be recited and acted out with the hands or other parts of the body. The teacher tells the rhyme or story all the way through, and then invites the children to follow. For example, make sure the children are all facing you and say, "We're going to have some fun with our hands today. Listen and watch what I do with mine." Then chant slowly and add the hand actions as you go along:

> I have ten little fingers,
> And they all belong to me. (*Hold hands in front.*)
> I can make them do things,
> Would you like to see?
> I can shut them up tight. (*Make tight fists.*)
> I can open them up wide. (*Spread fingers out.*)
> I can put them together. (*Clasp hands.*)
> I can make them all hide. (*Put hands behind back.*)
> I can make them jump high. (*Raise over head.*)
> I can make them fall low. (*Lower hands to knees.*)
> I can fold them like this,
> And hold them just so. (*Fold hands on lap.*)

After you finish, say to the children, "Show me that you can do this along with me. I'll say the words and you move your hands the way I do." Repeat the chant and add the motions together with the children. Depending on their interest, you may want to repeat the rhyme one or more times, encouraging the children to say the words that accompany the actions: "That surely was fun! Let's try it one more time, and this time try to say the words with me. . . . Let's go."

Action rhymes are shared in a like manner, except that body parts other than hands or fingers are involved. For example, this rhyme invites creative body movements:

> Away up high in the apple tree, (*Point up.*)
> Two red apples smiled at me. (*Form circle with fingers.*)
> I shook that tree as hard as I could; (*Shake entire body creatively.*)
> Down came those apples,
> And m-m-m-m-m, were they good! (*Rub tummy.*)

Children enjoy fingerplays and action rhymes; their delightful rhythm, rhyme, and movement characteristics foster overall language growth.

Poetry

Poetry is an intensive language experience rich in imagery and powerfully conducive to eliciting an individual's deep thoughts and feelings. Theresa M. Brown and Lester L. Laminack state the following:

> By making poetry an integral part of young children's literary environment, we empower them with rich language and beguile them with its beauty. When we encourage children to play with words, to taste them in their minds, they soon come to realize the wonderful nuances of words.[7]

Poetry should be introduced to the children aurally; you should read appropriate poems in a pleasant, expressive voice. Poems should be selected carefully, with the children's interests and needs in mind. Betty Coody identified these characteristics of appropriate poems for young children:

- *Rhythmic language.* Poetry for young children must constantly have words and phrases that sound melodious and harmonious. Lilting language sets poetry aside from other literature. An appropriate poem for young children must have rhythm and melody in its language.
- *Emotional appeal.* Poetry elicits emotional reactions from its listeners: sadness, delight, reflection, empathy, or anger. A poem can stimulate the young children's emotions. Teachers should mirror their feelings about the poem.
- *Familiar theme.* Poetry for young children should be related to children's life experiences. Young children tend to favor poems that tell a story or are about animals, people, [seasons, nature,] or places that are fun, humorous, and nonsense.
- *Sensory appeal.* Poetry should provoke the children's senses of touch, taste, smell, sight, and sound.[8]

First poems should reflect Coody's characteristics and be short in duration. One poem that quickly becomes a child's favorite is the following:

> A peanut sat on the railroad track,
> His heart was all a-flutter;
> The railroad train came rushing by—
> Toot! Toot! Peanut butter!

Another humorous poem that should be part of every teacher's repertoire is the popular rhyme, "Higglety, Pigglety, Pop!"

> Higglety, pigglety, pop!
> The dog has eaten the mop.
> The pig's in a hurry,
> The cat's in a flurry,
> Higglety, pigglety, pop!
>   —Samuel Goodrich

Surely, humorous poems are among those most enjoyed by young children, but many forms of poetry appeal to them and contribute to their overall language development. Using poetry in the classroom provides all of the following benefits:

1. It raises children's general level of language development.
2. It heightens children's awareness of word sounds and rhythms.
3. It increases children's sensitivities to the wonders of their physical and social worlds.
4. It helps children relate to special feelings and emotions.
5. It empowers children's creative responses to a language frame rich in imagery, often encouraging children to form free-verse poetry of their own.

Poetry's magical language can be used to enrich all areas of the early childhood curriculum. Consider the following example (from *A Child's Garden of Verses*), which applies to self-awareness and even to concepts related to the physical environment. Search through collections of poetry to find others that can be used for areas such as weather, transportation, community helpers, playground activities, or animals.

MY SHADOW

I have a little shadow that goes in and out with me.
And what can be the use of him is more than I can see,
He is very, very like me from the heels up to the head,
And I see him jump before me when I jump into my bed.

—Robert Louis Stevenson

Many successful teachers of the very young have memorized a number of poems that they gaily offer children, often at times when they don't even realize it. Such spontaneity communicates to the children that the teacher thoroughly enjoys the poems, and encourages the children to accept the use of poems naturally. In time, you may find that children will learn to repeat favorite poems, much as they repeat favorite fingerplays or songs.

A number of fine collections of children's poetry will serve to enrich your professional library. Among these are:

Animal Poems for Children by E. Conyers, ed., (Racine, WI: Western Publishing Company, 1982).
The Complete Nonsense Book by E. Lear, (New York: Dodd & Mead, 1912).
Hailstones and Halibut Bones by M. O'Neill, (New York: Doubleday, 1961).
A Light in the Attic by S. Silverstein, (New York: Harper & Row, 1981).
A New Treasury of Children's Poetry by J. Cole, ed., (Garden City, NY: Doubleday, 1984).
Oxford Book of Poetry for Children by E. Blishen, ed., (New York: Franklin Watts, 1963).
The Random House Book of Poetry by J. Prelutsky, ed., (New York: Random House, 1983).
Where the Sidewalk Ends by S. Silverstein, (New York: Harper & Row, 1974).

Table 8–2 Language Assessment Checklist

_____

Child's Name _____

Time _____ Date _____

Observer _____

(Check items you see child performing. Use "N" to mean "no opportunity to observe.")

1. Confidence
   - _____ Is confident enough to speak freely in surroundings other than home
   - _____ Speaks in normal tone of voice so others can easily hear
   - _____ Identifies himself/herself verbally by name
   - _____ Starts conversations sometimes

2. Articulation
   - _____ Speech is clear to other children
   - _____ Speech is clear to adults

3. Language production
   - _____ Speaks in simple sentences
   - _____ Asks questions; makes requests
   - _____ Converses informally at play or meals
   - _____ Responds to questions with more than one word
   - _____ Takes part in conversation

4. Vocabulary
   - _____ Uses names of people and things around him/her
   - _____ Uses simple verbs (come, go, see, etc.)
   - _____ Uses simple pronouns (me, him, her, etc.)
   - _____ Uses simple adjectives (big, little, red, etc.)
   - _____ Uses simple prepositions (in, out, up, etc.)

5. Communication
   - _____ Communicates wants and needs with words
   - _____ Talks with adults
   - _____ Talks with children
   - _____ Talks to animals, dolls, toys

6. Language understanding
   - _____ Follows teacher's simple directions
   - _____ Responds appropriately to another child's question or request

7. Word play
   - _____ Makes up nonsense words
   - _____ Enjoys doing finger plays; can repeat words
   - _____ Enjoys playing word and sound games
   - _____ Has favorite stories or songs he/she wants repeated

8. Listening skills
   - _____ Sits still and listens to someone talking or reading stories
   - _____ Can identify words and sounds which are alike or different
   - _____ Can find teacher when he/she calls from another room
   - _____ Can remember words and sounds when they are repeated

_____

Reprinted with the permission of Merrill, an imprint of Macmillan Publishing Company, Inc., from _Skills For Preschool Teachers_ by Janice J. Beaty. Copyright © 1992 by Macmillan Publishing Company.

ASSESSING LANGUAGE GROWTH

As with every other aspect of the preschool program, the children in your classroom will vary widely in their oral language skills. The assessment checklist shown in Table 8–2 is a list of behaviors that most children with no physical or mental disability should be able to accomplish by the end of their kindergarten year.

This checklist is considered an informal assessment tool teachers might use to help verify indications—gained through regular classroom observations—that some children may be in need of special help with language development. Such knowledge can be used to accurately identify areas of language strength as well as areas in need of strengthening. Once this information is acquired, activities to help develop the areas of need can be prescribed.

THE ONSET OF LITERACY

Children develop spoken language early in life as they accumulate experiences within their linguistic environment. From infancy, they rapidly learn that oral communication is a means of interacting with others. And by the beginning of their second year of life, many children start to realize that the random sounds they playfully uttered earlier can be combined in ways that mean something to others. Frank B. May explained how children achieve this capability:

> They observe and listen to people speak, to be sure, but they also observe how people react when they, the children, do the speaking. Do Jamie's parents get him a little round sweet thing when he says "cookie"? Do they rush him into a special little room whenever he utters a sound like (pŏt′ē)? Do they pick him up and cuddle him and coo in his ear when he utters nothing more than "up"?[9]

Children learn words by trying out sounds and noticing their effects on others. If "gloppins" doesn't get him what he wants, the child drops it from his repertoire and experiments with other sounds until he reaches his goal. In the same way, children continue to experiment and learn until they are able to string together a series of words into phrases or sentences. All the while, children naturally uncover the rules and concepts of their language by interacting with and adapting to the language environment in which they are immersed. No structured or formalized lessons in oral language are given—interactive life experiences are the matrix for oral language.

Children progress through an orderly and predictable sequence of natural growth, during which experimentation is stimulated within a developmentally appropriate, language-rich environment. The child's motivation for learning to speak is based on a natural desire to communicate with others and to make sense out of his or her surroundings. Myna M. Haussler tells us: "For these same reasons, young children become aware of the print around them. It is the need to communicate with others and make sense out of printed language which motivates young children to begin reading. . . . Young children in our society, prior to formal schooling, are aware of print, understand the functions of written language, and are naturally beginning to develop reading strategies."[10]

Learning to read evolves naturally from experiences accumulated in a language-rich environment.

Children's motivations to learn about and reproduce the print they see around them are the same as their motivations to learn about and reproduce the speech sounds in their environment. They must therefore be encouraged to learn about written language through the same processes as they learned about spoken language— by observing and experiencing others as they read or write, by constructing their own written products for others to read, and by continued life experiences that help foster language growth. Marjorie V. Fields, Katherine Spangler, and Dorris Lee stress the importance of continuing the types of experiences children have had while learning to talk as they become motivated to learn to read.

> Children learn oral language without formal instruction but are bombarded with as-
> sistance in learning to read. Ironically, oral language is actually the greater intellectual
> feat of the two.... Learning to read is less difficult than learning to talk, as reading
> merely builds on what the child has already learned about language. In acquiring
> oral language, children must first discover the existence and purpose of language,
> then master its sounds and structure, and finally learn the multitude of oral symbols
> which constitute vocabulary. In learning to read, children can build on their previous
> knowledge of their language as they figure out the written symbol system used to
> represent it.[11]

Written language should be thought of as a natural extension of oral language. Carol Chomsky's research has indicated that children acquire written and oral language through the same process—by constructing their own rules and concepts rather than by being told about them. Does this mean that we stand aside and allow the child to do whatever he feels necessary to learn to read? No. That method would be analogous to throwing a nonswimmer into the pool and leaving him to his own resources—the "sink or swim" technique. This chapter offers suggestions for what adults should do to help children deal with written communication.

The type of approach we will be considering is commonly referred to as a "whole-language" program. These programs try to introduce children to literacy in a holistic and natural manner, including an emphasis on the integration of all four language processes: speaking, listening, writing, and reading.

EMERGENT LITERACY

Literacy (learning to read and write) is viewed today as a natural part of the child's ongoing language development. This means that a major goal of early childhood education is not only to help children become capable speakers and listeners, but also to aid them in becoming readers and writers. In its influential report, *Becoming a Nation of Readers,* the Commission on Reading stated that, "all of the uses of language—listening, speaking, reading, and writing—are interrelated and mutually supportive. It follows, therefore, that school activities that foster one of the language arts inevitably will benefit the others as well."[12] The interrelatedness of the language arts can be visualized within this classroom scenario:

> ▶▶▶▶▶▶▶
>
> Mrs. Testa's 12 children enter the classroom excited to share the important things that have happened in their lives since their last visit to school. Hands fly into the air during circle time in eager anticipation of who will be the first to speak. Teri's words explode forth as she tells about helping her father plant a dozen tomatoes in the backyard garden plot. Robert's eyes sparkle with enthusiasm as he describes the new furniture that arrived at their house yesterday ("A beautiful yellow sofa, just beautiful!"). Wendy sadly recounts her family's heavyhearted task of saying good-bye to its 10-year-old beagle who was struck down by a speeding car the day before. Enrique happily describes the party his family organized in celebration of his fifth birthday.
>
> After each child has an opportunity to share an event, Mrs. Testa asks the children to offer one sentence to summarize each child's contribution. She writes the sentences on a sheet of chart paper and adds a simple illustration to highlight each. Mrs. Testa then reads back to the children the collection of sentences, pointing to each word and encouraging the children to help her read.

Another way of characterizing the concept of emergent literacy is to explain what it is *not*. In the past, one way of thinking about reading and writing was to perceive them as skills isolated from the worlds of language and thought, as if they had no relationship to listening and speaking. The preschool and kindergarten years were believed to be "times of readiness" when specific skills related to prereading and prewriting were stressed. Evelyn B. Freeman and J. Amos Hatch explain this position:

> Reading readiness assumes the existence of a set of skills that are necessary pre-requisites to formal reading instruction. Reading is viewed as a process distinct from writing (composing). Writing should not be encouraged or "taught" until children can read and spell. These reading skills, which are charted sequentially, can be learned through direct instruction and assessed by formal testing. Tests such as the Metropolitan Readiness Test are commonly given to kindergarten children to determine their readiness for formal reading instruction. Examples of specific types of readiness skills include auditory memory, rhyming, letter recognition, visual matching, listening skills, sound-letter correspondence, initial consonant sounds, visual and auditory discrimination.[13]

Emergent literacy does not see eye-to-eye with this traditional view of reading readiness. Instead of thinking of the reading and writing acts as phenomena occurring only after children acquire a preset, adult-imposed sequence of skills, children are seen as being in a process of becoming literate from a very young age while actively engaged as constructors of their language system. Hall noted that "developmental tasks take place within the child...emergence is a gradual process: it takes place over time...for something to emerge there has to be something there in the first place ...things usually only emerge if the conditions are right."[14]

Lloyd O. Ollila and Margie I. Mayfield characterize just what those "right conditions" might be:

> Max is 4 years old. His mother thinks he's marvelous. Yesterday, she found him curled up on the sofa with Snuffy, his favorite teddy bear, "reading" Snuffy *The Pokey Little Puppy*. It wasn't important that he didn't get all the words right. In fact, she knew he had memorized most of the story. Just two months earlier, he learned to print his name, and now he writes it on everything. Max has watched her write letters to relatives, and he wrote one to Grandma. He announced he was going to write her about his new puppy. The letter had misshaped letters, wavy lines, scribbles, and drawings, but it was signed Max and he was very proud of it. So were his mother and father as they listened attentively while he read them his letter. Thinking back to his infancy and toddler years, his mother could see signs that Max was going to excel. She talked and read to him daily in those years. Even as a baby, he seemed to really enjoy those conversations. He picked up new words easily as his mother talked with him while she went about her daily routine. She would sing little songs and nursery rhymes, and soon Max would join right in with her. He and his sister, Maria, were always building things with legos and little logs or making sand cakes and racing tracks in the sandbox with the neighbors. His mother could hear them chattering happily as they played. Even when Max was alone, she could often hear him talking to himself, playing different characters with his stuffed animals. His mother knows he is going to do well in school.[15]

Max's literacy development began even before he set foot in school. He developed language as a natural process during infancy by watching and listening to his parents; he also learned that his cries elicited desired reactions from his parents. Eventually, he copied his parents' speech and tried new ways of making language work for him. As with his spoken language, Max developed interests and abilities with print as it became an integral part of his daily activities. He observed others using print and sought meaning from its use—all literacy experiences were derived from warm, meaningful events in Max's life.

As in the case of Max, children "become aware of print as a natural, functional aspect of their environment as they observe adults interacting with, discussing, and using print, both in reading and writing, to fulfill their needs or their communication intentions."[16] When teachers accept this emergent literacy philosophy, the question often arises: "What can I do in my classroom to enhance and deepen the children's development of reading and writing that began so naturally so early in life?" The type of program advocated by early childhood specialists today is commonly referred to as a "whole language" program, a plan that introduces youngsters to literacy in an integrated, natural manner.

The whole language perspective offers early childhood teachers unending opportunities to capitalize upon the child's tendencies for playfulness, experimentation, and freedom of expression. Major support for its use was obtained in 1986 from a joint statement issued by the International Reading Association, the Association for Childhood Education International, the National Association for the Education of Young Children, and a number of equally influential professional organizations. The statement urged teachers to facilitate optimal pre–first grade literacy through many meaningful, functional language experiences. Their recommendations included the following:

1. Build instruction on what the child already knows about oral language, reading, and writing. Focus on worthwhile experiences and meaningful language rather than on isolated skill development.
2. Respect the language the child brings to school, and use it as a base for language and literacy activities.
3. Ensure feelings of success for all children, helping them see themselves as people who can enjoy exploring oral and written language.
4. Provide reading experiences as an integrated part of the broader communication process, which includes speaking, listening, and writing, as well as other systems such as art, math, and music.
5. Encourage children's first attempts at writing without concern for the proper formation of letters or correct, conventional spelling.
6. Encourage risk-taking in first attempts at reading and writing, and accept what appear to be errors as part of children's natural patterns of growth and development.
7. Use materials for instruction that are familiar, such as well-known stories, because they provide the child with a sense of control and confidence.
8. Provide a model for students to emulate. In the classroom, teachers should use language appropriately, listen and respond to children's talk, and engage in their own reading and writing.
9. Take time regularly to read to children from a wide variety of poetry, fiction, and nonfiction.
10. Provide time regularly for children's independent reading and writing.[17]

A second statement of major significance targets the types of whole language strategies considered essential to offering developmentally appropriate practice. NAEYC, the developer of the statement, contrasts appropriate practices with inappropriate practices (see Table 8–3).

Table 8–3 Integrated Components of Appropriate and Inappropriate Practice

Infants	
Appropriate Practice	Inappropriate Practice
• Adults engage in many one-to-one, face-to-face interactions with infants. Adults talk in a pleasant, soothing voice, and use simple language and frequent eye contact.	• Infants are left for long periods in cribs, playpens, or seats without adult attention. Adults are harsh, shout, or use baby talk.
• Infants are held and carried frequently to provide them with a wide variety of experiences. The adults talk to the infant before, during, and after moving the infant around.	• Infants are wordlessly moved about at the adult's convenience. Nothing is explained to infants.
• Adults are especially attentive to infants during routines such as diaper changing, feeding, and changing clothes. The caregiver explains what will happen, what is happening, and what will happen next.	• Routines are swiftly accomplished without involving the infant. Little or no warm interactions take place during routines.
• All interactions are characterized by gentle, supportive responses. Adults listen and respond to sounds that infants make, imitate them, and respect infants' sounds as the beginning of communication.	• Adults are rough, harsh, or ignore the child's responses.
• The caregiver frequently talks with, sings to, and reads to infants. Language is a vital, lively form of communication with individuals.	• Infants are expected to entertain themselves or watch television. Language is used infrequently and vocabularies limited.

Toddlers	
Appropriate Practice	Inappropriate Practice
• Adults engage in many one-to-one, face-to-face conversations with toddlers. Adults let toddlers initiate language, and wait for a response, even from children whose language is limited. Adults label or name objects, describe events, and reflect feelings to help children learn new words. Adults simplify their language for toddlers who are just beginning to talk (instead of "It's time to wash our hands and have snack," the adult says, "Let's wash hands. Snack-time!") Then as children acquire their own words, adults expand on the toddler's language (for example, *Toddler*—"Mary sock." *Adult*—"Oh, that's Mary's missing sock and you found it.").	• Adults talk *at* toddlers and do not wait for a response. Adult voices dominate or adults do not speak to children because they think they are too young to respond. Adults either talk "baby talk" or use language that is too complex for toddlers to understand.
• Adults respond quickly to toddlers' cries or calls for help, recognizing that toddlers have limited language with which to communicate their needs.	• Crying is ignored or responded to irregularly or at the adults' convenience.

Table 8–3 *(Continued)*

Toddlers

Appropriate Practice	Inappropriate Practice
• Adults frequently read to toddlers, individually on laps or in groups of two or three. Adults sing with toddlers, do fingerplays, act out simple stories like "The Three Bears" with children participating actively, or tell stories using a flannelboard or magnetic board, and allow children to manipulate and place figures on the boards.	• Adults impose "group time" on toddlers, forcing a large group to listen or watch an activity without opportunity for children to participate.
• Sturdy picture books are provided. Pictures depict a variety of ages and ethnic groups in a positive way.	• Books are not available because they get torn or soiled. Pictures are cartoons or other stereotypes.

3-Year-Olds

Appropriate Practice	Inappropriate Practice
• Adults encourage children's developing language by speaking clearly and frequently to individual children and listening to their response. Adults respond quickly and appropriately to children's verbal initiatives. They recognize that talking may be more important than listening for 3-year-olds. Adults patiently answer children's questions ("Why?" "How come?") and recognize that 3-year-olds often ask questions they know the answers to in order to open a discussion or practice giving answers themselves. Adults know that children are rapidly acquiring language, experimenting with verbal sounds, and beginning to use language to solve problems and learn concepts.	• Adults attempt to maintain quiet in the classroom and punish children who talk too much. Adults speak to the whole group most of the time and only speak to individual children to admonish or discipline them. Adults ridicule children's asking of rhetorical questions by saying, "Oh, you know that."
• Adults provide many experiences and opportunities to extend children's language and musical abilities. Adults read books to one child or a small group; recite simple poems, nursery rhymes and finger plays; encourage children to sing songs and listen to recordings; facilitate children's play of circle and movement games like London Bridge, Farmer in the Dell, and Ring Around the Rosie; provide simple rhythm instruments; listen to stories that children tell or write down stories they dictate; and enjoy 3-year-olds' sense of humor.	• Adults limit language and music activities because children sometimes become too silly or loud, OR they include story time and music time only as a whole group activity and require children to participate. Adults discipline children for using silly or nonsense language.

Table 8–3 (*Continued*)

4- and 5-Year-Olds	
Appropriate Practice	Inappropriate Practice
• Teachers move among groups and individuals to facilitate children's involvement with materials and activities by asking questions, offering suggestions, or adding more complex materials or ideas to a situation.	• Teachers dominate the environment by talking to the whole group most of the time and telling children what to do.
• Children are provided many opportunities to see how reading and writing are useful before they are instructed in letter names, sounds, and word identification. Basic skills develop when they are meaningful to children. An abundance of these types of activities is provided to develop language and literacy through meaningful experience: listening to and reading stories and poems; taking field trips; dictating stories; seeing classroom charts and other print in use; participating in dramatic play and other experiences requiring communication; talking informally with other children and adults; and experimenting with writing by drawing, copying, and inventing their own spelling.	• Reading and writing instruction stresses isolated skill development such as recognizing single letters, reciting the alphabet, singing the alphabet song, coloring within predefined lines, or being instructed in correct formation of letters on a printed line.

Source: Sue Bredekamp, Ed., *Developmentally Appropriate Practice in Early Childhood Programs Serving Children From Birth Through Age 8* (Washington, DC: NAEYC, 1987), pp. 34, 35, 40, 42, 45, 49, 55.

Helping the very young, then, is best addressed with the advice that, "Learning to become literate ought to be as uncomplicated and as barrier-free as possible."[18] The key is to offer environments, activities, and interactions that enable children to develop naturally as listeners, speakers, readers, and writers.

INFANTS AND THE READING PROCESS

One of the discoveries verified over the last few years is that the first steps in the reading process begin shortly after birth, when infants hear the language all around them. Nancy Larrick has stated, "The time to begin [reading] is with the first feeding, pampering, and bathing, when the parents' singing or chanting and gentle conversation begin to set the stage for the infant's participation only a few months later."[19] Linda Leonard Lamme asserts that such intimate physical and language contacts serve an important function in the parent-infant bonding process. When books are added to these warm encounters, the child will associate pleasure with reading. Infants enjoy warm physical contact, and when they are able to see that books accompany the encounters, a positive attitude toward reading is developed long before the children are even one year old. If made an integral part of the daily routine, "books become an accepted part of their world, and reading time is anticipated with joy."[20] Lamme has identified the reading skills that can be learned before age one:

> Through much interaction with books, infants become aware that pictures have meaning. They begin to use their eyes to discriminate between different objects in the picture, as someone points them out and names them. They develop listening skills and the ability to differentiate among sounds. They also learn to turn the book's pages and become aware that books have a right side up. Each of these skills will help establish a sound foundation upon which future learning can build.[21]

What kinds of books are appropriate for infants? The most popular is the sturdy picture book. Usually constructed of heavy, plastic-coated cardboard, these books contain colorful, clear, uncluttered pictures about things familiar to most infants: toys, animals, food, family members, vehicles, and so on. These books are especially good for infants because they are strong enough for the infant to turn the pages by himself and resilient enough to withstand his wet hands. Some infant picture books are made of cloth or paper, both of which are somewhat less desirable, at least as first books.

Of course, we want the infant to handle the books, but they have trouble with cloth books and often tear paper ones. When sharing any picture books with children, you play a critical role. Judith A. Schickedanz recommends a particular language format to follow.[22] First, focus the baby's attention on the picture by saying, "Look!" or "Look at that!" Then ask the question, "What's that?" or "What do you see there?" At this point, the baby may smile, attempt to vocalize in some way, or stare blankly at you with an expression indicating that she hasn't the foggiest notion of what in the world the object is. In any case, the baby and adult should provide an answer to the question. If the baby answers with a smile or incomprehensible gurgle, you must typically say something like, "Yes. That's a cup. It's a cup, just like yours." In short, the format is: (1) get the baby's attention, (2) ask a labeling question, (3) wait for the baby to answer, and (4) provide feedback. Because the baby's productive language is so limited, the adult is responsible for nearly all the dialogue during these book encounters.

Although sturdy picture books are most appropriate for babies, they should not be considered the only reading material to which our budding readers may be exposed. Ida Santos Stewart has reminded teachers that print surrounds the infant each day: "Television with entertaining commercials, cereal boxes with eye-catching names, colorful calendars around the house, newspapers with bold headlines and endless billboards quickly and naturally introduce children to written language."[23] In examining the infant's early reading behavior, authorities have become aware that children learn much about words and meanings long before they enter first grade.

YOUNG CHILDREN AND THE READING PROCESS

The pleasurable experiences with books during infancy pave the way for increased involvement and growing skills during later childhood. Leo Lionni, a popular author of children's books, explains how a child's early contacts with books expand throughout the early years:

> It is [with the picture book] that, through the mediation of an adult reader, he will discover the relationship between visual and verbal language....The meaningless signs that accompany the pictures, from which adults can extract meaningful sounds, vaguely enter his consciousness....Little by little, the scribbles appear to be related to the explicit meanings of the illustrations....The child learns to read and write.[24]

Books stimulate the young child's vivid imagination and serve to establish a strong relationship between words and creative images. M. W. Aulls describes how this process evolved with Tommy, age four, as he listened intently to his father's reading of Max's adventure in Maurice Sendak's *Where the Wild Things Are*.[25]

> Tommy's pudgy finger points to a word....."Here, Daddy. You begin here." "Thank you, son. '...and an ocean tumbled by with a great boat for Max and he sailed off through night and day and in and out of weeks and almost over a year to where the wild things are.' " Tommy sighs and mumbles to himself, "r-r-r-r-," in anticipation of the next line.[26]

Although Tommy had listened to *Where the Wild Things Are* several times before, he once again became absorbed in its plot and illustrations. But, even more than the book itself, Tommy relished the intimate, personal interaction of the situation where the reading took place. The youngster was comfortably sprawled alongside his father on Tommy's bed, head nestled contentedly on his father's shoulder. Tommy looked forward to this evening ritual; it was one of the most cherished parts of his entire day (as it was for his father). Furthermore, because the story ended with a few words of conversation, a good-night hug and kiss, and a special tucking-in ceremony, the story-reading interaction became a highly nurturant experience.

Strong positive feelings about books and the reading process result from such tender encounters between adult and child. If initial book experiences are enjoyable, the feelings associated with written words are quite likely to be positive. This is as true for the preschool environment as it is for home. The development of a positive outlook toward books and reading may be one of the most important contributions the preschool curriculum could make for future reading growth.

Developing Early Reading Behaviors with Books

Whether at home, at school, or both, children need to get turned on to good books. As they encounter good storybooks, preschoolers will often exhibit some readily apparent developmental trends in reading behaviors. The first stage actually begins during infancy and toddlerhood as children initially develop strategies for making sense of stories. One such strategy involves recognizing that objects in pictures have names and are labeled. Consider a portion of the dialogue between Mikey and his father as they shared a picture book on transportation. Mikey was twenty months old at the time of this interaction.

Teachers should tell children stories that both fascinate them and arouse their sense of curiosity and wonder.

Mikey:	(*Brings the book to his father, sits on his lap, and focuses on the book as his father turns from page to page.*)
Father:	"Oh, look! What kind of boat does Mikey see on this page?"
Mikey:	(*Gazes at the picture and points to the boat.*) "Bar-juh." (*Looks up at his father.*)
Father:	"Yes, Mikey, that boat is a barge. Do you know someone who builds barges?"
Mikey:	"Grandpa!" (*Looks up at father again.*)
Father:	"Grandpa builds big barges." (*Hugs Mikey and turns to the next page.*) "Let's see if we can find out what's on the next page."

The dialogue demonstrates that Mikey's exposure to books and meaningful interactions with his parents helped him get something out of pictures that made sense to him. Mikey knew the pictures were meaningful and that he could get information out of them. He seemed to confirm this notion as he repeatedly looked at his father to observe his reaction.

In other words, Mikey's father helped him during the early stages of reading by relating the key words from the book to Mikey's own life experiences. We call this the *life-to-text* instructional model.

From the age of two through the preschool years, new reading behaviors emerge and prosper as children are provided frequent, enjoyable experiences with books. Judith A. Schickedanz detailed those crucial early behaviors in this manner:[27]

1. *Children become increasingly able to retell the text more accurately.* The simple, predictable nature of children's stories, along with repeated readings of favorite books, often leads children to learn several lines of story by heart. This activity is actually the beginning of the process of learning to read. Although young children are not yet able to unlock the abstract nature of print, they are forming an understanding that print and speech are somehow related. Experiments of this type usually continue for many months until the child discovers the actual relationship between print and speech; the oral rendition of a story is often known very well before conventional reading emerges.

2. *Children move from thinking the pictures are read to knowing that print can be read without reference to the pictures.* Very young children seem to think that the reader looks at pictures to know what the book says. But, as their experiences multiply, they realize that it is the print and not the pictures that a reader reads; pictures provide clues about the story. Adults are able to determine whether a child thinks a reader needs pictures by asking some simple questions: "Where should I look to start to read this book?" or "Where do you think my eyes look while I read the book? Show me."

3. *Once they are aware of and interested in print, children develop a more accurate understanding of how the print and speech relate.* Later on during the preschool years, children who have experienced books widely begin to match their oral telling of a story to the actual print in the book. First attempts are global—children initiate sweeping movements across the page indicating, in general, that they understand the print represents what is being read. Since adults often run a finger under the text when reading, children mimic this action in their story-reading behavior, too.

   Once children begin to match actual words in print to specific verbal utterances, a new era has begun. A child usually experiments for many months with associating print to oral language before the actual puzzle is completely solved and the act of reading words in print begins.

4. *Children change from having almost complete interest in the pictures and meaning of the story to interest in the features of the text.* Toddlers and young preschoolers often ask questions of the following variety during story-reading sessions: "Where's his mommy?" "Why he sad?" But, as children experience deeper language skills and become more aware of print, they

begin to ask questions such as, "What does this word say?" or "What does it say?" Children's familiarity with a book (if they know it by heart) is an essential ingredient for their interest in exploring print; that is, the better a child knows a story, the more interested she will be in the print as opposed to the pictures or story meaning.

This developmental sequence of the reading process does not come about through immersion in phonics skills or in the mechanized forms of word analysis. Isolated drilling and practicing of specific skills often transforms a natural, pleasurable childhood act into a bewildering array of meaningless exercises. Instead of repeated drills, teachers should offer extensive experiences with good storybooks and words-in-print in various situations. As children see words repeatedly, they develop the ability to associate spoken words with print. Categories of activities specifically designed to achieve this literacy goal include: *story reading, book sharing, language experience stories,* and *labeling activities.*

Story Reading

Throughout this chapter I have stressed the developmental appropriateness of story reading to emerging literacy. Its value should be considered so great that it cannot be compared to any single influence. For that reason, pleasurable story-reading experiences should be offered to the very young in all group settings on a daily basis.

Successful teachers seem to weave a magic spell during story time, and you might be tempted to emulate good storytellers you observed in the past. However, what worked for that individual may not work for you. It is important to be yourself—personality and charm are made part of the story only if the children know that the storyteller is the same person who is with them during other parts of their day; periodic personality changes only confuse and unnerve the children. These suggestions for telling and reading stories may be helpful:

1. *Prepare carefully for each story you read.*
   - Read your story silently to get an overall idea of the plot.
   - Read the story aloud so you can develop a "feel" for its mood. Read it two or three times on a tape recorder and analyze each of your readings. Be especially watchful for "uhs" and "and-uhs."
   - Sit or stand in front of a mirror. Try to communicate openly a feeling of comfort and interest while reading aloud.
   - If you possibly can, practice your story in front of a friend and request honest criticism of your technique.
2. *Plan a good introduction so children are able to get an idea of what the story is going to be about.* Be careful not to get too involved with highly detailed

descriptions of characters or events, but give the children an idea of the main story characters and what their major situation will be. Some teachers find it useful to establish a motivating technique to encourage children to listen to the story. Some suggestions follow:

- Play a special little tune on the piano indicating to the children that story time is at hand.

- Use a favorite hand puppet to announce that story time is ready to begin. Then, a simple little dialogue between teacher and puppet can introduce the story to be shared. For example, a simple message from Ellie the Elephant encourages the children to listen, and also helps develop interest in the forthcoming story: "Hello, boys and girls. It's so nice to see you again today here at the story time corner. Miss Alley is going to tell us an exciting story today about a brave little boat named Little Toot. Let's all listen carefully to Miss Alley because I think she's about to start." Miss Alley may then thank Ellie and begin the introduction to the story. When using puppets in this manner, look at the puppet when *it* is "speaking" and look at the children when *you* are speaking.

- Capitalize on the children's creative imagination by engaging them in a simple role-playing experience. For example, the children can be asked to pretend that they are all taking a walk in the woods. Point out some interesting features and have the children imagine that they are actually seeing them: "Oh, look at that tree—it's so tall. Look at how tall it is. Let's all stretch ourselves and try to be as tall as that tree" or "There goes a little rabbit—watch it hop through the grass. Let's all hop like the rabbit." After sharing three or four such experiences, you may all pretend to be getting tired from the long walk and decide that it would be a good time to find a safe, cool place to rest. Ask everyone to pantomime looking for a place to rest. As the children look around the "forest" for a suitable place, you find a little meadow in the trees that would be a good spot. So no dangerous bears or lions will hear them, encourage the children to gather as quietly as they can into a compact group and sit in the meadow. After the children are quietly gathered in their safe little area, you may begin to tell them the story. Depending on the type of story to be told, the children can be similarly led to swim across a river to a safe island where a story is told, build a safe treehouse, and so on.

3. *Use your voice effectively.* Speak naturally, but be aware of the ways in which loudness or softness and fastness or slowness can affect the mood of a story. For example, suspenseful parts may call for a soft, slow, mysterious tone while happy parts may call for livelier, louder, joyous tones. Your voice can be used to add surprise, sadness, question, or fear to the story, but remember not to get overdramatic. If you do, you will shift the focus from

the plot to the storyteller, and you will interrupt the children's interest and concentration.

4. *Anticipate questions and minor interruptions during the reading or storytelling period.* Handle children's questions or comments tactfully so the trend of the story is not interrupted. For example, one child became so absorbed in a story that he blurted out just before the climax, "Oh, I wonder how the kitten will be saved." Another child insightfully offered the actual solution, "I know—the mama cat will save her." Although the storyteller could have become flustered at the revelation of the story's ending, she remained composed and simply commented, "Your idea was very good, Robin, but let's all listen and see if you were right." The children, in this case, were drawn right back into the story. Often, teachers themselves cause unnecessary interruptions by throwing out questions or explaining new words along the way. Such digressions add nothing to the story and mainly serve to lessen interest or to interrupt continuity of the plot. Never interrupt the flow of a story yourself except in case of extreme necessity.

Share pictures throughout the story if they help clarify or illustrate the evolving sequence of events. By sitting on a low chair or on the floor, you will be in perfect position to hold up the book for the children to see. Hold the book open all the way in a steady position. Some teachers, when reading a story, prefer to hold books at either side; others find it more comfortable to hold them in front. Whatever the position, be sure that all children can see the picture without having to crane their necks or move unnecessarily. If the children are seated in a semi-circle, you may have to move the picture so they all can see. In these cases, it is important to hold the book and pause so the group seated to your left can focus their eyes on the picture; hold and pause at the center; and hold and pause to your right. Some teachers share poorly by holding the picture so the children on the left are able to focus and then slowly sweeping to the right without stopping the picture along the way. It is difficult for the children in the center to focus on the moving picture, and they may not be able to see it properly. Short sweeps and pauses are necessary so the focal point can remain fixed for a short period of time.

Basically, children respond at three levels when they read and interpret pictures: a *low level*, where they are able to identify the objects in a picture; a *middle level*, where they are able to describe what is happening; and a *high level*, where they are able to communicate personal feelings and establish relationships among objects or events. Most preschool children operate on the low level, but since your goal is to encourage increasingly mature patterns of thought and language, you will want to insert higher-level questioning. Thus, the children can experience challenges and successes at individual levels of ability while, at the same time, being exposed to higher levels of thought through the comments and observations of their peers.

Help the children look for a variety of things in discussion pictures by guiding their observations along the lines of these questions:

Low Level

"Tell how many . . . ."

"Tell me what you see . . . ."

"Tell me about the picture . . . ."

"What color is the _____ ?"

"What _____(animal)_____ is in the picture?"

Middle Level

"What is _____ doing?"

"What kind of _____ do you see?"

"How far from the _____ is _____ ?"

"How large is the _____ ?"

High Level

"What will _____ do next?"

"What kind of _____ do you think _____ is?"

"Why did _____ happen?"

"What title can you give this picture?"

5. *Talk about the story.* Whether at home or at school, the adult-child interaction process is essential to the reading experience; children must be given many opportunities to talk about the stories read to them. In an attempt to discover what happens during typical book-reading encounters, Ninio and Bruner found that the events consisted of three essential elements: *attentional vocative, query,* and *label.*[28] *Feedback* from the parent was often present in the cycle. An example of such an interactional pattern follows:

Mother: "Look." [**Attentional vocative**]

Child: [*Attends to picture.*]

Mother: "What's that?" [**Query**]

Child: "Cow!" [**Label**]

Mother: "Yes, it is." [**Feedback**]

In her study of literacy practices, Shirley Brice Heath found that book-reading episodes with young children were played out similarly to the pattern described by Ninio and Bruner. However, she also found that, for older children, the nature of the interaction was different.

When children are about three years old, adults discourage the highly interactive participative role in bookreading children have hitherto played and children *listen and wait as an audience.* No longer does either adult or child repeatedly break into the story with questions and comments. Instead, children must listen, store what they hear, and on cue from the adult, answer a question.[29]

Such findings have important implications for research into the relationship between being read to and literacy development. We must maintain the strong interactive nature of book reading as the children continue developing through the preschool years and into the elementary school grades. To anyone who has ever spent time with youngsters, this conclusion makes great sense. Children learn about their world through relentless explorations and by asking countless questions. We can help them apply these energies to the act of reading by teaching them that questions are important; they help us think and get real meaning from the printed page. Reading is not just saying words. A study by Leslie Morrow indicated that using guided discussion with children promotes comprehension, helps them develop a sense of story structure, and increases the complexity of the children's oral language.[30] Morrow suggested that discussion questions focus on the following areas:

1. Setting.
   a. Time and place of the story.
   b. Characters in the story.
2. Theme: the goal or problem facing the main character.
3. Plot episodes: the sequence of episodes that lead to the main character reaching his or her goal or solving his or her problem.
4. Resolution.
   a. The way in which the main character reached his or her goal, or solved his or her problem.
   b. The story ending.

After the story is completed, then the children may enjoy discussing the main characters or plot for a short period. This will not always be the case, but if you find that interest is high, guide the discussion with questions like these:

- Tell us what you liked (or didn't like) about the story.
- If you had been (story character) how would you have felt when _____ happened?
- In what other way could (character) have solved this problem?
- Which character from the story would you most like to meet? Why?
- How do you think (character) felt when _____ happened?
- What story character would you most like to be? Why?
- Why do you think (character) did what he did?
- Did someone in the story change his mind about something? What was it? Why did he do it?
- What do you think happens to (character) now after the story ended?
- Have you ever had a problem like (character)? What did you do about it?

- Did you like the story? Why? Why not?

- Which picture did you like the most? Why?

- What things happened in the story that could really happen? That could not really happen?

- What would you change about the story?

- Do you know another story like this one? What is it? How are the stories alike?

There is no particular number of recommended questions to ask following a story. Sometimes children will want to talk about a story for five to ten minutes and at other times will only want to reflect on it quietly. Don't extend a discussion and run it into the ground by prolonging it. Remember that we are using story time as an emotional experience. We can ruin it with too many questions. Look at it this way—how would you feel when, after watching a great movie, you were forced to sit in your seat and answer a string of questions once the lights came on?

The Shared Book Experience

The shared book experience, introduced by Don Holdaway as a technique for influencing the teaching of literacy in New Zealand and Australia, is another key component of the whole-language program.[31] The experience incorporates the following characteristics:

1. *Repetitive materials.* These may be stories, songs, poems, or chants in which key words are restated several times.
2. *High predictablity.* The story events are especially easy to anticipate and recall. Repetition and rhyme contribute to the predictability of children's books.
3. *Strong rhythm.* The kind of sentence stays basically the same throughout the book, but just a few rhyming words change throughout the verses.

The shared book experience is similar to the book-reading experience, except that it is more directly concerned with reading instruction. Usually found in kindergarten classrooms, the shared book experience consists of repeated readings of the same story. Judith K. Cassady outlined the basic format of a shared book experience.[32]

Read the Book Aloud First, read the book to the group in a warm, enjoyable way. Settle the children comfortably around you and be sure the children are able to see both the text and the pictures. Follow the words with your finger so the children can see exactly what you are reading. In this way, children learn how print and speech are related; realize that words in print are collections of letters set off from others by space; understand that print is arranged in a left-to-right, top-to-bottom arrangement on pages; and know that the print (not the picture) tells the story in a book. Therefore, terms such as "word," "sentence," "page," and "story" should be used freely and naturally as the story is read—for example, "Isn't *corduroy* an interesting word?"

Big books, or enlarged copies of standard children's storybooks, are useful for the shared reading experience. The big books are so large that they are often placed on an easel, ensuring that every child is able to see the picture and print without trouble.

Try to select stories that have a great deal of *repetition.* When words or phrases are often repeated, children are able to *predict* what words will come next or what might happen on the next page. For example, in Bill Martin, Jr.'s book, *Brown Bear, Brown Bear, What Do You See?* a group of animals parade across the pages accompanied by words following the pattern described in the box below.

The repetition will aid in what transpires during the next phase of book sharing: rereading.

Read the Story Again   Most children enjoy the familiar; when they acquire an interest in reading, they will often seek to have stories read over and over again. They have begun to discover the relationship between speech and print through these repeated readings, often offering to "read" the story back. (Repeated readings are actually memorized by the child as she proudly "reads" it back to anyone who will listen.) During the second reading, invite the children to chime in as you elicit responses

> "Brown bear,
> Brown bear,
> What do you see?"
>
> "I see a redbird
> looking at me."
>
> "Redbird,
> Redbird,
> What do you see?"
>
> "I see a yellow duck
> looking at me."
>
> "Yellow duck,
> yellow duck..." [33]

from them. One particularly successful strategy is to read a short text segment and then use a rising vocal intonation followed by a pause to invite the children to supply a missing word or phrase. For example:

"Brown bear,
Brown bear,
What do you see?"

"I see a _____

_____ ."

A third reading could be a choral experience with groups of children reading alternate parts. Another reading might invite children to dramatize the characters by mimicking their actions.

Involve the Children in Further Exploration   This phase involves the children themselves reading and rereading the story from standard size books or the big book if they are interested in using it. The story can be a resource of activities for further learning. For example, draw their attention to the phrase "looking at me." Have the children suggest other words for "looking." Some children might enjoy a cooperative rewriting of the story. Have the children think of other animals, for example, that might be added to the original version of *Brown Bear*. The children's versions may range from very simple adaptations to stories more complex than the original. Accept all ideas and enjoy the rewriting experience with them. Some children may want to get together to produce an illustrated book of their own. Make their cooperative effort a part of the classroom library.

To foster independence, encourage children to listen to a tape-recorded version of the story. Some children will be able to handle paired reading, that is, reading to each other.

Despite the guidelines, you must realize that there is no single correct method of book sharing. A wide variety of reading material available to children exists, and each has its unique possibilities for appropriate early experiences. Therefore, the important consideration is to provide experiences with book reading much like the warm, intimate encounters found in language-rich families.

The Language Experience Approach

A second technique that assists the natural reading process is the *language experience approach (LEA)*. The LEA capitalizes on children's desire for involvement by using their own oral language production to create reading selections instead of sharing picture or storybooks. It encourages the children to express their own ideas and then invites them to observe their thoughts being written down on paper.

The first step in creating an LEA is to make sure that the children have had an experience interesting enough to stimulate lively discussion. A trip to the zoo, the

Field trips are fun, and they provide children with experiences that stimulate lively discussion.

hatching of a chick, a film, a new class pet, or last night's trick-or-treat adventures are examples of topics that are sure to generate a great deal of talk. Some authorities suggest that an LEA can be created with groups as large as fifteen to twenty children, but I prefer to limit the size of four-year-old or kindergarten groups to six or seven. Lower numbers get more children involved.

Have a general discussion of the experience before writing about it. Good ideas usually flow from these discussions as one child's thinking stimulates another's. When you feel the children have communicated an adequate sense of the experience, you can begin to write down individual ideas. Most teachers prefer to use a black marking pen or crayon on a large tagboard chart ($18'' \times 36''$) attached to the wall. Start with a question like "Who can give us a sentence that reminds us of what we've been doing right now . . . James?"

James offers, "We have a pet hamster. His name is Fluffy."

"That's good, James. I'll write that down. As usual, I'll start at the top left and begin with a capital letter."

Say each word as you write it, and then read the entire sentence back to the children: "James said, 'We have a pet hamster. His name is Fluffy.' " Be sure to point to each word as you say it, emphasizing the left-to-right progression.

When writing down children's ideas, be very careful not to correct or edit their contributions. If the child uses a colloquialism like "y'all," write it down. Even if the child says, "The hamster pooped," you should write it down. You want the LEA to be a total language experience in which the child learns to see his ideas communicated orally and in writing. This concept of natural language usage is much more important during early reading than using correct grammar or speech patterns. Do not break the *link* between speech and writing. If we constantly correct children for such "errors," they may become reluctant to share their ideas. Spelling should be proper, however. If a child says "goin' " for "going," spell the word correctly and let the child pronounce the word the way he likes as he reads it back. The only other modification a teacher should make is to ask a child to rephrase the rare comment like, "I didn't like the damned hamster." Words you would not normally accept in your center or school (swear or curse words) should not be displayed on the chart.

> **OUR HAMSTER**
>
> James said, "We have a pet hamster. His name is Fluffy."
>
> Joan said "He has brown fur and big brown eyes."
>
> Carmen said, "Fluffy is a funny hamster."
>
> Jackson said, "He always scratches and digs."
>
> Faith said, "We love Fluffy."

Another reason to keep the numbers in an LEA group to six or seven is that you do not want to make the story more than six or seven sentences long. Have the children choose an appropriate title when the chart is completed. Now the chart is read several times both by the teacher and the children, each time in a slightly different way:

1. After each child has had an opportunity to contribute, the teacher reads the entire story back to the group.
2. The teacher may ask the children to read from the chart. Some may read only the title or a word. Others may be able to read the entire sentence they contributed as the teacher points to each word.
3. The teacher may use follow-up activities:
   a. "Find the sentence that Sharon told us."
   b. Hold up a card containing a key word in the story and see if anyone can recognize it on the chart.
   c. Ask questions to check on comprehension: for example, "What color are the hamster's eyes?"

No word is more special to learn than a child's own name.

Some children may want to illustrate the story when it is complete. The teacher should write the story title and the child's name at the top of the paper. After illustrating, the child may want to tell a related story. Write down the words as the child says them in the space below the illustration or on a separate piece of paper.

Illustrated experience stories from either the chart paper or individual drawings make interesting "library books" when they are given attractive covers and placed in an area where they are readily available to the children.

The experience chart holds great appeal for young children because of their involvement in formulating it. Their names and their thoughts are on the chart, and so, too, may be their artistic contributions. But most importantly, the children have had an experience that illustrates concretely how speech is recorded in print.

Labeling Activities

Children are greatly motivated to read by a lively LEA program, and their growing interest in words can be further encouraged by casually labeling many items in the classroom. Start by placing labels on some of the more commonly used items—

plants, aquarium, water, rest room, chair, table, and so on. Give each of the children a matching word card and ask them to find the corresponding label. Ask them what the word is. Other labeling activities include these:

1. On the first day of school you may want to construct name tags for each child. Cut silhouettes (of fish, birds, kittens, and so on) out of construction paper, print each child's name on one, and pin it to the child. Children take great pride in their name tags and enjoy comparing their tags.

2. Label each child's storage box, locker, or coat hook with his or her name. On the first day of school, you may want to take each child's photograph with an instant camera, mount it on tagboard, print the child's name under it, and scatter all the labeled pictures on the floor. Ask the children (one at a time) to find their own tag and take it to the locker where an aide can hang it. This procedure can be extended by informally including other reading skills—for example, "Jana did a wonderful job finding her name. Now, let's have someone whose name begins just like Jana...J...J...find his or hers. That's just great, Jimmy, you really did fine."

3. Write the child's name on a piece of finished artwork. Repeatedly exposing the child to his name is sure to help him in recalling it, and the child takes pride in seeing his name on something he created. When labeling, try to put the name in the upper left-hand corner so that the child will get used to looking at that part of a page whenever he begins to read.

4. Label objects in the classroom during their period of greatest popularity. For example, if new gerbils are brought into the classroom, and the children's interest in them is high, you may wish to print the word "gerbils" clearly on a bright piece of paper and attach it to the shelf on which the gerbil cage is placed. Discuss the word with the children. If the children decide to name the gerbils, you may want to print their names on labels and place them near the cage as well. Labels like this can be made for a flower, a fish, the book area, and so on. Instead of simply placing the labels on the wall and seeing them receive no further attention, periodically take them away, and see if your children are able to find out where each should be returned.

5. At times, children in a dramatic play area may ask you to provide certain labels for them as they try to make their play a bit more realistic. For example, one group of children set up an ice cream store and were about to open for business when they realized they needed a name for their store and a list of flavors. The teacher made the sign and the list: chocolate, vanilla, strawberry, and butterscotch. This variation of a labeling activity had real meaning for the children involved.

6. For snack time, use place mats made from wallpaper samples and label each mat with a child's name. Change the location of the place mats daily, and encourage the children to find their own. As the children begin to recognize each other's names, they may (one or two at a time) take turns arranging the place mats for the entire group.

7.   When you are all taking a walk, call the children's attention to signs around the school. An exit sign will probably be the first they see. Stop signs, names of stores, or advertising signs may be read. Indicate the word you want the child to read by placing your hand under it, if possible, and moving your hand from left to right.

8.   Bring the children's attention to labels on cereal boxes, clothing, candy, toys, soap, record jackets, or even pictures from magazines.

The process a young child goes through during the early stages of literacy is a complex one that has frustrated and challenged experts for years. However, one idea that has met with rather widespread agreement is that early instruction should focus on *oral language* development in conjunction with beginning *reading* and *writing*.

Literacy: The Reading–Writing Connection

The preschool years are an exciting time of an individual's development. The children's world expands in so many different directions as fresh experiences lead to the development of new understandings, skills, and sensitivities. Among the most wondrous of these new acquisitions are the skills of reading and writing. Reading and writing have a common element—written language—and are both activities that involve *meaning-making*. For the purposes of this text, early literacy is defined as the purposeful efforts that children make to *get meaning from written symbols* and *convey meaning with written symbols*. Literacy is related to other meaning-making activities, including talking. Because of this connection, reading and writing efforts in the preschool environment should be initiated and sustained by teacher interactions that are supportive and encouraging. Teachers create situations that offer the same chance-taking spirit to young readers and writers as parents and caregivers extend to infants as they begin to talk. When a baby refers to water as "wa-wa," we do not initiate a remedial lesson during which the infant is given repeated practice until she comes close to the adult pronunciation, "water." Instead, we are thrilled that the child has identified the name of something and show our joy by interacting with her in a way that bestows loving support. We encourage infants and toddlers to take these chances, for if they are constantly corrected and criticized, they may become hesitant to try out new skills and abilities as they grow older.

When a child experiments with writing, however, and puts down "BT" for "boat," adults often see such effort as error-prone and worry that the child's lifetime writing skills will be adversely affected if the "error" is not corrected. The focus is on error (the child doesn't yet know conventional spelling) rather than on a demonstrated effort to explore the system of written language. Why do some adults have confidence that children will develop accuracy in speech without constant correction, yet respond differently to beginning writers? Perhaps a major reason is that they see learning to write as a different process than learning to speak, and, therefore, one in need of a different approach. We must, however, view all language processes as interrelated. In doing so, we must provide opportunities for children to explore print and allow children to discover how the system of written language works.

Early Writing Efforts

Initial interactions with print are often referred to as scribble-writing and "invented" spelling. Children are scribblers from the time they hold their first crayon. At about the age of one year, children will grasp a crayon in a fist-grip and joyously make random marks on anything available. This stage is called *uncontrolled scribbling;* the child does not intentionally place marks on the writing surface, but randomly scatters them about. The purpose is definitely one of sensory pleasure rather than an actual intent to create something. This stage of scribbling has often been compared to the babbling stage of oral language production; the sound and mark are both made at random.

Gradually, after much playing with crayons, chalk, and markers, the child's scribbles become more controlled. The *controlled scribble stage* ushers in a time when children gain more control over their efforts and become increasingly systematic in their attempts. They often create circles, squares, or triangles; lines go deliberately up and down, and dots are often diffused throughout the display. This is when young children first begin to demonstrate an understanding of the function of print. Their horizontal, linear efforts represent the writing they see in their everyday world. We can clearly see that children distinguish between drawing and writing by looking at a sample of each, produced by a three-and-a-half-year-old child, on the same piece of paper. Jeff's picture of a volcano and his story about it appear in Figure 8–1. The "story," even though it contains no recognizable letters, appears at the top. Notice that it looks linear and more like writing than the circular picture immediately below. The story and the picture were related. This is the story Jeff told: "The volcano had a big fire and lots of smoke." Words often burst forth like a volcano erupting from the young child who is encouraged to represent ideas with written symbols. Many

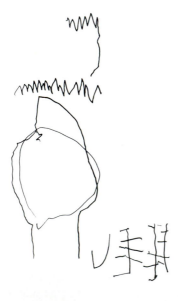

Figure 8–1

Figure 8–2

children at this stage enjoy attempting to personalize their picture story by signing it with their names. Can you find Jeff's signature in the lower right-hand corner?

As children accumulate more experiences with writing, they usually begin to closely approximate the form of real letters—although they scribble most of the time (see Figure 8–2). When Jeff was four, some of his designs looked like letters (notice the uppercase M, O, and N) in the writing sample, but a great deal of his effort resulted in scribbles. It is very common to find letters and other forms (or even names) mixed in with scribble-writing during this transition stage.

With added experience and encouragement, children become aware of how lines can be formed and combined to make real letters; their efforts contain less scribble-writing and more mock writing (letter-like forms). A sample of mock writing is shown in Figure 8–3. Here, only actual letters, or close approximations of them, are displayed. Notice that matters of orientation (the O is much larger than the other letters) and accuracy in the use of lines (the E and F are inaccurate) are not yet under complete control.

Figure 8–3

Figure 8–4

During the kindergarten year, children can produce writing that resembles standard forms very closely. Many have learned to create mature letter forms and are beginning to understand spatial placements. They often place their writing above or below a picture to tell a story (see Figure 8–4). The effort seems to communicate, "I'll draw a picture and then write a story about it." This brings us to one of the most mature forms of preschool expression—drawing, talking, and writing to communicate meaning. Even when children reach this stage, however, they still may use forms of scribble- or mock-writing. One kindergarten teacher experienced this when she saw Martin's scribble-writing as shown in Figure 8–5. Martin had regularly demonstrated an ability to follow accepted writing conventions, so his teacher was mystified by the seeming regression of skills. After talking with Martin, however, she discovered that Martin wasn't regressing, but experimenting with what he called "big people" writing (cursive writing). Look carefully at his sample and you will see some actual cursive letters mixed in with the scribbles. Despite the fact that they have achieved a basic skill in writing, many children will continue to experiment.

Figure 8–5

Learning to Write Words

The mechanical aspect of children's writing, then, progresses through a series of scribble stages to the point where youngsters create fairly good approximations of letters of the alphabet. The second aspect of children's writing picks up from here. Once children discover the sounds of the letters, learn how to print, and understand that oral language can be made into written words, they become extremely excited about making words of their own. Some will still enjoy copying words from signs and labels in the room (e.g., copying "crayon" from a box of crayons), whereas others will prefer to create their own stories—especially if they have had a stimulating experience. Judy displayed strong motivation for story writing after going on a field trip with her class (see box below).

Whatever the children's motivation, they will demonstrate some interesting early story creations. One of Mike's early story creations is shown in Figure 8–6. He proudly read his story to the teacher: "One day a little rabbit came hopping along the path. Then he saw that he had went the wrong way. Oh, oh!" Mike's story is an example of writing first words and stories; children's first stories contain many words that do not resemble conventional spellings. This is a process commonly referred to as *invented spelling*.

Rhea Paul has divided invented spellings into four stages.[34] The *most elementary stage* involves writing the first letter or phoneme (sound) of each word or syllable. "*F*" is quite satisfactory for "*Friday,*" for example. In the *second stage* the child adds the final phoneme to a word or syllable, still omitting short-vowel sounds: "*HL*" for "*hill*" or "*WZ*" for "*was.*" At this stage, long vowels seem to appear: "*FIR*" for "*fire*" and "*BOT*" for "*boat.*" Paul maintains that it is in the *third stage,* when children begin to separate short-vowel sounds from surrounding consonants, that the most interesting results appeared. She found that children appeared to be consistent in the vowel they choose to represent each vowel sound, even though it may not have been the "correct" vowel. For example, "BCUZ" ("because") and "CUZN" ("cousin") were

▶▶▶▶▶▶

A group of five-year-olds had just returned from a trip to the zoo. The teacher knew they were still intensely interested in what they saw, so she conducted a very lively discussion. When all contributions were exhausted, the teacher asked the class to draw a picture of their favorite part of the trip. All the children began working busily except Judy. Puzzled by this reaction of a normally active student, the teacher walked over to Judy to assess the situation. Judy informed her teacher with wide-eyed determination, "I think I'll write about my favorite part instead of draw it."

The teacher, pleased with Judy's enthusiasm, took her to a work table and gave her a large sheet ($18'' \times 24''$) of newsprint and a marker. Judy grasped the marker and began to write her first word.

Figure 8–6 Story with invented spellings

written with the same vowel sound by one child. This shows that even at an early age, before any formal teaching of vowel sounds, children seem to recognize that vowel sounds are separate from surrounding consonants, and attempt to represent them in a regular way. In the *fourth stage* of invented spelling, spelling moves closer to standard forms—sight-vocabulary words are spelled correctly, and stories tend to be a little longer.

Donald J. Richgels recommends that such experimentation be encouraged because it is a step leading to the reading act itself.

> It is important to note that children experiment with writing by scribbling, by drawing letterlike forms, by incorporating writing in pictures, and by using letters in a nonsystematic way (which is not spelling, invented or otherwise) before they begin using invented spelling. And these experimentations should be accepted and encouraged. Teachers should not try to hurry children beyond this stage so that they can get to more readable invented spellings.[35]

Invented spelling, then, is an important phase of development during which children work out the real meaning of letter-to-sound correspondences.

Young children's early writing efforts should be supported with plentiful writing materials.

Watching preschool or kindergarten children write their own words or stories is a lesson in unshackled creativity. They diligently attack each challenging word with great determination, often coming up with such unique solutions that teachers have been heard to comment, "Look at that word. I would never have thought of spelling it that way, but when you come to think of it, all the basic sounds are there!" Actually, the children involve themselves in the process of invented spelling to the same degree that they become involved in any other classroom activity that encourages them to express their own ideas. Rhea Paul explained:

> Just as at first they often are more concerned with spreading the paint or smearing the paste than with what the final picture looks like, it is the act of figuring a word out that intrigues them far more than the conclusion they come to. . . . The product—the way they actually decide to spell the word—appears to be greatly subordinate to the thinking process that leads to the decision. . . . [But] as soon as children learned the standard spelling for a word, they would spontaneously substitute it for their own.[36]

Through the use of spontaneous writing, we offer children a chance to use their almost intuitive knowledge of the English language before they begin formal reading instruction. Recall that this is the way most experts also explain the child's acquisition of the spoken language: They use creativity to produce words and sentences. For both the oral and the written aspects of language learning, early instruction should build on the children's strengths and on the unique way that those strengths can be involved in using reading and writing as tools of communication.

Through observation of children at work and active interaction with them, you will become sensitive to their levels of development and be able to plan appropriate learning experiences for writing. Your writing program should provide:

1. Daily opportunities for children to express themselves naturally and creatively through writing
2. A writing center where children obtain writing tools (pencils, crayons, watercolor markers, and both lined and unlined paper) to record their thoughts on paper
3. Other tools to use while experimenting with writing—a typewriter, word processor, or wooden and magnetic letters
4. Bank forms, memo pads, prescription pads, school forms, order pads, and other items to encourage writing at the play center in your classroom

SOME FINAL THOUGHTS

One of the most wondrous phenomena of early childhood is the emergence of language. Within a short time youngsters accumulate words and put them together into sentences. They acquire language in such mystifying ways that some professionals have labeled children "linguistic geniuses." Children seem to recognize patterns of language and internalize them into their own system of communication, regardless of the fact that they tend to over-generalize English grammatical patterns. (I have five toes and two foots.") Children's use of language tells you how they think. They attach word labels to actions and objects, using words to think. Children learn words through interactions with their environment. What does this mean for teachers?

Specifically, you enhance language development by serving as a model and stimulator of good language. You create a climate that promotes free, informal discussion; use stories, conversations, and other planned activities. You do not pressure the children into mature patterns of speaking until they are ready, for such pressures often cause children to develop anxieties that can lead to stuttering or stammering. Children who are not allowed to progress at their own rate may even eventually lose the urge to talk in the classroom.

The experiences we provide for reading and writing are much like those we provide for children as they learn the spoken language. We offer chances to act on the environment and to build knowledge through experience. Literacy thrives on a natural approach that begins during early years, as parents read to their children and allow them to handle books. These "lap techniques" are the single most important factor in early literacy. The roots of literacy are in early experiences with books and print, practically from the time children are born. The interest and skills children acquire through such natural involvement with books should continue in school, where teachers read aloud children's favorite books, often over and over again.

Similarly, early literacy benefits from programs that expose children to print. Meaningful language experience materials, word labeling, and correlating writing and reading are three major recommendations. Many teachers presently offer excellent natural reading programs, but pressures exerted by various sources have forced some to add developmentally inappropriate experiences. As a result, some programs stress isolated word drill with dittos and workbooks that have little or no meaning for young children. In designing your program, keep in mind that a developmentally appropriate program should be language-centered. It must capitalize on existing language competence and consider the conditions that foster literacy development.

NOTES

1. Robert D. Armstrong and W. J. Gage, in L. M. Logan, V. G. Logan, and L. Paterson, eds., *Creative Communication: Teaching the Language Arts* (Montreal: McGraw-Hill Ryerson, 1972), p. 9.

2. Kornei Chukovsky, *From Two to Five* (Berkeley, CA: University of California Press, 1968), p. 7.

3. David McNeill, "Developmental Psycholinguistics," in Frank Smith and G. A. Miller, eds., *The Genesis of Language* (Cambridge, MA: MIT Press, 1966), p. 36.

4. Alvina T. Burrows, "Children's Language," in Paul S. Anderson, ed., *Linguistics in the Elementary School Classroom* (New York: Macmillan, 1971), p. 90.

5. Marjorie J. Kostelnik, Laura C. Stein, and Alice P. Whiren, "Children's Self-Esteem: The Verbal Environment, " *Childhood Education, 65,* no. 1 (Fall 1988): 29–30. Reprinted by permission of Kostelnik, Stein, and Whiren; and the Association for Childhood Education International, 11501 Georgia Ave., Suite 315, Wheaton, MD. Copyright © 1988 by the Association.

6. Marjorie V. Fields and Dorris Lee, *Let's Begin Reading Right* (Columbus, OH: Merrill, 1987), p. 29.

7. Theresa M. Brown and Lester L. Lammack, "Let's Talk a Poem," *Young Children, 44,* no. 9 (September 1989): 49.

8. Betty Coody, *Using Literature With Young Children* (Dubuque, IA: William C. Brown, 1983).

9. Frank B. May, *Reading as Communication,* 2nd ed. (Columbus, OH: Merrill, 1986), p. 173.

10. Myna M. Haussler, "A Young Child's Developing Concepts of Print," in Angela Jaggar and M. Trika Smith-Burke, *Observing the Language Learner* (Newark, DE: International Reading Association, 1985), pp. 73–74.

11. Majorie V. Fields, Katherine Spangler, and Dorris M. Lee, *Let's Begin Reading Right: Developmentally Appropriate Beginning Literacy,* 2nd ed. (Columbus, OH: Merrill/Macmillan, 1991), p. 29.

12. R. C. Anderson et al., *Becoming a Nation of Readers: The Report of the Commission on Reading* (Washington, DC: The National Institute of Education), p. 79.

13. Evelyn B. Freeman and J. Amos Hatch, "Emergent Literacy: Reconceptualizing Kindergarten Practice," *Childhood Education, 66,* no. 1 (Fall 1989): 22.

14. N. Hall, *The Emergence of Literacy* (Portsmouth, NH: Heinemann, 1987), p. 10.

15. Lloyd O. Ollila and Margie I. Mayfield, eds., *Emerging Literacy* (Boston: Allyn and Bacon, 1992), p. 3.

16. Shirley C. Raines and Robert Canady, *The Whole Language Kindergarten* (New York: Teachers College Press, 1990), p. 4.

17. "Literacy Development and Pre-First Grade." Brochure from the International Reading Association (Newark, DE: International Reading Association, 1985). Reprinted with permission of the International Reading Association.

18. B. Cambourne, *The Whole Story: Natural Learning and the Acquisition of Literacy in the Classroom* (Auckland, New Zealand: Ashton Scholastic, 1988), p. 4.

19. Nancy Larrick, "Home Influences on Early Reading," *Today's Education, 64,* no. 4 (November/December 1975): 77–79.

20. Linda Leonard Lamme, "Reading with an Infant," *Childhood Education, 56,* no. 8 (April/May 1980).

21. Ibid.

22. Judith A. Schickedanz, *More Than the ABCs: The Early Stages of Reading and Writing* (Washington, DC: National Association for the Education of Young Children, 1986), p. 31.

23. Ida Santos Stewart, "Kindergarten Reading Curriculum," *Childhood Education, 61,* no. 5 (May/June 1985): 356.

24. Leon Lionni, "What a Child Sees in a Picture Book," *The Disney Channel Magazine* (March 1–April 11, 1987): 40.

25. Maurice Sendak, *Where the Wild Things Are* (New York: Harper & Row, 1963).

26. M. W. Autlis, *Developing Readers in Today's Elementary Schools* (Boston: Allyn and Bacon, 1982), p. 3.

27. Judith A. Schickendanz, *More Than the ABCs: The Early Stages of Reading and Writing* (Washington, DC: National Association for the Education of Young Children, 1986), pp. 51–59.

28. A. Ninio and J. S. Bruner, "The Achievement and Antecedents of Labeling," *Journal of Child Language, 5,* (1978): 1–15.

29. Shirley Brice Heath, "What No Bedtime Story Means: Narrative Skills at Home and School," *Language in Society, 11,* no. 1 (April 1982): 49–76.

30. Leslie M. Morrow, "Reading and Retelling Stories: Strategies for Emergent Readers," *The Reading Teacher, 38,* no. 9 (May 1985): 870–875.

31. Don Holdaway, *The Foundations of Literacy* (Sydney, Australia: Ashton Scholastic, 1979).

32. Judith K. Cassady, "Beginning Reading with Big Books," *Childhood Education, 65,* no. 1 (Fall 1988): 18–23.

33. From *Brown Bear, Brown Bear, What Do You See?* by Bill Martin, Jr. Copyright © 1967, 1983 by Holt, Rinehart and Winston. Reprinted by permission of Henry Holt and Company, Inc.

34. Rhea Paul, "Invented Spelling in Kindergarten," *Young Children, 32,* no. 3 (March 1976): 195–200.

35. Donald J. Richgels, "Experimental Reading with Invented Spelling (EIRS): A Preschool and Kindergarten Method," *The Reading Teacher, 40,* no. 6 (February 1987): 523.

36. Rhea Paul, "Invented Spelling," pp. 199–200.

CHAPTER 9

Motivating Creative Expression Through Art

Art experience in the preschool classroom is a creative process that encourages self-expression and original thinking. Because young children enjoy this opportunity to express original thought naturally, lines, squiggles, circles, human heads with arms growing out of the face, and even hands containing seven fingers characterize the drawings or paintings of the very young. Youngsters are not concerned about "inaccuracies"; they are absorbed in the *doing,* not the done. Good schools for young children provide varied art experiences not because they want children to conform to adult standards of what is good in art, but because they understand that the originality and inventiveness involved in the activity contributes greatly to the child's total development. This chapter deals with art as a valuable avenue of creative self-expression and suggests strategies for helping develop natural art tendencies at each developmental level. As you read, use the following questions to guide your thinking.

- How have Lowenfeld and Brittain categorized the separate stages of children's artistic development? How can we apply their ideas to early childhood art programs?

- How can art experiences contribute to cognitive growth?

- In what ways do free art expressions contribute to the child's emotional world?

- What are some popular types of art activities commonly offered in early childhood classrooms?

- How do teachers offer guidance in an area like art, where freedom of expression is so important?

An Episode to Ponder

Before the children arrive, Ms. Walls checks the easel area that was so popular among the children yesterday. She makes sure the materials are fresh and clean. There must be containers of clean paint—red, blue, green, yellow, black, and white—at each easel. Ms. Walls checks the supply of paper and examines the brushes to make sure they are ready to go.

During free play, Jerelene approaches the easels, grasps a brush and begins to experiment with the paint. Ms. Walls stops by to watch for a minute. Then she says, "The colors you chose make me feel so restful and calm." Jerelene smiles and tells Ms. Walls, "Green and blue are my favorite colors." Ms. Walls nods and adds, "They are very pleasant colors to look at."

Everyday, in preschools around the country, lucky young children experience the delight of allowing their imagination and creativity to flow freely. They are eager originators—always willing to try new ways of doing things. They find comfort and joy in expressing their inner existence, especially when they are offered encouragement in their exploration by wise, understanding adults.

Artistic expression is an excellent avenue through which children release their creative abilities. Youngsters enjoy the possibilities presented by various media and love to experiment with form and color; some children may simply engage in sense-pleasure play without concern for the depiction of people or things. They become involved in art experiences as easily as they breathe. You may find that some children are content to swish their hands pleasurably through finger paints, whereas others are more concerned with representing clouds, grass, the sun, or trees. Whatever the individual inclination, children revel in the use of paints, markers, clay, scissors, crayons, paper, and other art media and tools.

To some adults, however, whatever the children do with art materials is messy—their scribbles or exploratory activities seem to be only unimportant blobs or meaningless jumbles of line and form. E. Eisenstadt gives one preschool teacher's account of a parent's reaction to her child's "water painting":

> I gave back a water painting today. The water had dried, so basically, what Adam proudly presented to his mother was a wrinkled piece of white paper. She asked him what it was. When she received no answer, she said, "Adam, there's nothing there at all, so let's throw it out and take home one that has a pretty picture on it. Can you make me a pretty picture tomorrow?"[1]

Believing that the visible end product is what art is all about, such parents or teachers fail to understand or appreciate free-form expression. They resort to supplying patterns, follow-the-dot books, coloring books, or dittoed forms to ensure a recognizable, "pretty" outcome. Such material, though, can hinder the creative freedom that youngsters seek and give them the mistaken idea that there is only one

Freedom to express oneself creatively is the overriding goal of early art experiences.

correct way to express oneself artistically—the way identified by the teacher or adult. Sydney Gurewitz Clemens takes great exception to this damaging approach:

> Why no precut or patterned activity? It doesn't promote creativity for us all to make the same product. Each of us needs to make a different statement about who we are and how we see the world. How about giving children a circle for a cat's body and another circle for the head and a tail and having them glue the pieces together? Is that an art experience? Projects of this sort are designed to please adults. What they teach children is that their own work is not valuable. They could never make a cat as tidy as the one you precut. They could never draw a house as realistic as the one on the ditto. So, little as they are, in the face of these projects they give up, knowing they can't do art for themselves. Child-centered teachers avoid such projects. Knowing that freeform art is a wonderful means for people to express and heal themselves, we make sure to give children materials that will take any child's imprint and rejoice with the children over the beauty and differences in their creations.[2]

Clemens asserts that free-form art should be a cornerstone of the daily program and that, "A daily program that immerses children in the arts is *developmentally appropriate*."[3] (The italics are mine.) Instead of imposing a set of standards children cannot hope to reach, teachers must help children come alive and express their own feelings and ideas uniquely. Olive R. Francks adds a final thought about encouraging creative expression through art:

> We must tread carefully within the realm of art at these early stages, from infancy to ages five or six, so that children may work out their own thoughts and feelings without the constraint of evaluation. We should provide time, space, place, materials for children, and then allow them the dignity of "doing their own thing." We should be patient, learn to wait generously, and be prepared for whatever evolves. Above all, we can be happy for the child creator, even if he or she does not create what we would like to have created for us.[4]

If for no other reason, children should be offered art experiences in your preschool classroom because they love it. If you give children access to good materials, the time to explore, and the respect to encourage free exploration, your classroom will burst with glee, self-confidence, and imagination. The child's total personality emerges as she becomes involved in artistic endeavors. But before you plan to offer art experiences to youngsters, you must be informed of *how* children develop their abilities and *what* they portray in their finished products. Such knowledge helps you interpret the child's work and set realistic expectation levels for it. Likewise, this knowledge guides you in selecting and planning your teaching strategies and materials.

DEVELOPMENTAL STAGES OF CHILDREN'S ART

Fortunately, most early childhood teachers today understand the importance of children's early free-form artistic creations. They are able to look at art with appreciative eyes, thanks to the efforts of two respected scholars—Viktor Lowenfeld and W. Lambert Brittain. These influential researchers have examined uncounted examples of children's art and categorized developmental stages of progression—from using art media for the pure sensory pleasure it brings to actually creating recognizable representations. A summary of their findings follows.

Lowenfeld and Brittain describe developmental stages in art as following this predictable sequence.[5]

The Scribbling Stage

We can make the analogy that scribbling is to drawing as babbling is to speech. It is an early form of expression during which observable marks are usually random and disorganized. The child experiments without even knowing how to hold a crayon to make marks during his initial efforts. The crayon may be held upside down or sideways, but always with a clenched fist. Holding it in whatever position pleases him, the child then sweeps his arm in large arcs over the paper until a disordered collection of lines appears, creating a pattern called **disordered scribbling.** The child scribbles mostly for the sensory pleasure it brings and often draws a continuous line without removing his crayon from the paper. He does not even think of trying to represent something. Adults should not try to encourage children to draw something during the scribble stage.

Following repeated disordered scribbling experiences spread over about six months, children begin to sense that there is a connection between what their arms are doing and the marks appearing on the paper. They start to exercise visual control over the marks they are making. They are still not able to draw objects in their environment, but that is of no concern to them. Children will energetically exercise their new discovery by repeating horizontal or vertical lines or circles. They no longer keep the crayon on the paper from start to finish, but pick it up to start each new line. And because they pick up their crayons from the paper, children like to try different colors. Because the child has begun to master scribbling, this phase is accordingly labeled **controlled scribbling.**

The third scribbling stage is referred to as **naming of scribbling,** a period usually beginning at about three-and-a-half. The child's drawings are virtually identical to controlled scribbles, but they are given descriptive names. The child may say, "This is my cat, Mickey" or "I am sleeping in my bed," although his lines portray no hint of such scenes. This phase is important because it signals a beginning of the understanding that marks on paper have a relationship to the real world. Up to this time, scribbling has been primarily an enjoyable sensory activity. Now it is understood as a symbolizing medium involving deeper mental activity.

The Preschematic Stage

From about the age of four until about the age of seven most young children attempt to make their first representations of their environment. Drawing becomes an exciting experience for these youngsters—the concept of reality in art is appearing. Their first representational efforts are usually people with whom they have had repeated or significant contact. Objects of special meaning are also drawn: pets, trees, houses, or flowers. People are usually shown with only a round head and two stick feet, and other objects may be randomly scattered on the paper, but as the child matures details gradually are included.

The Schematic Stage

The final stage of immediate concern to early childhood practitioners starts when a child is about seven and lasts until he is about nine. Here children represent parts of their environment with quite accurate symbols. The human figure remains central in most children's drawings and now becomes readily recognizable. Features also become differentiated—fingers and toes are no longer "sunbursts" and the eye shapes are different from nose and mouth. The child becomes quite conscious of order in his drawings and places everything deliberately on a *base line* (a horizontal line representing any base on which a person is standing or an object is placed). If the child draws an outdoor scene, a blue line at the top of the picture usually represents the sky. This is a joyfully spontaneous age during which children's art becomes quite decorative.

For an illustration of artwork done by children during each developmental phase, refer to Figure 9–1. Despite the fact that their drawings made at about three-and-a-half to four years of age represent people and objects, most children are not yet concerned that their creative products conform to adult expectations or standards. For example, body parts may be jumbled. Parts of the face may not be arranged accurately, or the arms may grow from the head. The sky may be green, not blue. Children do not feel the adult need to conform to stereotypes for their art, and do not much care whether a sky is blue or green. One kindergarten child, for example, proudly brought home a finished springtime ditto that his teacher had asked the class to color in as she expected—a yellow chick that had orange feet and beak and was carrying a blue umbrella. However, this youngster was puzzled about one thing: "Why didn't my teacher like my picture? I think it's beautiful." The boy had received

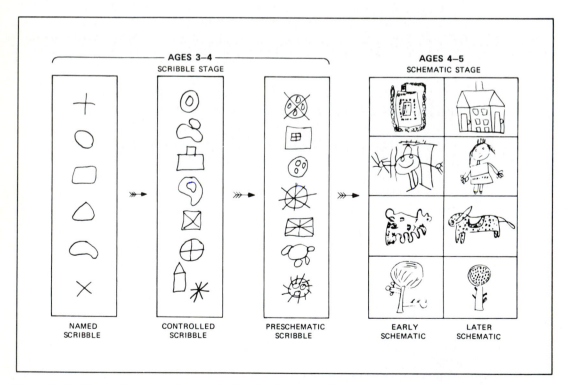

Figure 9–1 Shape, design, and stages in the development of children's drawing. Reproduced by permission of John Wiley and Sons, Inc., New York, N.Y., from *Development of the Child* by David Elkind and Irving B. Weiner, 1978.

a smiley face at the top of his paper (indicating need for improvement) rather than a star (good work) and didn't know why.

"I think your picture is beautiful, too," replied his father. "Did you ask your teacher why she gave you a smile face?"

"She said I didn't use the right colors," answered the child. Probing further, his father learned that the youngster had used brown and tan for the chick and red for the umbrella—instead of the colors expected by the teacher. "Why didn't you color it the way the teacher asked you to?" asked the father. "Because the other kids had all those crayons and there weren't any for me. I like my brown chick better, anyway."

Olive R. Francks advises teachers not to place such constraints or unrealistic expectations on children. "They have not yet reached the stage of artistic development when 'reality' is perceived as the adult perceives it. . . . The child's world is filled with objects that change shape and form while they are being created."[6] By restricting children's natural need to express themselves creatively, we run the risk of having

Art materials should encourage children to explore and express their ideas freely.

children become so obsessed with correct form and design that they lose interest in art. Diane Papalia and Sally Olds elaborate:

> Usually after the first few years of school a child who once happily drew with crayons abandons all interest in art. Thus, we have a sad irony. As children develop better control of their hands, their interest in putting the growing skills to use wanes.[7]

Lowenfeld and Brittain have claimed that passage through each of the developmental stages is a natural phenomenon—children must pass through one stage before they can attain the next. However, such movement is stimulated not by overt "teaching," but by providing an open environment in which the children freely bring forth and exercise what they already possess. When given opportunities to do so, they naturally progress through the developmental levels. In effect, the children are left alone to draw what they like, while the teacher acts as a guide and inspiring force. Any application of external standards or patterns is considered a constraining force producing only inhibitions and frustrations. Rhoda Kellogg states:

> The child is a very experienced master of self-taught art. . . . In fact, Picasso said that adults should not teach children to draw but should learn from them. . . . Children left alone to draw what they like, without the interference of adult guidance, usually develop a store of gestalts, which enable them to reach the culminating stage of self-taught art. From there, if they are especially gifted, they may develop into great artists, unspoiled by the stenciled minds of well-meaning adults.[8]

Creativity, then, is justification enough to emphasize a developmentally sound art program that provides a variety of art materials within an atmosphere of free-form expression. Other benefits are discernible, as well, such as *emotional expression* and *cognitive growth*.

EMOTIONAL ASPECTS OF CHILDREN'S ART

A major aspect of children's art is the dimension of *feeling*, a view that contends that children's artistic products reflect their emotions. Katherine Read, one of the leading proponents of this idea, offers the following lucid explanation of how art is related to children's emotions:

> Experiences in the graphic and plastic arts offer [an] avenue through which individuals release their feelings and find satisfactions. It is [an] avenue of expression which may serve as an outlet throughout the life of the individual. . . . The anxious attention on the *product* [italics mine] rather than the *process* [italics mine], the coloring books, and other "patterns" that were imposed on us have all served pretty effectively to prevent most of us from expressing ourselves through art. Yet art is an important means of expression and of draining off feeling as well as a source of satisfaction. . . .

> As we ourselves work with children, we must try to safeguard their use of art media as a means of self-expression. For every child, art can serve as an outlet for feeling if the process is emphasized more than the product. It does not matter that there are differences in ability just as there are in music. Given an easel, paper, and paint, and no directions, every child will paint. For some children painting will remain an important avenue through which they can express feeling all through their lives.[9]

Read, therefore, advocates the use of free, unstructured painting as the major avenue of emotional release through art. Through such activity, she believes, we gain a great deal of insight into what children are feeling.

However, you should resist the temptation to act as an amateur psychologist as you review your children's artwork. We are not trained psychologists and have not had the level of professional training to allow us to interpret children's art accurately. One teacher, for example, became highly concerned when looking at a child's explosive picture, a picture with small bursts of color laid over a foreboding, eerily dark easel painting. Wondering just what this representation "meant," the teacher's interpretations ran the gamut from the child's possible deep-seated hatred of someone to his feeling of extreme anxiety about some condition at home or school. Finally, she decided to approach the child and ask him to tell her about the painting. His response: "This is a hurricane. I saw one just like it on TV yesterday." Relieved, this teacher discovered that most children's art has easy explanations.

COGNITIVE ASPECTS OF CHILDREN'S ART

This feature of artistic development asserts that children's art grows and develops in direct relationship to their ability to conceptualize, that is, to internally (mentally) represent objects and events. By age two, this representational ability has evolved in the sensorimotor capacity, which enables children to understand the permanent existence of objects. This means that the child is able to understand that objects continue to exist even though they cannot be seen. However, according to Barry J. Wadsworth, "There is no evidence of the existence of images in the mind of the sensori-motor child."[10] As the sensorimotor child moves into preoperational thought (two to seven years), she not only acquires the ability to form mental images, but also gradually develops the skill to represent those images symbolically. Because these internal (mental) representations of objects and past experiences are not yet accurate perceptions, children's drawings bear very little resemblance to what they are intended to represent. It is not until children pass into the stage of concrete operations (age seven to eleven) that they are able to form accurate mental images and represent all of the salient features of objects or events.

These stage-associated thought processes explain why the preoperational child's use of crayon, pencil, brush, or marker amounts to basic scribbling. At first, there is no thought given to representing something through drawing. Over the course of the preoperational years, as the ability to form increasingly precise mental images evolves, children attempt to represent things through their drawings, and their efforts become more realistic. Artistic expression appears to evolve through stages as described by Brearly:[11]

1. *The stage of synthetic incapacity.* The child neglects the size proportions, distance orientation, and perspective relationships. This stage is normally found to last up until the ages of six or seven and is accounted for by the child's inability to completely "pull together" all the elements involved in his mental images.

2. *The stage of intellectual realism.* The child represents what he knows rather than what he sees. For example, children will often drawn a human figure completely clothed, but with a circle placed on the skirt or blouse. Since the child becomes very sensitive to navels at this age (six to nine years) he paints his "bellybutton" even though he cannot see it. He knows it is there and feels compelled to represent it.

3. *The stage of visual realism.* The child, beginning at age nine or ten, begins to show a more complete understanding of spatial relationships. He draws only those objects or parts of objects that can be seen and shows a more sophisticated knowledge of size and space.

Cognitive theory emphasizes that the child's ability to represent objects and events through art develops primarily to the extent that she has been able to actively experience things within her environment. These direct experiences are transformed into mental images and gradually those images are converted into their pictorial representations. This evolution of artistic expression has direct application to Piaget's conception of language acquisition. Piaget views the child as progressing from the need to interact with real objects (sensorimotor) into a period of life when the child creates and expresses mental images of those objects (preoperational). Through those periods and into the concrete operations stage, the child's accumulated experiences lead to a third level of representation—*sign*, or words. These three types of representation are referred to as *signifiers*:

1. *Index:* The child has a pure visual perception of an object. When an individual views a pencil, for example, his perceptive abilities operate on it— that is, eyes focus on the pencil, perceive its form, detect its color, and so on. The mental image formed from such a process is a true picture of something directly observed, and meaning comes only from such direct observation.

2. *Symbol:* The child deals not with the object itself, but with representations of objects. Piaget refers to this process as "internal imitation." For example, the child may signify his driving of a car by imitating the sound of a honking horn, or may use tempera paint to symbolize his idea of a flower. The child does not need the real object, but forms an intellectual construction of it.

3. *Sign:* The most abstract representation of an object, this level relies on systems of words and language to communicate ideas. Index and symbol representations are considered *personal* signifiers because they communicate individual interpretations of objects, whereas sign representations are considered *social* signifiers because they utilize abstractions (words) that must be mutually agreed upon in order to have meaning. Sign signifiers are more abstract. The word *pencil,* for example, bears no resemblance to the real thing.

These three key Piagetian terms are illustrated in Figure 9–2.

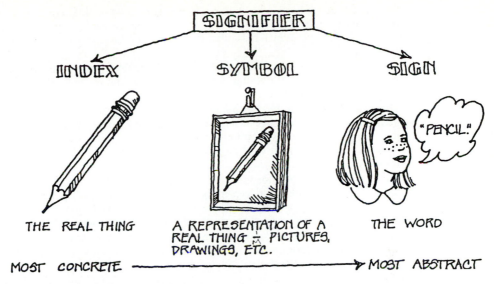

Figure 9–2 Piaget's levels of representation

To summarize, internalization of real things (*index*) or experiences allows the child to create *symbols*. The child then assimilates the objects and their symbolic representations into his mental schemes, and these eventually grow into the most abstract expression of thought—the *word (sign)*.

The educational implications of the cognitive developmental theory of art development are similar to those of the theory as it is applied in all other areas of the curriculum: (1) provide the child with rich experiences so that their mental images can be more accurately formed (bringing content to the child's expression), and (2) furnish a wide variety of materials so that the children acquire skills in using the media. With a combination of these two considerations, the cognitive developmental art program is designed to offer a developmental sequence of experiences that relate to each other and that lead to increasing depth of skill and understanding.

Children use art, then, to display their interpretations of the phenomena encountered in the world around them; these interpretations become more detailed and complex as adults interact appropriately with the children. Sylvia F. Burns closely examined typical preschool art experiences and identified many opportunities for learning. Her recommendations follow.

Crayons: Initial color perceptions, use of small muscles, perceptual-motor development, space and shape relationships, pictorial representation of the child's world. Counting, matching, grouping of colors, whole-part relationships, use of crayons for rubbings (paint over with thinned tempera—scientific learning that some things do not mix).

Paint: More complex medium than crayons involving another approach to perceptual learning. A constantly changing medium good for scientific learnings; looks different wet than when dry; opaqueness can be covered over (What is underneath the visible color?). Variations in texture, fluidity, different textured effects depending upon brushes used. Can be mixed to change color, dripped into another color. Can be used on materials other than paper (Is the result the same?). Excellent vocabulary builder.

Paper collage: Size relationships, shape discrimination, whole-part concepts, arrangement (design). A two-dimensional experience for reading. Problem solving (choosing from offered materials). Beginning math (classifying, counting shapes).

Three-dimensional collage: Separating and putting together of items. Bringing together shapes and elements in the world (important for beginning reading). Sorting, comparing, seeing similarities in items, classifying items of same shape and/or material. Use of items in new ways (seeing alternatives). Problem solving (how to fasten).

Clay: Sensory-tactile perceptions via shaping, rolling, pulling, pounding. Representation of personal ideas and perceptions of things in the world. Concepts of mass, change, relationship of parts to whole, fractions (whole, half, quarter). Math (many, few, larger, smaller, more), may also be used for addition and subtraction.

Finger paint: Compare consistency, motor development, change of form, development of control (not confined to small area). Visual-motor coordination, figure-ground perception. Vocabulary builder.[12]

The great variety of benefits associated with developmentally appropriate art programs can tempt us to push the child, to accelerate the process. Preschool teachers do not do this; we do not "teach" art, but set the conditions that allow children to explore and experiment naturally without the threat of adult intervention. We give children beautiful materials, arrange an appropriate art environment, and turn the children loose to create and to make new discoveries. Then, we stand back and exult in the splendor and variety of their creations.

PAINTING EXPERIENCES

Easels

Easel painting is among the most popular of all early childhood art experiences. Children enjoy experimenting with tempera paint and brushes as they freely express their concepts and emotions.

The easels should be located in a quiet, uncluttered part of the room, preferably near a sink—important in the case of accidental spills. (I like to set up the easels outdoors whenever the weather is nice.) Newspaper or long sheets of butcher paper should be spread on the floor to catch drips and spills. Make sure each child is protected with a plastic apron, smock, or parent's discarded shirt. If the child uses a parent's old long-sleeved shirt that buttons down the front, make sure it is worn backward with the sleeves rolled up.

If it is the children's first experience with painting at an easel, you may want to start with only two or three children while explaining how to use the materials. Use your own language, but a suitable introduction might go something like this:

"I wonder if you can guess what we're going to try today. We are going to paint. This is called an easel. It holds the paper we will paint on. Here is the paintbrush."

(Allow each child to hold a brush and examine it.) "I'll dip mine into the red paint, like this. See how I got paint on the bristles?" (Give the children a chance to do the same.) "Now I'll put my paint on the paper. Oh, look at my red line. It's your turn now. Dip the brush into the paint... get the paint on the bristles. Good, now you are ready to paint. Paint anything you like.... What can you do with your paintbrush?"

The children should be encouraged to experiment freely with brush and paint. I usually recommend only one color during the first painting experiences—children become so excited by the sensory pleasure of the activity that they often don't care whether there is one color or more than one. After a few easel experiences, however, new containers of paint could be introduced, each with its own brush. You do not want to have the children use the same brush for all colors. Dipping brushes in and out of the different colors would certainly muddy each. Do not expect the child to paint a "picture." This will come later—at first she is most interested in painting the colors and experimenting with a variety of lines and shapes. Some children, especially the shiest ones, will need a little encouragement to get started. You might want to assist in those cases, making sure not to interfere unless absolutely necessary. Consider the following dialogue.

Teacher: You painted the whole paper green, Paul. It must be one of your favorite colors.

Paul: Yeah, I like green color.

Teacher: I wonder how your painting would look if you added dots of another color.

Paul: How do you make dots?

Teacher: Let me show you. (*On another piece of paper the teacher shows Paul how to use his brush to make dots.*)

Paul: I want to make red dots.(*Paul experiments a bit with the red paint and makes some large, irregular dots. After some time he proudly announces that he has finished his painting.*)

Such informal instruction opens the door to new possibilities for the child and helps him increase his creative skills. In the same way, children can be led to experiment with thick lines, thin lines, circles, swirls, and various color combinations.

As the children complete their paintings, you should print their names using upper- and lowercase letters in the upper left-hand corner. This informally teaches the children to look at the upper left-hand corner when beginning to read pages in a book. Now you know which painting belongs to each child when it's time for them to go home. Placing the child's name on the painting also provides the child with a certain degree of recognition—knowing that the painting is truly hers. Children are very pleased with their artwork at this age and take pride in any special recognition they receive for it. They will often freely talk about their paintings, giving you an opportunity to write a title on the picture along with the child's name. However, don't demand that the child tell you about the picture. And don't ask the child what the painting is; usually children paint for the sheer pleasure of it and do not have a representation in mind. The child will take even more pride in her work if it is attractively displayed in the room.

Include the children in the cleanup process when they are finished at the easel. Arrange four labeled buckets in order to tell the children how to proceed. Bucket one

Easel painting helps give children satisfaction and self-confidence.

should be illustrated with paint-covered brushes and filled with soapy water. This is the wash bucket. Bucket two should be illustrated with clean brushes and filled with clear water. This is the rinse bucket. A tray for clean brushes should be next to the rinse bucket. Bucket three should be illustrated with a pair of paint-covered hands and filled with soapy water. This is for washing the hands. Bucket four is illustrated with clean hands and is filled with clear water for rinsing. A stack of paper towels completes the cleanup arrangements (see Figure 9–3).

Figure 9–3 Organizing an easel painting cleanup process.

Finger Painting Experiences

Finger painting is a second type of unstructured art activity that youngsters especially like because of its sensory appeal. Some children will want to draw pictures with the finger paint, but that is not the primary goal of the activity—you want to encourage free exploration and sensory pleasure. In order to do this, it is important to show the children how to use the finger paint in a pleasurable and stimulating way.

Begin by asking the children to put on their protective clothing, and then show them the special paper they will be using. They will be surprised by the slipperiness of the glazed surface. Commercially available finger paint paper is best, but adequate substitutes are easy to come by. The glossy surface of freezer paper is one option, or oilcloth or an enameled table top can be used as it is. After they have explored the painting surface, you will want to have them wet it in preparation for actually

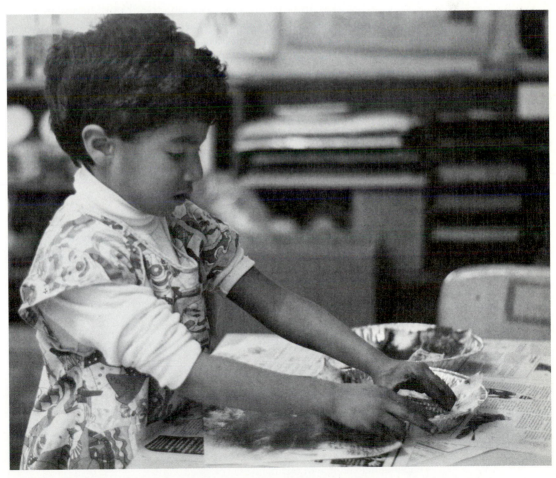

The slick, smooth feel of finger paint is a fun-filled, likable sensation.

using the finger paint. Demonstrate how to use a sponge to saturate the paper completely—this is almost as much fun as the painting itself! Now introduce the paint and demonstrate its use. Dip your fingers into the paint and perform a few long sweeps on the wet, glazed surface. Demonstrate how you can use fingers, palm, back of the hand, side of the hand, knuckles, fingernails, or even elbows and arms in the process. Encourage the children to go ahead and paint with their fingers and hands. Most children will enjoy finger painting, but occasionally you will run into a reluctant child. Try to encourage shy ones, but do not force them. Other types of painting–for instance, sponge painting or printing—may be a more satisfactory substitute.

Finger paint can be bought commercially, but teacher often prefer to mix their own with the children. Here is the formula:

Mix: 1 cup laundry starch with enough water to form a smooth, thick, creamy paste.

Stir: 1/2 cup soap flakes into the mixture. Continue to stir until lumps are gone.

Add: food coloring or powdered tempera paint for different colors.

For a change of texture, add sand, salt, coffee grounds, or fine sawdust to the finger paint.

For variation in color, put powder paint in salt shakers and let children shake their own colors onto wet, uncolored finger paint. This will help them learn color names, color concepts, and the concept of mixing colors to create new colors.

Other Painting Activities

It is important to encourage children as they explore and create. Saying, "You made zigzags with your finger," reinforces what the child has accomplished and calls other children's attention to a new observation. Merely saying, "Oh, that's nice," or "How wonderful!" offers less stimulation to the individual child and little to the awareness of other children. As you sense the children's interest to move into new painting challenges, the ideas suggested in the Painting Activities box on pages 322–323 may be introduced.

▷▷▷▷▷▷▷

PAINTING ACTIVITIES

- *Ink blots:* Prefold paper; drop thick paint onto paper from tongue depressors; refold; open. Several colors may be used to produce interesting designs.

- *String painting:* Dip short lengths of string into bowls of paint and let them fall on paper. Paper may also be folded, then string pulled out while the paper is held shut with one hand.

- *"Block" printing:* Dip objects into bowls of paint and press or rub on paper. Objects may be spools, corks, sink stoppers, sponges, jar lids, small blocks, scrub brushes, potatoes cut in shapes, combs, Q-tips, and so on.

- *Dry powder painting:* Put dry powder tempera paint in dishes at the easel or on the table, and use wads of wet cotton. Dab the dry paint onto a paper that has been completely moistened with a sponge and water.

- *Textured paint:* Mix a textured substance with paint for different effects, adding a little glue to ensure sticking. Use salt (which sparkles when dry), sand, fine sawdust, coffee grounds, or soap flakes.

- *Spatter painting:* You will need small wire screens on wood frames, toothbrushes, pans of thin paint, and various designs to set under the screen on protective paper. Objects may be paper silhouettes, leaves, cookie cutters, or a variety such as keys, forks, spoons, scissors, tongue depressors, and so on. Dip the toothbrush into the paint and run it over the wire screen. The paint will produce an interesting effect on the object below.

- *Table painting:* Use bowls of paint and short-handled brushes for a variety of individual painting activities.

- *Fancy paper:* Cut easel paper into unusual shapes to stimulate more elaborate design painting on children's part: circles, triangles, free form, Easter eggs, Christmas trees, houses, and so on.

- *Different types of surfaces may be painted:* Paper towels, colored construction paper, printed newsprint, finger-paint paper, cardboard boxes, egg cartons, wallpaper, magazine pages, dry-cleaning bags, wooden blocks, cloth, wood, clay, dried dough, seashells, stones, branches, paper bags, oil cloth, pine cones.

- *Window painting:* Bon Ami or Glass Wax may be colored with dry paint powder and used to paint windows.

- *Soap painting:* Whip soap powder and add dry paint powder. Paint on colored or white paper with brushes.

- *Crayon and paint:* Draw on paper with light-colored crayons, then cover with a wash of dark paint. Paint will not cover the crayon.

- *Detergent paint:* Paint mixed with detergent can be used to paint on glazed paper surfaces, plastic, aluminum foil, and glass.

- *Mixing colors:* The children can mix their own paints to be used at the table or easel. Put out colors in small amounts in paper cups or muffin tins and allow the children to mix. Mixing primary colors teaches pastel tints and grayed tones.

- *Water painting:* Large brushes and small pails of clear water can be used either outdoors or indoors to "paint" fences, walks, tricycles, sides of buildings, and so on.

DRAWING EXPERIENCES: CRAYONS, CHALK, AND MARKERS

The materials we choose for children are important not only for their usefulness in helping express thoughts, but also for helping children strengthen the fine-motor skills necessary for future school-related pursuits. Crayons, chalk, and marking pens are important parts of the curriculum because they offer a combination of such experiences—children not only create things; they also refine their small muscles in order to use the tools.

Because most children have probably used these tools at home, they are among the first art materials offered in an early childhood setting. Place these materials on a large table along with an ample supply of drawing paper, so that children are free to use the materials to create their own designs. When given such freedom, young children use crayons and related media in the same natural way as they paint.

Crayons

In general, young children's **crayons** are fat and come in eight basic colors. Manila paper is especially good for crayon work because it is durable, and the rough surface is especially suitable for giving a stronger, bolder color. Smooth paper tends to concentrate the waxy crayon deposits and not blend the colors as nicely. Encourage your children to experiment with crayons—a light touch gives a light color, more pressure gives a deeper color, several colors may be combined in one area, broad strokes with the side of an unwrapped crayon will cover wide areas quickly, and short strokes will tend to produce grassy or furry looks.

In addition to the major purpose—experimentation—crayons are used with young children in two other popular ways: crayon rubbings and crayon resists. **Crayon rubbings** are made by rubbing the side of a crayon over a sheet of thin paper covering any of a number of special textured shapes (cut paper, coins, wire screening, leaves, and so on) so that a silhouette of the textured material shows on the thin paper. **Crayon resists** are made with the idea that a waxy surface will repel water. The child begins by drawing a crayon design on manila paper with sufficient pressure so that a minimum of paper shows through. Most areas are crayoned, but the entire sheet should not be covered. Apply water paint freely over the entire paper, but do not scrub. The paint will adhere to all uncovered areas and make the crayon work stand out in brilliant contrast. Children react in awe to this process as they watch the crayon design magically appear from under the water colors.

Colored Chalk

This is a fascinating art tool for young children—the large, sturdy, comparatively soft sticks are enjoyable when used either wet or dry. Suggestions for use are similar to those for paints and crayons, so the same freedom of expression should be expected. Some special variations include:

- *Wet paper.* Paper dipped in water permits chalk to slide more easily, gives more fluid motion to drawing, and makes colors more brilliant. Construction paper or paper towels may be used.

- *Wet chalk.* Chalk is dipped in a bowl of water before being used on dry paper. The effects are similar to those of dry chalk on wet paper.

- *Buttermilk or diluted plastic starch.* Apply these liquids to wet paper. The chalk will stick to the paper after it dries.

- *Fixative.* This may be sprayed on dried chalk drawings or added to water for wet paper drawings. It prevents chalk dust from rubbing off. Common fixatives include hair spray, liquid starch sprayed from a bottle, or special fixatives purchased from school supply stores. Be sure to use these away from the children.

- *Chalkboard.* This large surface encourages expansive, sweeping motions. Children love to draw with chalk on the chalkboard.

Felt-Tip Markers

Markers have become a drawing tool that most children prefer, even more than crayons. The colors are bolder and the instrument glides more easily over paper. It is not surprising to watch children choose markers over crayons when given a choice of drawing implements.

Perhaps the greatest frustration in dealing with markers, however, is persuading the children to keep the markers capped. Be sure to stress this responsibility as you outline the appropriate procedures for using the markers. If you prefer, Crayola™ now makes a handy wooden storage rack that encourages children to return the markers to their caps when they are not using them.

COLLAGE MATERIALS (AND SCISSORS)

Little did Picasso and other prominent early 20th-century artists realize that their innovative technique of pasting scraps of cloth, discarded newspaper, string, and other materials on canvas would give birth to one of the most intriguing art mediums for young children today—the **collage.** Beginning collage experiences should center on the correct way to paste. Place some precut shapes on the table along with some paste. Show children the paste that you have put in an unbreakable dish, and invite them to pick some up and feel it. Talk about its texture and its stickiness. Then tell the children how it will be used: "We will use the paste to stick some of these shapes on a large sheet of paper. Take any shape you want and put some paste on the back. Be very careful; the glue is strong and you don't need too much." Demonstrate if necessary, since youngsters have a tendency to glob on excessive amounts at first, thinking that more paste ensures better sticking. "Pat on just a little like I am doing and be sure that it sticks." If you choose to use white school glue in squeezable bottles instead of paste (it sticks better and lasts longer), you will want to demonstrate it in a similar fashion. Encourage the children to keep using other shapes until they have a product they like. You don't need cut paper for these first collages—cloth scraps or a variety of junk materials do very well: velvet, burlap, fur scraps, seeds, twigs, weeds, feathers, styrofoam packaging popcorn, patterned gift wrap, paper doilies, aluminum foil, sponges, bottle caps, string, tinsel, cork, buttons, rice, eggshells, tiny pebbles, sequins, or glitter.

Once the children have some gluing or pasting skills, you may want to invite them to create their own shapes for a collage by tearing or cutting with scissors. *Tearing* is usually done by younger children but often persists in an art program even after the children have learned to cut. Cutting with scissors requires a much more refined level of eye-hand coordination than does tearing.

Young children enjoy using *scissors* (5″ blunt-ended scissors with rubber-covered handles should be provided) but may find them hard to use at first. For that reason, their first cutting experiences should be directed not to cutting out patterns or cutting along lines, but to random explorations with varieties of materials—construction paper, cloth, string, newspapers, magazines, tissue paper, and so on—using sharp scissors. Make sure that whatever material you choose can be cut easily. Poster paper and butcher paper are especially good beginner's papers. Most children will cut by holding the paper still and moving the scissors. But they may find it easier to hold the scissors steady and move the *paper*. Try it yourself and see if you agree. Children take special pleasure in the cutting actions and will not be too concerned about the final product at this stage of development (about age three or four). Cutting activities help children get used to handling scissors and develop the hand and finger muscles necessary for opening and closing the scissors. When these skills become fairly refined (about age four or five), the child is ready to cut out something he has thought about. For example, Carlos had come to the cutting table from the creative dramatics area, where he had been role-playing different scenes that fascinated him on a recent field trip. "I'm gonna make a punkin," he announced, and proceeded to cut out a figure crudely approximating an orange circle. The teacher held it up for the others to see and announced to the other children, "Maybe some of you would like to make pumpkins." Then he moved around the table and watched as several children gleefully cut out round, oblong, and squiggly-shaped pumpkins. Whatever the shape, though, the teacher was careful to praise and reassure each child for his cutting efforts.

From these preliminary cutting experiences, children are often led to practice cutting along preplanned patterns to refine their skills—wavy, jagged, straight, and curved lines seem most popular. Practice with these different patterns encourages finer eye-hand coordination and motor skills. Such maturity aids the child who wants to cut special shapes or important parts of pictures to add to his collage.

MODELING MATERIALS

Working with clay and other modeling media is a pleasant experience for all children. They love to squeeze, roll, thump, pat, pull, pinch, and play with these pliable materials in many creative ways. And that's what the child's first experience with this expressive medium should consist of—play and experimentation. Children will pull apart, add to, and experiment with all kinds of shapes— snakes, pancakes, balls, dishes with fragile edges, cups, and whatever else they can think of at the moment. Later these pieces will be combined in different forms. Most teachers provide Play-Doh (or a similar brand) for these early experimentations because it is among the most pliable of the modeling materials.

Although much of the dough used in early childhood classrooms is commercially manufactured, many teachers make their own. It is not only cheaper but often superior in quality. You can make a superior substitute for commercial dough by following this recipe:

2 cups flour
1 cup salt
2 tablespoons cooking oil (for a smooth texture)
1 tablespoon alum (optional—retards spoilage)

Method: Mix the flour and salt thoroughly. Add dry tempera paint for color or water with food coloring. Add enough water slowly so that the dough can be formed into a ball. Knead on a floured surface until pliable but not sticky.

Pushing, squeezing, and pounding dough and clay are engaging, expressive experiences for young children.

Children will enjoy playing with the dough by itself, but they often like other activities with it, too. Offer a rolling pin to roll the dough and cookie cutters to form the dough. Watch them make a batch of "cookies" with these materials! Some children may become interested in forming clay or dough figures. Again, there is no one right way to proceed. Some children will have definite ideas of what they want to make, whereas others may simply manipulate the clay until an emerging shape reminds them of something. A few children may work together to make various parts of a figure. Animals and other objects of all descriptions emerge as they give form to their ideas.

PRINT-MAKING ACTIVITIES

The printing process involves using paint and things that can form patterns to repeat a design over large pieces of drawing or butcher paper. The teacher prepares a printing area by first putting out several shallow pans and laying sponges or folded towels in the bottom of each. Then he pours heavy paint into each pan, so that a kind of printing pad is formed. The children press their printing tools on the pad and stamp their repeated designs on a piece of paper. Some of the printing tools available for preschool youngsters are listed below. If an object looks too thin to print with, glue a small piece of wood to it to serve as a handle.

- *Food printing:* Cut potatoes, green peppers, corncobs, celery, apples, or other fruits or vegetables in half to make natural printing stamps. Special designs may be cut into solid vegetables like potatoes or carrots.

- *Miscellaneous:* Use thread spools, hair curlers, cotton swabs, corks, forks, keys, coins, cookie cutters, the round ends of paper towel rolls, cotton balls, carpet scraps, bottle caps, and other common scraps to make effective printing tools.

- *Rolling-pin printing:* Rolling pins, cardboard tubing, or metal cans are all effective for this activity. Glue yarn or string to the rolling pin, dip the printing tool into the paint, and roll it over a surface.

- *Sponge printing:* Dip sponge pieces into the paint and stamp them onto a surface.

- *Button printing:* Glue buttons to dowel sticks and use them for printing.

Early printing experiences should be experimental. Items are selected and printed at random with little concern for arrangement. The important consideration is that the child gains confidence in his abilities and enjoys what he is doing. Once children understand the printing process, they may become interested in planned arrangements and patterns. Such designs are often used for wrapping paper, greeting cards, booklets, notepaper, or place mats for special gift-giving occasions.

GUIDING ART ACTIVITIES

The teacher's role in guiding art activities basically involves two tasks: (1) arranging the environment with equipment and materials, and (2) supervising the work in a warm and friendly manner. While *arranging* the room for creative art activities, you should always remember that children grow best when they are allowed to explore freely in a challenging setting. Such a setting has an adequate amount of space, so that children are able to work comfortably alone or in small groups. Materials and equipment should be easily obtainable at the area where the work is being done. Children must be unhurried and free to plan and carry out special projects in their own ways. Some suggestions follow.

- In addition to an easel painting center, which should be basic to nearly all preschool settings, arrange a large table that features a special *art center*. Art center activities may include finger painting, collage work, cutting and pasting, or any other individual or small-group project that the children can do as part of their daily planned program.

- Design a bulletin board or display area that can effectively exhibit the children's creations. Display the work at their eye level rather than at yours (see Figure 9–4).

- Play some soft music in the art area. Young children may use the rhythm to move their brush across the paper, moving freely.

- Make handy various cleanup materials such as a sponge, water, or mops so that the children can easily clean up when they are finished or if there is an accident.

You should follow a number of guidelines as you *supervise* the children during their creative art endeavors:

1. Offer encouragement and praise while the children work. Let them know how much you value their efforts. As you observe their work and talk to them about it, do not pressure them to describe what they are doing. They may be merely exploring with the art media and may not be able to express anything in particular about their product. You may wish to show interest and appreciation by commenting about the color, shapes, sizes, or design of the product. You should, however, refrain from forcing conversation when none seems constructive. Avoid comments like "What is it?" or "What are you making?" when children are engaging in media explorations. However, you can perfectly well lead off with the open-ended request, "Please tell me about your picture." Refrain from being too critical about accidents. Just as we would never admonish a houseguest for spilling a drink by complaining,

ON BULLETIN BOARDS OR OTHER WALL DISPLAYS

ON VARIOUS LEVELS OF DISPLAY BOXES

ON ORDINARY CLOTHESLINE WITH CLOTHESPINS

ON VARIOUS KINDS OF SHELVES

TACKED TO A BOARD AND LEANING AGAINST THE WALL

ON FREE-STANDING CORRUGATED CARDBOARD

Figure 9–4 Some ways of displaying children's art

"Oh, you are so clumsy!" we must also never admonish children for their honest accidents.

2. Resist using patterns, outlines, or guides whenever possible. Of course, some special projects will demand such structures, but excessive use of them limits freedom of expression.

3. Help children and encourage their efforts, but refrain from yielding to requests—for example, "Will you draw a dog for me right here?" Do not allow the children to become dependent on you—encourage them to think about ways in which they can accomplish their goal themselves. Requests for help usually come from the desire to produce a "masterpiece" to please a teacher or parent. Let the children know that what they create should be pleasing to them. It is their own—not the teacher's.

4. Resist the temptation to display only the "best" works. Remember that your enthusiasm should be extended to all within your room, so an undue emphasis on the work of only a few children will soon discourage the rest.

5. Allow the children to take their productions home. Children often get frustrated when they are not allowed to share their artwork with their parents, so a question such as, "Do we get to take our pictures home tonight?" should not go unheeded. Encourage parents to value their children's artistic development and to display their children's work in a prominent place.

6. Beware of unsafe art materials. Sydney Gurewitz Clemens identified these hazards:

   - Powdered clay. It is easily inhaled and contains silica, which is harmful to the lungs. Use instead wet clay, which can't be inhaled.
   - Paints that require solvents such as turpentine to clean brushes. Use instead water-based paints.
   - Cold-water or commercial dyes that contain chemical additives. Use instead natural vegetable dyes, made from beets, onion skins, and so on.
   - Permanent markers, which may contain toxic solvents. Use instead water-based markers.
   - Instant paper-maché, which may contain lead or asbestos. Use instead black-and-white newspaper and library paste or liquid starch.
   - Epoxy, instant glues, or other solvent-based glues. Use instead water-based white glue.[13]

When appropriate classroom arrangements are provided and free, creative exploration is encouraged, there is great value in children's art activities. In such environments, we find a burst of individualism, self-expression, and confidence. Children naturally enjoy the sensory qualities of art and thoroughly delight in production. The enjoyment of creating, the fascination of working with art materials, and the creative processes involved in art activity all support the incorporation of a strong art program in the preschool curriculum.

CRAFT PROJECTS

Although the major emphasis of an early childhood art program should be on creativity, you may wish sometimes to lead the children in thematic craft projects. I do not encourage you to display 15 identical dittoed turkeys for Thanksgiving; the emphasis should be placed on creativity. In connection with holidays or other particularly significant days, these projects bring a special reward when they are completed and taken home to proud family members. Because these activities are more highly structured and teacher-directed than the ones discussed until now, they are not as widely recognized as suitable vehicles for the development of the child's imagination. Be sure that your directions for completing the project are clear and that the children possess the necessary physical skills, so that they enjoy and are not frustrated by the project. Also, be sure to offer special projects sparingly, so that the thrust of the children's art activities is toward sensory experiences that help them create and foster cognitive, social, and motor skills. Some suggestions are contained in the Special Craft Projects box.

▶▶▶▶▶▶▶

SPECIAL CRAFT PROJECTS

Spooky Pictures

Give the children orange and white crayons and ask them to draw a Halloween design or picture with them. Encourage the children to press hard because a thick layer of crayon is necessary. Then brush one coat of thin black tempera paint over the picture.

Rubbings

Furnish the children with a variety of objects with interesting textured surfaces—for example, keys, coins, doilies, combs, paper clips, and so on. Have the children put a piece of paper over the object and rub over it with a crayon.

Hairy Pumpkin

Scoop the seeds and meat from a medium-sized pumpkin. Place a styrofoam block or cylinder into the pumpkin so that it extends about two or three inches above the top. Encourage children to bring in colorful leaves from the playground or fall flowers (such as mums) from home. Stick the leaves and flowers into the styrofoam until a pleasant arrangement results.

Variation: You may wish to have each of your children make an individual pumpkin of this type to take home as a centerpiece gift. In this case, visit pumpkin farms and encourage children to search for small pumpkins for the project.

Snowman

Beat equal amounts of Ivory Snow and water until the mixture is very stiff. The children should take turns mixing. Have the children spoon the mixture onto a cardboard snowman shape and spread it evenly. Allow the snowman to set overnight.

The next day the children can decorate their snowman by painting on facial features and buttons with black tempera paint. They may wish to tie a fabric strip around the neck to serve as a scarf and add a construction paper top hat.

Easter Chicks

Cut apart several cups from styrofoam egg containers so that each child has one cup. Have the children cut two eyes from black construction paper and one orange triangle for the beak. Then have them dip a cotton ball into glue and set it into the cup. Brush the eyes and beak with glue and set them in place on the cotton ball.

Easter Eggs

Fill a large jar three-quarters full of liquid starch. Punch a hole in the lid. Place a ball of twine in the starch, thread one end through the lid, and place the lid back on the jar. Pull the string through the hole while a child wraps it around an inflated balloon. Encourage the child to wrap the balloon in several directions with phrases such as "around and around," "up and down," and so on. Once the balloon has been wrapped several times, have the child finish his wrapping at the top so the string can later be used as a hanger. Allow the balloon to dry overnight.

If the balloon has not popped by itself on the next day, prick it with a pin. The children can then push Easter basket grass through the openings in the yarn until the egg is full.

Tub Turtles

Gather a number of used plastic margarine tubs. Have the children paint pieces of styrofoam packing material for the legs, tail, and head of a turtle. Glue the styrofoam pieces to the tub as illustrated.

Turkey Ties

At Thanksgiving time, solicit some old neckties from the parents of your children. Make the basic turkey shape from construction paper and staple it to a bulletin board or mount it on heavy tagboard. Have the children staple or glue the old neckties onto the paper turkey to make the tail. The ties can then be used to discuss concepts related to size, shape, color, and so on.

Paperweight

Take the children on a nature walk and ask them to find a medium-sized stone. Bring the stones back to the classroom and wash them off. Have a variety of tissue paper available and have the children cut or tear the tissue paper into small pieces. First, the children brush a mixture of one-half water and one-half white glue on a small part of the stone. They cover this area with tissue paper and cover the paper with white glue. They repeat this procedure until the entire top of the stone is covered, overlapping the pieces to make it more attractive. Wait until the top is dry before covering the bottom in the same way.

Caterpillars

Cut apart enough cardboard egg cartons so that each child can have one three-cup section. Punch two holes in the first section. Make available pipe cleaners and three or four different colors of tempera paint. Have the children make caterpillars by painting the egg carton sections and putting pipe cleaner antennae through the punched holes.

SOME FINAL THOUGHTS

Young children enjoy drawing, painting, and expressing themselves through a variety of art media. Because most preschool children are not yet inhibited by adults' having imposed a right or wrong way to scribble and draw, their artistic expressions are often freely and openly generated. Starting with simple scribbles, often done for sheer sensory pleasure, and progressing through stages until they begin to represent things—people, trees, houses, animals, or other objects close to them, children experience a means of expression without parallel in their lives. Researchers have studied young children and found that artwork, besides its obvious pleasurable aspect, can give us clear information about other areas of the child's development. The detail and accuracy shown in drawings gives us an indication of both the child's mental maturity and small-muscle control, and the content of the artwork can illustrate the child's moods and emotions.

Motivate your children to enjoy art by having enough materials and encouraging them to express themselves. Always provide well-organized areas of the room where they can work without worrying about being messy. Show interest in the children's work, but try to refrain from pressing them to explain it. Your major concern is to encourage creative artistic expression—a foundation upon which growing skill and aesthetic sensitivity can be built.

NOTES

1. E. Eisenstadt, "Young Children's Art," in Olive R. Francks, "Scribbles? Yes, They *Are* Art!" *Young Children, 34,* no. 5 (July 1979):21.

2. Sydney Gurewitz Clemens, "Art in the Classroom: Making Every Day Special," *Young Children, 46,* no. 2 (January 1991):5.

3. Ibid., p. 4.

4. Olive R. Francks, "Scribbles? Yes, They *Are* Art!" *Young Children, 34,* no. 5 (July 1979):21.

5. Viktor Lowenfeld and W. Lambert Brittain, *Creative and Mental Growth,* 8th ed. (New York: MacMillan, 1987), pp. 151–154.

6. Olive R. Francks, "Scribbles? Yes, They *Are* Art!" p. 18.

7. Diane E. Papalia and Sally Wendkos Olds, *A Child's World,* 4th ed. (New York: McGraw-Hill, 1987), p. 242.

8. Rhoda Kellogg, *Analyzing Children's Art* (Palo Alto, CA: Mayfield Publishing, 1970), pp. 12–21.

9. Katherine H. Read, *The Nursery School: A Human Relations Laboratory* (Philadelphia: W. B. Saunders, 1971), p. 235.

10. Barry J. Wadsworth, *Piaget's Theory of Cognitive and Affective Development,* 3rd ed. (New York: Longman, 1984), p. 74.

11. M. Brearly, *The Teacher of Young Children: Some Applications of Piaget's Learning Theory* (New York: Schocken Books, 1970).

12. Sylvia F. Burns, "Children's Art: A Vehicle for Learning." Reprinted by permission from *Young Children, 30,* no. 3 (March 1975), p. 201. Copyright 1975, National Association for the Education of Young Children, 1834 Connecticut Avenue, N.W., Washington, DC 20009.

13. Sydney Gurewitz Clemens, "Art in the Classroom," p. 7.

CHAPTER 10

Creating an Environment for Music and Movement

Children love music, whether in a planned period of creative activity or as incidental, spontaneous experiences. Anyone who has ever worked with children understands the joy and pleasure youngsters associate with music. They move their bodies naturally to the rhythmic sounds they hear around them and sing or hum extemporaneously as they play. Music and movement are fundamental to the lives of young children; for this reason they should be an important part of the early childhood curriculum. This chapter explains how teachers can plan and carry out music activities for the very young even though they may be nonmusicians themselves. As you read, use the following questions to guide your thinking.

- What are the goals of a developmentally appropriate music/movement program?

- Is there a predictable sequence of children's musical/movement development?

- How do teachers plan and carry out music and movement experiences with the very young?

- What different types of music and movement activities can be planned for preschool children?

- How do young children benefit from music and movement experiences?

An Episode to Ponder

One bright school-day morning, Mrs. Skurha gathered together her young children and began to sing a new song:

> "If you're happy and you know it,
> Clap your hands (clap, clap).
> If you're happy and you know it,
> Clap your hands (clap, clap)..."

The children quickly caught the pattern and joined in with the singing and clapping. Mrs. Skurha's energy and enthusiasm spread quickly through the group as they continued on with the verse:

> "...If you're happy and you know it,
> Then your smile will surely show it.
> If you're happy and you know it,
> Clap your hands (clap, clap)."

The children picked up the words and movements quickly, singing loudly and eagerly. Mrs. Skurha introduced several additional verses that used movements other than clapping—stamp your feet (stamp, stamp), pat your head (pat, pat), and toot your horn (toot, toot)—to complete each verse.

The song went on for some time as the children each had a chance to voluntarily contribute their own suggestions—touch your nose, flap your arms, wave bye-bye, and so on.

Why did the children respond so enthusiastically to this encounter? *First*, it was *fun!* The major emphasis in music in the preschool environment is on enjoyment rather than on any particular demonstrated skill or knowledge outcome. The most important reason we offer music in the preschool setting is for the pleasure it brings to the lives of young children. *Second*, it was appropriate in terms of *lyrics, rhythm*, and *melody*. The song was short, bouncy, tuneful, and completely understandable by the children. *Third*, it involved *action*. Music and movement go hand-in-hand; songs must give children an opportunity to move their hands and oftentimes their whole bodies. Realistically, the actions associated with a song will attract young children as much as the song itself. *Fourth*, it was a *voluntary experience*. Teachers should never force a child to participate but should wait for growing enjoyment to emerge; children will gradually join in. *Fifth*, it was *spontaneous*. The episode did not occur during a planned "music class," but at a time when the children were most highly motivated. Music should occur at any time of the day—arrival, free play, cleanup, snack, or even outdoor play. The children will respond more enthusiastically to movement/music experiences in a free, uncontrived atmosphere. *Sixth*, it invited *creative contributions*. The teacher started with standard lyrics and melody, but eventually invited the children to contribute their original ideas. Children surely enjoy the original compositions, but also love experimenting with words, rhythms, and movements.

MUSIC IN EARLY CHILDHOOD EDUCATION

Capturing the musical interest of young children is virtually an effortless task. All one needs to do is start something musical and watch the children join in. Music should permeate the early childhood environment; it allows children to develop in a number of areas, including these:

1. *Music helps children manage their feelings.* Music has the power to soothe and relax the child or to pick up her spirits. It offers opportunities to express feelings. A three-year-old, for example, dancing happily at the thought of a special visitor, tells a sensitive adult much about her thinking.

2. *Music helps foster cognitive development.* Music and movement, although naturally spontaneous in children, are not simple activities. They involve the ability to perceive the elements of music. Children distinguish differences in rhythm, tone, pitch, tempo, and volume while choosing the most appropriate movements or sounds to represent life experiences.

3. *Music helps develop physical fitness and motor skills.* Children exercise their bodies and improve their coordination while singing and playing musical instruments. Moving to different kinds of music helps children understand what they can do with their bodies.

4. *Music helps develop an appreciation of one's cultural heritage.* Because cultural, racial, and ethnic groups have distinctive styles of music and dance, children develop a sense of identity and pride when hearing music from their own backgrounds. Meanwhile, hearing music from other backgrounds helps to foster feelings of interest and enjoyment in other groups.

5. *Music helps encourage creativity and self-expression.* Children welcome opportunities to experiment freely with words, movement, and vocal expressions. Music is an excellent vehicle for promoting the natural need for freedom of expression by children of preschool age.

Teachers can capitalize on these benefits by providing a wide variety of musical experiences and by allowing for as much individual experimentation as possible. The goals of a sound early childhood music program have been enumerated by Sally Moomaw:

- Children should have many opportunities to explore music with their voices, through their movements, and by making sounds with instruments.
- They should have opportunities to express emotions through music.
- They should gain increased understanding of what makes different kinds of sounds.

- They should have opportunities to expand listening skills.
- They should develop increased awareness of body image and self-identity.
- They should develop increased enjoyment of music.
- They should explore their own creativity in music.
- Children should have experiences that reflect their developmental needs.
- They should have opportunities for group participation.[1]

In 1991 the Music Educators National Conference emphasized the role of music as a natural and important component of a young child's development with its position statement on music in early childhood education. The position statement declared:

> Music is a natural and important part of young children's growth and development. Early interaction with music positively affects the quality of all children's lives. Successful experiences in music help all children bond emotionally and intellectually with others through creative expression in song, rhythmic movement, and listening experiences. . . .
>
> Music education for young children involves a *developmentally appropriate program* [italics mine] of singing, moving, listening, creating, playing instruments, and responding to visual and verbal representations of sound. The content of such a program should represent music of various cultures in time and place. . . .
>
> Musical experiences should be play-based and planned for various types of learning opportunities such as one-on-one, choice time, integration with other areas of the curriculum, and large group music focus.[2]

Major recommendations for implementing such a program included devoting at least 12 percent of contact time with children to the teaching of music, retaining a music specialist qualified in early childhood education as a consultant, requiring at least one staff member in every center to have received formal training in music, and making available in every center a "music corner" or similar area where children have easy access to music materials.

The early childhood music program, then, is based on a philosophy that a natural delight in music leads to a program of personal expression with voice and body. Such delight begins during infancy, so:

> Music should be included daily for infants as well as for older children. The presence of music, whether through recording or the teacher's singing or playing, can awaken early responses to musical sound and can encourage infants to learn to listen.[3]

During infancy, the child appears to be primarily a *receiver* of music and, with this important prerequisite, quickly evolves into a *maker* of music. Because the infancy stage is a crucial foundation for later musical production, it will be discussed as a separate topic in this chapter.

THE BEGINNINGS: MUSIC DURING INFANCY

Babies are seldom thought of as singers, but their attempts at vocalizing often result in musical sounds such as trills and high-pitched squeals that are considered

Children enjoy all aspects of music; moving to the beat with creative dances is especially pleasurable.

akin to singing. Although there is no evidence that infants consciously mimic others in their environment as they produce these singing sounds, infant observations surely indicate that babies take much pleasure in listening to musical sounds. As a matter of fact, some of the most tender, loving moments of one's life take place during infancy as a parent or caregiver affectionately holds a baby in her arms and hums or sings a special song. The great American writer of children's books, Marguerite de Angeli, once wrote:

> I remember my mother, sitting in a low rocker, singing during a thunderstorm. What she was singing is not clear. It could have been "Sing a Song of Sixpence," "Rock-a-bye Baby," or any one of the familiar rhymes, or all of them, for there were many rockings and many comfortings. Later, when my younger brothers came along, I often sat in my mother's place and sang to them, choosing my own favorites and making up the tunes as I went. In those days we sang and rocked the children to sleep, and felt their dear heaviness when they finally gave up the fight to stay awake.[4]

Have you ever watched a baby in its parent's arms as she listens to a soft lullaby at sleep time? Her movements slow down, and with contented coos and gurgles she is eventually lulled to sleep. And what about the same baby as she hears a lively, rhythmic song on the radio? Again she becomes entranced; but instead of falling asleep, she often reacts by bouncing or rocking or moving about actively in some other way. The earliest evidence of musical interest in babies is their fascination with sound. Some have even suggested that this fascination begins before birth; mothers have reported a noticeable change in the activity level of their unborn babies as different kinds of music are played. As early as the third month of development, a fetus's heart rate often changes in reaction to external musical sounds. From the beginning, babies express their consciousness of music in a number of active ways.

Because the early months of a baby's life are spent responding to music in the environment, it is important to sing a soothing lullaby such as "Rock-a-Bye, Baby" or "Hush, Little Baby" when you wish to quiet him. Use faster-paced music when the baby can be more active. Your infant will show an active awareness of all musical sounds by turning his face toward the source. And musical sounds should not be thought of only in terms of hearing someone sing or play a musical instrument. Babies are captivated by all kinds of sounds; such musical toys as crib mobiles, trains, balls, music boxes, bath toys, squeeze toys, and push-pull toys all help enhance a baby's awareness of musical sounds in the environment. You will soon become fascinated by hearing a baby trill and coo while he begins to create musical sounds of his own.

At this early age, children are particularly interested in highly repetitive songs, chants, fingerplays, and nursery rhymes—forms of expression that link rhythm to words and sounds. "Pat-a-Cake," "This Little Piggie," and other games delight babies and often encourage charming movement participation.

Highly repetitive songs provide interesting musical experiences for infants. "Old MacDonald," "Are You Sleeping?" "Row, Row, Row Your Boat," and "The Farmer in the Dell" are but a few of the standard favorites.

These songs become even more enjoyable if you insert the baby's name whenever possible. For example, "Lori had a little lamb, little lamb...." Spontaneously created songs or *chants* are obviously enjoyed by infants, too. Babies love to hear you sing or talk rhythmically in many situations, and you will not find an already composed song or rhyme for each. Rhythmical chants like the following are easy to make up as you go along with whatever you are doing at the moment.

> Rub-dub, rub-a-dub,
> We're bathing baby in the tub.

The baby will gurgle in glee as you repeat the verse over and over again either with or without an added tune.

Some *simple fingerplays* are another source of experience in rhythm and song. Sit the baby facing you and share a popular fingerplay or action song such as the one shown at the top of page 343. Clap the baby's hands or do other actions that are appropriate to the developmental capabilities of the baby.

Nursery rhymes add rhythm and bounce to your chanting experiences. Hold the baby on your lap and clap her hands while you say such nursery rhymes as:

Clap, Clap, Clap, Your Hands

American Traditional

Key: F
Starting tone: F

Clap, clap, clap your hands, Clap your hands to - geth - er.

Clap, clap, clap your hands, Clap your hands to - geth - er.

JACK, BE NIMBLE

Jack, be nimble,
Jack, be quick,
Jack, jump over the candlestick.

HICKORY, DICKORY, DOCK

Hickory, dickory, dock!
The mouse ran up the clock;
The clock struck one, and down he ran,
Hickory, dickory, dock!

TO MARKET, TO MARKET

To market, to market, to buy a fat pig;
Home again, home again, jiggety jig.
To market, to market, to buy a fat hog;
Home again, home again, jiggety jog.

HUMPTY-DUMPTY

Humpty-Dumpty sat on a wall;
Humpty-Dumpty had a great fall.
All the king's horses
And all the king's men,
Couldn't put Humpty together again.

FIDDLE-DE-DEE

Fiddle-de-dee, fiddle-de-dee,
The fly shall marry the bumblebee.
They went to church, and married was she;
The fly has married the bumblebee.

Repetitive songs, simple fingerplays, and nursery rhymes certainly form the bulk of the infant's interactive experiences, but to limit an infant's musical involvement only to these episodes would limit the potential of this developmental period of life. Infants should be exposed to many forms of music; they appear to enjoy great variety:

- *Folk music.* Repeated verses and simple melodies attract children.
- *Jazz.* Bouncy rhythms are especially good during active times.
- *Classical music.* Louder, faster-paced varieties of classical music attract most youngsters (Bach's Brandenburg Concerto no. 2, for example).
- *Lullabies.* These soothe and calm children during periods of quiet rest or prior to sleep.
- *Children's records.* A large variety of records on wide ranges of subjects (patriotism, other languages, basic academic skills, animals, community workers, and so forth) are offered by such popular children's recording artists as Ella Jenkins; Miss Jackie; Raffi; Tom Glazer; Hap Palmer; Steve Millang and Greg Scelsa; and Sharon, Lois, and Bram.

These are but a few examples of the kinds of music that can be shared with infants (and young children, too). Collect suitable rhymes, chants, and songs from other sources and use them regularly. By creating an environment in which music is freely and pleasurably offered, we provide the first important step toward enhancing the natural affinity for music that children bring into this world with them.

MUSIC AND MOVEMENT ACTIVITIES FOR YOUNG CHILDREN

A good music program for young children fosters a love and appreciation of music while emphasizing the fun and satisfaction that active participation brings. Precise performances are not the goal; instead, it is hoped that the type of involvement provided will become an enjoyable part of each child's daily experiences. Many different kinds of music and movement activities can be offered to preschool children; we will classify them into these categories for ease of discussion: singing, listening, experimenting with rhythm, using musical instruments, and encouraging creative movement.

Singing

From the pleasurable vocal play episodes of infancy and into the early years of childhood, children enjoy experimenting with their voices and the sounds they make.

They love to sing; youngsters chant, chirp, croon, and hum when they are happy. Teachers must do all they can to capture this natural love and enthusiasm for song; avoiding practices that destroy it or turn it into a chore is a must for good early childhood teachers.

Informal Singing   To help communicate a positive regard for singing, it is critically important to serve as a positive adult role model and to use songs frequently and informally throughout the school day. You must show your appreciation and enjoyment of songs.

Perhaps the greatest impediment to this teaching responsibility is the lack of confidence many of us have in our own musical abilities. Skittish about the quality of our own voices, we usually shy away from situations that call upon us to sing.

Why do we feel that way? Is it a product of our own experiences as students with music in the schools? If so, we owe it to our children to overcome our externally imposed inhibitions and to avoid making those same mistakes we experienced in the past. If we feel awkward singing in the classroom, we will probably make the children feel the same way.

Sing in the classroom. If you find it difficult to carry a tune, don't worry; most children can't either. Children are not music critics and rarely, if ever, say anything like, "Your singing sure stinks, teacher." They don't care if you have the sweetest voice in the world or sound like an old foghorn. What is important to children is to see that you are having fun singing with them. They appreciate your efforts to make their day more enjoyable.

Show the children how much fun music is by finding good excuses to sing throughout the day. One type of song to start with is a narrow-range chant. Use minor inflections as you vocalize short verses, not necessarily to any melody:

Picking up the blocks,
Putting them away.
Make them neat and ready
For another day.

Clap or tap your feet as you chant. The children will catch your spirit and soon join in the "music" and the cleanup activity. These informal music experiences can be done any time you feel like it—for brushing teeth, going outside, getting back from a group activity, starting the day, or for anything that makes you happy. You use the song or chant because it makes you feel good and you have a strong need to express your positive emotions. Can such a spirit be contagious? You bet! Children love to sing when they are happy, too. Your chants will eventually become more melodious as you create your own original songs about the children and their activities. Songs of greeting, songs for calling children to the large group meeting area, songs for putting away the toys, songs for washing up, or songs for going to the playground— all of these can be adapted from standard children's tunes to add zest to your day. One teacher, for example, sings a special rendition of "Happy Birthday" as the children come into the room to start the day. The children eagerly join in as they put away their wraps and start on their way to the various play areas:

> Good morning to you.
> Good morning to you.
> Good morning, dear friends.
> Good morning to you.

What other routines or situations can you brighten up with songs or chants? How about the child who needs help with his clothing? One teacher adapted "Twinkle, Twinkle, Little Star" as she offered assistance:

> Let me help you if I may,
> We'll get that shoe tied today.

You can compose simple lyrics to accompany other enjoyable activities. For example, this song (to the tune of "Clementine") was composed by a teacher during a cooking activity:

> Cut the carrots,
> Cut the carrots,
> Cut the carrots, one by one,
> Our soup needs lots of carrots,
> Isn't this a lot of fun?

Singing or chanting directions can be used in a variety of situations. This song was sung to the tune of "Row, Row, Row Your Boat":

> Brush, brush, brush your teeth.
> Brush them nice and clean.
> Brush, brush, brush.
> Scrub, scrub, scrub.
> Get them nice and clean.

The most important advice for you in dealing with music as an informal part of your daily program is to have confidence in your musical ability, drop your musical inhibitions, and have fun. If you are accustomed to singing more complex works, say, Bach arias, go ahead and sing them. Just break them up into manageable chunks and repeat. The children won't like them less, and it will be more interesting for you. Children are not music critics—they will enjoy listening to you more than they will to a recording of a famous singer because they like you, know you are there, see you are having fun with them, and appreciate your efforts to make routines enjoyable. Their response to your efforts will be gratifying and professionally rewarding.

So, ready or not, music will be a part of your program because children bring it to school with them. They cannot leave something that is so much a part of their lives out on your doorstep until the end of the day. You must learn to make spontaneous music a shared activity, and try to overcome any unpleasant memories or fears you may have developed about music. Prepare to have fun *with* children. As Mary Jalongo and Mitzie Collins point out: "Remember that you sing *with* children, not for them. When you view yourself as a participant rather than as a performer, you can relax and concentrate on the activity, not on yourself."[5] Do not think of musical development as the domain of a specialist who is trained as a music teacher. Music is part of the child's natural makeup and grows from everyday spontaneous interactions.

Group Singing   Informal singing dominates most of the day, but good preschool programs must also provide opportunities for children to learn and sing favorite early childhood songs. Naturally, these experiences must be comfortable and informal; they should not be offered in an atmosphere that says, "Now we're going to learn a new song." Plan a scheduled music time of approximately 15 to 20 minutes, during which the children gather together to discover a new song. They may meet at a rug, at the book center, or at the block building area. The song may be introduced after hearing a story or in connection with a play activity or field trip to the farm. Whatever the situation, singing new songs should occur in a relaxed atmosphere rather than one so formal as to require children to sit quietly in chairs or on designated marks around a circle.

When introducing a new song, be sure to help the children understand what the song is about. For example, "Pawpaw Patch" is a popular song traditionally sung by preschoolers for decades. It is fun and the children enjoy singing it. But, how many *know* what they're singing *about*? How many of *us* know what a pawpaw is? "Kumbaya" is another childhood favorite; what does it mean? You might want to share an appropriate object or picture to clarify unclear or unknown concepts before the song is sung and to motivate the children. Or, some introductory conversation might be helpful. For example, showing the children a toy stuffed spider she majestically pulled out from a drawstring bag, one teacher asked: "Have you ever seen a real spider? How does it move?" After the children shared their ideas, the teacher invited them to listen as she sang the following song all the way through and made appropriate wiggling movements of her fingers for the rain falling and for the spider going up the spout:

> The eency weency spider went up the water spout,
> Down came the rain and washed the spider out,
> Out came the sun and dried up all the rain,
> And the eency weency spider went up the spout again.

Following the initial singing, the teacher may repeat the song several times. The children are invited to sing along when ready or insert their own movements where appropriate (or duplicate those of the teacher). Most will do so, but some preschoolers are somewhat shy at first and may not immediately join in. They should never be forced to participate; if the music time is fun, their growing enjoyment will lure them in quickly. Refrain from comments such as "Everyone sing now," or "Alex knows the words already; listen to him sing" (a sure way to quiet anyone). Also, do not sing each separate line or phrase over and over again and ask the children to repeat until they have learned the entire song. If they have not learned the whole song by the time you have repeated the whole thing a few times, it is probably too hard for them and should be put away to be used another time.

Choosing a Song　Children's first songs should be action songs—rhythmic melodies that involve body movements. Often the hands may do the actions, but sometimes the whole body may be used. "Where Is Thumbkin?" (see box below) is an example of a popular song involving hand movements only.

Songs that call for children's movements have great appeal; vigorous action, especially with their whole bodies, attracts youngsters and encourages them to listen, sing, and respond. "Head, Shoulders, Knees, and Toes," shown at the top of page 349, offers one splendid example of songs that inspire various body movements.

The songs sung by young children should also be related to their experiences and interests. Choose songs about nature, animals, the weather, other children, transportation, games or activities, and concepts the children are learning about in school. However, the teacher need not explain *every* word of a song for the children to get meaning from it. For example, the song "Jennie Jenkins" includes the lines:

> I'll buy me a fol-de-rol-dy
> Til-dy-tol-dy seek-a-double roll
> Jennie Jenkins roll.

▶▶▶▶▶▶▶

WHERE IS THUMBKIN?

(Sing to the tune of "Frère Jacques")

Where is Thumbkin?	(Hide hands behind back.)
Where is Thumbkin?	
Here I am.	(Bring out hands. Extend thumbs.)
Here I am.	
How are you today, sir?	(One thumb bows to the other.)
Very well, I thank you.	(Other thumb bows to first.)
Run away.	(Hide one hand behind back.)
Run away.	(Hide other hand.)

Sing four more times substituting "Pointer," "Tall Man," "Ring Man," and "Pinkie" for "Thumbkin." The children may have difficulty getting the last two fingers to stand by themselves, but they have fun trying.

Head, Shoulders, Knees, and Toes
(Tavern in the Town)

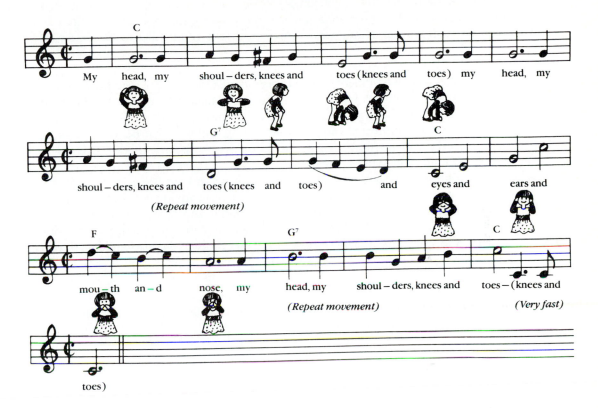

As mentioned many times in this chapter, the emphasis in singing is on the *process*—experimenting with sound, rhythm, and voice. Even though some parts of "Jennie Jenkins" are not understandable, the children get much fun out of the original tune and sayings.

Songs that appeal to the teacher are of great importance, too. A child's reaction to a song depends on how it is sung, so be sure to choose something that conveys your interest and enthusiasm. Try to recall some of your old favorites—nursery songs your parents used to sing, TV commercials, camp songs, hymns, folk songs. Or, how about an appropriate rock tune or rap selection? These sources are a great start for your singing repertoire. You'll also benefit from listening to children's tapes or records. They are excellent resources to help you learn new, appropriate songs to teach. Listen to the record and sing along; you'll learn the words quickly. Some teachers, however, invite the children to sing along with these records instead of participating with the children themselves. The joy of participation is bound to diminish as the children sing along with an impersonal record player instead of an active, expressive teacher who varies her voice, changes her facial expression, and laughs at humorous words. When used properly, these records contribute to the preschool program in ways that go beyond simply teaching new songs to a teacher. One beneficial use is to make them available at the music center, where the children can put on earphones and listen to them whenever they wish. Children, just as adults, like to hear a favorite song many times.

Instrumental Accompaniment   Some beginning teachers feel that their inability to play an instrument is a handicap for teaching young children to sing. However, children do not need musical accompaniment to enjoy singing—as a matter of fact, pianos or other instruments often distract young children. Unless you are skilled enough to play an instrument by ear, children may be helped more by having no accompanying music than by having it.

If you prefer musical accompaniment, there are two *chording* instruments that are fairly easy to learn and furnish delightful accompanying music for children's songs: the guitar and the Autoharp. The soft, simple chords produced by these instruments provide enjoyable backgrounds for songs. With the guitar, you will need to learn the finger positions required for basic chords. Because children's songs are relatively unsophisticated, though, you will need to learn only a few chords. The Autoharp is even more easily learned, since it uses preset chords. Three-year-olds often enjoy playing it. You only have to press down on a chord bar and strum the strings to produce the desired sound—the chord bar leaves the correct strings free while stopping all the rest. Each chord bar is marked on the Autoharp. Many books have chords marked for the teacher. Look at the chord designations at intervals.

London Bridge

1. Lon - don bridge is fall - ing down,   fall - ing down,   fall - ing down;

Lon - don bridge is   fall - ing down,   my   fair   la - dy.

As you can see, "London Bridge" contains only two different chords, F and C7, each repeated several times before the other is introduced. A few minutes' practice with guitar or Autoharp should make you ready to share this favorite song with your children. The Autoharp is manufactured by Oscar Schmidt International, Inc., of Union, New Jersey, and is available in most music stores for as low as $100.

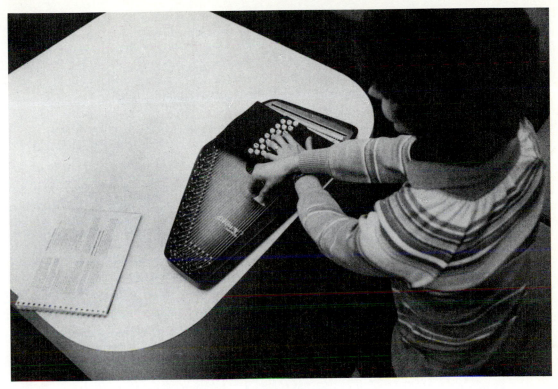

The Autoharp helps support group or individual singing.

The enjoyment aspect of music cannot be overemphasized, whether you are encouraging spontaneous singing throughout the day or choosing song material for a group experience. The ability to choose melodies for group experiences is a very important skill in maintaining the pleasurable aspect of your program. B. Joan E. Haines and Linda L. Gerber offer the following criteria for making good choices and ensuring successful teaching.

1. The song must appeal to the children:
    (a) through its clear rhythm,
    (b) through its pleasing, simple melody ... ,
    (c) through its singable range (very young singers do best in the limited range of middle C up to G),
    (d) through its content ... of interest to the children.
2. It must be well known to and well liked by the teacher.
3. It must contain a close relationship between the words and the melody so that it has unity. The meaning of the words should be reflected in the style of the music.[6]

Haines and Gerber further recommend that a good song for the children to learn often contains several of the following attributes, though they are *not* essential:

(a) It may be short or divided into several verses and a chorus.
(b) It may contain verbal or melodic repetition.
(c) It may suggest physical activity or instrumental accompaniment.
(d) It may deal with the familiar.
(e) It may stimulate the mind and imagination to new interests and knowledge.
(f) It may correlate with other areas of subject matter. (Or it may not—in fact, it may be nonsense!)[7]

Haines and Gerber recommend that when you choose songs, all the criteria in items 1, 2, and 3 be met. A song including some aspects of (a) through (f) is even more likely to be successful.

Singing Games   Kindergarten children often enjoy playing a game as they sing. Songs that have a game orientation usually require the group to form a circle with one or two children singled out for some specific purpose. Consider these two childhood favorites, for example:

Old King Glory of the Mountain   Arrange the children in a circle and designate one child to be "king." The king parades around the outside of the circle as the others stand and sing. As the words *first, second,* and *third* are sung, the king taps the shoulder of the child he is passing at the time. Only the *third* person, however, leaves the circle to follow the king on his parade. The song then begins again with the king choosing additional children for the parade. The song is repeated until all children are in the parade except one, who becomes the king for a new game.

Old King Glory of the Mountain

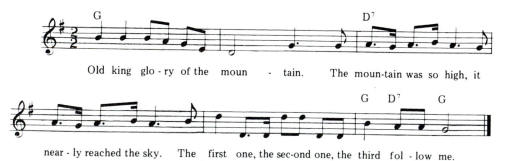

The Noble Duke of York   Form a circle and designate one child to be the "duke." The duke leads the other children during the first verse as they march in a circle.

During the second verse, the children stand in the circle and stand straight during the words "when they were up, they were up;" sit down during the words "when they were down, they were down;" and squat or kneel during the words "when they were only halfway up, they were neither up nor down."

The Noble Duke of York

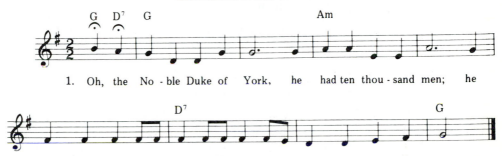

1. Oh, the No - ble Duke of York, he had ten thou - sand men; he marched them up to the top of the hill, and he marched them down a - gain.

2. And when they were up, they were up,
   And when they were down, they were down,
   And when they were only halfway up,
   They were neither up nor down.

Games with Rules   As the children grow into kindergarten and the primary grades, they reach a level of social maturity and physical skill that allows them to benefit from group games involving rules. These organized games should have few rules or directions, because children are more interested in the physical activity than they are in following the directions. Games most appropriate to kindergarten or primary grade play are loosely organized and are frequently of the circle type. The few rules guiding such games direct the activities.

Because the primary objective of games is to have fun, the actual playing time should be lively and relaxed. Do not become so involved in communicating rules to the children that your anxiety and desire for conformity reduce your children to boredom and gloom. Remember instead that excitement is part of the game and that the fun and thrill of playing are controlled only to the degree that game rules must be followed.

When introducing young children to games, remember to tell them that it is important for them to concentrate on your directions if they expect to play the game correctly. It may be advisable to give verbal directions while stressing the importance of listening carefully. It may likewise be advisable to demonstrate certain steps with some children so that the others will understand your directions more clearly. Go through each step carefully before you proceed to the next so that the set rules are clearly established. Here is one teacher's outline of how she organized a game with her kindergarten youngsters.

1. Group the children in a large circle and have them signal how they feel about being there.

2. Have the children use their arms to draw a letter (or numeral) as large as they can in space. Ask them to think about other parts of their body that they can draw with and have them do so.

3. As the children to choose partners and form a letter (or numeral) with their bodies on the floor or in a standing position.

4. Form a large letter on the floor with heavy yarn. Then, for example, encourage the children to move around a big *B* "buzzing like a bug or bouncing like a ball."

5. Give each child one letter. Then begin this rhyme and ask the first child to make his letter in space as big as he can:

   This is what I can do.
   Everybody try it, too.
   This is what I can do.
   Now I pass it on to you.

   After the verse is complete, ask the other children to mimic the action and tell what letter (or numeral) was shared. Repeat for each child.

Most games involve a great deal of physical activity and mobility, as in the preceding example. Games can be played indoors or out, but keep in mind that the playground often gives you more area, allowing for greater freedom of movement. These games are enjoyed by kindergarten and primary grade children.

Most children's games should be chosen for fun ("Here We Go 'round the Mulberry Bush" or "Ring around the Rosy"). Their enjoyment comes from the active movement and singing involved in the activity. Winning and losing are not part of these games—their value lies in the action and togetherness they provide. There are other favorite early childhood games that do not end as predictably as these—"Duck, Duck, Goose" is a good example. It is a game that could involve winners and losers, but children often assign a different meaning to winning and losing than do adults. For example, consider Ryan, age four. His class was playing the game, and he was "it." When he touched Belinda on the shoulder and said, "Goose!" she didn't pop up and chase him. Rather than run full speed to his original place in the circle and rejoice in winning, however, Ryan took a few steps, hesitated, and slowed down. With prodding from the other children, Belinda finally jumped up and chased Ryan. Ryan enjoyed this part so much that instead of stopping at his original spot in the circle, where he would be safe, he continued going around, squealing with delight. Like most children his age, Ryan was in no hurry to end an enjoyable activity—the fun was not in the winning or losing but in the activity.

As they get caught up in the excitement, children may alter rules without a firm grasp on a game's goal. It is not until the child is seven or eight that he understands rules and the need to follow them in order to determine winners or losers. Until that time, watch your children for cues. Notice the aspects of children's games that interest them, and allow for the child to simplify or add variations to the games that make them more pleasurable. The best advice you can follow is to give your children the freedom and opportunity for play. Other suggestions for using games effectively are:

1. Use your time efficiently. As a rule of thumb, young children's attention spans during intense activities are about one or two minutes more than their age.

2. Keep groups as small as possible. This provides greater opportunity for maximum individual effort, with careful guidance from the teacher.

3. Concentrate on only one or two skills in any game session. More than that number may confuse or frustrate some children.

4. Give clear, simple directions and make sure the children understand how the game is played. Demonstrate the actions of the game to give a clear idea of how to play.

5. Do not force each child to play. Try to encourage all to participate, but you will find that the activity will go much better if the children join of their own free will rather than because of the teacher's demand.

6. Keep a watchful eye on the children. Stop the game when their interest wanes, and move on to something else. Don't overdo it—too much of a good thing will eventually tire the children of nearly anything.

Listening

Children should have regular opportunities for purposeful hearing of music; listening carefully to the music they hear is an important ingredient of music appreciation and helps children understand how listening to different tunes can make them feel. Listening to music can be both soothing and enjoyable, so many different types of music should be made available each day: children's songs, classical, marches, lullabies, jazz, folk songs, rock, or rap. Because the music you choose will definitely affect their mood and energy level, the children should be encouraged to respond to these songs with creative body movements—dancing, marching, or the playing of instruments, real or imagined. Be judicious in the type of music you choose during the day, however, for a lively march would certainly cause problems during naptime, but could enliven the group during cleanup time.

Listening experiences can be offered at music centers or as background during specific routines. For example, records or tapes and a record or tape player (with earphones) should be placed in an area of the room to be operated by the children themselves. Put out a small selection of music at a time, changing the choices frequently. Additionally, appropriate music can be played during routines such as snack, free play, art, or rest time.

Special interest in music is often generated when parents or siblings come to school to play an instrument or sing for the children. Some may be extremely talented—one mother played lead violin in a prestigious symphony orchestra, for example. She played some selections as the children listened intently; afterwards she invited the children to pull a bow over the strings as she changed the notes. Others may be interested in sharing their musical hobbies. Imagine the excitement as one father shared his interest in bagpipes with a preschool group. Gospel singers, Spanish flamenco dancers, American Indian songs and dances, and other listening experiences can enliven and enrich a child's cultural awareness.

Opportunities such as these not only develop an appreciation of music, but also sharpen the children's listening skills. A richer program results when you, the teacher, provide your children with a variety of music listening experiences.

Experiments with Sound Part of a good music listening program is encouraging children to experiment with sounds related to music. Play guessing games where the children listen carefully to sounds with their eyes closed. Ask them which sound is louder or softer, or which two out of three sounds are alike. Teacher- or child-made instruments also are effective in helping children understand how musical sounds are made. For example, you might want to work together with the children to construct a string guitar as shown in Figure 10–1. Tighten and loosen the fishline as the children pluck out notes. They will enjoy touching the line and feeling its vibrations. Jointly made drums can be constructed from oatmeal boxes, coffee cans, or large vegetable cans (see directions in Figure 10–1). Have the children experiment with sounds by making drums of different sizes. Rattles, shakers, and chimes can be used in the same way.

Children's involvement in music should stimulate rich creativity. Relate these teacher- and child-made instruments to real ones so the children can understand how items can be beaten, plucked, or blown into to create various sounds. Children learn many things through experimenting with instruments—how different materials make different sounds, the way they play the instrument affects the sound, and the way the size of the instrument affects the sound. Concrete experiences help children develop basic musical concepts and gives children opportunities to express themselves creatively through the sounds they make.

Rhythm

Rhythmic activities offer children opportunities to explore the pulse and flow of musical sounds. Even some of the games most enjoyed by infants involve rhythm; one of the first games babies love to play is pat-a-cake, a relatively simple exploration of rhythm. Young children, too, are quite uninhibited; they freely match movement with music through a wide range of rhythmic action, both musical and nonmusical.

Capitalize on this natural, spontaneous response to music and encourage your children to move in response to the rhythm around them. Do so spontaneously during transitions—cleaning up, for example. Marches are quite good—move freely among the children to the beat of the song. Explain to the children, "This music is so lively it makes me want to move. I'm going to move the way the music makes

Wood Chimes   Hang different materials from a straight bar or a triangular wooden frame or a circular band of metal stripping so that they will strike each other when they are moved by the wind. For a variety of sounds, use different sizes and kinds of materials, such as nails, metal scraps, pieces of glass, strips of wood, dowels, pieces of bamboo, and pieces of pipe.

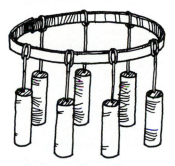

Wood Block Tambourine   You will need blocks of wood about ¾ inch × ½ inch × 6 inches, bottle caps, and nails with wide heads. Remove the cork from the bottle caps. Place a bottle cap on the wood block and hammer a nail through the cap and partway into the wood block. Make sure the hole is wide enough so the cap will slide freely along the nail. (Maybe make the hole in the cap first—with a larger-sized nail—then attach it to the wood.) Use as many nails and as many caps on each nail as desired.

Nail Scraper   You will need blocks of wood about 2 inches × 2 inches × 8 inches and nails of different sizes. Hammer a few nails into a block of wood so that they are all the same height. Leave a space and repeat the process with different sized nails—or use the same size, but hammer them in deeper. To play, run a large nail along the separate rows of nails.

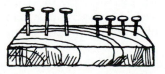

String Guitar   This is the most complicated instrument to make. You will need a strip of wood about 2 inches × 24 inches × ¾ inch, two screw eyes, 36-inch nylon fishline (squidding is best), two popsicle sticks, and a large nail for each one.

1. Insert a screw eye near each end of the wood strip.
2. About 1½ inches from each end of the wood strip, saw a ¼-inch deep groove across the strip for the popsicle stick.
3. Insert the popsicle stick sideways into the grooves, and tie the fishline between the two screw eyes.

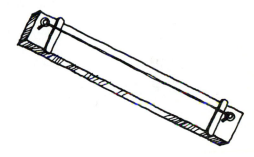

4. Tighten the fishline by turning one of the screw eyes with the large nail.
5. Use as a rhythm instrument, or make several string guitars (each tuned to a different note).

Drums   Use old coffee cans or large vegetable cans that can be obtained from the school cafeteria. Cover the open end with inner tube rubber as tightly as possible and secure it with heavy cord or wire. A drumstick is easily made with a dowel rod and piece of foam rubber at the end.

Kitchen Cymbals   Collect discarded kettle lids (with knobs on top) and use them as cymbals.

Rattles   Some containers you might use are paper cups, plastic bottles, small plastic boxes and cans, wooden match boxes, and metal bandage cans. These can be partly filled with one or more of the following: dried beans, peas, grain, or seeds; table salt; rock salt; marbles; pebbles; feathers; sand.

Figure 10–1   Hand-made instruments (Many of these homemade musical instruments are based on the ideas of two creative teachers, Pearl Bailes and Mary Alice Felleisen.)

me feel. . . . Come and move the way the music sounds to you." You may find that the children will imitate you during their first efforts, but that's okay. They often feel more comfortable doing that. Watch for children who create new patterns, however, and encourage others to try something a bit different by saying, for example: "Loretta has thought of a way to twist her body that is very interesting. I think I'll try that. . . . I wonder who else could think of a different way to move to the music?"

The preschool or kindergarten day is full of chances for spontaneous rhythmic experiences. For instance, while pushing the child on a swing, chant:

Ashley goes u-u-u-p, and
Ashley goes do-ow–ow-own!

Bouncing balls, hopscotch games, and teeter-totters offer you similar opportunities. With your hands, clap the rhythm of a child's name. Ask the group to guess any child's name represented by that rhythm. Or turn a wastebasket upside down and, using a wooden spoon as a drumstick, ask the children to go to the playground with a movement suggested by the beat you provide.

Spontaneous music is often expressed through movement as well as through singing or playing musical instruments. As children develop better muscular coordination, they become very interested in experimenting with all types of movement. Hopping, bouncing, dancing, climbing, and galloping are but a few activities that they try enthusiastically. For some children, the need to express themselves through energetic body movements may be so strong that those movements may make up the main mode of personal expression. These children move more than they speak. Many children combine this urge to move with their spontaneous chants (rhythmic use of their voice) or humming while playing in another classroom area. A soft, comforting lullaby may accompany rocking a doll, or a vigorous "vroom-vroom-vroom" may go with rolling a toy car. Children seem to respond to sounds naturally with spontaneous rhythmic movements.

Encourage such spontaneous expression in your classroom, but do not become so involved in what the children are doing that they become overdependent on you for approval or ideas. A very young child cannot comfortably respond to a rhythm imposed upon him by adults. If care is taken, though, a response will quickly develop and serve as a firm foundation for a planned musical program. During spontaneous movement, however, children should not be constrained to seeking a "right way" to express themselves rhythmically, nor should there be competition or requests to share their musical creations with others. If at some point the child wants to show what she has originated with someone, it will be for the sheer joy of wanting to share her creation, and not to "show off." Think of musical expression as being like all other forms of creativity—children benefit not only from the products, but from the *process*.

Rhythmic expression, then, should at first be encouraged through spontaneous activity. Allow the children opportunities to move rhythmically in their own ways for short periods of time during the day. Often children will do so if different kinds of music are played on the record player. You will find them clapping or tapping as they attempt to keep time to a regular beat. Other children will be content to twirl and move to the music. Still others will enjoy holding colorful scarves in their hands and allowing them to trail as they glide smoothly to the beat of the music. Such random bodily movements eventually become more controlled as children are exposed to planned rhythm experiences. These initial experiences should involve steady rhythmic patterns that are not necessarily from songs. For example, you may steadily beat on a drum or tambourine as the children walk in a circle. You may ask the children to alter their gait as the beating is either speeded up or slowed down. Chants associated with popular early childhood games, including jump rope chants, should be used to help children explore rhythmic movement. A popular jump rope chant follows:

> Teddy Bear, Teddy Bear, go upstairs.
> Teddy Bear, Teddy Bear, say your prayers.
> Teddy Bear, Teddy Bear, turn out the light.
> Teddy Bear, Teddy Bear, say good-night.

Many aspects of rhythm, from clapping musical rhythms to using instruments, can be carried out effectively in a planned group experience.

Another feature of the beginning phase of developmental music programs is to encourage verbal and physical reactions to rythmic and repetitive chants. These responses are natural to young children, and they are also an integral part of music. Begin by relating the musical experience to something they already know. You may, for instance, say to the children: "I am going to show you something. Who can tell me what it is? . . . A pail, that's right! . . . Yes, bucket. What are buckets used for? I know a song about a little boy and a little girl who used a bucket to carry water." (Sing the nursery rhyme "Jack and Jill.") "I'm going to sing the song once more and clap as I sing. Please help me sing." (Sing the rhyme once more, clapping at each syllable.) "This time I'm going to sing and clap again. You can sing and clap along with me if you like."

Teach rhythmic responses for the enjoyment they bring to children. The rhythmic and repetitive pulse of nursery rhymes ideally matches the clapping, drumming, or stomping actions that should be present as the children develop initial musical awareness.

It's not difficult to get children involved in these rhythmic activities, for they are naturally conscious of rhythm and enjoy moving to the beat of action rhymes and musical selections. Evidence of this interest can be seen as children play in unstructured settings: they chant in rhythm as they swing or jump rope; experiment with words or sounds such as "quack-quack" or "bow-wow"; twirl in a circle while "dancing" to a favorite song; or sway and tap when a catchy tune is heard. These and many other forms of rhythmic movement can be easily seen if the environment is one of freedom and acceptance, where children can express their feelings openly.

Children's natural rhythmic responses to music bring much enjoyment to daily activities.

Musical Instruments

As the children gain opportunities to experience creative rhythmic activities, they will enjoy using rhythm instruments such as drums, triangles, rhythm sticks, or tambourines. If the instruments are all brought out at one time, you will probably find that the children become too excited about them. It is best to introduce one or two instruments at a time, so the children will have opportunities to experiment with them thoroughly. Of course, there will be some noise at first, but if you alternate instrument use between outdoors and indoors, most problems can be overcome. At this point, you should talk informally with the children about their instruments, focusing on the sounds they make. Identify the instruments for the children by using the appropriate terms: say "triangle," for example, instead of "clang-clang." Show the children the triangle and play it while they listen. Talk about the sound it makes. Then hand out several triangles and allow the children to play them. As the children explore the instruments, you may help them discover the proper way to hold them. Have a child tap a triangle while holding it by one side as he had been doing and then tap it while holding it by the string. Don't say, "See, you were holding it wrong," but keep your comment open ended: "Which way sounds better?" As the children become used to playing all the rhythm instruments properly, you can ask them to furnish the rhythmic pattern in rhythm activities.

As such informal, creative experiences are provided for young children, they will slowly become able to manipulate the instruments properly and will gain sufficient control for group experiences. If you choose to group your children as a "rhythm band," you will at first need to develop sections of instruments. The instruments most popularly used in preschool settings include *triangles, drums, rhythm sticks, cymbals,* and *bells.* Give each section enough time to work together so that they are able to coordinate their efforts. Rarely should you expect all sections to play together in unison—the responsibility of playing together in a section is demanding for preschool youngsters. Only at the end, for one or two beats, can you expect all the children to play together. The following is one way to organize a rhythm band experience:

1. Choose a record with an appropriate beat, or select a suitable song to be played on a musical instrument.

2. Decide on the sequence in which each instrument will be played. For example, our ever-present Ms. Carpenter developed this plan for "Jingle Bells":

Jingle bells, jingle bells (*bells only*)
Jingle all the way (*triangles only*)
Oh, what fun (*cymbals only*)
It is to ride (*drums only*)
In a one-horse open sleigh. (*rhythm sticks only*)
(*Repeat verse exactly as before.*)
"Jingle bells!" (*everyone together*)

3. Develop cues with which to signal each group to enter the song. You may choose to hold up the instrument to be played, show the children a picture of the instrument, use a cue word such as "cymbals," or simply point to the next group to play.

As the children gain coordination and skill in using these rhythm instruments, you will be able to supplement your total program in many ways. Rhythmic responses to music are a natural part of most childhood activity. Children don't express themselves in those ways because someone has told them to, but because they want to. Ms. Carpenter capitalizes on this childhood joy by encouraging the rhythmic expression as the children indicate a need to express them.

▶▶▶▶▶▶

In Ms. Carpenter's kindergarten classroom, music was looked upon as something natural and spontaneous—it could be expected to come at any time from anyone. Bea walked into school this morning and began to sing her favorite seasonal song to the aide: "Jingle bells, jingle bells, jingle all the way...." Some other children soon caught the pattern and chimed in, "Oh what fun it is to ride...." The aide sang along with the children, and all ended the song with a great deal of laughter and excitement.

Later on in the morning, the children returned from a trip to a toy store—a part of the teacher's seasonal activity. During free play, Ms. Carpenter observed a boy marching in a circle pounding an imaginary drum as he went along. He was chanting, "See the drummer boy, boom...boom... boom!" in rhythmic movement. He was an especially outgoing youngster, so Ms. Carpenter offered him a drum from her set of percussion instruments, and he continued to imitate the toy drummer boy he had seen at the toy store. Ms. Carpenter then went to the piano and added a soft, marching rhythm accompaniment to the boy's activity. Other children began to join the marching activity with other kinds of rhythm instruments. The marching continued for several minutes while the children's attention remained high.

Of course, Ms. Carpenter did not always become directly involved in the children's musical experiences. Such a practice is neither appropriate nor advisable. This illustration is only a single example. On most occasions all you need is space, materials, and encouragement—the children will take it from there. And they will find music in the most surprising places:

▶▶▶▶▶▶

Dalena always enjoyed participating in the learning activities in the room, and today was no exception. Moving to the science area, she quickly became engrossed in the manipulation of sound jars (glass containers filled to different levels with water to demonstrate a science concept). Each container, when struck with a small mallet, produced a different pitch. Dalena experimented with the jars for some time until she discovered a pattern. Running to the teacher and asking her to come, she proudly announced, "Listen; here's the song we were singing before—I learned a song, I learned a song!" and plunked away at the first few notes of "Jingle Bells." "Oh, that's a very interesting discovery, Dalena," replied the teacher, "How did you learn?" "It was easy," Dalena smiled, "I just figured it out."

Music is all around early childhood teachers. We cannot escape it. For that reason alone, music should be an integral part of the early childhood program.

CREATIVE MOVEMENT

Early childhood is a fun time of life; young children are dominated by a strong desire to move. Growing muscles enable youngsters to initiate and refine some very important accomplishments—walking, running, jumping, and so on. Parents and caregivers are quite captivated by the toddler's persistent efforts to push, pull, pound, and tug. They watch with interest as the very young prance about with a favorite stuffed animal held tight to their chests or dump a container full of toys to the floor in a strong drive to find a favorite one. Children are charged with physical energy; the relative passivity of infancy has been transformed into strong locomotor drives. Never again are such dramatic advances in physical appearance and motor abilities experienced as during the first five years of life. Arms and legs lengthen; the soft, round, cherubic cheeks of infancy slowly begin to disappear; muscular strength and coordination make walking, running, jumping, and a number of other amazing physical feats possible. The adventurer who takes her first solitary walking journey at 15 months soon uses her stubby little legs to ascend the steps of a climber and speed down the slide. Those same legs welcome new challenges along the way—making the pedals on a tricycle work or finding firm footing atop a boulder. Great leaps in development likewise occur in the ability to coordinate the efforts of small muscles and the eyes: "How do I get this crayon to go where I want it to go?" Guiding scissors around an outline, rolling a lump of clay into a "worm," and pasting one piece of paper on the exact spot one would like it to go are all intricate skills that take much practice to master. Propelled by an intense need to be active, children continually perform the climbing, running, jumping, balancing, cutting, pasting, coloring, and grasping activities of childhood that provide the movement and stimulation necessary to help them grow and gain mastery of their bodies. Fraiberg commented on the intensity of a young child's need for physical movement:

> The discovery of independent locomotion and the discovery of a new self usher in a new phase in personality development. The [child] is quite giddy with his new achievements. He behaves as if he had invented his new mode of locomotion... and he is quite in love with himself for being so clever. From dawn to dusk he marches around in an ecstatic, drunken dance, which ends only when he collapses with fatigue. He can no longer be contained within the four walls of his house and the fenced-in yard is like a prison to him. Given practically unlimited space he staggers joyfully with open arms toward the end of the horizon. Given half a chance he might make it.[8]

This urge to move should be capitalized upon in preschool programs. Certainly, teachers must be sensitive to the spontaneous movements that children display nearly all the time. They must also be aware of opportunities to provide planned experiences in body movement. Poest, Williams, Witt, and Atwood advocate a planned program to move from the spontaneous, unplanned movements engaged in by young children toward the refinement of skills associated with these three categories: (1) *fundamen-*

tal movement skills, (2) *physical fitness,* and (3) *perceptual-motor development.*[9] Such a program should be designed to help children develop patterns of coordination and control as well as to foster continued creativity in body movements.

Fundamental Movement Skills   Fundamental movement skills are those basic movements that children are developmentally ready to refine and develop during the preschool years. Among those most commonly associated with the early childhood years are the following:

- *Walking.* Walk fast; walk slow; walk backwards; walk on tiptoe; walk on heels; walk sideways; walk with hands on head; walk with hands on hips; and so on. Play games like Follow the Leader or encourage the children to walk like favorite animals.

- *Standing.* Stand on tiptoe for a count of five; stand on right foot for a count of five; stand on left foot for a count of five; stand in each of the previous ways with eyes shut.

- *Balancing.* Get a $2'' \times 4'' \times 8'$ board for these activities. First ask the children to stand on the board to see if they can control their bodies. This ability to balance is basic to other activities. When children display good balance, ask them to walk with one foot on the board and one foot on the floor. Then encourage them to take short series of steps with both feet on the balance board. Gradually children will learn to walk forward on the balance board. Then ask them to walk slowly (forward); walk sideways (first the dominant side leads and then the other leads); walk with a beanbag on their heads; walk slowly (backward); walk backward with a beanbag on their heads.

- *Running.* Run fast; run slowly; run on tiptoe; run with hands behind their backs; run with long or short strides; run toward the teacher; and so forth.

- *Jumping.* Jump up and down in place; use only one foot while jumping; jump forward; jump backward; jump into the air and make a quarter turn; jump with eyes closed; and so on. Jump from a low height onto a mat or landing pad. Children can be encouraged to become frogs, grasshoppers, or jumping jacks.

- *Galloping.* Help children learn this skill by showing them the correct procedure. Play some background music appropriate for galloping and invite the children to become galloping ponies or reindeer. Then show them how to gallop—step forward on one foot and bring the other foot up beside it. Then step forward on the first foot again and bring the second beside it. Gradually encourage the children to repeat the process to the music until they achieve a smooth, galloping gait.

- *Skipping.* Skipping is perhaps the most difficult body movement for young children to master. For that reason, you must spend a good deal of time instructing them in this skill. Tell the children to step forward on one foot

These "tightrope walkers" are having fun and developing crucial movement skills at the same time.

while holding the second foot in the air (you may want to hold it up for the child). The first foot then makes a hop and the second foot steps forward. The children are led to step and hop on one foot, step and hop on the other, and so on until the step-hop sequence becomes smooth and natural.

- *Playing with a ball.* Throwing, catching, kicking, punting, hitting, bouncing, volleying, dribbling, rolling, and trapping are basic skills associated with ball playing.

Some teachers feel that the only thing we need do to help children acquire these skills is to wait until they are physically ready. Surely, physical maturation plays a major role in skill development, but practice and instruction, too, help children attain competency in movement. Most of the movements above can best be encouraged with the use of musical accompaniment—a recording or the use of drums and tambourines add special challenge and pleasure to the program. The fundamental movement skills listed above can serve as organizational themes around which to plan daily experiences. Set up your play equipment each day to challenge the children's competency and creativity. Offer activities that spur the children's imagination—walking like a spider (on all fours), pulling themselves like seals, squatting and jumping like a kangaroo, waddling like a duck, crawling like a snake, kicking like a mule, plodding like an elephant, or swimming like a fish. Other suggestions are offered in the accompanying box.

▶▶▶▶▶▶▶

CREATIVE BODY MOVEMENT ACTIVITIES

Freeze

Play lively music on the radio or tape recorder. Invite the children to move freely as the music is playing. Every so often, quickly turn off the sound and ask the children to "freeze." See if they can hold the position for two or three seconds, and start up the music again.

Shadows

Two children work together. One child performs a basic body movement and the other child must imitate what was done. They take turns being the leader.

Rope Games

A long length of rope should be placed on the floor or ground. Have the children who are able walk a straight line along the rope forward and backward. Make a circle from the rope and ask the children to walk the circle forward or backward. With the rope in a straight line, have the children hop over it and then hop back again. Make curves in the rope and have the children run or hop so each step will be taken in a new curve. As the children to invent a new way of moving with the rope.

Tightrope Walker

Establish a straight line about 10 feet long on the floor of your classroom. Invite the children to walk along the line as far as they can without ringing a small bell held in their hand. For variety, try making a curved line, a circle, and other shapes.

Wings

Especially on days when winds are brisk and steady, invite the children to don a variety of wings and run about as imaginary butterflies, birds, superheroes, or anything else that jogs their creativity. Some effective wings include an old sheet; crepe paper streamers stapled onto a cloth strip; and a plastic garbage bag slit to form a large sheet. (Plastic bags can be dangerous, so children playing with them should be closely supervised.)

Going to the Zoo

To encourage creative movements of many kinds, gather the children in a group and invite them to go with you on an imaginary trip to the zoo. On this special trip, the children must choose an animal to imitate as their means of getting there. Lead them by saying, for example: "We're going to the zoo. How is Diana going to get there?" "I'm going to fly like a bird," says Diana. Encourage the rest of the children to follow the first child's lead and perform the actions described in the previous activity—flying like birds, hopping like frogs, waddling like ducks, swimming like fish, crawling like snakes, and so on.

Circus Time

Arrange the children in a circle formation, seated on the floor. Select one child to stand in the center to act as "ringmaster." The ringmaster passes out one slip of paper to each child, each slip picturing an animal with a distinctive movement, such as a horse, elephant, bird, and so on (or hang the picture around the child's neck). When signaled by the ringmaster, the child steps to the center of the circle and pantomimes the animal on his slip. After the ringmaster has given each child a chance, she organizes a parade in which the children move in a circle, pantomiming their respective animals.

Balloon Bat

Give each child in your group an inflated balloon. Give the children a signal to start, whereupon they throw their balloons into the air. The children see how long they can keep the balloons in the air by tapping them back when they begin to come down.

Jack, Be Nimble

Make several potato chip canister "candlesticks" (make a slit in the plastic top and pull a red kerchief through it). Place one in front of each child in your group. Say the nursery rhyme "Jack, Be Nimble," and have the children jump with both feet over the candlesticks as the last line is recited. (You may wish to encourage the children to jump one-by-one over their candlesticks by substituting each name for "Jack.")

> Jack, be nimble,
> Jack, be quick,
> Jack, *jump* over the candlestick.

Say the rhyme again, this time jumping backward over the candlestick: Continue with variations such as jumping sideways or with arms stretched in front.

Action Verses

Compose a set of verses by which you can encourage various body movements. For example, while playing outdoors, these rhymes can be used:

> Little frogs, little frogs,
> Hop to the wall;
> Little frogs, little frogs,
> Please come back, I call.
>
> Little lions, little lions,
> Run to the door;
> Little lions, little lions,
> Give a great big roar.
>
> Little ducks, little ducks,
> Waddle to the gate;
> Little ducks, little ducks,
> Hurry—don't be late.
>
> Little birds, little birds,
> Fly to the swings;
> Little birds, little birds,
> Flap and flap your wings.

Physical Fitness   Physical fitness refers to one's health development and functional capacity—cardiovascular endurance, muscular strength, muscular endurance, flexibility, and body leanness. Although this has been a popular topic for adults, little research has been directed toward the area of preschool fitness. Poest, Williams, Witt, and Atwood report, however, that "young children are especially weak in the areas of muscular strength, cardiovascular endurance, and body leanness. The research seems to show that children are in worse physical condition now than 20 years ago."[10]

Planned daily fitness activities should encourage continuous, fast-paced movement. Participate in the activities yourself; you will serve as a good model for the children to emulate. Some suggestions follow.

- Take a brisk, daily walk with the children.

- Include a daily run or gallop to music, either indoors or out. Encourage the children to push themselves a little bit farther each time: "Try to keep running until the music stops." Gradually increase the length of the musical selection.

- Include creative movement activities in your fitness program. As mentioned earlier, encourage children to hop like frogs or crawl like snakes. Similarly, they can speed around the playground like police cars with sirens blaring, or flop about on the rug pretending to be clothes in a dryer.

- Use a variety of music to encourage cardiovascular endurance. Avoid recordings or activities that call for group calisthenics or structured exercise routines. These are developmentally inappropriate techniques for young children.

Perceptual-Motor Activities   Perceptual-motor activities involve the processes of "monitoring and interpreting sensory data and responding in movement."[11] Many children enter the preschool setting with good coordination and muscle control. These children benefit from continuing opportunities to improve their skills through the informal exercise we have been discussing. Others are less proficient and need positive encouragement to achieve greater success. Your role is to structure short indoor or outdoor practice activities in which the children can work on developing their muscular coordination. Such activities, combining creativity and physical exercise, can be informal. Consider the example in the box below.

In addition to these informal experiences, teachers' programs are often carefully designed to help children practice their growing awareness of body potential. Operating by the motto, "Teach a little and play a lot," these teachers realize the importance of developing guided activities appropriate for the age level of their children. At the same time, though, they realize the need for youngsters to do it their way. "I can do it" and "Watch me" are frequent exclamations of children exhilarated by their greater control over their movements. Your ability to perceive the world of the child and to see things from that point of view is a necessary prerequisite to sharing happy play experiences like those described in the section on page 370.

▶▶▶▶▶▶▶

Ada and her friend Terri made an interesting discovery while on the playground one day. They went down on their hands and knees and watched in fascination as a large frog hopped erratically in the tall grass at the edge of the play area. Soon several other children joined the two girls and called to their teacher to observe their discovery. After encouraging the children to comment on the frog's bumpy skin and bulging eyes, the teacher was pleased when the children began to discuss how it hopped and jumped. "Gee, look how far it hopped!" "It jumped so high." Suddenly, Terri kicked up her legs and supported herself with her hands. "Watch me," she called, "I'm a frog. Watch me hop." Soon the other children joined Terri and hopped along with each other. The teacher, alert to the situation, began to lead the children in a rhythmical chant. "Hippity hop, hippity hop, watch us jump and flip and flop. Hippity hop, hippity hop...."

Knowledge of Body Parts

1. Ask the children to identify parts of the body by touching them. Start by touching the different parts of your body as you say, for example, "I'm touching my nose. Touch your nose." Continue with the ears, eyes, chin, mouth, shoulder, neck, arm, elbow, knee, stomach, toes, back, side, ankle, and hand.

2. A number of traditional early childhood songs stimulate children to recognize body parts and their relative movement properties. Some examples are shown in the accompanying box.

3. Use variations on the first activity:
   - Touch the parts with eyes closed.
   - Touch the parts with two hands.
   - Touch the body parts with a body part other than the hand or finger. For example, "Touch your elbow with your knee."
   - Touch a body part with an object in the environment; for example, "Touch your knees to the floor," or "Touch the tree with your foot."
   - Invite the children to take turns leading the activity.

4. Establish relationships of body parts. Say, for example, "See if you can move your hands far away from your feet (or shoulders)," or "Move one foot behind the other," or "Stand next to a partner," or "Wave your hand above your head."

5. Use fingerplays (examples are in the accompanying box) to help identify body parts.

▷▷▷▷▷▷▷

BODY PARTS SONGS

Traditional Tunes

To the tune "Hokey Pokey," encourage the following movements:

> Put your right hand in. (toward center of circle)
> Take your right hand out.
> Put your right hand in, and shake it all about.
> We'll shake it in the morning or we'll shake it after noon.
> That's what it's all about.
> (second verse) . . . left hand . . .
> (third verse) . . . right foot . . .
> (fourth verse) . . . left foot . . .
> (fifth verse) . . . head . . .
> (sixth verse) . . . whole body . . .

Put new words to familiar tunes as children are encouraged to exercise. This is one of many possible variations on the tune "Jingle Bells."

Clap your hands, clap your hands,
Clap them loud and long.
Oh, what fun it is to clap,
And sing this happy song,
(second verse) Touch your toes ...
(third verse) Stretch up tall ...
(fourth verse) Walk in line ...
(fifth verse) Row your boat ...
(sixth verse) Throw the ball ...

"Looby, Loo" is a favorite circle song that encourages children to move different parts of their bodies creatively.

(chorus)   Here we go looby, loo,
Here we go looby, light,
Here we go looby, loo,
All on a Saturday night.

Verses follow with:

I put my left hand in
I put my left hand out
I give my left hand a shake, shake, shake,
And turn my self about.
(chorus)   Here we go looby loo ...

Continue with right hand, left foot, right foot, round head, and whole self.

Small-Muscle Control   Perceptual-motor development involves not only knowing the body parts but also having the ability to gain control over them. We examined how this can be done by exercising the large muscles; now we will see how small muscles (fine motor) development can be enhanced. In the realm of fine motor activity, children are given experiences in manipulating puzzle pieces, holding paintbrushes, using scissors, and drawing with crayons and markers. All of these experiences are planned to develop perhaps the most important of all fine motor skills—precise hand control. Some common developmental patterns of hand control are shown in Table 10–1.

To encourage these fine motor skills, you should offer a variety of materials with which the children can experiment. There are many opportunities for children to refine small muscle skills during daily routines. We have talked about some of these in other chapters: pouring, cutting, building, drilling, mixing, putting together puzzles,

Table 10–1   Patterns of Fine Motor Development in Preschool Children

Age	Fine Motor Abilities
1–2 years	Can hold large pencil or crayon Can pull off shoes and socks Can begin to drink from a cup and feed themselves with a spoon
2–3 years	Can scribble with pencils or crayons Can open boxes and other simple containers Can begin to use knives and forks when feeding themselves
3–4 years	Can use pencils or crayons to copy circles or simple lines Can print large capital letters Can use modeling clay, make cookies, and sew Can feed themselves well and even wash and dry dishes Can cut paper
4–6 years	Can copy some simple geometric figures: circles, squares, triangles, and rectangles Can print their names, entire alphabet, and numerals from 1 to 20 Can build crude models from wood and other materials Can bathe themselves, brush own teeth and hair Can dress themselves completely Can cut following a line

pasting, buttoning, screwing on bottle caps, drawing, zipping, mailing, painting, lacing, scribbling, and using tools.

Such activities are not only inherently pleasing to young children, but they also ready them for the eventual mastery of handwriting and related skills. Before young children can be expected to write, for example, they must be able to hold a pencil properly and control movements of their wrist and finger muscles. They gain this control through the activities listed in the preceding paragraph. As children develop small-muscle skills, they learn to coordinate the hand and eye (eye-hand coordination). Children who hammer a nail straight or follow a path with their pencil demonstrate eye-hand coordination. All of these actions help increase the children's intellectual growth.

Equipment designed to foster small-muscle control is rich and varied. Some common small-muscle equipment is listed below.

- *Stacking rings.* Children stack the colorful plastic rings in order.

- *Snap-lock beads.* These colorful plastic beads snap together and pop apart.

- *Puzzles.* Simple wooden or durable cardboard puzzles should be easy enough for the child not to frustrate him. For two-year-olds, use one- or two-piece puzzles with handles. For three-year-olds and older, use puzzles of up to eight pieces.

- *Shape toys.* Children put three-dimensional plastic shapes into appropriate openings in a special box.

Gaining control over one's small muscles and coordinating movements are important developmental skills.

- *Wooden beads.* Children pick up the beads and either string them or plop them back into the can.

- *Dressing frames.* Children refine their skill at lacing, tying, buttoning, zipping, and snapping on small practice frames.

- *Art supplies.* Children can be helped to train their small muscles through such creative art media as fat crayons, fat pencils, felt-tip markers, note pads and paper, glue, clay, blunt-pointed scissors, brushes and paint, and yarn.

- *Small plastic figures.* Children enjoy playing with animals, farmers, firefighters, police officers, and other small plastic figures.

You should be aware of the importance of providing chances to refine gross and fine motor skills. As the children experience learning opportunities in curriculum areas, they do so in physically active ways. Children *need* physical activity during the preschool years. You will find that, except for short periods of quiet (during story time) or rest (after vigorous play), nearly all activities during a typical preschool day involve the children in physical activity. It is important that you individualize your program and make it developmental. All children develop at different rates, and

The best puzzles suit the child's degree of fine-motor coordination and ability to concentrate.

opportunities for muscular exercise should range from the simple (running, jumping) to the more demanding (cutting, printing). Your ability to plan a range of activities will help children develop to their full potential.

SOME FINAL THOUGHTS

Music, like art, should be an enriching part of each day for preschool youngsters. Whether included as a pleasurable accompaniment to daily routines (washing up or dressing, for example) or simply as a means of channeling energy by moving freely to the rhythm, informal music can bring a special sense of well-being and joy to you as well as to the child. Don't be afraid to make up your own times or words to songs as you fit them to almost any activity the child is involved in. You will be astonished at how skilled you become at this and gratified to see how young children are drawn to your spontaneous efforts.

Although children differ markedly in their ability to make music, nearly all respond to melody and rhythm and want to sing as well as to dance. Some do prefer to listen, though. Whatever the case, music experiences should be provided for the very young. You need not read music, play an instrument, or sing like a Grammy award winner in order to bring music into your classroom. After all, you don't have to be Picasso in order to set up an easel painting area in your room. The single most important requirement for a good preschool music program is the teacher's sense of enjoyment in singing and dancing. Your spirit—not a perceived bad voice or clumsy dance movement—is what will register with the children. If you augment your program with simple songs, basic musical instruments, and well-chosen records, your children will be eager to explore music and movement, and their creativity will flourish. Music is an important vehicle for physical development, too. Even during infancy, physical (or sensorimotor) musical play stimulates the child's simple, repetitive actions. These play behaviors gradually give way to more sophisticated motor responses during toddlerhood and the early years. By being knowledgeable about and sensitive to children's specific physical abilities, you can extend and enrich their musical play and encourage growth from one developmental level to the next.

It is important to remember that physical growth is greatly enhanced through creative movement experiences within stimulating, challenging musical environments. Offer many daily opportunities where children can develop large and small muscles as well as perceptual skills in a pleasurable, developmentally appropriate manner.

NOTES

1. Sally Moomaw, *Discovering Music in Early Childhood* (Boston: Allyn and Bacon, 1984), p. 7.
2. "MENC Position Statement: Early Childhood Education," (Music Educators National Conference, 1902 Association Drive, Reston, Virginia 22091), 1991: p. 1.
3. Dorothy T. McDonald with Jonny H. Ramsey, "Awakening the Artist: Music for Young Children," in Janet F. Brown, ed., *Curriculum Planning for Young Children* (Washington, DC: National Association for the Education of Young Children, 1982), p. 187.
4. Marguerite de Angeli, *Book of Nursery and Mother Goose Rhymes* (Garden City, NY: Doubleday, 1954), foreword.
5. Mary Renck Jalongo and Mitzie Collins, "Singing With Young Children," *Young Children, 40*, no. 2 (January 1985): 17.
6. B. Joan E. Haines and Linda L. Gerber, *Leading Young Children to Music: A Resource Book for Teachers,* 4th ed. (Columbus, OH: Merrill/Macmillan, 1992), p. 124.
7. Ibid.
8. S. Fraiberg, "How a Baby Learns to Love," *Redbook* (May 1971): 123–133.
9. Catherine A. Poest, Jean R. Williams, David D. Witt, and Mary Ellen Atwood, "Challenge Me to Move: Large Muscle Development in Young Children," *Young Children, 45*, no. 5 (July 1990): 4–10.
10. Ibid., p. 6.
11. Ibid., p. 6.

CHAPTER 11

Advancing Interest in the Social Environment

A traditional goal of early childhood education has been socialization—helping children understand and appreciate their roles in society and transmitting our culture to them. Basic to this mission is a strong emphasis on helping children develop a sense of their individuality, their uniqueness as persons. It is only after the child can accept and appreciate herself as an individual, unique and competent, that she can be motivated to seek relationships with others and to want to learn about others. The early childhood environment must be one that first encourages learning about oneself and then progresses to learning about other people as individuals with their own interests, strengths, weaknesses, and feelings. This chapter deals with the daily experiences that help promote knowledge of self and others. Such experiences form a basis for encouraging children to explore new social worlds that arouse their curiosity. As you read, use the following questions to guide your thinking.

- Why is a teacher's sense of wonder essential for working with young children?

- What is meant by a child's *social world*?

- How do teachers help promote positive self-concept and an appreciation of others?

- What body of information do educators draw on as they help children learn about the world around them?

- What is the teacher's role in helping children discover learnings related to their social world?

An Episode to Ponder

I will go very far,
farther than those hills,
farther than the seas,
close to the stars,
to beg Christ the Lord
to give back the soul I had
of old, when I was a child,
ripened with legends,
with a feathered cap
and a wooden sword.

—Federico Garcia Lorca

The essence of teaching is wonder. The spirit of wonder is a glorious gift that is bestowed upon all of us at childhood—an endowment of unbridled energy and excitement for exploration and discovery. For many, this gift lasts a lifetime; for others, it regrettably flickers and fades away through the years. Part of being a teacher of young children is to keep that prize—to maintain the glorious gift of wonder and joy in making new discoveries. A "child-like" eagerness to discover new knowledge of the world with children should form a major part of every teacher's personality, and bring them as much sincere pleasure in unlocking the world's mysteries as it does their children.

Albert Cullum advises teachers to maintain a rich quality of childhood exuberance and imagination. If this can't be done, teachers will find it impossible to encourage those qualities in the children they teach.

> As teachers we should be constantly searching for our lost feathered caps and our lost wooden swords, for they are the only entrees we have to the world of children. If we can't enter their world, we can never reach them. Try donning a feathered cap, wave a wooden sword. . . . (and create an exciting atmosphere for learning).[1]

Our children's understanding of their social world involves all they learn about themselves, others, and the environmental phenomena that influence relationships between themselves and others. This awareness begins during infancy as babies experience their first **social interaction** with the adults responsible for their care. Social interactions are evident while an adult hums a soft tune during feeding time, buzzes her lips on the baby's tummy, or plays a rollicking game of "peek-a-boo" with the baby. Social interactions are all the special exchanges between adult and child that contribute to positive interpersonal responses. From these early positive experiences, children progress through special growth experiences referred to as **social development** The term *social* refers to the establishment of relationships between two or more individuals, through which they influence each other's behavior.

THE SOCIAL WORLD OF INFANTS

After the first three to four weeks of the baby's life, pleasant social interactions such as gentle touches, humming, cooing, stroking, tickling, or rocking often result in the first positive social responses—social smiles. Adults are quite delighted at the emergence of a social smile, for it is not only an enjoyable phenomenon, but also socially significant. It is the first obviously positive social response offered by babies. Gradually, during the next two to three months, the baby expands the constituency with whom she shares a social smile—even strangers may be granted this special treat. T. G. R. Bower explained how young babies, even in their first days of life, react so positively to the social endeavors of others:

> One of the more spectacular demonstrations . . . is the fact that babies less than a week old will imitate other people. If the baby's mother, or some other adult, sticks out her tongue at the baby, within a relatively short time the baby will begin to stick his

One of the most heartwarming facets of early adult-child interactions is to be the object of a child's social smile.

tongue back out at her. Suppose she then stops sticking her tongue out and begins to flutter her eyelashes, the baby will flutter his eyelashes back. If she then starts to open and close her mouth in synchrony . . . the newborn actually seems to enjoy engaging in this mutual imitation game. . . . And all these (imitative) capacities are bent toward what is clearly, I think, a social purpose. The newborn enjoys social interaction with adults. Imitation at this stage is a social game. The responses are quite specifically directed toward human beings and seem to me to be testimony that the newborn considers himself human too. . . . The newborn baby imitates the facial gestures of the adults around him for no reward other than the pleasure of interacting with them.[2]

Therefore, through interactive games, the infant begins to participate in **socialization experiences**. These experiences are most fruitful if they happen spontaneously, when both adult and baby are relaxed and receptive.

Often the person who cares for the infant most will become the object of most highly positive social exchanges. That person is able to soothe and comfort the baby when others are unsuccessful. It is to this person that the baby turns, gives the most special smile, or stretches out its arms in an appeal to be held. According to Gladys G. Jenkins and Helen S. Shacter, "There are indications that babies thrive best when there is one central caregiving person to whom they form an attachment by the middle of this first year. This attachment provides the feelings of security and trust which make it possible for the baby to grow into warm relationships with other people all through life."[3]

Babies must receive abundant attention and human contact in order to build active, affectionate relationships with their families or primary caregivers. As babies experience interactions with other people, they develop strong attachments to them. They gain interest in the company of adults and in familiar interactive games with others. At about the tenth month, they are able to participate in more advanced social games such as pat-a-cake. (As hard as they may try, though, it is difficult for babies to clap palms together. Their first motion in a pat-a-cake game is clapping their fists together instead of their palms. Eventually, they are likely to clap their palms together, but they won't make clapping sounds.) Slowly, infants begin to understand simple commands and requests, along with special cue words for familiar games and daily routines. These patterns of socialized play indicate a stable pattern of social growth. Children are fascinated with repetitive play and enjoy duplicating their new experiences many times—to the point where it often becomes monotonous for an adult. Don't lose your patience when this happens, but keep in mind that children behave like this because they are thrilled with their new discoveries. As they are continually encouraged by adults to extend their interests, their growth is stimulated and reinforced. Several kinds of social play are described in the box on pages 381–383.

Many caregivers, especially beginners with little or no experience with infants, want to encourage their baby's development but feel awkward or uncertain about how to do it. Because infants cannot walk, talk, or play the way they will do later in life, some people think they are unintelligent or "blank slates." That is not true; babies are intelligent and extremely social, and they love to communicate with and respond to others.

The key to effective interaction is to relax and allow the child within you to emerge. Don't be inhibited; go ahead and touch, smile, sing, and laugh. In no time, you'll enter freely into the child's world and will completely understand his mode of communication. This is especially true after about the second month, when he responds to you with even more profuse smiles and laughter. There is no single "best" style of interacting with babies. Some people, for instance, have a strong physical style that emphasizes such vigorous interactions as "bicycling" the infants' legs, lifting them into the air, or laughing loudly as they are hugged. Others tend to interact in a quieter, more soothing manner: singing, talking, or rocking. Your baby's individual moods, temperament, and preferences will often dictate how you interact. Your baby will let you know when he's received the appropriate stimulation. He may turn his body away from you, arch his back rigidly, cry, or push away a toy that's offered to him. Your system of interaction will certainly change because of these reactions. Surprisingly, both types of loving expressions (strong or soft) elicit positive responses from babies. The reason for this is that babies are individuals and need different amounts, as well as different kinds, of love. They are responsive and develop trust in you only as you are reliable and consistent in the types of affection you offer. Be yourself. You, too, are an individual, and you have your own ways of expressing real affection.

As you interact positively with the infant, your attachment will become stronger and the infant will become enthusiastic, confident, cooperative, socially oriented, and curious about his surroundings. Infants feel emotionally secure in their newly developed social environment, and they seek to keep close contact with those they trust. This developing confidence encourages further explorations into new relationships and a healthy progression to more mature stages of personality development.

▷▷▷▷▷▷▷

SOCIAL PLAY FOR INFANTS

Mimicking

The caregiver encourages the baby to imitate gestures or sounds. Waving "bye-bye" or stretching out the arms to indicate "so big" are favorites. Coughing, sniffing through the nose, or making simple sounds such as "ahr-r-r-r" amuse the infant for great periods of time.

Drop and Fetch

Babies seem to drop things at first simply to see what happens. They hear the noise and turn to see what transpired. Their great joy comes, however, when the caregiver becomes involved and picks up the object. This soon becomes great entertainment; the baby drops and the caregiver fetches. To some caregivers, this repetition seems pointless and boring. However, when we consider the social play resulting from this interaction, we realize that the game is an important source of learning about the world.

Peek-a-Boo

Babies enjoy this traditional adult-infant participation game. The caregiver begins the game by hiding his face in back of his hands or a blanket, suddenly showing his face, and saying, "Peek-a-boo. I see you," to the baby.

Pat-a-Cake

This simple rhyme is greeted with enjoyment by infants long after the caregiver may become tired and bored with it.

> Pat-a-cake, pat-a-cake, baker's man. (*Clap baby's hands together.*)
> Bake me a cake as fast as you can.
> Roll it (*Roll baby's hands.*)
> And pat it (*Pat baby's hands.*)
> And mark it with a B (*Make a letter "B" on baby's tummy.*)
> And put it in the oven for baby (*or baby's first name*) and me!

Action Games

Traditional favorites are jiggling the baby above one's head, swinging him from the chest to between the knees, tickling the baby's trunk, or bouncing him on a knee to a familiar rhythmic verse. Here are two rhymes to accompany the bouncing activity:

> TO MARKET, TO MARKET
>
> To market, to market, to buy a fat pig;
> Home again, home again, jiggety jig.
> To market, to market, to buy a fat hog;
> Home again, home again, jiggety jog.

> FIDDLE-DE-DEE
>
> Fiddle-de-dee, fiddle-de-dee,
> The fly shall marry the bumblebee.
> They went to church and married was she;
> The fly had married the bumblebee.

Sound Games

Interaction with infants is greatly enhanced when the caregiver plays sound games involving parts of the body. Games combining movement and rhymes include these popular selections:

> BABY BUMBLEBEE
>
> I'm bringing home a baby bumblebee.
> (*Cup hands together.*)
> Won't my mommy be so proud of me?
> I'm bringing home a baby bumblebee.
> OUCH! (*Clap hands.*)
> He stung me!

> KNOCK ON THE DOOR
>
> Knock on the door. (*Tap on baby's forehead.*)
> Peek in. (*Lift up an eyelid.*)
> Open the hatch. (*Pretend to turn baby's nose.*)
> And walk right in. (*Tickle baby's lips.*)

Give and Take

This is a popular favorite, which begins with the caregiver giving the child a favorite toy and saying, "Now I'll give it to you." Back-and-forth activity is encouraged as the caregiver says, "Now you give it to me."

Gotcha

Once the baby is able to creep or crawl, he or she enjoys the challenge of moving away and being chased to a warning, "I'm gonna getcha." The caregiver should let the baby crawl for a while and grab him or her, exclaiming, "Gotcha!" The baby should be given a big hug or tickle after each episode.

Hide-n-Seek

Babies laugh with glee as their caregivers repeatedly call their names while searching behind doors or in wastebaskets or drawers for the "lost infant."

Facial Examination

Older infants punctuate their growing social awareness by showing an interest in a caregiver's facial features. The baby may grab the nose, grasp eyeglasses, touch an ear, or poke at one's eyes. By guiding the infant with words such as "Easy, easy," the caregiver informs the baby that such exploration must be done carefully. One may want to name each feature as the child touches it, eventually encouraging the child to touch the same feature on his or her face. By continually following this pattern, the child may be able to respond appropriately by the end of the first year when asked to "Show me your nose (or other feature)."

THE SOCIAL WORLD OF TODDLERS

During infancy, children demonstrate certain temperaments while eliciting responses from parents and caregivers. These early mutual interactions between adult and child begin to shape the child's personality. If those interactions are constructive, children will, by age two, have established trust and confidence in their world and strive to take their first complex steps toward independence and initiative. When they begin to do this, they retain the individuality so strongly evident during infancy. The more outgoing, aggressive child will yell, hit, bite, or throw things when frustrated in an attempt at some hopeless task, whereas a more tranquil child may suck his thumb or whimper. One child may jump headlong into any new situation, whereas another prefers just to watch the others. The "scientist" enjoys taking things apart to see how they work, while the "performer" prefers the dramatic delight of the housekeeping area. Some are energetic and bold, others timid and shy. Some conform readily to behavioral norms that others strongly resist. Some respond to social situations, and others do not. Some are serious; others smile a lot.

Although toddlerhood is marked by individuality, it is also a time of rapidly shifting behaviors—toddlers are known for their quick changes in mood. The time of growing independence—"I want to do it myself"—is also a time of "no." Children who used to smile and help as you got them dressed now shriek, "No! No!" as you attempt to put on their jackets to go outdoors. During free play time, he may not want to play with blocks, but ten minutes later he is screaming because he does not want to stop. She may be hungry and ready to eat, but place the dish in front of her and she balks. Children who accepted things congenially until about the age of two now almost constantly seek to exert their growing independence.

"How much work a toddler can be!" the teacher often thinks to herself as she follows them from one end of the room to the other yelling, "No! No!" or "How many times do I have to ask you not to do that?" Realistically, toddlers must be told many times—they must experiment and learn from their mistakes before we can expect them to become competent at managing their own behavior. All children need to learn how to act in order to get the approval they seek. Teaching them management skills is an important part of the preschool curriculum.

We must remember that these characteristics only emphasize the fact that every child is different. Our role is to know how to treat each child. Katherine Baker and Xenia Fane express this idea well:

> We help children most when we accept them as they are. We all need to feel that we are loved for what we are. This feeling gives each of us the courage to grow and improve. We are likely to want to change at our own rate and in our own way. It makes us uncomfortable or even unsure of ourselves to be pushed. Being pushed often makes it harder to change. Children feel the same way. . . . Each one wants to be accepted and liked for what he is. Each needs to be helped to grow in his own way and at his own rate.[4]

Toddlers must be allowed to establish their independence within an environment that offers many opportunities for making decisions and for doing things independently. This feature in itself is a difficult professional task, but it is further complicated by the fact that you must consistently step in and extend decisive control whenever toddlers make poor choices or become too headstrong in their pursuits. Balancing these two components of a quality early childhood climate is important. The children must experience freedom, but at the same time they need to know that they can depend on their teacher to furnish sensitive guidance within a trusting environment.

As toddlers are allowed to explore the environment, to act, and to create, they grow into young children capable of planning their own activities, attempting new challenges, and becoming part of a group. If they are given conditions in which they can fulfill these developmental needs in comfort and trust, they will feel good about themselves and will be likely to exhibit cooperative, positive behaviors. On the other hand, children who are discouraged while initiating plans and taking action will not feel good about themselves, will be unhappy, and will often demonstrate disruptive behavior.

THE SOCIAL WORLD OF YOUNG CHILDREN

As children grow into their third year and internalize the many experiences within their environment, their social growth enters a new phase of development. They become engaged—with every fiber of their existence—in being young children. They rush out into the world briskly and eagerly. In the next two or three years, their horizons widen and, if given trust and confidence, they will develop an interest in learning about others and will begin to sense their place in the mysterious world in which they find themselves.

In short, young children are on their way to achieving **social competence.** What is social competence? Essentially, it is the ability of an individual to respond to or interact effectively with others in the environment and to manage interpersonal circumstances in ways that prompt positive outcomes; it is the process through which children acquire behaviors appropriate for individuals of their age, gender, and culture. Children become socially competent when they understand and appreciate the traditions, rules, and beliefs of a culture, as well as its behavioral expectations for group membership. How do youngsters achieve social competence?

The first step in achieving social competence began during infancy and toddlerhood as children's **self-understanding** (perception of their unique character) unfolded. The infant's self-understanding may have been limited to **self-recognition.** That is, the baby, by about 18 months, perceives herself as a distinct part of the envi-

Sharing thoughts and ideas is strong evidence of deepening social skills.

ronment. A four-year-old, however, demonstrates self-understanding in a much more complex way. For example, he begins to distinguish himself from others in either of two ways: (1) **physical** or **material attributes** ("I'm different from Anton because he has blonde hair and mine is black," or "I'm different from Donna because she has a horse and I don't") and (2) **active attributes** ("I can jump farther than Sheldon"). In summary, children's self-understanding during the early childhood years is described in terms of one's physical self or active self.

A second major step in achieving social competence is the development of a positive **self-concept,** or self-esteem. For example, a child not only perceives himself as a dancer, but as a *good* dancer. Another understands that she is not only a runner, but a *splendid* runner; she is flushed with success, for example, because no one caught her today in a game of "Duck, Duck, Goose." Of course, not all evaluations of one's self are positive. The same four-year-old who perceived herself as a splendid runner may feel upset that she cannot yet name the basic colors. Children make evaluative judgments about all aspects of their lives; they may see themselves as good in physical skills and bad in academic skills, for example.

Each day you contribute to the formation of children's self-concept as you help strengthen their confidence in themselves as individuals who can feel happy, sad, helpful, or angry. These children know that someone is near who can help them cope with feelings without feeling overwhelmed. The comfort and trust generated in a secure classroom environment helps fill a child with pride and self-accomplishment. Children begin to see themselves from the perspective of others, which is a characteristic greatly affecting their personalities as they grow. Children internalize their interactions with others in the environment and begin to form feelings and ideas regarding their worth. Figure 11–1 illustrates the sophisticated process of the self-concept.

Teachers exert a tremendous influence on a child's self-concept when they interact verbally during the various daily routines. One teacher realized this fact when she needed to decide whether to allow a child, Vanessa, to climb the steps to the top of the playground slide and glide down all by herself. The teacher spent a great deal of time hovering over Vanessa, worrying about whether she would fall and hurt herself. Even though the teacher taught Vanessa how to grip the guardrail carefully as she climbed the steps and sit firmly before starting down, she just couldn't bring herself to let the little girl try it alone. The teacher appeared to communicate the message "You're not good enough to do that by yourself," a message damaging to a positive self-concept. Charles Horton Cooley is famous for his theory of the *looking-glass self,* which is related to this idea.[5] The theory can be summarized as "I am what I think you think I am." Closely related to this theory is R. K. Merton's famous concept of the *self-fulfilling prophecy.*[6] He pointed out that what people learn to think about themselves from the messages they receive from others will eventually come true. For example, if Vanessa is constantly told that her efforts are certain to end in failure, she may eventually avoid all challenges for fear of possible injury or failure.

Vanessa helped alter her teacher's approach one day through her sudden and straightforward statement, "I don't want you to help. I want to do it myself!" The

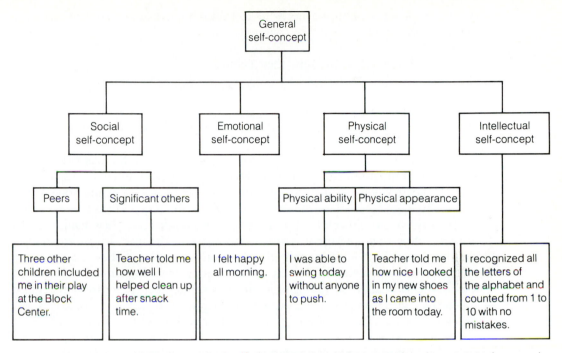

Figure 11–1 Factors influencing general self concept. Adapted from F. J. Shavelson, J. J. Hubner, and G. C. Stanton, "Self-Concept: Validation of construct interpretation," *Review of Educational Research,* 46, 1976, 413. Copyright American Educational Research Association, Washington, DC. Reprinted by permission.

teacher backed off and suffered inwardly, but the result was positive. Vanessa is now nearly four years old and hasn't had an accident yet. She was ready for this new experience, but the teacher wasn't! It is important to keep an eye on your children but also to realize that children don't know what they can do until they are at least allowed to try.

The self-concept of an individual is a direct result of daily experiences. But it is even more important to note that the very young child appears to react to those experiences not primarily on the basis of whether he or she was successful. Instead he bases his reaction on what the important people in the environment seemed to think of his efforts to accomplish something. The views that people appear to have of children are revealed through their reactions to the children's behaviors—through reward or punishment, love or withdrawal of love, approval or disapproval, acceptance or nonacceptance. From the very earliest years, children learn to read messages from such reactions. They learn how capable they are at activities deemed important by people of significance and how "valued" they are as individuals. Therefore, if a teacher communicates to a child that specific behaviors or skills are important but reacts in ways that indicate that the child is incompetent, the child forms a negative self-concept. Because of strong needs to feel important, children may react to the situation in ways that are not even conscious:

- They may hide or disguise their failures.

- They may minimize the importance of the activity.

- They may make it apparent that they will no longer extend an effort toward accomplishing a behavior or skill because of the possibility of failing again.

With the current emphasis on early formalized academics, for example, kindergarten children often learn that ability to read or recognize numbers is socially desirable. If they try and fail at these pursuits, however, they may assume one of the postures listed above. Because the second posture is the most difficult to maintain, children may choose either of the remaining options—to hide their failures or to quit trying altogether. Because it is nearly impossible to conceal such shortcomings, youngsters are often forced into the third option—to act as if they are not really trying. They may show lack of interest, refuse to participate in planned activities, be careless, or state a hatred of reading or mathematics. But if teachers learn to recognize competence in areas other than academics and help them to recognize successes, the children will stand a better chance of developing a positive sense of self and gaining the confidence to learn more. From there, they will take pleasure in attempting further learnings. The role of self-concept is important in all areas of development, not only in the realm of social competence. The self-concept plays a vital role in the total picture of what eventually forms each child's personality.

ENHANCING THE SOCIALIZATION PROCESS

Because what young children learn depends a great deal on outside factors, opportunities to learn come from a wide variety of materials and experiences. The young child's life is enriched by a wide circle of people important to him. His social world expands rapidly; the family remains important, but a growing exposure to peer groups, increasing involvement in worship groups, watching television, being read books, and, perhaps, attending preschool or child care introduce new interactive experiences to the child's life. For children in preschool, these new experiences may be quickly labeled "social studies" as a convenient tag under which to classify related learnings. However, I am hesitant to classify learnings in this way. As I explained in Chapter 6, it is difficult to categorize young children's learnings according to subject matter designations like we find in elementary schools. The child's awareness of the social environment is not something that grows only during "social studies class"—it evolves throughout the day's events. Given the lack of consensus among scholars as to what the term *social studies* means, I have chosen to accept the advice of Arthur Bestor (at least as it concerns the field of early childhood education), who once commented that, "This label [social studies] has itself contributed so greatly to educational confusion and stultification that it ought to be abandoned forthwith."[7]

Instead of adding to the confusion and labeling as "social studies" what we do to bring young children to an understanding of how their world functions, I have chosen to use the term "socialization". And, for the remainder of this chapter, the term "socialization" will be used to designate the means by which culture is transmitted to the very young.

The young children's environment includes the **culture** in which they find themselves. *Culture* is a difficult term to define, but we will consider it to be an inclusive term describing the sum of all the traditions, beliefs, values, habits, skills, arts, and institutions of any given group of people. *Socialization* is the process by which children acquire behaviors that are considered by a culture to be appropriate for their age and sex. The way that a culture is transmitted from one generation to the next is of critical interest to early childhood educators; in the following sections we will look at some of the important processes involved in socialization.

Teachers play a critical role in promoting the socialization of young children. Through their early relationships with teachers in the preschool environment, children learn what behaviors are expected of them in society at large. If they have been loved and accepted, and if you meet their needs as swiftly and consistently as possible, children will acquire a sense of security that will help them get along with peers, teachers, and other adults.

Teachers have many roles in this process, but for organizational purposes in this text, I have chosen to specify them as (1) encouraging play and social interaction, (2) helping children become autonomous, (3) participating in shared activities, and (4) promoting an understanding of and interest in the child's culture.

Encouraging Play and Social Interaction

One of the most obvious ways to help children acquire social behaviors is to provide them plentiful opportunities to play together during the day. Many social learnings take place during interactive play; the roots of a child's personality are deeply embedded in the process. **Social play** is any play that takes place between two individuals— stacking a tower of building blocks alone in a corner of a room is an example of solitary play; directing a friend to park her toy car in a block "parking garage" is a cooperative, or social play activity. In Chapter 3 you read about Mildred Parten's classifications of social play, which are categorized according to the type and amount of peer interaction involved: solitary, onlooker, parallel, associative, and cooperative play. Younger children prefer to play alone but gradually acquire a host of interpersonal interests and skills that make it possible for them to help one another in play activities requiring shared goals.

One especially important feature of social play is the drama children enact during their efforts to interpret and deal with the real world. Sarah Smilansky calls this type of play **sociodramatic play.**[8]

Sociodramatic play always involves themes that appeal to the children; it is of critical importance that the children have had a direct experience as a base for relating to the roles and behaviors required in the play situation. For that reason, the most common roles taken by preschoolers during dramatic play episodes are parent-child or mother-father roles. As children gain experiences outside the home, they begin to adopt representational roles that interest them the most. Therefore, the wiser teacher encourages play within a "firefighter" theme after a visit to the firehouse. On the other hand, the teacher who tries to stimulate her children to play the roles of astronauts or airline pilots can offer them no chance to directly experience their duties. Therefore, in most preschool programs, field trips (see pages 410–413) are considered an important part of the program because they not only provide the children with new and enriching social experiences, but also establish a sound foundation upon which to launch sociodramatic play. In their play episodes, then, children have fun playing out familiar themes, meanwhile participating in meaningful opportunities to practice skills of social interaction, develop cooperative behaviors, and express their ideas imaginatively.

Helping Children Become Autonomous

As we read in Chapter 3, one of the important theories of social competence was that advanced by Erik Erikson. Erikson described the child's development in terms of a series of stages, each characterized by opposing conflicts, or desires.[9] The first three of his stages begin during infancy and span the preschool years. To review, the first stage (*trust* versus *mistrust*) lasts through the first year of life. During this time the child learns to have faith in the world, so that she is able to confidently launch an active exploration of all of life's mysteries. The second stage (*autonomy* versus *shame and doubt*) lasts to about three years of age. After gaining trust in a parent or caregiver, children discover that their behavior is their own. That realization leads to a strong drive for independence, or autonomy. The third stage (*initiative* versus *guilt*) emerges during the rest of the preschool years. As their social world broadens, children learn that purposeful behavior is needed to cope with new challenges. They must learn to accept responsibility for their bodies, their behavior, and the cleanliness and order of their surroundings. Learning to handle such responsibilities increases initiative; irresponsibility often causes feelings of anxiety or guilt.

Although no single theory by itself can explain all the complexities involved in attaining social competence, Erikson's ideas have been quite prominent in guiding preschool practices. Early childhood educators view social maturation as a process of developing self-governing individuals capable of behaving in socially effective ways. Social competence is greatly facilitated by the confidence and skill children attain as they are allowed to actively explore the environment physically and socially (e.g., peppering the teacher with questions about everything they handle). The overall goal is to achieve positive growth throughout the developmental stages; growing through the first three stages results in developing an autonomous self—an individual who behaves effectively and is capable of assuming a constructive role in society.

Erikson believed that two of the most effective processes by which children become socialized are *imitation* and *identification*. Children not only imitate models and adopt their values and beliefs but also, in a sense, strive to be just like a desirable model. It is reasonable, then, to suppose that social imitation and identification can be influential in both the acquisition of personal behaviors and the attainment of cultural values and traditions. Infants, for example, may copy the behavior of a warm caregiver but, as social experiences increase (movies, books, television, trips, etc.), newer models become powerful influences on children's behavior.

The role of the teacher in such a setting is critical; she helps foster the children's self-concepts and social competence by acting as a mediator between the child and his emerging social world—family, peers, and other significant others. She helps the children make a transition from their self-centeredness to an expanded social world, while also helping to preserve the positive values of family and culture. The preschool teacher does all of this in a nurturing way, becoming a figure of trust who helps the child know that his world is safe and accepting. She opens the child to new experiences, encouraging and supporting endeavors beyond the familiar. She seeks to create self-control within each child—helping him know when to hold onto something important and when to let go and share.

In an effort to help children achieve autonomy, teachers must provide as many positive experiences as possible for the children to learn by example. They must convince children that they are respected as competent individuals as they grow and seek to become independent. For example, are you really helping children by pouring their juice during snack time? Are they really becoming autonomous when you hang up their jackets in the cubby? What message do you really send to young children when you tell them not to operate the tape recorder; that you will push the buttons for them? Certainly, many young children will have difficulty with some of these tasks, but their teacher must be willing to spend the time necessary to monitor children until they can do these things independently. Otherwise, the children may sense an attitude that they are expected to be little and helpless while they are in the preschool classroom.

Teachers can help children become autonomous by acting as good examples in the classroom. They show children they respect their rights by modeling positive aspects of cooperation and sharing. Think about the following scenarios. Which do you think describes a situation most appropriate for encouraging the growth of positive attitudes toward cooperation and sharing?

▶▶▶▶▶▶▶

Maja has been pulling around some rocks in the outdoor play area with her toy truck. Shortly, Kimberly arrives and demands the truck: "Gimme the truck, I want to use it." Maja counters, "No, it's mine. You can't have it!" The teacher observes the situation, walks over, and says, "My goodness, we seem to have a problem here. I think we can fix it by taking turns. Maja, you may have the truck for three more minutes; then it will be Kimberly's turn."

▶▶▶▶▶▶

The same problem arises, but this time the teacher walks over to the girls and says, "Kimberly, it's okay to want a truck just like Maja's. But screaming doesn't help you get it. You need to ask if Maja is ready to stop playing with it. Or, let's see what else you can use to carry rocks with."

Some teachers handle similar situations as the first teacher did. But, think of the message the child receives from those teachers: "I know you have the toy now. But, someone else wants it so you'd better get ready to hand it over to her. I'll decide when that should be done because you're too little (or too stupid) to know." The problem with that approach is that Maja might not be able to reach a fulfilling completion of her play activity that she alone initiated because an outside force (the teacher) controlled the decision-making process for her. This does not help Maja develop inner controls for her behavior.

Other teachers approach such situations by making sure each child has had an opportunity to get the most out of the experience. Therefore, they would not limit Maja's time with the truck, but allow her to keep playing until she was done. (It would be wise to prevent such situations from developing by offering duplicates of popular toys.) If another child expresses an interest in the toy, these teachers would respond much as the teacher in the second scenario. Ideally, Maja would complete her play activity and remember to tell Kimberly that the truck was available. The teacher should then commend Maja for her thoughtfulness: "Kimberly is very happy that you remembered to give her the truck. She's loading rocks on it, too. I guess you really started something." Hopefully, as the children become more autonomous, they might be able to rectify the situation without teacher intervention. The teacher might say, for example, "Maja, Kimberly really wants to use the truck, too. Is there any way we can work this out?" If the girls cannot arrive at a solution, it would be best to take the approach illustrated in the second example. In all childhood centers, youngsters should be encouraged and expected to recognize the rights of others and to help each other out. Growth in this ability does not happen when children are *told* what to do, but when they are offered positive guidance by a respectful adult.

Positive guidance is not yelling at children in a loud "discipline voice," but a way of delivering a message to children that focuses on the real issue. Those statements should be very clear and contain the following elements:

1. *A statement of the problem:* "Alissa, you've used your rolling pin two times this morning to change a part of Emily's play dough."
2. *A description of acceptable behavior:* "The rolling pins are for rolling your own dough. Leave Alissa's alone."

3. *An assertion of unacceptable behavior:* "I cannot let you use your roller on Emily's play dough.'"

4. *A suggested solution:* "You must use your own lump of play dough. Or, you can ask Emily if she wants to do something together with the play dough."

The words teachers use when they offer positive guidance to young children help promote self-discipline and autonomy. More information on positive guidance is offered in Chapter 13. Descriptions of Thomas Gordon's *Teacher Effectiveness Training* will be of particular interest; they help teachers approach conflicts in a respectful, mutually satisfying way.[10] Gordon's approach helps build children's self-esteem by allowing them to express their own needs and feelings within an environment grounded in acceptance, respect, and positive guidance.

Participating in Shared Experiences

The preschool classroom should offer many opportunities for children to share and cooperate. This can be done as teachers encourage children to help each other ("If you ask Todd how to use the toy, I think he will let you."), to help resolve their own conflicts ("Okay, I'll be the baby today. But I'm not gonna drink milk from the stupid baby bottle."), or by modeling positive interaction techniques ("Please use our red paint with your class today, Ms. Kuhn. We have plenty. I'm sorry yours ran out."). These techniques help children develop a positive sense of self, understand others, and relate to others in a helpful, positive manner. Successful teachers know that these efforts are important, but understand that special routines also have a direct effect on the social behaviors of children as they live, play, and work together.

At the start of any school year, young children enjoy participating in activities emphasizing the idea that everyone is special. Before the start of the first day at school, for example, decorate your room with stuffed bears, pictures of bears, and books about popular, likable bears such as teddy bears, Winnie-the-Pooh, Paddington, Corduroy, or the Berenstain Bears. Prepare simple bear-shaped name tags and arrange the tags, each not yet displaying a child's name, on a colorful bulletin board captioned, "A Beary Special Group." Introduce the children to a special bear puppet, "Teddy the Magnificent... Teddy for short." Have Teddy greet the boys and girls with a nonthreatening roar and then, "Good morning boys and girls. I am so happy to see you today and you all look so nice. I was lonely without you. We'll have fun each day playing, talking, and learning." Then, making Teddy appear startled, have him say, "Good gracious, I've never seen so many bears in my whole life! A room full of little bears!... Quickly, bears, tell me your names." Then, making Teddy look at each child and perhaps shake their hands (paws), say, "Please tell me your name." The teacher can then ask the children to introduce themselves to Teddy as she writes each name on a tag. (Remember to use upper- and lowercase letters.) Pin each tag on the child's shirt and say, "Now this is better. Each of the bears has a name." Teddy roars, "Now the school year can begin!"

After this introduction activity, you may want to play a short action game with the children, keeping your bear theme central. Tell the children that bears are lots of fun and that school will be fun this year, too. Ask Teddy if he is happy to be in this classroom and have him respond a cheery, "Roar, roar." Then, encourage the children to join you in the action song, "If You're Happy and You Know It" by using these phrases: "... say roar, roar ... clap your paws ... do them both. ...!" The following days at school can expand on this aspect of individual understanding. Now, while the children are together in a group, you may wish to read a book about bears and the first day at school. *The Berenstain Bears Go to School* by Stan and Jan Berenstain is one possibility. Some teachers prefer to extend group time during this first day of school by helping the children become familiar with each other through an enjoyable nursery rhyme or fingerplay. Such activity helps develop a spirit of camaraderie on this very important day. For example, say, "Let's have some fun together. Listen and watch what I do." Before you start, make sure the children are all seated and facing you. Place your hands behind your back and sing the following song (to the tune of *Frère Jacques*):

Where is Thumbkin? (*Hands behind back.*)
Where is Thumbkin?
Here I am. (*Right hand out, thumb up.*)
Here I am. (*Left hand out, thumb up.*)
How are you today, Sir? (*Right thumb "bows."*)
Very well, I thank you. (*Left thumb "bows."*)
Run away. (*Right hand behind back.*)
Run away. (*Left hand behind back.*)

"Now, where are your thumbs? Can you make them Thumbkins by pointing them up like this? Very good! Let's sing the song together and this time you be Thumbkins, too."

Repeat the song as many times as the children show interest. Be sure to allow extra time for the children to move their thumbs to the song's actions. As the children gain confidence in future sessions, add verses for "Pointer," "Tall Man," "Ring Man," and "Pinky" following the actions indicated.

On the second day, some teachers prefer to adapt the initial "Thumbkin" activity by using children's names. For example:

Where is (child's name)?
Where is (child's name)?
There she is. (*Child stands up.*)
There she is.
How are you today, Ma'am? (*or "Sir"*)
Very well, I thank you. (*Child bows.*)
Run away. (*Child sits down.*)
Run away.

Repeat the song several times, using each child's name and inviting the children to stand and sit according to the verse. The introducing phrase of the routine can be extended on the third day with an activity called "This Is My Friend." The game begins with the children seated in a circle, holding hands. The puppet starts things off by covering his eyes with his hand and saying, "Peek-a-boo. Who are you?" Uncovering his eyes, Teddy looks at a child while the child gives his name. The game continues until all the children are introduced.

At the start of the year, young children enjoy participating in activities that emphasize the uniqueness of each individual and in those that stress the contributions of each individual to the welfare of the entire group. Some traditional favorites include:

Classroom Helpers   Individual contributions to group welfare can be effectively demonstrated by assigning helpers for specific classroom duties. Deciding who the helpers should be can be done on a daily or weekly basis, but it should be a consistent part of the schedule. There are several ways to organize this facet of your program; the following suggestions may prove helpful (also see Figure 11–2).

- Start off the year by utilizing concrete materials to indicate individual responsibilities. For example, a child's photograph and a sponge may be placed next to each other on an "Our Helpers" bulletin board to indicate who is responsible for cleaning the table after snack. A straw matched to a photograph indicates the straw arranger, a napkin and photograph for the napkin passer, and so on.

- As the children begin to recognize their names, print them on smiley faces and follow the preceding procedure by associating the smiley faces with the

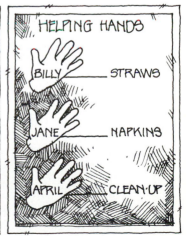

Figure 11–2   Classroom helpers bulletin board

labeled concrete object. A "Happy Helpers" bulletin board is an attractive way of organizing the materials.

- As a final stage in this developmental process, organize a "Helping Hands" bulletin board, on which one hand is labeled with the classroom responsibility and the other identifies the child assigned to it. To avoid disagreements as to whose turn it is to do what job, print each child's job on the back of the hand with her name.

Children enjoy assuming responsibility in the classroom and enthusiastically meet their tasks each day, especially if they are motivated by colorful charts or bulletin boards.

Attendance Charts Charts designed to record who is present or absent each day help young children recognize that separate individuals compose their group and aid them in recognizing each other's names.

- Mount the children's photographs or small self-portraits on red construction paper apples labeled with their names. Make a large apple tree from green and brown construction paper. As they arrive at school each day, the children find their apples and place them on the apple tree. The children can look at the chart during large-group time and determine who is absent that day.

- Mount library book pockets on a bulletin board, each pocket illustrated with the child's photograph or self-portrait. Print each child's name on a card large enough so that when the card is placed in the pocket, the child's name can be read. As the children come to school each day, they place their name card in the corresponding library pocket.

- To promote counting skills, make a series of cardboard dolls representing the boys and girls in your classroom. Label each doll with the child's name. As they enter the classroom, the children place their dolls in the "Here Today" row; when everyone has arrived, you take the absent children's dolls and place them in the "Absent Today" row.

Using similar techniques during large-group time, you may help the children count the number present, the number absent, the number of boys present, girls present, boys absent, or girls absent (see Figure 11–3).

Birthdays One of the major highlights of the school year is the celebration of special days, but no party or experience seems to bring as much excitement as the planning and execution of a birthday party. Most preschool teachers set aside a special time during the day when the birthday child is allowed to share his special day with the others. Some suggestions follow:

Figure 11–3   Attendance chart

- Paint a special chair with bright paint and decorate it. This is a "Birthday Chair" to be used by the birthday child only on his or her birthday.

- Make a crown from construction paper, decorate it, and label it with the child's name, date, and age. He may wear it during the birthday party and keep it to take home as a souvenir.

- Wrap a large shoe or hat box, top and bottom separately, with festively decorated paper, and glue a bright bow to the top. Inside the box, place a packet of materials for making a birthday hat (paper, trinkets, stickers, glitter, glue, etc.). Bring out the box ceremoniously on each child's birthday and let the child choose the materials for the birthday hat that you (or an aide) and the child can make together.

- Decorate a box similar to the one described above and fill it with small trinkets—erasers, pencils, small cars, or animals. Have the birthday child choose a gift from the box.

- Offer special privileges to the birthday child—being first in line, running errands, leading a routine, and so on.

Birthday celebrations are happy times that help to elevate a child's self-esteem.

- Recite a poem, such as the following, to add significance to the child's birthday.

  FIVE

  Say, everybody, look at me,
  For I am five-years-old, you see.
  And nevermore will I be four,
  Never, never, anymore.
  I won't be three, or two, or one,
  For that was when I'd just begun.
  Now I'll be five for a while and then—I'll be
  something else again.

  —Author unknown

- Have children make birthday cards for each other. The birthday child can take them home and share them with his family.

Promoting an Understanding of and Interest in the Child's Culture

Before children can form adequate relationships with others, they must be able to accept themselves as autonomous, competent individuals. This is an important first step toward social competence, for only after children have developed an awareness of their uniqueness as individuals and experienced a growing positive self-concept, can they be expected to form relationships with others and develop an understanding of their roles in an expanding social world.

As the child's interest in her expanding world begins to expand, a wealth of stimulating learning experiences can be employed to help children make new discoveries of the world around them. Many of these experiences are integrated throughout typical daily experiences—taking on the role of a mail carrier during free play, listening to the story of Ping from distant China, and waiting for the traffic signal to change before crossing the street are all examples of social/cultural learning experiences. Topics of more planned instruction vary; they are determined mainly by the children's interests, individual abilities, community needs, children's backgrounds, school policy, or teacher's interests. Some popular topics and sample areas of interest for preschoolers include these:

- *The family.* What are the various family compositions in the classroom? How are family tasks and responsibilities divided? What family traditions are observed by the children in our classroom?

- *The school staff.* Who works at our school? What skills are used on the job?

- *The neighborhood.* What are the major buildings in our immediate neighborhood? What changes are occurring—new building construction, street repair, and so on?

- *Community helpers.* What are the goods and services provided by the workers in our community? How do our needs and wants get met by these people?

- *Environmental education.* What observations could we make of the natural environment? What is our role in helping to prevent abuse of the natural environment?

- *Holidays.* What major holidays are celebrated by families in our room—in our country—around the world?

Building a Thematic Web

In effect, children's natural learning is more effective if it takes place across a theme of interest. Teachers can create a quality early childhood curriculum by identifying a theme of interest and building a thematic web to show how important learnings are integrated into that theme.

All that is required to construct a thematic web is to take a single idea and let your mind explore it freely. Throughout the process, it is important to record your ideas in a systematized way—not in a list form, but in an expanding web. Write the word or words describing your theme in the middle of a sheet of paper and draw a circle around it. Then, draw lines connecting to it anything that is related. It might be best to think of how the theme covers your entire curriculum: language; mathematics; science; social studies; art; and movement, drama, and music. Let us suppose we choose a cooking activity to serve as our integrating theme. Dozens of learning outcomes exist; the first step is to discern what they are. As you come up with possibilities, try to organize them around a web as depicted in Figure 11–4. The web is a visual representation showing whether there might be too much emphasis in some areas and not enough in others.

Webs can be created for endless numbers of themes, but among the most popular and traditional of all theme categories is *holidays*. This tradition is so much a part of our early childhood culture that teachers often unconsciously create themes around holiday celebrations. Why? It seems that children's excitement and interest are highest during holiday times, so it is only natural that child-centered teachers seek to

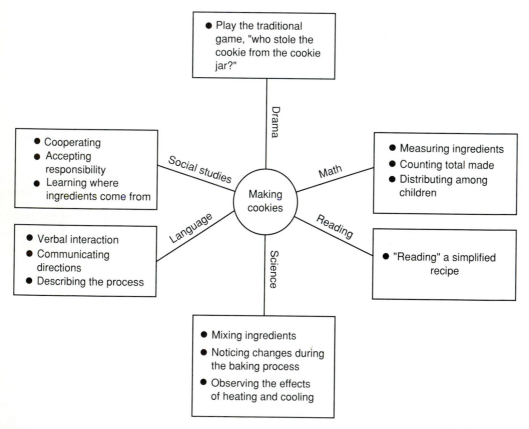

Figure 11–4 A thematic web

capitalize upon them. A sample web for Kwanzaa, an African-American celebration of heritage, is depicted in Figure 11–5.

As popular as holiday themes are, however, they should not be overdone. Jeanette C. Nunnelly elaborates:

> Turkeys are in November; Santas are in December; snowmen are in January; and hearts are in February. Depending on the time of year, visitors to child care centers, nursery schools, and kindergartens will see these seasonal objects hanging from the ceiling, taped to the walls, and displayed on shelves. [These]...consistent themes... have various activities connected with them and yield their own products. Year after year, children cut, glue, draw, paint, and eat the same traditional theme elements.[11]

To seek alternatives to such traditional fare, brainstorming for *innovative* topics should occur at least twice a year. No idea should be considered inappropriate; a teacher's imagination should be allowed to run free, without limitation. Teachers should be allowed to recall their past childhood interests or those of their own children. "Hot Air Balloons" was chosen as a theme by one teacher, for example, after her own children developed a strong interest in them. Once the central theme

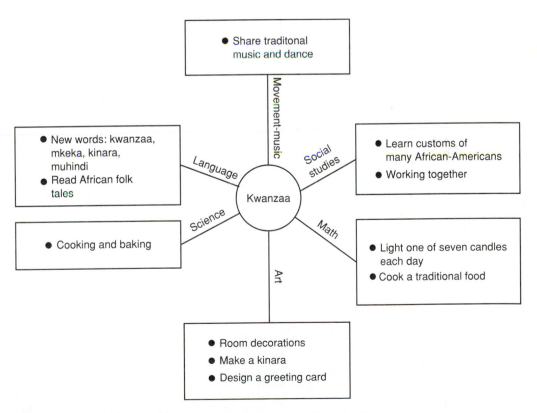

Figure 11–5 A holiday web

is chosen, every possible learning experience, no matter how ordinary or improbable, should be listed on a thematic web. Some traditionally popular seasonal themes are shown in Figure 11–6.

The next phase involves narrowing down the list of ideas to form a feasible plan. Some ideas may stand out as ideal, whereas others will show a need for refinement. Examine each possibility carefully to ensure that it is appropriate for the developmental level of the children intended. Activities should be varied: Some should be planned to take place in interest centers; others during group times; several should occur outdoors. Commercial idea books may offer some help in planning activities, but they *rarely* have enough ideas to complete full exploration of your own children's interests. Therefore, many learning experiences must be of your own design. To see what a test this is, take the theme of "Hot Air Balloons" and create a web describing the possibilities for developmentally appropriate learning experiences.

Thematic webs are useful planning strategies for organizing learning experiences in preschool, child care, and kindergarten classrooms. They can be used to plan the delivery of either traditional or innovative topics. The steps described in this section can be used for any age group—even infants. The planning strategies stay the same; only the activities will vary. The possibilities for selecting social/cultural content for preschool programs are enormous; however, holidays always make popular and exciting topics of choice.

September	October	November
Self-Concept	Pumpkins	Signs of Fall
Making Friends	Halloween	Native Americans/Pilgrims
Colors	Christopher Columbus	Thanksgiving
Shapes	Apples	
First Day of Autumn		
The Farm		

December	January	February
Christmas Around the World	Animals in Winter	Presidents' Day (Washington and Lincoln)
Hanukkah	Martin Luther King, Jr.	Valentine's Day
Las Posadas	Brotherhood	Chinese New Year
Kwanzaa	Winter	Groundhog Day
Signs of Winter		

March	April	May
First Day of Spring	Easter	Mother's Day
Wind, Clouds	Rain	Memorial Day
St. Patrick's Day	Animals in the Spring	Plants and Seeds
Kites	Five Senses	

Figure 11–6 Traditional themes in preschool classrooms

These kindergarteners take great pleasure in sharing what they have learned about their own holidays and those of other cultures.

Holidays

Children are naturally interested in holidays. They learn much about their social environment as they experience the customs and traditions of various cultural groups: their art, music, institutions, beliefs, celebrations, and so on. Although the preschool child's world centers around himself, his home, and his school (the things close to him), he is also beginning to be fascinated by the lives of other people—people from backgrounds similar to his own, as well as those whose backgrounds are quite different. Such motivation may come from exposure to a diversity of backgrounds within the preschool center or from within the child's own neighborhood. Regardless of its cause, however, the important consideration is that the child's interest is beginning to grow.

Although holidays are associated with fun, colorfulness, delight, and companionship, the challenge of celebrating holidays in the preschool can be a potent one. Victoria Jean Dimidjian elaborated on this challenge as she described two popular, although potentially problematic, approaches to the treatment of holidays.

Distorting the term "holiday," Dimidjian described the alternatives as "hollow days" and "wholly dazed." In the first alternative, "hollow days" are "characterized by ceremonies performed perfunctorily, words recited by rote, actions that seem mechanical, faded decorations pulled from closets where they have been stored for a year, or glitzy commercial decor ordered from school supply catalogues."[12] In contrast, "wholly dazed" approaches often "add unnecessary and potentially overwhelming stimulation to children who may already experience holiday hype from the media...."[13] Dimidjian further explains that some programs cause children to become "wholly dazed" by the pace and number of days for holiday activities. This leads to the danger that the "wholly dazed" approach can be

> just the busywork of cutting and pasting cardboard "Indian headdresses," paper chains, or Easter baskets.... Holiday activities are often done on a rote, product-oriented basis, offering children little developmental challenge, information, or opportunity to develop individuality. The danger of emptiness in such an approach is epitomized in a little boy's response when asked why he was painting a play-dough Christmas ornament: "She said I had to so I could play blocks."[14]

As an alternative to the "hollow days" and "wholly dazed" approaches, Dimidjian suggests a "holidays" or "holy days" approach. A "holidays" concept stresses nonreligious aspects of the celebration. Schools choosing a "holiday" approach would generally be a nonreligious school concerned with protecting parent's rights to offer whatever religious training is desired. In contrast, schools selecting a "holy days" approach tend to consciously recognize and transmit a religious tradition. A public school, for instance, constitutionally barred from celebrating holy days, would most likely choose a "holidays" approach. When December comes, such a school may focus on the commonalities and differences among winter celebrations and what the associated rituals mean to those who observe them. Las Posadas, Christmas, Hanukkah, and Kwanzaa are examples. The "holy days" school, such as in a Jewish community center, would focus on a particular holiday (Hanukkah) and straightforwardly study its tradition. "Holy days" schools have greater latitude in celebrating the holidays they have chosen because one of their main purposes of existence is to convey a particular belief system of traditions and rituals. "Holiday" schools, on the other hand, must refrain from endorsing specific religious traditions. They may, however, focus on comparative study of various manifestations of holiday celebrations.

Commercialized holidays such as Christmas and Easter pose especially difficult dilemmas to teachers. Nonreligious schools recognize the popularity of these days, but must refrain from recognizing them as religious holidays. In cases where nonreligious schools want to focus on a particular religious-based holiday, but not stress its religious rituals, related themes (e.g., rebirth, new life) and seasonal characteristics might be appropriate. Mary Rivkin contrasted the "holiday" and "holy day" approach to Christmas. Her concepts are shown in Table 11–1 (pages 406–407).

Multicultural Sensitivities and Experiences

As we discussed earlier, children's self-concepts affect how they relate to other people. Therefore, teachers should build from a strong self-concept base the idea that everyone is worthy of dignity and respect, regardless of racial, ethnic, or religious background. Thus, all preschool programs have the responsibility to help children become understanding individuals who feel comfortable with their identities and sense their unity with other people. Some people believe that this goal can best be accomplished through the study of holiday celebrations of various cultures; however, the responsibility of the preschool program goes far beyond that. A program designed to help children expand their world to include others in an unprejudiced way is often called a multicultural curriculum. Joanne Hendrick contrasted the "holiday" approach of helping children learn about others to a true multicultural approach:

> Many teachers seem to think this is all there is to multicultural education, whereas it is actually only the beginning. We must realize that the basic purpose of providing multicultural experiences is not to teach the children facts about Puerto Rico or Japan, or to prove to the community that the teacher is not prejudiced. *The purpose of multicultural curriculum is to attach positive feelings to multicultural experiences so that each child will feel included and valued, and will also feel friendly and respectful toward people from other ethnic and cultural groups.*[15]

Everyone has a culture—you, your children, your friends, and the people in your neighborhood. All individuals who share a sense of group identification have a culture. According to Ina Corrine Brown, culture is made up of

> all the accepted and patterned ways of behavior of a given people. It is a body of common understandings. It is the sum total and the organization or arrangement of all the group's ways of thinking, feeling, and acting. It also includes the physical manifestations of the group as exhibited in the objects they make—the clothing, shelter, tools, weapons, implements, utensils, and so on.[16]

Culture is universal, but how a culture meets people's needs varies. Donna M. Gollnick and Philip C. Chinn illustrate this fact by considering foods; food is needed by all cultures to survive, but which foods are perceived as edible varies from culture to culture:

> Many Americans reject foods, such as horses, dogs, cats, rice, mice, snakes, snails, grasshoppers, caterpillars, and numerous insects, consumed by other cultural groups in different areas of the world. At the same time, other cultural groups reject foods that are normal to many Americans. Muslims and Orthodox Jews do not eat pork. Hindus do not eat beef, some East Africans find eggs impalatable, and some Chinese do not drink milk. . . . Do you remember the foods included on the Basic Four charts learned in elementary school? Often we find it difficult to believe that not everyone has a diet that includes the basic four food groups seen on those charts.[17]

Kluckhohn offers this vivid example of the ways in which food habits of one culture are viewed with distaste by another:

> Guests who came her way were often served delicious sandwiches filled with a meat that seemed to be neither chicken nor tuna fish yet was reminiscent of both. To queries she gave no reply until each had eaten his fill. She then explained that what they had eaten was not chicken, nor tuna fish, but the rich white flesh of freshly killed rattlesnakes. The response was instantaneous—vomiting, often violent vomiting. A biological process caught in a cultural web.[18]

Table 11–1 Christmas in Religious and Nonreligious Schools

"Holiday" or Nonreligious School Exploring Symbols	"Holy Day" or Religious School Using Symbols
Symbol: Christmas tree	
Have children smell and feel fresh evergreen boughs to experience their fragrance and beauty. Talk about why people might want in a cold, dark season to bring bright boughs and trees inside and decorate with lights.	Decorate a Christmas tree and talk about the evergreenness of the tree being like ever-lasting life. Talk about Christians in southern climates not using Christmas trees because they don't grow there. Enjoy the tree, its fragrance and beauty. Read stories around it. Sing carols near it.
Symbol: Lights	
Burn oil and candles. Sit in a darkened room and light a candle. Talk about feelings, watch the candle go out, talk about feelings. Talk about lights on trees, how the symbols combine.	Explore the symbol as in "holiday" schools but talk about Jesus's birth being like a light that cheered people. Talk about stars; make stars. Tell the story of the manger and the star that guided people to it.
Symbol: Gifts	
Have each child find something in the room to present to another child, wrapped or unwrapped. The experiences of thoughtfulness and pleasure in receiving a gift will be encouraged, as will empathy. Talk about feelings, why we give gifts on birthdays.	Make gifts to take home or to share at school to celebrate Jesus's birthday in the same way that many people celebrate other birthdays.
Symbol: Baby Jesus	
If a baby can visit the class, children can look at the baby and talk about what it might be when it grows up. Explain that Christmas is about a baby that grew up to be a leader.	Construct a creche that children can play with. Talk about the baby's growing up to be the Jesus we pray to, what a special baby he was.
Symbol: Sweet food	
Make cookies, date bread, etc., to experience the sweetness that is like the sweetness of life and of people's happiness when a new baby is born.	Make cookies, date bread, etc., as in "holiday" school, linking it to the birth of Jesus as a special new baby to be happy about.

Table 11–1 *(Continued)*

"Holiday" or Nonreligious School	"Holy Day" or Religious School
Exploring Symbols	Using Symbols
Keeping perspective	

Because Christmas is so widely and thoroughly celebrated in America, children who do not celebrate it often feel envious of those who do. These feelings can be eased by talking about the value of all traditions, looking at a globe to show that Christmas is celebrated chiefly in Europe and the Americas, which means lots of other people don't observe it.	Because Christmas is so widely and thoroughly celebrated in America, children who celebrate it may think that those who do not are odd or unworthy. Talk about the fact that other people have happy celebrations too, and that Christmas is celebrated mainly in Europe and the Americas.
Sometimes people celebrate Christmas just because they think it is fun or because their neighbors do it. That is all right too.	

Source: Mary Rivkin in Victoria Jean Dimidjian, "Holidays, Holy Days, and Wholly Dazed," *Young Children, 44,* no. 6 (September 1989): 74–75.

As with food, people often have a difficult time accepting the special practices and beliefs of other cultures; they often feel their culture is superior to any other. Understandably, culture becomes the filter through which its members judge the world. Gollnick and Chinn believe that this is both a positive and a negative characteristic:

> It is an asset for the culture to be viewed by its members as the natural and correct way of thinking, acting, and behaving. At the same time it often solicits feelings of superiority over any other culture. The inability to view another culture through its cultural lens ("filter") prevents an understanding of the second culture. This inability usually makes it impossible to function effectively in a second culture.[19]

Cultural insularity is especially dangerous today in light of the need for interdependence among countries and the importance of establishing positive ties among all cultural groups in the United States. Although America is mythologized as a great "melting pot," the virtues and achievements of the dominant Anglo-American sector of society have historically been revered, whereas those of the African-American, Native American, Hispanic, and Asian-American populations have been neglected. These four groups have consistently been restricted from full participation in social, economic, political, religious, and educational life in the United States. According to William Joyce, "Our nation's experiences in minority group relations demonstrate that the proverbial American melting pot has been a colossal fraud, perpetrated by a dominant majority for the purpose of convincing society at large that all cultural groups, irrespective of race or ethnic origin, were in fact eligible for full and unrestricted participation in the social, economic, political, and religious life of this nation."[20]

Teachers who believe that cultural awareness is part of the child's early developmental processes are in a strong position to plan for the incorporation of multicultural activities into the preschool curriculum. Patricia Ramsey identified these reasons for doing so:

1. To help children develop positive gender, racial, cultural, class, and individual identities and to recognize and accept their membership in many different groups.

2. To enable children to see themselves as part of the larger society; to identify, empathize, and relate with individuals from other groups.

3. To foster respect and appreciation for the diverse ways in which other people live.

4. To encourage in young children's earliest social relationships an openness and interest in others, a willingness to include others, and a desire to cooperate.

5. To promote the development of a realistic awareness of contemporary society, a sense of social responsibility, and an active concern that extends beyond one's immediate family or group.

6. To empower children to become autonomous and critical analysts and activists in their social environment.

7. To support the development of educational and social skills needed for children to become full participants in the larger society in ways that are most appropriate to individual styles, cultural orientations, and linguistic backgrounds.

8. To promote effective and reciprocal relations between schools and families.[21]

Multicultural education is not something we isolate in Black History Month, Hanukkah, Chinese New Year, Puerto Rican Awareness Day, Las Posadas, and the celebration of Martin Luther King, Jr.'s birthday. Certainly, those events are important, but limiting a multicultural program to specific events does not make the issue of ethnicity an important segment of the entire program. Multicultural sensitivities can be reflected throughout the daily program in the books that are read to children, in the songs they sing, or in the active experiences offered to the group. Edith W. King believes that the arts are an excellent source of integrating multicultural studies into the young child's program:

> Music, art and literature know no national or cultural boundaries. The common expressions of human feeling found in these forms can be used effectively by the teacher to develop children's capacities to identify with other groups and other societies—indeed, the totality of [humankind]...
>
> Aesthetic experiences, embodied in the arts and humanities, provide ways of giving the individual an opportunity to try on a situation—to know the logic and feeling of theirs—even though these others [are remote to the lives of the school population].[22]

It is never too early to introduce young children to the arts of various cultures. Songs, rhymes, chants, and fingerplays elicit enthusiastic responses from the very young. Stories, pictures, books, arts and crafts, stage plays, puppets, dance, and other forms of creative expression add zest to childhood. Children should be helped to understand that the arts reflect culture, and that one cannot fully appreciate the value of any art without some understanding of the cultural matrix from which it emerged. Conversely, one cannot fully appreciate a culture unless one values the creative efforts of its individuals.

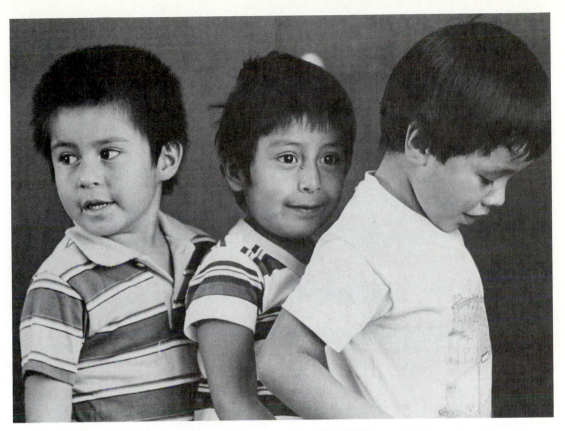

All early childhood programs must respect each child's personal and cultural dignity.

The Arts and Multicultural Concepts

Children who have many opportunities to express themselves through dance, paintings, or crafts will easily understand and appreciate the art of others. Some examples of how art can contribute to the multicultural experience include:

- Visiting museums, especially those specifically associated with various cultural groups.

- Attending a dance or music show that reflects special cultural characteristics—African chants, African-American spirituals, Yiddish folk tunes, square dances, Ukrainian folk dancers, for example.

- Learning to perform dances of different cultures—the German dance "Landler" or the Yiddish dance "Cherkessia," for example.

- Singing songs of various cultures—set up a separate area in your classroom for music and dance. Display large, attractive pictures or photographs of dancers or musicians from various cultures. A record player or tape recorder and a variety of music can be made available. First, a listening experience might be appropriate (music from various cultures as well as classical music—Beethoven's Fifth Symphony is a favorite); a box of scarves or other props can be used for later dance experience.

- Listening to and observing someone demonstrate a special craft or art technique—a Navajo jewelry craftsperson, Japanese garden construction, or Amish quilt making.

- Inviting someone who speaks another language to visit the class. The visitor should teach the children a few phrases of the language.

- Good books for young children featuring people of various racial, ethnic, and home backgrounds. Use these resources to present various cultures in unbiased ways.

INSTRUCTIONAL RESOURCES

Certainly, real experiences with concrete materials are the best way for learning to take place during the early years, but vicarious experiences are important vehicles for learning, too. Examining pictures or photographs; watching a film, videotape, or filmstrip; listening to a story; or hearing folk songs, chants, and other music are adequate substitutes until the time when children can be easily transported, for example, from rural Kentucky to the beaches of California. But, of all the resources available to children, none can be as potentially valuable for young children as a field trip. James Hymes commented that, "A field trip is clearly the best way of providing a stimulus. Young children cannot read but they can see. A field trip is a prize stimulus for learning at any age. We can almost thank God for the young child's illiteracy. It forces us to do the very best thing—take him on a firsthand experience."[23]

Field Trips

On her way to school one day, Miss Romano saw workers digging up a piece of land and planting flowers. She stopped and asked them if she could bring her group of four-year-olds to watch. The workers agreed and, as soon as the children all arrived at school and used the rest room, they were off on their excursion.

Trips are an important part of the preschool experience. Children love the excitement and adventure of trips; the firsthand experiences are necessary components of learning about one's culture. It is one thing to read a story about farmyard animals, and quite another for children to be at a farm where they have the opportunity to see, feel, and hear for themselves.

It is best not to plan trips outside of school until the children have been there for at least one month. Allow them first to get used to the teacher, other children, and surroundings. Once they have become a cohesive group and are familiar with the adults, a brief trip not far from the school might be taken first. A walk around the block, for example, might be a good place to start. Even the most obvious things are worth pointing out, because your goal is to help the children develop an awareness of the environment and articulate the things they see and hear. During one such episode, for example, a rabbit hopped out from among some bushes as the children walked by. The children watched its movements and had fun doing so: "Look at it hop," "Look how long the back legs are," and other comments were made. The teacher encouraged their animated discussion and occasionally inserted questions, such as "Did you see its fluffy tail?" to guide their observations. The children's interest was evident—several youngsters began hopping along the street to their next adventure. It is important to encourage such dialogue at this age because it establishes the groundwork for active thinking about what the children will see. On future trips, you will notice many interesting things in the landscape: traffic lights, fire hydrants, mailboxes, bus stops, telephone booths, and parking meters. It is also exciting to see less common activities such as loading and unloading of trucks; and repair work on streets involving exposed pipes, open manholes, or large cranes. During the spring it is fun to notice the leaves coming out on trees on the street and in parks. Keep in mind that first trips should have many familiar elements; this makes it easier for children to associate newly learned concepts with the established ones. One frequently overlooked source of learning outside the classroom is the world directly outside—nature. Take frequent trips outdoors to walk through a field of flowers or to listen to the noises of a busy street. Stop for a moment to watch a caterpillar crawl along the pavement or a rainbow fade into the blue sky. Nature includes the sights, sounds, smells, and tastes all around us. Help the children learn about nature by taking a nature walk, and try these activities:

- *Listen*. Sit down in a park, near the street, or anywhere else, and listen quietly for one minute. Ask the children not to talk or move. Listen to the sounds: birds chirping, wind whistling through the trees, airplanes flying overhead, automobiles driving by, other people talking, insects buzzing, construction equipment hammering, and a multitude of other sounds to talk about.

- *Look*. Children love to look for colors. How many different colors do they see? How many shades of the same color are there? How many basic shapes (circles, square, triangle, rectangle) do they see in nature?

- *Feel*. Find objects that are round, smooth, soft, furry, cold, warm, wet, or dry. Discuss how they feel.

- *Smell*. How many different things can the children smell? How does the freshly cut grass smell? How about a bakery? What does the air smell like after rain?

Before returning to the classroom, ask each child to pick up three "treasures" to bring back. What are some possibilities for using their "treasures" in teaching situations?

As the children become comfortable with short walking trips, "bigger" trips can be planned. There is a tremendous wealth of possibilities here; a few are listed below:

Farm	Supermarket	Truck terminal
Museum	Post Office	Cultural event
Department store	Camping area	Zoo
Historical site	Pond	Repair shop
Airport	Public buildings	Bakery
Railroad station	Bus terminal	Concert
Factory	Shopping center	Construction project
Newspaper building	Planetarium	Orchard
Fire station	Children's theater	
City Hall	Public library	

It is essential that all field trips, especially those involving the need for transportation, be handled with great care. Before they are taken on their first trip, be sure the children are able to listen and follow directions. Communicate all procedures carefully, being sure the children are able to understand them. Typical procedures include staying together; walking behind the teacher; staying together with a designated friend; keeping on the sidewalk, path, or side of the road; crossing streets only on signal from the teacher; and walking at all times. Be sure to send home a permission slip to be signed by a parent or guardian giving approval for each trip. Figure 11–7 shows a sample form that may be used.

Some additional considerations to keep in mind follow:

Adequate supervision (at least a 5:1 child-adult ratio). Color- or shape-code sturdy name tags so each adult volunteer can keep track of her own children: "Mrs. Chandler, your children are all wearing *red* name tags." The name and phone number of the school should be included in case the child gets lost.

Toileting. Everyone goes before you leave.

Emergency materials. Band-Aids, tissues, safety pins, change for the phone.

Clothing. Extra clothing for winter, rain gear, and so on.

These first experiences away from the classroom must be handled with great care. You should know the location to be visited and have a distinct purpose for your visit. Don't just go on a trip for something to do. Be sure to establish secure feelings in the children by telling them where they will be going, what they will see, and what they will hear or taste or smell. Don't be too informative, though, because you do not want to keep the trip from being a learning experience in itself. In deciding whether or not a trip will be beneficial for your group, it is important to consider factors such as the following:

```
Dear Parents,

     The four-year-olds will be taking a trip to the Acme Brick

Factory on Monday, March 31, at 10:00 A.M.  Transportation will be

furnished by volunteer drivers.

     The children will return to school at 12:00 noon. Please pick up

your child at 12:30.

     Four parents have volunteered to assist the children.  Your child

will be properly supervised.

     Please sign the form below if you grant permission for your

child to participate in this field trip. Return it to your child's

teacher by Wednesday, March 26.

---------------------------------------------------------------


_____ has my permission to go on a field trip to the
       (Child's Name)
Acme Brick Factory on March 31.



_____              _____
        (Parent's Signature)                      (Date)
```

Figure 11–7   Sample field trip permission form

- Is the length of time involved appropriate for the age of the children? Will they become overly tired?

- Are the concepts to be acquired appropriate for the maturity level of the children? Could they be gained more effectively in some other way?

- Have the children had an opportunity for this experience with their families?

Resource Persons

Resource persons are individuals either within or outside the school who have expertise, experience, skill, or knowledge in a field of special interest to the class. Generally children enjoy contact with outside visitors and the contributions and in-

Classroom visitors enlighten and enrich the children's experiences.

teresting materials they share. When studying topics related to the neighborhood or community, for example, you can invite persons who provide goods or services in the specific area: police officers, firefighters, farmers, delivery people, construction workers, doctors, nurses, newspersons, bakers, industrial workers, store workers, craftspersons, lawyers, bankers, clergy, government officials, and so on. When introducing children to different cultures or ethnic groups, you can ask people with appropriate backgrounds to provide information and answer questions. As with field trips, careful planning is essential for a successful visit by a resource person.

1. Determine whether inviting a visitor is the best way to get the intended knowledge and information.
2. Determine whether the speaker's topic and style of delivery are suitable to the maturity level of the children.
3. Inform the speaker about such matters as the children's age level, their needs, the time allotted for the presentation, and the facilities available.

4. Follow-up and discussion related to the speaker's presentation should be provided. Discussion, art projects, dramatization, and storytelling are all suggestions for summarizing and extending the information.

5. A letter of thanks is highly recommended as a gesture of appreciation and gratitude.

▷▷▷▷▷▷▷

Visitors to the classroom can provide the children with exciting experiences because they offer important adventures in a very personal way. One day, for example, Ms. Graham heard a discussion about fire fighters among a small group of children while they were examining a book in the reading corner. She listened as the children expressed wonder at the big rubber boots and hard red hats the fire fighters wore. Seizing the moment, she suggested that a fire fighter might be invited to visit their classroom. "Would he really come to see us?" asked Michael. "I'd like him to come here," offered Sarah. "How can we ask him?" Ms. Graham had no doubt that her intentions were appropriate and called the fire company to ask if a fire fighter could visit the children. She was informed that not only was such a visit possible, but that arrangements could be made for two fire fighters to bring a small fire truck to the school.

The next day the children eagerly waited at the school parking lot for the truck to arrive. Their anticipation grew into excitement as the bright red and silver truck motored up the winding entrance. Keeping the children well in control, Ms. Graham reminded them to stay behind her until the fire truck came to a halt. When it did, the children gingerly approached the vehicle. The fire fighters came out to show the children all their paraphernalia and explain their jobs. "The truck is so shiny," remarked Rebecca. "Yeah, and look at all those big hoses!" shouted Ben. "One of the firemen is a lady. Wow, a lady fireman," said Denise, all agog. "Do you have to go to college to learn how to be a fireman?" asked Oren. The children watched, listened, commented, and asked questions as they tried on the hard hats and floppy boots, watched the brilliant lights, and listened to the fire fighters talk. The most adventuresome youngsters even accepted an invitation to climb up into the cab and sit in the fire truck. All this wonderful activity culminated in a well-supervised short trip around the parking lot on the back of the truck. Ms. Graham was rewarded by the fact that this informal learning experience was thoroughly enjoyed by the children and that they had learned a great deal about a valuable community service.

After the fire fighters left the school, Ms. Graham assembled the children as a group and invited them to share their thoughts. As the children spoke, Ms. Graham recorded their comments on an experience chart. Later the children dictated a thank-you note that was mailed to the firehouse.

▶▶▶▶▶▶

Mrs. Greene, on the other hand, handled her visit by a resource person in quite another manner. Upon learning that a parent of one of her children was a skilled wood-carver, Mrs. Greene invited the parent to give a short demonstration of his skill. When the wood-carver arrived at school, Mrs. Greene quickly admonished the children, asking them to move from their free play and join together in a group to meet him: "Quickly, children, put away your materials and join us on the rug. Show Mr. Champion what good boys and girls you are." Promptly and efficiently, the children put away their materials and grouped themselves on the rug, hands folded and eyes directed toward Mr. Champion. "Weren't they just terrific?" commented Mrs. Greene, as if attempting to convince the parent of her superlative control. The children, unsure of why Mr. Champion was there, listened as Mrs. Greene continued with a lengthy introduction of the visitor. Finally Mr. Champion had a chance to talk, explaining his craft in such minute detail that even the most mature child's interest began to wane. Nervous glances from Mrs. Greene informed each fidgety child that certain behaviors were not to be tolerated. At the end of the long presentation, Mrs. Greene eagerly thanked Mr. Champion for coming, and warned the children of the danger of going close to any of his materials. Ending with the comment, "Let's all show Mr. Champion how much we enjoyed his visit by clapping for him," Mrs. Greene lined up the group and led them to the rest room.

Compare and contrast the techniques of Ms. Graham and Mrs. Greene. What were the obvious strengths in Ms. Graham's style? What were the apparent flaws in Mrs. Greene's approach?

Speakers are usually very willing to share their accomplishments with children. One problem, though, is that teachers often do not know where to find them. Many teachers solve this problem by sending questionnaires home with their children soliciting parents to speak. The questionnaire should ask for name, address, phone number, area of knowledge, preferred age level, days available, and hours available. It should also ask if the speaker is willing to come to the classroom or if the class should visit the speaker.

Many times, interested schools or parent-teacher organizations keep a central card file of persons from the community who are willing to share their expertise. These persons might include some who can help break down stereotypes, such as senior citizens with special skills or hobbies, women carpenters, male nurses, and so on. The card file can be organized by subject listing, and all teachers can use it as a ready reference. Care must be exercised, though, in the way contributors are solicited as possible classroom speakers. The practice of sending request forms to everyone in the community, for example, can cause problems, because a small number of persons who have little or no immediate usefulness may volunteer. Public relations dilemmas can result when these persons are never called upon to speak. The safest approach seems to be requesting recommendations from other teachers, involved parents, and other school personnel. In this way, you will be able to select speakers who will inform and motivate your children about a variety of new jobs and experiences.

Teachers should never complain about the lack of suitable learning materials for children's social/cultural learning experiences. After all, teachers have the whole world and all its people at their disposal. It remains up to caring teachers to use their professional skills to identify, locate, and evaluate the possible resources to stimulate and enrich the children's learning. The classroom should be a special place for young children, containing the resources to foster an unbiased view of humanity. However, the cornerstone of social/cultural learning is direct experience. Children learn best through interaction with their environment.

SOME FINAL THOUGHTS

Children have a deep interest in their world; they eagerly explore and experiment while satisfying their curiosity about all its wonders. Our children must be given every opportunity to channel this interest through developmentally appropriate activities. We do not teach "subjects" as we plan learning opportunities; rather, we open up the world to the children, allowing them to experience worms, ants, trees, fire trucks, mesquite, and other enthralling features of our environment. These experiences not only help fulfill a deep quest to learn, but also stimulate further interests as the children gain a growing awareness of their world.

An integrated approach to learning—in which children are offered challenging experiences free of subject matter delineations—can be especially productive. Teachers have always paid attention to this idea by arranging special experiences—excursions to the firehouse, police station, apple orchard, farm, supermarket, or construction site. But now, teachers realize that much more needs to be done to help children achieve social competence. They understand that social competence is rooted in the child's self-concept. Children must be guided by trustful, respectful adults who allow children to think and act as children do. The environment invites the child to experience childhood to the fullest without fear of undue criticism or repression; the teacher's role, meanwhile, is to invite children to accept as much responsibility for their own actions as is developmentally appropriate.

Once the children feel confident in themselves as being lovable and capable, they openly seek to establish constructive relationships with others and strive to learn about others in an unbiased, unprejudiced way. Many opportunities, real and vicarious, open up the children's inquiring minds to the wonders of the social and cultural world. Play, activity, and doing are the bases for such learnings—most of which take place when the curriculum is integrated with other areas. Teachers in a developmentally appropriate program must embrace the idea that children's curiosity is natural and spontaneous; thus, they must be professionally skilled in seizing opportunities that arise spontaneously as well as in planning learning episodes designed to awaken new interests and delights. Teachers of young children must be highly flexible, for teaching young children is never predictable.

NOTES

1. Albert Cullum, *Push Back the Desks* (New York: Citation Press, 1967), p. 21.
2. T. G. R. Bower, *A Primer of Infant Development* (San Francisco: W. H. Freeman and Company, 1977), pp. 28–30.
3. Gladys G. Jenkins and Helen S. Shacter, *These Are Your Children* (Glenview, IL: Scott, Foresman, 1975), p. 48.
4. Katherine R. Baker and Xenia F. Fane, *Understanding and Guiding Young Children* (Englewood Cliffs, NJ: Prentice Hall, 1971), p. 21.
5. In R. Bierstedt, *The Social Order,* 4th ed. (New York: McGraw-Hill, 1974).
6. R. K. Merton, *Social Theory and Social Structure* (New York: Free Press, 1968).
7. Arthur Bestor, *Restoration of Learning* (New York: Alfred A. Knopf, 1955), p. 126.
8. Sarah Smilansky, *The Effects of Sociodramatic Play on Disadvantaged Pre-school Children* (New York: John Wiley and Sons, 1968).
9. Erik H. Erikson, *Childhood and Society* (New York: Norton, 1963).
10. Thomas Gordon, *T.E.T.: Teacher Effectiveness Training* (New York: Peter H. Wyden, 1974).
11. Jeanette C. Nunnelly, "How to Plan Innovative Curriculum Themes," *Young Children, 46,* no. 1 (November 1990): 24.
12. Victoria Jean Dimidjian, "Holidays, Holy Days, and Wholly Dazed," *Young Children, 44,* no. 6 (September 1989): 72.
13. Ibid., p. 72.
14. Ibid., pp. 72–73.
15. Joanne Hendrick, *The Whole Child*, 5th ed. (Columbus, OH: Merrill/Macmillan, 1992), p. 283.
16. Ina Corrine Brown, *Understanding Other Cultures* (Englewood Cliffs, NJ: Prentice Hall, 1963), p. 3.
17. Donna M. Gollnick and Philip C. Chinn, *Multicultural Education in a Pluralistic Society,* 3rd ed. (Columbus, MO: Merrill/Macmillan, 1990), p. 6.
18. C. Kluckhohn, *Mirror for Man: The Relation of Anthropology to Modern Life* (New York: McGraw-Hill, 1949), p. 9.
19. Donna M. Gollnick and Philip C. Chinn, *Multicultural Education,* p. 13.
20. William W. Joyce, "Minority Groups in American Society: Imperatives for Educators and Publishers," in Jonathan C. McLendon, William W. Joyce, and John R. Lee, eds., *Readings in Elementary Social Studies: Emerging Changes,* 2nd ed. (Boston: Allyn and Bacon, 1970), pp. 289–290.

21. Patricia G. Ramsey, *Teaching and Learning in a Diverse World: Multicultural Education for Young Children* (New York: Teachers College Press, 1987), p. 3–5.

22. Edith W. King, *The World: Context for Teaching in the Elementary School* (Dubuque, IA: William C. Brown, 1971), pp. 5–6.

23. James L. Hymes, Jr., *Teaching the Child Under Six* (Columbus, OH: Merrill, 1968), p. 89.

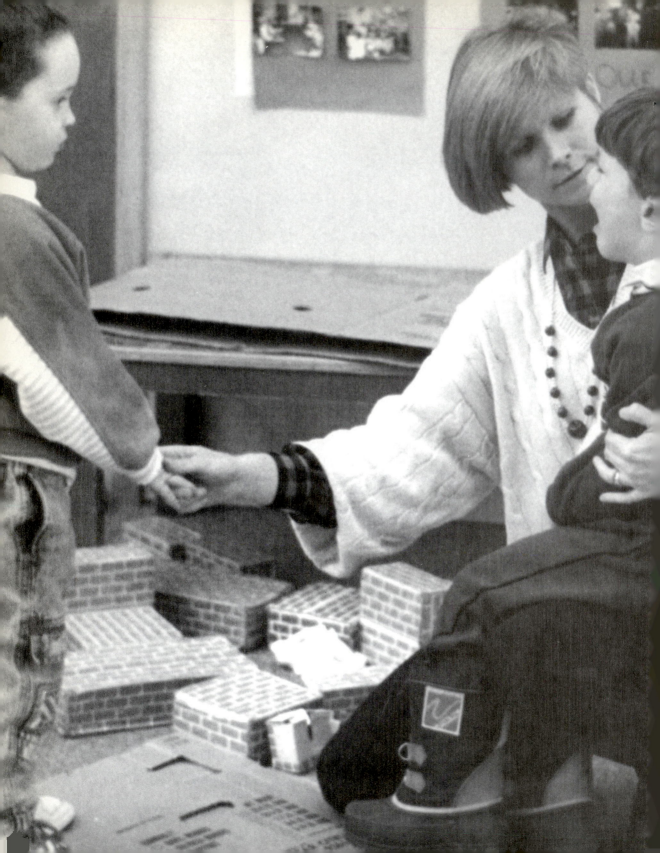

CHAPTER 12

Guiding Young Children

An affectionate bond between teacher and child is fundamental to all aspects of early childhood programs; it is especially critical as an element of good discipline. Discipline is a word that appears to have a special aura for prospective teachers—I can't think of a more pervasive concern among my students. Their worry is justified, however, because there is probably no other teaching responsibility requiring greater conscientiousness than discipline. They fear that too much discipline will cause children to hate them, whereas too little discipline will give the impression of timidity and a lack of clear direction. Beginning teachers implore, "How do I get children to do what I want them to and still maintain an appropriate relationship?" This chapter addresses that concern by suggesting strategies to help children move from adult-imposed controls on behavior toward self-controls. As you read, use the following questions to guide your thinking.

- What is a democratic approach to behavior management?

- What are some dangers of using punishment to control the behaviors of young children?

- What is the difference between punishment and discipline?

- What rules are commonly required in early childhood settings? How are they best communicated to the children?

- How should teachers handle situations in which children break established rules?

- Do teachers ever use techniques of physical guidance with young children?

An Episode To Ponder

Lori, a student teacher of four-year-old children, relates the following tale of a "difficult" child:

"I remember one child. His name was Paul—a student teacher's nightmare. He just wouldn't listen to me or do much of anything I asked. One time I asked him to clean up the blocks.

'Just a second,' he replied, 'I want to finish this tower.'

But then he brought over a toy truck to the blocks and added it to his play activity. A few minutes later I asked him again to clean up the blocks.

'I'm still playing this game,' he claimed.

I got angry and insisted that he do what I said.

'I don't want to,' he replied belligerently.

I threatened him with staying in during outdoor play, but he just looked at me defiantly and said, 'I don't care.' Again, I tried other threats—all of which I knew I couldn't enforce—but he just sat there and refused to help. I knew I couldn't *make* him do it . . . nothing I tried worked. I remember wanting someone to come along and take that kid away!"

Such extreme distress is not new to adults entering the early childhood profession. Despite the fact that children are usually very sensitive, kind, happy, and cooperative—they have a great inner drive to please, to be accepted, to be approved of, and to be loved—there will be moments when they misbehave or find it difficult to follow established house rules. "What do you do when children misbehave?" is a serious query when adults know they should intervene but are not quite sure how to do it.

Some teachers respond to the children's behavior in an overly permissive manner. They react with little discipline, allowing children to attempt regulating their own actions and impulses completely. Permissive teachers feel that any restrictions might inhibit the child and cause the youngster to fear and resent their power. They may believe they might lose the children's love or become unpopular with the children. To counter these fears, they permit children to "rule the roost" by giving them the freedom to do as they wish. Not unexpectedly, permissive classrooms are quite loud, confused, and disheveled. When teachers become so easygoing and weak as to allow children to "walk all over them," they invite a sure loss of respect, and are quite likely not to be liked or trusted. In the long run, children develop real concerns such as, "Who will protect me?" or "Will I be safe here?" A child who cannot trust an adult may eventually display anxiety, distress, and avoidance (and some may even become quite aggressive).

On the other hand, some teachers are over-controlling. They have many classroom rules, strict expectancies for behavior, and a demand for deference to authority. Sometimes these "authoritarian" teachers become extreme in their behaviors and employ harsh disciplinary measures to control children. Their classroom management style usually involves two forms of control: *verbal criticism* and *punishment*. Verbal criticism involves all the language that teachers use to denounce children's behaviors; such criticism may cause children to feel bad, stupid, deceitful, or irresponsible. Thomas Gordon categorized a number of these hurtful comments:[1]

1. *Ordering, commanding, directing.* By giving children direct, forceful orders ("Stop that!" "I don't want to hear one more word about it.") teachers often produce fear of their power.

2. *Warning, threatening.* These messages are much like commanding, but consequences are added: "If you don't learn to wait your turn, I'm going to keep you in from the playground all week."

3. *Moralizing, preaching.* These messages communicate to students that the teacher is all-wise, and, because of this wisdom, the children should rely on the teacher's judgment: "You have to learn one important thing: Good boys never hit others."

4. *Judging, criticizing.* Characterized as putdown messages, these statements tear down the student and chip away at self-esteem: "You're acting like a bunch of wild animals today," or "You're always the one who starts trouble around here."

5. *Name-calling, ridiculing.* These verbal comments have a hurtful effect on children: "You'll always be klutzy, Adam," or "I can't believe you actually forgot your jacket today. You're so forgetful!"

6. *Probing, questioning.* Sometimes questions are used to convey a lack of trust or to put the children out on a limb before sawing it off: "How long did it take you to wash your hands?" . . . "Well, no wonder they look as if you were still playing in the mud."

7. *Being sarcastic, humoring.* When children have a problem, they need to talk about it and are generally serious about it. They need respect in these cases, and when facing distractions, will take their problems elsewhere: "Are you a clown today, Al? Well, fold up your tent and take your act elsewhere."

Certainly, there are some serious hazards associated with these comments. Children are made to feel unworthy, incompetent, insignificant, or unloved as the adult conveys attitudes of hostility, haughtiness, disrespect, and insensitivity. Such encounters hurt children and unremittingly chip away at their tender shell of self-esteem. A good beginning in developing a sense of personal worth is critical in the lives of little children, for it motivates each young individual's drive to develop and maintain meaningful personal attachments with others. The seed of self-esteem cannot sprout and thrive in a hurtful environment; rather, it must be nurtured through loving interactions, encouragement, and support.

A second authoritarian response to children's misbehavior, other than hurtful language, is punishment. Some ill-advised adults believe that children best learn "right from wrong" by being pushed, pulled, shaken, or smacked. The "giant" adult often

Most days find young children involved in activities where they are cooperative and caring.

defends her actions by saying that punishment is the only thing that works. "They're asking for it," or "It sure works," are common statements of justification. Actually, harsh physical treatment may superficially succeed because most young children are terrorized by an adult's imposing size, but each incident leaves the child angry and with a slightly lower sense of self-worth. Those who are wise enough not to physically punish children often use another form of punishment that damages tender self-concepts—the "time-out chair." Teachers employing this technique discipline children by removing them from activities and forcing them to sit in an isolated place some distance from the center of the action. The children are given an opportunity to rejoin the group after an interval of time the teacher determines appropriate and only when the child is ready to follow the rules for appropriate behavior. Ann S. Clewett denounced the use of time-out chairs as hurtful:

> [the children's] self-concepts may be diminished and their reentry into the group painful. . . . The very existence of the chair causes anxiety in some children. Others are mystified and hurt when they are sent to take time out for behavior consistent with their own experiences at home, for which they know no alternative. Others suffer humiliation upon being sent to the chair because of misunderstanding. Further, there are children who make a game out of the time-out chair. They intentionally transgress and accept the penalty innumerable times during the day in a test of wills with adults.[2]

James L. Hymes examined the effects of all types of punishment, and concluding that punishment is, in general, not consistent with effective behavior management:

1. Punishment is subject to "inflation." For example, you may choose a punishment such as making a child sit while the others play and it seems to have a tremendously positive initial impact on controlling misbehavior. Then, at some point, the child may say, "Aw, that doesn't bother me anymore," and you've got to control his behavior with a new punishment that hurts him even more than the original.

2. Punishment opens up a "bargaining" process. The child soon learns she has a choice: is the right to misbehave worth the punishment that results? Soon, your classroom may assume the character of an auction, where children are not guided by a sincere desire to adopt socially acceptable behaviors, but by whether or not their misbehavior is worth a degree of mental or physical pain that results.

3. Punishment jeopardizes positive adult-child relationships. Youngsters are intimately dependent upon the love and support of nurturing adults. An angry face, a cross word, a sharp voice, or a caustic glare all strike more fear into young children's hearts than we can ever imagine. Our punitive expressions of displeasure to their behaviors hurt children deeply because they need our understanding, patience, and approval so much.[3]

Alice S. Honig adds an important consideration to the Hymes list. She asks us to recall the peddler in *Caps for Sale* (a book by Esphyr Slobodkina) whose caps are taken by mischievous monkeys while he sleeps.

When he wakes up, the monkeys have climbed a nearby tree and refuse to return his caps. The angry peddler shakes his fingers at the monkeys, and the monkeys shake their fingers back at him. He stamps his feet at the monkeys, but they just stamp their feet back at him. Then in disgust the peddler throws down his only cap. Even if you don't know the story, you can guess what happens next: The monkeys throw down their caps, too.

This delightful classic is a good reminder that much like those monkeys, children imitate our behavior. When we shout in anger, tenderly comfort a child, cringe at the sight of a spider . . . , our children are likely to follow our example.[4]

Discipline, then, cannot involve yelling, shouting, or hitting. We cannot teach children not to yell by yelling at them any better than we can teach them not to swear by swearing at them. Instead, it must embrace the soundest teaching strategies we know. Beneficial disciplinary techniques recognize that behaviors take a long time for children to develop, starting from birth. A fundamental emotional need of babies is to know that they can trust us. Do we come quickly when they cry? Do we relieve their hunger, discomfort, or loneliness? Are we tender and loving? From our interactions with babies, we help establish a groundwork of trust. When babies learn to trust those they must depend upon for love and care, they start to accumulate the experiences that help them learn to trust as they grow older. As the babies grow into toddlerhood and gain the physical skills and desire to explore their surroundings, they become more independent and assertive. Their lack of experience, however, often gets them into trouble. How do they know, for example, that the delicious-looking red marking pen isn't an appetizing snack? Why should they share the toys that were once exclusively theirs? We must understand that this is the toddler's perspective: curious but unexperienced. We must examine early behaviors from a developmental perspective, for good guidance can help the child turn typical behaviors into learning experiences. Eventually the independence of toddlerhood transforms into the social consciousness of young children. They are eager to make friends and play with one another. During these times, children need to move freely. There is a buzz and a spirit in classrooms that allow them to do this. Children react to freedom with happiness and mirth. They giggle, laugh, talk, and shout; they see themselves surrounded by friendship and security. But sometimes children are sad: They cry; they hurt. Now and then they may hurt themselves, and occasionally they hurt others. Most of the time the children are happy. When there is a problem, they usually don't stay distressed for long. Their hurts are diminished by a warm environment designed to help them feel good about themselves. Self-regulated conduct and responsibility will grow from the establishment of positive, respectful surroundings, because there is a close relationship between how children feel about themselves and how they behave in the classroom.

DEVELOPMENTALLY APPROPRIATE GUIDANCE

Throughout their preschool years, children do not naturally understand a great deal of what constitutes acceptable behavior. They must be taught. Teaching or guiding the acquisition of acceptable behavior is often called **discipline.** What is discipline? In its statement regarding developmentally appropriate practice, NAEYC equates discipline to self-control and advises that children learn self-control when they are treated with dignity. Acceptable discipline techniques include the following:

1. Guiding children by setting clear, consistent, fair limits for classroom behavior; or in the case of older children, helping them to set their own limits.
2. Valuing mistakes as learning opportunities.
3. Redirecting children to more acceptable behavior or activity.
4. Listening when children talk about their feelings and frustrations.
5. Guiding children to resolve conflicts and modeling skills that help children to solve their own problems.
6. Patiently reminding children of rules and their rationale as needed.[5]

In short, developmentally appropriate discipline (guidance) is based on respect for children. Discipline helps children to understand and grow through the acquisition of patterns of self-control. Such acquisitions are fostered by caring adults in an environment replete with positive helping interactions. Dan Gartrell advises emerging early childhood educators not to expect such nurturing skills to appear in their professional repertoires overnight—after all, the process requires much work:

> These processes take commitment and practice. They deal with the young child's need to feel safe and secure, through personal acceptance, sensible limits, gentle corrections, and genuine encouragement. They address behavior that needs addressing but respect the feelings of the child: This is the essence of a positive approach.... By establishing the habit of regularly reading books and articles on childrearing and early childhood classroom practice...and of applying and practicing sensible ideas in...work with children, each of us can develop a positive discipline philosophy and an accompanying collection of approaches to implement it.[6]

Essential to good behavior management is a caring adult who is attentive
to children's moments of crisis.

Despite the fact that the positive discipline philosophy is widely recommended by early childhood specialists, each new teacher will initially apply its principles in quite unique ways. Some teachers, uncomfortable and uncertain with its use at first, may sometimes feel professionally inadequate. Others may offer too much help; some may take no action at all. These are all natural reactions to beginners struggling to develop sophisticated skills in such a sensitive area of professional responsibility as behavior management. Professional growth can be an awkward process; making errors is an important part of learning to teach. That is why guides for action are so important. Such guidelines are gleaned from the experiences of others and furnish the supporting framework that, combined with your own experiences, help you build relationships with children in highly individual ways. Time is required for you to build an individual process of working with children, and time is necessary for establishing relationships with children. Each of you will do this in your own way; that is part of what makes early childhood education so exciting. Although there are many important guides for professional behavior, each individual teacher is able to personalize them into his or her own unique plan of action.

For our supporting framework, we will use the NAEYC principles for developmentally appropriate practice as the concept applies to self-control and discipline. But, before we examine each area separately, one basic that overrides this list must be discussed: determining why a misbehavior occurred.

DETERMINE WHY A BEHAVIOR OCCURRED

The basic goal of developmentally appropriate guidance is self-control. Therefore, teachers should know when to step into a situation and when it is most helpful to remain an observer. Every child must have an opportunity to help herself, so teachers should study situations carefully to determine the type and amount of assistance required. Because each child is an individual, the type of guidance we offer must vary from situation to situation. It is human nature to want to have all the answers when you face situations involving the behavior of young children. In some instances, however, you will simply not know enough to resolve a problem situation. However, you shouldn't stop trying to discover the cause when something is simply not right. Search for clues to the behavior. Conscientious observation yields valuable information about the cause of misbehaviors, and also helps provide the basis for handling the situation. Think, for example, of an infant who suddenly cries. She is clearly exhibiting a behavior you wish to change, but what do you do about it? Certainly you know not to yell at her, give her a scowl, or, even worse, hit her. Your training and sensitivities tell you that much. You must find out what is causing the behavior before you can do anything about it. Is the baby hungry, sleepy, or sick? Does she have a rash? Does the diaper need to be changed? Was the baby burped after the most recent feeding? Was she possibly frightened or startled by something? Did you lay her on a small toy? Is she in discomfort? You consider the possibilities and, if you find the apparent cause, deal with the situation accordingly. If you can find no cause for the baby's crying after you examine all the possibilities, you will probably try your last resort: pick her up, cuddle her, and croon a soft, soothing lullaby. Older children also benefit from such reassurance and love when they face complicated problems having to do with emotions.

You must examine many causes when searching for the factors that encourage certain behaviors among toddlers and young children. And if your first hunches are not on target, you search for alternatives rather than inflicting punishment or withdrawing affection. Your goal is to help eliminate the problem.

Here is an example: You see Tara, a four-year-old, assume leadership in the housekeeping area. The children appear to enjoy playing with each other until Tara hits Doreen. Hitting is a behavior that cannot be allowed in your classroom. You approach Tara, explaining the rule she has broken and why she should not hit. However, despite all your well-intentioned talking, you become aware that Tara's penchant for hitting is becoming a habit. Now what do you do?

Just as physicians know that a fever is caused by many different health problems, teachers must understand that misbehavior is caused by a variety of reasons, too. Before physicians treat the fever, they must observe it and ascertain its cause. The teacher, too, must be observant and aware so that he can discover the causes for misbehavior in his classroom and use his knowledge as a base for altering that behavior. This observant teacher would try to find out such things as:

- Did Doreen take something from Tara?

- Was Tara frustrated in the situation?

- Was Tara provoked in some way?

- Did excessively crowded conditions contribute to Tara's behavior?

- Were the blocks age-appropriate for Tara and her playmates?

- Does a particular home situation have Tara upset?

In order to avert hitting in the future, you must know the reasons for Tara's behavior. If crowded conditions provoke Tara (and they do some children), you will need to rearrange the block area so that more space is available. If Tara hits because she has difficulty sharing her toys with others, you will need to stress the positive value of sharing. From your informal observations you may find a simple remedy for your problem. But if you always treat the symptom (hitting) and never the cause (Tara was provoked), you may regularly be frustrated in trying to address problem behavior.

The way you handle situations involving children's feelings is important to the development of healthy personalities and budding social relationships. You must always use constructive methods to cope with the various stumbling blocks that can affect positive growth.

Let us now look at the DAP proposals as a guide to establish a process of positive discipline. Our overall goal will be to acquire the behaviors and sensitivities necessary to carry out helpful interactions with youngsters—so that they are able to move toward self-discipline as well as to continually develop increasingly deeper positive self-concepts.

SETTING CLEAR, CONSISTENT, FAIR LIMITS

Most teachers are aware that the physical environment of the classroom as well as the daily schedule contribute a great deal to the behavioral climate of the early childhood facility. These two facets of classroom management are critical in establishing a warm, productive setting for youngsters; busy, happy children are less likely to misbehave. However, even the most ideal physical environments can be ineffectual if the children are not informed of the general behavioral standards expected within that environment. To start your program of positive discipline, study all of the classroom routines that will constitute the children's day and then identify the general behaviors expected within each.

List the routines you want your children to learn: using the bathroom, getting ready for snack, going home, and so on. The list should include every established routine that is part of your program. Once the list is completed, you must systematically outline the *procedures* for carrying through each routine. For example, when children depart for home, they put away all their school materials, gather up articles to be taken home, put on their sweaters or coats, and so on. You must consider all components of the routines and decide how to teach them to the children. Usually it is best to demonstrate the routine, invite the children to join you to practice, and

Table 12–1   Planning Chart for the Introduction of a Classroom Procedure

Procedure:	Children put away all toys after they are finished using them
Justification:	Children learn social responsibility and self-discipline. They enjoy helping out.
Introduction:	Most children know how to put away the toys. For those who don't, the procedure at each center will be broken down into small steps.
Signal:	I will play the same short tune on the piano each day. The children know to put things away when they hear the tune. If needed, a direct statement will help inform children who do not respond: "It's time to put away the toys so we can get ready for snack."

observe the children to see whether or not any are experiencing difficulties. See Table 12–1 for an example of how one teacher planned to help her children with one special routine.

Each special routine, then, has a set of specific expectancies, or standards of behavior. Limiting the number of children on the ladder of the playground slide at one time is a safety procedure that is designed to protect the children. Is it okay to take the wheel toys off the asphalt surface? The children need to know. Do not overburden the children, but at the same time, maintain an environment where they know what is expected. Some early childhood specialists have organized and communicated their procedures so carefully that they are able to have only one "rule" for classroom conduct: "Everyone and everything in our room must be treated with respect." Established procedures satisfy the child's need for safety. They inform the children what will happen next and, if their expectations come true, the youngsters feel safe. They will seek to explore the environment and learn from it.

These established procedures sometimes become endangered, however, when a child (for whatever reason) varies from normal classroom expectations and threatens to harm others or create a disturbance. When an established procedure is violated, it is your responsibility to communicate to the child how he should behave with regard to the established routine. For example, Matthew understands that the usual procedure for storing the hollow blocks is to pick up each block with both hands and stack it in a corner, but today he picked one up and dropped it on top of Tracey's unit block building. Matthew's behavior clearly violated an established procedure and called for intervention on the part of his teacher. Her responsibility would be to make Matthew stop, because he had violated a procedure that was established to guarantee the respect of everyone in the room. Out of concern for the safety of the other children or for the materials, the teacher must communicate an established guide for action: "I cannot allow you to destroy other children's things. Put the large block in the corner and come back to help Tracey rebuild her structure." Firm limits accompanied by a simple explanation are all that is usually required.

Children need much practice in learning procedures; the teacher must be patient with them. Learning a behavior or procedure is basically no different from learning anything else in an early childhood setting. You would probably agree that an initial recitation of the alphabet is not the sole experience children need to internalize the names and order of the letters. Much reinforcement and repetition of related skills are required. Likewise, learning procedures for carrying out routines and rules for behavior requires many learning opportunities before children can be expected to become completely competent at self-management.

MISTAKES AS LEARNING OPPORTUNITIES

Lawrence Kohlberg's popular ideas of moral development have given early childhood educators evidence to support a developmental philosophy of behavior management.[7] By carrying out intensive studies of children around the world, Kohlberg found that, despite differences in cultural, social, economic, and religious backgrounds, individuals progress through a common series of stages in moral development. Although Kohlberg never assigned age designations to his stages, it is basically accepted that most children through the kindergarten year operate at stage one. This is a period of development during which children believe that to be "well behaved" means blind obedience to an adult authority figure. Children do not understand why certain behaviors are expected of them—they determine "goodness" or "badness" of an act solely on the basis of whether an adult will reward or punish them. If we interpret Kohlberg properly, we realize that a unilateral respect for the behavioral expectations of adults is an unavoidable stage in the development of children. For this reason, they call out for guidance from adults and require that behavioral standards be established. However, those standards must be chosen thoughtfully, for children do not completely understand the reasons for your choices. Their complete trust is in you.

Although we could interpret this as indicating a need for strict classroom authority, the only way a child can move from the initial stage to more mature stages is through experience—not through authoritarian leadership. Children can gain experience by being involved in understanding both the motives behind behavioral expectations and the reasons for the rules. We thereby help them progress to increasingly mature patterns of self-guided behavior. The children, then, move from the least mature behavioral motivation—being concerned about reward or punishment for their actions—toward a higher Kohlberg stage, such as behaving in ways that take into consideration other people's feelings and what a "good" person should do. For example, when Erin decides that she should share the cookie cutter with Luis because that is what a "good person" does in the classroom, she displays a higher level of moral development than if she were merely expecting a reward or reprimand from the teacher.

The young child, then, is moving from a "wanting-to-please-others" orientation of behavioral motivation toward becoming an independent person. He will want to test out new situations while moving in this direction and, sometimes, his experimentation will involve doing things in ways other than he has been told. He is "testing the waters"—seeing what it is like to be a self-directing person. This attitude should not be construed as anti-teacher, but as a healthy, important component of growth and development. A child needs to know that it is important to live within certain restrictions and limitations, but also that it's okay to assert his independence safely. For example, a young child may withdraw from circle time, refusing to listen to a story her teacher had prepared to read. Instead of interpreting this conduct as obstinacy, the wise teacher waits. She understands that it is important for the youngster to assert her independence, knowing that the little girl will soon come back and continue with the regular routine. She knows this will happen because she understands the child and the reasons for her behavior. No one can grasp all the aspects of a behavioral event the moment it happens, but this teacher has learned enough about the child to know that (1) she wasn't trying to get on the teacher's nerves, (2) she was not a social isolate, (3) she enjoyed listening to stories, and (4) the weather wasn't a factor (a rapid change in weather often triggers disruptive behavior). The teacher knew that the little girl's family had recently had a new baby. The little girl was asked to assume more independence and responsibility at home; she enjoyed trying to do so at school, too. The teacher understood this; her knowledge helped her to choose the type of child guidance most appropriate for the situation. Seeking to understand the situation and allowing the child to test new behaviors were important components of her positive approach to guidance and discipline.

Sadly, though, the idea of punishment is often the first solution to rush into some people's minds—especially if the misbehavior tends to be repeated. "What else can you do?" they ask in frustration. Before that question can be answered effectively, let us start with the premise that your actions should be in direct proportion to the severity of the misbehavior. Minor misbehaviors that neither disturb others nor threaten their safety or well-being are often best ignored. For example, Jeffrey, a calm, easygoing child, rarely displayed open signs of intense emotion. One day he accidentally knocked over a container of paint and blurted out, "Damn!" The teacher saw that the other children were unaffected and Jeffrey had started to clean up his accident. She decided it would only embarrass him if she brought attention to this short-lived infraction. So she ignored it. The same teacher observed signs of apparent misbehavior as personality growth in other children. For example, Michael entered his kindergarten classroom at the beginning of the year as an intense, behavior-conscious youngster who idolized his teacher and loved school, but he was somewhat rigid in his conduct. One day, Michael began slowly to swing his backpack above his head on the way to the bus—a behavior that might not normally be approved. Instead of asking Michael to lower the backpack, his teacher smiled to herself and saw the action more as a sign of growing personal confidence and relaxation than as a type of behavior in need of reproof. Reminding Michael to bring the bag down might have caused more harm than good. The ability to know your children and to understand which behaviors should be controlled and which tolerated is the mark of an extremely mature professional.

REDIRECTING CHILDREN

Redirecting children's behavior involves drawing a child's attention away from a problem situation to an act or object of equal interest or value. If he's throwing a pail, for example, we can suggest, "Use the pail in the sandbox; if you want to throw something, you can use this ball." Of course, knowing why the child is throwing the pail helps us to determine how his actions should be redirected. If he is angry, we can suggest other ways of draining his feelings—pounding nails, for example. If he simply enjoys throwing, however, we can substitute the ball for the pail.

Detouring the child (changing the environment in which the behavior takes place and substituting something of equal value) is often an effective means of dealing with unacceptable behavior. Let us suppose that one child is busily digging in the sand with a large shovel. Another child decides she wants the same piece of equipment and suddenly grabs at it. The teacher takes a helpful stance when she suggests: "It's Carl's turn to use the shovel now, Jean. You can use this big rake to smooth out a special road while you're waiting for your turn." Teachers must face the situation directly and offer an activity of equal value when redirecting attention.

Be sure to redirect children only if the strategy is appropriate for the situation. A teacher who sees a child threatening someone with a rolling pin while rolling dough at the art center does not help by saying, "Come over here and help mix the pancake batter now." Such an attempt at redirection does not address the problem. She helps the child more by saying, "The rolling pin is for rolling the dough. Keep it on the table." Likewise, if two children want to read the same book, you'll help when you say, "It is Debbie's turn to read *The Hungry Caterpillar*. You can read *The Very Busy Spider* while you're waiting for it." Redirection shows the child an avenue of problem solution; it does not attempt to avoid the problem altogether.

LISTENING TO THE CHILDREN

A supportive environment is one that not only involves sensitivity in the teacher's choice of actions and words, but also encourages an openness to the thoughts and feelings of the children. We can learn much about children's behavior by listening to them. One of the most popular programs designed to help teachers tune into the feelings of children is Thomas Gordon's *Teacher Effectiveness Training (T.E.T.)*.[8] Gordon's program is based on the idea of creating a classroom climate in which teachers actively listen to children. He claims that when children are upset or troubled teachers often do not listen at all; instead they tend to moralize, preach, criticize, or give advice. When children appear upset, a teacher's frequent approach is: "Oh, come on. If at first you don't succeed, try and try again," or "Stop crying. You're no baby," or "That wouldn't have happened if only you were more careful." Gordon refers to these statements as *roadblocks to communication,* responses that often obstruct further communication.

Active listeners communicate a sincere desire to open up lines of communication with children.

Instead of the roadblocks, Gordon advises that teachers demonstrate *acceptance* through a willingness to relate to and listen to the children. When children have problems, they need teachers to *listen*—not talk—to them. "But I *do* listen to my children," most teachers claim in response to such a remark. Surely listening does help children open up and share their inner feelings, but T.E.T. proposes an even more effective strategy: *active listening*. It is a way of responding to the child that is new and at first strange to many teachers. What active listening involves is actually hearing and accepting the child's communication. To understand active listening, we must first examine the communication process.

For instance, anything a person says can be interpreted as a coded effort to describe the speaker's inner state. What the listener hears is the listener's *personal interpretation* ("decoding") of the sender's message. [See Figure 12–1(a)].

In the example, the teacher "heard" the child's statement as a neutral request for information. Actually, however, this child is feeling anxiety. He fears alligators

Figure 12–1 The process of active listening

and realizes he may have trouble if forced to observe them. Obviously, he must communicate this fear by going through the process of *encoding*, or selecting verbal symbols to describe an emotional state. The child chose the verbal code represented in Figure 12–1(a). The receiver of the coded message then must attempt to decode it—in order to understand the meaning of the message and respond accordingly. [See Figure 12–1(b)]. Although the receiver *infers* the meaning of the message, he cannot be sure whether he is right or wrong because he cannot read the sender's mind. Therefore, he must determine the accuracy of his decoding effort. This determination is the heart of active listening. All you need to do is *feed back* the results of your decoding as in Figure 12–1(c). Such a paraphrased "feedback" of the child's message is designed to open up lines of communication by creating a safe psychological environment in which the child realizes that his needs are heard, that the teacher wants to hear more, and that his concern will be dealt with. Hearing the teacher's feedback, the child may say, "No, I don't want to go. The alligators are too mean." The teacher's feedback, then, helps clarify the child's reason for asking the question and leads him into a direction where the conversation goes something like this:

Teacher: Oh, you're worried that we'll stop at the alligators.

Child: Yes. I don't like to look at them. They're scary.

Teacher: When we get to the alligator house you can stay with Mrs. Martin at the tigers. Is that okay?

Child: Thanks!

The skill of active listening takes much practice, but it is an extremely valuable technique for conflict resolution. It provides a model of joint problem solving within a democratic environment where people are free to think, explore, and share feelings.

Although Gordon speaks of active listening in the context of finding out what is bothering a child, it can be a useful way of responding to children when they share any feeling with you. Suppose a child comes to you and says, "I'd like to be a fire fighter some day." How do you respond? An active listener would either ask a question or paraphrase the child's comment as an invitation to say more. For example, "When did you first get such an idea?" The child may then go on to say, "I guess since my daddy took me to the firehouse and I saw all the big yellow trucks." Active listening responses do not follow any rigid formula, but they do contain a number of common elements:

- Do not criticize or evaluate the child's response.

- Put the responsibility on the child to look at his own ideas and think for himself.

- Do not try to do big things. The purpose of your response is to set a mood. Each response is only one of many; its effect is cumulative

- Do not intend for the response to develop into an extended discussion. The idea is for the child to think, and he usually does that best alone. Allow for two or three rounds of dialogue and then offer to break off the conversation with some honest phrase, such as "It was nice talking with you," "I see what you mean now," or "Your idea was very interesting. Let's talk about it again some other time."

- Do not respond to everything everyone says or does in the classroom.

- Direct responses are to individuals whenever possible. A topic about which Henry needs clarification may be of no interest to Mac. Issues of general concern may warrant a general response to the entire class, but even here the individual must ultimately do the reflecting for himself.

- Use responses in situations where there are no "right" answers, such as in situations involving feelings, attitudes, or beliefs. Your responses should never be used to draw a child's thinking toward a predetermined answer.

Responses that paraphrase a child's statement must be used creatively and with insight. Some questions that are possible to use in an active listening situation include:

"How did that make you feel?"
"Did I understand you to say that . . . ?"
"Is that the first time you ever tried that?"

GUIDING CHILDREN TO RESOLVE CONFLICTS

In spite of our most sincere intentions, we often compound or complicate matters by failing to allow the child to express his emotions or by misinterpreting his intentions.

Strong emotions that go unexpressed or unrecognized may eventually be expressed in highly destructive, hostile ways. For example, recognizing that Arnie slammed his paper cup on the table because he was thirsty and impatient, the teacher may say, "It's hard to wait for your juice when you're thirsty, isn't it, Arnie? You want your juice right now." Arnie may answer, "Yes, I wish Judy would hurry." The teacher may suggest, "Then you should tell her. I cannot allow you to slam your cup like you did. Please tell Judy what you want." Arnie may now go on to express his desires to Judy and receive his juice in return. You should describe the child's feelings only if you can identify them accurately *and* give a description of the situation that goes beyond a simple statement such as "You're feeling angry, aren't you, Arnie?"

By allowing the children to seek solutions to personal problems, you not only help them discuss their point of view and remedy disagreements, but also serve as a positive model of conflict resolution. There are all kinds of ways to help children, but those that offer the children chances to take responsibility for their own behavior help them more to grow by themselves than those where the teacher assumes most responsibility. We should avoid doing unnecessary things for children; still, we should give the help the child wants and needs.

REMINDING CHILDREN OF ACCEPTABLE BEHAVIORS

Children need boundaries or limits for their behavior. They expect guidance from adults; they seek someone to be in charge and to lead the way. As teachers, we must furnish that leadership—to try our best to recognize problems and to communicate responsibly about them. You communicate responsibly when you are able to employ well-chosen words and a tone of voice that promote self-discipline. When children are led by someone who communicates rules and limits appropriately, they feel safe and secure, and are more willing to assume responsibility for their own actions.

The following examples and suggestions illustrate some techniques used by teachers to get ideas across to children. They often illustrate special statements; do not consider these as models per se. You will certainly develop your own way of saying these things and resolving problem situations. Examine these ideas as a useful framework and search out the ideas of other educators in order to develop your own form of verbal guidance. No single recipe will ever teach you how to guide *all* children; you need to understand the child, the situation, and the reasons behind the behavior.

Use an Appropriate Tone of Voice

Teachers normally communicate with pleasant, casual, or soft tones during the day. When something goes wrong, however, some teachers change and assume a louder, harsher, or "drill sergeant" type of voice. This might be especially evident in situations where limits or procedures are endangered. We do not need to change our voice dramatically when such situations arise. Granted, it may be necessary to speak in a firmer voice, but do not yell or become gruff when children make mistakes. Children need to feel competent even if they err. A gruff voice communicates a message of rejection and dislike; children strive for acceptance and love. By using consistent patterns of communication, children will recognize you as a sincere, sensitive guide who can be trusted with the responsibility to protect them.

Speak to Children Privately

Whenever possible, come to the child; squat, sit, or kneel down; look into the child's eyes; reach out and gently touch the shoulders; and talk about the situation in a quiet, firm tone. Do not shout or use words to make the child feel sad or angry. By coming to children and speaking in precise, positive ways, you help to maintain positive self-respect and guide them along the road to self-discipline.

Give Directions in a Positive Way

In other words, try not to say "no" or "don't." We confuse children when we tell them what *not* to do ("no running!") because they are unsure what the acceptable behavior is. Although youngsters must learn the meaning of "no," "stop," "don't," and other words that are necessary for immediate attention, constant use of such words makes children feel bad and fails to help them learn to handle situations through positive means. So instead of saying, "Don't leave the book on the floor," or "No running in the room," you might say. "Put the book back on the shelf," or "Walk in the room. You may run outside."

When a particularly frightful situation arises, a negative statement, followed by a clear explanation of an acceptable alternative, may be called for. For example, "No pushing on the slide; someone can get hurt. First Richard, then Jenny, then Loretta." This technique sets firm limits in respectful tone and words.

State the "But" When a Child May Be Doing the Wrong Thing

Whenever two children have a conflict over such concerns as wanting a toy or waiting one's turn, for example, it is wise to step in and say: "I know you want to ride the trike now, Bradley, *but* Lamont is using it. Use the tractor until he's done." This lets the child know that you understand his problem but realize that others have needs, too. Sometimes "but" statements are useful when a potentially dangerous situation arises. For example, Tara enjoys jumping out of the seat while swinging at home, and wants to try it at school. Her teacher says, "I know you like to jump off the swing when it gets real high, Tara, *but* you may fall and get hurt; it's my job to keep you safe." Statements like these demonstrate that you understand the child's desires. As a competent, trustful leader, though, you must let the child know that there are some considerations that take precedence over their own wishes. This will help you acquire the child's respect and faith.

Direct Your Comments to What Has Happened, Not to the Child

You should disapprove of the behavior, not the child. Avoid labeling the child as "bad," "stubborn," or as an "attention-seeker." Which of the following comments would tear down the child's confidence if used to handle a classroom situation? (1) "You spilled the water on the floor. Why must you be so clumsy?" (2) "Water makes the floor very slippery and someone could fall. Take this mop and try to wipe it up." By using positive guidance, you help children not only to change behaviors, but also to understand the consequences of their actions.

Give Choices Only When You Mean It

"Do you want to come indoors now?" the teacher calls to the children as she waits by the door for the children to come in from the playground. "Do you want to eat your snack now?" and "Would you like to clean up now?" are the kinds of questions that back us into a corner because they give children a choice that we are not willing to accept. How would a teacher react if the children replied "No," in response to each? Was she really inviting the children to make a choice? What will children think if the teacher constantly offers choices with alternatives the teacher will not accept? An example like "You may either swing or ride the trike" offers the children a choice— either of which the teacher can accept. Such a choice also helps children understand that their decisions are important and valued by the teacher.

Offer Sincere Encouragement

There is no question that young children prosper in environments where they receive positive signs of approval. Comments and other signs of acceptance not only enhance self-esteem, but also serve as important reference points for behavior. For years, teachers have been advised to establish supportive, warmhearted environments in which they openly offer statements of praise as a means to enhance a positive self-concept or to promote autonomous behavior: "Good for you, Carlos. I like the way you're eating your snack." The basis of such advice is rooted in behavioral psychology:

Special words of encouragement help the child develop an inner drive to succeed.

Children learn more when they are rewarded for good behavior. The rewards might be tangible ones such as gold stars or candy, or they might be social ones such as a smile or word of praise. Verbal feedback ("Great job. . . . You did it!") is intended to provide the positive reinforcement necessary to enhance positive individual or group behaviors.

Randy Hitz and Amy Driscoll examined this traditionally popular use of praise in early childhood education and found that it may not be as beneficial as we have thought. One of their major concerns is that teachers have used praise ineffectively. Examining Jere E. Brophy's influential classroom interaction studies,[9] Hitz and Driscoll concluded that:

> verbal praise is usually accompanied by negative affect in nonverbal expressions. For example, the teacher may say, 'That's good, Jody,' while looking in another direction instead of looking the child in the eyes. . . . When they do praise, they tend to use pet phrases, little animation, and body language that contradicts the verbal message. In other words, such praise often lacks credibility.[10]

Hitz and Driscoll are further concerned about the fact that praise is often incorrectly used to motivate children's behaviors through extrinsic (external) rewards rather than through intrinsic (internal) rewards. In intrinsic motivation, the personal satisfaction of accomplishing a task is reward enough to bring a child to perform that task. When children are praised, on the other hand, they may be encouraged to focus on the praise they receive rather than on the reason it was given. Carried to an extreme, praise can even lessen self-motivation by creating an overreliance on external rewards.

A third concern of Hitz and Driscoll is that teachers use praise as a method of managing children, although it is not necessarily effective in this role. For example, a teacher may make a statement such as, "I like the way Ryan is sitting," not primarily as praise for Ryan, but as a way to influence other children to conform to the same behavior. Hitz and Driscoll condemn such practices because they often lead to resentment and anger and because they are blatantly manipulative in nature. They point out that preschoolers may conform to such practices initially because they want to please their teacher and not be classified as "bad," but eventually their resentment may grow to such a degree that praise no longer contributes to effective classroom management.

With these important considerations swirling about in your mind, you may be asking, "If all this concern about praise is valid, what else can be done to communicate approval or admiration to the children I teach?" The answer offered by Hitz and Driscoll as well as by Brophy is to use *effective praise* (called *encouragement* by some professionals).[11] Their guidelines for effective praise follow.

- *Encouragement is specific.* In order for praise to be most effective, we must give specific feedback to the children. Instead of saying, for example, "Regina, you played very well with the children in the block corner today," you must highlight exactly what it was that made you think that Regina played well. A specific statement such as, "You put the blocks back on the shelf where they belong when you were done with them. Now they're ready for someone else to use," informs the child exactly about the behaviors that you approve of. Notice that the specific statement did not include a judgment such as "That's positively fabulous" or "I'm proud of you." The judgment about the quality of her play is left to the child alone.

- *Encouragement is teacher initiated and usually takes place in private.* You read earlier that ineffective praise makes the children feel resentful because they sense the teacher's attempt at manipulation. By talking privately, however, a teacher increases the potential for a child to see her words as an honest exchange of ideas. In such a context, the child is free of implied comparisons with other children. The child realizes the praise is meant only for him because he is on a one-to-one basis with the teacher and she is not attempting to motivate others by using him as an example.

- *Encouragement focuses on improvement of process rather than evaluation of a finished product.* A teacher's comments should be directed at the effort a child has expended toward completing a product rather than on the finished product itself. For example, instead of saying "Good work, you did such a nice job setting the snack table today," it might be more appropriate to say: "Thank you for helping set the table today. You put a cup at everyone's place."

- *Sincere, direct comments delivered with a natural voice are encouraging.* Earlier, you read that ineffective praise is often delivered in a matter-of-fact manner with gestures or facial expressions that often contradict the verbal message. In addition, teachers often employ words or phrases such as "Terrific," "I'm proud of you," "It's beautiful," or "Wow" in such an overused way that they often lose their effectiveness. Effective praise, on the other hand, should be communicated with honest feelings; they are more direct and honest and they are spoken neither overdramatically nor in a deadpan manner. Obviously, the direct, honest comment (e.g., "Danny, you rode your trike around the bench. You were careful not to knock it over.") can be said in an enthusiastic manner with appropriate physical feedback, too: a smile, nod of approval, hug, or pat on the back.

- *Encouragement helps to stimulate intrinsic motivation for behavior.* Ineffective praise such as, "Lucy, you always do such a great job of putting away your toys," is somewhat difficult for many young children to accept repeatedly because they know they are not *always* nice or good. Instead, use a statement that will allow Lucy herself to determine whether or not her deed was good: "Lucy, you put the puzzles back where they belong. When you do that we all can come together for a story much sooner." This statement is not value-laden; it invites the child to internally determine the worth of her actions. Overreliance on timeworn statements such as "I like the way you cleaned up," or "You did a wonderful job," inform the child that her actions are valued because they please the teacher, not because they are rewarding themselves.

These ideas are certainly valued and represent a critically important area of innovation in early childhood education today. However, it is my feeling that many of the overused terms and phrases are nearly impossible to eliminate from a supportive, friendly environment. Although Hitz and Driscoll recommend that these repeated comments be banished from the early childhood environment, I feel that the abuse lies more in when and how the words are used than in the words themselves.[12] Certainly, if we overuse any strategy exclusively, its effectiveness is likely to diminish. Traditionally popular words of praise are not immune to that phenomenon. Children thrive on variety. Therefore, the solution appears to be one of applying the principles of *effective* praise as described by Hitz and Driscoll, while utilizing the traditionally overused words of praise judiciously. It is a rare person—adult or child—who does not thrive on being told, for example, "You did a very nice job today." If such a statement is heartfelt and not said to satisfy either of the questionable purposes described earlier, the effects can be quite beneficial.

Employ Humor

All teachers who enjoy what they're doing must have and use a sense of humor in appropriate situations. Joking and "silliness" can achieve an instant rapport between you and your children. An angry, stubborn toddler, for example, refuses to wash his hands before lunch and won't let you do it either. Your frustration grows and your temper is about to flare, but instead of lashing out at him, you say: "My, oh my, Oscar the Grouch. What dirty hands you have! Did you play in the mud all day? . . . the garbage? Oh, Oscar, you mixed anchovies and ice cream together with your hands? We'd better get them clean!" Most children will react to this approach and giggle their way through scrubs. By kidding around, you've gotten a child to do something that might have otherwise been difficult for him.

Learning how to joke and kid around with children requires special sensitivity. Watch for special verbal and nonverbal reactions—a child's face is easy to read. Her reactions will reveal whether your joke amused her or hurt her, whether your humor was understood or went over her head. Once you have acquired this sensitivity, you will be free to enjoy yourself and enjoy laughter with your children.

When Necessary, Show the Child What You Mean

Whenever confusion, miscommunication, or refusal to comply characterize the encounter, it might be useful to demonstrate how to do something or how to do it in a better way. For example: "Gently drop the eggs into the dye. Let's put one into the cup together" (the teacher lends a hand), or "Pour the juice carefully. Here, I'll hold the cup while you fill it," or "I'll hold your hand while you try to climb onto the tree stump. You let me know when you're ready to try it by yourself." Be careful, however, not to give too much help in situations like these—it is often tempting to do things for the children rather than helping them do it. Children's self-confidence and growth in problem solving are increased when they know everyone in the classroom operates as a team instead of as adversaries.

Inform Children of the Logical Consequences of Their Behavior

What causes some children to choose misbehavior over positive behavior? What do they hope to accomplish? According to Rudolf Dreikurs, what they want usually corresponds to one of these four goals: (1) to get extra attention, (2) a quest for power, (3) to get revenge for real or imagined hurts, and (4) to avoid repeated failure.[13] Whether a child misbehaves for attention, power, revenge, or failure avoidance, teachers must respond accordingly; they must interact in some way. If we're able to identify the goal of the misbehavior, we can redirect the misbehavior by matching long- or short-term intervention techniques to the behavior. For example, the child misbehaving because he wants to avoid failure should be offered much long-term encouragement to help build self-esteem. With time, the child will learn to feel capable, wanted, and valued.

Dreikurs advises the use of "logical consequences" as a short-term intervention strategy. Logical consequences are statements made to the child to clarify the outcomes of his behavior. For example, if one child spills another child's paint during an art activity, the teacher says: "You must clean up the paint with a sponge and water. Then you'll need to share your paint with Christopher because he doesn't have any." Or, if a child refuses to put on a coat before going outside on a chilly day, the teacher would say: "If you do not wear a coat, you must remain indoors."

Logical consequences are communicated in a genuinely friendly manner, directly as the misbehavior occurs. This way, misbehaviors are treated as mistakes rather than serious transgressions that will bring disgrace to the child. Logical consequences must be reasonable: A reasonable consequence is directly proportional to the misbehavior. For example, suppose Wally scribbled over the bathroom door with a washable marker. A reasonable consequence would be to have him wash the door; an unreasonable consequence would be to have Wally wash every door in the classroom. Although the latter would leave an indelible impression on Wally, it would not justify the damage to his psyche that would likely result. We want to foster cooperation with this strategy, not antagonism.

The entire area of handling personal behavior management is extremely sensitive. Katherine H. Read supported this view when she said that guiding the young child requires a great deal of personal insight: "Overdirection may distort his development; so may the lack of direction. He needs time to learn through suitable experiences. He is sure to make some mistakes in the process of learning. . . . If we deal calmly and confidently with unacceptable behavior, we will create the kind of climate in which the child is helped to master his impulses and to direct his own behavior. We will be using authority in constructive ways."[14]

Problems Still Arise

Despite our best efforts to arrange a developmentally appropriate physical environment and daily schedule, in spite of our most sincere attempts at positive discipline, there will be situations when adults (regardless of how skilled they are) will throw up their hands and ask, "Now what do I do?" Sometimes it is necessary to blend a number of guidance techniques in order to be effective whenever discipline seems to go flying out the window.

BLENDING GUIDANCE TECHNIQUES

Let us suppose that some children are playing indoors at the puzzle table and Minh has begun to misuse the materials, dumping the puzzle pieces on the floor. Your first option might be to communicate a firm, brief statement (perhaps with a "but") reminding Minh of the behavior expected at the table: "It's fun to play with the puzzles, Minh, but you must keep the puzzle on the table so the pieces don't get lost." Let us suppose you get no response. Your next step could include restating the behavioral expectancy, but adding a second feature—physical help! "There's a special way to use the puzzles, Minh, so the pieces won't get lost. I'll hold your hand in mine while we put the puzzle piece on the puzzle."

By this point, young children often become absorbed in the activity and forget to resist. However, for those who persist, you might try active listening: "What is the matter, Minh?" The child may have a reason he can communicate. Let him know you are sincere in your efforts to help him out.

If a reasonable solution does not emerge by this time, you need to clearly inform the child of the logical consequences for his behavior. In this case, it might be either

Sometimes children need a break from the stimulation of a special activity.

taking the puzzle away for a short time or removing the child from the situation. If you try taking the puzzle away, you must explain why: "I'll put the puzzle here until you're ready to keep the pieces on the table." You may permit the child to stay in the puzzle area, but he may not use a puzzle until he indicates readiness to follow established procedures. He may ask immediately for another chance, but before you allow him to take the puzzle back, the child must tell you how it is to be used.

For some children, time away from the interest center might be most constructive. In extreme cases, when a child resists all other efforts or when the child's presence annoys other children, he may have to take time away from the group. Do not demean or frighten children with a time-out chair (or, as one misguided teacher did, make the child hold a baby bottle to signify his "immaturity"), but provide a short breather to gain control before returning to play. In this example, you calmly approach the child, take his hand, and guide him to the outside of the puzzle area. Tell the child: "Please stand (or sit) and watch how the other children use the puzzles." Do not do this in a humiliating way, but be helpful and supportive. After a minute or two of watching, you should turn to Minh and say: "Did you see how the children used the puzzles? Can you tell me what they did?" If the child can state the appropriate behavior, let him return. Be sure to comment on the child's ensuing effort: "You kept the pieces on the table and finished the puzzle. Now you have time to try another one or to visit another center."

In rare instances, children may lose their composure when requested to leave an activity they are disrupting. When this happens, assure the child that you'll help him work out this situation: "I'll hold you until you're feeling better." Sometimes children become involved in the throes of such intense emotion that their actions may cause harm to themselves or others. Children who lose control need help to regain it before they can be allowed to do anything else: "You are angry now, and you need to calm down before I can give you back the puzzle." Many children will cry loudly and call you hurtful names, but you must remain firm until the child gains control. At times, the tantrums may be so intense that the child will kick and flail his arms in frightful ways. At these moments you must provide firm, supportive help. Hold the child close to you, facing outward if possible, and support him while his tantrum begins to subside. Don't try to moralize about the condition that resulted in the tantrum; the child may only start again. As soon as he gains control, however, let him become involved in some alternative activity. Talk calmly about the conditions causing the outburst, and remind him of the behavior required in that situation. Your understanding and support must be there when the child needs them. The child needs to come out of this crisis knowing that you can be trusted and that you are near to help when control is lost.

COPING WITH DISLIKE FOR A CHILD

Programs for young children should be centered on the faith and hope we have in the individuality of children—in the belief of accepting each as they are. Our caring attitude should help create an affectionate environment where youngsters are not afraid to be openly evaluated. Such an environment does not reward blind conformity with manipulation and insincere praise. Rather, as Joanne Hendrick informs us, the ideal childhood environment is one that provides individual acceptance, the keystone of building self-esteem:

> [Individual acceptance] is the ability to feel and project what Carl Rogers terms *unconditional positive regard*. This kind of fundamental acceptance and approval of each child is not contingent upon his meeting the teacher's expectation of what he should be, but simply depends on his being alive, being a child, and being in the group. A good test of being accepting or not is to become aware of what one is usually thinking about when looking at the children. Ask yourself, "Am I taking time to enjoy the children, or am I looking at each one with a critical eye—noting what behavior should be improved?" If you catch yourself habitually noting only what should be changed, this is a sign you are losing sight of half the pleasure of teaching, which is to appreciate the children and enjoy who they are right now, at this particular moment in time—no strings attached.[15]

There is no substitute for acceptance of each child. Part of that acceptance is the idea that each child has a right to be different and is loved regardless—not because he is livelier, brighter, or friendlier than another child, but because he is himself.

Most of your feelings toward young children are pleasurable, accepting, affectionate, and caring. You want to make their lives as lovely as possible. Whenever you think of outstanding teachers, you probably imagine those qualities. Would you add feelings such as jealousy, dislike, ambivalence, fear, or anger to that list? Probably not—yet teachers do have those emotions, and children frequently are the cause. Despite this fact, teachers are usually reluctant to admit their feelings, especially the important one we shall consider here: dislike for a particular child. Guilt often accompanies the realization of dislike, and teachers agonize as they attempt to repress it. It is a human reaction, and one that H. M. Greenberg states should be accepted as a normal emotion: "It is impossible to feel the same way toward all children. Human beings react uniquely or specifically to other human beings. [Teachers] have had a lifetime to form personal likes and dislikes. [They] cannot shed them in class."[16] Although, as caring professionals, we find it difficult to admit dislike for any single child, it is important to recognize the fact that such an emotion may exist in our professional life. *Only through such recognition can we expect to cope with the situation.* W. K. Fordyce offers these coping strategies:

1. *Pinpoint the specific reason for disliking a child.* Is it the physical appearance such as obesity or a constantly running nose? What about specific mannerisms such as biting or hair pulling? A list of these specific behaviors could stretch out for pages. After identifying the irritating behaviors or characteristics, you should accept them as problems to be solved.

2. *Analyze why a personal chord has been struck.* Once you have pinpointed the bothersome behavior, try to understand why it is so dominant in your attitude toward the child. Is it because the behavior itself is so foreign to your own behavior repertoire? Can it be that the behavior is so much like you, for example, a quick temper? By discovering this source of personal aggravation, you can begin to direct strong feelings away from the child.

3. *Recognize which characteristics or behaviors are genuinely liked.* Try to look beyond your dislikes and develop a well-rounded view of the child, searching for positive characteristics. For example, you may strongly dislike a five-year-old clinging to his mother upon arrival to school, but may truly enjoy his creative play at 9:20. These feelings of delight will help you overcome your dislikes and form a more well-rounded view of the child.

4. *Determine whether the disliked behaviors are actually age-appropriate.* Be sure to solidify your knowledge of child development so that you can establish realistic expectations. Rather than labeling a two-year-old "restless" because she is unable to participate in a whole-group activity for twenty minutes, you should understand that such behavior is characteristic of all children at that level. Understanding this developmental stage can be an excellent way to displace dislike.

5. *Share your concerns with a colleague.* Although you may be "turned off" by a child, a coworker may feel differently. You can then be assured that the child will get fair and objective treatment from that coworker who enjoys the child's company.[17]

Dislike for a child is but one extreme emotion you can expect to surface as you begin a career with young children. There are many others, of course, but let us now consider a feeling exactly the opposite of dislike—strong positive regard for a child. Sometimes one child is held in such high esteem by a teacher that feelings interfere with sound judgment. This teacher might unknowingly accept the child's impulses and actions even though they would not be considered appropriate if demonstrated by other children. Similarly, the teacher in such a situation might exert very little guidance and control, offer inequitable attention for accomplishments or successes, or address routine situations by displaying distinct favoritism toward the highly esteemed child. For example, the teacher might say, "I like the way A. J. is sitting [even though the majority of the class is sitting the same way]. He will be the line leader again today." Such strong feelings, if they exist, should be examined, recognized, and analyzed in an objective manner similar to that used in dealing with a child who is disliked. Only by doing so can you expect to offer a classroom that is sensitive and responsive to the unique developmental needs of all children.

PARENTAL COOPERATION FOR PERSISTENT PROBLEMS

Very few persistent behavioral problems will be solved if you do not develop a plan that is consistent with parents' actions. Home interaction patterns must parallel those of the school. Most parents are willing to cooperate in such a venture and to establish parent-child relationships similar to the teacher-child relationship. This home-school connection is essential to reinforcement of your practices, because the parent-child relationship is normally far deeper than the teacher-child relationship.

Some parent-child ties cause problems, however, for they sometimes prevent parents from perceiving a situation with the same objectivity that you have. For example, some parents in your child care facility may become upset because they want a program stressing group conformity in behaviors, while you value individual pursuits more highly. In these instances, you need to resolve differences by thoroughly discussing them in a professional manner. In other words, explain your philosophy of guidance so that the parents can see the value of your beliefs. They need to understand your position completely if their concerns are to be relieved. Also, remember that your discussion with the parents must be a two-way process. Listen to what they have to say. Perhaps the way they act is based on deep convictions, such as cultural expectations, very different from your own. In these cases you must take the time to understand and respect the parents' concerns—a quick resolution is rarely possible. Instead of forcing your beliefs on the parents and risking the alienation of them and of their community, try to empathize with their position and work out an amicable agreement. This takes skill to accomplish, but you won't win them over with a take-it-or-leave-it attitude. You can't provide the best situation for their children if you can't offer the type of program you think is soundest—it can become a real dilemma. Take the case of young Charles, for example. Charles was brought up in a rough neighborhood and was taught by his parents to fight whenever possible to protect his possessions. Naturally, when playing in the child care setting, Charles frequently protected his toys and games with physical force. Concerned for the safety of the other children, Charles's teacher approached his parents. The parents refused to support any of the teacher's suggestions for changing Charles's behavior because they felt it was a necessary quality for survival in their neighborhood. Thoroughly perplexed, the teacher realized that any techniques used in school would not be carried through in the home, so she decided that her responsibility was to do the best possible job at school. Whenever Charles resorted to punching or hitting, she would immediately step in and sternly say, "I cannot allow you to hit other children *in school*." Respecting the parents' feelings, the teacher did not warn the child that his behaviors were wrong in *all* situations, but she did communicate the limits of his behavior in the classroom in a firm, direct way. You should become familiar with the various techniques of parent-teacher cooperation, because a partnerlike relationship between parent and teacher is essential to solving social-emotional problems and helping a child grow.

SOME FINAL THOUGHTS

Throughout recorded history, authorities of various reputations have suggested ways to reduce misbehavior among young children. Some have offered "magic lists," whereas others have advanced "simple rules to follow." I have entered into the tumult by writing this chapter about the management of children's behavior. Despite all our technological advances, though, no one has yet formulated a surefire method for getting children to do something as seemingly uncomplicated as eating their vegetables. It would be comforting for parents and teachers to have a book of recipes, so that whenever one child bit another, for example, one could look in the index and find under "Biting, toddlers," a precise, constructive way of eliminating the behavior. But no writers, regardless of their prominence in the field, can yet provide us with such information. Many have made valiant efforts, but not one has succeeded...yet.

Regardless of how well you've planned your classroom, established your daily routine, and formed positive bonds with your children, there will certainly be times of conflict. Some teachers will have less difficulty handling those situations than others. The reasons for those differences are varied, but the personality of the teacher and the composition of the class are certainly major factors. Yet they are not the only ones—sound knowledge of child development and of generally accepted principles of behavior management must be mastered and practiced. Whatever combination you find appropriate for your situation, discipline must be accompanied by understanding and compassion. Children are learning—they will make mistakes. We must accept these mistakes as signs of growth; a classroom where children never make mistakes is one in which they never get an opportunity to manage failures as well as successes. We want children to try out new behaviors, and they will fail at times. They must know that, when they do fail, an understanding leader will be near to help.

NOTES

1. Thomas Gordon, *T.E.T.: Teacher Effectiveness Training* (New York: Peter H. Wyden, 1974).
2. Ann S. Clewett, "Guidance and Discipline: Teaching Young Children Appropriate Behavior," *Young Children, 43,* no. 4 (May 1988): 27.
3. James L. Hymes, Jr., *Teaching the Child Under Six,* 3rd ed. (Columbus, OH: Merrill, 1981), pp. 139–140.
4. Alice S. Honig, *Love and Learn* (Washington: National Association for the Education of Young Children, 1987), p. 1.
5. "NAEYC Position Statement on Developmentally Appropriate Practice in Early Childhood Programs Serving Children From Birth Through Age 8," in Sue Bredekamp, ed., *Developmentally Appropriate Practice in Early Childhood Programs Serving Children From Birth Through Age 8* (Washington, DC: National Association for the Education of Young Children, 1987), p. 11.
6. Dan Gartrell, "Punishment or Guidance?" *Young Children, 42,* no. 3 (March 1987): 55.
7. Lawrence Kohlberg, "The Claim to Moral Adequacy of a Highest State of Moral Judgment," *The Journal of Philosophy, 70,* no. 18 (October 25, 1973): 631–632.
8. Thomas Gordon, *T.E.T.: Teacher Effectiveness Training.*
9. Jere E. Brophy, "Teacher Praise: A Functional Analysis," *Review of Educational Research, 51,* no. 1 (January 1981): 5–32.
10. Randy Hitz and Amy Driscoll, "Praise or Encouragement?" *Young Children, 43,* no. 5 (July 1988): 8.
11. Ibid., pp. 6–13.
12. Ibid.
13. Rudolf Dreikurs and Vicki Soltz, *Children: The Challenge* (New York: Dutton, 1964).

14. Katherine H. Read, *The Nursery School: A Human Relations Laboratory* (Philadelphia: W. B. Saunders, 1971), pp. 108–109.

15. Joanne Hendrick, *The Whole Child: Developmental Education for the Early Years,* 5th ed. (Columbus, OH: Merrill/Macmillan, 1992), p. 128.

16. H. M. Greenberg, *Teaching with Feeling* (New York: Macmillan, 1969).

17. W. K. Fordyce, "A Worm in the Teacher's Apple," *Childhood Education, 58,* no. 9 (May/June 1982): 287–291.

CHAPTER 13

Organizing and Managing the Classroom Environment

If given a choice between a superior teacher in a poorly equipped room or a weak teacher in a glorious room, which would you take? Most of us, I presume, would choose a superior teacher in a poorly equipped room. We realize that there is no substitute for the person who uses sound theory as the basis for providing challenges and experiences for her children. The ideal, though, is an early childhood program that reflects a combination of the two—a good teacher who is able to equip an early childhood classroom with material suited to the developmental needs and interests of her children; a teacher who knows what materials to offer daily and what to hold back; a teacher who knows the precise point at which the materials stimulate but do not overexcite; a teacher who knows how to pull the most out of the materials so that optimal growth is stimulated. The aims of this chapter are to describe some of the materials one would expect to find in a desirable early childhood setting and to discuss how those materials can best be arranged and utilized. As you read, use the following questions to guide your thinking.

- What materials are basic to a well-equipped nursery for infants in a group setting?

- What are some popular *classroom* activity centers into which teachers often organize materials for young children?

- How should the centers be arranged and managed in order to ensure the maximum benefit from them?

- How do teachers organize a schedule that informs the children of what is happening when?

An Episode to Ponder

Ms. Johnson looks around the classroom. Most children are involved in worthwhile play activities, but a few are acting confused and frustrated. Mark is on his hands and knees trying to find a cylinder block from a jumbled pile on the floor. Veronica and Jenny race across the room from the sand table to reach a large box where balls are kept, but Jenny trips and falls. Tears begin falling—more from the shock of the accident than from injury. Kim winces and drops her broom at the housekeeping center as Basil's wheel toy careens around the corner and just misses hitting her. "Something is clearly wrong here," thinks Ms. Johnson, "the classroom needs some careful organization." First, she arranges the blocks on shelves according to shape so the block builders can easily get what they want. Ms. Johnson also involves the children in helping to clean up and organize the blocks when the activity is finished for the day. She rearranges classroom furniture to cut off open spaces that seem to invite running. Additionally, Ms. Johnson moves the large wheel toys to an area isolated from less physically active pursuits. She reminds the children about the procedures for playing with blocks, moving from one area to another, and riding wheel toys.

Ms. Johnson was extremely perceptive in realizing that her children were being affected by the classroom environment, and that certain practices needed change. It was easy for her to see how and what specific adjustments were needed to make everyone's day run more smoothly. Environmental factors are highly influential in determining quality of early childhood programs; teachers must be especially careful to plan and organize the classroom in ways that work *for* rather than *against* them. A well-planned and carefully organized classroom helps make the teacher's job easier, the child's day more enjoyable, and the engagement with activities and materials more productive and challenging. A well-equipped and effectively managed program gets the children's wheels turning; it makes for an atmosphere of anticipation, delight, inspiration, magic, challenge, and charm. NAEYC's Guidelines for Developmentally Appropriate Practice reinforce this thought:

Children of all ages need uninterrupted periods of time to become involved, investigate, select, and persist at activities. *The teacher's role in child-chosen activity is to prepare the environment* [italics mine] with stimulating, challenging activity choices and then to facilitate engagement. In developmentally appropriate programs, adults:

1. Provide a rich variety of activities and materials from which to choose....
2. Offer children the choice to participate in a small group or in a solitary activity.
3. Assist and guide children who are not yet able to use easily and enjoy child-choice activity periods.
4. Provide opportunities for child-initiated, child-directed practice of skills as a self-chosen activity.[1]

To prepare and manage a developmentally appropriate environment involves many responsibilities, among which decision making related to equipment and supplies is the most encompassing. As a manager, your decisions will often involve careful judgments such as these:

- Selecting the most developmentally appropriate equipment and supplies

- Arranging the equipment and supplies in an organized way

- Creating a daily schedule with consistent routines and smooth transitions

Managing the child's physical environment is a primary professional responsibility that begins long before the children set foot in your classroom.

Equipping and arranging the indoor environment are among the most exciting activities beginning teachers encounter. Most of you have experienced the thrill of planning your own dorm room, apartment, or other living space; it grew and developed into a special place of your own as you begged, borrowed, or bought the items that added a personal touch to its creation. As the living space evolved, you determined your interests or needs and obtained the right equipment and supplies: Kitchen facilities were needed to prepare food or refreshments; a separate, quiet area was necessary for studying; stereo equipment or a television set may have been selected to provide relaxation; and sheets, blankets, and other bedding were essential. Other considerations were addressed, of course, and the result was satisfying because you were able, perhaps for the first time in your life, to originate a living space of your very own. Likewise, the selection and arrangement of classroom materials and supplies must be yours. They should, however, also stem from a knowledge of the general characteristics, interests, and needs of young children.

THE INFANT ROOM

Babies' most important needs are physical care, comfort, sensory and motor stimulation, and emotional security. Caregivers meet these needs by providing many opportunities for affectionate exchanges. Loving responsiveness to the baby not only promotes sound emotional health, but also gives the baby the confidence necessary to explore the environment. The caregiver is important but does not operate alone—babies also need a warm, safe environment.

In setting up your child care nursery, it is wise to follow a few basic rules. Babies spend a great deal of time sleeping, so they should have a place to themselves that is airy, clean, and quiet enough so that they can sleep undisturbed. It is best to have a separate sleeping area or a remote, private niche that can be closed off from the main room. Infants operate on different timetables, so it is inappropriate to expect them all to lie down and sleep at exactly the same time. Some may need to play in the main room while the others sleep, so separate rooms for napping and playing are very important.

Furnishings should be simple in construction, practical, and easy to clean. If you must use second-hand furniture, make sure the paint is lead-free before repainting it. It's a good idea to obtain a large hardwood crib with a firm, snug mattress. Use fitted sheets and waterproof mattress pads to ensure the baby's comfort. No pillow is necessary. The side rails should have a plastic teething guard on the top slats, childproof releases, and rails with gaps no wider than two and three-eighths inches. Safety bumper pads should run around the entire crib. A small chest of drawers for baby shirts, booties or socks, coveralls, and other items of clothing is desirable. Babies require between ten and twelve diapers per day as well as cotton shirts, stretch suits, waterproof pants, socks or booties, and shoes (to protect feet while walking). Both you and your baby will enjoy a rocking chair for feeding and any other cozy moments you share.

Other essential nursery equipment includes a refrigerator for the baby's milk or formula, diaper pail, clothing hamper, changing table, portable baby swing, and toy storage box. Also very important is a high chair with a strong tray latch, crotch strap to prevent sliding, adjustable footrest, padded seat back for head support, and raised-edge tray to catch spills. You may wish to add a playpen with hinges that lock tightly; firm, foam-padded floor support; mesh netting; and padded rims. A good stroller provides easy transportation for daily walks. Be sure it has wide-diameter wheels for stability, a padded seat, shock-absorbing suspension, easy-to-operate brakes, and no easily removed wing nuts or other easy-to-swallow parts.

Limit your bathing supplies to simple, necessary articles: mild soap and shampoo, brush and comb, towels and washcloths (three or four of each per child), cotton swabs, baby nail scissors, baby thermometer, and common toiletries such as moist towelettes.

Feeding supplies include presterilized nurser kits (or eight bottles per child and a sterilizer kit), bottle warmer, baby dishes and utensils, food strainer, food warmer, and bibs.

At about six months of age, babies will need room to creep, roll, and crawl. They need floor space to kick, squirm, and work arms and legs. Mattresses, pillows, or furniture cushions placed on the floor add interesting challenges for the babies as they go through, over, or under them. Offer the children safe, easy-to-clean floor coverings such as mats or pads, on which to practice their emerging skills. These are desirable for their cleanliness, convenience, and economy.

As they crawl, babies enjoy reaching for things and looking at moving objects or bright patterns. Infant care facilities should offer stimulation related to these interests—colorful floor coverings and large, bright, plastic-laminated pictures of animals, nursery rhyme characters, flowers, or popular childhood characters, as well as unbreakable mirrors mounted on the walls at floor level.

Finally, your nursery should provide a variety of infant toys. The educational value of such toys is much emphasized these days; however, it does not follow that the toys have to be intricate or expensive. Toys must be fun—babies will lose interest if they are not. Also, they must be within the child's developmental capabilities. First toys, for example, must be large enough for the baby to handle comfortably and be made from materials that can be thoroughly washed—plastic, rubber, or smooth wood with rounded edges. Be sure there are no sharp edges or corners, and no easily removable parts that could be swallowed. Keep an especially watchful eye out for small wheels, little bells, or loosely attached eyes on small stuffed animals. Be certain that no toys are painted with lead-based paint. Most toy packages specify the age group for which the toy is most appropriate, so check the labels carefully.

The toys enjoyed most by the youngest babies are those that they can grasp easily in order to bang, wave, or place in the mouth. Later, as their manual dexterity improves, they need "do-something" toys—buttons to press, handles to turn, dials to spin, items to build up and tear down, or things to take apart and put together. These toys not only help reinforce and develop emerging physical skills but also develop the baby's intelligence and imagination. Babies acquire countless skills through play with well-selected, developmentally appropriate toys.

THE YOUNG CHILD'S ROOM

Nothing outdoes a large, bright, well-organized, clean room for greeting the children in their "home away from home." A room that meets licensing requirements for space (usually between 35 and 50 square feet per child) is only the beginning. The wise teacher understands that the room must be carefully planned well before the first day of school in order for the children to work and play most productively. For example, we know that young children are physical. If we crowd their room with furniture and do not leave enough space for physical activity, we run the risk of creating a stifling environment. If there are too many open spaces, though, the children may run aimlessly from one play area to another. We also know that young children vary in social responsiveness. Are there areas where children can play together? Is there a private nook where a child can go off and be alone? How the space is planned and filled is at least as important as how many square feet are available.

The room you occupy may not be specifically what you had in mind as you planned for a career teaching young children. Some may have been specifically designed for preschool children, but others will be found in such unlikely places as abandoned stores, church basements, or private homes. There may be no low windows (if there are windows at all), dull walls, and a dearth of ground that could serve as a playground or be turned into a garden plot. Such an environment often upsets beginning teachers with its uninviting, drab appearance, but with a bit of ingenuity it can be transformed into an efficient, usable space. Walls decorated with colorful, light paint or with favorite story and cartoon characters can brighten the room. Lamps add to its attractiveness and comfort. Low shelves or screens can be arranged as boundaries for a private dramatic play corner, carpentry area, or book nook. Live plants placed on shelves or tables and in hanging baskets provide attractiveness as well as excellent learning opportunities. Large wooden or metal boxes filled with dirt and placed in a sunny area of the playground make splendid outdoor planters for flowers and vegetables. Don't be frustrated by the initial appearance of the place where you will be teaching. It is far more rewarding (and demonstrates greater skill) to make acceptable and comfortable a room that originally seemed dingy than it is to organize an already ideal space. Meeting the needs of your children calls for certain equipment essential to all programs—a large rug, chairs, tables, storage shelves, and cots or mattress pads for full-day programs. A *large rug* serves as the congregation point for stories, discussions, or any other activity that may involve the entire group. It should be big enough to accommodate up to 20 youngsters and be made of a material that can be easily cleaned. The *tables and chairs* should be child-size but sturdy enough to carry an adult's weight. Children will sit at tables while they have a snack or lunch, work with craft materials or puzzles, or look at books. *Storage shelves* should be child-size so that children are able to get toys and other materials comfortably when they need them. In full-day groups, where rest or napping is necessary, cots or mattresses are a necessity. Cots and mattresses should have washable covers and be lightweight enough to be stacked for storage. In addition to these essential features, most teachers—regardless of their philosophical orientation—divide their rooms into several clearly defined areas that are organized thematically and filled with a variety of related materials.

ACTIVITY CENTERS

Classrooms for young children are divided into separate thematic areas called *activity centers* (sometimes *interest centers*). Teachers do this for two main reasons. First, young children function more efficiently in small groups. By creating separate areas of activity, you limit the number of children who can play together at one time. Second, a subdivided classroom offers children opportunities to make choices. An area set aside for books, for example, invites a child who might presently prefer a quiet activity, whereas a block building area would appeal to a child who wants to play more actively. Developmentally appropriate classrooms, then, are divided into separate activity centers, giving children clear choices of where they wish to play. These centers were discussed comprehensively in Chapter 5.

ROOM ARRANGEMENT

Choosing thematic equipment for the classroom centers is just the beginning—it is now important to consider how the centers will be arranged so that young children will obtain the greatest benefit from them. For example, an unappealing block center located in a confined area encourages few children to play and increases the possibility for conflict, but a large-motor center with plenty of room encourages many children to play together and offers opportunities for positive social experiences. A mixture of manipulatable toys and art materials is confusing and can lead to abuse of the involved items. The impact of room arrangement is obvious: Each area is separate and distinct yet important for the total program. Children cannot work or play adequately in a chaotic environment.

Figure 13–1 shows a floor plan designed by one teacher of a group of four-year-olds. Note that storage shelves are placed against the walls and tables are located in the middle of the room. Many beginning teachers approach the design of their first classroom similarly. If we analyze the arrangement, we find that the room could be chaotic and counterproductive to the goals of the program. For instance, the open spaces in the middle may invite children to run around from one activity to another.

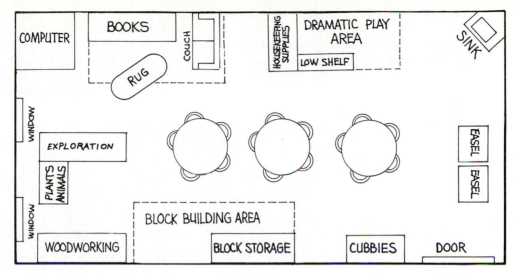

Figure 13–1   Floor plan for four-year-olds

The easels are open to the rest of the room and in a direct line with the door. The block center is right next to the cubbies—you can imagine the anger generated as block structures are toppled by eager youngsters leaving their cubbies to visit another classroom center.

Teachers will want to rearrange centers to be like Figure 13–2 so that running space can be cut down and children offered well-defined areas in which to work

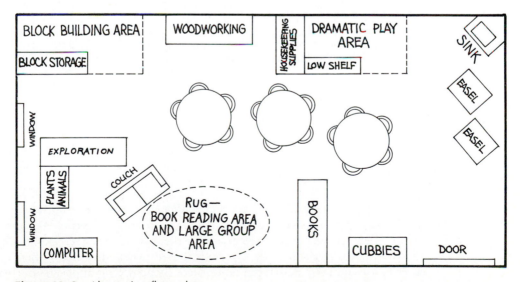

Figure 13–2   Alternative floor plan

and play. Notice how the shelves have been brought away from the walls and used as dividers to set off as many specific areas as possible. Children playing in highly active areas such as blocks or housekeeping will feel protected from other activities, while those choosing a quiet area such as books will be secluded enough not to be distracted. The new arrangement should also make it easier for children to get from one area to another without interfering with others as they play. The advantages of well-organized space are that it eliminates unproductive behavior and that it helps children pursue activities with a sense of security, confidence, and trust.

The quality of your classroom, then, depends greatly upon how the space is arranged into centers. There is, however, a second major organizational factor involved—the techniques used to display the materials within the centers. If the materials are not displayed properly we run the risk of having the children misuse them. What message do we send to the children, for example, when we clutter shelves with as many toys as possible? The most obvious is: "Here you go, children. Use these in any way you wish!" Good teachers understand that unspoken messages may be communicated to children through the ways items are displayed. With such understanding, they follow some very important guidelines:

- *Introduce equipment and materials deliberately.* It can be dangerous to over-stimulate young children with many new materials. The children may become overwhelmed by everything around them and demonstrate two basic behaviors: (1) withdrawal from all activity because of too much stimulation too soon, and (2) uncontrolled darting about from one part of the room to another in an attempt to experience as much as possible in the shortest amount of time. Lori Fisk and Henry Lindgren illustrate this concern with the following example:

  Introducing a number of [classroom materials] all at once produces a situation in which children's cognitive systems collapse under an "overload of input," as my computerized friends and colleagues would say. Once, as a teenager, I babysat for a day, while the child's mother attended a conference. As she went out the door, she paused for ninety seconds and told me how to run the dishwasher, washing machine, clothes dryer, garbage disposal unit, and toaster oven. Before I could open my mouth to say, "Just a minute, you're going too fast!" she was gone, with a cheerful, "Have a good day!" Needless to say, I touched none of these household devices during her absence, since I was afraid that I would do something to break them. Children are of course less mature than teenagers and can absorb even less information if it is delivered all at once.[2]

  Introduce only a few materials at the beginning of the preschool year and gradually add others as time goes by to maintain a comfortable, challenging environment.

- *Give young children time to adjust to group life outside the home before you expect them to share.* As you know, young children are egocentric. We cannot expect their self-centeredness to disappear the moment they set foot in your classroom, so let them enjoy a period of time when they know their desires to use certain materials can be satisfied. By providing duplicates of basic materials like table toys or kitchen utensils, we help children adjust to a new situation without fear of being left out or disciplined for taking something another child is using.

- *Encourage children to understand that every item has its place.* Draw pictures or take photographs of each item, mount them on durable cardboard, and laminate them for protection. Tape these labels to the appropriate storage shelves, and put each item on its represented place. All materials now have special locations for storage, and children will learn to return items to the proper locations when they are finished using them. The child's attitude becomes, "This is my classroom, and I care about it." More skillful children do not need photographs or pictures to help them; gross outlines of items like cooking utensils, cleaning utensils, eating utensils, or art supplies can be displayed for them. In this way, the children are not only contributing to classroom organization, but they are practicing the skill of matching and grouping.

- *Help children plan what they want to do.* Construct a planning display at the beginning of the year to help the children make choices about what they want to do. Mount close-up photographs of each child on tagboard cards and glue a clothespin to each card. Large tagboard signs depict the various areas within your classroom. Clip the photos to a sign to indicate the area to which each child will move during small-group activity periods (see Figure 13–3).

A cozy, undisturbed period of rest is all some children need to recharge drained energy.

Figure 13–3 Display indicating movement among small-group activities

After a conference with you, the child takes her photo and clips it to a picture representing the area where she will play. How the child will move from center to center will most probably follow one of four patterns:

Pattern 1: You assign all children to centers by pinning their pictures to the center designations. This approach would most probably result in too much child dependency upon adults.

Pattern 2: You provide the child with two or three alternatives and the child chooses from among them.

Pattern 3: The children and you confer and make a joint decision after considering several choices.

Pattern 4: The children have free choice of all center possibilities. This pattern is most likely to result in greater opportunities for growth of personal responsibility.

The most appropriate planning strategies for preschoolers appear to be those in which the children can make choices of some type. Those choices can be communicated by the child to the teacher through techniques as simple as pointing to the reading area or as complex as picking out props and costumes desired for some fantasy play. The exact pattern of planning is not as important as the consideration that each child gets some chances to select activities that interest her and, with the help of an adult, plan how she will go about doing it. Why is child planning important? Nancy Altman Brickman and Lynn Spencer offer these reasons:[3]

- It helps children see that they can make things happen for themselves. They develop a sense of control over their own lives and take responsibility for their own choices.

- It helps children develop a better understanding of time by requiring them to anticipate the future and to think about what can be accomplished in a given time period.

- It helps children develop language skills, because they learn new words and phrases as they choose their activities and identify the materials and processes they plan to use.
- It gives children opportunities to acknowledge and use their own moods and feelings in constructive ways. If a child comes to school excited about a visit from his grandparents, for example, you might help him clarify his feelings and make appropriate plans: "You might like to make an airport so you can watch grandma and grandpa's plane come in."

Because planning is so important, it's worth some extra effort to help the children get started. As adults, we are fully aware of how difficult it is to organize time, so don't expect preschoolers to plan smoothly at the first attempt. They will need much help and preparation.

- *Allow the room to be the children's.* The physical space should reflect the interests, needs, and talents of the children. It becomes theirs when shelves, tables, chairs, and storage facilities are at the children's eye level so that displays and materials are easily accessible. It becomes theirs when there is a place for display of the children's artwork and other products. It becomes theirs when individual lockers (cubbies) are designed for the children's personal use. Youngsters take comfort in knowing that a special part of the room is for them; they enjoy assuming responsibility for keeping it neat and orderly. It becomes theirs when we decorate and equip the space with an aesthetically pleasing decor—warm colors, draperies, flooring appropriate to the activity area (tile for the art center, carpeting for the book center), and washable, durable surfaces. It becomes theirs when the children feel at home!

THE OUTDOOR ENVIRONMENT

From the earliest nursery schools of McMillan to today's diverse preschool alternatives, all early childhood educators have accepted the idea of having a well-equipped playground where young children can not only get fresh air and exercise, but also gain experiences contributing to all areas of development, including intellectual goals. In essence, every developmental goal that is attainable in the classroom is likewise attainable outdoors. Early nursery school educators such as McMillan perceived the outdoor environment with such esteem that they often left one side of the school open to nature—a play area or garden, for example, where children would spend most of their day. The indoor environment was used primarily as a shelter from inclement weather. Today, NAEYC, in its statement of Developmentally Appropriate Practices, reiterates the importance of a carefully planned, quality outdoor environment:

Because their physical development is occurring so rapidly, young children through age 8 need daily outdoor experiences to practice large motor skills, learn about

Children should have opportunities to play outdoors whenever the weather permits.

outdoor environments, and experience freedom not always possible indoors. Outdoor time is an important part of the curriculum and requires planning; it is not simply a time for children to release pent-up energy.[4]

The outdoor environment contains possibilities for individual growth going far beyond physical gains; it gives the child opportunities to develop and refine growing social, emotional, intellectual, language, and creative abilities, too.

Outdoor Safety

The teacher's role in the outdoors is two-fold: (1) to use time and equipment in ways that provide for the children's physical, social, emotional, and intellectual needs; and

(2) to protect the children with a safe environment. Teachers should be constantly aware of the children's activity as well as of the safety of the equipment. However, proper care and supervision begins before the children take their first steps into the outdoor environment. Be certain to select and use equipment that is safe. Use the following general criteria in making your judgments:

1. *Will the children enjoy the equipment?* The equipment should be challenging, yet not frustrate or defeat the children.

2. *Are the materials safe?* Check the material for sharp corners or edges and exposed nails or screws. Make sure it is constructed of materials that would be harmless when used in normal ways. Check whether the paint, varnish, or other finish is nontoxic. Make sure small pieces are securely fastened so they cannot be swallowed or poked into eyes or ears.

3. *Are the materials durable?* Be sure that the materials are strong and resilient. They should be able to withstand extreme weather conditions and hard use.

4. *Are the materials versatile?* Look carefully to see if the materials can be used in a variety of ways. Balls, blocks, wagons, and ropes are but a few of the many items that are appropriate.

5. *Will the equipment provide balance to my collection?* Assess the materials you presently have, and evaluate whether you are overloaded with one or more of these types of equipment: solitary play (as opposed to group play); creative activity (as opposed to closed-ended activity); motor equipment (as opposed to intellectual or social-type equipment).

6. *Is the material attractive?* Determine whether the children will be attracted or repelled by the color, form, or sound of the equipment. Equipment should have a high overall appeal for children.

7. *Will the child be actively involved in its use?* Many times equipment is manufactured to appeal to an adult rather than to a child. After all, adults buy the equipment. Be wary of gimmicky equipment designed to entertain. It makes the children passive observers.

8. *Is the material developmentally appropriate?* Check to see that the size is correct and that the equipment is suitable for the age level of the children.

9. *Am I buying this equipment because the children need it or because I like it?* Be careful to avoid impulse purchases. Decide what your needs are and stick to your purchase plans. Do not be enticed by sharply reduced prices, flashy displays, or smooth sales pitches.

To find out about, or to report a playground product you think might be hazardous, call the United States Consumer Product Safety Commission's toll-free hotline: 800–638–CPSC. They can send you pamphlets on the purchase, maintenance, and proper use of toys and children's play equipment. Additionally, Penny Lovell and Thelma Harms have developed a useful playground improvement rating scale that offers many helpful suggestions on how to make playgrounds safe and help expand children's play (see Figure 13–4 on pages 466–468).

Program _____

Number of children _____ Date _____

Ages of children _____ Rater _____

Number of staff _____

Score each item: 3—outdoor play area meets this goal very well
2—outdoor play area needs to be improved to meet this goal
1—little or no evidence that outdoor play area meets this goal

ACTIVITIES AND EQUIPMENT
(Examples of items to look for are listed in parentheses.)
Range of activities

_____ 1. The equipment provides appropriate and stimulating levels of difficulty for all the age groups served (infants, toddlers, preschool children, school-age children).

_____ 2. A variety of equipment is provided to stimulate different types of physical activity (balls, balance beams, wheel toys, swings, climbing equipment, jump ropes, ladders, planks).

_____ 3. Some of the equipment and materials invite cooperative play (outdoor blocks, rocking boat, dramatic play props).

_____ 4. Creative materials are readily available for children (clay, carpentry, paints, water, sand).

_____ 5. Some of the equipment is flexible so that it can be combined in different ways by the children, with adult help if necessary (planks, climbing boxes, ladders).

_____ 6. The climbing equipment incorporates a variety of spatial relationships (through tunnels, up or down ramps, over or under platforms).

_____ 7. There is a suitable place for gardening (window box, tubs with soil, garden plot).

_____ 8. There are enough options for the children to choose from without unreasonable competition or waiting.

SAFETY AND HEALTH

_____ 9. The equipment is substantially constructed (anchored climbing structures and swing frames).

_____ 10. Cushioning is provided under swings and climbing apparatus (loose sand or tanbark at least one foot deep within a containing edgeboard, rubber padding).

_____ 11. Swing seats are made of pliable material.

_____ 12. Swings are separated from areas where children run or ride wheel toys.

_____ 13. Protective railings prevent children from falling from high equipment.

_____ 14. Equipment is well maintained (no protruding nails, splinters, flaking paint, broken parts, frayed ropes).

_____ 15. The play area is routinely checked and maintained (trash picked up, grass mowed, good drainage).

_____ 16. The health hazards from animal contamination are minimized (sand box covers, fences, children wash hands after playing outdoors).

ORGANIZATION OF PLAY AREA

_____ 17. The play area is well defined (fence that cannot be climbed).

_____ 18. There are clear pathways and enough space between areas so that traffic flows well and equipment does not obstruct the movement of children.

_____ 19. Space and equipment are organized so that children are readily visible and easily supervised by teachers.

_____ 20. Different types of activity areas are separated (tricycle paths separate from swings, sand box separate from climbing area).

_____ 21. Open space is available for active play.

_____ 22. Some space encourages quiet, thoughtful play (grassy area near trees, sandbox away from traffic).

_____ 23. Blocks and props can be set up outdoors for dramatic play.

_____ 24. Art activities can be set up outdoors.

_____ 25. The area is easily accessible from the classroom.

_____ 26. The area is readily accessible to the restrooms.

_____ 27. A drinking fountain is available.

_____ 28. Accessible and sufficient storage is provided.

_____ 29. A portion of the play area is covered for use in wet weather.

_____ 30. An adequate area is sunny in cold weather.

_____ 31. An adequate area of shade is provided in hot weather.

VARIETY OF PLAY SURFACES

_____ 32. A hard surface is available to ride wheel toys, play group games, or dance.

_____ 33. Soil, sand, and water are available for digging and mud play.

_____ 34. A grassy or carpeted area is provided.

_____ 35. Good drainage keeps all surfaces usable.

SURROUNDING ENVIRONMENT

_____ 36. The fence creates an effective screen for the playground by blocking out unpleasant or by admitting pleasant aspects of the surrounding environment. It protects children from intrusion by passers-by.

_____ 37. The setting visible from the play area is pleasant.

_____ 38. The location is relatively quiet (little noise from railroads, traffic, factories).

SUPERVISION AND USE OF PLAY AREA

_____ 39. A sufficient number of adults supervise the children during outdoor play.

_____ 40. Responsibility for specific areas is assigned to staff to assure that the entire playground is well supervised.

_____ 41. Teachers focus their attention on and interact with the children to enhance learning and maintain safety (adults do not talk together at length or sit passively when supervising children).

_____ 42. Children are guided to use the equipment appropriately (climb on ladders instead of tables).

_____ 43. The daily schedule includes morning and afternoon active play periods for all age groups, either outdoors or in suitably equipped indoor areas.

_____ 44. The schedule for use of the play area minimizes overlap of the age groups to avoid conflicts, overcrowding and undue competition for materials.

_____ 45. Special activities are planned for and set up in the outdoor area daily (games, painting).

(continued)

———— 46. Teachers add to or rearrange large equipment at least every six months (spools, crates, tunnels).

———— 47. Teachers encourage and assist children in rearranging small flexible equipment (ladders, planks, boxes).

———— 48. Most of the children are constructively involved with the equipment and activities in the playground.

———— 49. Children help clean up the area and put away equipment.

———— **Total Score**

Figure 13–4 Playground improvement rating scale. Source: Penny Lovell and Thelma Harms, "How Can Playgrounds Be Improved? A Rating Scale." Reprinted by permission from *Young Children, 40* (March 1985), pp. 7–8. Copyright © 1985, National Association for the Education of Young Children, 1834 Connecticut Avenue, N.W., Washington, DC 20009.

A storage shed is ideal for keeping outdoor play equipment well organized.

Most of the equipment described until now probably appeared to you most appropriate for outdoors on the playground in fair weather. However, poor weather and limited-access outdoor play areas should not hinder your children's large-motor activity, for this is a very important area of your children's growth. This awareness has led manufacturers to develop durable, flexible, safe equipment appropriate for indoor and outdoor play. Usually built of durable plastic or a hardwood like maple, this equipment is made so that it is easily transportable between the playground and classroom. Jungle gyms, slides, and other equipment can be used indoors on stormy days and returned to the playground a week later when the weather turns. Such flexibility allows you to use the same play equipment over and over again for different activities.

CREATING A DAILY SCHEDULE

The children's security and confidence in school grow from the positive experiences they have with the routines established during the first day and continued throughout the year. After the introduction to school activities, children begin to become familiar with a structure of daily routines. These regular daily events help bring comfort and order to their rapidly changing lives by informing them *what* is happening *when*. Many of these routines may differ from home, so you must spend plenty of time at the start of the year introducing and teaching these routines. Some of the more common routines found in early childhood programs are outlined below; detailed discussions are offered throughout the remainder of the text.

- *Arrival.* The teacher offers a warm greeting to parent and child and encourages the parent to help the child undress and place items in a cubby. Spending a few minutes with the parent and child helps ease the transition from home and get the day off to a positive start. As the children organize their belongings, they get involved in any of a number of free play activities that interest them.

- *Free play.* Most early childhood programs schedule a free play time block immediately after the arrival time, because so many children will have already been involved with block building, dramatic play, puzzles, and other independent activities as they arrive. Each adult classroom staff member is responsible for a separate area: One may be in charge of helping children at a table where activities with Play-Doh are offered; another may be responsible for the large wheel toys; and a third may supervise any of several dozen other possible activities in which the children choose to become involved.

  It is difficult to say how long this time block should be. It may vary from day to day, depending on the children's mood. If they are restless, the period should be diplomatically cut short. If they are working in harmony, the period may be extended to half the daily session. You must observe the children carefully and decide.

The teacher's role during free play is mainly supervisory. He interacts with the children whenever he can but is careful not to interfere. He makes sure the children have ample materials to complete their activities successfully. He ensures the safety of each child by making sure that all established rules and procedures are followed carefully. And he encourages children to help clean up and organize their area before they move to another. Self-care and responsibility are major goals of this time block. Adults respond to the child's initiative and allow the child to take the lead.

- *Toileting.* Elimination is a natural, significant part of the child's life. Children come to school at different levels of toileting skill. Some two-year-olds have achieved bowel and bladder control, whereas some four-year-olds are unable to stay dry and clean. Most teachers recognize these individual differences and understand the significance of toileting routines in the child's life. They observe their children carefully and learn to establish a schedule to fit each child's rhythm. This may involve approaching individual children to check diapers or help them to the toilet, but such an effort must be made to ensure the child's security. Once the child is secure, she will feel free to approach the teacher when she needs to use the toilet.

Story time and other group activities help teachers achieve multiple objectives.

- *Group activity time.* Most early childhood programs schedule at least one large-group session daily. It may be offered immediately after the arrival period, when the children gather together on a rug to discuss the day's routine, birthdays, the weather, current events, or important happenings in the lives of the children. The large-group session may be a set time during the day when art activities, craft projects, music experiences, movement activities, special learning projects, or stories are shared. Sometimes two or more activities are offered in separate areas of the room during the time slot, and adults have responsibility for specific activities. For example, one-third of the children may do a finger-painting project while another third listens to a story and the final third participates in a counting game. Whatever the arrangement, the essential feature of this time slot is that the entire group be offered activities at the teacher's discretion. Sometimes teachers prefer to schedule a large-group session just before the children go home. During that time, the teacher leads the children in a discussion of the day's events as an evaluative tool: "What did you like most about being here today?" If teachers listen carefully to the children's responses they can gain valuable insights into the children's preferences and make appropriate program adjustments.

- *Meal or snack times.* Healthy children require the nourishment provided by midsession snacks (and lunch if it is a full-day program) to maintain their energy levels. They come to school with individual eating habits, so the type of food and the expectations during mealtimes differ enormously. Our goals are to maintain the children's enjoyment of food, to interest them in nutritionally sound foods, and to have them practice acceptable social behaviors at the table. Accomplishing these goals takes much time, understanding, and patience. Most early childhood programs schedule snacks as a group experience in the middle of the morning or afternoon (immediately after rest or nap), depending on the nature of the program. Some see the need for snacks to be individually determined—the children should themselves choose when and how much they will eat. Whatever pattern you choose, try to involve the children in setting and cleaning up for snack time. They enjoy counting cups or napkins, sorting cookies or crackers, pouring milk or juice, throwing away the disposables, and sponging down the table. Snack time becomes more enjoyable when children are given opportunities to participate actively.

- *Rest or nap time.* While all other routines are normally greeted with childhood enthusiasm, rest is something many children often oppose. They find it very difficult to slow down and be quiet after a morning or afternoon filled with play and other delightful experiences. However, every program must have a period of rest if the children are to be kept from getting overtired. Half-day programs may offer a rest time after a physical workout when children sit quietly on single rugs or mats and look at books, work on puzzles, or listen to music. Children in full-day programs will often require a nap time and be encouraged to sleep on cots or mattresses. This does not mean that all children *must* nap; some three- and four-year-olds cannot function late in the afternoon without a nap, whereas others have outgrown it. Nap time must be arranged for those who need it and other arrangements planned for nonsleepers in an area where they can be quiet and not disturb the others.

- *Outdoor play.* Quality early childhood programs demand provisions for regular outdoor play. In fact, programs located in warm climates can carry out most of their day in the out-of-doors. The value of outdoor play lies not only in the promotion of motor development, but also in its ability to contribute toward social, emotional, and intellectual development. Children use outdoor time to plan things together (social); to pull, push, balance, and lift (physical); to throw balls, run vigorously, and shout loudly (techniques to drain off strong feelings); and to explore and make observations (intellectual). One need only witness the joy expressed in the children's laughter and squeals to understand the contributions of regularly planned outdoor play.

- *Departure.* As the session winds down, adults should emphasize slower, quieter activities. Before the children leave, you should provide a time during which children put away their toys and work together with the adults to straighten up the activity areas. As the parents arrive, you will have an excellent opportunity to share special information or interesting anecdotes about their child's day. This is especially appreciated. Refrain from communicating problems, however. Children need to feel good about their day and look forward to their next visit with pleasure and anticipation. Save any major problems for another time, for a positive ending to the child's day is just as important as a positive beginning. Signaling a happy, satisfying day with a cheery, "Goodbye, Eddie. See you tomorrow," not only informs the child that you value him as an individual, but also sets a positive tone for tomorrow.

Transitions between Routines

A major management responsibility related to establishing daily routines is knowing what to do as one period comes to a close and the next period begins, or when children must move from one location to another. If you do not tell the children what you have in mind at these times, you may find them bickering because of a longer wait than can be tolerated or bumping into each other as they try to put away materials in an unreasonably short transition time. Careful planning, however, will ensure the greatest possibility for the children's moving through the day's routine with confidence and ease. Here are some useful techniques for moving children through transition times.

- Signal the children with a special tune played on the piano or other instrument. Such a tune need not be longer than five or six notes. The children should know that when you play it, they have a responsibility to bring their activity to a close and begin to move to the next one.

- Ring a bell or set an egg timer to go off at a special time. This will let them know that cleanup should begin.

- If you are moving from a large-group activity to a snack, for example, play a simple concept game with the children. You might say, "The children wearing red (polka dots, stripes, etc.) may go to snack now" or, on another day, "Tell me the opposite of *up,* and you may go to snack."

- Adapt a familiar rhyme or song to move the children from one activity to another. One teacher adapted "Twinkle, Twinkle Little Star" to inform children when it was their time to move:

  Snack is ready,
  Girls and boys,
  Time to put away
  Your toys.

- Ask children to decide in pairs how they will move from one activity area to another (hop, skip, etc.).

- Choose three animals that make distinctive sounds—for example, bird, dog, and cow. Whisper an animal's name into each child's ear, and ask him or her to make the sound of that animal. Be sure that one-third of your group is assigned each animal. The children then make the sounds until they have all grouped themselves according to the animal you assign.

These are but a few of the transition possibilities for young children. Add your own ideas as you see what works particularly well with your children. Using creative transition techniques both makes for orderly changeovers and creates continuing interest in regular routines.

Planning a Daily Schedule

As you become sensitive to your group's interests and needs as well as the school's policies, you will be able to set up a daily schedule flexible enough to adjust to special circumstances but balanced enough that certain routines are carried out at specific times. The dynamic nature of young children and the necessities of programming for them will periodically result in minor changes to the daily routine—going on a full-morning field trip, for example. A flexible schedule invites creativity and initiative on the part of the teacher and the children. So in developing your daily schedule, establish time blocks for the "essentials" as presented above, but keep some freedom, so that particular interests and needs can be satisfied in special ways. In general, your time blocks should (1) balance active times with less active times, (2) alternate quiet and noisy periods, and (3) offer large blocks of time for play. See a sample half-day schedule in Figure 13–5.

In full-day programs, lunch is usually followed by a brisk walk or large group activities. Naps or periods of extended rest (planned according to children's individual

9:00– 9:15	*Children arrive.* The teacher greets the children and helps them put their belongings in the cubbies.
9:15–10:50	*Free play.* Children have the freedom to use materials in the various activity centers.
10:50–11:00	*Toileting and handwashing.*
11:00–11:15	*Snack.*
11:15–11:45	*Large group time.* Stories, singing, fingerplays, creative movement, and arts and crafts projects are experienced.
11:45–12:15	*Outdoor play.* If weather permits, children play outdoors daily.
12:15–12:30	*Group meeting.* Children get ready to go home or, if present all day, have lunch. Conversations about the day's experiences or other topics of interest should be shared.

Figure 13–5   Sample half-day schedule

needs) usually last until about three o'clock. A snack often follows this quiet time; free play, either indoors or out, culminates the day's schedule.

The preschool schedule, then, defines the events of the day, shows how the activities will flow, and specifies the approximate time parameters for each. No one single schedule works for all groups or for all teachers, so it is important to remain flexible and respond to the children's natural rhythms as each day progresses.

SOME FINAL THOUGHTS

Each setting for young children is special, for it reflects the needs, interests, and talents of the teacher and children who will live and learn there. Just as no two teachers and no two children are exactly alike, each room is distinct. If the teacher gives the classroom and outdoor space thought and creativity, the children will have fun and respond with spirit and delight. In fact, the children's attitude toward school depends, to a large extent, on the mood that the overall setting presents.

Young children need plenty of quality space. They need room for vigorous play, space to play with others, and a place to be alone. But these spaces must be well-organized. Ask yourself these questions: (1) Are there separate play centers? (2) Will the children see how to get from one area to another? (3) Can the teacher see what is going on in each center without having to walk about the room? (4) Will the children be able to help put materials away? By properly utilizing the available indoor and outdoor space, teachers are able better to serve the needs and interests of the group and control unproductive behavior.

The setting must say to the children, "I am yours...have fun." The children make an indoor or outdoor space come alive; there is nothing quite so bleak as an early childhood setting after the children have left. Nearly as discouraging, however, is the attractive setting whose policy is, "Hands off, you might ruin something." Children must be able to explore, manipulate, move, and learn—they should be motivated to say to themselves as they come and go each day: "What a great place to be!"

NOTES

1. "NAEYC Position on Developmentally Appropriate Practice in Early Childhood Programs Serving Children From Birth Through Age 8," in Sue Bredekamp, ed., *Developmentally Appropriate Practice in Early Childhood Programs Serving Children From Birth Through Age 8* (Washington, DC: National Association for the Education of Young Children, 1987), p. 7.
2. Lori Fisk and Henry Clay Lindgren, *Learning Centers* (Glen Ridge, NJ: Exceptional Press, 1974), p. 58.
3. Nancy Altman Brickman and Lynn Spencer, eds., "Child Planning: Why It's Important, How to Get Started," in *Extensions, 1,* no. 1 (September/October 1986).
4. "NAEYC Position on Developmentally Appropriate Practice," p. 8.

CHAPTER 14

Preparing a Safe, Healthful Environment

Early childhood educators, more than any other single group of teachers, understand the importance of sound health and safety practices. They know that the related habits and attitudes formed during the early years last a lifetime. They realize that sound health and safety practices not only help the children feel secure and cared for, but also ensure conditions that help promote optimal growth and development. Therefore, early childhood teachers strive to provide children with many formal and informal opportunities to learn about their personal health, the health of others around them, and valuable safety practices. This chapter describes the many ways good teachers promote beneficial health and safety practices. As you read, use the following questions to guide your thinking.

- What are some key considerations in formulating a sound health and safety program?

- How can toileting routines be handled in a healthful manner?

- What are some causes of toileting accidents in early childhood settings?

- How do teachers treat the interest boys and girls have in each other's bodies in a constructive way?

- How important is washing and keeping clean as a consideration for teachers of young children?

- How do teachers forestall the onset of fatigue among their children?

- What are some guidelines for establishing sound nutritional practices for infants and young children?

- What are some common illnesses and injuries that occur in early childhood settings? What important measures should be initiated to prevent or treat them?

- Why is knowledge of child abuse an important component of good teaching?

▶▶▶▶▶▶

An Episode to Ponder

Lois and Evan are four-year-olds who attend a suburban nursery school. They both enjoy playing outdoors—and the messier the activity, the more they enjoy it. After a short swing and a climb on the jungle gym one day, the two youngsters moved to the garden plot, where they began to dig excitedly for worms. After uncovering four or five of the wiggly creatures, they decided to put worms and dirt into a small pail so their new discoveries could be shared with the teacher when it was time to go inside.

In a little while, the teacher signaled the children to return to the classroom, where they were to remove their wraps and prepare for a short snack. Lois and Evan rushed up to the teacher and showed the worms they had found. The teacher congratulated the youngsters on their fine work and invited them to tell the others about their worms during group time after the snack. But first, she reminded the two that they had to wash their hands. Into the bathroom went Lois and Evan, where they giggled their way through the hand-washing experience, mixing the soap and water to make bubbles. Finding it necessary to use the toilet, Lois and Evan both stopped to urinate before returning to the classroom.

Lois and Evan returned and joined the other children at the tables for a short, healthful snack. Today the teacher had prepared their favorite: milk and oatmeal cookies. When the snack was finished, the teacher invited the children to join her in a group for a short, quiet period of sharing. This group period not only gave the children a chance to express themselves to the others but also provided them with an opportunity to relax and regain some of the energy they had expended on the playground. Of course, Lois and Evan beamed as they shared their story of digging up the worms from the school's garden plot.

This brief vignette describes a fairly typical sequence involving a teacher's ability to arrange a safe, healthful environment. How did the teacher deal with health and safety concerns? Here are some examples.

1. Outdoor activity encouraged healthful exercise.
2. Proper clothing was worn to meet the demands of the weather.

3. Cleanup experiences were an integral part of the plan.
4. Toileting was encouraged in a warm, accepting environment.
5. Nutritious snacks helped fulfill basic physical needs.
6. A short period of rest helped balance active and quiet times.

Health and safety education in the preschool is not normally taught through *formal* lessons, but is generally *informal* in nature. It evolves from activities that are basic to daily living rather than from formally planned learning episodes such as lectures or discussions. Children must experience one-to-one contact as much as possible while becoming involved in activities that address their immediate needs and interests. Most health and safety programs for preschoolers begin with the development of a pattern of cleanliness and self-care. Skills and attitudes related to these areas must be stressed so that children develop a positive attitude toward them and begin to look forward to increasing competence in establishing and maintaining self-care. Young children must learn how to care for their physical selves.

CREATING A HEALTHY ENVIRONMENT

Early childhood professionals are careful to create a nurturing environment for children. Affection, love, and a respect for children are essential characteristics of teachers of the very young. In addition to these traits, however, teachers must be highly motivated to maintain a healthy environment; they must be energized to prevent illness through proper health supervision. Basic to a healthy environment is to establish policies that will control the spread of infectious diseases.

PERSONAL CLEANLINESS

Cleanliness is an important consideration for all young children and those who work with them. Good sanitation practices help prevent or decrease the spread of communicable diseases. Robin Lynn Leavitt and Brenda Krause Eheart explain that, "Researchers tell us that the number and severity of illnesses among children in day care are related to sanitary practices and personal hygiene. For example, the most thoroughly documented information we have on potentially dangerous infections and diseases such as hepatitis in centers is that they are most often spread by the fecal-oral route, especially in centers where children are not yet bowel trained. Meticulous handwashing has been shown to diminish the spread of such illnesses."[1] Routine washing of the hands—both the children's and the adults'—should be established as a routine for adults and children at various times throughout the day.

Hand Washing

Hand washing is the first line of defense against infectious disease. Adults and children should always wash their hands at least at the following times:

- Before eating or preparing food
- After using the toilet
- After diapering (both child being diapered and adult)
- After any contact with a body secretion (nasal fluids, urine, vomit, blood, stool, or sores)
- After handling or feeding animals
- After playing in dirt or sand

Routine washing of the hands—both the child's and the adult's—should be done with warm running water about 110 to 120 degrees Fahrenheit, using soap, preferably liquid. The hands should be scrubbed vigorously for at least 15 seconds, making sure that a good soapy lather has been worked up and that the palms, backs of hands, wrists, and areas between fingers and under nails have been scrubbed. Rinse thoroughly under running water. Hands should be dried with disposable towels. Because the sink faucet itself is a likely place to pick up germs, it may be wise to turn off the water using the paper towel instead of bare hands. Some recommend sinks with elbow- or foot-operated faucets for cleanliness. Concern for cleanliness should be stressed not only for adults but for the children, too. It is a habit youngsters will develop, especially if motivated by an adult model they respect and admire. The procedure may need to be altered somewhat, however, to suit the developmental needs of the children. For example, you will need to wipe the infant's or toddler's hands with a damp paper towel moistened with a liquid soap solution. Then you will need to rinse off the soap with a paper towel moistened with clear water. Finally, dry their hands with a clean paper towel. Young children should be fairly adept at hand washing, but may need you to squirt the liquid soap on their hands. As you teach younger children to carry out the hand washing routine, they will eventually master the entire procedure on their own.

Diapering

Toileting is one of the most basic physical needs of young children—a need requiring extra care and support. Learning to use the toilet facilities is a major accomplishment for children during the preschool years. Most children tend to be nearly fully toilet trained by the age of three, but toddlers and infants cannot, in most cases, be expected to control their body functions. So you must assume a supportive role in caring for them. This role can become very complicated if all the mechanics of such care are picked up on a trial-and-error basis. The following suggestions are presented for those of you who will work with infants. Hopefully, then, the tricks of diapering will more quickly become a part of their repertoire and result in more pleasurable child care experiences.

- Set up the diapering area in a section of the room exclusively designated for that purpose.

- Use a flat, sturdy, safe changing surface, making sure it is about at your waist level. Be sure the surface is clean and waterproof; it should be covered with a nonabsorbent, disposable cover (shelf paper, freezer paper, or disposable squares available from medical supply sources). Add a guardrail or safety strap for extra safety.

- Be sure all supplies are ready and within reach.

- Lay the child on the changing surface. If you use them, put on disposable gloves now.

- Remove the soiled diaper; fold disposable diapers inward and reseal the tapes.

- Place soiled disposable diapers in small plastic bags and tie them. Dispose of the bags in a covered step-container lined with a disposable plastic bag designated for soiled diapers only.

- Put each soiled cloth diaper into separate plastic bags, tie them securely, and collect them in individually labeled larger plastic bags to be taken home by respective parents.

- Clean the baby's bottom with disposable wipes; wipe front to back using the wipe only once; pay particular attention to skin folds. Pat dry with a paper towel. Do not use any type of baby powder; it may be dangerous if inhaled by the baby. Also, talc—the basic ingredient of many baby powders—has been shown to be chemically related to asbestos, a known carcinogen.

- Dispose of the wipes in the lined step-container. If you used disposable gloves, dispose of them now, too.

- Clean your hands with a disposable wipe. Dispose of it in the lined container.

- Diaper the child. Wash his hands.

- Remove the disposable covering from the changing surface. Each day, make a solution of one-quarter cup bleach per gallon of water (or one tablespoon per quart if you want a smaller amount) and keep it handy in a spray bottle. After you discard the disposable cover, spray the bleach solution thoroughly over the surface.

- Wash your hands thoroughly. This helps prevent the spread of such potentially dangerous diseases as hepatitis.

- Sing or talk to the baby as you change him. Make the situation one that is comfortable and relaxing so that baby is encouraged to develop control.

Learning to Use the Toilet

At some time between the ages of eighteen months and three years, the child gains some understanding of her body functions and begins to develop control of the sphincter muscles and bladder—when to hold on and when to let go. She may show a readiness for this control when, still wearing diapers, she says, "I just made a BM" (or whatever term she learned to use at home). This is an indication of awareness—a sign that the child is understanding the meaning of the physical sensations that occur when the need to defecate or urinate is coming. When you hear these comments, you can accept them as signals that the child may be ready to use the toilet. Don't rush the child, though. Starting to use the toilet is an enormous learning experience, so allow it to occur in a relaxed way. Let the child establish her own pace. Simply ask if she would like to try the toilet. Some children are insecure on adult-size toilets, so a toilet seat adapter would be appropriate. Adapters are relatively inexpensive; they are washable plastic, child-size seats that fit over the regular toilet opening. Because of hygiene problems, potty chairs (small, child-size toilets) are not recommended by experts.

Try to help the child relax on the toilet. Some soft music or a book to look at may help the child feel more comfortable and allow his sphincter muscles to release more readily. Provide ample time on the seat, but don't be discouraged if first efforts fail. Children usually greet their first successful attempt at using the potty with much excitement, so let them know you are proud of them, too. Don't be too demonstrative, though, for the child may be confused by your excitement over this natural physical act. A few words of praise as you admire the product of the child's effort—she'll want to see what came out—and a clean wipe of the behind are usually all that is needed. Be sure to help the child wash her hands after a successful toilet experience. Use the procedure outlined in the previous handwashing section.

Control of the bladder follows sphincter control—they do not occur simultaneously. Knowing this will keep you from placing too much pressure on the child to achieve full toileting control before he is ready. Most children do not sense the need to urinate in the same way they do to move their bowels, so they often are not aware until afterward. When they realize that wetness is associated with the need to urinate, bladder control measures can be initiated. Observe the child—if he is going longer and longer periods of time staying dry, it may be advisable to substitute training pants for diapers. When the child reaches a regular urinating schedule, suggest that he try urinating on the toilet. Keep a record of each child's urinating schedule so that he can be reminded or encouraged to use the toilet before an accident happens. Don't insist if she refuses; just try again at another time.

Even when youngsters gain control of their bladders and sphincters, they still have some accidents. Learn to accept them—they are typical of the eighteen-month- to three-year-old age group—and avoid communicating feelings of repulsion at the sight of a child's accidental excretions. If you show queasiness or disgust to the child, you may make him ashamed and confused instead of comfortable and secure in the situation. If a child is told, for example, "Change into these dry pants and you'll feel better," instead of "Oh, not again—aren't you ashamed of yourself?" he will gain self-assurance and learn to control his own needs, knowing that you understand. Under no condition should a child be made to feel ashamed for a toileting accident in school. Such an attitude can only breed conflict and resistance. Meet incidents with a matter-of-fact attitude and direct your attention to the child's successes rather than to his failures. If accidents do happen, institute hygienic measures like those described in the diapering section.

Children often wait until the very last moment to use the toilet, so be constantly watchful and look for signs of a toileting accident. Often the last child to let you know of such incidents is the one who has the problem. If you don't discover it quickly, the other children in the room are bound to do so. And their reactions will often be unintentionally shattering: "Ugh, Kelly just peed in her pants!" If this happens often enough, the child will soon develop feelings of disapproval or shame about her toileting failures.

It is useful to request a change of clothes for each child so that proper cleanup can be done after accidents. The extra set can be kept in a shoebox labeled with the child's name and placed on a shelf or in a closet. Some teachers have found, too, that keeping a few sets of unisex clothing on hand is either preferable to keeping track of separate clothing for each child or handy should a child have a second accident.

FRESH AIR, EXERCISE, AND REST

It is important to maintain standards of personal cleanliness as a safeguard against the spread of infectious disease, but equally as important is the availability of fresh air, exercise, and rest.

Fresh Air

Infectious diseases pass more easily from one child to another if children are confined in small, poorly ventilated spaces. Open space and good ventilation minimize the passage of germs among the children.

The best source of fresh air is the outdoors. Children should have an opportunity to play outside each day, even in winter, except in cases of inclement weather. Outdoor play is a basic necessity of early childhood programming, for it not only minimizes the spread of infectious disease, but it also provides ample opportunity for large-muscle exercise.

Indoors, the facility should provide adequate ventilation, humidity, and temperature control. If it does not, children's resistance to illness may be lowered. In winter, for example, dry, hot air robs their skin and mucous membranes of moisture. In summer, on the other hand, hot, humid air prevents children's bodies from cooling off efficiently. Therefore, careful attention must be paid to the air quality of preschool settings. NAEYC has encouraged early childhood educators to follow the guidelines shown on page 484.

Children need daily opportunities for fresh air and exercise to stay healthy.

- Keep the air temperature between 65° and 75° F in winter and between 68° and 82° F in summer if at all possible.
- *Open the windows in every room every day* to circulate fresh air, even in winter (except in centrally air conditioned or ventilated buildings). Windows must be screened from exiting.
- Offer more liquids and sponge bathing in extremely hot weather to prevent over-heating and dehydration. Use sprinklers outside for toddlers and preschoolers. Young children, especially infants, become dehydrated more easily than adults.
- Provide extra clothing during cold weather to maintain body heat.... (Shared clothing must be washed between uses by different children.) Hats should never be shared.
- Use a humidifier or cool air vaporizer to add moisture to dry air. Do not use a steam vaporizer. Wash and sanitize the humidifier regularly according to the manufacturer's instructions. Otherwise, germs can collect in the water and be spewed back into the air....
- Avoid strong odors. Some people, including children, have allergic responses to smoke, perfume, and room deodorizers.
- *Do not allow cigarette smoking in spaces that children will use. An even better policy would be to prohibit smoking in the child care facility at any time.*[2]

Exercise

Children of all ages need exercise; exercise promotes health in many ways. Susan S. Aronson explains:

> It builds stamina for stressful situations and, as a lifetime habit, contributes to the prevention of heart disease, high blood pressure, lung disease, and obesity. It also benefits children with chronic illnesses such as asthma, diabetes, and diseases of the nervous system. . . .
>
> The size and development of muscle mass and the amount of body fat are significantly affected by exercise throughout the period of growth. In addition, exercise affects joint mobility and the strength of bones.[3]

As we discussed in Chapter 11, opportunities for exercise must occur naturally in a stimulating environment. Such exercise is not structured and does not use adult manipulation to coerce specific movements. Safe, closely supervised activity that allows for creative movement is most appropriate. Running; jumping; kicking, throwing, and catching balls; dancing, riding wheel toys, hopping, skipping and other activities that promote gross motor skills and endurance should be provided at least "twice a day for 30–45 minutes each time."[4] It is important to offer regular daily periods of enjoyable physical exercise, for the habits we encourage during the early years often last a lifetime.

Rest

To avoid fatigue, children need an individualized program of sleep, relaxation, and activity. Naturally, not all children need the same kind or amount of rest, so the program should be flexible enough to allow individuals to relax in whatever manner they choose, so long as it is not disturbing to others. Some children may need a long nap in a dark, quiet room. Others may rest on their cots, read a book, or play quietly with a toy. Whatever the choice, young children should be given an opportunity for rest or relaxation periods, especially in a full-day program. Many teachers arrange a schedule that allows for frequent changes of pace. These changes alternate quiet periods with more active ones, and follow concentrated, rigorous activities with more relaxed ones.

Day-long programs normally include a period of rest or relaxation in the afternoon: a quiet, relaxed period of about one hour for those children not needing sleep, and a longer period of time for those who do. The half-day program normally includes only a short period of relaxation—usually about ten minutes—during which the children rest from a vigorous outdoor or indoor activity. During this time, the tables may be prepared for a snack while the children listen to pleasant, soft music. The success or failure of any rest period rests squarely on the shoulders of the teacher. It is his responsibility to create the proper atmosphere for relaxation and to help the children settle down whenever a comfortable, quiet interval is needed. This responsibility—as uncomplicated as it may sound—is one of the most challenging that teachers face in their daily programs, for although rest is needed by all children, it is resisted by many. Often the situation becomes a battle of wills, with one side firing, "Do what I say is best for you," and the other responding, "I dare you to try and make me!"

If you have determined that an extended period of reclining rest or sleep is needed by your children (this can differ from one preschool setting to another), the following guidelines may be of use.

1. Rapidly growing children need a great deal of sleep. For example, an eighteen-month-old child needs approximately sixteen hours of sleep per day, whereas a two-year-old may need only twelve; a three- or four-year-old may need eleven-and-a-half hours; a five-year-old, eleven. Daytime naps, of course, help children meet these average sleep requirements. Children up to age three, then, undoubtedly require additional sleep in the preschool setting, whereas three-, four-, and five-year-olds may have received all the sleep they needed the night before. It must be emphasized that the *amount* of sleep is much less important that the *quality* of sleep. A good rest period for those in need of one—with a comfortable cot, a darkened room, and an emotional climate of comfort and happiness—may be the last quiet, relaxing period before bedtime.

2. Make the restless child feel comfortable and reassured. Some children need more time to quiet down than others, so help them along. Walk quietly over to the child and whisper a reminder to him or comment about a particularly enjoyable experience that both teacher and child can remember with pleasure. Perhaps some gentle stroking on the back will soothe and relax the child. Often a favorite stuffed animals or blanket will help these children to rest.

3. Help the children who are afraid to sleep because of unreasonable fears. Encourage them to talk about what bothers them, and let them know you care. However, be careful not to make comments that will help perpetuate the fears. For example, a child who fears falling asleep because "the monsters will get me" will have his beliefs reinforced by the answer, "Don't worry, I'll stay here and chase them away when they come." Instead, reassure the child that there is nothing to be afraid of, that there are no monsters (or whatever), and that you will be near if he needs you.

4. Allow the children to sleep for as long as they like, but remember that each child has a natural sleep tendency. Some parents will not want their children to have a long afternoon nap because a longer nap than necessary tends to delay their falling asleep at night. With experience, you will be able to judge each child's needs and adjust their rest times as necessary.

5. Before the nap and immediately afterward, provide for a period of toileting, face washing, and clothing change. After the nap, children often look forward to a snack.

6. Remember your valuable role as a model for the children. As you supervise the rest time, assume a position of rest yourself. Stretch out on a cot or relax

in a chair, but be careful to avoid record keeping, busy room preparation duties, and any other activity that says, "Do as I say, not as I do."

If you set the right conditions, children will regulate their sleep to the amount they need. But to do this, they must be free from strain, pressure, nagging, and the like. The teacher must find a way to combine freedom, reasonable restrictions, and guidance so that the nap period will be a valuable experience for each child. You can do this primarily by getting to know your children and becoming familiar with their needs.

GOOD NUTRITION

Involved in the responsibility of maintaining a healthful environment is providing a program of sound nutrition. Perhaps the most obvious product of poor nutrition is an overweight or underweight child. The reasons why a child becomes overweight may be either hereditary or environmental (eating too much). Many authorities today, however, feel that our affluent society and its proliferation of junk foods has contributed more to the problem than any other source. Soda pop, candy bars, cakes, cookies, and fast food restaurants (often referred to as "franchised malnutrition") appeal to children and parents so much that America's caloric intake is at an all-time high. Related nutritional benefits have not increased proportionately. Concern about this situation has become so intense today that complaints from special-interest groups have pressured food manufacturers and advertisers to modify their approach to marketing "empty calorie," fatty, and sugary foods. We still have a long way to go, but such public reaction helps to alleviate a situation that some authorities view as a major health problem of young children.

Less well recognized are the problems of underweight children. These children, too, need to be understood, for they may suffer as much as overweight children. Adverse reactions from others can cause these children to become shy and sensitive about their condition. Also, they may lack the stamina to engage in some of the more active games.

Both severely underweight and overweight children are usually victims of poor nutrition, but in some cases the problem may be physical. If you are in doubt, check with a physician to see what weight is best for the child and to what extent the condition is physical or psychological.

According to Diane E. Papalia and Sally Wendkos Olds, a rule of thumb to follow in determining whether or not a child is growing normally is that physical growth is most rapid during the first three years of life and slows down thereafter. For instance, the baby doubles its birth weight at about five months of age—from an average of about $7\frac{1}{2}$ pounds to 15 pounds. By one year, the average baby triples its weight to about 22 pounds. By two years of age, the child's weight nearly quadruples from the birth weight, to about 28 pounds. From there, typical children will gain about four to six pounds per year until puberty. Height increases rapidly and predictably, too. During the first year, it increases between 10 and 12 inches, so that by age one the average child is about 30 inches tall. During the second year, height increases four or five inches, and during the third, three or four. From there, until puberty, typical children experience height increases of approximately two inches a year.[5]

Early child care requires better nutritional practices not only for physical and behavioral advantages, but also because of the relationship between early diet and the fulfillment of a child's mental capabilities. Roger Lewin has argued that "an infant deprived of nutrition or stimulation will never develop to full capacity."[6] Dorothy Rogers substantiates this claim:

> The infant's brain has reached 25% of its final weight at birth; and by 6 months it is halfway there. By contrast, total body weight at birth is only 5% of its final weight and reaches the halfway mark only by age 10. As a group, severely malnourished children lag behind in language at the age of 6 months. If both *adequate food and supplementary schooling* are provided children by the age of $3\frac{1}{2}$, deficiencies attributed to early malnutrition may be overcome. However, if these children do not get the additional foods until after that age they do not show such gains, because the critical brain-growth period has passed [italics are mine].[7]

Similar observations have been made over the years, but only recently have early childhood professionals so strongly stressed the relationship between inadequate diet and reduced learning power. We have become concerned because of our commitment to provide opportunities for optimal development and functioning. Herbert Birch and Joan Gussow report that *the most important factor* in determining the child's growth and functioning is probably nutrition. They go on to explain that "there is no question that the child's ability to respond appropriately to significant stimuli in his environment is retarded during the period of chronic malnutrition; and that continued malnutrition is accompanied by progressive behavioral regression."[8]

Mealtime

Child care centers should recognize the importance of sound nutrition both in their mealtimes and in their educational programs. Sound nutrition is as important to the success of a complete early childhood program as any other component. The following guidelines should be carefully considered by child care facilities catering to infants.

GUIDELINES FOR INFANT NUTRITION

1. Feed infants when they get hungry. They develop many of their feelings of trust by being fed when they are hungry. Most healthy babies want six to eight feedings per day by the end of their first week of life. By about one month, the schedule becomes about five feedings per day, and at about four months the child can be expected to want to be fed at regular adult intervals.

2. Because breast milk is the best source of nutrition for infants, mothers who have chosen to breast-feed their babies should be given support by

your program. Offer a private, quiet, comfortable place where the mother is able to nurse at arrival, departure, or during convenient times of her day. If she cannot nurse during some daily feedings, be sure to offer safe facilities for the storage and handling of expressed breast milk. Make sure that the bottle is labeled with the child's name and date and that it is kept refrigerated at a temperature lower than 45° F.

3. Whether the child is fed iron-fortified formula or breast milk, the feeding experience should be a nurturing one. Hold the baby comfortably during feeding. He will understand that the world is a safe place and that you can be trusted. Never simply prop up a child alone or allow children to go to sleep while sucking on a bottle.

4. Smile, chat, and respond to the infant as he is fed. Make the feeding experience a pleasant one.

Caregivers must select meals and snacks that contribute to the child's nutritional demands.

5. Have a well-trained nursery attendant in charge of one or two infants, and allow each child to determine his own feeding schedule.

6. Keep in constant touch with the home to see when the baby is beginning to indicate an interest in solid foods. It is helpful if the baby is able to sit relatively well and push away or reach for food before introducing solid foods. The Committee on Nutrition of the American Academy of Pediatrics presently recommends that children begin eating solid foods somewhere between four and six months of age.

7. Most pediatricians recommend that, when solid foods are introduced, iron-fortified, single-grain cereals like rice be started first. These are not only palatable but also kind to delicate digestive systems.

8. At six or seven months, babies begin to show preferences for various foods, so the diet should be planned to agree with the baby's tastes. Introduce the baby to new foods by encouraging him to explore a variety of foods—soft-cooked, salt- and sugar-free vegetables followed by fresh and soft-cooked fruits. Strained meat and eggs may be added at about nine months. Soon after this time, solid vegetables or fruits may enter the infant's diet. Bread or dry cereal pieces may also be introduced. *Close supervision* is required, however, and all food must be cut into swallowable-size pieces.

9. When a baby indicates a readiness for solid food, hold her in your lap in a familiar and comfortable position. This position should be about the same as that used for bottle feeding, but a bit more upright. Put a small amount of the new food on a spoon and place it on the baby's tongue. The baby may either accept it or spit it out. The baby is not being ornery or showing dislike of the food if she rejects it. She may just be unsure about the new sensation is her mouth. Whatever happens, react in a calm manner. Usually the baby will accept the food and you will have no problem. If the food is repeatedly rejected, however, be patient enough to remove it and try again another time. If the same thing occurs then, you may want to wait several days or weeks before trying again.

10. When the child moves toward eating solid foods, a new challenge awaits you—getting him to use eating utensils. Follow these suggestions:
    - Allow the child to use his fingers during feeding time, but remember that he will be messy. This is an important initial step in getting the infant to feed himself.
    - Give the infant a spoon to play with as you feed him. Soon you will be able to help him fill the spoon and put it into his mouth. Naturally he will miss the target a few times at first. Have patience: He will improve with practice.
    - Let the infant play with an unbreakable empty cup while you are feeding him. When he seems to be in control of it, fill the cup with a few drops of a favorite liquid and let him try to drink it. Again, there is bound to be some spilling, so give a small portion at a time and

allow plenty of practice. Interest and skill in using a drinking cup is usually acquired between the ages of five and eighteen months.

11. Attention to food safety is crucial once children learn to eat solid foods. Whole pieces of round firm foods can lodge in the airway and result in choking. Young children under three or four years of age should not be offered these foods: nuts, popcorn, whole grapes, or chunks of round hot dogs.

Toddlers and young children attending child care facilities may need one or several mealtimes during the day: breakfast, midmorning or midafternoon snack, lunch, and, in some cases, dinner. These meals should be carefully planned, preferably by a qualified nutritionist, and prepared by capable cooks in clean, sanitary kitchens. The number and kinds of meals, of course, depend on how long a particular child spends at the preschool. For example, a child attending a center for a half-day may be given only breakfast and a snack; a child attending a full day may require all meals. Whatever the case, each menu should be planned around a sound nutritional base. The U.S. Department of Agriculture and the Department of Health and Human Services have published guidelines intended to promote good nutritional practices for all Americans. Some of the guidelines follow:

- Eat a variety of foods.

- Avoid too much fat, saturated fats, and cholesterol. Choose lean meat, poultry, fish, dried beans, and peas as protein sources.

- Use skim and lowfat milk and milk products for preschoolers. Whole milk is recommended for children from six months to about two years; skim and lowfat milk thereafter. Whole milk is more healthful during the two years because it contains sufficient calories for growth.

- Broil, bake, or boil rather than fry.

- Eat foods with adequate starch and fiber—whole-grain breads and cereals, fruits and vegetables, and dried beans and peas.

- Avoid excessive sugar—white sugar, brown sugar, raw sugar, honey, and syrups. If sugar, sucrose, glucose, maltose, dextrose, lactose, fructose, or syrup is the first ingredient on a label, then the product contains a large amount of sugar.

- Limit the use of sodium (salt).

Preparing Their Own Food (Cooking)

Adequate nutrition during the early years is essential for good health. Further emphasis on food and nutrition can be employed in the early childhood classroom by involving children in the preparation of food. Preparing food is a learning activity that not only fulfills the goal of feeding children, but also explores the emotions and attitudes surrounding food. Children come to the early childhood setting with experiences in being fed, but with little or no personal involvement in helping prepare food. Thus, we must offer cooking experiences that help children acquire sound nutritional concepts and attitudes.

When creating a cooking program, keep in mind a principle central to nearly every theory of learning: Start with the simple and move to the more complex.

Serving their own food and eating a nutritional meal are important daily experiences for these young children.

Beginning cooking experiences should contain activities in which all young children can participate with a reasonable degree of success. These activities, usually referred to as *precooking activities,* can be characterized as tasks that help children become familiar with the various skills necessary to cook. The following list describes some precooking activities you can have the children do.

1. Scrub vegetables (carrots, celery) with brushes.
2. Spread peanut butter on a half-slice of bread.
3. Measure and pour dry ingredients (rice, popcorn) from a cup into a bowl.
4. Measure and pour liquids (water, milk) from a cup into a bowl.
5. Blend together two ingredients (water and flavored gelatin powder).
6. Shake something (cream to make butter).
7. Roll something with the hands (cookies).
8. Use cooking utensils: butter knives (cut soft foods), hand grinder (peanut butter), hand grater (cheese, carrots), rolling pin (cookie dough), egg beater (pudding ingredients), scraper (peeling carrots or potatoes), hand juicer (oranges), food chopper (nuts).

Beginning activities like these help familiarize children with cooking. If they are properly guided, most youngsters become excited about their accomplishments and are highly motivated to enter into more complex cooking projects. However, successful cooking projects don't happen by chance—they must be carefully planned in advance to derive the maximum learning potential from them. Keep the following ideas firmly in mind as you plan any cooking project with your young children.

1. Allow all children who want to do so to participate actively.
2. Require that children wash their hands and faces before the cooking project starts.
3. Sanitize the cooking counter with a water and bleach solution before the cooking activity begins.
4. Encourage children to experiment as they work with the food (smell, taste, chop, and so on).
5. Emphasize the many areas of learning as the cooking project evolves.
   - Following directions (e.g., "pour the milk into the bowl").
   - Listening (following verbal directions: "Roll the dough").
   - Learning new words ("knead" the dough).
   - Working as a group member (help to peel the apples).
   - Learning about foods (where they come from, how they grow; their nutritional value).
   - Understanding changes in states of matter (liquid to gelatin).
   - Measuring ingredients (one-half cup, one teaspoon).
   - Developing muscle control (mixing, pouring, grasping).

6. Maintain a safe environment.
   - Discuss safety measures for appropriate projects.
   - Use care while working at a hot stove or with hot liquids. Keep handles turned toward the back of the range. Adults should do all the cooking that involves hot burners on a stove. Children may, however, assist if the cooking is done in electric fry pans.
   - Sharp metal knives should not be used by young children. Choose either serrated plastic knives or blunt knives for youngsters as they learn to cut bananas, cooked eggs, or other soft foods. One child should work with a knife at one time while the teacher guides his hand. Position hard items steadily on the cutting surface.
   - Move any sharp tool out of reach when it is no longer in use.
   - Young children can handle only one task at a time. If you want a child to stir something, you should hold the handle while she stirs.
   - Beware of the children's clothes. Droopy sleeves, for instance, can catch fire if allowed to flap near the burner.

7. Allow children the opportunity to have fun and enjoy the cooking experience. The time should be one of pleasant socializing rather than of stony silence or petty arguments.

8. Cooking can be more fun if the children prepare foods they have grown themselves. Beans, spinach, peas, and lettuce are all easily raised in a small garden plot and provide sound, nutritious meals.

9. Most educators advocate doing away with junk foods containing sugars, saturated fats, and large amounts of starches. A back-to-nature approach is gaining strength—a program that emphasizes natural fruits, vegetables, nuts, and dairy foods rather than prepackaged foods, cake mixes, pudding, candy, and other sweets.

Initial cooking projects should be fairly simple—many teachers begin with gelatin, popcorn, vegetables, and the like. Increased interest and skill will gradually lead to more complex undertakings. Be careful, though, to suit the project to the level of the children. If it is too difficult, too long, or has too many steps to follow, children may become distracted and frustrated with the idea, "Here's another thing I can't do!" The anecdote in the box on pages 496–498 illustrates how one teacher combined all of these suggestions in creating a cooking experience.

Enthusiasm for Mrs. Hollister's project (see box on pages 496–498) soon reached the children's homes. Parents contacted her and made comments such as, "What kind of salad did you make in school? Billy never wanted to eat salad before, and now I can't feed him enough of it." This examples illustrates how much teachers can influence good nutrition in the home. Mrs. Hollister decided to take advantage of the parents' interest by sending home a recipe letter each time a new recipe was created in her class. See the sample letter in Figure 14–1.

1988

Dear Parents,

　　We made a tasty tossed salad today and would
like to share our recipe with you. You will need these
vegetables:

　　　　2 cups iceberg lettuce
　　　　1 cup raw spinach
　　　　1/2 thinly sliced carrot
　　　　1/4 sliced cucumber
　　　　1/4 diced onion
　　　　2 sliced radishes
　　　　1/4 diced green pepper
　　　　1 sliced tomato

Wash or scrub all of the vegetables. Tear the lettuce and
spinach leaves and place them into a large bowl. Add each
of the other ingredients. When all have been added, toss
them until the salad is evenly mixed. Store the salad in
the refrigerator until it is to be served. Then prepare
this dressing and pour it over the top.

　　　　Mix 2 cups mayonnaise
　　　　　　1 cup sour cream
　　　　　　4 tablespoons finely chopped green onion

The salad was delicious!

　　　　　　　　With love,

　　　　　　　　Mrs. Hollister's Five-Year-Old Group
　　　　　　　　Sunnydale Child-care Center

Figure 14–1　Sample send-home note

▶▶▶▶▶▶▶

Mrs. Hollister, a teacher of five-year-olds, had already done some basic food preparation activities and seen the children respond favorably to them. Now she was encouraged to try making a tossed salad with them. In developing the project, Mrs. Hollister found it useful to complete a planning form (similar to the one illustrated in Figure 14–2). This task helped her to organize her thinking and kept the project moving along in a confident, purposeful manner.

Mrs. Hollister served as the "cooking coordinator," the person responsible for guiding the efforts of four small groups of children. The groups, lo-

---

COOKING PROJECT

Date _____   Project _____

    Whole group activity   Small group activity

1. Purpose for the project:

    ☐ New food experience   ☐ Observing texture changes in
                                        cooking
    ☐ Fun experience   ☐ Noting similarities and differences

    ☐ Language development   ☐ Small muscle skills

    ☐ Following directions   ☐ Learning about different foods

    ☐ Cooking skills   ☐ Encourage experimentation

    ☐ Sensory experience   ☐ Listening experience

    ☐ Observing changes in matter   ☐ Social experience

2. Cooking supplies needed:

    _____   _____   _____
    _____   _____   _____
    _____   _____   _____
    _____   _____   _____

3. Ingredients needed:

    _____   _____   _____
    _____   _____   _____
    _____   _____   _____
    _____   _____   _____

4. Step-by-step procedure:

    a. _____   f. _____

    b. _____   g. _____

    c. _____   h. _____

    d. _____   i. _____

    e. _____   j. _____

Figure 14–2 Planning form for a cooking project

cated at four separate tables, each worked with volunteer "cooking mothers." Each group used its time to do a specific task leading to the completion of the salad. At one table children busily washed and tore lettuce and spinach. Similarities and differences between the two vegetables were brought out as the cooking mother encouraged the children to observe the dark green spinach leaves and compare them to the lighter green lettuce leaves. The children were also asked to compare differences in texture, size, taste, and other features. As the cooking mother asked questions about the leaves' growth and their other uses, the children were motivated to theorize about the answers.

In much the same manner, cooking mothers at other tables sparked conversation about their tasks. At the slicing table, children talked about how cucumbers, tomatoes, and radishes change in appearance from outside to the inside. At the grating table, children discussed the smell and texture or appearance of the carrots and cheese as they were grated. Meanwhile, a fourth group of children made a simple salad dressing that would eventually turn the salad creation into a masterpiece! The children at each table were guided by the cooking mothers and a simplified recipe to tell just how much of each ingredient was needed for the salad. (Sample children's recipe guides are illustrated in Figure 14–3).

As the children worked along toward the completion of their separate projects, Mrs. Hollister and the cooking mothers observed them to determine levels of motor skill development (eye-hand coordination, manipulation of utensils, and so on), perception, listening skills, ability to follow directions, and concept development (quantity, texture, time, and so on).

Figure 14–3 Children's recipe guides

When each table had completed its task, the children were brought together by Mrs. Hollister at a fifth, central table where all the ingredients were combined. As each table's ingredients were added to a large bowl, the children were asked to talk about what their group did so the whole group could learn to appreciate the efforts of small groups in a large community activity.

When the salad was eventually completed, Mrs. Hollister asked them to sit at their tables and then passed out a small bowl of the finished product to everyone. "Yumm, it smells so good," and "This is the best salad I ever ate" were the comments generally heard. However, one or two hesitant children couldn't be convinced to try the salad. They were simply asked, "Please stay and keep the rest of us company." Mrs. Hollister chose to capitalize on the children's pride of accomplishment for this project by making an experience chart later in the day. In this way all the experiences were summarized in a meaningful beginning reading activity. Those who wished to do so added illustrations for the story during the quiet time that followed.

PREVENTATIVE HEALTH CARE

The wellness of each child must be closely monitored in order to detect conditions that might be in need of medical attention. Early identification and treatment are necessary to keep children functioning at their best and help prevent permanent problems. It is crucial that children's health be periodically assessed by health experts to provide important information about risks for future disease.

Observation

Because most young children find it difficult to tell you how they feel, your careful observation usually furnishes the most direct evidence when something is wrong. Signs of illness often consist of (1) a fever with temperature of 101 °F or higher, (2) vomiting or forceful emptying of the stomach, (3) frequent loose bowel movements with strong odor, (4) unusual irritability or drowsiness, (5) an unusual rash, (6) breath odor, and (7) the sound of a cough.

These signs may indicate that a child has become infected with a contagious disease. Infectious diseases are "illnesses caused by infection with specific germs— viruses, bacteria, fungi, or parasites. *Contagious or communicable diseases* are infectious diseases that can spread from one person to another.... The germs that cause infectious and contagious diseases are spread in four main ways:

- Through the intestinal tract (via the stool)
- Through the respiratory tract (via fluids from the eyes, nose, mouth and lungs)

- Through direct contact or touching
- Through blood contact[9]

The germs that cause contagious diseases thrive in warm, moist, stuffy environments; they have difficulty growing in clean, dry environments where there is an abundance of fresh air. So, be sure to follow the basic cleanliness suggestions outlined earlier in this chapter: Wash hands properly, ventilate the room daily, and clean and sanitize areas used for toileting. In addition, you will want to teach the children how to cough or sneeze properly with disposable tissues.

Perhaps the two most common infectious diseases are the **common cold** (most preschool children have between five and eight per year) and **influenza** (flu). The more contact a child has with other children, the more colds he is likely to get, so expect to have many in your classroom. Children with colds are contagious only during the acute stage—usually the first three or four days. After that the body's natural resistance overcomes the virus, and all that usually remains is a cough or a runny nose. The child with a *persistent* cough or runny nose—the one who always seems to have a cold—could, instead, have an allergy. Frequently teachers and parents mistake allergic symptoms for colds. Influenza is more of a concern to teachers than the cold because its symptoms are more severe than those of a cold. Chest pain, fever, chills, muscle aches, and diarrhea often occur, causing much discomfort and

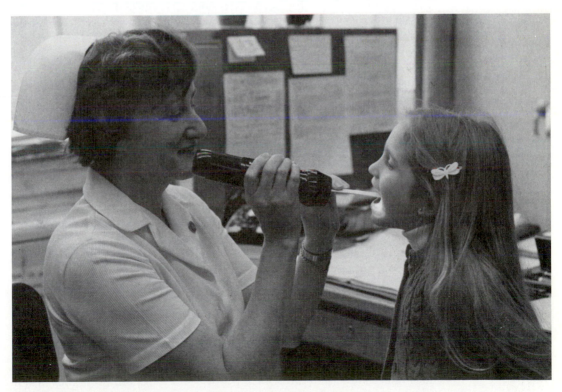

Sound medical data is crucial to a healthy early childhood setting.

difficulty. There is little one can do to prevent influenza from infecting the children—vaccinations are not normally recommended for children. A case of the flu usually lasts from three days to a week.

A third condition that results in fussiness among young children, especially infants and toddlers, is **otitis media.** Although there are a number of different types of otitis media, they all involve a middle-ear inflammation and infection, and they often accompany colds or allergies. Symptoms include ear pain, fever, and headache; if you have an irritable, fussy child who pulls at his ears, you may suspect a case of otitis media. In severe cases, there is nausea, vomiting, and loss of appetite.

Be aware of these common childhood respiratory infections, but be careful not to rush to the phone and call the parent every time a child coughs or sneezes. You may be overreacting to a cold. But because of the frequency of other, more serious infections, you should constantly look for warning signs that indicate conditions a parent should know about. Very often—for mild or noncontagious illnesses—the child will remain in the center so that parents will not be forced to leave work. These children need not be isolated, as exposure to their illness has already taken place. Just be sure *not* to administer *any* medicine—that includes any over-the-counter drug—unless the medicine has been prescribed by a doctor or you have a physician's note requesting that medication be dispensed to the child.

Once the specific infection has been determined, parents and teachers are often concerned about whether or not the infected child should be allowed to remain in school. Susan S. Aronson advises:

> There is no evidence to suggest that the exclusion of children with respiratory infections from child care makes any difference in the wellness of others in the group. The decision about permitting a child with respiratory illness to remain in child care should depend on the availability of the parent to provide the needed care and the ability of the child care staff to provide the extra attention that an ill child requires. On the other hand, most programs find it prudent to exclude a child with frequent loose infectious stools because stool running out of a diaper or let out by accident in a child's underwear poses a significant risk for spread of infectious disease if the ill child remains in the program.[10]

Although most common respiratory ailments do not warrant exclusion from school, one somewhat common condition does—head lice. Head lice are tiny insects that live on a person's scalp and hair. They hatch from small eggs (nits) that firmly attach themselves to individual hairs near the scalp. Symptoms include itching and irritation, often with a rash on the back of the neck. But proof of lice infestation can best be obtained by carefully examining the child's hair or clothing for signs of lice. Look for the *nits*—which have the appearance of little flakes of dandruff or grains of sand clinging to a hair shaft—hiding behind the ears or gathering around hair roots near the nape of the neck. Small crawling adult lice may be observed on the scalp or in the seams of the child's clothing, too. Persistent scratching of the head should arouse your suspicions.

The idea of lice infestation turns some people's stomachs, but no serious health problems can be documented as related to lice infestation. Certainly, though, lice are undesirable—you'll want to wipe them out quickly. Refer any child who may be infested to a health care provider who will determine what kind of medicine to use. After shampooing the hair with the recommended medicine, all nits must be removed. This is a difficult process because nits are stubborn and cannot be easily removed. A solution of vinegar and water often helps in loosening the nits; a special, fine-toothed, nit-removal comb is also necessary. Continue to check for nits daily for the next seven to ten days. Repeat the treatment if new nits are observed. Children should not be allowed back to school until they have been treated.

Except in cases of unusual diseases, children should be allowed to remain in the early childhood facility as long as their condition does not disrupt all other activity or overburden the resources available to other children in the group.

Immunizations

The first line of defense against potentially more serious infectious diseases is immunization. Childhood immunization involves protection against eight major diseases: diphtheria, tetanus, pertussis (whooping cough), polio, measles, mumps, rubella (German measles), and Haemphilus infections (Hib). Immunizations strengthen the immune response against disease, thereby improving resistance to certain germs. All children entering your program should be immunized unless they are exempted by your state laws for religious or medical reasons. Figure 14–4 shows a childhood immunization schedule typically recommended by public health departments. You must not accept children who are not properly immunized.

Routine Health Assessment

The goal of preventative health care is to keep the children well rather than treat them after they become sick. An integral part of that process is to maintain a comprehensive and regularly updated health history. It is crucial that young children are seen regularly by health care providers so potential health problems can be minimized or corrected through early detection. Routine health examinations usually include these procedures:

- *Measurement of physical growth.* This consists of measurement of height and weight (and head circumference for children up to one year of age). These figures are compared to normal growth patterns.

- *Blood pressure measurements.* Children with measurements in the upper ranges of normal for their age may be at risk for hypertension and associated diseases.

- *Sensory screening.* Vision and hearing impairments must be caught at an early age in order to prevent long-lasting effects.

	DTP	Polio	MMR	Hepatitis B*	Haemophilus	Tetanus-Diphtheria
Birth				✓		
1-2 months				✓		
2 months	✓	✓			✓	
4 months	✓	✓			✓	
6 months	✓				◆	
6-18 months				✓		
12-15 months					◆	
15 months			✓		◆	
15-18 months	✓	✓				
4-6 years	✓	✓				
11-12 years			(✓)			
14-16 years						✓

(✓) Except where public health authorities require otherwise.

◆ As of March 1991, two vaccines for *Haemophilus influenzae* infections have been approved for use in children younger than 15 months of age. The schedule varies for doses after 4 months of age depending on which vaccine for *Haemophilus influenzae* infections was previously given.

* Infants of mothers who tested *seropositive* for hepatitis B (HBsAG+) must also receive hepatitis B immune globulin (HBIG) at or shortly after the first dose, a second hepatitis B vaccine dose at 1 month, and a third hepatitis B vaccine injection at 6 months of age. Pediatricians may decide that infants of mothers who tested *seronegative* begin the three-dose schedule after the baby has left the hospital.

Figure 14–4 Immunization schedule recommended by the American Academy of Pediatrics. From "Immunization Protects Children," copyright © 1992 by the American Academy of Pediatrics.

- *Developmental and behavioral assessment.* This assessment checks for mental retardation, learning problems, and emotional disturbances that can be seriously disabling.

- *Physical exam.* At a minimum, the health care provider should check body build, maturity, posture, gait, and coordination. Likewise, the provider should examine the ears, eyes, nose, mouth, neck, chest, abdomen, genitalia, extremities, head, and back. In addition, tuberculin testing, anemia screening, cholesterol and blood lipid screening, and urinalysis could be a part of a checkup visit.

It is important to be aware of each child's health. Children do get sick; you cannot prevent that from happening all the time, but you can take knowledgeable precautions to minimize the risk of illness and to care for and manage sick children. An excellent resource of related information has been published by NAEYC:

Abby Shapiro Kendrick, Roxane Kaufmann, and Katherine P. Messenger, eds., *Healthy Young Children: A Manual for Programs* (Washington, DC: National Association for the Education of Young Children, 1991).

In addition, valuable health information can be received from *Guidelines for Health Supervision* (1988) available from:

American Academy of Pediatrics
Publications Department
P.O. Box 927
Elk Grove Village, IL 60009

INDOOR AND OUTDOOR SAFETY

Accidents (69.2 deaths per 100,000) are by far the leading cause of death in children between one and four years of age.[11] Young children are accident-prone for several reasons:

> First, these young children are now mobile; they can walk, climb, and reach many objects that were not accessible earlier. Second, their small muscle development allows them to grasp and open containers that they previously could not have explored. Third, they are curious, persistent, and eager to gather information through all of their senses. Many interesting things go into their mouths, despite taste or appearance. And, fourth, they lack the experience and ability to predict dangerous outcomes of situations. It is no wonder, then, that the possible risks of young children are staggering.[12]

The potential for accidents cannot be entirely eliminated, but the probability that they will occur can be reduced if we provide careful supervision of all children during their entire school day. The watchword for safety is *vigilance*. Be sure to adhere to the recommendations offered in the previous sections, and be sure every member of the school staff is constantly wary of conditions that might cause illness or injury to a child. This is extremely important, for as a teacher you automatically acquire certain legal responsibilities related to what takes place during school hours. Robert Hess and Doreen Croft explain:

> In essence, the administration and staff become liable for the health and safety of the students and, if legally challenged, must provide suitable explanation for the way they met this responsibility.

> Nursery school liability is essentially different from that of other schools, because when a young child is injured, there is deemed to be no contributory negligence on his part. If older children are injured, lost, kidnapped, or in some other way harmed while at school, the courts hold that they may conceivably have contributed to their condition. In cases involving nursery schools, however, the law is clear that young children are not expected to take care of themselves. Because caretaking, not education, is interpreted to be the primary purpose of a nursery school, a special burden is placed on the school and its teachers.[13]

Your legal responsibility is referred to as *tort liability*. Specifically, within the area of tort liability is a category referred to as "unintentional acts," or those acts defined as an unintentional breach of legal duty leading to injury or damage. According to Polly K. Adams and Michael K. Taylor, as a trained professional, you become negligent in your duties and therefore liable for damages if you do not take positive action in establishing responsible rules and regulations, providing adequate supervision, employing trustworthy staff, maintaining safe playgrounds, and ensuring safe conditions throughout the center.[14]

Because of your liability, you should take careful and deliberate steps to check on the overall safety of the physical plant. Space limitations prevent the presentation here of all the safety standards and practices necessary to be licensed, but you can create a safe environment by following these basic guidelines:

- Be alert to hazards both indoors and outdoors and eliminate or avoid them.
- Look at the world through the eyes of a young child—it is colorful, mysterious, and has new places and objects to experiment with and explore. Get down on your hands and knees to see what a child sees. You may be surprised at what you find!
- Conduct regular safety checks. Each room should be checked at least once per month....
- Encourage all staff to participate in conducting the checks and planning ways to deal with hazards. Parents and older children can help too. [Check the standards established by your state licensing agency or consult the previously recommended NAEYC publication, *Healthy Young Children: A Manual for Programs*.]
- Know what you're buying or what is being donated to your program. Read labels and instructions carefully. If you have any questions or complaints about the safety of a product, call the Consumer Product Safety Commission at its toll-free number: *800-638-CPSC*.[15]

Accidents and injuries are sometimes a part of a day's unscheduled activities regardless of your diligence and care. Because the responsibility for meeting these situations normally falls on the teacher, it is up to you to select and maintain safe equipment and enforce safety measures in and around school.

Regardless of your safety efforts and vigilance, however, accidents are bound to happen. As the teacher, you will probably be the first adult on the scene of the emergency. If the injury is a serious one, telephone the doctor at once. Diagnosis and treatment should be left to professionals, but many common problems can be effectively handled with common medical knowledge and basic first-aid supplies. Whatever the situation, you must try to remain calm and in control. A frightened child cannot be reassured by a tense or hysterical adult. Table 14–1 lists some common injuries and what to do about them. Further first-aid instructions can be obtained from these resources:

American Academy of Pediatrics
P.O. Box 927
141 Northwest Point Boulevard
Elk Grove Village, IL 60009
(*AAP First Aid Chart*)

Susan S. Aronson, *First Aid in Child Care Settings*
(Washington, DC: American Red Cross, 1988).

It would be helpful to take the certified child care course from the American Red Cross. Contact a local chapter first, or use the following address:

American Red Cross
17th and D Streets, N.W.
Washington, DC 20006

Table 14–1   Treatment of minor injuries

Minor Injury	Condition	Guideline
Abrasion	Oozing blood, as from a scraped knee	Clean out with soap and water; bandage if necessary.
Laceration	Deep cut that bleeds more freely than an abrasion	Apply pressure to wound; clean with soap and water; bandage; notify medical personnel.
Burn	Redness of skin or blistering	Keep under cold running water or wrapped in towel soaked in cold water; if blistering, get medical help.
Sprain	Swollen and discolored joint	Keep pressure off the injured joint; apply cold packs; elevate the arm or leg; contact medical personnel.
Fracture	Difficulty moving arm or leg; swelling; hard to distinguish from sprain unless bone punctures skin	Do not move the child; summon medical help at once.
Head injury	Sometimes no apparent signs of injury; bump or bruise often accompanies	Calm the child; apply cold pack to minor bumps; seek immediate medical assistance if child is unconscious or drowsy, experiencing convulsions, unable to move any body part, oozing blood or watery fluids from the ears or nose, or complaining of a severe and persistent headache.
Foreign object in eye	Burning eyes; watery, turning red	Keep child from rubbing eye; wash eye with cold water; summon medical help.
Bee sting	Part of body red, swollen, and warm to touch; if allergic, child may have difficulty breathing, become cold, feel clammy, or even become unconscious	Apply a cold pack; if child is allergic, get medical help at once.
Fainting	Loss of consciousness due to insufficient supply of blood to the brain	Keep child lying down and raise legs; summon medical assistance if the child does not regain consciousness after a few seconds.
Nosebleed	Trickle of blood from the nose	Keep child quiet. Place in sitting position, leaning forward if possible. If that is not possible, place victim in a reclining position with head and shoulders raised. (Do not tilt head back. The swallowed blood causes nausea.) Squeeze the nostrils between the thumb and index finger for at least five minutes.
Choking	Foreign matter lodged in air passage	Use the Heimlich maneuver. *For adults and children over one year:* 1. Stand behind the victim or victim's chair (if sitting). 2. Wrap arms around victim's waist. 3. Place fist with thumb side between victim's navel and rib cage.

(continued)

Table 14–1 *(Continued)*

Minor Injury	Condition	Guideline
Choking *(continued)*		4. Place other hand over fist and make a quick upward thrust, exerting pressure into victim's abdomen. 5. Repeat if necessary until the foreign body is expelled. *For infants:* 1. Put the baby face down on your arm with her upper chest and jaw in your hand. 2. Deliver four sharp blows between the baby's shoulder blades. 3. Turn the baby quickly to be face up on your other arm and give four quick, careful chest thrusts using two or three fingers. *Be careful*—too much pressure may injure the baby's spleen or liver. 4. If the object is not removed, open the mouth and search for the foreign body. Remove it with a sideways sweep of the finger. *Never* poke your finger straight into the throat. 5. Rapid transport to a medical facility is required if these measures fail.
Convulsions	Child falls unconscious; muscles stiffen, relax, and so on, in a series of rhythmical contractions	Make sure breathing passages are open; keep child from bruising self; lay on side with head lower than hips; put *nothing* in the mouth.
Poisoning	Change in behavior; stains or burns near the mouth; vomiting or stomach pains; unconsciousness; drowsiness; convulsions and/or rapid breathing	Try to identify the poison; call the poison control center, hospital, doctor, or paramedic unit immediately. Do *not* induce vomiting except on professional advice; call the poison center for instructions.

SOME FINAL THOUGHTS

The years between birth and six years are times of tremendous physical growth accompanied by great strides in the refinement of physical skills. Adults are often enthralled by the rapid development children make during those years. One needs only to watch the way parents place pencil marks along a door jamb to follow their child's changes in height, or view their unreserved joy at a toddler's first step. They are sure to keep detailed baby books that record major changes in appearance as well as milestones like creeping, crawling, standing, walking, running, and catching a ball. And most parents understand that well-planned provisions for proper health and safety are necessary in order for their children to experience optimal growth in skills and physical development. Of course, when parents send their children to settings away from home, they expect that teachers will provide a healthful, safe environment and establish a sound program to enhance physical development.

Early childhood programs have many opportunities to promote the general health and safety of young children. All children who enter through the doors of any facility must be assured that they will be protected from infection and injury; they must know wholeheartedly that affection, warmth, and a sincere regard for their lives permeate the environment. The promotion of health and safety measures, then, includes such considerations as:

- Encouraging personal cleanliness
- Learning to use the toilet
- Providing fresh air, exercise, and rest
- Maintaining a program of sound nutrition
- Instituting preventative health care measures
- Promoting sound indoor and outdoor safety considerations

You must follow the recommendations for each of these considerations and function as a role model, protector, and teacher as you offer opportunities for children of all ages to interact with the environment, other children, and adults.

NOTES

1. Robin Lynn Leavitt and Brenda Krause Eheart, *Toddler Day Care* (Lexington, MA: Lexington Books, 1985), p. 101.
2. Abby Shapiro Kendrick, Roxane Kaufmann, and Katherine P. Messenger, eds., *Healthy Young Children* (Washington, DC: National Association for the Education of Young Children, 1991), pp. 24–25.
3. Susan S. Aronson, *Health and Safety in Child Care* (New York: Harper Collins, 1991), p. 11.
4. Ibid., p. 13.
5. Diane E. Papalia and Sally Wendkos Olds, *A Child's World,* 4th ed. (New York: McGraw-Hill, 1987), p. 144.
6. Roger Lewin, "Starved Brains," *Psychology Today, 9,* no. 4 (September 1975): 30.
7. Dorothy Rogers, *Child Psychology,* 2nd ed. (Belmont, CA: Wadsworth, 1977), p. 89.
8. Herbert G. Birch and Joan D. Gussow, *Disadvantaged Children: Health, Nutrition and School Failure* (New York: Harcourt, Brace and World, 1970), p. 39.
9. Abby Shapiro Kendrick, Roxane Kaufmann, and Katherine P. Messenger, *Healthy Young Children,* p. 217.
10. Susan S. Aronson, *Health and Safety in Child Care,* p. 157.
11. Sandra Anselmo, *Early Childhood Development: Prenatal Through Age Eight* (Columbus, OH: Merrill/Macmillan, 1987), p. 242.
12. Ibid., p. 242–243.
13. Robert D. Hess and Doreen J. Croft, *Teachers of Young Children,* 2nd ed. (Boston: Houghton Mifflin, 1972), p. 353.
14. Polly K. Adams and Michael K. Taylor, "Liability: How Much Do You Really Know?" *Day Care and Early Education, 8,* no. 3 (Spring 1981): 15–18.
15. Abby Shapiro Kendrick, Roxane Kaufman, and Katherine P. Messenger, *Healthy Young Children,* p. 45.

CHAPTER 15

Involving Parents in the Program

You have many complex and time-consuming responsibilities as a teacher—for example, planning daily activities, providing motivating materials, organizing the curriculum, keeping records, and attending meetings. These and many other duties fill your day as you plan and carry out a sound early childhood program. Your professional world revolves around the children you teach, and you take great pride in knowing you have done your job well. But in order to have a high-caliber program, you cannot limit your thoughts to the children. Teachers must effectively involve families and be totally committed to the concept that the school and family should work together in meeting the emerging developmental needs of all children. This chapter's goal is to help you learn how to join forces with the family to make the child's educational endeavor a rich and valuable one. As you read, use the following questions to guide your thinking.

- Why is parental involvement so important to a good early childhood program?

- How can parents be involved in their child's program?

- What can a teacher do to help parents feel comfortable with their involvement?

- What goals are considered important for a parent-involvement program?

Giving advice is risky business, but an essential part of sound early childhood programs. There are many instances when teachers need to explain what they think is best for a child—times when they *have* to speak up. *The child* is the reason for the program's existence. Teachers form an intricate partnership with parents to help nurture children's growth and development. But this partnership is not instinctive; parents and teachers will often disagree on methods. They both want what is best for children, and each takes much pride in providing, in their own way, for essential health, welfare, and educational needs. Much tension and frustration can occur when either party feels its perspective on how best to address these needs has not been fully grasped or appreciated. It is when you encounter such situations that some of the most tense, frustrating facets of teaching will enter your professional life. Penny Hauser-Cram, for years a teacher and director, commented about two roles teachers should avoid in keeping parent-teacher relationships from escalating into emotionally charged encounters:

> based on my years as a teacher and director, I have come to believe that there are at least some roles that teachers can't and shouldn't fill. Two roles that I have seen cause tension and hard feelings come immediately to mind: the role of family therapist and the role of parenting expert.
>
> Parents need and want other adults in each of these roles. Since teachers and parents share an intimate, ongoing relationship centered on children they both care about, it is tempting for all sides to move from educational and developmental issues to personal, and even therapeutic ones. A big challenge for teachers is to help parents find the help they need, without adopting those helping roles themselves.[1]

HOME-SCHOOL RELATIONSHIPS

What are the characteristics of a wholesome home-school partnership? NAEYC addressed that question in its renowned position statement, "Developmentally Appropriate Practice in Early Childhood Programs Serving Children From Birth Through Age 8." Its recommendations were that early childhood teachers must work in concert with families to achieve individually appropriate programs for young children. Such programs were to be built on these bases:

A. Parents have both the right and the responsibility to share in decisions about their children's care and education. Parents should be encouraged to observe and participate. Teachers are responsible for establishing and maintaining frequent contacts with families.

B. Teachers share child development knowledge, insights, and resources as part of regular communication and conferences with family members.

C. Teachers, parents, agencies, programs, and consultants who may have educational responsibility for the child at different times should, with family participation, share developmental information about children as they pass from one level or program to another.[2]

Because children are so dependent upon their families for care and nurturing, strong communication ties between families and teachers are crucial. Mutual sharing of information and insights help both the family and the program by recognizing and acknowledging different points of view. Mutual respect emerges from honest, open sharing; sharing ensures a program better able to promote well-being among the children. Teachers who have established effective relationships with parents often indicate that they were able to do so only after acquiring a basic background of knowledge about working with parents. But all the knowledge in the world will not keep you from worrying about communicating with parents, and some issues can be worked out best only with experience. You may now be thinking:

"What? Me give advice to parents? Why, I'm young enough to be their child. . . . Why would they listen to me?"

"How am I supposed to give advice to parents? I was never one myself, so how can I expect them to listen to me?"

"Tell a (African-American, Anglo, Korean-American, Native American Indian) mother how to raise her child? I don't know anything about their culture—how could I explain what she should do?"

These and similar concerns often seem to surface when teachers first begin to involve parents in the education of their children. These teachers understand the value of parental participation but fear that they will create a variety of other insecurities or anxieties during contact with parents. However, remember that parents often *want* help in raising their children—even those parents who seem to be able to answer the whats, hows, and whys of child rearing. The unschooled parent, of course, wants to learn the best methods of child rearing, and the knowledgeable parent often seeks professional reassurance about previously acquired information. Regardless of the type of program in which you work, participation with parents is essential for its success. Such participation can be found in many forms; the most popular of these are described in the following sections.

INITIAL CONTACTS WITH PARENTS

Effective parent-teacher relationships begin with a clear parental understanding of general information about the school or center. Preschools and child care centers must explicitly communicate their philosophy and curriculum to parents so that parental expectancies correspond to what the facility actually offers. That way, for example, parents who prefer a developmental program can look elsewhere if the facility they are considering publicizes an academic program. Program philosophies and other general information such as curriculum, tuition, hours, accreditation, and so on can be productively communicated with fliers or brochures. These printed sources of information offer an initial perception of the school or center and—if parents become interested—lead the way to a preenrollment visit. The purpose of this initial visit is to allow parents to actually observe the teachers and children as they carry out the daily activities to determine whether or not they want to enroll their child. By offering such a visit, the school or center conveys two important messages: (1) "We recognize the extreme concern you have for your children," and (2) "We are proud of what we do and are delighted to share it with others." Should the parents eventually enroll their child, the school or center opens up wider channels of communication. One of the most important is the parent/ child orientation meetings.

Parent/Child Orientation Meetings

A parent/child orientation meeting shortly before the opening of school, usually made by appointment, helps parents and children to become familiar with the new setting and to feel more at ease in the teacher's presence. Such meetings provide information about daily procedures, school events, and other pertinent details. Here are some suggestions for this important meeting:

- Call the parent on the telephone to set up a time for the meeting. This gives a personal touch to the arrangement and, unlike a written invitation, allows for questions or comments.

- Arrange the room with displays, materials, and furniture much as they will be on the first day of school. Since the purpose of this meeting is to establish a smooth transition between home and school, you will want to assure the child that the new environment will look the same upon his or her return to your room. A drastic change from this meeting day to the first day will only create confusion in the young child.

- Plan a comfortable seating area where you can sit and talk with the parent. Refrain from sitting behind a desk and asking the parent to sit on a chair in front of you. Such a practice establishes roadblocks to good communication by setting up an artificial barrier between you and the parent. Instead, arrange two or three child-size chairs facing each other, or sit around a children's table. Try to have a beverage (coffee, tea, or milk) for the parent along with a small snack. A small nutritious snack along with juice or milk might be available for the child.

- Arrange a separate display area with photographs of activities from the school program, advertising brochures, program descriptions, and other informational materials concerning items such as health policies, field trips, meals, fees, and so on, for the parents. These hands-on items usually create good topics for discussion and often serve as excellent means to break the ice conversationally.

- When the parent and child arrive, emphasize the idea that the program and setting are there for the *child* by directing your first comments to the child: "Good morning. You must be Charles, and this is your dad. Hello, Charles, and good morning, Mr. Goodwin. Please come in; I've been expecting you. This is where you will come to school, Charles."

- Extend your initial comments to the child by calling his attention to the play materials arranged about the room. Try not to overwhelm the child with too much, but have popular materials such as puzzles, books, crayons, blocks, or other items that require a minimum of supervision with single children. Lead the parent and child on a short walking trip around the room pointing out these items for the child. End the tour at your prearranged conversation area, inviting the child to return to an area he seemed to be attracted to on the walking tour: "Charles, your dad and I will sit at this table and talk for a little while. We have a Mickey Mouse puzzle you can play with, or you might like to draw with crayons. They're right here at another table. They are two kinds of things children like to play with at school. Your dad and I will be right at that table if you need us."

- If the child appears distressed when asked to leave his parent (most will leave), do not force him to go. Just say, reassuringly, "Charles would like to stay and listen to us talk. That's okay, too. But, if you want to visit the blocks in just a short while, Charles, we'll all go and you can show us how to build with them." When you actually do this, try to get the parent to help interest the child in the blocks. If that fails, simply bring a puzzle, book, or toy to your conversation area and let the child play there as you talk. Or walk from one display to the other as you hold your conversation with the parent; the child may become interested in one or another as you move along.

- Briefly discuss your program along with special policies (arrival, departure, birthday celebrations, meals, fees, and so on). Most of this information should have come to the parent through the mail (see Figure 15–1 for a sample letter). The visit should focus on questions parents may have had about the mailed information and on the child—special needs, interests, hobbies, talents, and so on. Encourage parents to center on positive aspects

Dear Parents,

    It is a pleasure to welcome you and your child to Happy Day Nursery School. Being four, your child is among a group of other children at the magical age when they are full of questions, just loving to get into things. They are full of boundless energy! We want to capitalize on their spirit and do things with your children, explore with them, encourage them to solve problems. To meet this goal, your children have to experience things - so there are times your children may become wet, or dirty, or messy, or rumpled. Becoming involved often means these things.

    To help your children, send them to school in clothes-for-fun. Please try not to send them in clothing accompanied by "Don't get them dirty," but dress them in durable wash-and-wear items that are able to withstand the challenges of childhood.

    (Other policies inserted here)

    As a final note, occasionally your children will be asked to bring home special messages like this, perhaps pinned to their clothing. Please read them in the company of your children so that they understand your interest in their school. By the way, please compliment your children on being good messengers!

    Thanking you in advance, I remain

                Sincerely yours,

Figure 15–1 Sample introductory letter to parents

A cuddly friend or special toy helps youngsters adjust to new surroundings.

at this initial meeting. Some will criticize the child or want to talk about a special problem. Indicate interest in such concerns, but schedule a later meeting to discuss them at greater length.

- Plan to spend about 30 minutes for each visit. This allows sufficient time to talk with your visitors as well as to make any preparations for the next. You may want to jot down a few special notes while the parent talks with you or wait until the end of the visit to record special information. On the one hand, taking notes during the visit formalizes the process; on the other, waiting until the end of the day often causes confusion and incompleteness.

- End your visit with something personal for the child. Go with the parent to where the child is playing and say, "Charles, I know you're having fun, but it is almost time to leave. You may play with the crayons again when you come back to school." You may want to have Charles's cubby name tag ready and direct him to the place that will be his. To do this, prepare a set of name tags beforehand along with a variety of pictures of the same size (animals, vehicles, cartoon characters, story characters, and so on). Make sure you have different ones for each child. Invite the child to choose from among the pictures one that he would like to have on his cubby. (The child who cannot yet recognize his name in print will remember the picture he chose as he tries to find his cubby on the first day of school.) Then see if he can select his name tag from a group of three or four. If not, reassure him that you can help. Attach the picture along with the name tag to the child's cubby. Prepare a duplicate set so the child can take it home (a *special* gift) and bring it back to school on the first day. Then the child can match either his animal or his name tag in order to find his cubby. This should establish a link between the introductory visit and the first day of school.

First Day Separation Procedures

Orienting the parent and child to the school or center is one major consideration; another is to establish a healthy separation process during the first day of school.

The Easy-To-Adjust Child   Many youngsters, especially by kindergarten age, will eagerly manage the great adventure of the first day at school and enthusiastically greet it as a sign of growing up. A few, however, may not be so responsive and may protest the fact that they are going to be left alone in the new situation. The sight of the teacher, the unfamiliarity of the physical setting, and the strangeness of all the other children may cause them to resist rather than participate. As soon as the parent prepares to leave, the child may cling tightly to a leg. If the parent tries to pull away and says good-bye, the little youngster may then break into tears. For those who adjust well, you need only exchange a few casual remarks with the parent and child. Then the parent can assure the child that she will be picked up at session's end, and the child is encouraged to join in with the others at one of the interest centers you have arranged. The parent should be advised to depart quickly so that the child is able to participate with her new "school family." For instance, the parent may say, "I'm going to go now, but I'll be back in a while and we'll go home together."

The Lingering Parent   It is easier for the enthusiastic child to adjust to his new setting when he is not torn between school and parent, as is the case when parents linger with their children. Often, when parents stay, the child will actually become confused, soon refuse to leave the parent, or become involved in such a way that he looks for the parent's approval with every action. Sometimes, the child may even become embarrassed at his parent's lingering presence. One kindergarten mother, for example, appeared especially apprehensive upon delivering her child at school. Bending down and peering directly into her son's eyes, she asked, "You're not going to cry when I leave, are you, Frankie?"

"No," responded Frankie confidently.

"It's okay if you want to cry," offered the mother. "Remember how we talked last night about crying and how people feel better when they cry. So, cry if you think it will make you feel better."

"I really don't want to, Mommy," blurted the youngster.

"I'm sure going to miss you, Frankie. It will be lonely at home without you," added the mother.

"Oh, Mommy. You're treating me like a baby," Frankie said. "I think you better go home now."

With Frankie's admonition, his mother gave him a big hug and went on her way, although somewhat reluctantly. Frankie eagerly went about sizing up his new situation. This scenario—variations of which occur each year—indicates that separation problems may sometimes be greater for the parents than for the children. The parents fear losing the central role they have held in their children's lives up to this time.

It is easy to be critical of protective parents, but there are some very good reasons why a parent fears separation. First, the bond between parent and child is very strong. As such, there is a great conflict between wanting to hold onto the child and giving the child the opportunity for independence. Second, parents may be apprehensive about the experience itself (some, by necessity, must leave their children for full days as early as three or four months of age). You must encourage these parents and reassure them to support their children at this very critical time.

The Reluctant Child   At the other extreme, we find an even greater professional challenge. Here we have a child so timid, so insecure, and so inexperienced that it would be just short of emotional abuse if we forced him to stay during the first day without a parent. The popular temptation (and practice) for some parents and teachers is to have the parent silently sneak away at the first sign that the child is becoming interested in a puzzle, toy, or other activity. Their justification for such a tactic is that the parent's anxiety will actually compound the child's if the parent stays. Also, it is argued that interrupting the child to say good-bye will make him stop playing and resume his clinging, cranky behavior. Perhaps these parents and teachers are correct in their observations, but consider what the child may do if, a few minutes after the parent has left, he searches and cannot locate him or her. We must realize that, with his protesting manner, the child is attempting to communicate a feeling in ways that words cannot express. He is not ready to be left alone, but he does not possess the mental maturity to translate his anxieties to us in any other way. Both parents and teachers must be aware of the hesitant child's needs and join together in a psychologically safe plan to help the child make the adjustment from home to school. You may consider these steps in setting up your program.

- Ask the parent (or someone designated by the parent) to stay at least during the first whole session.

- Encourage the parent to leave for a short while if the child becomes engrossed in an activity. Don't suggest that the parent steal away. He or she could approach the child and say, "I'm glad you are building with the blocks. I'm going to leave for ten minutes, but I'll be right back to see how you're doing." (It is a good idea, when using phrases like "ten minutes," to give the children a point of reference. Have a cardboard or plastic clock on which the hands can be moved. Show the child how that clock indicates the same time as the classroom clock. Then move the hands to show when the parent will return.) Some children may stop playing at this point and hold onto the parent in an effort to keep him or her from leaving. The parent should then be instructed to sit down near the child's play area and say, "Okay, I'll watch just for a short while before I go." After a few minutes, the parent should leave with a message such as, "It's time for me to go. You finish playing with the blocks, but I'll be back in ten minutes (or a short while) to see what you've built."

- At times, parents will not be able to progress through these suggestions because of uneasiness or their own separation anxiety, so you may need to be near to initiate the conversation. Should that be necessary, you might say, "Your mother (father) will be leaving for ten minutes. I will be near if you need me."

- Meanwhile, insist that the parent leave immediately but return exactly as promised. You must give the child every reason to trust you and the parent during this often traumatic transition period.

- Once the parent returns to the classroom, he or she can go straight to the child and comment about the progress he has made. Then the parent and teacher can come together to discuss the child's reaction to this initial separation. If the child continued playing with little or no negative reaction, you might encourage the parent to try leaving until the end of the session. On the other hand, if the child seemed uneasy or anxious during the departure, you should plan a subsequent exit-return sequence. This sequence should be continued for as long as it takes the youngster to become acclimated to his new environment.

Some children will adjust in one day. A rare child may take as long as two weeks. The key to the entire process, however, is joint parent-teacher planning and execution within a confident, unpressured sequence of exit-return strategies. Successive positive experiences in which the child observes parent and teacher working as partners will form the foundation of adjustments and help him assimilate into his new group.

CONTINUING CONTACTS WITH PARENTS

Some schools maintain a strong parent component by inviting periodic parent visits throughout the school year. Scheduled by the teacher with the consent of the parents, these visits keep parents in tune with regular routines and patterns of interaction. Other than providing opportunities for parents to watch the teacher work with their children, teachers often employ various techniques of communicating with parents: parent-spaces, parent-teacher conferences, group meetings, telephone conversations, duplicated messages, parent workshops, and home visits.

Parent-Spaces

Marian C. Marion recommends the use of "parent-space" as a technique for making parents feel more welcome at their child's school. Her concept of a parent-space involves a special area in a room or the hall that could be reserved for the use of parents. Marion explains:

> To create this "parent-space" [even] when a separate room is not available, all that is needed is a bulletin board, a small table and a chair or two. The space should be inviting—adequate lighting, comfortable chairs, a vase of flowers and attractive paper or burlap on the bulletin board. It should also be well defined. To do this, print with large letters on the board: PARENTS' BULLETIN BOARD. The parent-space should be readily visible when the parents enter the building. One school's parent-space is located near the area in which the children are received. The parents stop to read the board and any available material while their child is being checked in. If the parent-space happens to be separated from the classroom, a parent may stay to read or browse through books without interruption.
>
> Materials placed in the parent-space depend on the needs of a particular group of parents. If teachers want parents to stop, look at and read the materials they present, then the teachers themselves must stop, look at the needs of their parents and listen for clues to these needs. The clues are often given in casual comments made by parents in day-to-day conversation with the teacher; e.g., "I really have a hard time finding good books for Kim to read. I don't know if I pick the right ones." This mother could use some guidelines for choosing children's literature. Clues also come from the children; e.g., "I like play-dough. Can I take some home? My mom don't know how to make it." Perhaps a display of playdough and recipes is in order[3]

A parent-space may also function in the following ways:[4]

1. *As an information center to announce vacations, tuition costs, parking information, and so on.*

2. *To introduce parents to activities in school that can be carried on in the home.* Such activities include finger painting, cooking, reading stories, and making puppets and other toys. Simple recipes or guidesheets can be included along with sample materials for the parents to manipulate.

3. *As a follow-up to parent meetings or study groups.* If your parents' interests on a particular subject were stimulated during a large-group meeting, you may wish to use the parent-space to display or loan out additional material on the subject.

4. *To inform parents of personnel and activities in the classroom.* The parent-space can be used to advise parents of the various activities in which their children are involved during the day and to indicate which activities will be supervised by volunteers, aides, and the teacher.

5. *To inform parents of community events especially planned for children.* Information presented in a parent-space can extend beyond school matters to issues of community interest. Special free or inexpensive events sponsored by the Red Cross, local libraries, or recreation departments may be brought to the parents' attention. A check of your community may supply the names of these and other agencies that offer special programs for young children.

Parent-Teacher Conferences

Special individual conferences should be periodically arranged with your parents to discuss their child's growth, development, or special problem areas. During these conferences it might be a good idea to share items from the child's cumulative folder, samples of his artwork taken over a period of time, or results of special tests administered to the children. In sharing this information with the parents, it would be wise to follow these guidelines, many of which are based on the ideas of Katherine E. D'Evelyn.[5]

1. Help the parents feel comfortable by establishing a warm, friendly environment. Arrange chairs in a good conversational setting (don't sit behind a desk!) so that you and the parents enjoy equal status; serve coffee and doughnuts if possible; allow parents time to browse around the room upon entering.

The most common form of parent involvement is the parent-teacher conference.

2. Project a positive attitude toward the parents during the conversation. In order for conferences to be successful, recognize the parent as a valued person with his own needs and feelings. Accept parents' feelings even though they may differ from your own. Avoid displaying a "know-it-all" attitude. It will serve only to hinder communication.

3. Create a nonthreatening environment where parents are free to speak what they feel. Develop the skill of *active listening,* making it clear that all ideas are welcomed during the conversation. As you listen, look at the person directly and let him know you are not only hearing the words being said but are truly aware of what is being said. You can communicate this feeling by

   - *Establishing favorable body language.* Your facial expressions (smiles, frowns, looks of surprise, and so on) and posture (looking like you're at the starting gate waiting to get out, for example) communicate to the speaker the degree of your interest.

   - *Rephrasing what was said.* By paraphrasing what the speaker said, we invite the person to tell us more. For example, restating the parent's statement as closely as possible, "You don't feel that Julio should be playing with dolls," invites the speaker to go on from that statement to an elaboration of his feelings.

   - *Feeding back feelings.* "You feel that Julio is becoming a sissy if he plays with dolls. . . . Would you like him to play outdoors more?" In this way we acknowledge the parent's strong feelings and encourage him to tell us more.

4. It is a good idea to arrange for no interruptions during a conference. Nothing is more disturbing to the serious efforts of trying to think through a problem than to be interrupted at a crucial moment.

5. Responsibility for the success or failure of a conference rests primarily with you. Make an effort to establish rapport by (a) expressing good points about the child, and (b) giving the parent the feeling that you are sharing with him the responsibility of meeting the child's problems.

6. Be as specific and direct as you can during the conference. Speak as clearly as possible and show examples of the child's work to support your information and suggestions (but be careful about making comparisons with other children or other families).

7. If a parent gives what she thinks is the reason for a child's behavior, accept it—but lead the discussion on to the consideration of other possibilities. Remember that behavior is the result of many factors, rarely of only one.

8. If a parent suggests a plan of action for handling a particular problem, try to accept it. It is often more satisfying for parents to try their own ideas than to be forced into one of yours. A major goal in any parent-counseling session is to get the parent to take the initiative. If the parent's plan fails, it is always possible to suggest others that may strike nearer to the root of the difficulty.

9. Help reassure the parents that they are part of a partnership with you and that you are willing to cooperatively plan and carry through measures that are in the best interests of their children. Above all, don't communicate the feeling that you are trying to "teach" the parents how to deal with their children. You are there simply to work along with them.

10. Resist the temptation to assume an authoritative position if conflicts arise. Such a position gives parents the idea that you know best and that your ways must always be accepted.

11. Don't speak "educationese" at the conference. For example, instead of saying, "Your child's auditory memory skills appear to be maturing," say, "Your child is getting much better at listening to a pattern and repeating it." Educational jargon often creates a barrier between parent and teacher, so phrase your questions and comments in terms that nonprofessionals understand.

12. Be ready to answer the questions most often asked by parents at conferences: "How is my child doing in his schoolwork?" "Does my child behave?" and "Does my child get along with the other children?"

13. Dwell on the positive aspects of the child's growth and development. Just as we all become affected by constant negative comments about ourselves, so do parents when they hear that their child is not doing well. This does not mean that you should avoid telling parents about their child's shortcomings. It does suggest, however, that you let the parents know that you value the many positive virtues of their child and that you want to help with any problem he may be having.

14. Approach the parent about helping to come up with a cooperative solution to the child's problem (if the child has one). Be sincere about such an offer as you jointly plan a positive course of action. Most parents heartily want to do the best for their children, and if they are involved in such decisions they will work more willingly toward solutions.

15. End the conference on a positive tone. Review the important points of the conference, and let the parents know that you are looking forward to working with them toward mutual goals.

What follows is a list of open-ended, nonthreatening questions that you can use during school visits, conferences, or other contacts. This is just a partial list, and it may spur you on to develop your own.

1. "How does _____ feel about school?"
2. "How does _____ help with duties around the house?"
3. "How does _____ get along with his brothers and/ or sisters?"
4. "What special interests or skills does _____ have?"
5. "Have there been any sudden, upsetting experiences (illness, death, and so on) affecting _____?"

6. "Does _____ seem to enjoy participating in activities with other children?"

7. "How does _____ let you know when he's angry? happy? sad? interested? frustrated?"

8. "What do you and _____ enjoy doing most together?"

9. "What have you found to be the most successful way of controlling _____'s behavior?"

10. "What do you think _____ should be doing in school?"

11. "What would you like _____ to be when he/she grows up?"

12. What things do you do with _____ at home that you would like to see continued at school?"

Group Meetings

Many preschool centers plan regular large-group meetings (usually monthly) to bring together parents and teachers. Such meetings can be designed to introduce parents to the school program, to inform them about new ideas in child rearing, or to collect their ideas about various other areas of interest such as fund-raising enterprises or special activities. Some important guidelines to remember in planning such meetings include:

1. Plan the first meeting to familiarize the parents with your daily program. Rather than talking to the parents about the program and its policies, plan and develop a slide and tape presentation that shows its major characteristics. This will mean more and will hold the interest and attention of the parents more effectively (especially if their children are pictured in the slides).

2. Solicit help from the parents through a short questionnaire, or form a parent committee to make suggestions for future meetings. Repetitious meetings or topics in which few parents are interested soon lead to low attendance and a lack of interest. Some topics that have created enthusiasm among parents in our child care program included: preparing for the arrival of a new baby, nutrition and your child's behavior, teaching the preschool child at home, and helping children cope with death.

3. Plan alternative sites for the meeting. Parents enjoy the school setting, but other successful group meetings can take place at dinner affairs, family picnics, swimming parties, and the like.

4. Encourage the parents to assume a major role in planning and carrying out the group meeting. By gaining "psychological ownership" of the meeting, the parents will be more interested in its success and will work harder to involve others.

Telephone Conversations

The telephone can be an extremely valuable tool for furthering positive parent-teacher relationships. Some parents, despite (or because of) our most enthusiastic efforts, may remain timid about approaching the teacher at school. The telephone allows such parents to engage in dialogue with the teacher without facing the threat that a school setting may impose. Encourage these shy parents to telephone you, for this may be your only source of confidential information about their child.

You can further develop effective parent-teacher relationships by calling the parent to convey a positive report. All too often calls are made to report problem behaviors like a child's uncooperativeness or tendency to destroy property. These calls should be made infrequently—a face-to-face discussion is more appropriate in such circumstances. Calls reporting such incidents as the following help develop positive and confident relationships with parents: "Hello, Mrs. Dougherty. I thought you'd like to know about something that Kevin did today. He sat down at the drawing table this morning and wrote his name with crayon for the first time. Naturally, I praised him for his wonderful accomplishment, but I just wanted to let you know, too, just how happy I was. I'll make sure to send the paper home with Kevin." If positive attitudes are allowed to grow through such telephone calls, parents will soon feel comfortable enough to discuss their concerns and ideas openly with you.

Duplicated Messages

The importance of parental involvement in the child's education often leads preschools to prepare periodic messages—usually in the form of a newsletter—as a communication link between home and school. Such newsletters serve three basic objectives: (1) they keep parents informed about routine classroom activity; (2) they help stimulate the parents' interest in their children's activities; and (3) they provide suggestions that help reinforce and extend school learnings at home. The content of preschool newsletters varies, but the following topics have been used successfully:

1. Names, addresses, and phone numbers of other children and their parents in the group
2. Suggestions for activities similar to those tried in school
3. Short lists of appropriate books for young children
4. Recipes for finger paints, Play-Doh, paste, or food projects the children have experience with
5. Words to favorite songs or fingerplays
6. Short suggestions on such topics as dental health, thumb sucking, sleeping problems, fears, or personal grooming
7. Ideas for promoting reading, mathematics, and other cognitive skills
8. Toy buying guides—especially around the Christmas season

9. Suggestions for activities that can be undertaken during vacations, car trips, or other situations where children need extra stimulation

10. Information regarding fees, health services, the school calendar, school policies, and special activities planned for the school year

A sample newsletter is illustrated in Figure 15–2.

PLAYTIME NEWSLETTER

Playtime Bulletin Board

October 21 at 8:00 P.M.

Parent-teacher meeting in all-purpose room. Slides will explain your child's school program.

October 23 at 4:00 P.M.

Storytime at City Library. Puppet show: "Pinocchio."

October 24

The class will be going on an all-morning field trip to the zoo. Please have your child bring a jacket to school.

DID YOU KNOW?

Did you know the dangers involved while your little child is a passenger in your car? For example:

• A 30 m.p.h. head-on crash exposes your child to the same force as a fall from a three-story building.

• Holding a young child in your lap is not an effective safety measure. The child's weight is multiplied by 10 to 20 times by the force of a crash. A 20-pound child may hit the windshield or dashboard with the force of a 400-pound weight in a crash.

What can you do? Besides spending hundreds of dollars for power windows or other optional equipment on your car, make an investment for a good child restraint. It may be worth it in the long run.

TALK ABOUT FUN!

Here's a game that we played in school. The children enjoyed it very much so I thought you might like to try it at home.

Here's how: The first person says "Ha." The second person then says "Ha Ha." Then the first person (or the third) says "Ha Ha Ha," and so on back and forth, each player adding one more "Ha." The "Ha's" must be said WITHOUT LAUGHING (which isn't easy) and the player who manages to keep a straight face the longest is the winner.

Figure 15–2 Sample format for a preschool newsletter

Parent Workshops

Special workshop sessions can be planned to introduce your parents to the techniques they can use to reinforce at home what has been done in the classroom. Some groups plan workshop programs in which parents are actually involved in manipulating the materials used by their children: finger paints, Play-Doh, puzzles, and so on. The purpose of such activities is to help parents understand the experiences their children are having in school and to encourage them to organize similar experiences in the home. Other sessions may train parents to offer a wide variety of home-learning topics. One session might include the sharing of basic parental skills, such as those described in the following list:

1. Talk to your children—even infants love to hear your voice.
2. Listen to your children—they need to talk to you and know that you are interested in what they have to say.
3. Read to your children—a child who is read to is more eager to learn to read himself.
4. Take your children places—point out interesting things and give them exposure to a variety of new experiences.
5. Buy books for your children when you can afford them—a child who owns a few good books will be more interested in reading.
6. Praise your children when they do a good job—praise reinforces learning.
7. Keep your children in good health—provide plenty of rest, exercise, and good nutrition.
8. Show a genuine interest in your children—your attitude is usually the child's attitude.
9. Plan opportunities for nonpressured play—it gives your children an opportunity to try out new things in a safe manner.
10. Play with your children—provide appropriate playthings and a cheerful place to have fun.

Remember that your parents are probably your most important coworkers. The extent to which they effectively carry out educational practices in the home influences the rate and direction of your preschool program. Through on-site parent workshop sessions, you are able to inform parents of practical strategies for the home. In doing so, the two of you reinforce and extend the child's experiences and growth—the primary goal of a sound parent-teacher relationship.

Other Ideas

1. Acknowledge parents who are making valuable contributions to your program. Let them know that their help is appreciated by thanking them pub-

SMILE-GRAM from Mrs. Turner

Dear Mrs. Thompson,
    Brenda did a much better job recognizing her colors today because of the help you gave her last night. Thank you for taking the time to help Brenda and me.
                                            Sincerely,
                                            Joan Turner

Figure 15–3   Thank parents for their efforts

licly at a parent-teacher group meeting, sending them a note, citing them in a newsletter, or holding a thank-you party for them at the year's end.

2. Send a special "Smile-gram" to parents for their efforts with their children. See Figure 15–3.

3. Declare a "Parents' Day" to let your parents know how much you appreciate their cooperation. American Education Week (usually the second or third week in November) would be a great time to send thank-you notes from your entire class, hold a thank-you party, or do an art project just for the parents.

4. Take field trips to visit parents. Members of your class may be thrilled to see each other's parents in action—be they homemakers, mechanics, nurses, service station attendants, business people, or bakers. Take pictures of your trip and mount them on a career bulletin board. Be sure, though, that you convey the feeling that each parent's job is interesting and important. Some teachers adapt this kind of visiting experience by taking class trips to the homes of each child in the room. Parents normally enjoy activities like this and often prepare simple snacks or activities for when the children arrive.

Home Visits

Some schools and child care centers enhance the parent-teacher relationship by arranging for home visits. The major purpose of the home visit is to introduce the child and parents to the teacher in familiar surroundings, and to help the teacher learn more about the child's home activities. The most important benefit, though, is that it is a comfortable place for parents to meet with the person they entrust with the care, nurturing, and education of their child. Home visits can provide you with:

1. *Information about the child.* Casual observations and conversations can reveal facts about the child's interests, fears, attitude toward schooling, eating habits, comfort, cognitive stimulation, and other concerns.
2. *Information about the parent.* The home visit can reveal information about the parent, including attitudes about school, disciplinary techniques, educational background, perception of parent and teacher roles, and the like.
3. *Information about the family.* Home visits provide valuable cues regarding lifestyle, roles of family members, sibling relationships, leisure time activities, and other special characteristics.

Home visits are especially useful when they are arranged beforehand. Contact the parents so they will be able to cooperate in establishing a visitation time. When deciding the time with the parent, try to arrange it so the child is home when you arrive. You will be able to gain greater insight into the home life of the child if he is there when you visit. Most teachers try to arrange home visits with parents at three particular times:

Before the start of the school year. These visits help to make the child, as well as the parent, feel more comfortable on the first day of school, because they have already met with you in their home in a relaxed social situation.

At regular intervals during the school year. Some teachers organize three or four visits during the school year; others go so far as to schedule weekly visits. Regular visits help establish a sound view of the child's home activity during the school year and help maintain a continuing partnership between the parent and teacher.

On special occasions. All too often, teachers make special home visits only when a severe problem arises in school. However, the special home visit should be used more frequently for positive reasons. For example, a favorite toy or book can be brought to the children on their birthdays. Some teachers bring get-well cards from classmates to the homes of sick children. Such visits help parents and children feel important and encourage them to feel secure as the year unfolds.

Initiating a home visitation program can sometimes be awkward because parents, as well as teachers, may feel awkward about them. Doreen J. Croft has suggested these reasons why parents may be reluctant to have teachers visit their homes:

1. The house is a mess, and the parents do not want the teachers to see their poor housekeeping habits.
2. Parents are fearful that teachers will judge them and get bad impressions.
3. Teachers are intruding on the parents' lives.
4. The family culture or way of life may be so different that the teacher would never understand it.
5. Parents' past experiences with home visits are all negative. If the teacher comes over, it's only because the child has been bad.
6. Parents do not see any real value in teacher visits.
7. Teachers try to change the parents and tell them how to be "better" with their children.
8. Parents are too busy to bother.[6]

On the other hand, teachers may sometimes feel that they are intruding on the parents, that they are "out of place" in the home (especially if it is ethnically, culturally, or socioeconomically different from their own), or that they are being forced to take time from their families or busy schedules. These concerns will diminish once you truly understand the values of home visits and appreciate the results they bring. If you find that home visits can be made in your situation, here are some suggestions that may help change the attitudes of reluctant parents.[7]

1. Get acquainted with the parents on neutral territory, such as the school playground or a nearby park. These opportunities can result from group picnics or simply through informal meetings.
2. Establish a friendly relationships during such informal chats.
3. Be clear about your reasons for visiting the home. Tell the parents what you want to talk about and how long you want to stay.
4. Learn about the lifestyle of the parents. By showing empathy and understanding, teachers establish trust and nonthreatening avenues of communication.

PARENTS AS PARTICIPANTS IN THE PROGRAM

Parents can add to the school program in many ways if they know you are interested in their help and welcome and respect their skills. There are two basic ways that family members can become involved in your program: (1) as volunteers in the classroom and (2) as decision makers in relation to certain policies and program concerns. Whatever the role, however, they must know that their efforts are sincerely wanted and appreciated. Without them, your program won't be as effective as you would like it to be.

Parent Volunteers

When you decide to encourage and accept volunteers in the classroom, you must determine what their roles will be. In many instances, you will have parents who are professionally competent and able to help with instructional activities. You may have other parents who possess no particular professional skills but are willing to help with noninstructional tasks—making bulletin boards, getting supplies ready, helping on field trips, and the like. Both groups must be accepted by you and given assignments suitable to their abilities and talents. Remember that assigning professionally competent persons to do functions "below" those they normally do may be demeaning to them. Likewise, unreasonably high expectations may make nonprofessionals feel uncomfortable. If roles are defined to the parent volunteers and choices made available to them, they will, almost without exception, assume the one best suited to their interests and abilities and be comfortable with it.

Once parent volunteers have been accepted into your program and their roles have been cooperatively defined, they must be totally involved in the classroom routine. The first step in this process is to plan an orientation session in which the following considerations are communicated:

1. The philosophy of the school
2. Your personal philosophy of learning
3. The school program
4. The policies of the school
5. Methods of discipline and control, especially the defining of limits

When the parent enters the classroom for the first time, there are several things you should do:

1. Introduce the parent to the children and allow them to interact if there seems to be sufficient interest.
2. Ask the parent to simply observe during the first day or so—this will help him understand the levels and types of classroom interactions and activities.
3. Make the parent feel welcome. Comment on special things that need to be pointed out and maintain a positive attitude throughout the day. As the parent's self-image is enhanced, he will gain more confidence in his ability.

George S. Morrison summarizes the impact of a sound parent volunteer program by stating these advantages:

1. The teacher becomes more effective and efficient when parents make materials, handle routines, or tutor children.
2. Children benefit from having social interactions with a wide variety of adults who bring rich cultural backgrounds, diverse skills, and different points of view.

Grandparents are often eager to volunteer their help. Youngsters find their visits delightful.

3. The sense of self-worth through involvement is enhanced in the parent. As they are meaningfully involved, they gain increasing confidence in their child-rearing abilities.

4. Often, there is an enhanced relationship between the family and child in the home as a result of involvement as a school volunteer.

5. Teachers become more empathetic toward the role of a parent. They can begin to see children from a parent's point of view.[8]

Parents as Decision Makers

A second major opportunity for parent participation involves making decisions regarding the policies and curriculum directions of the children's school. This goal can be achieved in several ways.

Parent Advisory Committees   Find three or four parents who are particularly interested in their children's school, who reflect a cross section of the children, and who can work closely with you. Ask them to meet with you periodically to discuss relevant problems, preview upcoming activities, and advise you on possible directions of action on pertinent topics. This group can help set or review policy as it acts as a liaison between home and school.

Ad Hoc Parent Committees   A popular technique in many preschools is to establish temporary parent committees, which are brought together to accomplish a specific task and are then disbanded. For example, parent volunteers could be asked to design plans for a fund-raising carnival to be held on the playground, to review a special piece of equipment for purchase, or to design and build a new area for storing art supplies. This one-time-only form of participation on an ad hoc committee is attractive to many parents, especially those who are too busy to make a long-term commitment.

Parent Cooperatives   Parent interest and involvement in their children's education is the major reason for the growing popularity of cooperative preschools around the country. In a co-op, parents agree to work a certain amount of time per week in the classroom and to attend regular planning meetings. Though they serve as an advisory group to the teacher, the parents normally assign the major responsibility for curriculum decisions and teaching techniques to the director or teachers. However, co-op parents do have a voice in determining how the school operates and what parent education activities it offers.

Parent participation, then, should be encouraged and used in preschool programs. If used effectively, such participation can help the school and its teachers maintain a line of communication that keeps them in tune with the desires of the parents, and keeps the parents informed about the successes and needs of their children. By maintaining two-way communication, we encourage the type of cooperation that helps create the best educational program possible.

POTENTIAL PROBLEMS OR COMPLICATIONS

Changing Family Styles

Families and child-rearing techniques have undergone radical transformations during the past few decades. It was not long ago that a typical family could be characterized as having a mother, father, and combination of children. Today this image is no longer predominant; there are many kinds of families. Certainly, someone assumes a parenting role in each, but more than 50 percent of American youth today can expect to spend at least part of their childhood in a nontraditional family. Their families may take any of several forms:

1. *Nuclear family.* This is the traditional family—two parents and children.
2. *Extended family.* This is an enlarged nuclear family that often includes one or more of the following relatives: grandparents, aunts, uncles, or cousins.
3. *Single-parent family.* This is a family that has only a mother or father living with the children. Primarily because of the rapid increase in divorce rates

today (one child in three has parents who are divorced; the divorce rate is presently at 50 percent), single-parent families are the fastest-growing family type. Although divorce accounts for the greatest numbers of single-parent families, factors such as unwed pregnancies and choosing single-parenthood (through avenues such as adoption, artificial insemination, or other procedures of reproductive technology) also affect this trend.

4. *Blended family.* This is a family that is reconstructed from two others—when two people with children marry and merge into a single unit, they form a blended family.

5. *Foster family.* This is a family consisting of parents who accept and care for children who are not their own. Sometimes foster parents adopt the children they care for, but normally the arrangement exists temporarily.

This variety of family styles must be recognized because each has special needs that require early childhood teachers to be especially vigilant. There are many ways that teachers can lend a hand, but paramount among their efforts is to be supportive of the family's own efforts to help its children. Many families, of course, whether traditional or nontraditional, will be headed by a successful parent or set of parents. However, you will also encounter situations where the family is faced with great challenges—for example, a single parent overwhelmed by everything that needs to be accomplished both at home and at work, a stepparent attempting to assimilate new members into a blended family, or a nuclear family awaiting the birth of a new baby. In each family situation, parents must be assured that someone is near to lend a "tender ear" to their circumstances. Sometimes an eager, professionally respected listener empathetic with the family condition can assist parents with their problems. In especially troublesome situations, however, teachers may wish to be more direct in their assistance. It may be necessary to refer parents to specialized agencies or counselors who focus on family matters.

Poverty

One prevailing problem related to changing family patterns is poverty (especially among partnerless women). Certainly many mothers have chosen to work for reasons other than economic need; however, the need for money is still the biggest reason for mothers seeking gainful employment outside the home. Female-headed families, for example, are three times as likely to be in poverty as two-parent families. In fact, one in three families headed by a woman is in poverty, compared to one in ten headed by men and one in nineteen headed by two parents.[9] Obviously, mothers who are alone have a more compelling reason to work than families in more economically privileged circumstances: They must work to survive.

This increase of women in the work force has produced about two million children who receive formal, licensed child care. Additional millions are looked after by unlicensed babysitters—whether they offer quality services or simply a place to stay to pass the time of day. A wave of fundamental social change is underway in America today, and child care finds itself increasingly involved. Change in family structure is one major factor that has contributed to the need for expanded child care services. You should assume a positive advocacy role for increased quality child care services, working to relieve the stress of parents struggling to "make ends meet."

Poverty is not confined to female-headed households. Although women compose a large portion of this group, many families living in poverty come from racial or ethnic minorities. Almost 36 percent of African-American families and 30 percent of Hispanics fall below the poverty line. As a result, millions of children are affected by poverty each year—22 percent of our nation's children are members of low-income families.[10] This situation has serious ramifications; numerous studies have shown that children from low-income homes have many more school-related problems than do children from homes with higher incomes. These children may drop out of school earlier, adjust poorly to school routines, achieve on a lower scale, and generally underestimate the value of their schooling.

It is important for every teacher to study the family backgrounds of all children in the program, including those children who might be met with prejudice or fear. For example, because I was brought up in a neighborhood that included many "culturally different" youngsters, I had friends whose homes were dilapidated and torn—some even had dirt floors. Later, as part of my professional training, I took a course titled "Disadvantaged Youth." The course instructor had obviously never lived in a culturally different setting as a youngster—nor did she seem to have visited many as an adult. Before a trip to a poor, rural home, she warned, "Be careful not to drink coffee or eat food while you're there. Remember that these people are not very sanitary." When we arrived, the mother welcomed us by offering coffee and a cake that she had baked especially for our visit. After hearing polite refusals from the others in my group (including the instructor), I eagerly answered, "I'd enjoy some," remembering my friends' parents and the pride they took in their ability to cook. The mother's response, as you might suspect, was precious. My biggest reward of the entire visit, though, came when the father delivered a sign that indicated total acceptance of a visitor in his home—he shared his hunting rifle with me. This experience is included to illustrate how preconceived ideas, even from professionals, can lead either to damaging or to improving self-concepts among children and their families. When you use a term such as my instructor used—*culturally different*—to classify a child, think of who was actually culturally different in the vignette and what the resulting actions and words were.

Work toward understanding all children and their families. Volunteer some time as a student assistant in preschool programs designed for children from socio-economic conditions different from your own. Visit local community groups or neighborhood associations, talk to teachers, read about the particular culture in which you are interested, and observe different children in their preschool setting or home environment. When you experience the rich culture and the pride that people of all cultural groups have, you will find that your apprehension quickly disappears. Children and parents will sense that you accept them—you will gain added value in their eyes because of your words and actions.

It is unreasonable to expect teachers to solve all the problems facing today's alternative family styles and poverty. However, sensitivity to the nature of family situations and acceptance of parenting styles foreign to your own are perhaps the most important ways you can lend encouragement and support.

Child Abuse

Being in a loving, caring profession such as early childhood education, it is often difficult to face the fact that not all children are brought up by parents who love or enjoy caring for them. Our idealized concept of the child-family situation is characterized by harmony and joy; sadly, this is not always the case.

Nearly every preschool or child care center has children with histories of parental neglect and abuse. Over one million cases of child abuse are reported each year, but this number may represent only a fraction of the maltreatment that occurs. Surveys on the extent of child abuse tend to focus primarily on the more injurious forms of violence, so we have no accurate idea of the total range of maltreatment experienced by children. One disturbing report estimates that, "Eighty-five percent of the children abused are under six years of age, 75 percent under four years of age, 25 percent under one year and 16 percent under six months."[11]

Identifying Abused Children Being able to secure meaningful data regarding the extent of child abuse is complicated by the fact that child abuse is defined differently from state to state; reports may therefore be categorized differently. But, because of the swelling tide of public concern, increasing numbers of agencies and advocacy groups have worked diligently to do something about the identification, treatment, and prevention of the child abuse problem. Currently, Public Law 93–247, the Child Abuse Prevention and Treatment Act, defines child abuse as, "The physical or mental injury, sexual abuse, negligent treatment, or maltreatment of a child under the age of eighteen by a person who is responsible for the child's welfare...."[12] If children experiencing any of these forms of abuse are identified when they show the first symptoms, they may be helped when their problems can be most readily solved. However, too often problems are not recognized until they become acute and devastating. By then it may be too late to salvage the child or the home. Table 15–1 offers a comprehensive list of symptoms of possible neglect and abuse. These signs by themselves do not absolutely identify an abused child, but they do offer teachers and caregivers a general idea of when to be concerned about any child. Children should be observed over a period of time to determine whether or not their appearance or behavior may indicate symptoms of abuse.

Table 15–1 Guidelines for Detecting Abuse and Neglect

Kind of Abuse	Child's Appearance	Child's Behavior	Parent or Caretaker's Behavior
Physical	Unusual bruises, welts, burns, or fractures Bite marks Frequent injuries, explained as "accidental"	Reports injury by parents Unpleasant, hard to get along with, demanding, often disobeys, frequently causes trouble or interferes with others; breaks or damages things; or shy, avoids others, too anxious to please, too ready to let other people say and do things to him/her without protest Frequently late or absent, or comes to school too early or hangs around after school Avoids physical contact with adults Wears long sleeves or other concealing clothing Version of how a physical injury occurred is not believable (doesn't fit type or seriousness of the injury) Seems frightened of parents Shows little or no distress at separation from parents May seek affection from any adult	History of abuse as a child Uses unnecessarily harsh discipline Offers explanation of child's injury that doesn't make sense, doesn't fit injury, or offers no explanation Seems unconcerned about child Sees child as bad, evil, a monster, etc. Misuses alcohol or other drugs Attempts to conceal child's injury or protect identity of responsible party
Emotional	Less obvious signs than other types of mistreatment; behavior is best indication	Unpleasant, hard to get along with, demanding; frequently causes trouble, won't leave others alone Unusually shy, avoids others, too anxious to please, too submissive, puts up with unpleasantness from others without protest Either unusually adult or overly young for age (e.g., sucks thumb, rocks constantly) Behind for age physically, emotionally, or intellectually	Blames or belittles child Cold and rejecting Withholds love Treats children unequally Seems not to care about child's problems

Table 15–1   *(Continued)*

Kind of Abuse	Child's Appearance	Child's Behavior	Parent or Caretaker's Behavior
Neglect	Often dirty, tired, no energy	Frequently absent	Misuses alcohol or other drugs
	Comes to school without breakfast, often does not have lunch or lunch money	Begs or steals food	Disorganized, upset home life
		Causes trouble in school	Seems not to care what happens
		Often hasn't done homework	Isolated from friends, relatives, neighbors
	Clothes dirty or inappropriate for weather	Uses alcohol or drugs	Doesn't know how to get along with others
	Alone often, for long periods	Engages in vandalism, sexual misconduct	Long-term chronic illnesses
	Needs glasses, dental care, or other medical attention		History of neglect as a child
Sexual	Torn, stained, or bloody underclothing	Withdrawn or engages in fantasy or babyish behavior	Protective or jealous of child
	Pain or itching in genital area	Poor relationships with other children	Encourages child to engage in prostitution or sexual acts in presence of caretaker
	Has venereal disease	Unwilling to participate in physical activities	Misuses alcohol or other drugs
		Engages in delinquent acts or runs away	Frequently absent from home
		Says has been sexually assaulted by parent/caretaker	

Source: United States Department of Health, Education and Welfare, Office of Human Development Services, Administration for Children, Youth and Families, Head Start Bureau, Indian and Migrant Programs Div., *New Light on an Old Problem,* DHEW Publication No. (OHDS) 78-31108 (Washington, DC, 1978), pp. 8–11.

Reporting Suspected Cases of Child Abuse   Once you have reason to suspect child abuse, it is important to report the case directly to your immediate supervisor or to a protective agency, depending on the regulations of your child care facility. Such a procedure is no longer the humanitarian gesture it once was; it is now a matter of professional responsibility. In several states (including California and Pennsylvania), professionals may be guilty of a misdemeanor if they fail to report incidents of suspected child abuse to the proper authorities. You should be aware of the official policy and specific reporting procedures of your school, and you should know your legal obligations and the protections from civil and criminal liability specified in your state's reporting law. All states provide immunity for mandated, good-faith reports.

Many teachers, however, fail to report suspected cases of child abuse because the condition is foreign to their own personal lives or beliefs about parenthood. They tend to block it out and try to pretend it isn't there. Others refuse to report suspected cases because they fear personal harm from angry parents. However, if our concern for the total welfare of children is genuine, we must be willing to confront cases of child abuse and try to do something about them. All children have the right to be treated with dignity and respect, so we must be willing to notice and take action on any conditions that indicate a child's welfare may be in jeopardy.

Teachers who do report such cases rarely, if ever, get involved beyond this point. The protective agencies normally contact the parents, find out the facts of the case, and assess the type and quality of service needed to rehabilitate the home—all without ever bringing the teacher into the picture. This rehabilitation philosophy is based on

> a "reaching out" with social services to stabilize family life. It seeks to preserve the family unit by strengthening parental capacity and ability to provide good child care. Its special attention is focused on families where unresolved problems have produced visible signs of neglect or abuse and the home situation presents actual and potentially greater hazard to the physical or emotional well-being of children.[13]

Many parents, after having their initial anger or resentment calmed by a caseworker who convinces them that he is there to help and not to punish, are willing to undergo therapeutic intervention. Strange as it may sound, they are willing to do so because their neglect and abuse were probably not willful or deliberate. Their treatment of their children commonly results from frustration with their perceived inadequacy or inability to live up to parental roles. If they are, for example, unable to control their child's behavior, their frustration builds, and they may feel that severe physical or mental abuse of the child is the only solution. The role of the protective agency in such a case is to educate these parents and help them become more skilled and confident in their parenting responsibilities.

Causes of Child Abuse   Although many parents abuse children because of a poor knowledge base, stress is a major contributing factor. Illness or injury, loss of job, employment problems, income, divorce, and a number of other pressing conditions often build extreme tension and cause parents to lose patience and self-control with their children. Richard J. Gelles and Ake W. Edfeldt identified these additional factors often associated with violence toward children:[14]

1. *Age.* Younger parents are more likely to use violence towards their children than older parents.
2. *Marital status.* Single parents are at a greater risk for abusing their children due to stress and low incomes.
3. *Education.* Those parents with the highest (at least some college) and lowest (no high school) levels of education were the least likely to use violence.

4. *Parents' backgrounds.* Parents abused as children were more likely to abuse their own children.

An additional cause of child abuse has been increasing in recent years—*substance abuse.* George S. Morrison reported on this severe problem:

First and foremost, substance abuse creates a chaotic environment in which children cannot tell what to expect from their parents. Second, children of alcohol- or drug-using parents are often neglected because the parent is emotionally absent when drunk or high, or physically absent. Substance-abusing parents are the kind of parents who forget to go to the store to buy food for a week. Because children of drug-using parents may not be physically abused, the signs of abuse may be subtle. A teacher might pick up clues that something is wrong at home if the child...is wearing the same clothes over and over again, or wearing clothes that don't fit, or wearing worn-out shoes because mom and dad haven't noticed that new ones are needed. In general, drug use renders parents dysfunctional and unable to adequately care for their children.[15]

By working together with the proper agencies, you can help children in need of protection from their parents. If help is provided in time, the emotional damage of serious neglect and abuse can be avoided, and the blocks that inhibit the development of a whole child can be removed. For more information contact:

National Center on Child Abuse and Neglect
Children's Bureau
Department of Health and Human Services
P.O. Box 1182
Washington, DC 20012

National Child Abuse Hotline
(800) 422–4453

SOME FINAL THOUGHTS

Young children are greatly dependent on the significant adults in their lives to love and protect them—to foster feelings of security and self-worth. Parents and teachers, of course, are of key importance here. Parents begin the nurturing process by initiating warm, long-lasting emotional attachments in the home. These attachments help the child develop a secure base of trust and confidence from which to respond to other environmental phenomena. When the child moves on to an appropriate early childhood setting, this base becomes broadened and extended to other adults responsible for her care. From this point on, a partnership of adults from home and school establish a continuity of experiences to help widen the child's circle of love and trust.

Certainly, this partnership becomes stronger if the relationship between home and school is wholesome. Programs flourish when the continuity between parents and teachers remains unbroken and when each party makes sincere efforts to reach out in understanding of the other. Teachers must communicate a message that says, "I care about your child, not because I'm an expert but because I am a member of a partnership responsible for your child's health and happiness." Such a message will serve to evoke reciprocal communications from parents, as a foundation of trust and mutual respect unfolds.

In practice, you cannot expect unfailing success with any single approach to parenting, including this one. Any endeavor involving complex human personalities will have its failures. However, if you reach out openly and honestly to parents, you will be rewarded with many fulfilling experiences that help you understand your efforts are respected and productive.

NOTES

1. "Backing Away Helpfully: Some Roles Teachers Shouldn't Fill," (Comments Based on an Interview with Penny Hauser-Cram), in Mary A. Jensen and Zelda W. Chevalier, eds., *Issues and Advocacy in Early Education* (Boston: Allyn and Bacon, 1990), p. 341.

2. "NAEYC Position Statement on Developmentally Appropriate Practice in Early Childhood Programs Serving Children From Birth Through Age 8," in Sue Bredekamp, ed., *Developmentally Appropriate Practice in Early Childhood Programs Serving From Birth Through Age 8* (Washington, DC: National Association for the Education of Young Children, 1987): 12.

3. Marian C. Marion, "Create a Parent-Space—A Place to Stop, Look and Read." Reprinted by permission from *Young Children, 28* no. 4 (April 1973), pp. 221–224. Copyright 1973, National Association for the Education of Young Children, 1834 Connecticut Avenue, N.W., Washington, DC 20009.

4. Ibid., pp. 222–24.

5. Katherine E. D'Evelyn, *Individual Parent-Teacher Conferences* (New York: Teachers College Press, Columbia University, 1963).

6. Doreen J. Croft, *Parents and Teachers* (Belmont, CA: Wadsworth, 1979), p. 50.

7. Ibid., pp. 50–52.

8. George S. Morrison, *Parent Involvement in the Home, School, and Community* (Columbus, OH: Merrill, 1978), pp. 150–152.

9. Valora Washington and Ura Jean Oyemade, "Changing Family Trends," *Young Children, 51,* no. 1 (September 1985): 13.

10. Ibid.

11. Lola Sanders et al., "Child Abuse: Detection and Prevention," *Young Children, 30,* no. 5 (July 1975): 334.

12. *Statutes at Large,* Vol. 88, pt. 1 (Washington, DC: U.S. Government Printing Office, 1976), p. 5.

13. V. deFrancis, "The Status of Child Protective Services," in R. E. Helfer and C. H. Kempe, eds., *Helping the Battered Child and His Family* (Chicago: University of Chicago Press, 1968), pp. 130–131.

14. Richard J. Gelles and Ake W. Edfeldt, "Violence Towards Children in the United States and Sweden," in Mary A. Jensen and Zelda W. Chevalier, eds., *Issues and Advocacy in Early Education* (Boston: Allyn and Bacon, 1990): 137–138.

15. George S. Morrison, *Early Childhood Education Today,* 5th ed. (Columbus, OH: Merrill/Macmillan, 1991), p. 445.

APPENDIX A

Certification Standards for Teachers of Children From Birth Through Age Eight

The Association of Teacher Educators and the National Association for the Education of Young Children believe that every state should adopt certification standards for teachers of children from birth through age eight. In order for professionals to act, it is impossible to separate knowledge, abilities, dispositions, values, and attitudes, one from the other. Therefore, statements of understanding and ability necessarily incorporate dispositions, values, and attitudes. The certified early childhood teacher will demonstrate professional knowledge, abilities, dispositions, values, and attitudes regarding growth, development, and learning; family and community relations; curriculum development, content, and implementation; health, safety, and nutrition; field experiences and professional internship; and professionalism.

I. GROWTH, DEVELOPMENT, AND LEARNING

This group of standards includes understanding of the various domains of development of infants, toddlers, and preprimary and primary-age children, and the processes by which these domains are integrated. It also includes understanding of how learning and developmental processes interact and the influences of sociocultural and other ecological factors on learning and development. It further includes the ability to appropriately assess the development of children from birth through age eight who come from a range of sociocultural backgrounds and who may be at risk for developmental delay. Specifically, it addresses the teacher's understanding and ability regarding the following:

A. physical development of young children, including variable growth and behavioral patterns during prenatal, perinatal, infant, toddler, preprimary, and early primary years

B. cognitive development and the relation of children's early experiences to their individual differences in cognitive development

C. receptive and expressive communication, speech, and language development in the young child

D. emotional, social, and moral development, including emergence of identity and development of self-esteem in the young child

E. integration of various developmental domains and ways in which individual differences affect development in all areas

F. the importance of play and of active involvement in sensory and motor development and their influence on later cognitive, perceptual, and language skills

G. biological and environmental factors that promote wellness and sound nutrition and that influence development of and exceptionalities in children's motor, sensory, cognitive, and psychosocial development

H. recognition of signs of emotional distress, child abuse, and neglect in young children and knowledge of responsibility and procedures for reporting known or suspected abuse or neglect to appropriate authorities

I. observation and recording of young children's behavior and conducting of accurate and meaningful assessments in order to be aware of individual differences that occur among young children

J. utility and limitations of developmental screening tests administered to young children

II. FAMILY AND COMMUNITY RELATIONS

This group of standards encompasses understanding the vital role of the family and the community in the care and education of infants, toddlers, preprimary children, and primary-age children, and primary-age children. It stresses the teacher's ability to cooperate with family and community systems in an effort to build upon the child's sociocultural background and, with support staff, to work with families and children who have special needs. Specifically, it addresses the teacher's understanding of and ability regarding the following:

A. explaining to parents the fundamentals of child growth, development, and learning; articulating the rationale for developmentally appropriate education programs for young children and the need for community support for such programs

B. articulating the concept of developmental delay and the rationale for early intervention services for children who are developmentally delayed or at risk of developmental delay

C. services that provide information and support for families and children and the role of related disciplines in supporting young children and their families

D. roles of parents as primary caregivers and informal teachers of young children, understanding the importance of parents' expectations for their children, and acknowledging the collaborative role of parents and teachers in early childhood programs

E. how young children affect and are affected by parents, siblings, extended family, and community

F. working cooperatively and supportively with families, especially those that have special educational needs, including those in which English is not the dominant language

G. including families in assessing a child's development, reporting assessment results in a clear and supportive manner to family members and other appropriate professionals, and identifying strengths and needs when setting goals

H. special education community services for the young child, including prevention, early intervention, integration into mainstreamed environments, and referral to specialized programs

III. CURRICULUM DEVELOPMENT, CONTENT, AND IMPLEMENTATION

This group of standards includes understanding of planning for and facilitating learning by infants, toddlers, preprimary children, and primary-age children in the content areas of language, literacy, mathematics, science, social studies, the arts, and health and safety. It also includes understanding of planning for and facilitating interactions in appropriate environments. Finally, these standards emphasize the importance of assessing children's abilities and the importance of sociocultural background for the planning of environments and experiences that meet the needs of all children, regardless of cultural background or special needs. Specifically, it addresses the teacher's understanding and ability regarding the following:

A. observing, recording, and assessing young children's behavior for the purpose of planning appropriate programs, environments, and interactions

B. using theories of development, learning, and assessment in planning appropriate programs, environments, and interactions

C. planning and implementing learning environments including the physical and psychosocial environments; management of time, space, and material; and adjusting for children's age, cultural background, and special needs

D. physical growth and development and implementing developmental approaches to large and small motor skills

E. developing and implementing an integrated curriculum that focuses on children's developmental needs and interests; incorporating culturally valued contents and children's home experiences

F. using play, themes, and projects in planning experiences that integrate all developmental domains (emotional, physical, social, and cognitive)

G. creating and managing a learning environment that emphasizes direct experience, active manipulation of concrete materials, child choice and decision making, exploration of the environment, and interaction with others

H. using developmentally appropriate methods that may include play, open-ended questioning, group discussion, problem solving, cooperative planning, and inquiry experiences to help young children in developing intellectual curiosity, solving problems, making decisions, and becoming independent learners

I. using group and individual guidance and problem-solving techniques to assist the construction of knowledge and nurture prosocial interactions among children, to encourage interpersonal problem solving, and to develop self-control and positive self-esteem

J. supporting children's actions that increase the likelihood that children will be mentally alert, curious, confident, and honest in expressing their views; encouraging them to take initiative in generating ideas, problems, questions, and relationships

K. assisting young children in developing decision-making and interpersonal skills necessary to promote good health and personal safety

L. integrating multicultural/antibias themes, literature, and experiences in all curricular areas

M. participating and assisting other professionals in family-centered assessments and in developing and implementing individualized service and educational plans for young children with handicaps

N. adapting curriculum content to meet the needs of all young children, including those who may be gifted, handicapped, developmentally delayed, or at risk for developmental delay

IV. HEALTH, SAFETY, AND NUTRITION

This group of standards addresses understanding of managing an environment that provides for the health, safety, and nutritional well-being of infants, toddlers, preprimary children, and primary-age children. Teachers should be able to apply this knowledge regardless of children's sociocultural background and should be aware of the special needs of children who may have disabilities that put them at risk. Specifically, it addresses the teacher's understanding and ability regarding the following:

A. basic health, nutrition, and safety management procedures for infants, toddlers, and young children; also, basic health and safety management procedures regarding childhood illness and communicable diseases

B. using appropriate health appraisal procedures and recommending referral to appropriate community health and social services when necessary

C. identifying hazards, assessing risks and taking appropriate corrective steps in early childhood settings

V. FIELD EXPERIENCES AND PROFESSIONAL INTERNSHIP

This group of standards includes understandings needed for implementation of a quality program for infants, toddlers, preprimary children, and primary-age children, and an appreciation for differences in sociocultural backgrounds and special needs. It includes 300 clock hours of experience serving children in two of these age groups in various early childhood settings, including supervised interactions with families and children from a variety of cultural and socioeconomic backgrounds and varying degrees of special needs, and experience working with interdisciplinary teams of professionals, where appropriate. Specifically, it addresses the teacher's understanding and ability regarding the following:

A. integrating theory and practice through field work in conjunction with coursework and professional consultation

B. assuming the full range of teaching duties in exemplary early childhood settings

C. accepting and reflecting upon supervision from on-site as well as other clinical personnel

D. analyzing, evaluating, and discussing field experiences in seminar meetings with supervisors and colleagues

VI. PROFESSIONALISM

This group of standards includes understanding of the importance of continued professional growth and of working with others in the profession and in the greater community to advocate for infants, toddlers, preprimary children, and primary-age children. It further includes an appreciation and advocacy for children and families with diverse sociocultural backgrounds and special needs. Specifically, it addresses the teacher's understanding and ability regarding the following:

A. articulating a personal philosophy of early childhood teaching and demonstrating interest and commitment to young children's development, learning, and well-being

B. how historical, philosophical, and social foundations of early childhood education affect current practices and future trends

C. current issues, trends, legislation, and other public policy affecting children, families, and programs for young children and the early childhood profession

D. value issues and the need for incorporating codes of ethics in professional practice

E. working cooperatively with colleagues to organize, supervise, and lead staff and volunteers in planning and maintaining a safe, appropriate group environment for young children's development and learning

F. participating in advocacy activities on behalf of sound programs and services for young children and their families and enhanced professional status and working conditions for early childhood educators

G. the importance of career-long growth and development activities for professional early childhood educators, e.g., active membership and participation in early childhood professional organizations and activities

Source: "Position Statement: Early Childhood Teacher Certification," *Young Children, 47,* no. 1 (November 1991): 16–21. Reprinted by permission.

The National Association for the Education of Young Children Code of Ethical Conduct

PREAMBLE

NAEYC recognizes that many daily decisions required of those who work with young children are of a moral and ethical nature. The NAEYC Code of Ethical Conduct offers guidelines for responsible behavior and sets forth a common basis for resolving the principal ethical dilemmas encountered in early childhood education. The primary focus is on daily practice with children and their families in programs for children from birth to 8 years of age: preschools, child care centers, family day care homes, kindergartens, and primary classrooms. Many of the provisions also apply to specialists who do not work directly with children, including program administrators, parent educators, college professors, and child care licensing specialists.

Standards of ethical behavior in early childhood education are based on commitment to core values that are deeply rooted in the history of our field. We have committed ourselves to:

- Appreciating childhood as a unique and valuable stage of the human life cycle

- Basing our work with children on knowledge of child development

- Appreciating and supporting the close ties between the child and family

- Recognizing that children are best understood in the context of family, culture, and society

This Code of Ethical Conduct and Statement of Commitment was prepared under the auspices of the Ethics Commission of the National Association for the Education of Young Children. The Commission members were Stephanie Feeney (Chairperson), Bettye Caldwell, Sally Cartwright, Carrie Cheek, Josué Cruz, Jr., Anne G. Dorsey, Dorothy M. Hill, Lilian G. Katz, Pamm Mattick, Shirley A. Norris, and Sue Spayth Riley.

- Respecting the dignity, worth, and uniqueness of each individual (child, family member, and colleague)

- Helping children and adults achieve their full potential in the context of relationships that are based on trust, respect, and positive regard

The Code sets forth a conception of our professional responsibilities in four sections, each addressing an arena of professional relationships: 1) children, 2) families, 3) colleagues, and 4) community and society. Each section includes an introduction to the primary responsibilities of the early childhood practitioner in that arena, a set of ideals pointing in the direction of exemplary professional practice, and a set of principles defining practices that are required, prohibited, and permitted.

The ideals reflect the aspirations of practitioners. The principles are intended to guide conduct and assist practitioners in resolving ethical dilemmas encountered in the field. There is not necessarily a corresponding principle for each ideal. Both ideals and principles are intended to direct practitioners to those questions which, when responsibly answered, will provide the basis for conscientious decision making. While the Code provides specific direction for addressing some ethical dilemmas, many others will require the practitioner to combine the guidance of the Code with sound professional judgment.

The ideals and principles in this Code present a shared conception of professional responsibility that affirms our commitment to the core values of our field. The Code publicly acknowledges the responsibilities that we in the field have assumed and in so doing supports ethical behavior in our work. Practitioners who face ethical dilemmas are urged to seek guidance in the applicable parts of this Code and in the spirit that informs the whole.

SECTION I: ETHICAL RESPONSIBILITIES TO CHILDREN

Childhood is a unique and valuable stage in the life cycle. Our paramount responsibility is to provide safe, healthy, nurturing, and responsive settings for children. We are committed to supporting children's development by cherishing individual differences, by helping them learn to live and work cooperatively, and by promoting their self-esteem.

Ideals:

I-1.1—To be familiar with the knowledge base of early childhood education and to keep current through continuing education and in-service training.

I-1.2—To base program practices upon current knowledge in the field of child development and related disciplines and upon particular knowledge of each child.

I-1.3—To recognize and respect the uniqueness and the potential of each child.

I-1.4—To appreciate the special vulnerability of children.

I-1.5—To create and maintain safe and healthy settings that foster children's social, emotional, intellectual, and physical development and that respect their dignity and their contributions.

I-1.6—To support the right of children with special needs to participate, consistent with their ability, in regular early childhood programs.

Principles:

P-1.1—Above all, we shall not harm children. We shall not participate in practices that are disrespectful, degrading, dangerous, exploitative, intimidating, psychologically damaging, or physically harmful to children. *This principle has precedence over all others in this Code.*

P-1.2—We shall not participate in practices that discriminate against children by denying benefits, giving special advantages, or excluding them from programs or activities on the basis of their race, religion, sex, national origin, or the status, behavior, or beliefs of their parents. (This principle does not apply to programs that have a lawful mandate to provide services to a particular population of children.)

P-1.3—We shall involve all of those with relevant knowledge (including staff and parents) in decisions concerning a child.

P-1.4—When, after appropriate efforts have been made with a child and the family, the child still does not appear to be benefitting from a program, we shall communicate our concern to the family in a positive way and offer them assistance in finding a more suitable setting.

P-1.5—We shall be familiar with the symptoms of child abuse and neglect and know community procedures for addressing them.

P-1.6—When we have evidence of child abuse or neglect, we shall report the evidence to the appropriate community agency and follow up to ensure that appropriate action has been taken. When possible, parents will be informed that the referral has been made.

P-1.7—When another person tells us of their suspicion that a child is being abused or neglected but we lack evidence, we shall assist that person in taking appropriate action to protect the child.

P-1.8—When a child protective agency fails to provide adequate protection for abused or neglected children, we acknowledge a collective ethical responsibility to work toward improvement of these services.

SECTION II: ETHICAL RESPONSIBILITIES TO FAMILIES

Families are of primary importance in children's development. (The term *family* may include others, besides parents, who are responsibly involved with the child.) Because the family and the early childhood educator have a common interest in the child's welfare, we acknowledge a primary responsibility to bring about collaboration between the home and school in ways that enhance the child's development.

Ideals:

I-2.1—To develop relationships of mutual trust with the families we serve.

I-2.2—To acknowledge and build upon strengths and competencies as we support families in their task of nurturing children.

I-2.3—To respect the dignity of each family and its culture, customs, and beliefs.

I-2.4—To respect families' childrearing values and their right to make decisions for their children.

I-2.5—To interpret each child's progress to parents within the framework of a developmental perspective and to help families understand and appreciate the value of developmentally appropriate early childhood programs.

I-2.6—To help family members improve their understanding of their children and to enhance their skills as parents.

I-2.7—To participate in building support networks for families by providing them with opportunities to interact with program staff and families.

Principles:

P-2.1—We shall not deny family members access to their child's classroom or program setting.

P-2.2—We shall inform families of program philosophy, policies, and personnel qualifications, and explain why we teach as we do.

P-2.3—We shall inform families of and, when appropriate, involve them in policy decisions.

P-2.4—We shall inform families of and, when appropriate, involve them in significant decisions affecting their child.

P-2.5—We shall inform the family of accidents involving their child, of risks such as exposures to contagious disease that may result in infection, and of events that might result in psychological damage.

P-2.6—We shall not permit or participate in research that could in any way hinder the education or development of the children in our programs. Families shall be fully informed of any proposed research projects involving their children and shall have the opportunity to give or withhold consent.

P-2.7—We shall not engage in or support exploitation of families. We shall not use our relationship with a family for private advantage or personal gain, or enter into relationships with family members that might impair our effectiveness in working with children.

P-2.8—We shall develop written policies for the protection of confidentiality and the disclosure of children's records. The policy documents shall be made available to all program personnel and families. Disclosure of children's records beyond family members, program personnel, and consultants having an obligation of confidentiality shall require familial consent (except in cases of abuse or neglect).

P-2.9—We shall maintain confidentiality and shall respect the family's right to privacy, refraining from disclosure of confidential information and intrusion into family life. However, when we are concerned about a child's welfare, it is permissible to reveal confidential information to agencies and individuals who may be able to act in the child's interest.

P-2.10—In cases where family members are in conflict we shall work openly, sharing our observations of the child, to help all parties involved make informed decisions. We shall refrain from becoming an advocate for one party.

P-2.11—We shall be familiar with and appropriately use community resources and professional services that support families. After a referral has been made, we shall follow up to ensure that services have been adequately provided.

SECTION III: ETHICAL RESPONSIBILITIES TO COLLEAGUES

In a caring, cooperative work place human dignity is respected, professional satisfaction is promoted, and positive relationships are modeled. Our primary responsibility in this arena is to establish and maintain settings and relationships that support productive work and meet professional needs.

A—Responsibilities to Co-Workers

Ideals:

I-3A.1—To establish and maintain relationships of trust and cooperation with co-workers.

I-3A.2—To share resources and information with co-workers.

I-3A.3—To support co-workers in meeting their professional needs and in their professional development.

I-3A.4—To accord co-workers due recognition of professional achievement.

Principles:

P-3A.1—When we have concern about the professional behavior of a co-worker, we shall first let that person know of our concern and attempt to resolve the matter collegially.

P-3A.2—We shall exercise care in expressing views regarding the personal attributes or professional conduct of co-workers. Statements should be based on firsthand knowledge and relevant to the interests of children and programs.

B—Responsibilities to Employers

Ideals:

> **I-3B.1**—To assist the program in providing the highest quality of service.
>
> **I-3B.2**—To maintain loyalty to the program and uphold its reputation.

Principles:

> **P-3B.1**—When we do not agree with program policies, we shall first attempt to effect change through construction action within the organization.
>
> **P-3B.2**—We shall speak or act on behalf of an organization only when authorized. We shall take care to note when we are speaking for the organization and when we are expressing a personal judgment.

C—Responsibilities to Employees

Ideals:

> **I-3C.1**—To promote policies and working conditions that foster competence, well-being, and self-esteem in staff members.
>
> **I-3C.2**—To create a climate of trust and candor that will enable staff to speak and act in the best interests of children, families, and the field of early childhood education.
>
> **I-3C.3**—To strive to secure an adequate livelihood for those who work with or on behalf of young children.

Principles:

> **P-3C.1**—In decisions concerning children and programs, we shall appropriately utilize the training, experience, and expertise of staff members.
>
> **P-3C.2**—We shall provide staff members with working conditions that permit them to carry out their responsibilities, timely and nonthreatening evaluation procedures, written grievance procedures, constructive feedback, and opportunities for continuing professional development and advancement.
>
> **P-3C.3**—We shall develop and maintain comprehensive written personnel policies that define program standards and, when applicable, that specify the extent to which employees are accountable for their conduct outside the work place. These policies shall be given to new staff members and shall be available for review by all staff members.
>
> **P-3C.4**—Employees who do not meet program standards shall be informed of areas of concern and, when possible, assisted in improving their performance.
>
> **P-3C.5**—Employees who are dismissed shall be informed of the reasons for their termination. When a dismissal is for cause, justification must be based on

evidence of inadequate or inappropriate behavior that is accurately documented, current, and available for the employee to review.

P-3C.6—In making evaluations and recommendations, judgments shall be based on fact and relevant to the interests of children and programs.

P-3C.7—Hiring and promotion shall be based solely on a person's record of accomplishment and ability to carry out the responsibilities of the position.

P-3C.8—In hiring, promotion, and provision of training, we shall not participate in any form of discrimination based on race, religion, sex, national origin, handicap, age, or sexual preference. We shall be familiar with laws and regulations that pertain to employment discrimination.

SECTION IV: ETHICAL RESPONSIBILITIES TO COMMUNITY AND SOCIETY

Early childhood programs operate within a context of an immediate community made up of families and other institutions concerned with children's welfare. Our responsibilities to the community are to provide programs that meet its needs and to cooperate with agencies and professions that share responsibility for children. Because the larger society has a measure of responsibility for the welfare and protection of children, and because of our specialized expertise in child development, we acknowledge an obligation to serve as a voice for children everywhere.

Ideals:

I-4.1—To provide the community with high-quality, culturally sensitive programs and services.

I-4.2—To promote cooperation among agencies and professions concerned with the welfare of young children, their families, and their teachers.

I-4.3—To work, through education, research, and advocacy, toward an environmentally safe world in which all children are adequately fed, sheltered, and nurtured.

I-4.4—To work, through education, research, and advocacy, toward a society in which all young children have access to quality programs.

I-4.5—To promote knowledge and understanding of young children and their needs. To work toward greater social acknowledgment of children's rights and greater social acceptance of responsibility for their well-being.

I-4.6—To support policies and laws that promote the well-being of children and families. To oppose those that impair their well-being. To cooperate with other individuals and groups in these efforts.

I-4.7—To further the professional development of the field of early childhood education and to strengthen its commitment to realizing its core values as reflected in this Code.

Principles:

P-4.1—We shall communicate openly and truthfully about the nature and extent of services that we provide.

P-4.2—We shall not accept or continue work in positions for which we are personally unsuited or professionally unqualified. We shall not offer services that we do not have the competence, qualifications, or resources to provide.

P-4.3—We shall be objective and accurate in reporting the knowledge upon which we base our program practices.

P-4.4—We shall cooperate with other professionals who work with children and their families.

P-4.5—We shall not hire or recommend for employment any person who is unsuited for a position with respect to competence, qualifications, or character.

P-4.6—We shall report the unethical or incompetent behavior of a colleague to a supervisor when informal resolution is not effective.

P-4.7—We shall be familiar with laws and regulations that serve to protect the children in our programs.

P-4.8—We shall not participate in practices which are in violation of laws and regulations that protect the children in our programs.

P-4.9—When we have evidence that an early childhood program is violating laws or regulations protecting children, we shall report it to persons responsible for the program. If compliance is not accomplished within a reasonable time, we will report the violation to appropriate authorities who can be expected to remedy the situation.

P-4.10—When we have evidence that an agency or a professional charged with providing services to children, families, or teachers is failing to meet its obligations, we acknowledge a collective ethical responsibility to report the problem to appropriate authorities or to the public.

P-4.11—When a program violates or requires its employees to violate this Code, it is permissible, after fair assessment of the evidence, to disclose the identity of that program.

Source: "The National Association for the Education of Young Children: Code of Ethical Conduct," *Young Children, 45,* no. 1 (November 1989): 25–29. Copyright © 1989 by the National Association for the Education of Young Children. Reprinted by permission

Photo Credits

All photos were taken by Elizabeth A. Maxim, except for the following.

On p. 34, the photo appears courtesy of Culver Pictures, Inc.

On p. 49, the photo appears courtesy of the Child Development Council, Head Start Program of Columbus, Ohio.

On p. 97, the photo appears courtesy of Tom Hutchinson/Macmillan.

On p. 351, the photo appears courtesy of Larry Hamill/Macmillan.

On p. 360, the photo appears courtesy of Michael Hayman.

On p. 379, the photo appears courtesy of Anne Vega/Macmillan.

On p. 409, the photo appears courtesy of Gale Zucker.

On p. 508, the photo appears courtesy of Anne Vega/Macmillan.

Index